Negro Politics in America

Edited by

Harry A. Bailey, Jr.
TEMPLE UNIVERSITY

Charles E. Merrill Books, Inc.
Columbus, Ohio

To Harry, III and Larry

Printed in the United States of America

Preface

During the years since World War II, the Negro in America has made greater inroads into the political system than at any time previously. Beginning with the Supreme Court decision in 1944 outlawing the white primary as a private club's election,[1] glacial changes have been taking place in Negro political behavior in the South and throughout the United States. And as politicians continue to "socialize conflict,"[2] it is expected that a greater number of Negroes, especially in the deep South, will be brought into the political arena. More than that, though, Negroes are themselves assisting in the socialization of conflict movement, as evidenced by the Negro revolution which is said to have begun with the Alabama bus boycott of 1955 and accelerated with the North Carolina sit-ins of 1960.[3]

The dramatic events of the past two decades have heightened interest in Negro political behavior and in its subsequent impact on the "authoritative (governmental) allocation of values."[4] This book is an effort to fulfill a felt need for an empirical and systematic explanation of Negro politics in America. Throughout my teaching of American government and politics I found that there were available excellent single volume books on *some* aspects of Negro politics but that what I considered the best studies of Negro political behavior were scattered among articles in various journals. They are here brought together, along with two chapters from two excellent books on Negro politics, for the convenience of teachers and students seeking to explore the nature of Negro participation in the policy-making process. In addition, two federal laws and a state supreme court decision are presented

---

[1] See *Smith* v. *Allwright,* 321 U.S. 649 (1944).

[2] To "socialize conflict" is meant the process of inviting a larger audience to participate in the quarrel as opposed to keeping conflict private or restricted to a small audience. Expanding the number of people who may vote, for example, is one way of socializing conflict. For an excellent discussion of the socialization of conflict and the widening of the political arena see E. E. Schattschneider, *The Semi-sovereign People: A Realist's View of Democracy in America,* (New York: Simon and Schuster, 1964).

[3] For perhaps the most concise histories of the Negro revolution in America see Louis Lomax, *The Negro Revolt,* (New York: Harper, 1962) and William Brink and Louis Harris, *The Negro Revolution in America,* (New York: Simon and Schuster, 1964).

[4] Values are allocated to the society by government whenever it, among other things, passes a law. See David Easton, *The Political System,* (New York: Alfred A. Knopf, 1953), pp. 131-141.

iii

to show something of the impact of Negro politics on the American political system.

This book of readings does not and obviously cannot exhaust all the areas of Negro participation in American politics. The role of Negro interest groups, the place specifically of a Negro leader such as Martin Luther King, and the significance of an Edward Brooke* in Massachusetts politics where Negroes constitute only two per cent of the population are not included. Indeed, some areas of Negro participation in politics await study and hence are not available for a reader.

My aim throughout the book has been to select readings which combine both theory and evidence to produce knowledge about an increasingly significant force in American politics. A deliberate decision was made at the outset to exclude material of a polemical nature and to utilize only those studies which have no axes to grind and no causes to support. In the main, all the readings are the product of sound social science research.

All the readings are rather recent and cover the crucial period of the Nineteen Fifties and Sixties when enormous political and social changes were taking place in the nation.

Brief introductions have been provided for each part, but they are not intended to be exhaustive. They are primarily included to assist the student in relating these materials to the larger reality which is *American* government and politics.

The editor is grateful to the Department of Political Science, Temple University, which made possible much of the time devoted to this anthology. The editor is particularly grateful to his colleagues at Temple University, Professors Raymond Short, Daniel Elazar, and Stephen Whitaker for having read and commented on several portions of the manuscript; to Professor Gerald Pomper of the Department of Political Science, Rutgers University, for his good advice; and to the various contributors and publishers who granted permissions to reprint papers. The editor is also indebted to Misses Joan Cimino, Dolores Chiolo, and Linda Scherr who typed or retyped portions of the manuscript. Last, but not least, the editor would like especially to thank Mary Bailey, without whose aid none of his work would be realized. Needless to say, the editor accepts full responsibility for his selection of the materials and for the views he expresses herein.

Harry A. Bailey, Jr.

Temple University
Philadelphia, Pennsylvania
1967

*Recently elected United States Senator from Massachusetts.

Contents

Part 1

The Negro Sub-Community
and the Political System*

Close to twenty million, or ten per cent, of America's citizens are Negro. In this fact alone Negroes would appear to possess a great deal of political power, since ours is a nation of immigrants in which numerous ethnic groups

*The use of the term sub-community to refer to the Negro community is borrowed from Floyd Hunter, *Community Power Structure*, (Garden City, New York: Doubleday & Company, Inc., 1963), Chapter 5. The term is interpreted to mean a functional community within a larger community; the larger community sets the prevailing standards and values of the society. The activities of a sub-community, such as the Negro community, are to some undefined extent exclusive of the activities of the general community. It has its own leadership, professional organizations, churches, fraternities, etc. The Negro community is perhaps the most distinctive sub-community in America because its racial identity is an element in all equations.

1

make possible the politics of pluralism. Negroes, however, have stood outside of the political arena until recently, because the society created and dominated by whites, in the main, did not see Negroes as equals and therefore worthy of citizen participation. To be sure, America's efforts to count the Negro in began a long time ago. However, the legal progress made in keeping with America's ideals was also reversed by practice in favor of what many Americans continue to feel: that Negroes ought still to be kept out of the mainstream of American life. Indeed, in spite of the great changes taking place in Negro political behavior, Negroes remain the most inactive minority because, as James Q. Wilson succinctly puts it, "powerful constraints work against Negro influence in civic and political affairs—race prejudice, class differences, geographic concentrations, and a weak economic position. . . ."[1]

The readings in this section will try to show the general relationship of the Negro sub-community to the larger community. What emerges is a picture of why Negroes, in the past, have been politically weak, and why politically Negroes are presently gaining increasing strength.

Until Lincoln's Emancipation Proclamation in January, 1863, and the end of the Civil War in 1865, most Negroes were slaves in American society. With the legal barriers to their participation removed, approximately four and a half million newly freed Negroes became a political power in many places in the South. That Negro political power was real can be seen in the fact that between 1869 and 1901 twenty Negroes from eight Southern states were elected for a total of sixty-eight years to the U.S. House of Representatives. During this same period two Negroes were elected to the U.S. Senate from the state of Mississippi.[2] Not since this time have Negroes been able to match this record of federal elective officeholding.

The Civil War amendments — the Thirteenth, Fourteenth and Fifteenth to the Constitution — did not prove adequate to protect the Negro's new found freedom and political power. What had been the custom in the deep South could not easily be changed. As Alexis de Tocqueville put it many years ago: "There is a natural prejudice that prompts men to despise whoever has been their inferior long after he has become their equal. . . ."[3] With the Hayes-Tilden compromise of 1876 in which Hayes promised to withdraw all federal troops from the South in return for Democrats not contesting his election to the Presidency, Southern whites moved to reestablish the subordination and exclusion of Negroes from the Southern mainstream. Poll taxes and literacy tests were established as criteria for voting. In almost every sphere of social and economic life segregation became the custom or was legislated into

[1]*Negro Politics: The Search for Leadership,* (Glencoe, Illinois: The Free Press of Glencoe, 1960), p. 6.
[2]See the data compiled by Edward T. Clayton in *The Negro Politician: His Success and Failure,* (Chicago: Johnson Publishing Company, Inc., 1964), p. 32.
[3]*Democracy in America,* Vol. I., (New York: Alfred A. Knopf, 1945), p. 357.

reality. With the Supreme Court's separate-but-equal decision in 1896 sanctioning southern practices,[4] the southern way became the American way.

The history of Negroes in America since the turn of the century has been the drama of a weak minority struggling, sometimes alone, sometimes with assistance of members of the white community, to alter their position vis-à-vis the strong majority. Once the Negro population in America was thoroughly disfranchised, many observers of the social scene rationalized a solution for the Negro's plight in various ways. Some argued his plight was the result of his inherent inferiority and no solution other than segregation was forthcoming. Others suggested that the Negro's problem was just a matter of his becoming acculturated. Once this had become the case his position in American society would change. Some went on to argue that the application of Christian principles to the race problem would solve all the difficulties.

None of these solutions apparently were adequate. Sociological tracts denying racial inferiority did not alter substantially the views of white southerners (whose views were most important since at the turn of the century approximately ninety per cent of the Negro population in America lived in the eleven states of the old Confederacy). Nor did the advancement of large numbers of Negroes to middle-class status change things. And many southerners used their interpretations of Christianity to confirm the need for the perpetual subjugation of Negroes.

It is, however, with the present that we are concerned. The question is: how may we view the contemporary place of the Negro sub-community in the larger community? How much has changed? How much remains the same?

In the first article, Joseph S. Roucek suggests that we ought to start out by viewing white-black relations in America as simply another aspect of human power relations. People seek power over others — black, white, or otherwise. It is reasonable to expect, Roucek is saying, that the white majority will seek power over the black minority. The conclusion which emerges is that if Negroes in America have less power than other minorities have had in relation to the larger community, it can be attributed less to the fact of Negroes being Negroes and more to the fact that Negroes are a minority without the resources which accrued to other minorities which immigrated to this country. While one may wish to argue the validity of accepting Roucek's arguments *carte blanche,* there can be no denying that the question of who gets and keeps power is one important facet of the Negro's problem. To this extent, Roucek's arguments go a long way toward clarifying one of the problems which confronts minorities in most times and places.

The political status of Negroes in America has been changing substantively for the better. It would be presumptuous for us to try to list every factor which has been influential in this change, but one significant factor does

---

[4]See *Plessy v. Ferguson* 163 U.S. 537 (1896).

emerge from all others: the migration of Negroes from the South to the North and West.

In 1900, only ten per cent of all American Negroes lived outside the eleven states of the old Confederacy. By the beginning of World War II, twenty-seven per cent lived outside the South. At the beginning of the Korean War, well over thirty-seven per cent lived in the North and West. And by 1960, nearly fifty per cent or half of America's Negroes had moved into states outside the Old South. This change in the geographical location of Negro citizens in America significantly affects Negro political power. Negroes have moved into the North and the West, to be sure, where their right to vote is not usually questioned; but, more than this they have moved into such big-city states as New York, Pennsylvania, Illinois, and Michigan which carry large numbers of electoral votes. In these states the major city contains a Negro voting population whose ballots could mean the difference between success and failure in a national election.[5] Moreover, the increased significance of the Negro vote in the major urban centers of the North can be seen in the fact that there are presently in the Congress six Negro Congressmen: Augustus F. Hawkins (California), William L. Dawson (Illinois), John J. Conyers, Jr. (Michigan), Charles C. Diggs, Jr. (Michigan), Adam C. Powell (New York), and Robert N. C. Nix (Pennsylvania). All are Democrats and all serve from big city constituencies. In the second article reprinted in this section Robert E. Martin reviews the redistribution of the Negro population in the United States and discusses some of the implications for the political system made possible by the phenomenon of Negro migration from the South.

The new political power accruing to Negroes because of their strategic geographical location alone is obviously not enough to cause drastic changes in the political system. Learning to participate effectively in a dynamic political system with all the subtleties and nuances which go into value-making does not take place by simply changing one's location. People have to realize new possibilities and learn new roles. In the third article Dwaine Marvick discusses the roles learned by Negroes in the old non-participative order and the roles being learned by Negroes for the new participative order. In addition, he points up some of the tensions generated in Negroes in their accommodation to the new order.

Negroes do attempt to wield power under their present circumstances. And obviously where transition to a new order is not yet complete we can hardly expect that Negroes will be able to exercise political power commensurate

---

[5]See, for example, the arguments of Theodore H. White on the role of the Negro vote in the 1948 and 1960 presidential elections in *The Making of the President 1960,* (New York: Pocket Books, Inc., [Cardinal Edition] 1961), pp. 243, 279, 424.

with Negro population size and strategic location. In the fourth article James Q. Wilson discusses some of the attempts and means of the traditionally powerless Negro to wield power. He effectively illumines many of the problems facing the Negro sub-community and its leaders when they attempt to determine who gets what, when and how.

Minority-Majority Relations in Their Power Aspects

Joseph S. Roucek

Probably the most outstanding weakness of the numerous studies appearing yearly on the various problems of race and minority relations in the United States has been the insistence that in the final evaluation of the available evidence, a solution must be found in the ideological area rather than within the framework of the empiric facts. There has been a never-ending flood of literature engulfing us with a rehash and repetition of the old formulas—traditional answers and cliches, the seemingly self-confident declarations of the "practical" man—all insisting that the answers to the difficulties lie in "ifs"—"if all men were behaving like Christians," "if we would just realize that this or that minority would not be so obnoxious if given half a chance," and so on, ad nauseam. This dominant school is headed by Gunnar Myrdal, whose interpretation of Negro-white relations in the United States is but a good illustration of believing that the acceptance of the creed will solve the facts; Myrdal makes the violation of the American Creed in our treatment of the Negro a basic point; for him "the status accorded the Negro in America represents nothing more and nothing less than century-long lag

Reprinted from *Phylon*, Vol. 17, (First Quarter 1956), pp. 24-30 with permission of the publisher. Copyright 1956 by Atlanta University.

of public morals."[1] Yet, in spite of all the previous and more recent proponents of Myrdal's thesis, this "lag of public morals" has continued to operate most efficiently and persistently; evidently the Myrdal tribe has an attractive ideology for its believers, but its appeal has influenced little, if at all, the non-organized and organized promoters of race hatred.[2]

The same situation exists in regard to the other minorities in America. How, otherwise, can we explain the support given to the survival of such numerous organizations as the National Conference of Christians and Jews, Common Council for American Unity, the Department of Race Relations of the Federal Council of the Churches of Christ in America, the Congress of Racial Equality, the American Council on Race Relations, etc.? Obviously, all these organizations operate in a situation "where, if the ideal were followed, the function of the institution could not be performed."[3] In other words, the very number of these organizations indicates the failure of their humanitarian appeals, and their fight against the practices counter to their abstract ideal is often met by ceremonials "designed to create enthusiasm, to increase faith and quiet doubt. It can have nothing to do with the actual practical analysis of facts."[4] Furthermore, the ceremony or the literature surrounding such institutions need not be "consistent, logical, or rational because of the inherent nature of the psychological forces which bind men together in groups."[5]

Yet, the budgets of these organizations reach million dollar figures; they all use similar techniques: propaganda and educational indoctrination; exhortation, stimulation of contacts, workcamps, community self-surveys, workshops, personal therapy; some of them even use threats or the application of anti-racial discrimination laws.[6] Just like Myrdal, all these devices seem to operate on the basic premise that the survival of our democracy automatically necessitates the experimentation of such efforts to handle the problem.

It can be hardly argued that the survival of American democracy is the supreme goal not only of these professional reformers but also of every sociologist who is more interested in the deterministic aspects of intergroup

[1]Gunnar Myrdal, *An American Dilemma* (New York, 1944), p. 24.

[2]According to the American Jewish Committee, *Anti-Semitic Activity in the United States* (New York, 1954), the anti-Semitic movement, for instance, reached its lowest ebb in 1947, but since then has seen "changing trends in dynamics and tactics." One can only wonder whether the Supreme Court's ruling of 1954 that segregation in the nation's public schools is unconstitutional will produce another wave of race hatred. Disregarding the legal dictum, Governor Herman Talmadge of Georgia said: "I do not believe in Negroes and whites associating with each other socially or in our school systems, and, as long as I am governor, it won't happen." Governor James F. Byrnes had taken a similar position: "South Carolina will not now nor for some years to come mix white and colored children in our schools."

[3]Thurman W. Arnold, *The Folklore of Capitalism* (New Haven, 1950), p. 375.

[4]*Ibid.*, p. 379.

[5]*Ibid.*, p. 376.

[6]*Minorities* (New York, 1953), pp. 647-720.

relations than in the "if and when" variety of approaches. But why is it that in spite of the money granted to these idealistic efforts, and even in spite of some research promoted by them, little has been accomplished in the improvement of the whole area of majority-minority relations? We grant also that no scientist can look for a total and a final solution; that the social relations cannot be viewed only in their majority-minority aspects; and that the interactive and cumulative nature of the social forces influencing intergroup relations cannot be always successfully isolated. But we should be also fair enough to realize in the overall view of group relations that most of the social operators in this field seem to confuse objectivity in scientific analysis with unlimited cultural relativity as a desirable attitudinal approach. This fallacious equation is, of course, a familiar one — but it has been plaguing the sociologists in spite of the growing maturity of this area of social science. In fact, it can be even brutally said that the reform movements, as well as their sociological supporters, can be classified more often as symptoms of the whole problem rather than molders of changing accommodations.

Part of the trouble has been due to a definite disinclination to view majority-minority relationships as another aspect of human power relations.[7] In spite of the insistence that "democracy" is the basic proposition involved, the fact remains that all the claims propounded by either the majority or minority groups (or as individuals representing the groups or the claims of these groups) are primarily weapons in power struggle.

When we observe the life of men around us, we cannot fail to be struck by two facts: that every man, as a rule, desires to have his own way, to think and act as he likes; and, at the same time, everyone cannot have his own way, because he lives in society. Each human being's desires, from the very day of his birth, conflict with those of other human beings. The relations of the individual members of society with one another, therefore, are regulated by all the devices of social control, including the supreme control exercised by the government.

It need not be elaborated that each individual and group benefits or loses by observing, disobeying, or manipulating this order of relationships in human society. From his very first day on earth, the child is dominated by his parents; but he is also dominating his parents, by such ageless techniques as crying, smiling, kicking, or gurgling. The parents do not have to be taught to manipulate the child by feeding it, scolding it, punishing it or frowning at it. Social control may range, as the child continues growing, all the way from the rule of tradition and crude coercion to the influence of rational guidance. The reaction of those subjected to social control varies a great deal; their obedience

---

[7]The latest book in this field, Simpson & Yinger, although steadily skirting around the power-relationships involved, uses the word "power" only once in the introductory chapter; the concept is not listed in the index at all. *Ibid.,* p. 26.

may be unwilling and forced, but it may be also automatic and unquestioning (a conditioned reflex). In this never-ending ebb and flow of human relationships, the conformity or non-obedience to the social control methods satisfies or thwarts the desires of the individuals and groups involved. The appeal of the parents to the ancient formula, "Nice children don't do such things" may or may not bring results. If it does, the parents will be happy but the child might not. If it does not, the parents might adopt sterner measures, since they have power to adopt them, consisting not only of the "parental authority" rooted in the age, the ability to manipulate verbal and other symbols, but also in coercion, bodily restraint, and even violence; yet, at the same time, the child has its own reserve of power to display — sulking, crying, screeching, weeping, appealing to the "other" parent for support, etc. Hence, power is more than the average person thinks; it is more than mere brutal force. It is the ability to influence and to impress other persons, even if it be ever so faint. Erotic skill, artistic attraction, technical competence — all those can be sources of influence, and thus of power, not to speak of the ways of exploiting one's prestige, or lack of sympathy, of promoting the ideologies of "brotherhood," "equality," "constitutional rights," and of printing such ideologies and indoctrinating them through formal and informal channels, individual as well as mass.

The possession of and the ability to use power, therefore, allow the individuals to achieve their ideological wishes and goals in varying degrees. On the group level, social power is the sum total of all those capacities, relationships, and processes by which compliance of others is secured; this compliance may be voluntary or involuntary, conscious or unconscious, beneficial or detrimental — but always for ends determined by the power holder; the power subject is frequently dimly conscious of the imperfection, unreasonableness, or even iniquity of social power. Since in a power relationship the power holder uses power for his purpose in a discretionary if not outright arbitrary way, there can never be an equality between the parties; the exercise of power is accompanied by domination on the one side, and subordination and dependence on the other. Both behavior patterns may vary a great deal in intensity. But only the grave marks the boundary of power — although power can be exerted even beyond the grave (the reputation, the last will provisions, etc.).

If we accept this formula for explaining majority-minority relationships, then we shall more readily perceive the real problems involved here. Every act involved in this relationship has some specific value and goal which is, however, usually hidden within the acceptable ideological framework. Anti-Semitism, for instance, cannot be directly propounded in most parts of America because of the existence of a political democracy and the important role that many Jews play in the civil life. But the Jewish culture patterns and Jews' reputed ability to be successful competitors in economic life sometimes lead to the blocking of Jewish entry into the "social" life of the upper class and

thereby restricting Jewish ability to compete.[8] No amount of appeals to the
constitutional or democratic ideology will do much here, since the real issue
is not the constitutional and democratic ideology but the power relations
involved: the resentment of the Jewish culture pattern and the desire to
restrict Jewish ability to compete. Interestingly enough, the minorities concerned play this game in the same way when the situation is reversed. While
the Jew has found that the insistence on the ideology of "tolerance" and
"equality" and of the guaranteed minority rights makes an undebatable ideological weapon, he is just as willing to disregard this ideological stand when
the power relationship is in his favor. How many voices of American Jews
have been heard on behalf of the eight hundred thousand Arabian refugees
from Israel, who lost out because of the Israeli-Arab war? But they have done
nothing else than what the American Negro did to the white man in the
South after his liberation during the Civil War. Elsewhere, on the international scene, the situation is even more glaring. The Congress Party of India,
over a period of more than half a century, sought to establish the principles
of equality in regard to Britishers; but once India became free, in spite of
Gandhi's constant and eloquent appeals to his countrymen to refrain from
hatred and violence, the continued slaughter between Indians and Pakistani
has characterized the sub-continent of India. Or scarcely a week passes without some news of armed warfare between British colonials and the Mau
Maus of Kenya, or the bloody riots between the East Indians and Bantus
in the cities of South Africa.

Another critical aspect of these conflicts in the contemporary world is
that the range of their influence always extends beyond the local community
in which they take place. An attack upon the East Indians in Durban or
Port Elizabeth immediately evokes an official protest in New Delhi, and
in the United Nations. Soviet propaganda always uses such incidents with
its interpretation as evidence of "capitalistic exploitation" of "suppressed
races." In fact, the colonial world has seen communism associated with the
movements of natives or racial minorities for political independence from
their "white oppressors." Indeed, the Soviet master minds, in charge of
propaganda, have capitalized on the growing abyss between the words and
moral promises and the "facts of life" by paying lip service to the high
moral ideals, while, at the same time, carrying out all their realistic goals.
To show a deadly example: the word genocide was coined for a United
Nations convention which attempts to prevent acts intended "to destroy,
in whole or in part, a national, ethnical, racial or religious groups." Its
author, Professor Raphael Lemkin, estimates that twenty million persons
have perished during the twentieth century as victims of this politically
motivated crime. The United Nations Pact has been in the process of ratifica-

---

[8]Carey McWilliams, *A Mask for Privilege* (Boston, 1948), pp. 18-22.

tion for six years. In May, 1954, the Soviet Union became the 44th nation to deposit its ratification. What an ironic gesture, when we recall the destruction of three Baltic nations — Lithuania, Latvia and Estonia; previously, at least six ethnic groups in the Soviet Union had been wiped out (the Volga Germans, the Crimean Tartars, the Chechens and Ingushes, the Kalmyks, the Karacha, and the Balkars). In 1922-23 and in 1929-1930, priests of the Orthodox Church and their followers were shot by the thousands and ninety percent of Russia's fifty thousand churches were destroyed or closed. The Church has survived, it is true; but only as a servile organ of the state.

At the end of 1948, Ilya Ehrenburg, *Pravda's* propagandist, launched an attack on Israel and Zionism; this blast ignited anti-Zionist campaigns in all the satellites, and quickened the strangulation of independent Jewish cultural life. But Soviet Russia was glad to sign the Genocide Pact!

Obviously, the power relationships vitiate most of the efforts of the organizations or states promoting the solution of the majority-minority problems since their efforts are more in the field of "ought" and "if" than in the area of empiricism; they fail to appreciate that a coincidence of all human interests is a utopian belief, that self-interest is the backbone of all majority-minority struggles, that the demand for the sacrifice of self-interests is more than many individuals and groups are willing to even consider. Equally ineffective are the efforts based on Bentham's famous formula: "The greatest happiness of the greatest number," since they insist on promoting the interests of the spokesmen who will benefit by this utility principle, and not the self-interests of those who are to make the sacrifices on behalf of this principle.

It is true also that even all power relationships cannot disregard completely the expressions of altruism; there are many individuals and groups which are making sacrifices. But, even here, the skeptic can ask, how much of the sacrifice is really virtue? especially the gratification afforded by this benevolence. And above all, this power relationship can be better understood by appreciating Bentham's hedonism: "There has been among moralists a vehement disposition to shut out the influence of the self-regarding principle from the mind. Why this reluctance to admit, as a motive, that which is and must be the strongest of all motives — a man's regard for himself? Why is not self-love to be brought into the field? It is from a sort of bashfulness — a disposition to consider the principle to which all the actions and passions of men owe their birth, as the *partie honteuse* of our nature."[9]

---

[9] Jeremy Bentham, *Deontology; or, The Science of Morality*, Vol. I, p. 163. The very term *partie honteuse* appears also in Nietzsche's *Zur Genealogie der Moral* and exactly in the same evaluative sense; Nietzsche praised it as a special merit of English moralists of the 19th century to have done far more justice to the *partie honteuse* of human nature than other European ethicists. For the best survey of Bentham, see: David Baumgardt, *Bentham and the Ethics of Today* (Princeton, 1952).

In fact, we shall advance in our understanding of all minority problems if we shall appreciate more the ethnical importance of power and of self-regarding impulses, as frequently vindicated by Bentham: "Power, in all and every shape, is the sole instrument of morality, and the struggle for it, within the limits of prudence and benevolence, so far from being worthy of reprehension, is perhaps the very strongest of all excitements to virtue."[10]

But the depreciation of the power approach to all social relations has been quite fashionable in America. We have tried so hard to separate politics from power politics, and politics from social life. Yet, all the evidence shows that the struggle for power is universal in time and space and is an undeniable fact of experience. Even those peoples who want to be free from the desire for power are playing power politics, because they give more opportunities to others to promote their power interests; especially the power-hungry individuals and groups welcome the lack of aspirations for power among others. Majority-minority relationships are but another aspect of the universal struggle for power, modified only by the different conditions under which this struggle takes place on the local scene. In view of the ceaseless struggle for power in all social relations, and on all levels of social organization, is it surprising that majority-minority relations are of necessity power relations — and that they have to be evaluated as such?

It is true that a great deal of time and energy are now spent on efforts to improve group relations. But only a small proportion of this investment is spent on empiric research; and even less is spent on the analysis of the "brutal facts" involved in these tense situations. Most students of this area of human relations are not only confused but morally threatened if they want to deal with the "facts of life" which do not conform to the prevailing ideological principles and norms. Improvements in the situation will come only when the scientist will be allowed to carry on his empiric research and able to declare his conclusions unqualifiedly that this or that is "true facts" — regardless of "ifs" and "ought to be."

---

[10]*Ibid.*, p. 51.

The Relative Political Status of the Negro in the United States

Robert E. Martin

The political status of the Negro in the United States has undergone basic change during the past decade. His improved position stands out in sharp contrast with the situation which existed in the 1930's, and especially with that of 1900. As the twentieth century dawned the shortlived political career of the Negro had gone into almost total eclipse. After a long period of relentless assault upon Southern Negro suffrage — ranging from outright fraud, intimidation and violence to evasion and cunningly constructed legislative[1] and constitutional devices which shrank the black electorate,[2] the Negro had been reduced to a position of political impotence. Shortly after having been catapulted into the political arena and becoming a most controversial element, the Negro had been generally abandoned by the federal government. Indeed, the disillusioned freedmen could find no refuge in their hour of great need; they faced enemies within and without. In the pithy

Reprinted from *Journal of Negro Education,* Vol. XXII, (Summer 1953), pp. 363-379 with permission of the publisher.

[1] W. A. Dunning, "The Undoing of Reconstruction." *Atlantic Monthly,* 88: 437-449, 1901.
[2] Paul Lewinson, *Race, Class and Party.* (New York: Oxford University Press, 1932), especially Chapter V, pp. 79-97.

words of Du Bois, ". . . it was a losing battle, with public opinion, industry, wealth, and religion against them. Their own leaders decried 'politics' and preached submission. All their efforts toward manly self-assertion were distracted by defeatism and counsels of despair, backed by the powerful propaganda of a religion which taught meakness, sacrifice and humility."[3]

By 1910 most Southern states had effectively eliminated the Negro voter. Moreover, the organic law of most of these states had been revised to the end of formalizing and legalizing the de facto situation of Negro disfranchisement and also for the avowed purpose of preventing Negroes from ever achieving political importance in the future.[4] Acting cautiously at first, later this was done boldly and without equivocation, especially after the "Mississippi plan" of disfranchisement survived judicial scrutiny without difficulty. Aware that they need not fear judicial opposition to their nullification of the federal Constitution, a delegate at the Virginia Constitutional Convention candidly stated that "we came here to sweep the field of expedients for the purpose of finding some constitutional method of ridding ourselves of it [Negro suffrage] forever; *and we have the approval of the Supreme Court of the United States in making that effort.*"[5]

One of those actively engaged in furthering the movement for black disfranchisement gave a frank evaluation of the situation:

> It is an open secret that the Negro's vote is rendered nugatory wherever it is sufficiently large to endanger white supremacy. If he votes enough to be effective, the white race circumvents him by the easiest method— fraud, if possible, force, if necessary.[6]

Anticipating the complete elimination of the colored elector, an influential

---

[3]W. E. B. DuBois, *Black Reconstruction.* (New York: Harcourt, Brace & Co., 1935), p. 692.

[4]For the story of how this was accomplished in Virginia see Robert E. Martin, *Negro Disfranchisement in Virginia.* (Washington, D. C.: Howard University Studies in the Social Sciences, 1938).

[5]*Proceedings and Debates of the Virginia Constitutional Convention.* 1901-02, Vol. II; emphasis not in the original. As pointed out in my study of Virginia politics, "Reference was probably being made to the case of *Williams v. Mississippi* in which the Supreme Court upheld clearly disfranchising sections of the Mississippi constitution on the grounds that its 'understanding clause did not actually discriminate against the Negro' and that 'it has not been shown that their actual administration was evil, only that evil was possible under them.' This case, 170 U. S. 231, was the first in which the Justices of the United States Supreme Court sanctioned the revision of southern constitutions for the purpose of disfranchising the Negro." Martin, *Negro Disfranchisement in Virginia,* p. 157.

[6]A. F. Thomas, *The Virginia Constitutional Convention and Its possibilities.* (Lynchburg: J. P. Bell Co., 1901), p. 22.

Richmond newspaper, after demanding repeal of the 15th Amendment, editorialized:

> The people of the South have determined that the Negro shall not continue to be a disturbing factor in their politics, *and they are going to disfranchise him whether or not the 15th Amendment be repealed* ... Virginia is taking steps to accomplish that end. The Fifteenth Amendment *will soon be a dead letter so far as the Southern States are concerned.*[7]

This was no exaggeration. All through the Southland Negro political power disappeared and Negro office-holding ceased. In Virginia the number of registered Negro voters, having stood at 147,000 in 1900, fell to 21,000 in 1904.[8] In Louisiana Negro registration plunged from 130,344 in 1896 to 5,320. So it went all through Dixie. Thus ended the first era of Negro voting and officeholding in national and local government—an era in which 22 men of color served in Congress.

As the Negro walked wearily into the twentieth century, therefore, his political future looked bleak and foreboding, indeed. Yet, hope was not entirely abandoned. Small groups of Negroes clung to the ballot here and there, a few in the South but most of the remnants were in the North — where only a part of the colored population lived. Like the torch of learning in the West during the Middle Ages, the Negro's political aspirations flickered only faintly for a long while, awaiting a new day.

The past decade has brought the dawn of that new day. The Negro is again in politics. Growing steadily and undergoing significant re-distribution, his vote is becoming a powerful force with which to reckon — North and South of the Mason-Dixon line. Again represented in Congress, Negroes are now serving in considerable numbers in state legislatures. They have won seats in more than two dozen municipal councils, of particular significance being several in the South. High appointive offices, on both national and local levels, are being made available to Negroes in unprecedented numbers. The Negro vote, more independent than ever before, is now being courted as never before, especially in local contests — North and South.

This new situation is of great importance, having basic significance not only for the over-all status of Negroes in American society but also for the larger political process in the United States. These recent developments are the product of a variety of factors. The remainder of this essay is devoted to an analysis of these factors. In doing so, efforts will be made to ascertain what has happened, to isolate the major causal forces, and to determine what this portends for the future.

---

[7]The *Richmond Times,* May 6, 1900; emphasis is not in the original.
[8]The *Times-Dispatch,* Ap. 1, 1905. The number of white men registered was 276,000.

Important Recent Developments

Renaissance in Negro Political Interest

Ultimately the importance of Negro political participation must be demonstrated in terms of results at the polls. Of greater significance in the initial stages of this new movement, however, has been the development of a deep-running and expanding interest among Negroes in things political; a veritable renaissance has taken place. After two generations of what amounted to almost a political blackout, there is in process a resurgence of political discussion and action.

The atmosphere has become charged with a heavy political content. Negroes are "talkin' politics" as never before, not only at civic clubs, mass meetings, and barber shops but also in homes, churches, schools, and on the street corner—anywhere people gather. No longer do most Negroes regard politics as a thing apart, forbidden territory. As the writer traveled in the South a few years ago, he was told many times: "Us colored folks use to think that politics was white folks business. But now we feel like it's for us, too, that we have a right to be in it."[9]

It has not been easy to develop this new political climate. Efforts to do so conflicted with an opposing tradition of long standing and ran head on into stultifying lethargy born of long, bitter, and unsuccessful struggle to maintain the political rights of a people searching for a place in freedom's promised land. Sustained efforts are now being made by Negroes to escape from the stagnant backwater of Southern life. Long quiescent, they now are aggressively attacking the innumerable barriers which have frustrated them for so long. Renewed interest is the vital key to this whole new situation. Without it little of importance could have happened. It has made possible large scale registration—often under most trying circumstances, and also large turnouts at the polls—all leading to a reexamination of the southern political status quo.[10]

Growth in Registration and Voting

The administration of registration is highly decentralized in the South and most southern states have no reliable registration and election statistics. The

---

[9]Interviews in North and South Carolina, 1945-46, while collecting data for my doctoral dissertation.
[10]See the searching analysis of the Southern scene made in V. O. Key, *Southern Politics*. (New York: A. A. Knopf, 1949).

result is that for information on Negro participation it is necessary to use estimates made by local observers and local studies.[11]

As a result of being barred from the "white primary" in most Southern states until after 1944, the main Negro voting in this section was in general and nonpartisan elections and in local referenda on bond issues, etc.[12]

As the extensive field research of the Myrdal investigators revealed in 1940, "For all practical purposes, Negroes are disfranchised in the South."[13] In the eight states of the Deep South (Alabama, Georgia, Mississippi, Louisiana, Florida, Texas, South Carolina, and Arkansas), Bunche estimated that only about 80,000 to 90,000 Negroes voted in the general election of 1940, and more than half of these were in Texas.[14] For all eleven states below the border states, Bunche estimated that less than 250,000 Negroes were voting in 1940,[15] and most of these were concentrated in a few urban areas. The small increases which took place in the late '30's and early '40's occurred primarily in the Upper South and border states. The legal proscription of the white primary was a powerful stimulus to the slowly growing political tide among the black people of the Southland. This rising ferment greatly impressed the writer in the course of his political investigations in the South during 1945-46. By the time of the 1946 elections, the number of southern Negroes who had qualified to vote had risen to around 600,000, an increase of more than 300 per cent over the previous decade.[16] The Political Action Committee of the C.I.O. estimated that by 1948 the number of Negro voters in the eleven southern states had risen to about 750,000, indicating that ". . . Negro political activity jumped by leaps and bounds

[11]Most Southern states do not have records of registered voters by race. General practice in the South is to identify the name of Negro registrants with "colored" but often this is not done accurately; and these local records are not summarized into county and state totals. In my study of voting in two counties in the Carolinas, it was necessary to get access to the registration books and carefully pick out the names designated by "c."

[12]An important exception has been Negro voting in the AAA referenda, in which Negro participation has been heavy and significant. See: Robert E. Martin, "The Referendum Process in the Agricultural Adjustment Programs of the United States." *Agricultural History*, 25: 34-47, Ja. 51.

[13]Gunnar Myrdal, et al, *An American Dilemma.* (New York: Harper and Brother, 1944), p. 475.

[14]Because of the relatively smaller size of the Negro population in Texas, and other factors, opposition to Negro voting has not been as virulent there as in some other parts of the Deep South.

[15]Myrdal, *op. cit.,* pp. 487-88.

[16]On the basis of local reports, the NAACP in its Bulletin of November, 1946, placed the figure at 603,000, with Texas and Georgia leading. Professor Luther P. Jackson set the figure at 595,000 in 1947; see his "Race and Suffrage in the South Since 1940," *New South, Je.-Jy.,* 1948. The untimely passing of Dr. Jackson was a great loss; few people have devoted so much time to the systematic study of politics or have done so much to encourage constructive participation in politics by Negroes.

in the 1940's."[17] On the basis of considerable field work, Heard estimated that the total had grown to around 900,000 by 1950.[18] Utilizing reports of persons actively engaged in registration drives in the South, Moon estimated that 1,257,000 Negroes had succeeded in registering by August, 1952, in the eleven southern states[19] — and the drives were continuing in the six states in which the registration books were still open.

SOUTHERN NEGRO VOTERS: POTENTIAL AND ELIGIBLE, 1940-1952

State	1940 Potential Voters	1940 Eligible[a] Voters	Per Cent	1947[b] Eligible Voters	Per Cent	1952 Eligible[c] Voters	Per[d] Cent
Alabama	521,080	1,500	0.30	6,000	1.2	50,000	9.68
Arkansas	270,995	8,000	3.00	47,000	17.3	60,000	25.84
Florida	316,640	10,000	3.20	49,000	15.4	150,000	40.89
Georgia	580,751	10,000	1.71	125,000	18.8	125,000	20.07
Louisiana	473,562	2,000	0.42	10,000	2.6	130,000	27.01
Mississippi	563,754	500	0.09	5,000	0.9	40,000	8.04
North Carolina	493,175	50,000	10.14	75,000	15.2	97,500	17.73
South Carolina	383,686	1,500	0.39	50,000	13.0	130,000	33.33
Tennessee	309,456	50,000	16.15	80,000	25.8	155,000	48.62
Texas	540,788	50,000	9.24	100,000	18.5	200,000	34.31
Virginia	364,411	20,000	5.49	48,000	13.2	70,000	16.56
Totals	4,818,298	203,500		595,000		1,207,500	

a. Estimates of Ralph Bunche based on extensive interviews by him and associates on the Myrdal study. Myrdal, *op. cit.,* pp. 486-88.
b. Estimates by Luther P. Jackson, "Race and Suffrage in the South Since 1940," *New South,* Je.-Jy., 1948, p. 4.
c. Estimates by Henry L. Moon, Director of Public Relations for the N.A.A.C.P., in his "The Negro Vote in the South: 1952," *The Nation,* 175, Sept. 27, 1952, p. 248.
d. These percentages are calculated on the basis of population figures for 1950.

The changes in Negro voting between 1940-1952 are given by states in Table I. These figures indicate that, while the number of eligible Negro electors in the South is still considerably less than one-third of their total potential vote, highly significant progress has been made. Though smaller in some areas than in others, this progress is southwide in extent and is one of the most important factors at work fundamentally reshaping the southern political process. Important recent developments in two basic areas of this process, the poll tax and the white primary, will now be examined.

---

[17]Alexander Heard, *a two-party south?* (Chapel Hill: The University of North Carolina Press, 1952), p. 181.
[18]*Ibid.,* pp. 181 and 302-03.
[19]Henry L. Moon, "The Negro Vote in the South: 1952." *The Nation,* 175, Sept. 27, 1952, p. 248; Negro registrants in Okla. were estimated at 60,000.

The Poll Tax

The poll tax is probably the most publicized instrument of disfranchisement in the South. Although its effects have been somewhat exaggerated,[20] it has been quite useful in bulwarking the one-party system and conservative control by southern Bourbons and their allies.[21] Although "sold" to whites as a device for use against the black electorate, the poll tax, more importantly, was developed as a weapon for use against uprisings like "the radical agrarian movement which swept the West and parts of the South" near the end of the 19th century — a "movement which threatened for a time to unite the poor white and black masses against the ruling classes in the South."[22]

Since there were other more effective ways of deterring Negroes from voting, the poll tax has been more useful against poorer white southerners. With personal income relatively much lower in the South, especially among the agricultural masses, this tax has harmful effects upon both races — particularly in those states where it is cumulative.[23] As a result of the poll tax and other obstacles to voting, participation in presidential elections fell by an average of 35 per cent in southern states.[24]

The poll tax has long been under attack. The effort to abolish it has taken three forms: action in Congress, in the courts, and on state and local levels. Attempts to get Congress to enact a bill outlawing this tax in federal elections have been frustrated by southern filibusterers — many of whom were beneficiaries of the poll tax system. In 1945, as in 1943, the House of Representatives passed an anti-poll tax bill, even though less than 10 per cent of the Democrats from poll tax states voted for it, as compared with more than 80 per cent of the Democrats from other states and more than 90 per cent of all Republicans. The bill was filibustered to death in the Senate.

Efforts to get the courts to void the poll tax were made in two recent cases. The Southern Conference for Human Welfare and the United Mine Workers brought the issue before the courts in 1940 in *Pirtle v. Brown,* involving the election laws of Tennessee. The arguments against the tax were (1) that the suffrage is one of the privileges and immunities protected by the 14th Amendment; (2) that the right to vote for members of Congress arises

---

[20]Key, *Southern Politics,* pp. 599-617.
[21]G. C. Stoney, "Suffrage in the South." Part I, "The Poll Tax," *Survey Graphic,* 29: Ja., 1940, pp. 5-9, 41-43. Eleanor Bontecou, *The Poll Tax.* Washington: American Association of University Women, 1942.
[22]Robert E. Martin, "War on the Poll Tax Front." *Opportunity,* 20: Ap., 1942, p. 100.
[23]National Committee to Abolish the Poll Tax. *The Poll Tax Fact Sheet.* (Washington, D. C., 1945); Bontecou, *op. cit.*
[24]R. G. Lloyd, *White Supremacy in the United States.* (Washington, D. C.: Public Affairs Press, 1952), pp. 1-19. It is impossible to determine precisely how much of the reduction was due to the poll tax.

from the federal Constitution and thus elections to fill these offices are
federal functions; and (3) that the functions of the national government
are not subject to taxation by the states; therefore the poll tax, as a levy
on voting in federal elections, is unconstitutional. This was denied, however,
by both the District Court and the Circuit Court of Appeals.

Calling on the opinion of the United States Supreme Court in *Breedlove* v.
Suttles (1937),[25] the Circuit Court held that requiring payment of poll taxes
as a prerequisite to voting does not constitute a violation of the 14th Amend-
ment because suffrage is a "political right" and "is not derived from the
United States, but is conferred by the state, and save as restricted by the
Fifteenth and Nineteenth Amendments and other provisions of the federal
Constitution, the state may condition suffrage as it deems appropriate."[26]
The Supreme Court declined to review the case.

In 1950 Mrs. Jessie Butler, a Negro woman of Virginia, brought suit
challenging the legality of the poll tax of that state. She demanded to be
registered without paying the tax, contending that such a requirement violated
the 15th Amendment, the Virginia Constitution of 1867, and the 1870 act
of Congress giving the state congressional representation.[27] District Judge
Albert Bryan held that "no immediate question of race or color" was raised
in the case, and that the complaint did not charge election officials with
"conspiracy or misconduct" or maladministration of the poll tax.[28] The suit
was dismissed on the grounds that the legality of state poll taxes had been
established by the Breedlove case in 1937. A special three judge federal
tribunal upheld the decision of Judge Bryan and the case went to the nation's
highest court. The Supreme Court, with only Justice Douglas dissenting,
affirmed the findings of the lower courts without issuing an opinion.[29] The
poll tax, therefore, appears to be safe from judicial condemnation, at least
for a while longer.

The most successful efforts to secure poll-tax reform have taken place
in the states. Opponents of this device have sprung up all over the South.
Leadership has been provided by many liberal individuals and organizations
such as the Southern Electoral Reform League, Southern Regional Conference, Southern Conference for Human Welfare, Southern Women's Committee to Abolish the Poll Tax, the C.I.O., the A. F. of L., and the N.A.A.C.P.,
to name only a few.[30] Agitation has led six states to abandon this prerequisite

---

[25]302 U. S. 277, 1937; this case dealt with the Georgia poll tax.
[26]118 F. 2d218 (1941).
[27]The *Washington Post,* June 3, 1950.
[28]*Ibid.* Jl. 25, 1950.
[29]*Ibid.,* My. 29, 1951.
[30]For a fuller list of individuals and organizations active in the poll tax repeal movement,
see W. M. Brewer, "The Poll Tax and the Poll Taxers," *Journal of Negro History,* 29:
260-99, Jl. 1944.

to the franchise: North Carolina in 1920, Louisiana in 1934, Florida in 1937, Georgia in 1945, and South Carolina in 1950. The tax was repealed by the Tennessee legislature in 1943 but this action was voided by the state supreme court as a violation of the state constitution.[31] Nevertheless, the fight for repeal continued; Tennessee in 1949 exempted women and veterans from the tax and abolished it as a requirement for voting in party primaries. Two years later the legislature, in order to get around the requirement of the state constitution that a voter must have paid the poll taxes "assessed against him for such preceding period as the legislature shall prescribe," limited the tax requirement to the payment of taxes levied for the year 1871.

As a result of repeal in six states, there are only five remaining poll-tax states: Alabama, Arkansas, Mississippi, Texas and Virginia; and agitation for abolition continues in these. A strong movement against the tax developed in Virginia, only to be frustrated by the Democratic machine.[32] Arkansas voters amended the state constitution in 1948 so as to permit the use of a registration system in anticipation of a federal law outlawing the poll tax. In a referendum in 1949 Texas voters came within 10 per cent of passing an anti-poll tax amendment to the state constitution.[33]

The struggle against this indefensible impediment to political democracy goes on, for "The poll tax can be justified only by outright denial of democratic values."[34] Liberals of both races are determined to carry on until this device has been killed completely for they know that "Fundamentally it is a weapon against progressive politics, against the economic and political reforms which the South needs so desperately."[35]

The White Primary: Decline of an Era

The passing of the white primary was one of the most significant political developments of the past decade, ranking second in importance only to the sharp recrudescence in political interest among all strata of the Negro population — and it was the most powerful catalytic agent activating this development. It opened the most crucial area of the southern political process to

---

[31]*Biggs v. Beeler,* 173 S. W. 2d144, 1943; for a discussion of this complex and amazing situation, see Jennings Perry, *Democracy Begins at Home.* (Philadelphia: Lippincott, 1944).
[32]The *New York Times,* N. 8, 1949. *The Washington Post,* N. 4 and 6, 1949 and F. 22, 1952; *The Richmond Newsleader,* D. 6, 1951; The Richmond *Times-Dispatch,* Ja. 3, 1950; amazing enough the proposed substitute for the poll tax requirement in Virginia was worse than the poll tax itself; see editorial, "Virginia Booby Trap," in *The Washington Post,* N. 4, 1949.
[33]The *New York Times,* N. 9, 1949.
[34]William H. Riker, *Democracy in the United States.* (New York: The Macmillan Co., 1953), p. 62.
[35]Martin, "War on the Poll Tax Front," *op. cit.,* p. 102.

Negroes and also is a striking example of how legal action, persistently applied, can make major changes in the status of disadvantaged groups in a democratically oriented society. It is ironical indeed that the primary, which was born in a great struggle for democracy,[36] should be used to subvert democracy for Negro Americans. This dramatic story of the determination of a people to have a voice in their government began in 1927; it could well be recounted wherever political lethargy is a problem.

The fact that in the one-party South the Democratic primary was the real election discouraged many Negroes from trying to take part in politics. Being excluded from this primary, voting in the general election amounted merely to an ineffective expression of protest or a ratification of the obvious. If the franchise was to have meaning and effectiveness, the Negro had to get into the Democratic primary in large numbers at any cost; the battle was joined in Texas.[37] A Texas statute excluding Negroes from the Democratic primary was brought up to the federal Supreme Court which voided it, saying that ". . . color cannot be made the basis of a statutory classification affecting the right set up in this case."[38]

To evade this decision, the Texas legislature passed a law granting to the executive committees of political parties the authority to determine the qualifications for membership; the state Democratic Executive Committee forthwith adopted a rule excluding Negroes. The Court held the statute unconstitutional since it delegated to party committees powers which the state could not exercise.[39]

Deciding to achieve their purpose without state assistance, white Democrats called a convention which passed a resolution barring Negroes from membership. The party rule came up for judicial testing after R. R. Grovey, local leader in politics and labor, was refused a primary ballot. The Supreme Court held that a political party, being a private association, could exclude Negroes from membership without violating the Constitution.[40]

It seemed, therefore, that the Negro would not be able to crack this vital barrier to political effectiveness in the South. In 1941, however, the Court, with some new members and fresh points of view, decided that the primary was "an integral part" of the electoral procedure and thus subject to the provisions of the federal Constitution.[41] Though it did not involve Negroes,

---

[36]C. E. Merriam and H. F. Gosnell. *The American Party System*. (New York: The Macmillan Co., 1949), pp. 304-09.

[37]Of course, some Negroes had voted in the Democratic primary for a long time. While all Southern states, except Florida, North Carolina, and Tennessee, formally excluded Negroes by state party rules, yet local application of the rule varied from state to state and also within states. See Myrdal, *op. cit.*, pp. 474-504.

[38]*Nixon v. Herndon*, 273 U. S. 536, (1927).

[39]*Nixon v. Condon*, 286 U. S. 73, (1932). These cases were sponsored by the N.A.A.C.P.

[40]*Grovey v. Townsend*, 295 U. S. 45 (1935).

[41]*United States v. Classic*, 61 Sup. Ct. 103 (1941).

this case set the scene for a renewed attack upon the white primary. The
N.A.A.C.P. brought suit on behalf of Dr. L. E. Smith, Houston dentist,
who had been denied a ballot in the primary. Facing reality forthrightly,
the Court in 1944 reversed the Grovey decision, holding that the primary
was regulated by the state and was an integral part of the machinery for
choosing officials; the Democratic party was thus a public organization and
the exclusion of Negroes was a violation of the 15th Amendment.[42]
   This historic decision seemed to sound the death knell for the white primary. However, adamant South Carolina Democrats immediately set about
finding ways to maintain their party's racial exclusiveness. A special session
of the state legislature was called for the avowed purpose of repealing all
laws which regulated the primary. This, it was felt, would make the Democratic Party of South Carolina a private organization and thus legally able
to limit its membership as it saw fit. In a speech before the state senate,
Senator B. R. Maybank declared that: "regardless of any Supreme Court
decision and any laws that may be passed by Congress, we of the South will
maintain our political and social institutions as we believe to be in the best
interest of the people."[43]
   Addressing the special session of the legislature Governor Olin B. Johnson,
after a horrendous discussion of conditions during the "carpet-bag"[44] era,
made the following ominous statement:

   After these statutes are repealed, in my opinion, we will have done
   everything within our power to guarantee white supremacy in primaries
   of our State in so far as legislation is concerned. Should this prove
   inadequate, we South Carolinians will use the necessary methods to
   retain white supremacy in our primaries and to safeguard the homes
   and happiness of our people.[45]

   Repeal of all laws dealing with the primary, it was claimed, thus turned
the state Democratic Party into a completely "private club."[46] Membership
lists, called "Club Rolls," were kept in each community by local party officials, and became the basis for determining party membership and qualifications to vote in the Democratic primaries.
   All these elaborate efforts to keep the Democratic primary white were of
no avail. In a test case brought by George Elmore, a Columbia Negro, the

[42]*Smith* v. *Allwright,* 321 U.S. 649 (1944).
[43]The *New York Times,* Ap. 15, 1944.
[44]An old device of Southern politicos, one that has probably been more effective than
any other in maintaining the "Solid South."
[45]The *New York Times,* Ap. 16, 1944.
[46]The "club" idea had existed in the state for some time; it is discussed by Ralph Bunche
in his *Negro Political Status,* (unpublished manuscript in the Myrdal Study) Book IV,
pp. 1039-40.

South Carolina plan did not withstand judicial scrutiny. District Judge J. Waites Waring, native of the state, declared that

> I am of the opinion that the present Democratic Party in South Carolina is acting for and on behalf of the people of South Carolina; and that the primary held by it is the only practical place where one can express a choice in selecting Federal and other officials.
> Racial distinctions cannot exist in the machinery that selects the officers and lawmakers of the United States; and all citizens of this state and country are entitled to cast a free and untrammeled ballot in our elections, and if the only material and realistic elections are clothed with the name "primary," they are equally entitled to vote there.[47]

This opinion was affirmed by the Circuit Court and the Supreme Court refused to review it, thereby strengthening Judge Waring's admonition that "it is time for South Carolina to rejoin the Union. It is time to fall in step with the others and to adopt the American way of conducting elections."[48]

Although abolition of the white primary caused some resentment in South Carolina, there has been no substantial reaction. While doing research in the state, the writer found many whites who were not at all disturbed about Negro voting. Some county Democratic conventions had passed resolutions in 1946 urging the state Democratic convention to open the primary to Negroes. The resolution stated that such action would not only be just in the circumstances but would "tend to act as a means of preventing colored voters from going into Republican ranks."[49] This point of view regarded Negro voting as inevitable and felt that South Carolina should make the best of it. The writer encountered a former chairman of a county Democratic committee who had resigned his position primarily because of his opposition to the party's determination to continue its racial barriers. Several white farmers interviewed expressed the opinion that the primary should be open to all Democrats regardless of color.[50]

The scene of battle next shifted back to Texas where another serious attempt was made to resuscitate the white primary.[51] In Fort Bend County white Democrats utilized a lily-white voters' organization, the Jaybird Democratic Association, to hold "preprimaries" prior to the date fixed by Texas law for party primaries. Nominations and decisions made in the Jaybird

---

[47]*Elmore* v. *Rice,* 72 F. Supp. 516 (1947).
[48]*Ibid.*
[49]*The State* (newspaper), Ap. 15, 1946.
[50]The interviews were connected with a larger study by the writer, "Negro-white Participation in the AAA Cotton and Tobacco Referenda," made possible by a grant for field research from the Social Science Research Council.
[51]Because of the potentialities of this scheme, it merits rather full discussion.

primaries were accepted by the local Democratic party. White voters of
Fort Bend County were automatically members of the organization; county
voting lists, except for Negroes, comprised the membership.[52]
Suit was brought on behalf of a group of Negro citizens, contending
that exclusion from Jaybird primaries unconstitutionally denied them a voice
in the only election that had meaning, and that the Jaybird Association is
in fact the local Democratic party. For sixty years, the brief stated, the
local Democratic organization had submitted to the decisions of the Jaybird
group, accepting its choices without contest. The Jaybirds contended that the
15th Amendment applies only to elections or primaries held under state
regulation, that their association was not so regulated, and that it was not
a political party but a "self-governing voluntary club." This was a crucial
case for, if this scheme were successful, it could be used to restore the white
primary all through the South.
The District Court ruled Jaybird racial discrimination invalid[53] but the
Court of Appeals reversed, saying there was no constitutional or congressional bar to the admitted discriminatory exclusion of Negroes because
Jaybird primaries were not "action under-color of state law."[54] In a decision
announced as this essay is being written, the Supreme Court ruled that this
plan did illegally deny Negroes their voting rights; the Court, divided 8 to
1, issued four separate opinions. In giving the court's decision, Justice Black[55]
stated that

It is apparent that Jaybird activities follow a plan purposely designated
to exclude Negroes from voting and at the same time to escape the
Fifteenth Amendment's command that the right of citizens to vote
shall neither be denied nor abridged on account of race.[56]

After noting that success in the Jaybird primary was tantamount to county
election, Justice Black said further

For a state to permit such a duplication of its election processes is to
permit a flagrant abuse of those processes to defeat the purposes of the
Fifteenth Amendment. The use of the county-operated primary to ratify
the result of the prohibited election merely compounds the offense. It
violates the Fifteenth Amendment for a State, by such circumvention,
to permit within its borders the use of any device that produces an
equivalent of the prohibited election.

[52]The *Afro-American,* Washington edition, D. 26, 1952.
[53]90 F. Supp. 595.
[54]193 F. 2d 600.
[55]Speaking for himself and Justice Douglas and Burton.
[56]*Terry, et al* v. *Adams, et al,* 345 U.S. 461 (1953).

In a concurring opinion, Justice Clark[57] held that

> Quite evidently the Jaybird Democratic Association operates as an aux-
> iliary of the local Democratic Party organization selecting its nominees
> and using its machinery for carrying out an admitted design of destroy-
> ing the weight and effect of Negro ballots in Fort Bend County. To be
> sure, the Democratic primary and the general election are nominally
> open to the colored elector. But his must be an empty vote cast after
> the real decisions are made.

Calling attention to the state's responsibility, Justice Frankfurter in a closely
reasoned concurring opinion said that "State authority has come into play"
since "county election officials aid in this subversion of the state's official
scheme of which they are trustees, by helping as participants in the association's primary." Thus "the evil here is that the State, through the action
and abdication of those whom it has clothed with authority, has permitted
white voters to go through a procedure which predetermines the legally
devised primary." A striking example of judicial myopia, Justice Minton,
in dissent, regarded Jaybird elections merely as private "straw votes" designed
to ascertain the views of the county's voters and thus did not violate the
Constitution; this flight from reality hardly merits comment.

The decision in this case appears to be epoch making. For it is a very
broad and forthright application of the 15th Amendment and, moreover,
it seems to indicate that the Supreme Court will refuse to sanction *any*
scheme which disfranchises persons on racial grounds. The Court made it

quite clear that it is a violation of the 15th Amendment for any state "to
permit within its borders the use of *any device that produces an equivalent
of the prohibited election.*"[58]

Although efforts to evade the Court's action may continue, the prolonged
"battle of the primary" seems to have been won — and decisively. With
hundreds of thousands of Negroes now voting in the Democratic primary —
and all over the South — the situation has changed drastically from the
time when Lewinson reported that "the only place in the South where the
Negro had by 1930 made a real breach in the white primary system was
Memphis."[59] Thus it seems that the primary, created in the late 19th century
search for democracy, has itself been democratized.

---

[57]Joined by Justices Reed and Jackson and Chief Justice Vinson.
[58]From the opinion of Justice Black, emphasis is not in the original.
[59]Lewinson, *op. cit.,* p. 162.

Significant Population Changes: Growth and Dispersal

The two basic population trends among Negroes in the United States — steady, over-all growth and heavy regional shifts — have considerable significance for the Negro's political status. The total Negro population increased both relatively and absolutely between 1940-1950,[60] and so did the number of voting age. Of the 79,863,451 Americans old enough to vote in 1940, 7,427,938, or 8.8 per cent, were Negroes.[61] In 1950 Negroes of voting age numbered 9,208,116,[62] or about 9.5 per cent of the 94,802,019 Americans in this category. The decline in the proportion of Negroes among persons of voting age which occurred between 1930-1940[63] seems to have been checked.

Politically, the most significant change in the Negro population has been its redistribution. Whereas in 1900 almost 90 per cent of all American Negroes lived in the South, in 1940 the figure was down to 77 per cent; and by 1950 only about 67 per cent lived there. Comprising over 32 per cent of the South's population in 1900, Negroes formed only 20 per cent of it in 1950; as expected this has helped to reduce white fears as to the Negro voting potential.

The northern Negro population more than tripled between 1900-1940, rising from less than a million to almost three million; during the 1940's the number grew to 4,109,000, or almost 50 per cent in one decade. Michigan's Negro population, for example, more than doubled, whereas its white population increased only 17 per cent. The Negro population in the West has grown even more spectacularly, increasing by 41.8 per cent between 1930-1940 and by 74.3 per cent during 1940-1950. Thus in California the Negro population rose to nearly 700,000, an increase of 116 per cent, as compared to a 50 per cent increase among whites.[64]

As to the distribution of the total potential Negro vote: of the 9,208,181 non-whites of voting age in 1950, 5,693,181,[65] or 61.8 per cent were in the South — as compared with 70 per cent in 1940. In 1950 non-whites made

---

[60]See the sections of this issue of *The Journal* devoted to population for detailed data.
[61]These data are from reports of the Bureau of the Census and include only citizens.
[62]The 1950 figures include all nonwhites; all but about 5 per cent of nonwhites, however, are Negroes.
[63]This decline was due to the fact that in that decade Negroes 21 years old and over increased less rapidly than the white population of corresponding age.
[64]Only New York and 8 Southern states now have larger Negro populations than California.
[65]For precision, of course, these figures would have to be adjusted so as to exclude persons institutionalized for crime, mental illness, and those ineligible because of residence, poll tax requirements, etc.

up 4.8 per cent of the potential voters of the West, 5.1 per cent of the North, and 20.1 per cent of the South. Redistribution of the Negro's voting power is still underway as migration from the South is continuing.[66]

By 1950 Negroes had become predominantly urban, 61.2 per cent living in urban areas, as compared to 64.1 per cent of the white population.[67] Sectionally, about 47 per cent of southern Negroes and approximately 80 per cent of those in the North and West are now urban residents. Negroes are now becoming urbanized at a faster pace than whites; during 1940-1950 the white population in 168 standard metropolitan areas increased by only 20 per cent, as compared with 44.3 per cent for nonwhites. In the West the increase of nonwhites in metropolitan areas was 127.6 per cent, for whites 48.9 per cent.

In 1910 no city in the United States had a Negro population of over 100,000, but in 1940 there were eleven and, in 1950, sixteen such cities; there are now 27 cities with more than 50,000 Negroes. Rapid urbanization of the Negro is of great significance for every aspect of Negro life and culture, especially politics; for it is directly related to the compactness and cohesiveness of the Negro vote — which substantially condition its effectiveness. Resultant galvanizing shocks arouse group consciousness, focus minority opinion, and stimulate group leadership and demand on an unprecedented scale.

The Negro as Officeholder

Voting with no real racial handicap in the North and West — where their increasing population offered a new and powerful base of operation — Negroes have opened up a new era in officeholding, both elective and appointive. The 1940's saw the number of Negroes in political office grow at a rate unparalleled since Reconstruction. In 1944 about 26 Negroes were elected to legislative bodies, including two members of Congress, and two state senators. In 1946 at least 38 Negroes, 23 Republicans and 15 Democrats, were sent to legislatures.[68] In the last several elections approximately 40 Negro candidates were successful — as compared to only 1 or 2 in 1900. 1952 saw the first Negro woman elected to a state senate.[69]

Negroes have won election to a good cross section[70] of the country's state legislatures; about 17 in all, they range from Massachusetts to California,

---

[66]See Alain L. Locke and Robert E. Martin, "The American Negro." *The Encyclopedia Britannica*, Chicago: 1953, 16: 194-98.
[67]In 1940 only 48.6 per cent of Negroes were urban and in 1900 only 22.7 per cent.
[68]The *Pittsburgh Courier*, N. 16, 1946.
[69]Attorney Cora M. Brown of Michigan.
[70]Outside the South, of course.

and from Wisconsin to Missouri.[71] Their greatest electoral success has been in Illinois, Pennsylvania, and New York. During the past decade Negroes have won a considerable number of seats in municipal councils, in at least 20 cities;[72] in several instances Negro candidates received many white votes. Particularly significant is the fact that since 1947 several Negroes have been elected to office in the South. They won seats in the municipal councils of Richmond, Va., Winston Salem, Fayetteville, Greensboro, and Durham, N. C., and Nashville, Tenn. In addition a few Negroes have recently been elected as magistrates, constables, commissioners, and school board members in the South.[73] In May, 1953, two Negroes were elected to the 16 member City Executive Committee of Atlanta, which governs local elections.[74] Perhaps of greater importance than the small number of Negroes elected in the South is the rising frequency of their candidacy. They campaigned for congressional posts in several states and for the council in more than 40 southern cities. With Negroes forming 20 per cent of the South's potential voters and qualifying in unprecedented numbers, this situation portends much for the future of Dixie.

There are, of course, those who advocate caution, fearing that aggressive independent Negro political action might bring undesirable reaction. They suggest moving slowly until Negro voting has lost its novelty and the black electorate has gained more political experience.[75] As Carleton points out, however, "this time Negroes are in Southern politics for keeps. There will be no turning back. Southern liberals themselves claim that the time is coming when they will be integrated liberals, and they will be sustained by their Southern constituencies. They will not be broken on the race question."[76]

Appointive Office

In the wake of the political resurgence among Negroes has come unprecedented recognition in appointive positions. These have taken several forms:

---

[71]The states are: California, Colorado, Delaware, Illinois, Indiana, Kansas, Kentucky, Massachusetts, Michigan, Missouri, Nebraska, New Jersey, New York, Ohio, Pennsylvania, West Virginia, and Wisconsin.
[72]They include Chicago, Cleveland, Cincinnati, Detroit, East Chicago (Ind.), Englewood, N. J., Gary, Kansas City, Indianapolis, Los Angeles, Newark, Pittsburgh, Philadelphia, New York, and several in the South.
[73]The *Pittsburgh Courier* N. 16, 1946 and N. 15, 1952; The *Amsterdam News,* N. 16, 1946; the most recent victory was Dr. Rufus G. Clement, president of Atlanta University, who was elected to the Atlanta Board of Education in a city-wide primary in My., 1953.
[74]The *Washington Afro-American,* My. 16, 1953.
[75]See Heard, *op. cit.,* pp. 218-19; and Samuel Lubell, *The Future of American Politics.* (New York: Harper & Brothers, 1952), pp. 118-22.
[76]*St. Louis Post Dispatch,* My. 12, 1946; Professor Carleton recognized, however, that effective political participation of Southern Negroes would come progressively rather than by an immediate mass movement.

outstanding persons from many walks of life, and not primarily politicians, serving as political advisers to the New Deal — known at one time as the "Black Cabinet";[77] bright young Negroes brought into government service at all levels, with significantly increased representation in the administrative and professional classes;[78] and growing numbers of patronage jobs, national, state and local, opened up as a result of accelerated party activity.[79]

In recognition of the black electorate's new power, Negroes increasingly are receiving appointment to responsible positions in state and municipal administration.[80] A considerable number are working as attorneys, civil service commissioners, analysts, health and housing officials, tax commissioners, judges, magistrates, etc. The old practice of "window dressing" — using a few Negroes in jobs of no real function or responsibility — has diminished considerably; recent appointees are, for the most part, capable and aid in policy formulation and execution.

In Dixie, too, Negro ballots have brought important gains for the group. Better school facilities, improved municipal services — such as electric lighting, paved streets, trash disposal, recreational facilities, police protection,[81] etc. — badly needed and long overdue — have resulted from bargaining by enlarged, more active electorates in several communities. Thus, North and South, the past decade revealed that "There had taken place among Negroes a political regeneration that made it possible for them to demand a great deal of consideration from both major parties."[82]

The Margin of Victory: Balance of Power

The strategic position of the Negro vote has long been recognized. Though relatively small in size Negro ballots could provide the margin of victory in large, pivotal states where the vote is closely divided. Increase in the Negro voting potential, especially from migration and heavier registration, has caused them to be regarded as a crucial factor in some recent elections. In 1940 the presidential vote was quite close in several northern and border states where

[77]Although somewhat controversial, this group, many of them highly intelligent and devoted men and women, play a vital role in giving direction and momentum to the movement for Negro integration and equality in public service.

[78]Negroes, however, never got access to upper bracket jobs in anything like the proportions to which their members and training, as demonstrated by performance on examinations, entitled them; yet progress was outstanding. See L. J. W. Hayes, *The Negro Federal Government Worker*. (Washington: 1941).

[79]See Florence Murray, *The Negro Handbook*. (New York: Macmillan Co., 1946).

[80]See W. E. B. DuBois, "Race Relations in the United States: 1917-1947." *Phylon* 9, Third Quarter, 1948, pp. 234-47.

[81]Negroes have been added to the police force in several Southern cities.

[82]John Hope Franklin, *From Slavery to Freedom*. (New York: A. A. Knopf, 1950), p. 519.

[83]The states were Ill., Ind., Md., Mich., Mo., N. Y., Ohio, and Pa.

the bulk of Negro voters were found.[83] Wilkie carried only two of these states, although a small switch would have changed the results in all except Maryland. Victory in the 6 others would have given Wilkie 153 more electoral votes — almost enough to have defeated Roosevelt.[84]

Republican National Committee Chairman Brownell found that a shift of only 303,414 votes in 15 states outside the South would have meant victory for Dewey by 8 electoral votes in 1944.[85] A shift of only 5 per cent or less of the popular vote of 28 states would have thrown their electoral votes to the other major party.[86] "In twelve of these, with a total of 228 electoral college votes," as Moon points out, "the potential Negro vote exceeds the number required to shift the states from one column to the other."[87]

Walter White claims that, in 17 states with 293 electoral votes — 27 more than necessary to elect the president — there are enough Negro voters to determine any close election.[88] In addition to a close election, this would require the overwhelming majority of all potential Negro voters to be registered, highly organized and flexible. This is a large order, requiring most sharply drawn issues. Cohesiveness of the Negro vote increases greatly where his rights and aspirations are at issue. However, even though there is an unusually high feeling of group identity among Negroes, there are strong class differentiations and complete political solidarity is quite unlikely where both parties make any real effort to secure their support.

Even so, the increasing power potential of the strategically distributed Negro vote was dramatically demonstrated in recent elections. In 1944 Negro votes more than equalled Roosevelt's plurality in some states; at least 150,000 of them voted for him in Maryland, where his plurality was only 22,541. In some states, like Missouri and New Jersey, Negro ballots for Roosevelt equalled his margin over Dewey. In the closer 1948 election, California, Illinois, Ohio provided the margin of victory; in each state the Negro vote for Truman was several times larger than his plurality. As a result of the nature of American two-party politics, the crucial potential of an alert Negro electorate is quite obvious.[89]

Another development of basic significance for the Negro's political status is his emancipation from prolonged subservience to a vanished past. Out of the facts of Negro freedom and enfranchisement by the Republican party

---

[84]For an analysis of the Negro vote in this campaign, see Harold F. Gosnell, "The Negro Vote in Northern Cities." *National Municipal Review*, 30: My., 1941.
[85]The total major party vote for president was 47,608,783.
[86]In 18 states a shift of 3 per cent or less would have changed the winner.
[87]Henry L. Moon, *Balance of Power: The Negro Vote.* (Garden City, N. Y.: Doubleday and Co., 1948), p. 198.
[88]See his "Will the Negro Elect the Next President?" *Collier's* N. 22, 1947 and "Win Our Vote or Lose," *Look*, O. 7, 1952.
[89]See R. H. Brisbane, "The Negro's Growing Political Power." *Nation*, 175: 248-49. S. 27, 1952.

and the legends which grew up around them, developed a deep-rooted loyalty to the GOP. This spell was broken under the impact of several forces: continuing failure of the Republicans to supplement lip service with a constructive program for improving the Negro's lot, rise of the New Deal and its emphasis on broad social legislation, growing political sophistication among the group, to name more basic causes.

Events of the past decade clearly indicate that substantial progress in the political status of Negroes has occurred and that their influence and power potential have increased considerably throughout the United States. Though there is real cause for optimism, the future, however, must be viewed soberly and cautiously. There are still many roadblocks to full Negro political participation in the South. While the judicial process has done a splendid job recently in freeing the suffrage of major racial restrictions, effective impediments remain. And as the Southern Regional Council[90] states, "It is well-nigh impossible to find legal remedies for petty evasions, delays, and 'errors' of courthouse officials, disapproving frowns and veiled threats, purges of registration lists."[91]

The two most serious remaining obstacles to Negro political equality are discriminatory registration procedures in small towns and rural areas — where "a cold war of the ballot"[92] exists — and apathy towards politics by many Negroes.[93] Although much of this apathy is the product of a long, brutal struggle, it nevertheless reduces the Negro's overall bargaining power. The first obstacle will require, as a supplement to court action, enlightened, constructive and cooperative community action — ranging from education and moral appeal to intelligent political and pressure group tactics; it must not be forgotten that Negro progress has been accompanied by some racial antagonism.[94] Industrialization, political realignment and extension of the two-party system to the South may be a real boon to the Negro's political hopes.[95] The second roadblock must be resolved by in-group action — stimulation, education, responsible leadership and maturing political experience. Mutually beneficial alliances with broad liberal movements must be utilized — as is slowly happening. Although unsuccessful in preventing

[90]The Council is an interracial organization, made up of business men, educators, clergymen, labor leaders and civic workers in thirteen Southern states.
[91]The New York Times, F. 8, 1953.
[92]Ibid. Negro applicants often are required to have one or more written white character witnesses, meet severe property qualifications, pass strictly enforced literacy tests, spend long waiting periods when applying, face rejection because of alleged technical errors in filling out registration blanks, etc.
[93]It has been estimated that registration of Negroes for the entire region "is only about half as widespread as among white citizens." Ibid.
[94]See Lubell, op. cit., p. 120.
[95]See Heard, op. cit., especially pp. 227-49, and V. O. Key, "Solid South: Cracked or Broken," The New Republic, 127, Dec. 1, 1952.

adoption of the Boswell Amendment in 1946, liberal white and Negro groups in Alabama were stirred into cooperative action against a common threat.[96] Significantly, a somewhat similar device was defeated in Mississippi in 1952. As the Southern Regional Council reports:

> Economic growth and sweeping court decisions have put the South well on the way to surmounting the former roadblocks of poverty and official denial of constitutional rights. The challenge now is to build a common citizenship that can be achieved only by informed community action and the fullest and wisest use of the ballot.[97]

In the North the major political problems facing the Negro are the maximization of his growing strength through increased registration and voting, and the judicious use of the ballot to achieve broad group and civic purposes. It appears that Negro Congressmen will soon come from Pennsylvania, Ohio, Michigan and California. Moreover, census data indicate that Negroes can be of influence in 80 odd congressional districts in 19 Northern and border states — if well organized and active. Enlightened and responsible leadership must find the means to harness and direct the aspirations of the Negro masses into effective and constructive channels.

---

[96]This Amendment gave local registrars enough discretion in determining qualifications for voting — literacy, good character, employment — to hold down the number of Negro voters. It was declared unconstitutional in 1949. *Davis* v. *Schnell*, 81 F. Supp. 872, 1949.

[97]From one of the Council's periodic reports on Negro voting in the South.

The Political Socialization
of the American Negro

Dwaine Marvick

ABSTRACT: American Negroes perforce "came to terms" historically with a locality-circumscribed political world. A huge northward migration has occurred, and the younger Negro has gradually become aware of metropolitan as well as national American political processes as they affect him. Opinion-survey evidence reveals clear contrasts by region and generation in Negro attitudes toward public officials; it also suggests that Negro evaluations of political opportunity sometimes approach parity with matched counterpart groups of underprivileged whites. A shift has also occurred in Negro leadership, away from accommodationist civic dignitaries, tapped by whites as liaison spokesmen for the Negro subcommunity, to Negro professional politicians, negotiating from positions of pivotal electoral power both in Southern localities and Northern metropolitan districts. The middle-class leadership of the National Association for the Advancement of Colored People (NAACP)

Reprinted from *The Annals of the American Academy of Political and Social Science,* Vol. 361 (September 1965), pp. 112-127 with permission of the publisher and author.

and Urban League, moreover, has been supplemented and jostled into new militancy by the direct-action protest organizers of the Southern Christian Leadership Conference (SCLC), the Congress of Racial Equality (CORE), and the Student Nonviolent Co-ordinating Committee (SNCC). Full and mundane possession by Negroes of a reformulated place in the American polity depends, however, on the proliferation of community-level opportunities to learn new skills and roles in civic affairs.

In the middle of the twentieth century, the political socialization of the American Negro is rapidly and drastically changing. In part, the trends involve and reflect a massive migration from the rural South into Northern metropolitan slums. In part the trends are embodied in the perspectives of successive generations — those under forty today, whose awareness of American political life is therefore exclusively post-World War II, and their elders, who grew up in a prewar or wartime climate of opinion.

These key dimensions — migration and generation — will be repeatedly considered as we sift the findings available from recent research into how people are inducted into their political culture, which is what we mean by the phrase "political socialization." And because change is the outstanding feature in considering both dimensions, the findings raise questions about "resocialization" quite different from those involved in teaching civics to children or in other ways giving young people a "feel for politics." Protest, alienation, reconciliation, reintegration: these are all relevant terms when we examine how Negroes adjust to the rules and arrangements of American politics.

Political socialization refers to one's induction into a political culture, and perhaps one's capacity to change it. As a learning process, it needs to be seen as often painful, embarrassing, and even stultifying. It is a school of hard knocks for those on the receiving end as American Negroes are. It is not a pleasant academic routine of lessons learned and grades achieved in a civics class. It is the process by which adults come to learn what is expected of them as citizens and, perhaps, leaders.

Political socialization, then, is concerned with how a person "comes to terms" with the roles and norms of the concentric political worlds — local, regional, and national — into which he passes as he grows up. Necessarily it focuses on formative experiences — in the family, school, and primary group contexts of childhood — that shape ideals and give insight into political aspects of life. It requires consideration of a set of motivational factors — rooted in each individual's private problems of psychic management, including also the patterned goals and goads to which he responds with some regularity. Negro Americans in many ways are excluded from the dominant political culture of their community and nation, and are denied its rewards. Norms and roles for political performance are learned in a special Negro subculture, which is at present undergoing basic changes, creating for the next Negro generation new prototypes for political action, and creating also new tensions and new frustrations for the individual.

But the psychological transformation — the "internalized revolution" — in the way Negroes are being inducted into American political life still confronts the would-be "new Negro" with some practicalities that can make all the difference. The study of political socialization requires attention also to situational insights and beliefs — sets of ideological, group-oriented, or self-interested calculations made by a person which largely determine the level of his involvement and participation in any specific occasion or process. Attitudes of skepticism may be widely prevalent among Negro citizens, but they are surprisingly differentiated from person to person, and from situation to situation. And linked to these situational appraisals also is the question of what resources can be marshaled. A full analysis of the changes occurring in Negro political socialization would take into account a long list of capabilities — skills, knowledge, contacts, style, energy, strength, reputation, access, control of organizations — each of which is distributed unequally within the Negro population, and each of which implies control by an active intelligence to be effectively invoked.

Finally, political socialization is not simply the study of how people come to terms with the conventional practices and arrangements which are manifestly referred to as "political" or "governmental" in the institutional sense. It involves examination also of a set of functional equivalents, ways of doing indirectly what cannot be done directly. Because of the history of Negro exclusion — both nationally and in his residence localities — from active and accepted participation in the conventional processes of governance, it is especially relevant to look at his political education as it is functionally acquired, even though the ostensible processes are those of community-service groups, fraternal associations, or church affairs.

This, then, is a brief inventory of the range of problems embraced by the study of political socialization. Applied to an inquiry about the American Negro, it is, perhaps, a useful approach. But certain risks should be pointed out. First, learning what is expected and how to perform in either basic or specialized roles is an undertaking that seems to imply a rather homogeneous political culture, housed in monolithic institutions and with standardized induction norms. Second, it is likely to suggest that the things to be learned are, on the surface, straightforward, manifest political events and governmental patterns. Third, these, in turn, imply that learning depends upon the initiative of each student; some will get A's and others F's. Fourth, it conveys a rather static picture. Allowing for variations in milieu, the old textbook should continue to apply; if one is not politically inducted into the same culture, at least it is into a progressively unfolding political culture. These are all comfortable illusions. In any extensive society there is a plurality of political milieus into which a person coming to adulthood passes. They are not equally challenging, nor easy, nor stable. In the South, a Negro "knew where he stood" and what to expect — or he used to. In the North, impersonal treatment is functional on the surface. It means access to public accommodations, a chance to vote, due process of law, and so forth. It also means isolation, exclusion, hypocrisy, and ambiguity about where the Negro stands socially.

Change does not necessarily mean revolutionary change. The actions of those in a political culture *are* largely what reaffirm or modify its norms and practices, and incidentally serve to integrate or disjoin it from other political cultures. The accretion of small changes in political practice, moreover, includes not only innovations made on purpose and by forceful leaders, but the modifications as well that result from improvisation, from fumbling, from short-sighted maneuvers, from unwillingness to continue in familiar roles, and so forth.

To learn the political game only once is not enough, whether one treats it as a spectator sport, a hobby, or a vocation. Change is too basic; resocialization is too necessary. Especially is this so in the rapidly changing arenas of America's racial politics. Recent collective efforts at direct action have multiplied Negro opportunities for political experience; the organizational scaffolding of leadership and cadre roles has vastly increased the list of political tasks to be done at the same time that it has made those roles more desirable and more differentiated. New organizing skills, analytical abilities, and communication talents are being found and encouraged in the distinctive circumstances of "protest politics." Yet, in looking at the changing patterns of Negro role-playing and Negro skill-acquisition, it is still difficult to gauge the changes in Negro attitudes and motivations. It is necessary to remember the backlog of frustration, self-doubt, and anger which the neophyte must somehow control if he is to learn anything effectively. That he often fails, and in the process learns other lessons about himself and the political system, are other aspects of the problem.

This inquiry, then, becomes a case study in the use of a new conceptual paraphernalia — that of "political socialization" — applied to the complexity and recalcitrance of actual politicizing situations, as reported by Negro informants. Analyzing some of the available data in these terms is at least a way of highlighting the flimsiness of our theoretical apparatus in this area. And because it is impossible to consider the acquisition of political capacities, skills, and beliefs by a sizable segment of the population without asking what difference it is likely to make to the political system in which they will be used and are being used, this inquiry also links interpretation of Negro potentialities to the developmental prospects for the American polity. Let us turn then to a consideration of the resources and difficulties of Negro Americans in coming to terms with the political worlds that surround them.

The Noncompatibility of Negro and White Circumstances

In special ways as well as common ones, American Negroes occupy inferior statuses. Almost from birth they are discriminated against and made to feel inadequate, useless, and undesirable by the dominant white community. As a group also they tend to be poor, marginally educated, and maladapted economically.

In these latter respects, many whites living in the same localities are in similarly depressed circumstances. Some of the apathy and skepticism about American political life which we expect to find among Negroes is probably due to these socioeconomic disabilities. At the same time, the political viewpoints and roles of typical Negro citizens must substantially be seen as a response to the animosities and prejudices they experience because of their ethnic distinctiveness.

Within the Negro community as elsewhere, there is a spectrum of affluence and poverty, prominence, and ordinariness. It is increasingly hard to find a "typical" Negro. How old should he be? Does he live in a Northern city? Does he work at a menial job? Does he earn less than $5,000 a year? For every such Negro, an equal number can be found in contrasting circumstances.

Only a composite picture begins to convey at once the "central tendencies" and the "scatter" in Negro characteristics. Sample surveys, by interviewing representative cross-sections of the citizenry, secure just this kind of composite picture for the nation as a whole. Complications arise, however, when a segregated and disadvantaged subgroup like the Negroes in such a sample are compared with the larger majority-status sample of whites.

In the spring of 1960, the National Opinion Research Center (NORC) undertook a national survey of the United States, as part of a five-nation study of contemporary patterns of political socialization. Reported elsewhere, that project has disclosed many fascinating parallels and contrasts between American, British, German, Italian, and Mexican publics.[1] Many subsidiary problems were scarcely touched upon in their transnational study, although their data are directly relevant. One such problem area concerns the American Negro's past and potential induction into politics.

---

[1]Gabriel Almond and Sidney Verba, *The Civic Culture* (Princeton, N. J.: Princeton University Press, 1963).

TABLE 1

COMPOSITION OF NEGRO AND WHITE COUNTERPART SAMPLES
AND NATIONAL WHITE CROSS-SECTION (1960 SURVEY)[a]

(Cases)	Matched Subsamples		National White Cross-Section (870) %
	Negro (100) %	White (100) %	
1. Sex: Male	49	49	47
2. Age: Under forty	47	47	40
3. Residence: Big-city dwellers	53	53	42
4. Region: Southern	55	55	30
5. Income: Less than $5,000 a year	57	56	24
6. Rearing place: Rural or small town	50	55	54
7. Married	67	67	73
8. Dependents: Three+ children	38	38	35
9. Intend to stay in current locale	76	78	83
10. Birth region: South	89	50	27
11. Lived in current locale "always"	36	46	47
12. Occupation:			
Unskilled workers	37	30	20
Operatives and service workers	39	28	20
Craft and white collar workers	19	28	41
Business and professional	6	13	19
13. Education:			
Only some grammar	37	25	16
Full grammar (8 grades)	19	19	16
Only some high school	22	15	18
Full high school	16	24	29
Some college	6	17	21
14. Group membership:			
Belong to no organizations	41	57	43
Belong to one organization	36	23	24
Belong to several organizations	23	20	33
15. Interviewer: SES Rating: Low	48	37	15

[a]Data from NORC survey of American electorate in the spring of 1960 for Almond-Verba
five-nation project.

To investigate carefully those aspects of Negro political socialization that
seem distinctive for the ethnic group, and at the same time identify attitudes
and beliefs about political matters that equally characterize a set of whites
in comparable socioeconomic circumstances, a matching procedure was followed. One hundred interviews had been taken with Negro respondents, as
part of the NORC survey. These were now classified by region (South or
North), by urban or rural residence, by age (over and under forty), by
income levels (over and under $5,000 a year for family units), and by sex.
Invoking all five points of distinction as either-or dichotomies produced

thirty-two exclusive categories, each with two to five Negro respondents. The 870 white respondents in the national sample were then divided into the same thirty-two subsets. Random selection methods were used to choose as many white counterparts in each subset as there were Negro cases. Thus a composite group of one hundred whites was defined, deliberately matched with the Negro group on five dimensions.

In each component, hereafter called the Negro and the Counterpart groups, approximately half were male, under forty, big-city dwellers, Northerners, and earning over $5,000 a year. The other half were not. So far as the national white cross-section was concerned, proportions quite different from fifty-fifty were found on most of these same counts (Table 1).

A few other points of comparability deserve mention. In both Negro and Counterpart samples, approximately half grew up in rural, small-town, or farm environments. In both samples, two-thirds were married, and just under two-fifths had large families — three or more children. In both groups, also, at least three-fourths intended to stay in their current locality of residence.

On all of these points, moreover, the national white cross-section registered quite similar levels. Once having come to terms with a community, a young adult marries, raises a family, and intends to stay there. In all these respects, both the Negro and Counterpart groups are typically American.

Looked at from another vantage point, what sociologists call status-crystalli-zation operates in ways that are dysfunctional to the Negro's most elementary solution — to move. This is illustrated by the impossibility — using the kinds of matching procedures noted — of securing a good match between Negroes and their Counterparts on either occupational or educational counts; there were simply not enough whites in menial job categories or with limited educational backgrounds, once age, sex, region, income, and residence area dimension were stipulated.

Cumulative social constraints box in an American Negro. Unskilled or semi-skilled (76 per cent) and poorly educated (56 per cent), his problem is further exacerbated by the region and locality in which he lives and *wants to remain living.* Of the Counterpart group, only 58 per cent hold similarly low-status jobs, and only 44 per cent had comparable educational handicaps. For the larger white cross-section, these percentages dropped to 40 per cent and 32 per cent, respectively. The Counterparts are considerably closer to the Negroes on these counts than are most white Americans. Their disadvan-tages, nevertheless, are not so cumulative; they are not so "locked in."

The "first solution" — migration — is, of course, widely used by Negroes. In our sample, only half now live in the South, but nine-tenths were born there. Nearly half the Counterparts but only 36 per cent of the Negroes reported that they had always lived in their current locality.

The underlying point, however, relates to the generational aspect of the socialization phenomenon. For many Negroes, although not for all, "coming to terms" with a political world is almost irreversible. Basic life premises are involved. Some kinds of adult activity are so difficult, once foresworn, as to be impossible to undertake later in life. Some sets of events are so remote that they do not really touch one's daily life, however relevant, as news developments about public policy or group demonstrations, they may seem to the observer. Politics is the "art of the possible." And in school, on the job, in dealings with police or government officials, learning the art of the possible is not an abstract problem. Instead, it is a practical question of getting along with a specific teacher, a particular foreman, a well-known sheriff, a certain postal clerk or building inspector.

Consider the evidence in Table 2. Asked in 1960 whether government officials were likely to give them "equal treatment" in matters like housing regulations or taxes, 49 per cent of the Negro sample and 90 per cent of the white Counterpart group said yes. On a parallel question, asking about encounters with the police over traffic violations or similar minor offenses, a slightly reduced margin was found, with 60 per cent of the Negroes and 85 per cent of the Counterparts expecting "equal treatment."

Probing to learn what kind of treatment was expected, that is, how considerate and reasonable, the same patterns were found. Among both Negro and Counterpart groups, substantially fewer persons expected either bureaucrats or policemen to "give serious consideration" to their explanations. Counterparts are close to the scores registered on these counts by the larger white cross-section; the Negroes are about half again as likely to be pessimistic. This is a level of caution and distrust among Negro Americans toward representatives of the law with whom they have dealings which may well be substantially realistic.

It is when North-South contrasts and younger-older comparisons are made that the dynamics of Negro resocialization are suggested. While 60 per cent of the Northern Negroes expected equal treatment from officials in government agencies, only 40 per cent of the Southern Negroes were so optimistic. And, however equal the treatment might be, only 44 per cent of the Northern group and 18 per cent of the Southern expected agency officials to take their viewpoint seriously. Not only has the trek north to the metropolitan slums been accompanied by a measurable growth in confidence of equal official treatment, but also it represents a heightened feeling that the character of official treatment is not deaf or insensitive to their points of view.

Northern Counterpart whites, to be sure, are more confident (93 per cent) than Northern Negroes (60 per cent) of equal treatment. When the quality of that treatment is brought into question, however, they register only 49 per cent confidence of being listened to. The 44 per cent level on this point among Northern Negroes thus approaches parity.

If we look next at the parallel question of police treatment, the direction of change is just opposite. While only 47 per cent of the Northern Negroes expected equal handling by the police, 76 per cent of the Southern Negroes did. Moreover, this latter figure approaches parity with the level of confidence scored by the white Counterpart — and even the white cross-section. Only 29 per cent of the Northern Negroes expected the police to listen to their story. Here again the level of confidence registered by Southern Negroes (44 per cent) matches that found among the Southern Counterpart. In sum, in the South of 1960 a random sample, economically and socially, of Negroes and their white counterparts reported roughly equal treatment by the police in their home communities. Equally, too, they reported that treatment to be reasonable and considerate.

A glance at the generational breakdown on these points is useful. It is younger Negroes, not those over forty, whose confidence in the police had risen to a near parity with that registered by their white Counterparts. It is

TABLE 2

EXPECTED TREATMENT BY OFFICIALDOM: COMPARISONS OF NEGRO AND WHITE COUNTERPARTS, WITH REGIONAL AND GENERATIONAL BREAKDOWNS

	National White Cross-Section %	Matched Subsamples		Regional Breakdown[a]				Generational Breakdown[b]			
				Negro		White		Negro		White	
		Negro %	White %	N %	S %	N %	S %	Y %	O %	Y %	O %
1. Government officials would give equal treatment	87	49	90	60	40	93	87	57	42	89	91
2. Police would give equal treatment	88	60	85	47	76	84	87	77	47	87	83
3. Official would listen and take views seriously	50	30	45	44	18	49	42	36	25	43	47
4. Police would listen and take views seriously	58	36	48	29	44	51	44	45	28	55	42

[a]N = North,
  S = South.
[b]Y = Younger (under forty),
  O = Older.

younger Negroes, too, whose expectations of considerate attention from officials — although not equal treatment — had risen to a parity level.

The Negro Migration into American Urban Life

By 1960 half of America's Negro population lived outside the states of the old Confederacy, and nearly a third lived in the twelve largest metropolitan centers. More than half of the residents of Washington, more than a third of those in Detroit, Baltimore, and Cleveland, and easily a quarter in Chicago and Philadelphia were Negroes. In a ten-year period, a million and a half Negroes had left the South. No immigrant wave in American history was ever so large or came so quickly into the urban centers of the nation. In 1930, half of the Negro population lived in rural Southern areas and another quarter in the towns and cities of the South. By 1940, the ratio was one Northern to every two Southern Negroes. And while the proportion living in Northern localities went, decade by decade, from a quarter to a third to half, the size of the Negro population in absolute numbers had nearly doubled.

This massive influx of Negro citizens flooded the metropolitan slums with newcomers who, by reason of their opportunity-deprived upbringing, often lacked the incentives and goads to get ahead found among previous immigrant groups. Earlier ethnic minorities had come from culturally intact backgrounds in Europe which provided them with distinctive but, usually, well-defined standards of conduct for political life. The slave-period traditions for Negroes who had been field hands in the Delta, members of a domestic class in a plantation system, or personal servants for white masters in the urban South were quite disparate, but in all cases were heavily weighted in terms of imitating white patterns.

While this long spiral of migration continued, other trends were also at work. Technological advances in industry and commerce were displacing unskilled and semiskilled labor — Negro labor — at an accelerating pace. Metropolitan programs for meeting transportation, education, recreation, and housing demands were inevitably displacing families — both long-established and newly come — from blighted neighborhoods.

Table 3 provides some glimpse of the magnitudes involved in the attitudinal reorientation of Negroes toward local government. In 1960, asked how important was its impact on their daily lives, nearly the same proportion — one-third — of Negroes and whites felt that the answer was "great impact." Among Northerners, whites (41 per cent) were somewhat more inclined to this view than Negroes (29 per cent).

Asked to evaluate the contribution of local government, only 50 per cent of the Negroes, compared with 72 per cent of their Counterparts, felt it had generally been helpful in their lives. In the North, however, the 60 per cent scored by Negroes was rather close to the Counterpart figure of 69 per cent. On the other hand, only 42 per cent of the Southern Negroes made this evaluation, while 75 per cent of their white Counterparts did so. When generations are compared, the margin by which whites make more favorable evaluations is similar for younger and older sets.

Those interviewed were asked to consider what could be done to prevent the village or city council from adopting a regulation which "you considered very unjust or harmful." For the national white cross-section, only 24 per cent felt it was almost impossible for them to change a bad local ordinance. Somewhat more (31 per cent) of the Counterpart whites and fully 38 per cent of the Negroes felt this way. Asked whether they had, in fact, ever tried, 70 per cent of the national cross-section of whites and 73 per cent of the Counterpart whites admitted never having done so, but 86 per cent of the Negroes had never tried.

When attention is given to the regional and age breakdowns, again the attitudinal transformation can begin to be seen. Not alienation, but heightened involvement and substantial realism in the choice of methods and targets seem to be disclosed. While fully 53 per cent of the Southern Negroes felt that changing a bad local law was virtually impossible, only 20 per cent of the Northern Negroes did so — a figure rather similar to that of Counterpart whites. The contrast in optimism was correspondingly great also between younger and older Negroes, with "virtually impossible" being the reaction of 28 per cent and 47 per cent, respectively, a substantially greater age difference than registered by white Counterparts.

TABLE 3

EXPECTATIONS ABOUT LOCAL GOVERNMENT: COMPARISONS OF NEGRO AND WHITE COUNTERPARTS, WITH REGIONAL AND GENERATIONAL BREAKDOWNS

	National White Cross-Section %	Matched Subsamples		Regional Breakdown[a]				Generational Breakdown[b]			
				Negro		White		Negro		White	
		Negro %	White %	N %	S %	N %	S %	Y %	O %	Y %	O %
1. Local government has "great impact" on daily lives	35	31	37	29	33	40	35	36	26	38	36
2. Local-government actions are usually helpful	71	50	72	60	42	69	75	55	45	77	68
3. It is almost impossible to change a bad local regulation by own efforts	24	38	31	20	53	36	27	28	47	26	36
4. Very unlikely to try to change bad local regulation	26	43	38	31	53	50	27	34	51	26	49
5. Never have tried to influence local policy decision	70	86	73	76	95	76	71	89	83	68	77

[a]N = North,
  S = South.
[b]Y = Younger (under forty),
  O = Older.

As to whether they, personally, would actively try to change a bad local law if the occasion arose, sharp contrasts are found between North and South. More than half of the Southern Negroes felt it was unlikely they would ever try; only 27 per cent of Southern Counterparts were so passive. Conversely, only 31 per cent of the Northern Negroes felt they would never try to influence such a matter, but 50 per cent of the Northern Counterparts admitted their probable inaction. For both Negroes and Counterpart whites, the younger age groups showed markedly greater propensities toward local political agitation. And when the question was posed, had any actual attempt to influence a local ordinance issue ever been made, 95 per cent of the Southern Negroes said "never." On the same question, only 76 per cent of the Northern Negroes had ever tried, the same proportion as for Northern Counterparts.

The Locally Circumscribed Political World of American Negroes

In the study of American race relations today, intellectuals tend to assume that Negroes all along have felt oppressed and constrained at the mold of second-class citizenship, in 1895 as much as 1935 or 1965. Yet, little is known about their political socialization patterns, and a few cautionary points are pertinent. Ordinary Negroes lived mostly in the South. About 1890, open efforts began to disfranchise Negro voters and to impose Jim Crow circumscriptions with the force of law on Negro use of public facilities. By 1910 the political rules had been reformulated; the Supreme Court's "separate but equal" doctrine helped to quiet public concern about what was happening, while political realities ensured a steady deterioration in the public services and accommodations available in their home communities to Negroes. Incidental to this triumph of nasty-mindedness, much race hatred was preached and countenanced, apparently in part to reassure the poor whites that they were not the next target.

Frederick Douglass, the most militant national Negro leader, fought in vain after 1880 against the trend to disengage all national machinery capable of aiding the Negro. After his death in 1894, others founded the NAACP and the Urban League, conceived as instruments for rallying the racial elite, of training the "Talented Tenth" as race spokesmen and cadres for future struggles, of pursuing political goals not in political arenas but in academic, philanthropic, religious, and journalistic modes. Themselves the products of a selective social mobility process within the Negro world, most of the Negro publicists, lawyers, academics, and others on the national scene struggled to get and to keep open elite communication lines. Their efforts reflected a middle-class presumption that the Negro masses, when mobilized, would accept their lead. There is dignity and restraint, rather than anger and impatience, in the formulation of tasks confronting the NAACP by the militant leader, W. E. B. DuBois: "By every civilized and peaceful method, we must strive for the rights which the world accords to men."[2]

Nationally, the "accommodationist" style of Negro leadership was set by Booker T. Washington. The head of Tuskegee was a man of humble origins, a self-made man who had met the world on its own terms. He was realistic. Negroes lacked the skills and knowledge to succeed economically; education was the crucial resource needed, and education was provided by local governing bodies; Southern whites would only provide that crucial resource if the "products" were reliably docile.

Just when the use of governmental machinery to enforce disadvantages on the Negro was at its peak, Washington counselled submission. Work hard, in the service of the community, and you will become accepted in proper time. His advice and example were for Negroes to give up their interest in political power as a way of securing their rights. Industrial education and an appropriate station in the emerging industrial work of twentieth-century America, were the objectives he used.

De facto segregation in the North was not implemented by state laws and local ordinances as in the South; nor were prejudices so openly proclaimed by militant whites. But the Northern reception system has been a pale facsimile of its Southern prototype in many ways, and especially at the local community level.

Until the postwar years it can be argued that, North and South alike, Negro adults became politically socialized almost exclusively to the circumscriptions and indirect channels of the localities in which they lived. It was irrelevant to speak of national or even state-bestowed citizen status for Negro Americans. In the outlook of educated Negro elite figures, no doubt, an awareness of the life in the national and state superstructure of American politics existed. At the same time, it is quite understandable that most events occurring in the central institutional complex of American democracy would not touch the ordinary Negro American emotionally, nor arouse desires to participate. And for the Negro poor, during this whole century of segregation and lower-caste treatment, politics was white man's business; even in the local arenas of political life Negroes often could secure no electoral footing. The ambit of Negro influence was thus severely limited; it took only a primer to learn the rules of how to behave. Compliance with imposed norms was rudimentary but necessary, even when fellow-Negroes called it "Toming."

Myrdal's massive codification in 1942 of the circumstances of Negro life informs us about the extent to which Negroes of that and previous gener-

---

[2]Quoted in Charles E. Silberman, *Crisis in Black and White* (New York: Random House, 1964), p. 129.

ations were a minority harder than Italians, Poles, or Jews to assimilate.[3] His study stressed themes that continue to preoccupy discussion today. Myrdal believed that Negroes were "exaggerated Americans," who believed in the American Creed more passionately than whites, and who should exploit their common bonds of belief with white Americans more effectively. It would not be possible for white Americans to sustain their corporate belief system unless those who asked their due were granted it, once heard. Negroes had not strenuously asked their due; avoiding scenes and temporizing had been the style.

The Negro community was dependent on the white community; whites were committeed to their egalitarian, optimistic, democratic creed, as were the Negroes; by playing upon the beliefs of whites, Negroes could gain their objectives.

Did Negroes consciously or persistently aspire to full citizenship? Had they been politically socialized to want citizen status, but somewhat left untutored in how to manipulate and persuade whites to grant them what was due?

Or had they undergone a harsher socialization process, one which left them not prepared to believe that the American political system, for all its protestations, would support them in their aspirations?

The argument here is *not* that Negroes were passive, apathetic, and for generations unable to protest effectively because they had become disenchanted with the American Creed — alienated from American society. Probably more commonly, Negro adults had never allowed themselves to become enchanted with "democracy" in the first place, so far as their own community and private lives went. Traditionally, Negro civic leaders occupying symbolic positions of respect were "tapped" by leaders in the white community as contact points. The influence of such "anointed" figures often depended more on their near-monopoly over liaison channels to the all-important white community's decision-makers than on any spontaneous following within the Negro community which they might have generated. Undertakers, insurance men, bankers, teachers, a few professional men — above all, ministers of Negro churches: these were the men who traditionally were treated as spokesmen for their local Negro communities. Accommodationist, conservative, dignified, personally successful men: they have been for more than half a century the prime models for Negro children asking to be shown *local* "men of influence."[4]

[3]Gunnar Myrdal, *An American Dilemma* (New York: Harper & Brothers, 1944).

[4]See Silberman, *op. cit.,* chap. vii. Also M. Elaine Burgess, *Negro Leadership in a Southern City* (Chapel Hill: University of North Carolina Press, 1962); E. F. Frazier, *The Negro in the United States* (New York: The MacMillan Company, 1949), and G. Franklin Edwards, *The Negro Professional Class* (Glencoe, Ill.: Free Press, 1959).

With the mobilization of electoral strength, the decline of Negro ministers and leaders of fraternal organizations as sources for community leadership — whether in the liaison or symbolic sense — has steadily been taking place in Southern localities. "Street lights, sidewalks, and paved streets are more common in communities where Negroes vote in substantial numbers. Such things as Negro civic centers, bandshells, playgrounds, libraries, hospital annexes, and even swimming pools are found in increasing numbers."[5]

The dynamics of political *rapprochement* in Louisiana communities, according to Fenton and Vines, have occasionally involved an alliance of "shady white and underdog Negro" elements. Local politics centers around the sheriff's office. If a sheriff permits gambling, he is charged with corruption by middle-class residents of the community; to offset their electoral threat, the sheriff in such instances has catered to the marginal Negro vote for support. "The reward . . . is respect from the politicians and attendance at Negro political meetings, cessation of police brutality, and promises made and often kept regarding such matters as street improvements and better school facilities."[6]

Thus in Southern communities where voter registration has progressed to a point sufficient to create a substantial potential bloc, a new, self-taught, and white-tutored breed of professional Negro politicians has begun to emerge. Specifically equipped with the organizing and campaigning skills appropriate to electoral politics, these new political journeymen bargain with some effectiveness among the rival white politicians anxious for their vote.

In Northern metropolitan centers, too, professional Negro politicians have emerged, men who work inside the party machine dominating their city, men who accept the terms of political life laid down by white counterparts who are scarcely less ethnic-minded — Irish, Italian, Polish, Jewish, and Puerto Rican "spokesmen" also judged by their readiness and reasonableness in making bargains, and by their ability to deliver votes as promised. Considerable variations remain, of course, in style, in methods used, and in results obtained.[7] In Chicago, Dawson's political strength within the Democratic machine, like that of other ethnic politicians, has depended on the historical "fit" between ward boundaries and Negro ghetto limits. Working in a solidly Negro area, he deals in tangible and divisible benefits, few of which pose clear moral questions. In New York City, on the other hand, Powell's role is also system-specific, but here a much weaker and less unified

---

[5]H. D. Price, "The Negro and Florida Politics, 1944-1954," *Journal of Politics* (May 1955).

[6]J. H. Fenton and K. N. Vines, "Negro Registration in Louisiana," *American Political Science Review* (September 1957).

[7]See James Q. Wilson, *Negro Politics* (Glencoe, Ill.: Free Press, 1960) for a comparative inquiry which develops these points systematically.

alliance of politicians runs the dominant party apparatus. There is therefore scope for Powell's agitational style. He deals in moral questions, in intangible ideals and indivisible causes which must not be compromised. His dramatic skills link these to his personal leadership. Dr. Kenneth B. Clark, himself an occasional rival of Powell in Harlem, has this to say:

> In his flamboyant personal behavior, Powell has been to the Negroes a symbol of all that life has denied them. . . . The Negro masses do not see Powell as amoral but as defiantly honest in his protest against the myths and hypocrisies of racism. . . . He is important precisely because he is himself a caricature, a burlesque of the personal exploitation of power.[8]

The growth of militancy among Negroes — with the decline of "accommodation" — in the modal leadership style is a double-edged blade. On the one hand, it reflects a shift away from the habit of evaluating their social position primarily within the nonpolitical, "intramural" range of Negro rivals, and a shift toward evaluating it instead by explicit comparison to a counterpart group — their opposite numbers in the white middle class.[9] On the other hand, it is a behavior pattern which, once initiated, generates its own reputation. It is far more conspicuous than the older pattern of accommodationist leadership, and it is reinforced powerfully by the way in which other Negroes, both peers and elders, respond by endorsing and accepting it. The "accommodating" style is established by a sequence of occasions when aggressive confrontations were avoided; the "militant" style is more rhetorical, and tends to be *predicted* on the basis of even a very small set of occasions when aggressive leadership options are used. Negro leaders drift into the former; they assert the latter kind of role.[10]

The Skills and Habits of Citizenship

Learning about political life, then, is not a simple, static, or finished process. Instead, it is highly complex; it is dynamic and changing; and at best, it is imperfectly realized. Many Negro adults never become very effective at organizing and improving their daily lives. How much less likely that the methods used to socialize them to onerous predetermined political rules and arrangements should regularly be effective! Indeed, if Negroes had

---

[8]K. B. Clark, *Dark Ghetto* (New York: Harper & Row, 1965), p. 210.
[9]Ruth Searles and J. A. Williams, Jr., "Negro College Students' Participation in Sit-Ins," *Social Forces,* 40 (1962), pp. 215-220.
[10]See the insightful participant-observer case study by Allan P. Sindler, "Youth and the American Negro Protest Movement," prepared for the 1964 International Political Science Association Meetings in Geneva, Switzerland.

internalized the American dream and seriously wanted it for themselves, it is hard to believe they would not long since have been radically disenchanted and militantly alienated. Instead, it is only in recent years that a new generation of Negro youths begins to think seriously about claiming their birthrights.

In 1910, for a young Negro to study the program of the then-fledgling NAACP was not to review an impressive sequence of judicial victories, as the task is for his 1965 counterpart. The 1910 program was a recital of watered-down hopes and carefully worded aims. Even so, Booker T. Washington and William E. B. DuBois debated the proper goals and strategy for Negroes in polemical terms that made the former's call for self-improvement seem at odds with the latter's demand for Negro civil rights at once.

Today, also, there are rivalries and polemics among Negro leaders on the national scene, conflicts brought home to Negro citizens by television and radio rather than in exclusively Negro news media. But perhaps there is now a stronger sense of the need for a division of labor: the need for militant direct action protests, to arouse the Negro poor from apathy and self-hate, and the simultaneous need for persistent integrative efforts — through the courts, in union-management bargaining and in government personnel practices, in community service organizations, and through partisan political activities. Not only the symbolic struggles that eventuate in decisions to desegregate a school, permit voter registration, make public accommodations equally accessible, or create job opportunities, but also the practical tasks of implementing and consolidating each such victory are coming to be seen by the young Negro of 1965 as part of the political world with which he must come to terms.[11]

But what does it mean to "come to terms"? One view expects each generation to produce a distinctive style, seizing new opportunities which older generations have yielded or neglected. Another view, not necessarily incompatible with the first, expects realism. Systematic adjustment to changing circumstances seems mostly to come from the older people, while youth refuse to come to terms and instead appear idealistic and unreasonable.

Not many studies of political socialization have yet been made, of Negroes or any other grouping. We have examined some systematic evidence about the attitudes and self-conceptions held by adult Negroes and their white Counterparts concerning American politics. But we know little of how those notions were first acquired, when today's adults were growing up and were gradually coming to understand their place in a white democracy.

---

[11]See the sympathetic sketches by Howard Zinn, *SNCC: The New Abolitionists* (Boston: Beacon Press, 1964) and the careful case study of biracial co-operation and protest activities in a Southern community by Lewis Killian and Charles Gregg, *Racial Crisis in America* (Englewood Cliffs, N. J.: Prentice-Hall, 1964).

Neither for Negroes nor for other categories do we know much about the differentiation and attenuation of childhood attitudes and beliefs. Yet adults have to behave in response to situational insights, and adults have to acquire the experience and skills as well as the nerve and desire to mount fresh assaults on complacency and indifference.

Memorable experiences, for example, whether they arise in the midst of electoral campaigns, in moments of public crisis, or in the workaday context of civic co-operation, are hard to plan ahead of time. They tend to be memorable because of accidental and unexpected developments. The Montgomery bus boycott of 1955 began spontaneously when a weary Negro seamstress refused to yield her seat to a white. For more than a year, 17,000 Negroes refused to ride, cutting the bus line's patronage to a fourth of normal. From such unplanned rejection of roles and defiance of norms, in the ten subsequent years, boycotting has become a formidable political weapon for American Negroes. With notice spread by word of mouth or from the pulpits of Negro churches, the boycott has provided a community-level focus and has helped to create leadership-communication networks that are transforming Northern metropolitan slum areas as well as Southern colored quarters. In 1963, a third of a national cross-section of Negroes and more than two-thirds of a panel of Negro leaders reported that they had boycotted certain stores in their local communities.[12]

The syndrome of dejection, self-contempt, a sense of worthlessness, and hopelessness is what Kardiner and Ovesey called the Negro's "mark of oppression." It has been repeatedly noted in studies since their work dealing with Negro psychological adjustment problems.[13] The problems of Negro personality formation are often traced to the "identity crises" through which Negro children perforce must pass: the color-bias they develop even in pre-school play, often linked with a tense reluctance to acknowledge that they are Negro; the postpuberty estrangement of Negro youths from their white playmates, enforced by white parental racist fears of miscegenation; in young adulthood, too, after the relatively sheltered years of school and familiar neighborhood, "the full awareness of his social devaluation in the larger society" can cause severe emotional distress.[14]

Little is known about how the emotional wellsprings of love and hate, hunger and vitality are linked persistently to a set of socially "given" goals and goads. The levels of need achievement among Negroes vary substantially,

---

[12]William Brink and Louis Harris, *The Negro Revolution in America* (New York: Simon & Schuster, 1964), p. 203.
[13]A. Kardiner and L. Ovesey, *The Mark of Oppression* (1951); see also the comprehensive survey by Thomas F. Pettigrew, *A Profile of the Negro American* (Princeton, N. J.: D. Van Nostrand, 1964).
[14]*Op. cit.,* p. 8.

perhaps as much as among whites, although the standards of behavior, life-plans, and career objectives are manifestly different in the ghetto subculture into which most Negroes are born and in the American society which isolates them from awareness of those norms and denies them the rewards of compliance with those norms.

It is in interracial dyadic relationships that Negroes have usually learned manipulative strategies, situational tactics, and bargaining ploys. It has been in response to the emotional strain of interracial contacts that Negroes have generated double standards of fair play, humor, and even relaxation.

Almost every Negro adult — not only his organizational leaders — has been schooled in ways to get along in superior-subordinate relationships. Moreover, the picture he has acquired very commonly puts him in the latter role. The extent to which the mental outlook of oppressed people tends toward fantasies, childlike incompetence, and passive dependence is hard to measure; available evidence suggests that a pervasive pattern of such behavior has historically laid its imprint on Negro America.

But when people acquire skills and sensitivities in how to sense the mood of superiors, how to parlay advantages, how to conceal their emotions, how to accomplish a thousand political artifices, they often find such assets portable to new circumstances and applicable in quite unexpected situations. American Negroes learned these skills under persistent conditions of duress. Perhaps many never have mastered techniques that could be used on anyone but a white superior; many have probably repressed all sensitivities to similar opportunities in intraracial organizational relations. Even so, given this kind of schooling, American Negroes must often make very acute political followers, able to appreciate very well the difference between a leader's pretensions and his actual performances.

The Negro revolution in America has been manifest in headlines and news bulletins for more than ten years. It is tempting to speculate about the ways in which scenes of militant direct action, showing parental courage and group discipline in the face of mindless hatred, affect young Negro children today — in the choice of their ego ideals, in the games they play, the stories they read, the fantasies they have, the careers they want, the nightmares they endure, and in their heightened awareness of political rules and possibilities, now that such awareness carries an instrumental rather than an academic tag.

There is perhaps no single event that marks the watershed in American race relations better than the 1954 Supreme Court decision calling for "all deliberate speed" in desegregating the nation's schools. Yet it was ten years later, in the Birmingham riots of 1964, before the Negro poor entered the protest movement:

The riots . . . were waged not by the disciplined cadres of relatively well-educated "middle-class" Negroes but by the apathetic poor who had previously remained completely on the outside, and whose potential for violence frightened Rev. Martin Luther King's lieutenants as much as the whites.[15]

Moreover, the nonviolent direct action methods of the new protest groups — CORE, SCLC, SNCC — represent also only part of a ten-year prelude to the far more fundamental revolution that is coming in the politics of neighborhoods and communities, of school districts and residential blocks, a revolution that began in scattered localities during the 1950's and received large financial and directional support from the 1964 Civil Rights Act and the resultant antipoverty program of the Office of Economic Opportunity. In states of the South as well as of the North, and at county and municipal levels, biracial area human resources councils are being formed, to co-ordinate and sponsor programs for community action, establish and run youth job corps and urban centers, and encourage private nonprofit groups and universities to contribute to neighborhood improvement and adult education projects.

The importance of these experiences, both to acquire new skills and play new roles in civic affairs, can scarcely be overestimated. The full, genuine, and mundane "political resocialization" of American Negro citizens awaits the proliferation of such institutional scaffolding for public-spirited action.

---

[15]Silberman, *op. cit.*, p. 143.

The Strategy of Protest:
Problems of Negro Civic Action

James Q. Wilson

The logical and empirical elements of bargaining are receiving increased attention as the effort proceeds to fashion an analytical tool useful for better understanding the nature of controversy. In many of these discussions, the focus has been on those who enter into the bargaining relationship out of either necessity or hope of gain (4, 9). The notion of bargaining is simplified if one assumes that the need for or desirability of bargaining is given. This is the case when two businessmen, for example, seek goals which are partially incompatible but individually attractive. Each stands to gain if his end can be realized, and to realize it he must deal with the other fellow. There is, in short, an inducement for each to bargain.

Equally interesting is the situation in which one party seeks a goal which it can realize without obtaining concessions from a second party. The second party opposes the realization of that goal, but has nothing which the first party needs or wants, and hence finds it difficult to place itself in a position in which the first party must bargain. This might be called the problem of

Reprinted from *Journal of Conflict Resolution*, Vol. V, (September 1961), pp. 291-303 with permission of the publisher and the author. Copyright 1961 by the University of Michigan.

the powerless. It arises, for example, when a disfranchised group seeks a law giving it the right to vote but, lacking the vote, has difficulty recruiting lawmakers who will support its cause. The most important group today which must act from a position of near powerlessness is the Negro. This article will (a) sketch some of the logical elements involved in attempts by the powerless to wield power, (b) relate these elements to certain empirical factors characteristic of the Negro in large Northern cities, and (c) describe the consequences of this situation as revealed by issues implicating Negro interests which were studied in Chicago.

Bargaining

By *bargaining,* I shall mean any situation in which two or more parties seek conflicting ends through the exchange of compensations. The ends must not be wholly incompatible (if they were, bargaining would be impossible) nor need the compensations be tangible. Intangible compensations are of importance as well. Bargaining will be distinguished from those cases in which one party seeks its ends by simply persuading the other party to accede by argument or rhetoric. It will also exclude cases of compulsion, in which one party endeavors to use physical force on a second party or so rearranges his situation that literally no alternative is open to him other than the one desired by the first party. The essential element in bargaining is that concessions are rewarded. The task is to find a mutually agreeable ratio for the exchange of those rewards.

These rewards may be either positive or negative. Banfield distinguishes between positive and negative inducements by noting that a *positive* inducement is given "if action in accordance with A's intention is made absolutely more attractive to B . . . and not because other possibilities have been made less desirable." In contrast, a *negative* inducement is given "if action in accordance with A's intention, although no more attractive absolutely than before the change was made, is nevertheless more attractive relative to the other possibilities that now exist" (1, 2). All other courses of action are made more disadvantageous than the desired course, which is also somewhat disadvantageous.

Certain individuals and groups may wish to bargain, but they may lack the resources to do so — i.e., they may lack any stock of inducements (positive or negative) which they can use to influence other parties to act in accordance with at least *some* of their intentions. Others feel no need to bargain with these people. The question then becomes, how such a group (which I shall call the "excluded" group) can acquire a supply of compensations such that others will want to bargain. In the typical case, the excluded group is separated from others by differences in status, class, caste, or authority, and thus neither persuasion nor compulsion is available as a tactic of influence. Bargaining is not available because the excluded group has nothing the others desire, either in relation to the issue in point or to any future issue which might arise.

It is, of course, not sufficient that the excluded group have some compensations. The leaders of that group — the would-be bargainers — must show that they in fact control the resources and can "deliver" if they commit themselves. Negroes, for example, may represent customers or voters to businessmen and politicians, but if Negro leaders cannot alter the buying habits or switch the votes of their followers, the potential resources are useless. At this point, deception may become important. To the extent that Negro leaders are able to bargain at all, it is frequently a result of ignorance (or at least imperfect information) on the part of those with whom they are dealing. Since excluded groups (like Negroes) are often excluded precisely because of great status and class gaps, and because these gaps work to reduce information which each party has about the other, ignorance and deception can become very important factors in the strategy of Negro leadership.

Deception is of limited value, however, since it is easily exposed when the bargain is consummated. (It is nonetheless remarkable, the extent to which influence continues to be imputed to leaders of excluded groups even after their inability to deliver has been revealed. This may be a function of uncertainty as to their influence in future cases or a doubt as to whether the revealed failure was a valid test.)

Protest

The problem of many excluded groups is to create or assemble the resources for bargaining. Many often select a strategy of protest. *Protest* is distinguished from bargaining by the exclusive use of negative inducements (threats) that rely, for their effect, on sanctions which require *mass* action or response. Excluded groups often make up in number what they lack in resources, or their cause finds sympathizers among relatively large numbers of other groups. Bargaining might (as noted above) involve the use of negative inducements as compensation — i.e., a promise by one party *not* to act in a certain manner can be, relatively, a reward for the other party. This bargaining situation is based on protest only when these threats rely, for their effect, on the possibility of a mass response. The party against which the protest is directed values something which the excluded group can place in jeopardy. This could range from a certain reputation (which could be harmed by unfavorable publicity) to a business (which could be hurt by a boycott) and would include, in some cases, a desire to further some civic program without controversy.

There are various forms of protest action: verbal, physical, economic, and political. *Verbal* protest would include issuing denunciatory statements, mounting a campaign of adverse publicity, submitting petitions and memorials, holding mass meetings, and sending deputations to confront the other party. *Physical* protest would include picketing, sit-down strikes (as in places of business), "marches" (as the famous "March on Washington Movement" of 1940-41 [5]), and (in the extreme case) violence (as in the Harlem race riots of the 1930's and later, which, in contrast with many riots in other places, were often initiated by Negroes). *Economic* protest characteristically involves a boycott or threat of a boycott (as in the "Buy Black" and "Don't Buy Where You Can't Work" campaigns in New York and Chicago in the 1930's) or a strike. *Political* protest requires voting reprisals, taken either by the excluded group or others who are sympathetic to its cause.

The strategy of protest requires more than the possibility of mass action, however. First, there must be an agreed-upon goal on behalf of which mass action can be mobilized. Such goals may be either specific or general, defensive or assertive, welfare or status. The precise nature of the goal sought has important consequences for the kinds of incentives which can be distributed to generate and sustain mass action. A *specific* goal is more typical of successful protest (i.e., protest which in fact involved overt mass action and which thus created a situation with which other parties had to deal in some measure). The March on Washington Movement had the specific goal of securing the adoption of a fair employment practices law (or, failing that, an executive order to the same effect). The student sit-down strikes had the specific goal of inducing white proprietors to serve Negroes when seated at luncheon counters. Economic boycotts have the specific goal of inducing businessmen to hire Negroes or offer for sale products manufactured by companies which hire Negroes. At the same time, the specific goal is always related to a general, more vague principle. Each specific goal is the immediately sought application of some *general* notion concerning equality, opportunity, or status. This is essential, inasmuch as such principles are an essential incentive with which to mobilize large numbers of contributors to the protest action. Few will benefit personally from the attainment of the specific goal; therefore, general reasons of an ethical character must be offered to attract the support of the many.

The offering of general reasons for specific goals is an important constraint on the leaders of protest movements. It usually means that the specific goal is endowed with a moral or sacrosanct quality which renders it difficult to compromise. This suggests that the discretion of the protest leader to bargain after he has acquired the resources with *which* to bargain is severely limited by the means he was forced to employ in order to create those resources. Getting into a bargaining relationship for a leader of an excluded group often means, therefore, a reduction in his ultimate ability to bargain. This was revealed in the case of the Negro leader, A. Phillip Randolph, who organized the March on Washington Movement. He was heavily criticized by many Negro followers when the actual march was called off because President Roosevelt issued an executive order creating an FEPC. Some demands were made that the march be carried on for broader goals, demands which Randolph had to resist (5).

Goals may be either defensive or assertive. The excluded group may be seeking to defend itself against some maltreatment or injustice by seeking to block changes in the status quo (such as a land clearance project) or by demanding a redress of grievances (such as police brutality or racial violence). It may assert certain goals, such as a demand for certain jobs, public services, housing, an improvement in the quality of public facilities, or the passage of a law which will alter the status quo in favor of the excluded group.

Goals may involve either the welfare or the status of the group. Welfare goals refer to the direct, tangible improvement in the lot of the group or its members through providing some job, service, facility, or revenue. Status goals imply the elimination of barriers, the creation of opportunities which members of the group may or may not take advantage of. The choice between improving the quality of Negro schools and integrating all-white schools is an example.

A second requisite exists for protest action. There must be an identifiable group or agency or firm which is capable of granting the end sought. There must, in a sense, be not only a specific goal, but a specific *target*. An opportunity for bargaining cannot be created when the target of protest action does not have it in its power to respond to the demands made. A secondary relationship might, of course, be found. Demands might be made by A upon B through a protest strategy even though B cannot satisfy these demands. It may nonetheless be a valuable strategy if C can grant these demands and C is in a bargaining relationship with B. B, in effect, can be compelled to become an intermediary and extract concessions from C (on the basis of an exchange of rewards which B and C value) which are then made available to A.

The target of protest action must not only be capable of responding; there must be some likelihood that he can be induced to respond. Responses to protest can be conceived of as a weighing of the probable costs of enduring the protest against the probable costs of making the concessions. The cost of being the target of protest action depends on the situation. For government officials and politicians (at least in the North) it *may* mean the loss of votes from Negroes or from sympathetic whites, criticism by articulate elements in the community, adverse effects on the opinion of foreign allies, and so on. For private parties (businessmen, unions, etc.) the costs would involve a deterioration in public relations, a possible loss of business, a fear of government intervention, a loss of manpower, and the exposure to controversy and unpleasantness. (It should be counted as a gain for protest that it might enable some parties to implement goals they feel *ought* to be realized with the rationale that they were "compelled" to do it and hence should not be criticized by opponents of the protest group.)

Limits of Negro Protest

It is clear to anyone who has investigated the matter even casually that there is today among Negroes, in both North and South, a quickened sense of mission and a rising level of expectations. More and more Negroes are expressing a deep discontent with their lot as individuals and as a group. The voices advocating "gradualism" and unhurried change have become fewer and fewer (even though the opinions behind these voices have not, in many cases, been altered). As the Negro has progressed, he has come to expect more and more in terms of equal treatment and improved conditions. Yet for all this heightened sense of urgency, relatively little in the way of Negro protest activity seems to occur. Negro organizations such as the NAACP continue to press legal suits seeking an expansion of opportunity, while other organizations, such as the Urban League, endeavor to extract concessions by persuasion, re-education, and the dissemination of information. But few protest actions (in the sense in which I have been using the word) are evident. Paradoxically, it would seem that more protest movements are found today among Negroes in the South than in the North. The Montgomery bus boycott, the student sit-down strikes, and other incidents are without parallel in Chicago, Detroit, Los Angeles, and St. Louis. Sporadic outbursts occur in New York, but they seem to lack clear direction and firm leadership.

This situation offers an opportunity to apply an analysis of protest strategy to an empirical situation to see if reasons can be found to account for the relatively low level of organized protest among Northern Negroes. To begin, it is apparent that an improvement in the leadership skills and organizational resources of the Negro has occurred at a time when the goals of Negro public life have become less clear and the targets have become more uncertain. In Northern cities in the past, and in the South today, most Negro community goals were specific, defensive, and of a welfare character. The Negro community responded to what were regarded as manifest injustices and public outrages. Anti-Negro violence, police oppression, the denial of ordinary public services, and other oppressions represented specific causes. They tended to unify the Negro community. Few could doubt that they were injustices. They touched, in a visible, direct, and personal manner the lives of identifiable individuals. Verbal forms of protest were often effective in branding the injustice and, given its character, the offense was usually condemned by the norms of the community. Newspapers and civic groups could not defend such offenses. Common decency seemed to demand a redress, and by simply calling attention to it in a forceful manner, some corrective action could be had — or at least (and this is what is important in this paper) responsible officials could be induced to deal in some manner with the situation. They could not easily avoid bargaining. They sought compensation — the prevention or cessation of criticism from the spokesmen for the community's mores. In an extreme case (such as a race riot), Negroes might organize(as they did on one occasion in Chicago) a picket line around the City Hall in order to acquire bargaining resources in dealing with the police commissioner and the mayor.

Today, the ends which are receiving the greatest attention are those which are often general, assertive, and of a status character. Negroes seek changes in the status quo in their favor in the fields of housing and employment. The problems which are of most concern and which are frequently spoken of as appropriate issues for protest action involve an uncertainty as to specific goals. Nowhere is this more evident than in the field of housing. There is disagreement among influential Negroes as to the source of the problem, what ought to be done about it, and what can be done under the circumstances (12). There is considerable uncertainty as to what Negroes should protest *for* — liberalized mortgage requirements, more police protection in changing neighborhoods, the ending of restrictive real estate practices, legislation barring discrimination in sales and rentals, or some combination of all. Further, anti-Negro practices in real estate do not violate clear community norms as does violence or manifest oppression. In the great majority of cases, no moral stigma attaches to the man who refuses to sell his home to a Negro. The exposure of such acts, by public protest, rarely carries with it any effective sanction. Whites may grant that Negroes have a moral right to housing, but they usually insist with equal conviction that whites have a right to preserve the character of their neighborhoods.

Second, the targets of protest action have become unclear or ambiguous. In issues where the exercise of specific public powers or the making of definite private decisions were clearly adapted to the ends sought, the target was obvious. The police could be asked for protection, the hotel required to admit Negro guests, the bus line requested to hire Negro drivers, or the legislature asked to pass a law. As the goals of protest action become broader and more general, the targets of that action become similarly diffuse.

What is the target for protests aimed at "equal opportunity in housing?" One cannot picket, or boycott, or send deputations to all the real estate brokers, all the mortgage bankers, all the neighborhood improvement associations, or all the community newspapers. If one selects a single target — one house or one block in a certain neighborhood — one *may* gain concessions, but these concessions will be limited to the specific case and will represent no change in policy. Discriminatory practices in housing, in brief, are not the product of public or private decisions by some identifiable decision-maker. They are the result of an infinite number of social choices made by tens of thousands of home owners, landlords, realtors, bankers, loan officers, community groups, and individuals. Some practices undoubtedly can be curbed by legislation, but since the housing market involves many forces beyond legislative control (or any centralized control), laws would be of limited value. This is particularly the case if the goal is *integrated* housing and not simply *more* housing for Negroes. Individuals can be compelled to show that a refusal to sell to a Negro is not based on racial grounds, but they cannot be compelled to remain in the neighborhood and live side-by-side with the Negro.

Third, some of the goals now being sought by Negroes are least applicable to those groups of Negroes most suited to protest action. Protest action involving such tactics as mass meetings, picketing, boycotts, and strikes rarely find enthusiastic participants among upper-income and higher-status individuals. Such strategies often require recruiting, through intangible appeals, lower-income, lower-status groups that do not consider mass action beneath their dignity. This was not crucially important when the Negro community could respond, with near-unanimity, to indisputable outrages — when, in short, they sought specific, defensive, welfare ends. Many of the goals being sought today, such as access to desirable housing in middle- and upper-income neighborhoods and employment in supervisory, skilled, or professional jobs, do not involve rewards for groups not equipped, by income, training, or disposition, to avail themselves of such opportunities. Even when the goal can be made specific, it becomes difficult to mobilize the masses when (a) the end sought clearly benefits, at least immediately, only middle- and upper-class Negroes and (b) no general, principled rationale can be developed which will relate the specific goal to the aspirations or needs of the rank-and-file. Indeed, as some recent cases suggest, there may be an actual conflict of ends between upper-status Negroes who seek access for their children to desirable white schools with high-quality instruction and the possibility of integrated living and, on the other hand, lower-status Negro parents who desire, simply, more schools and teachers even if they are all-Negro (6, 8).

Fourth, many specific goals toward which action can be directed occur in situations that place a negative value on protest. For example, when (as happened in Chicago recently) a builder proposes constructing a tract of homes in a white community which will be sold to whites and Negroes on a non-discriminatory basis, an intense controversy is immediately precipitated. Whites offer resistance. A specific issue is at stake — will or will not the houses be built. In this case, Negro protest organizations often feel, with some justification, that mounting a protest campaign against the whites would only aggravate the situation and reduce the likelihood of getting the homes built by giving credence to white fears that the integrated homes are part of a "conspiracy" created by the NAACP and other Negro organizations to "force" Negroes into white areas. Similar problems arise when a single Negro family attempts to buy and occupy a home in a white neighborhood. Often public officials come to the conclusion that the family's chances of establishing itself are reduced if Negro protest is organized in its behalf. Inducing whites to accept one Negro family is difficult; inducing them to accept a family which the whites believe was "planted" by the NAACP and is, thus, the vanguard of a host of Negro families is much more difficult. To be sure, there are some Negro leaders who seize upon such explanations as a rationale for not doing what they have no taste for doing anyway. But in many cases the problem is genuine. Protest appears to be dysfunctional in just those cases where a specific goal exists to make protest possible at all.

Fifth, Negroes are not organized on a continuing basis for protest activity. The on-going voluntary associations to be found in a northern Negro community are almost always led by middle-class Negro business, professional or church groups, with a sprinkling of labor leaders (10). These associations invariably lack a mass base. Even more important, those leaders who do command mass organizations are often under clear constraints to avoid protest tactics. At least two of the three principal Negro mass organizations (labor unions and political organizations) are part and parcel of city-wide unions and political groups. They derive the incentives used to maintain their organizations (jobs, patronage, appointments to staff positions, money, slating for office, etc.) from sources controlled by whites. Negro labor leaders and politicians tend to reflect the character of labor and political movements in the city as a whole. It is only when the labor or political groups of the city are weak, divided, or faltering that Negro leaders in these organizations can act with some independence. (This is the case in New York, for example, in the relationships between Tammany Hall and Harlem.) It becomes very difficult to organize political or economic protest movements that require strikes or switching votes. To attempt this would involve challenging established leaders in these fields. Even assuming such leaders could either be induced to protest or somehow bypassed, it is not at all clear that traditional voting allegiances could be overcome in a manner that would permit protest leaders to threaten realistically election reprisals against public officials.

This means that Negro protest leaders, in dealing with white politicians, often must employ deception or rely on imperfect information when they suggest that they speak "for" Negro voters. Surprisingly, many politicians can be influenced, at least marginally, in this way. Doubts exist, if not as to which way Negroes will vote, then as to the size of that vote. Hopes exist of improving one's individual position with Negro voters. But these are minor bargaining resources. Usually both sides realize that no organization exists which can switch any significant number of Negro voters in a predetermined manner.

Problems of Coordination

If these observations are correct, the prospects of vigorous, extensive, and organized Negro protest in large northern cities are poor. The danger confronting the Negro community in many places today is not extremism, but impotence. However, these conclusions regarding the logic and nature of protest do not cover all cases. Opportunities remain for this strategy, but these opportunities are of a limited character and present problems in themselves.

Protest action is best suited to situations in which the goal sought is defensive, specific, of a welfare character, relevant to the wants of the Negro rank-and-file, and has an explicit target. Such opportunities are found in greater number in the South than in the North today, but they are by no means absent in the North. Discriminatory practices are still to be found in many hotels, hospitals, restaurants, and places of employment. Existing voluntary associations in many, although not all, Negro communities are not absorbed in these tasks. For a variety of reasons — including the kind of people recruited to these agencies, the interests of the professional staffs, and budgetary needs — many of these associations are more concerned with broader problems involving goals which are assertive, general, of a status character, having multiple targets, and relevant more to the interests of the Negro middle and upper class. (This is not to dispute the possible validity of the argument that gains for middle-class Negroes in the long run mean gains for Negroes as a whole, because of the precedent or symbolic value of such advances. But people are hard to mobilize for protest action aimed at goals which, for them, have only indirect or symbolic value.) This means that stimulating protest action may require, in many cases, focusing attention on goals of a lesser order than those now being discussed.

Further, it may well mean creating organizations specifically adapted to these protest ends. Neither the NAACP nor the Urban League, in almost any city, is equipped to engage in such activity as it is now organized. Persons with the necessary leadership skills would, of course, be hard to find, as most are already either (a) committed to an existing Negro association, or (b) indifferent to civic action, or both. Further, the resources — in terms of time and money — for civic action are very scarce, and a new organization would only intensify the competition for these resources. At present, the NAACP is competent to issue verbal protests, provide legal assistance, and initiate court fights on behalf of Negroes, while the Urban League is sometimes able to negotiate (although usually with few, if any, bargaining resources). Other forms of protest are typically outside the province of most existing Negro associations as they are generally organized.

The task is to create the possibility of meaningful bargaining on a whole range of issues by being able to offer other parties the compensation of ending a protest campaign. This implies a division of labor between protest leaders and bargainers. In some cases, such a division in fact exists. In New York City, for example, the Urban League often finds itself presented with opportunities for negotiation because an extremist leader, such as Rep. Adam Clayton Powell, Jr., has brought some city agency or private party under heavy fire. This is true even though many Urban League leaders often deplore Powell and his tactics; for them, Powell is a useful nuisance. An ideal strategy would include a protest organization campaigning against certain targets (a, b, and c) while another agency bargained for certain ends (A, D, and E). In one case, the target (a) and the goal (A) would be identical, and the strategy would be a *primary* one. If the goal (A) is conceded, the protest against the party which concedes the goal (the target, a) would be ended. In another case, the goal (D) differs from the target (b). Concessions from b would be extracted because b stands in some bargaining relationship with d, who can grant the goal (D). This would be a *secondary* strategy. For example, obtaining more middle-income public housing units might be the goal, but the target would be an urban renewal program which would displace Negroes. The campaign against urban renewal would be reduced if the goal were granted. The bargaining linkage here might be between the Negro association which induces the backer of the urban renewal project to prevail upon the city housing authority to construct the housing project.

Some approximation of this does, in fact, occur on occasion. The difficulty is that it places a great premium on coordination among Negro leaders and organizations. This coordination is rarely easy to obtain. First, the various leaders may not agree on what goals should be sought. The would-be bargainers, in a typical case, might very well find more Negro public housing an objectionable goal since it might easily result in the placing of lower-status Negroes in the neighborhoods of upper-status Negroes. Second, the protest association might well resist being "called off" for the price of a few housing units. This limited goal may not be sufficiently endowed with ideological significance to be the basis for mobilizing support for the campaign. The rank-and-file might feel that they were "sold out" by leaders who accepted such

a concession rather than fighting the urban renewal project to the bitter end.
The problem is to select a limited goal (so that there is some hope it can be
obtained and so that it can plausibly be the subject of bargaining) and imbue
it with enough significance so that it can provide incentives for action. Third,
the protest and the bargaining groups would be radically different in character and thus find it difficult to work together comfortably. Each would be
in competition with the other for scarce resources (personnel, contributions,
publicity, etc.). Further, each would recruit members and leaders from different
walks of life and differing temperaments and interests. There is no logical
necessity that would prevent these two groups from coexisting peacefully and
cooperating smoothly, but in fact cooperation (and sometimes even coexist-
ence) seem impossible.

This raises a point about which Negro leaders themselves often speak. It
is customary to assign to the NAACP and the Urban League, for example,
distinctive roles and equal credit. Each has its function and each deserves
support, one is told. One may prefer the League to the NAACP, but one
recognizes the need for the other group. These amiable statements, however,
often thinly conceal a great deal of tension between "League" types and
"NAACP" types, particularly if (as is often the case) the leaders of the two
organizations display strongly differing political styles (12). One group
tends to be suspicious of the other. Normal organizational rivalries are intensified by tactical and temperamental differences. Suspicions are aroused about
the motives and purposes of the other party. Cooperation becomes more
difficult because one group has grave reservations about the ends and tactics
of the other and thus finds a coordinated venture filled with uncertainties
and possible risks.[1]

---

[1]An apparent exception to the difficulty of coordinating protest action is the case of some
Southern sit-in demonstrations. In cities such as Nashville, Tenn., and Montgomery, Ala.,
the spontaneous student sit-in strategy caused deep concern among both white and "established" Negro leaders. The problem for the established Negro leaders (the lawyers, ministers, politicians, etc.) was to bargain with their white counterparts in order to gain some
concessions in policies governing white lunch counters in return for ending the
sit-in movement. Successful bargaining required that the Negro leaders be able to control
the student demonstrators. In Nashville and other cities, when some agreement was
reached, the sit-in strikes were in fact ended. This suggests a remarkable degree of coordination among Negro groups which, at the outset, were somewhat suspicious of one another
and which had few common goals or common organizational memberships. I am told
by certain Southern Negro leaders that the device by which the "established" Negro
leaders acquired control over the student strikers was the bail money which the arrested
students could not furnish themselves. In Montgomery, for example, a large sum was
apparently collected by Negro leaders to use on behalf of student strikers. It is reported
that when some students showed a reluctance to agree to tactical moves suggested by
adult leaders, a withdrawal of this financial support was threatened. The threat proved
effective in most cases. Some student leaders attempted to assert their independence with
the slogan, "Jail, Not Bail," but did not command a large following when it became
apparent that a jail sentence could be for as long as 30 or 60 days.

A strategy of secondary protest, with its attendant problem of coordination between two associations with differing end- and incentive-systems, points once again to the practical virtues of emphasizing narrow, specific goals with unambiguous targets. That such goals and such targets are to be found in abundance cannot be doubted. The immediate and tangible needs of Negroes, particularly for more and better jobs, are manifest. An argument can be made that increasing the net disposable income of a minority group is, over the long run, the best way to make possible those larger gains which seem to elude protest action at the moment. In part this can be justified by the fact that in some areas, opportunities for Negroes are appearing faster than Negroes can prepare to take advantage of them. This is particularly true in fields where specialized skills, or simply a relatively high level of education, is required. Further, such anti-discriminatory measures as FEPC laws (although of value insofar as they permit Negroes to enter formerly all-white occupations) have not always been equally successful in permitting Negroes to rise into better-paying jobs. Greater access to such positions is probably essential if net Negro income is to be increased substantially. In addition, increased income, held over time and in conjunction with other factors (such as education), will work in the long run to reduce the *class* differentials which account for part (although certainly not all) of anti-Negro feeling. If this has any truth, then there is some real reward in organizing, to the extent circumstances permit, protest action aimed at employment goals — goals which are specific, have a welfare pay-off and identifiable targets, and implicate the interest of the rank-and-file.

Negro Protest in Chicago

That this is the case in at least one Northern city can be seen from an examination of seventeen issues involving Negroes in Chicago during the period 1958-60. These issues, the details of which are reported elsewhere (12), ranged across all areas of public life, including housing, employment, medical care, police protection, and education. The case histories of these issues were for the most part incomplete, as the issues themselves tended to be "truncated" — they were either perennial issues which seemed to have no ending, or they were attempts to influence public policy which came to nothing. In general, Negroes exercised relatively little *intended* influence over public policy, although they exercised a great deal of *unintended* influence by being the objects of the concern of others. Thus, Negroes were important in the sense that others took their *presence* (but not their activity) into account in making decisions regarding, for example, whether and where to build a county hospital, a new school, or a housing project.

Few Negro-initiated proposals (such as FEPC or open occupancy housing laws) become public policy. Occasionally, Negroes were able to block the proposals of others. These "vetoes" were often effective, in such cases as the opposition to construction of a branch of the county hospital, because the simple act of raising the race issue injected sufficient controversy into the problem that it could not be easily disposed of by "civic leaders" who were anxious to maintain a non-controversial reputation (11).

Of the seventeen issues examined in Chicago, the problem was raised or created by whites and white groups acting on behalf of Negroes in three cases, by both Negroes and whites in seven cases, and by Negroes alone in seven cases. In nine cases, little or nothing resulted — i.e., Negro demands did not affect public policy or private actions. In four cases, minor changes were noted — the Mayor was interested in problems of private hospital discrimination, there was a slight improvement in police protection in Negro areas, there appeared to be a slight lessening of police maltreatment of Negroes, and relocation procedures in urban renewal were improved. In four other cases, there was a clear impact on public policy — a shake-up occurred in a district police station in order to intensify narcotics investigation, a new vocational school was constructed, the building of a county hospital branch was delayed significantly, and some Negroes were hired in a downtown bank.

Several aspects of these limited successes are of interest. First, the ends successfully attained rested for the most part on demands for public services or minimal standards of justice that are difficult for whites to deny publicly or reject. They seemed to be demands for things that any citizen is entitled to as a matter of obvious principle. They were, as compared to demands for equal opportunity in housing or employment, relatively easy to justify, although not easy to attain. Second, they were demands which, in most cases, involved only the Negro community and not the city as a whole. Relatively few whites would be affected by the attainment of such ends. In those cases where whites were significantly affected (the demand for Negro employees at a large white bank and the placement of Negro physicians, to treat Negro patients, in white hospitals), the greatest effort was required. In the former case, a picket line was organized over a period of many days. In the latter case, a sustained effort by a *white* organization (the Chicago Commission on Human Relations, a public agency in the Mayor's office) has thus far produced only an interest and some action on the part of the Mayor. Finally, most of the issues in which some progress was made were not part of the agenda of existing Negro-led voluntary associations. In the instances in which relatively dramatic and clear progress was made (the police district scandal, the bank picketing, the new vocational school, and private hospital discrimination), the effective agents of change were neither the NAACP nor the

Urban League. In the school and hospital cases, white groups (a citizen's committee in the former case and a public commission in the latter) took the lead, albeit with Negro cooperation and assistance. In the other two cases (the police and bank issues), the issue was waged by simple protest tactics by *ad hoc* groups of Negroes.

Although neither the NAACP nor the Urban League was indifferent to these matters, for a variety of reasons they tended to stay out of them. In the police and bank cases, the issue seemed to be in the hands of people of uncertain reputation, lower-class backgrounds, or dubious motives. In the other cases, the established voluntary associations were divided as to ends or tactics and hence constrained from acting vigorously.

It has been frequently observed that these on-going Negro organizations lack the capacity for mass leadership. Indeed, that is a continuing theme of Negro criticism against them (7). The importance of this lies in the possibility, which this analysis of the logic and data of a protest strategy suggests, that the emerging center of gravity in the Negro civic life — the voluntary associations — may be pursuing in great part ends which neither reflect the direct and tangible interests of rank-and-file Negroes nor represent the areas of most likely success. Other areas, of less interest to the associations, may be the most vulnerable points in the defense of the larger community. The "agenda" of the associations may well be significantly different from the agenda of the Negro community.

The Meaning of Apathy

Many Negroes and some whites frequently comment on the lack of "Negro leadership." The absence of effective Negro civic leadership is usually ascribed to apathy, indifference, or conservatism. Such "explanations" actually explain very little. They are, for the most part, merely another way of stating the problem. In this paper I have suggested that the apparent absence of concerted protest action among northern Negroes can be accounted for by the nature of the ends sought, the diffusion of relevant targets, the differentiation of the Negro community along class lines, and the organizational constraints placed on Negroes as they enter into partial contact with the white community. If these factors, rather than "apathy" or "Uncle Tomism" provide a plausible explanation, then additional research is called for into the manner in which the relationship between ostensible ends, organizational constraints, and social stratification will vary among Negro communities. The task would be to uncover the variations which exist between stated goals and existing incentives for action toward those goals in a number of cities.

Preliminary research (12) suggests that the reason for the higher level of protest activity among New York Negroes as compared to those in Chicago is that the formal and informal political leaders and the officers of prestige-conferring voluntary associations in New York feel they must reward, as a result of their own maintenance needs, vigorous Negro leaders. Negroes protest more in New York because the desired outcome of protest (i.e., entering into a bargaining relationship with the other party) is much more likely than in, say, Chicago. In turn, this outcome is more likely because target organizations in New York have a greater need for the compensations which Negro protest leaders can offer — a cessation of public criticism and controversy. To explain why these compensations are valued more in one city than another would take us too far afield here; the example is offered only to show the possible lines of theoretical and empirical research which emerge out of an examination of protest as a civic strategy.

REFERENCES

1. BANFIELD, EDWARD C. "The Theory of Manipulation." (Mimeographed by Department of Government, Harvard University, 1956.)
2. _____. *Political Influence.* Glencoe, Ill.: Free Press. (Forthcoming.)
3. CLARK, PETER B. "Notes on Bargaining." (Mimeographed by Department of Political Science, Yale University, 1960.)
4. DAHL, ROBERT A. and LINDBLOM, CHARLES E. *Politics, Economics, and Welfare.* New York: Harper & Bros., 1953.
5. GARFINKEL, HERBERT. *When Negroes March.* Glencoe, Ill.: Free Press, 1959.
6. GLAZER, NATHAN. "Is 'Integration' Possible in New York Schools?" *Commentary,* (September, 1960), 185-93.
7. LOMAX, LOUIS E. "The Negro Revolt Against the 'Negro Leadership,'" *Harpers,* (June, 1960), 41-8.
8. MANNES, MARYA. "School Trouble in Harlem," *Reporter,* (February 5, 1959), 13-19.
9. SCHELLING, THOMAS C. *The Strategy of Conflict.* Cambridge, Mass.: Harvard University Press, 1960.
10. SELZNICK, PHILIP. *Leadership in Administration.* Evanston, Ill.: Row, Peterson Co., 1957.
11. WILSON, JAMES Q. "Negro Civic Leaders." (A paper read before the annual meeting of the American Political Science Association, September 8-10, 1960, New York City.)
12. _____. *Negro Politics: The Search for Leadership.* Glencoe, Ill.: Free Press, 1960.
13. _____. "Two Negro Politicians: An Interpretation," *Midwest Journal of Political Science,* November, 1960.

Part 2

Political Leadership
in the Sub-Community

An inquiry into Negro politics in America, once the general position of the
Negro vis-à-vis the larger community is placed in perspective, must invariably
begin with an examination of Negro leadership. The role of the Negro leadership in the politics of the Negro community is crucial because "the civic life
of a community — the raising, agitating, and disposing of issues — is carried
on by civic leaders."[1] Stated in another way, it is the leadership of a community which must crystallize the issues and channel the efforts of the community to the solution of such issues. Moreover, the study of Negro leader-

---

[1] James Q. Wilson, *Negro Politics: The Search for Leadership,* (Glencoe, Illinois: The
Free Press of Glencoe, 1960), p. 7.

ship is all important since "to ask questions about . . . Negro political
leadership is to ask some basic questions about the nature of that leadership
and about the larger subject of Negro politics."[2]

Negro leadership, like white leadership, is a product of socio-economic
conditions and the push and pull of forces which stimulate the desire to
influence the allocation of values in the society. The problems which accrue
to Negro leaders are not peculiar to them alone. Similar problems confront
most men who seek to lead a community or any part of it. Leaders in the
larger community are circumscribed by the alternatives available to them. So
are the leaders in the sub-community. The result in the sub-community, as
in the larger community, is considerable variation of leadership patterns
determined in part by personality and in part by the structure of the situation.

Part 2 attempts to present a portrait of the general character of Negro
leadership and the various types and styles of Negro leaders which emerge in
a sub-system within the American political system.[3] Reprinted in this section
are six selections concerning Negro leaders and leadership in America. In the
first selection Thomas and Elizabeth Monahan survey the general characteristics of Negro leaders in America. With the exception of their finding that
Negro women play a larger leadership role in the sub-community than do
Caucasian women in the larger community, the characteristics of Negro leaders
in America do not differ considerably from those of leaders in the larger
community.

In the next four selections an attempt is made to assess the nature of
Negro leadership under varying conditions. Ernest A. T. Barth and Baha Abu-
Laban examine Negro leadership where the sub-community population is
small and where there is a lack of consciousness on the part of Negroes that
they constitute a racial community. In this sub-community there is little or no
significant Negro leadership.

In the third selection, Harold Pfautz examines Negro leadership where
the sub-community population is small but where Negroes do experience
considerable feelings of "separateness" from the larger community. In this
framework a significant Negro leadership is identifiable.

---

[2]Everett C. Ladd, *Negro Political Leadership in the South,* (Ithaca, New York: Cornell
University Press, 1966), p. 114.
[3]Wendell Bell, Richard J. Hill, and Charles R. Wright, *Public Leadership: A Critical
Review with Special Reference to Adult Education,* San Francisco: Chandler Publishing
Co., 1961 p. 87, distinguish between ethnic leaders who direct their activities to *intra-
group* leadership and those whose activities perform the *bridging* function of representing
the ethnic group in the larger community. It is the latter type with which this section is
primarily concerned. A third type ethnic leader could be postulated: the ethnic *intergroup*
leader who serves the entire community. Attorney General Edward Brooke of Massachusetts is an outstanding example. However, some aspects of Negroes in politics must await
further study.

Once a significant Negro leadership has emerged in the sub-community, for whatever reasons, distinctive types of leadership behavior begin to emerge. In the fourth selection, Jack L. Walker discusses two types of Negro leadership which have come about: that which favors the sub-community adopting a militant and aggressive stance vis-à-vis the larger community, and that which favors the adoption of a more conciliatory stance by the sub-community. Increasing Negro frustration with the pace of *de facto* change in American society in the face of *de jure* change has resulted in Negro leadership resorting more to protest than negotiation as a means of engaging the larger community. In the fifth selection, a study of a Southern community, Killian and Smith analyze the factors significant in bringing the new leadership to power, the extent of support for the new leadership, and the implications of such leadership for Negro politics throughout the United States.

The materials to be presented in this section, to this point, have been devoted to the general character of Negro leaders in America, the emergence of Negro leadership under varying community conditions, and the types of Negro leaders which emerge in the sub-community. Such leaders have not usually been of the "appointive" or "elective" variety to public office. That is, they need not have been appointed to political positions of power by public officials or placed into public office by the electorate. Concluding this section is a perceptive study by James Q. Wilson of the character and style of two Negro leaders who have been elected by the sub-community to formal public positions of power in the larger community. Both leaders have been elected to the United States Congress. Both leaders perform a *bridging* function: they represent the sub-community to the larger community. But their leadership styles vary considerably. Wilson tells us why and makes clearer the impact of the larger community on the Negro leadership style, the goals of elected Negro leaders, and the means they employ to achieve their goals.

Some Characteristics of
American Negro Leaders*

Thomas P. Monahan
Elizabeth H. Monahan

In less than three generations since their legal emancipation American
Negroes have achieved international eminence and fame. The *Dictionary of
American Biography* for the period 1927-1934 listed 613 Negro notables, or
4.5 per cent of the total.[1] In the 1949 edition of *American Men of Science*
one finds 128 Negroes listed; and in the 1950-1951 edition of *Who's Who
in America*, 141 outstanding living Negroes.[2] As was the case for new immigrant populations in the United States, the Negro is still underrepresented in
such directories.

Reprinted from *American Sociological Review,* Vol. 21, (October 1956), pp. 589-596
with permission of the publisher and authors. Copyright 1956 by the American Sociological Society.
*The writers hope to publish additional tabular material at a later date. A more complete
bibliography is available from the authors upon request.

[1]Rupert B. Vance, "The Geography of Distinction: The Nation and Its Regions, 1790-
1927," *Social Forces,* 18 (December, 1939), p. 168.
[2]This number represents an increase of 56 over the number found in the 1944-45 edition
of *Who's Who in America.* See *Negro Year Book, 1941-46,* Atlanta, Ga.: Foote and
Davies, 1947, pp. 15-16, and *Negro Year Book, 1952,* New York: William H. Wise,
1952, pp. 96-98, 359-360, both copyrighted by the Tuskegee Institute of Alabama.

The Society of Friends observed 100 years ago that improvement of the condition of people of color in the main must spring from within their own group.[3] Of late, more recognition is being given to this thought that in the achievement of social and political rights the principle of self-improvement should not be ignored. What do we know about the leaders of the Negro group, upon whom by example and precept their minority so much depends? What are the occupational, political, and religious affiliations of present-day Negro leaders? What is their family status, reproductivity, place of birth, and place of residence?

Partial answers to many of these questions have been derived from an analysis of the biographical data given in *Who's Who in Colored America* for 1950.[4] Undoubtedly, as is the case with all *Who's Who* data, there are a number of inaccuracies and omissions. Nevertheless, the biographies give considerable detail on nearly 3,000 Negroes not available in any other publication and the data should give a better understanding of these contemporary leaders and form a point of comparison for future studies.

In 1950 there were 15 million Negroes in the United States, almost two-thirds of whom were living in urban areas: 48 per cent of the Southern population and 94 per cent of those living outside the South were city dwellers. The percentage of Negroes living in the South has been declining; nevertheless, 68 per cent were still living there in 1950.[5]

Women Leaders[6]

For the past twenty-five years women have constituted about 6 per cent of all persons listed in *Who's Who in America*. In the literary field they once registered a high of 14 per cent of that profession (born before 1851). Among *American Men of Science* (1949) they comprised 6 per cent; among

[3]Friends Society of Philadelphia, *A Statistical Inquiry into the Condition of the People of Colour of the City and Districts of Philadelphia,* Philadelphia, Pennsylvania: Kite and Walton, 1849, pp. 43-44. Cf., Carter G. Woodson, *The Negro Professional Man and the Community,* Washington, D. C.: The Association for the Study of Negro Life and History, 1934, p. 28.
[4]*Who's Who in Colored America,* 1950, edited by G. J. Fleming and C. E. Burckel, Yonkers, N. Y.: C. E. Burckel and Associates, 1950.
[5]United States Bureau of the Census, *Nonwhite Population by Race, 1950,* Special Report P-E, No. 3B, Washington, D. C.: United States Government Printing Office, 1953, Table 2, p. 16.
[6]This study was designed and executed in 1951-1952, and includes detailed tabulations on the biographees of both men and women in *Who's Who in Colored America, 1950.* Because an independent study has since been published on the women, this part of the data will not be discussed here. See Preston Valien and Carrell Horton, "Some Demographic Characteristics of Outstanding Negro Women," *Journal of Negro Education,* 23 (Fall, 1954), pp. 406-420.

Social Science Research Fellows (1925-1951), 8 per cent; but among persons in the *Dictionary of American Biography* (1927-1934), only 5 per cent. The earlier editions of *Who's Who in America* gave recognition to a higher proportion of women, 8 to 9 per cent, but with subsequent additions and omissions since 1928 the figure dropped to 5.6 per cent by 1950.[7]

It has been found that among Negroes 36 per cent of all college graduates were women, as were 13 per cent of all Ph.D.'s.[8] Considering also the greater responsibility of Negro women in family life and community activities, it is not surprising therefore that 12 per cent of the 1608 persons listed in *Who's Who in Colored America* for 1928-1929 were women. This proportion has increased rather than decreased with time, so that in 1950 women comprised 16 per cent of all the biographees.[9] Negro women, therefore, seem to receive greater recognition than do white women in their respective groups; moreover, their role in Negro and community affairs seems to have increased over the years.

Characteristics by Age

That leadership and recognition are reserved for older persons is brought out in Table 1. About three-fourths of the men are 40 years of age or older, the median age being 49 years. These statistics are much like those for *Who's Who in America*. In Winston's earlier study (1928), about 50 per cent of the W.W.C.A. biographees were under the age of 45; and only 8 per cent 65 years and over. The 1950 biographees are now a slightly older group.

Certain background characteristics according to age appear in the data. The non-college group is an older group, as are the M.D.'s and other medical persons; whereas, those who possess an M.A. or Ph.D. degree are significantly younger. On the whole this betokens a greater educational achievement among the younger men. The men who do not specify a Protestant denomination,

---

[7] *Who's Who in America,* Chicago: A. N. Marquis Company, 1st edition, 1899-1900, and following, especially 1903-05, pp. xxvi-xxviii, xxiii; 1930-31, p. 25; 1932-33, p. 26; 1940-41, p. 2812; Edwin L. Clarke, *American Men of Letters, Their Nature and Nurture,* Columbia University Studies in History, Economics, and Law, No. 168, Vol. 72 (1916), p. 42; United States Bureau of Labor Statistics, Bulletin No. 1027, *Employment, Education, and Earnings of American Men of Science,* Washington, D. C.: Government Printing Office, 1951; Vance, *op. cit.,* p. 169; W. M. Kephart and M. Bressler, "Marriage and Family Patterns of An Academic Group," *Marriage and Family Living,* 16 (May, 1954), p. 121; Mary Jo Huth, unpublished M.A. thesis cited in C. Kirkpatrick, *The Family: As Process and Institution,* New York: Ronald Press, 1955, p. 153.

[8] Harry W. Greene, *Holders of Doctorates Among Negro Leaders,* Boston: Meador, 1946, pp. 215, 219; Charles S. Johnson, *The Negro College Graduate,* Chapel Hill: University of North Carolina Press, 1938, p. 56.

[9] Sanford Winston, "The Migration and Distribution of Negro Leaders in the United States," *Social Forces,* 10 (December, 1931), p. 244.

TABLE 1

AGE OF NEGRO MEN IN *WHO'S WHO IN COLORED AMERICA*, 1950

(N=2,389)

Age in Years*	Per Cent
Under 40	24.2
40–49	27.6
50–59	25.9
60 and over	22.3
Total	100.0
Under 45	38.8
45–64	48.5
65 and over	12.7
Total	100.0

*Median age, 49.1 years.

or who declare themselves to be Catholics, are also characteristically younger. If more Negroes are adopting Catholicism consequent to their migration to Northern cities, this could create such an age relationship. As regards politics it is interesting to note that those declaring themselves to be Democrats are younger than the Republicans.

Marital Status

Various studies of biographees have revealed proportions married which equal or exceed the prevailing proportions in the population at large. A number of studies of *Who's Who in America* revealed that 89 to 91 per cent had been married; eliminating Roman Catholic prelates and correcting for age raises the figures slightly more. *American Men of Science* (1949) were single in only 6.3 per cent of the cases; and S.S.R.C. fellows (1925-1951) who were 45 years of age or over were nearly always married (3 per cent single). As to remarriage, 5.9 per cent of the 1903-05 W.W.A. biographees were married two or more times.[10]

Examination of Table 2 indicates that the data on Negro biographees in W.W.C.A. corresponds closely to the findings for other groups. The proportion of college graduates reported by Johnson (1938) as single, 29 per cent, is probably a consequence of age and sex distortion in his study, because such

---

[10] *Who's Who in America, op. cit.,* 1903-05 edition, p. xvi, 1930-31 edition, pp. 24-28; a letter from Helen Wood, United States Department of Labor, on Bulletin No. 1027, *op. cit.;* Kephart and Bressler, *op. cit.,* p. 122.

bachelorhood is absent among W.W.C.A. men. It clearly appears that over
90 per cent of these Negro notables marry.[11]

TABLE 2

MARITAL STATUS ACCORDING TO AGE GROUP, NEGRO MEN IN
WHO'S WHO IN COLORED AMERICA, 1950

Present Age	Number	Not Married	Married Once	Married More Than Once
		Per Cent		
Under 45	924	14.5	84.5	1.0
45–64	1,162	9.2	85.7	5.1
65 and over	303	7.6	88.5	13.9
Not stated	78	21.8	74.4	3.8
Total	2,467	11.4	84.0	4.6

Age at Marriage

The Negro population as a whole, even in urban areas, has a lower age
at first marriage than the white group. However, among the whites in the
professional-owner-proprietor classes and among persons listed in *Who's Who*
directories, the average age at first marriage is considerably above that of the
general population. Rather consistently in all studies of *Who's Who* classes
the median age at first marriage has been found to be about 28-29 years, and
the mean age about 30 years. This is roughly three to four years later than
the age at first marriage found in the professional and proprietary occupational groups in general.[12]

This study shows the leaders in the Negro group follow closely the white
pattern in their age at marriage. It might have been supposed that they would
show a lower age at marriage in conformity with the Negro population as a
whole, or that they might show a lesser tendency to marry or greater delay
in marrying because of their struggle for leadership attainment. Neither of
these propositions is true. The average age at first marriage is about 30 years,

---

[11]Persons in *Who's Who in Colored America* in 1950 who reported no marriage were
counted as single although some of them undoubtedly were, or had been, married. See
Johnson, *op. cit.,* pp. 60, 152; and Woodson, *op. cit.,* pp. 116, 158, 248, etc.

[12]T. P. Monahan, *The Pattern of Age at Marriage in the United States,* Philadelphia:
Stephenson-Brothers, 1951, p. 259 ff. It should be noted that quite recent statistics on
marriages for *certain* states show only a small difference between whites and nonwhites
as to their median age at first marriage. See National Office of Vital Statistics, *Vital
Statistics of the United States, 1953,* Vol. I, Washington, D. C.: United States Government Printing Office, 1955.

80 per cent of the Negro men marrying after the age of 24 years. (See Table 3.)

TABLE 3

AGE AT FIRST MARRIAGE, ONCE MARRIED ONLY, PRESENT AGE 45 YEARS AND OVER, NEGRO MEN IN *WHO'S WHO IN COLORED AMERICA*, 1950

(N=1,169)

Age at Marriage*	Per Cent
Under 20	2.1
20	1.4
21–24	16.0
25–29	32.8
30–34	23.3
35–39	10.5
40–44	6.7
45–49	3.6
50 and over	3.6
Total	100.0

*Median age, 29.6 years; mean age, 31.5 years.

Children

In 1950, 20.2 per cent of *all* nonwhite women in the United States, married once, husband present (35-39 years of age and married 15-19 years), were found to be childless; for *urban,* nonwhite women the figure was 25.4 per cent. Another survey in 1952 showed that 23.1 per cent of nonwhite women (45 years of age and over) had no offspring, while 27.8 per cent had had five or more children.[13]

Probably as a result of delayed marriage and other occupational and leadership factors, persons who achieve recognition in *Who's Whos* are somewhat more often childless than the general population. *Who's Who* notables have averaged less than two children per person (well below the replacement level), with an average number of children per family-having-children only moderately above two. Even S.S.R.C. fellows, 45 years of age and over (ever married), were childless in 21 per cent of the cases.[14] It has been true that

[13]C. V. Kiser, "Changes in Fertility by Socio-Economic Status During 1940-1950," *Milbank Memorial Fund Quarterly,* 33 (October, 1955), pp. 415, 421; J. S. Siegel, "Natality, Mortality, and Growth Prospects of the Negro Population of the United States," *Journal of Negro Education,* 22 (Summer, 1953), pp. 260-261.
[14]Kephart and Bressler, *op. cit.,* pp. 125-126.

the upper occupational groups in the United States have hardly been replacing themselves *in the past* and the leadership groups have been behaving similarly. As the figures in Table 4 show, about 30 per cent of the W.W.C.A. married men (married once only) are childless, the average number of children among those having children is only 2.4 (at best), and large families are not common. The percentage of childlessness appears higher than expected, although the average number of children is approximately the same as for a

TABLE 4

NUMBER OF CHILDREN ACCORDING TO DURATION OF MAR-
RIAGE, NEGRO MEN IN *WHO'S WHO IN COLORED AMERICA, 1950,*
ONCE MARRIED MEN*

(N=2,073)

Number of Children		Duration of Marriage in Years			
	Total	0–4	5–9	10–19	20 and Over
0	32.0	56.9	29.4	30.6	29.1
1	25.8	31.5	30.1	24.6	23.5
2	22.4	9.4	27.8	27.5	20.4
3	11.3	2.2	9.0	11.2	13.8
4	4.7		2.4	3.6	7.3
5	3.8		1.3	2.5	5.9
Total	100.0	100.0	100.0	100.0	100.0
Average Number of Children					
All cases	1.5	.6	1.3	1.4	1.7
Those with children	2.1	1.3	1.8	2.1	2.4

*Excluding adopted children. Total includes 103 cases for which duration was not available.

comparable population in the nonwhite group. While conforming to the pattern of their class, and to that of other *Who's Who* groups, it is apparent that Negro leaders — as well as white leaders — are not replacing themselves through childbearing.

Education

In 1943 there were less than 400 living Negro Ph.D.'s in the United States, 95 per cent of whom were engaged in the field of education. In earlier days a large proportion of the Negro physicians, dentists, and lawyers possessed no academic degree.[15] A great change has been wrought in the past few decades. Five out of six W.W.C.A. Negro leaders have college degrees; 10 per cent have Ph.D.'s; and 17 per cent have a medical degree.

In retrospect it should be recognized that 46 per cent of the biographees in the first edition of W.W.A. had no college training (1899-1900) but later a college degree became almost a prerequisite for this kind of distinction. In the 1946-47 W.W.A., 12 per cent had no college training and another 12 per cent had only attended college (versus 7 per cent and 10 per cent respectively for the men in the 1950 W.W.C.A.). However, 27 per cent of the W.W.A. group (1946-47) were reported to have their doctor's degree.[16] Thus, while the W.W.C.A. biographees have achieved over the years a higher minimum degree of formal education, they have not yet advanced as completely into the graduate levels of training.

The level of educational achievement among Southern Negro leaders is slightly above that of those in the North. (See Table 5.) Probably this is associated with the fact that a large proportion of the Southern leaders are employed in Negro colleges in the South. In the North more non-college Negroes are given recognition. Oddly enough, there are more medically trained men of prominence in the North than in the South where two-thirds of the Negro population is found.

Religion

Several studies of *Who's Who in America* have demonstrated the leadership position of certain old Anglo-Saxon Protestant groups. It has been said of the Negroes in the South that in the upper classes Baptists and Methodists predominate, and in the cities of the North higher proportions are found in the Episcopal, Presbyterian, and Congregational groups. Several studies of church membership figures and of Negro college students suggest that two-thirds to three-fourths of the Negro leaders should be Baptists and Methodists.[17] Although these two religious groups predominate in W.W.C.A., they comprise only slightly more than half of the total number of cases of Negro leaders. The Methodists and Baptists are, it is true, somewhat more numerous in the South. In the North the Episcopalians, Catholics, and miscellaneous denominations are almost as numerous as the Baptists and Methodists.

---

[15]Green, *op. cit.*, pp. 22-26, 40, 46, 215, 368; Johnson, *op. cit.*, pp. 19, 121; Woodson, *op. cit.*
[16]*Who's Who in America*, 1948-49, pp. 13-14. Table 5 excludes honorary degrees.
[17]Ambrose Caliver, *A Background Study of Negro College Students*, Washington, D. C.: United States Government Printing Office, 1933, p. 96; Greene, *op. cit.*, pp. 227-228; Johnson, *op. cit.*, p. 347; R. I. McKinney, *Religion in Higher Education Among Negroes*, New Haven: Yale University Press, 1945, pp. 22-24, 107-108.

Only 13 per cent did not declare a preference, 9 per cent in the South and 16 per cent in the North. This is surprising because less than half of the Negro population as a whole are registered as church members, and over 50 per cent of W.W.A. biographees do not report a religious preference. Whether this indicates a great religiosity among the Negro leaders, or a reticence among the whites, cannot be decided on the basis of these figures. A higher proportion of physical scientists in the W.W.A. group might reduce the degree of church affiliation, as Fry has demonstrated.[18]

Occupation

Even as early as 1916 the old time "learned" professions were being replaced in *Who's Who in America* by scientists and others. Although we have no figures from which to derive such a conclusion for the Negro group, historical (and other) evidence points to a similar realignment of leadership. In the early days of emancipation the Negro preacher was often the only leader in his community. At the turn of the century 53 per cent of the college trained Negroes were found in the field of education, and 17 per cent in the ministry. Physicians and lawyers constituted another 11 per cent.[19]

Only 12 per cent of the 1950 W.W.C.A. biographees were clergymen, in the North or South. The teaching profession still is the preoccupation of 45.5 per cent of the Southern leaders (including the District of Columbia); but, in the North, where greater occupational outlets are available, only 9.8 per cent of the leaders are so engaged. In the North there is a greater dispersion of leadership among other professions and business, governmental, and civic personnel. For physical scientists or performers the North is the locale of this type of distinguished Negro. The urban and industrial areas of the North are undoubtedly places of opportunity for both whites and nonwhites. The fact that more physicians, attorneys, and businessmen are found in the North, which has only one-third of the Negro population, gives reason to believe that opportunity is greater in the North for the Negro in particular.

Politics

Some miscellaneous figures have been produced in the past to show that upper-class Negroes are mostly Republican in their preference. A public

---

[18]C. L. Fry, "Religious Affiliations of American Leaders," *Scientific Monthly,* 36 (March, 1933), pp. 241-249.
[19]W. E. B. DuBois, "The Talented Tenth," in Booker T. Washington, *et al., The Negro Problem,* New York: James Pott, 1903, pp. 52-53.

opinion poll in 1955 disclosed that there is a drift of Negroes away from
the party which championed their emancipation and toward the Democratic

TABLE 5

CHARACTERISTICS OF NORTHERN AND SOUTHERN NEGRO MEN
IN *WHO'S WHO IN COLORED AMERICA*, 1950

	Per Cent Distribution* Residence		
	Total	South	North
Education			
Non-college	6.6	2.6	9.8
Some College	9.7	8.4	10.9
College degree	33.4	31.9	34.9
M.A. degree	23.6	29.7	18.3
Ph.D. degree	9.9	12.9	7.2
D.D.S.	4.9	4.1	5.5
M.D.	11.9	10.4	13.4
Religion			
Baptist	28.1	33.6	23.6
Methodist	24.7	27.4	22.7
Episcopalian	12.7	10.1	14.8
Presbyterian	7.7	7.8	7.7
Congregational	4.8	5.2	4.5
Roman Catholic	4.2	3.0	4.9
"Protestant"	2.3	1.2	3.2
Miscellaneous	2.8	2.6	2.8
Not stated	12.7	9.1	15.8
Occupation			
Business and official	7.9	6.5	9.4
Editors and writers	3.7	2.7	4.5
Governmental	6.5	4.6	8.0
Civic and social	8.6	6.1	10.7
Ministerial	11.7	11.6	11.9
Attorneys	10.7	6.3	14.5
Physicians	12.0	10.3	13.7
Dentists	5.0	4.0	5.8
Physical scientists	3.5	1.9	4.8
Education: Grades	9.0	15.6	3.3
College	17.4	29.9	6.5
Artists and performers	4.0	.5	6.9
Politics			
Republican	24.6	17.2	31.6
Democrat	31.0	39.7	23.4
Independent	14.4	13.8	14.9
Not stated	30.0	29.3	30.1

*Each group adds to 100.0 per cent vertically (rounded). The total includes 23 cases
of Negroes residing abroad.

party as being "more sympathetic to their race" and the "party of the poor man."[20]

The balance is somewhat in favor of the Democrats among the W.W.C.A. men who declared a preference, but not nearly as great as the Gallup Poll has indicated for the general constituency. In both North and South 30 per cent made no declaration on this point, and 14 per cent more identified themselves with a third party or as Independents. In the North those who declared themselves to be Republicans proportionally outnumbered the Democratic affirmants by 3 to 2, whereas in the South the Republicans were outnumbered 2 to 1.

Occupationally, certain *sensitive* or mechanistic pursuits show high percentages who were noncommittal as to political preference: college personnel, government and military persons, editors, and physical scientists. Physicians, dentists, and the clergy were more often Republican; lawyers and businessmen about equally divided; and editors, civic workers, educators, and others tended toward the Democratic party. Because of regional and other influences these relationships for a study of this size are not definitive however, and reliable conclusions are not possible.[21]

TABLE 6

NEGRO MEN IN *WHO'S WHO IN COLORED AMERICA,* 1950, PER 1,000 NEGRO MALES*

Region	According to Birthplace† (1900 Population)	According to Residence† (1950 Population)
North	1.29	.55
New England	2.13	.90
Middle Atlantic	1.46	.69
East N. Central	1.18	.48
West N. Central	1.01	.55
Mountain	.77	.49
Pacific	1.99	.25
South	.44	.23
South Atlantic	.54	.29
East S. Central	.34	.17
West S. Central	.37	.17
Total United States	.53	.33

*United States Bureau of the Census, *Population, 1900, Part I,* p. 492, Washington, D. C.: U.S. Government Printing Office, 1901, and *Statistical Abstract, 1955,* p. 35.
†Total proportions do not include 142 foreign born, or 23 foreign resident Negroes. (The foreign born include 82 from the British West Indies, 18 from the Virgin Islands, and 27 from South America.)

[20]Gallup's Public Opinion Poll, *The Philadelphia Sunday Bulletin,* December 4, 1955.
[21]This paragraph and the one following are based on an analysis of unpublished tables.

An apparent shift stands out clearly as one goes up the educational ladder: those who merely attended college prefer the Republican party; a college degree, and then a graduate degree throws the balance increasingly to the Democratic fold. Although this Democratic preference prevails among the Ph.D.'s, a rather high proportion (44 per cent) declare no preference. The two medical groups express a greater preference for the Republican party.

Birthplace and Residence

One study of *Who's Who in America* disclosed that there was a drain of talent away from the South.[22] Other studies of W.W.A. have shown that, according to place of birth, the New England area formerly spawned a large proportion of the persons who achieved this kind of recognition, but that the birthplace of leadership was gradually moving westward toward the North Central states.

According to place of birth, as shown in Table 6, the Northern division produced (proportionally) three times as many Negro leaders as did the South, even though two high "producing" areas (District of Columbia, and West Virginia) are included in the South. Indeed, the contrast between the Middle Atlantic area and the deep South is four to one. In terms of residence, however, there are only about twice as many outstanding Negroes in the North, but as between some areas in the North and South the proportions are twice as far apart again, or four to one. The rather large number of prominent Negroes listed in the 1950 W.W.C.A. who were born in the British West Indies and the Virgin Islands is noteworthy.

The drift of Negro leaders to the North is brought out in Table 7, along with the more general mobility of this group. Although 74 per cent of the American born leaders in W.W.C.A. were born in the South, only 48 per cent resided there. Greater proportions of the Northern born continued to reside in the same city or in the same state than did those born in the South; or, 23 versus 9 per cent, and 41 versus 30 per cent, respectively.

The mobility was not entirely one-sided: 42 per cent of those born in the South moved to the North; yet 20 per cent of those born in the North (a smaller number) moved to the South. On the other hand, 11 per cent of the American born Negroes in W.W.C.A. who live in the South were born in the North and 61 per cent who live in the North were born in Southern states. Figures from the 1950 Census, for nonwhite males 40-59 years of age, indicate that 99 per cent of these Negro men residing in the South were born

---

[22]Wilson Gee, "The 'Drag' of Talent Out of the South," *Social Forces*, 15 (March, 1937), pp. 343-346.

TABLE 7

PLACE OF BIRTH AND PLACE OF RESIDENCE, AMERICAN BORN NEGRO MEN IN *WHO'S WHO IN COLORED AMERICA*, 1950*

	Per Cent Distribution	
Residence	Southern Born	Northern Born
Same City	(8.6)	(22.9)
Same State	(30.0)	(41.4)
Same Region	45.2	53.8
Different Region	12.6	26.3
Moved to North	42.2	. . . .
Moved to South	. . . .	19.9
Total	100.0	100.0

*Excluding all foreign born, or foreign resident cases.

there, whereas 75 per cent of the men in this age group in the North were born in the South.[23]

The great mobility of leadership to the North impresses one at first. But taking into account the overall mobility of the Negro as revealed by population figures it seems that the Negro leader may be slightly less mobile Northward than the rest of his group, and the Southward mobility of Negro leaders (proportionately but not numerically) is far more noticeable.

Mobility by Education, Religion, and Occupation[24]

Apparently those leaders who are born in the North and attain an M.A. or Ph.D. degree are drawn to the South, whereas men in lower educational levels and the medical men are more often attracted to the North from the South. The occupational data bear out the foregoing observation. Only 13 per cent of the men who were born in the South and who were engaged in the field of education migrated to the North. On the other hand 52 per cent of the men who were born in the North and employed as educators migrated to the South. The proportional trend of all other occupational groups was strongly Northward, even for those engaged in the ministry. Among the Southern born, attorneys least often of all stayed in the South.

The variations by denomination are not as divergent as for occupation and education. The Northward pull on the Southern born was least for the two major Southern denominations, the Baptist and Methodist. Oddly enough,

[23]United States Bureau of the Census, *Census of Population, 1950, State of Birth, Special Report* P-E, No. 4A, Table 21, Washington, D. C.: United States Government Printing Office, 1953.
[24]Based on an analysis of unpublished tables.

the Presbyterian, Congregational, and miscellaneous denominations of Northern born men seem to have moved more readily to the South.

Conclusion

The Westward trend of the white population and its leadership has a counterpart in the Northward movement of the Negro. The pattern found in 1928 by Winston persists. The Northern born Negro continues to achieve distinction to a much greater degree than the Southern born Negro, and only about half of those listed as born in the South have remained there. The flow of talent, however, resembles the tide of Negro migration as a whole.

Compared to other listings, Negro women receive greater recognition among their group than do white women, 16 per cent of the Negro biographees being women. The family relationships of the Negro leaders are much like those found for outstanding men in general; they marry to the same degree as the general population, but about six to seven years later; and, those who marry show a high proportion of childlessness and an insufficient number of children to replace themselves as families.

Politically these leaders seem to favor the Democratic party, rather than the Republican. Occupationally in the North no one professional group predominates, although nearly half of the Southern leaders are employed as educators. The clergy account for only about one-tenth of the whole. As for educational preparation, these men more often have graduated from college than persons in *Who's Who in America*, but they do not yet show as frequent an attainment of higher degrees.

There is some evidence of social adaptation in these data. Where opportunities are available in the North, the leaders' occupational pursuits are varied. In the South they are strongly for the Democratic party, whereas they lean to the Republican party in the North. In the North as compared to the South these leaders show greater affiliation with the Episcopalian, Catholic, Congregational, and other denominations. These contrasts suggest that in this Northward migration there has been an assimilation of Northern culture.

Should Negroes consider making their career in the South? Such a recommendation is surcharged with much personal and social sacrifice. That Negro leadership and talent is dislocated from its parent group is apparent in these data. Only 47 per cent of those listed in *Who's Who in Colored America* live in the South, but 68 per cent of the American Negroes are found there. The comparison is not really as sharp as it appears, because opportunity often begets (in the North) recognition and leadership, and the lack of it dissipates ability. Nevertheless, if, as was proposed at the outset, self-improvement among the Negroes is a goal to be sought after, in which leadership should play a part, then here is found a dilemma for the Negro group as a whole.

Power Structure and the Negro Sub-Community

Ernest A. T. Barth and Baha Abu-Laban

In this study the influence system in the Negro sub-community of "Pacific City" is related to other dimensions of the sub-community's social structure. The influential Negroes and Negro organizations were identified with a similar research design to that employed by Floyd Hunter in his study of "Regional City." This procedure provides a basis for comparing the findings of the two studies. The data indicate that the Negro leaders were primarily concerned with issues of an inter-racial nature. Their sub-community lacked large scale business and industrial organizations, and, consequently, no genuine power structure had developed. The investigation suggests the fruitfulness of a typological approach to the analysis of community influence systems. Use of such an approach would be most effective if carried out within the framework of a comparative research design.

Recently Bernard Barber noted that "a hard look at contemporary social science will show that there is very little consensus on a theory of influence and that there is also very little sound empirical research on which such a theory might be based."[1] Also, Roucek has commented that "there has

Reprinted from *American Sociological Review,* Vol. 24, (February 1959), pp. 69-76 with permission of the publisher and authors. Copyright 1959 by the American Sociological Society.

[1]Bernard Barber, *Social Stratification: A Comparative Analysis of Structure and Process,* New York: Harcourt, Brace, 1957, p. 234.

been a definite disinclination to view the field of minority-majority relations as another aspect of human power relations.[2]

This paper reports findings from a study of influence and power as these phenomena operate within the context of the Negro sub-community of a large Northwestern city. The project was designed to replicate Floyd Hunter's work in the sub-community of "Regional City."[3] Hunter presents one of the few exceptions to Roucek's criticism noted above. Such studies represent a major step in the direction of bringing the field of minority relations out of the special value context within which it has long been encompassed and placing it within the framework of general sociology.

A comparison of the findings reported in this paper with Hunter's permits the study of functional relationships between the structure of the influence system and other dimensions of community structure. Such case studies offer a valuable, if partial, approach to the comparative study of communities. For example, Pellegrin and Coates have investigated the relationship between absentee ownership of the major industries of a middle-sized Southern city and the structure of power relations within that community.[4] In a study of the structures of power in an American and a British community, Miller reports differences in the occupational distribution of power leaders in the two contexts, which are related to the differences in the value systems of the two nations reflected in different prestige rankings associated with similar occupations.[5] These researches demonstrate the fruitfulness of attempts to develop a typology of power structures within the framework of comparative community theory. In addition, they further the understanding of community process and structure.

The Negro Community in Pacific City

As Hunter's "Regional City" dominates the economic and political organization of the Southeast, so the "Pacific City" of this study dominates in the Northwest. The two communities are quite similar in total population and economic structure.[6] Stimulated mainly by the expansion of job opportunities during and following World War II, the Negro community of Pacific City

[2]Joseph S. Roucek, "Minority-Majority Relations in Their Power Aspects," *Phylon,* 17 (First Quarter, 1956), pp. 25-26.
[3]Floyd Hunter, *Community Power Structure: A Study of Decision Makers,* Chapel Hill: The University of North Carolina Press, 1954.
[4]Roland J. Pellegrin and Charles H. Coates, "Absentee Owned Corporations and Community Power Structure," *American Journal of Sociology,* 61 (March, 1956), pp. 413-419.
[5]Delbert C. Miller, "Industry and Community Power Structure: A Comparative Study of an American and an English City," *American Sociological Review,* 23 (February, 1958), pp. 9-15.
[6]*Ibid.*

has greatly increased in population within the past seventeen years. Federal Census data show that from a total of 3,789 in 1940, the Negro population of Pacific City expanded to 15,666 in 1950, an increase of 313.5 per cent for the decade. It is estimated that at present the population is in excess of 25,000. The pattern of residential location is similar to that of most major American cities: Negroes are generally centrally located and highly concentrated in "black belt" areas. Although the city prides itself on its "liberal" policies concerning race relations, the index of residential segregation is high in relation to other comparable cities.[7] Early in the 1940s Negro migrants to the city were characteristically young, male, unskilled workers. Available evidence indicates, however, that since 1950 the stream of migration has included an increasing proportion of more highly educated, married men engaging in professional activities.

There are some important differences between the Negro communities of Pacific City and Regional City. The 1950 Census data show that Pacific City's Negro population comprised a relatively small proportion of the total population (approximately 3.4 per cent), whereas in Regional City approximately a third of the population was Negro. As noted above, the Negro population in Pacific City more than tripled in the decade 1940 to 1950. The corresponding rate for Regional City during that period was about 16 per cent. The former dramatic increase has had a disturbing influence on the relatively stable pre-war Negro community of Pacific City. The incoming stream of migration has brought with it a large number of professionally trained Negroes of high occupational status; their leadership now appears to overshadow most of the "old time" community leaders. At the same time, many of the in-migrants came from Southern states, carrying the cultural characteristics of Negroes in that region, which, in many ways, were inconsistent with those of the Pacific City sub-community, resulting in some social disorganization.

The Negroes of Pacific City occupy somewhat more prestigeful and better paid jobs than those of Regional City. In 1950, a larger proportion of them were concentrated in service occupations, especially government jobs, as compared with the concentration of workers in the unskilled labor category in Regional City. These occupational differences are reflected in the income figures for the two communities. The Federal Census data show that in 1949 the median income for whites in Pacific City was 2,356 dollars as compared with 2,218 dollars in Regional City, while Pacific City's Negroes earned an average of 1,709 dollars in that year as compared with 1,045 dollars for Negroes in Regional City.

---

[7]Donald O. Cowgill and Mary S. Cowgill, "An Index of Segregation Based on Block Statistics," *American Sociological Review*, 16 (December, 1951), p. 825.

One index of the differences in the over-all patterns of interracial relations characteristic of the two cities may be seen in the legal structure of the two states. In Regional City the official policy of segregation in schools and other public facilities has long been supported by the law, while in Pacific City a state F.E.P. law has been in effect since 1949 as well as a longstanding "public accommodations" law. The state legislature recently passed an "Omnibus Civil Rights Bill" almost unanimously, with provisions for the protection of minority rights in housing as well as in public accommodations and employment. The schools of the community are officially non-segregated although the pattern of residential concentration has had its usual results: a high proportion of Negro children in relatively few schools.

Study Design and Methodology

Since this study was intended to replicate Hunter's work in Regional City, his research design was followed in so far as possible.[8] Therefore, during the initial stage of the project, in order to locate individuals characterized as influential within the Negro sub-community, lists of names of people who had held office in the major organizations of the sub-community, plus additional names gotten from interviews with Negro informants known to the authors, were obtained. The names of sub-community organizations through which influence might be channeled were taken from a list prepared by the Chamber of Commerce, supplemented by other organizations mentioned by Negro informants. Also, a list of "important issues for the sub-community" suggested by the informants was compiled. In addition, the local Negro newspaper provided other names of leaders, organizations, and issues. From these sources 154 potential influentials, 84 organizations, and about 12 issues were obtained.

Two questionnaires were constructed, one containing the names of the potential leaders and the other the organizations. A panel of ten Negro respondents, representative of the various institutional areas of the sub-community, was selected. In a personal interview each respondent reported how well he knew each potential influential and added names of others whom he believed to have been omitted. He then selected from the list the names of ten people he would choose "to help in a major project requiring a decision by a group of sub-community leaders." The interviewee also rated each of the organizations as "most influential," "influential," or "less influential" in initiating or supporting actions of importance to the Negroes in the city.

---

[8]Hunter, *op. cit.,* "Appendix: Methods of Study," pp. 262-271.

With information from the first ten interviews, the list of leaders was reduced to 33 names, each of which had received three or more choices from the ten previous respondents. The list of organizations was similarly reduced to a total of 27. These modified lists were submitted to six other Negro informants who, in turn, were asked to rate the leaders and organizations and to add the names which they believed to have been omitted. The resulting final lists consisted of 36 probable influentials and 27 organizations.[9]

A second phase of the field work involved interviewing the 36 probable influentials.[10] Each respondent was asked to fill out a questionnaire seeking information about his background and activities in the community.[11] The respondent was asked to indicate how well he knew each of the other influentials and to estimate his average monthly number of social and committee contacts with each; and, again, the respondents were invited to add the names of any leaders they felt had been omitted from the list. Each was asked: "If you were responsible for a *major* project which was before the community that required *decision* by a group of leaders — leaders that nearly everyone would accept — which ten on this list would you choose, regardless of whether they are known personally to you or not?"

Each influential also was asked to rate the 27 organizations on the three-point scale of influence, adding such other groups that he believed had been omitted. Finally, each was asked to name two issues or projects which he considered to be "most crucial" to the sub-community. The respondent indicated whether or not anyone had contacted him about each issue, whether he had contacted others, and what media of communications were used in these contacts.

The Findings

Sub-Community Leaders

This study is primarily concerned with the 36 probable leaders whose names received three or more mentions by the panel of 16 judges. The names of these leaders, their occupations, the number of votes each received as a "top leader," and the number of mutual choices each received, are listed in Table 1.

---

[9]Cf. Robert O. Schulze and Leonard U. Blumberg, "The Determination of Local Power Elites," *American Journal of Sociology*, 63 (November, 1957), pp. 290-296.

[10]All of the interviews were conducted by Baha Abu-Laban, a former resident of the Middle East, whose swarthy appearance stimulated short friendly chats with the respondents and comments concerning his ethnic identity. The interviews were characterized by a high level of rapport in our judgment.

[11]Twenty-nine of the 36 respondents returned these questionnaires.

Sixteen (or 44 per cent) of the leaders are women. This tends to confirm the popular belief, expressed by several of the leaders themselves, that women hold high positions in the leadership structure of the sub-community. Although two of the individuals high on the list in terms of number of votes are women, for the total group of 36 leaders women received an

TABLE 1

SUB-COMMUNITY LEADERS RANKED BY NUMBER OF VOTES RECEIVED FROM OTHER LEADERS IN LEADERSHIP POLL

Leader	Number of Votes	Number of Mutual Choices	Occupation
1. Walters	31	9	Social Worker
2. Taylor	27	7	Lawyer
3. Bassett	25	6	Small business (druggist)
4. Troy	25	8	Minister
5. Barner	24	9	Architect
6. Baldwin	22	6	Lawyer
7. Smith*	20	10	Housewife
8. Treat*	17	4	Social Worker
9. Moster	16	6	Minister
10. Willard	15	4	Retired
11. Williams	13	4	Small business (bail bond)
12. Stephens	12	2	Social Worker
13. Worth	12	2	Small business (real estate)
14. Hardy*	10	3	Social Worker
15. Fallsworth	9	1	Small business (photographer)
16. Dunham	9	2	Physician
17. Young*	9	3	Office Secretary
18. Parks*	7	4	School Teacher
19. Main*	6	4	Personnel Clerk
20. Barrier*	6	1	Housewife
21. Olaf*	6	2	Sales (insurance)
22. Ford	5	3	Small business (insurance)
23. Stone*	5	3	Unknown
24. Homer	4	1	Lawyer
25. Planter	4	2	Small business (nursing home)
26. McNeil	3	0	Dentist
27. Spear*	3	2	Small business (beauty school)
28. Masters*	3	1	School Teacher
29. Horne*	3	2	Unknown
30. Roberts	3	1	Physician
31. Moore*	2	0	Social Worker
32. Miller*	2	1	Sales (real estate)
33. Stewart	2	0	Lawyer (Pros. Office)
34. Taylor*	2	1	School Teacher
35. Sullivan	1	0	Small business (dry cleaning)
36. Gold*	1	1	Service Worker

*Denotes female leader.

average of 6.1 votes compared with an average of 13.9 for men. This generally lower position of women in the leadership structure is probably due to the nature of their participation in the organizational activities of the community. Although, on the average, female leaders belong to about as many organizations as do men (8.42 memberships for men and 8.25 for women), women far exceed the men in fraternal and "social" activities. In this respect, we find many more women participating in the leadership activities of the sub-community than did Hunter. Male leaders concentrate their organizational activities in civic and professional organizations.

The findings concerning the age distribution of the leaders differ from those of Hunter. The mean age of the 36 Negro leaders was 44.8 years; Hunter's comparable figure is 54.3 years.

About 52 per cent of the leaders in the Pacific City sub-community were self-employed, averaging about three employees under their supervision. Two leaders supervised more than ten employees: a nursing home operator supervised 18 employees, and an insurance executive supervised 16 workers. (No non-leaders employed a sizeable number of workers.) Again these findings differ markedly from those of Regional City, where Hunter found that the "top leader" supervised 1800 workers and that eleven others supervised 25 or more workers. The much smaller figures for Pacific City reflect the positions held by the top leaders in the occupational structure of the community. Eight of the 36 leaders were engaged in small business activities, including insurance and real estate brokerages, a drugstore owner, a beauty school, and a photography shop, while most of the leaders were professionals: five social workers, four lawyers, three physicians, three public school teachers, two ministers, and one architect. If power within the community derives in part from high positions in its economic or political structure, it is clear that none of these leaders in Pacific City's Negro sub-community possessed such power.

Only four of the 36 leaders were locally born (within the state). On the other hand, 60 per cent of them came originally from the South. These figures reflect the impact of migration on the leadership structure of the community. Although the leaders had been in Pacific City for 16.5 years on the average, only 80 per cent of them owned their homes. The leaders had also achieved a fairly high educational status, having completed about 16 years of school on the average.

The "Top Seven Leaders"

In an attempt to determine whether or not there was any "leadership clique" among the Negroes of Pacific City a special analysis was made of the seven persons who had been mentioned as "top leaders" by one half or more of the 36 people interviewed. These seven "elitists" were distinguished from the other leaders by superior educational attainment, *shorter* length of residence in the community, and by their sex, all but one being men. All of the top seven owned their homes and four of them were self-employed.

Hunter demonstrates that the "top leadership group in the Negro subcommunity tends toward closure" in two ways. First, almost all of the leaders were known to each other ("Ninety per cent of the leaders know each other 'well' or 'socially' ") and, second, his sociometric data show a correlation between the number of votes received as a top leader and the number of mutual choices.[12]

Acquaintanceship among the 36 leaders in this study was also very high, with 93 per cent of the leaders reporting knowing each other "well" or "slightly." Among the seven top leaders, all reported that they knew each of the others well. In addition, with the exception of "Smith-Baldwin," all of the top seven reported having both "committee and social contacts with each other regularly." These findings tend to confirm those of Hunter on this point.

Table 1 lists the names of the leaders, the number of votes they received, and the number of mutual choices they achieved. The well-known correlation between sociometric leadership standing and the number of reciprocated choices achieved as a leader holds for our top seven, for they received an average of 7.9 such choices whereas the remaining leaders averaged 2.0. A further indication of the formation of a "closed" top leadership group is the relationship between the actual number of mutual choices and the total possible number of mutual choices. Within the top seven, of the 21 possible mutual choices,[13] 13 (or 62 per cent) were actually made, and in only one case was there a reciprocal nonchoice.

These top seven were only slightly better known to the wider leadership group than were the others. Use of an "acquaintanceship score," with a range from zero (not known to any of the other leaders in the group of 36) to 105 (known well by all other members of the leadership group),[14] gave these seven an average score of 95.6 as compared with 90.9 for the remainder of the group.

One major differentiating characteristic of the top seven leaders is the degree to which they participated with others in organizational committee

---

[12]Hunter, *op. cit.*, pp. 119 ff.

[13]A "mutual choice" was defined as the instance in which there was a reciprocal selection as a top leader.

[14]Each respondent was asked to indicate "how well he felt he knew" each of the other members of the leadership group on a four-point scale ("Don't know," "Heard of," "Know slightly," "Know well"), with each response assigned a weight from 0 to 3.

activities. Their participation average with the other leaders was 16.7 as compared with 10.6 such contacts for the remaining 29. This supports the contention of several of the respondents that "the top leaders in this community got there because they were very active in organizational work." The belief was expressed that if such activity ceased the top leadership position would quickly be lost.

The top seven shared one other characteristic: each had taken part, at one time or another, in interracial activities in an "equal status" context in which he (or she) acted as a spokesman for the Negro community. Here, perhaps, is a case of "prestige drainage," with Negro leaders draining prestige from the white leaders with whom they were in contact.

Issues Confronting the Sub-Community

If the nature of the power process in the local community is to be fully understood, the types of issues that are most crucial to those who exercise this power must be analyzed. Each of the 36 leaders was asked: "What, in your opinion, are two of the major issues before the Negro community — either immediately past or current?" Table 2 lists the issues mentioned and the frequency of their mention.

From Table 2 it is apparent that the issues of concern to the leaders identified in this study were those associated with problems of interracial relations and the effects of minority group status, and more specifically, with attempts to change the existing social structure of the community. In spite of the presence of at least one organization of Negro businessmen and the fact that several of the leaders were themselves businessmen, their major concerns did not directly involve business problems (or most political programs). In their position as *leaders in the Negro sub-community,* they

TABLE 2

ISSUES BEFORE THE NEGRO SUB-COMMUNITY LISTED BY FRE-
QUENCY OF MENTION BY 36 SUB-COMMUNITY LEADERS

Type of Issue	Number of Times Mentioned
Minority Housing	33
Civil Rights Legislation	17
Concentration of Minority Children in the Schools	11
Parks and Recreational Facilities in Minority Residential Areas	4
Discrimination in Employment and Career Counseling for Children	4
Police Brutality	1
Unity in Action within the Sub-Community	1
No issues mentioned	1

were preoccupied with problems of the "Negro protest." In some measure, perhaps, this interest reflects the attitude that, lacking the needed power, their influence on major decisions concerning general economic and political policy in the community is minimal.

Community Organizations and the Structure of Power

The formal organizations and administrative agencies, as well as the less formal but relatively stable cliques, offer mechanisms through which community decision-making activities may be channeled. In Regional City, Hunter reports that, although the "top" and six other leaders in the sub-community did not generally work through formal policy committees, the majority did so.[15]

In an attempt to identify the organizations in Pacific City through which policy decisions flow, a list of the major organizations in the sub-community was drawn up.[16] Each of the 36 leaders was asked to rate each organization on a three-point scale as (1) most influential, (2) influential, and (3) less influential. These organizations are listed in Table 3 in order of the numbers of "most influential" votes.

In two respects this list is comparable to that reported in Hunter's study.[17] Although eight of the 27 organizations listed are of the Greek letter variety, none of these received more than two mentions as "most influential," indicating that at best they play a relatively minor role in the decision-making activities of the sub-community. And, again as in the case of Hunter's list, the organizations considered "most influential" (including the local Urban League, although its major function is community organization and case work) have a pronounced political content in their programs. With one minor exception, the churches, perhaps the most fully segregated of all sub-community organizations, were not mentioned — an interesting finding, especially in view of the fact that two of the top ten leaders are ministers.

Three further observations concerning these organizations are in point here. First, six of the top seven groups are directly concerned with interracial relations and "race betterment." Second, only one of the organizations on the entire list (ranking seventh) has as its principal interest the business organization of the sub-community. Finally, although union membership among Pacific City's Negroes is fairly widespread, only one union was mentioned, one that rated low in influence. This finding is consistent with the fact that, although there are several professional Negro union leaders

---

[15]Hunter, *op. cit.*, p. 125.
[16]The technique of obtaining this list of organizations is discussed above.
[17]Hunter, *op. cit.*, pp. 125-126.

TABLE 3

SUB-COMMUNITY ORGANIZATIONS RATED BY 36 SUB-COMMUNITY LEADERS, RANKED ACCORDING TO NUMBER OF "MOST INFLUENTIAL" RATINGS RECEIVED

Organization	Number of "Most Influential" Ratings
Urban League	33
N.A.A.C.P.	29
Jackson Street Community Council	17
Christian Friends for Racial Equality	17
Association of Colored Women	16
Eastside Y.W.C.A.	16
East Madison Street Commercial Club	16
Cosmopolitan Century Club	9
Eastside Y.M.C.A.	8
Prince Hall Masons	6
The People's Institutional Baptist Church	4
The Brotherhood of Sleeping Car Porters	4
Philorati Club	4
Mary Mahoney Registered Nurses	3
Fraternal Organization	2
Veteran's Organization	2
Fraternal Organization	2
Fraternal Organization	2
Fraternal Organization	1
Sorority	1
Fraternal Organization	1
Fir State Golf Club	1
Fraternal Organization	1
Church Club	1
The Elks	1

in the community, none of them was cited as a "top leader." It appears that the major concern of the Negro sub-community, as well as of its leaders, lies with issues centering around minority status and group protest.

It may be noted that no "luncheon clubs," "supper clubs," or other informally organized groups appear on the list of the influential organizations. Early in the field work, an attempt was made to discover any such groups, but only one, the "Sunday Night Supper Club," was mentioned. One informant, a recent migrant to the community and a highly trained educator, in citing this club, noted that several top leaders whose names appear in Table 1 were active members. However, the club was only recently organized and appears to be primarily a recreational group.

Summary and Conclusions

According to Mills, Hunter, Miller and others, the structure of power in American society and in American communities is derived in large part from the institutional structure of the society. The majority of the leaders identified by Hunter and Miller in their field studies were occupants of high positions in the economic organization of their communities. Mills argues that power resides principally in the realms of economic, political, and military organization, and suggests further, that the structure of the "power elite" is related to the rate and nature of social change in a society at any given time. The fruitfulness of a comparative approach to the study of power is suggested by these views. Such an approach would aim at specifying the conditions relevant to the type of power structure and processes in a community or society and would require a typology of community power structures.

Although the findings of this study do not, of course, make it possible to develop a systematic theory of power, the following conclusions are relevant to this purpose. First, it is evident that, although there is an identifiable structure of leadership in the sub-community of Pacific City at the present time, the leaders themselves are not "power wielders" or "decision makers" in the sense in which the terms are used by Hunter and Mills: they hold positions of little importance to the community's institutional structures; their decisions have no serious ramifications for the larger community.

In Pacific City there is an ecologically identifiable "Negro community" — why is there no genuine power structure of the type found in Regional City? This lack can be attributed in part to the relatively small Negro population, insufficient to support large-scale separate institutions; in part to the rapid expansion of the population in the sub-community (evidence from interviews indicates that the old-leadership structure [prior to 1940] was disrupted and almost wholly destroyed by the impact of the incoming migrants); and in part to the attitudes of the leading figures in the minority community, who have worked hard for liberal legislation, better education for Negroes, and better housing on an open market. In this work they have been remarkably successful, and prefer not to risk these gains by supporting segregated institutions.

Several of the respondents insisted that it is incorrect to speak of a "Negro community" in Pacific City, maintaining that most Negroes are not conscious of being members of a racial community as they are in many other cities. Perhaps this helps to explain why the Negro leaders are those who are active in "protest" organizations — for these may be about all that remain of a Negro sub-community.

In any event, the sub-communities of Regional City and Pacific City represent quite different types. The well organized, stable structure of power in Regional City is missing in Pacific City. Although leadership groups have certain similar characteristics, those in Regional City wield power *within* the sub-community and those in Pacific City do not. Leaders in Regional City are motivated, at least in some measure, to maintain their segregated sub-community, while in Pacific City the leaders seek opposite goals. These findings emphasize the importance of the general community context in the study of power relations.

The Power Structure of the Negro Sub-Community: A Case Study and a Comparative View

Harold W. Pfautz

In the contemporary setting of rapid change, clear-cut issues, and sometimes overt conflict in race relations in many American cities, studies of the power structure of the Negro sub-community come to have strategic value on both theoretical and practical grounds. In contrast to a traditional lack of solidarity and powerless leadership, recent events and studies demonstrate a growing ability to act together and to develop a leadership which can make effective demands on the dominant group.[1] This situation provides an unparalleled opportunity to observe the formation, modes of operation, and functional significance of community power structures. In addition, reliable knowledge concerning the nature and functioning of Negro sub-community leadership on all levels — community, region, and nation — is one *sine qua non* of a responsible and successful expedition of the desegregation process.

The present study of the power structure of a Negro sub-community furthers the comparative note struck by Barth and Abu-Laban.[2] To "Regional

Reprinted from *Phylon,* vol. XXIII, (Summer 1962), pp. 156-166 with permission of the publisher. Copyright 1962 by Atlanta University.

[1]Cf. eg., Lewis M. Killian and Charles U. Smith, "Negro Protest Leaders in a Southern Community," *Social Forces,* XXXVIII (March, 1960), 253-57 and Martin Luther King, *Stride Toward Freedom* (New York, 1958).

[2]Ernest A. T. Barth and Baha Abu-Laban, "Power Structure and the Negro Community," *American Sociological Review,* XXIV (February, 1959), 69-76.

City"[3] and to "Pacific City,"[4] it adds empirical data on Providence, Rhode Island, a New England community of moderate size with a long history of race relations, a formally liberal tradition, a significant degree of sub-community identity, a clear-cut sub-community power structure, yet an economically depressed Negro population and a recent past of accommodating leadership. After a brief consideration of the history of the Negro sub-community in Providence, its power structure will be described and compared with those of Regional City and Pacific City. Finally, some practical and theoretical implications of the findings will be discussed.

The Negro in Providence

The history of the Negro in Providence and in the state of which it is the capital goes back to the seventeenth century.[5] Its merchants not only played a prominent role in the early slave trade but also, motivated by their religious convictions, were largely responsible for the abolition of slavery in the latter part of the eighteenth century. Although an effective and viable anti-slavery tradition had an early development in Providence, the general body of its citizens were highly discriminatory in their acts and hostile in their attitudes toward the city's fifteen hundred "free people of colour." Negroes were legally declared ineligible to vote in 1822 and received the franchise only after a bitter struggle, two decades later.[6] Moreover, there were anti-Negro riots in 1824 and 1831, each of which involved the razing of the city's already segregated Negro settlements. Nevertheless, by the time of the Civil War, despite (and largely because of) the generally prejudiced environment, Providence Negroes had developed thriving community organizations of their own — churches, mutual aid societies, schools, and the like. Some among them amassed considerable property and began to provide community leadership, winning a long and drawn-out battle for non-segregated public education in 1866.

---

[3]Cf. Floyd Hunter, *Community Power Structure* (Chapel Hill, 1943), pp. 114-50. Regional City involved a long-established, relatively static and traditional Deep South urban situation with a clearly identifiable sub-community power structure.
[4]Cf. Barth and Abu-Laban, *op. cit.* Pacific City involved a relatively new and dynamic Northwest coast urban situation which, according to the researchers, lacked sub-community identity and clear-cut organization for power.
[5]The account of the early history of the Negro in Providence leans heavily on Irving H. Bartlett, *From Slave to Citizen* (Providence, R. I.: The Urban League of Greater Providence, 1954).
[6]This was the occasion of "Dorr's Rebellion," a suffragist movement which attained the proportions of a local civil war. Ironically, the working class Suffragists refused to include Negroes in their program, and the latter attained the franchise ultimately through the efforts of the "aristocratic" Legal Party. Cf. Bartlett, *op. cit.,* pp. 39-43.

Between 1865 and 1910 the state's Negro population almost doubled (from 4,087 to 7,529), largely through migration from the upper South. And, by the turn of the century, Rhode Island Negroes could look back on a period of solid accomplishment in the area of civil rights. From 1900 until the beginning of World War II, however, almost no real progress was made. The dynamic struggle for equal citizenship which had characterized the city's race relations in the nineteenth century was succeeded by a period of stagnation in the first four decades of the twentieth century. To be sure, a local branch of the National Association for the Advancement of Colored People was established in 1914, but it was able to make little headway against the conservatism of the local community and internal struggles for power within the organization.[7] During this era the sub-community leadership seemed primarily oriented to Negro society. It was vested in a small group of men who were content, for the most part, to play the role of accommodating leaders.

The Negro population of Providence continued traditionally unskilled, ill-housed, and poorly paid to such an extent that the "old" leadership was completely by-passed in a revolt of the younger elements just before World War II. In 1939 the "young Turks" went directly to leading white citizens and succeeded in securing the cooperation of the latter in establishing a local branch of the Urban League with a full-time, paid, professional director. The cleavages in the Negro community in general and in its leadership in particular that resulted from this development are still evident. Nevertheless, the League, in its two decades of operation, has come to be accepted as the official spokesman for Providence Negroes.[8] It has extended its activities throughout the state, has been moderately successful in opening up new skilled and white-collar occupations, and has been the informal organizing force behind movements to bolster the civil rights of local Negroes. A State Commission Against Discrimination was established in 1951; the Commission's directive was broadened to include the policies and practices of the city's Public Housing Authority in 1956; and, currently, there are lively grass-roots movements to secure fair housing legislation for the state as well as a human relations commission for the city.

---

[7]Leadership disputes within the branch continued through the Forties. In 1945 one election was voided through the action of the national office of the NAACP. Cf. Barbara Elizabeth Chandler, "The Position of the Negro in Providence" (unpublished B.A. thesis, Department of Sociology, Bates College, April, 1947).

[8]The community has (quite unconsciously) sought to turn the League into a social case-work agency. Whenever difficulties involving a "racial" factor develop in the schools, public housing, neighborhoods, etc., community officials immediately get in touch with the League on the unstated assumption that the League can "solve" the problem on an informal basis.

By 1950 Providence Negroes numbered 8,304 (see Table 1), and comprised 3.3 percent of a total population of 248,674. While the city lost population with a percentage decline of 1.9 during the decade 1940-1950, the Negro sub-community experienced a moderate increase of 30 percent.[9] As might be expected, the Negro population is residentially segregated: more than one-half of the Negro residents are concentrated in only two of the city's thirty-seven census tracts. In 1950 the "index of dissimilarity" between the Negro and white residential patterns was 65.[10]

Perhaps the most signal indicators of the minority status of Providence's Negro population are data on their occupational and income status which are reported in Table 1, together with comparative data on Regional City and Pacific City.[11] The relatively depressed and static situation of Negroes in Providence is suggested by its closer similarity to the Southern than to the Northwestern case. Whereas only approximately 10 percent of Providence and Regional City Negroes were in white-collar occupations, more than 15 percent of the Negro labor force in Pacific City were so employed. Moreover, approximately one-fifth of the Negro labor forces in the New England and Southern cities were still in traditional private household service occupations in contrast to only one-tenth of Pacific City's Negroes.[12]

Turning to the data on income distribution, the median income of Negroes in Regional City in 1949 was lowest ($1,045), followed by Providence

---

[9]According to the 1960 census, these trends have continued. Providence experienced a 17 percent decline in total population between 1950 and 1960; its Negro population increased 34.3 percent; and the latter now number 11,153 and constitute 5.4 percent of the total population. The population of Regional City increased 47.1 percent and that of Pacific City increased 19.1 percent during this same period. The percentage increases of the Negro populations for these two cities were 53.7 and 71.7 respectively. In 1960 the proportion of Negroes in Regional City increased to 38.3 and the correlative figure for Pacific City was 4.8 percent. Cf. U. S. Bureau of the Census, *U. S. Census of Population: 1960. General Population Characteristics.* Final Report PC(1)-12B, 41B, and 49B, Table 21 (Washington, D. C., 1961).

[10]The "index of dissimilarity" is defined as the sum of the positive (or negative) differences between two percentage distributions. It indicates the percentage of one group which would have to move to a different area to match that of the other on a proportional basis. The larger the value of the index, the greater the spatial separation. Cf. Otis Dudley Duncan and Beverly Duncan, "A Methodological Analysis of Segregation Indexes," *American Sociological Review,* XX (April, 1955), 210-17. Parenthetically, despite much civil rights activity in Providence during the past decade, the value of the index based on census data for 1960 has remained practically constant and now stands at 64.

[11]Data on the socio-economic characteristics of the population for cities, by race, has yet to be made available by the Bureau of the Census.

[12]Significantly, a comparative study of the process of school desegregation in a number of communities discovered that the proportion of Negro females employed in domestic service was highly and significantly inversely correlated with non-compliance. Cf. Harry V. Ball and George E. Simpson, "A Comparative Study of Compulsory School Desegregation in Fifty-two Selected Communities" (paper read at the 56th Annual Meeting of the American Sociological Association, St. Louis, Missouri, August 29-September 2, 1961).

TABLE 1

SELECTED DEMOGRAPHIC AND SOCIO-ECONOMIC CHARACTER-
ISTICS OF PROVIDENCE, R. I., REGIONAL CITY, AND PACIFIC
CITY AND THEIR NEGRO POPULATIONS,[a] 1950

Characteristic	Providence	Regional City	Pacific City
Total population (1950)	248,674	331,314	457,591
Percentage change (1940-1950)	—1.9	9.6	27.0
Total Negro population (1950)	8,304	121,285	15,666
Percentage change (1940-1950)	30.0	16.1	313.5
Percent Negro	3.3	33.6	3.4
Median income white (1949)	$1,824	$2,218	$2,356
Median income Negro (1949)	$1,150	$1,045	$1,709
Percent white collar (Negro)	9.7	9.4	15.2
Percent private household service (Negro)	18.4	22.2	10.5

[a]U. S. Bureau of the Census, *U. S. Census of Population: 1950. Characteristics of the Population* (Washington, D. C., 1952).

($1,150), while Pacific City Negroes had the highest median income ($1,709). Whites in Regional City earned, on the average, twice as much as Negroes; in Providence they earned 1.6 times as much; and in Pacific City they earned only 1.4 times as much.[13] Indeed, the picture presented by both the Southern and New England cases is that of a very small number and proportion of middle and upper-income recipients, complemented by a large mass in the low-income brackets.[14] On the other hand, the form of the income distribution among Pacific City Negroes involves significant numbers and proportion in the middle-income categories. Thus, whereas approximately two-thirds of all employed Negroes over fourteen years of age earned less than fifteen hundred dollars a year in Providence and Regional City (64.2 percent and 68.4 percent, respectively), less than half (44.5 percent) of Pacific City Negroes were in this class.

On the basis of these data, Providence Negroes clearly continue to be economically depressed and the object of considerable discrimination and prejudice. In part this is due to the small size and proportion of the Negro population in comparison to the dominant white group, a fact which inevitably minimizes the former as a political threat. Another factor is the generally depressed economic situation of the city and state which, in the nature

[13]Studies suggest that it is the relative difference rather than the absolute difference in income that is a valid indicator of the state of race relations in a community. Cf. *ibid.*
[14]As late as 1947, Chandler concluded that while there were distinctions between "old-and newcomers" and "East Side and West Side," among Providence Negroes, because of the small size and lack of economic development of the Negro sub-community, no social classes existed. Cf. Chandler, *op. cit.,* p. 113.

of the case, bears hardest on the minority members of the community.[15] Finally, the previously mentioned schisms within the Negro sub-community and its leadership have necessarily weakened its ability to present a solid front and successfully to make collective demands on the dominant group.

Presently, a series of already accomplished as well as proposed urban renewal and redevelopment programs will ultimately involve the relocation of approximately 80 percent of all Providence Negroes. The issues brought to the surface by this massive dislocation, plus the current pressures and climate of opinion connected with the desegregation process on the national level, will bring about, for better or for worse, a new era in local race relations. In this context the sub-community leadership is already engaged in an internal competition for power and status as well as in an external power struggle with the dominant whites.

The Negro Sub-Community Power Structure

Data for reconstructing the power structure of the Negro sub-community in Providence were gathered by a modified version of the methods employed by Hunter and Barth and Abu-Laban. A list of political influentials was compiled from a variety of sources including local clergymen, business and professional men, as well as a newspaper clipping scrapbook maintained by the local Urban League. In view of the small size of the Negro sub-community and the correlative assumption that all of the leaders were well known and known to one another, interviews were begun immediately with those on the list who were mentioned by at least three different sources — e.g., two individuals and the newspaper.[16] In addition to questions concerning his own social and economic characteristics, each interviewee was asked the following:

> If you were requested to choose a committee of ten Negro leaders in Providence (either men or women) who together would formulate a general policy affecting the Negro community as a whole, and you wanted to choose those individuals who, if they were to express their approval of a particular policy, would influence the greatest number of Negroes in the community to support it — whom would you choose?[17]

---

[15]Cf. Kurt B. Mayer and Sidney Goldstein, *Migration and Economic Development in Rhode Island* (Providence, 1958).

[16]The writer is indebted to Miss Marjorie Gaysunas for an extremely skillful and tactful series of interviews.

[17]Because of the small size of the community, not every informant was able to name ten different leaders.

The first ten interviews provided a list of thirty-eight different individuals, and six additional interviews added no new names. Since this suggested that the complement of perceived leaders had been exhausted, interviewing was stopped at this point. The Negro sub-community leaders with whom we will be concerned were arbitrarily defined as those among the thirty-eight mentioned who received at least four votes.[18] The final result was a list of sixteen top leaders, each of whom had been interviewed.[19] And, in Table 2, these leaders, ranked by the number of votes each received from his fifteen peers in the interviewers, are presented. Data on the number of mutual choices, age, occupation, and "social orientation"[20] are also included.

TABLE 2

SELECTED CHARACTERISTICS OF NEGRO SUB-COMMUNITY LEADERS IN PROVIDENCE, R. I., RANKED BY NUMBER OF VOTES RECEIVED IN LEADERSHIP POLL

Leader	Number of Votes	Number of Mutual Choices	Occupation	Age	Social Orientation
Young	15	10	Agency director	56	Integration
Stephens	15	7	Mortician	51	Integration
Masters	15	9	Maintenance superintendent	47	Middle-road
Stewart	8	3	Management analyst	44	Integration
Spear	8	5	Agency director	46	Middle-road
Roberts	8	5	Real estate	79	Middle-road
Moore	8	5	Lawyer	72	Segregation
Miller	7	4	Union official	40	Integration
Dunham	7	5	Post office clerk (ret.)	62	Middle-road
Hardy	7	3	Physician	71	Segregation
Dunham, Jr.	5	3	Lawyer	30	Integration
Stone	5	2	Minister	63	Segregation
Sullivan	4	2	Bank manager	39	Integration
Worth	4	1	Trucker	71	Segregation
Gold	4	4	Mortician	72	Segregation
Gold (Mrs.)	4	0	Housewife	72	Segregation

[18]Of the remaining twenty-two potential influentials, two received two votes and twenty received one vote in the course of the sixteen interviews.

[19]Both Hunter and Barth and Abu-Laban developed selected lists of influentials from which ten were to be nominated by the interview panels. Hunter obtained interviews from twenty-three sub-community leaders who voted for ten among a list of thirty-four potentials. Cf. Hunter, *op. cit.*, pp. 114-18. Barth and Abu-Laban interviewed thirty-six potentials who voted for ten among themselves. Cf. Barth and Abu-Laban, *op. cit.*, pp. 71-72.

[20]See below for a discussion of "social orientation."

Needless to say, the most striking characteristic of the list is the complete unanimity regarding the top three leaders, which is indicative of the clarity with which the power structure of the Negro sub-community is perceived. Parenthetically, these three men (Young, Stephens, and Masters) were not only mutual choices but also meet one another in a variety of contexts, both formal and informal, which allows for constant and efficient intercommunication. For example, all three serve on the Boards of the local branches of the Urban League and the NAACP; they belong to and have served as officers and Board members of the two oldest formally organized Negro men's social clubs in Providence; and they also engage in mutual home visiting and entertaining.

In Table 3 some selected characteristics of the power structures of the Negro sub-communities in the three cities are presented. In view of the already demonstrated similarity between the Southern and New England situations in regard to the socio-economic status of their respective Negro populations, it is not surprising to find a degree of similarity in certain dimensions of their sub-community power structures. In contrast to Pacific City, the Negro leaders of Providence and Regional City are older and more provincial. The age difference is approximately ten years; and, whereas almost 90 percent of the Pacific City leaders were born outside of the state,

TABLE 3

SELECTED DEMOGRAPHIC AND SOCIO-ECONOMIC CHARACTERISTICS OF NEGRO LEADERS IN PROVIDENCE, R. I., REGIONAL CITY AND PACIFIC CITY

Characteristic	Providence	Regional City[a]	Pacific City[b]
Size of leadership group	16	34	36
Average age in years	57.5	54.3	44.8
Range in years	30-85	40-73	—[c]
Average length of residence in years	45.5	—[c]	16.5
Percent born outside of the state	68.7	57.9	88.9
Percent born in the city	22.2	15.7	—[c]
Occupational Distribution			
Professional	37.5%	55.9%	50.0%
Managers and officials	31.2	5.9	—
Small business	25.0	32.3	22.2
Clerical and sales	—	—	11.1
Other	6.3	5.9	16.7
Total	100.0%	100.0%	100.0%

[a]Cf. Hunter, *op. cit.*, pp. 114-150.
[b]Cf. Barth and Abu-Laban, *op. cit.*, pp. 69-76.
[c]Data not available.

the percentages for Providence and Regional City are 58 and 69, respectively. On the other hand, the occupational status of the Negro leaders is quite similar in all three cities — essentially a matter of professionals, minor managers and officials, and small businessmen.

The functional significance of the observed demographic differences in the makeup of the sub-community power structures inheres in their social psychological implications. The greater age and provincialism of the Negro leaders in Providence and Regional City might involve an entirely different "political generation" from that represented by the Pacific City leadership.[21] This, in turn, suggests the risk of a "trained incapacity" to deal with the rapidly changing form and content of race relations in the former two situations. In addition, the lack of leaders in large-scale commercial and financial operations in all three cases makes not only for a relative lack of power, given the institutional concept of "men of power" employed by most students, but also a serious gap in available perspectives for formulating strategy and tactics in community power struggles.[22]

As previously noted, the Negro power structure in Providence was split in 1939 in connection with the establishment of a branch of the Urban League. This schism continues in effect today along generational, organizational, and orientation lines, tempered by the presence of a few "middle-roaders."

The Executive Director of the local Urban League, who has served in this capacity for more than two decades and who, perforce, has constant dealings with all sub-community leaders, was asked to rate each one according to the following types of "social orientation":[23] (1) integration: activities and concerns anchored in and identified with the total community; participates actively in integrated organizations; (2) segregation: activities and concerns anchored in and identified with the local Negro sub-community; participates actively in segregated organizations; (3) middle-road: active in both integrated and segregated organizations; identification vacillates between the total community and the Negro sub-community.

The clarity of the generational split between the "old" and the "new" leader is suggested by the data in Table 4 where the leaders have been arranged by "social orientation," age, and votes in the leadership poll. Six of the sixteen leaders were categorized as "integration" oriented; their aver-

---

[21]Cf. Heberle's discussion of "The Problem of Political Generations" in Rudolf Heberle, *Social Movements* (New York, 1951), pp. 120-27.

[22]Barth and Abu-Laban, for example, conclude that "no genuine power structure had developed" in Pacific City due to the lack of large-scale business and industrial organizations. *Op. cit.,* pp. 69 and 76.

[23]The writer is indebted to James M. Williams, Executive Director of the Urban League of Rhode Island, for his many kindnesses and active participation in this study.

age age was 43.3 years; and they received an average of 6.3 votes. In contrast, six others were categorized as "segregation" oriented; their average age was 70.2 years; and they received an average of 5.3 votes. There were four "middle-roaders" with an average age of 58.5, who received an average of 8.8 votes. In general, the younger, integration-oriented leaders are more active in and identified with the Urban League, whereas the older leaders tend to be more active in and identified with the local branch of the NAACP. Significantly, the two older "middle-road" leaders (Roberts and Dunham, Sr.) are the only members of their generation to play active roles in the "new" Urban League, suggestive of their "broker" role and function.

On the basis of these data, the sub-community power structure of Providence would seem to be more oriented to "integration" than to "segregation." The differences, however, are often accommodated by the presence of the middle-roaders. And the strength of the latter is suggested by the fact that

TABLE 4

NUMBER OF VOTES IN LEADERSHIP POLL AND AGE OF "NEW" AND "OLD" LEADERS OF THE NEGRO SUB-COMMUNITY IN PROVIDENCE, R. I., BY SOCIAL ORIENTATION

| Type of Leader | Social Orientation | | | | | | | | |
| | Integration Number of | | | Middle-Road Number of | | | Segregation Number of | | |
	Name	Votes	Age	Name	Votes	Age	Name	Votes	Age
Old				Roberts	8	79	Moore	8	72
				Dunham	7	62	Hardy	7	71
							Stone	5	63
							Worth	4	71
							Gold	4	72
							Gold (Mrs.)	4	72
New	Young	15	56	Masters	15	47			
	Stephens	15	51	Spear	8	46			
	Stewart	8	44						
	Miller	7	40						
	Dunham, Jr.	5	30						
	Sullivan	4	39						

their average number of mutual choices in the leadership poll was 6.0 in comparison to 4.8 among the "integration-oriented" and 2.5 among the "segregation-oriented" leaders. Indeed, while the local sub-community leadership in Providence is currently more militant than it has been in the past, it is typically a matter of "protest within the status quo."[24]

---

[24]Cf. Hunter, *op. cit.,* p. 128 and Oliver Cox, "Leadership Among Negroes," in Alvin W. Gouldner, ed., *Studies in Leadership* (New York, 1950), p. 270.

Discussion and Conclusions

A brief account has been presented of the history of the Negro and of race relations in a moderate-sized urban New England community, together with a picture of the power structure of the Negro sub-community. The latter, in turn, has been compared with studies made in Southern and Northwestern urban situations. A number of theoretical and practical inferences can be drawn from the data involved.

In the first place, it is worth noting that many of the recent criticisms which have been made of the so-called reputational approach to the study of community power structures have considerably less validity when applied to the Negro sub-community.[25] This tends to be true of the Negro sub-community in general and of places which involve relatively small numbers and proportions of Negroes in particular.

The high degree of consensus in regard to the top three leaders of the Providence Negro power structure suggests that there may be less of a gap between "reputation" and "behavior" in the case of Negro sub-community leaders. This, of course, is related to the "form" of the Negro sub-community social structure which is likely to be monolithic in character, involving a small, articulate leadership at the top and an undifferentiated and inarticulate mass at the bottom.[26] Further, despite tendencies toward differentiation of leadership types according to issues which have been observed in metropolitan centers with large Negro populations,[27] there is only one issue in the final analysis: the ubiquitous race question. Thus, in Providence, despite the intense competition between generations and organizations for sub-community power and status, one of the most "segregation-oriented" and competitive "old" leaders voluntarily substituted himself for one of the "new" and younger leaders who failed to appear in court on time in connection with an injunction suit the latter had filed in protest against an urban renewal plan which would force the relocation of a large number of Negro families.

We would also point out that the institutional formulation of "men of power" espoused by Hunter and others is not without its ideological implica-

---

[25]Cf. e.g., Robert A. Dahl, "A Critique of the Ruling Elite Model," *American Political Science Review*, LII (June, 1958), 463-69; Nelson Polsby, "The Sociology of Community Power: A Reassessment," *Social Forces*, XXXVII (March, 1959), 232-36 and "Three Problems in the Analysis of Community Power," *American Sociological Review*, XXIV (December, 1959), 796-803; Peter H. Rossi, "Theory and Method in the Study of Power in the Local Community" (paper presented at the Conference on Metropolitan Leadership, Northwestern University, April, 1960; mimeographed); and Raymond E. Wolfinger, "The Study of Community Power," *American Sociological Review*, XXV (October, 1960), 636-44.

[26]Cf. Rossi, *op. cit.*, pp. 37-38.

[27]James Q. Wilson, *Negro Politics* (Glencoe, Illinois, 1960).

tions when it comes to social action.[28] Being "counted in" in community decision-making necessarily involves "protest within the status quo." Direct action outside of the institutionalized distribution of power (the social movement), however, is an increasingly obvious alternative for Negro leaders. To date, vested interests in segregated economic, political, and social markets, the saliency of "respectability" for the Negro middle class, as well as the lack of formal and visible barriers to equality in Northern urban centers (which minimize opportunities for dramatic protest), all conspire to favor being "counted in." In Providence, for example, the Urban League has become such an efficient "minority group" casework agency and locus of control and communication in local race relations that it is always consulted by white community leaders in connection with policy decisions affecting the community. On the other hand, it often finds itself unable to press its demands on the dominant group power structure lest it risk its hard-won formal respectability and social work "trouble-shooting" effectiveness. To the extent that Negro leaders become aware that the status gains which result from being formally counted in often involve the risk of being informally and effectively "counted out" or neutralized in the power struggle, militant protest outside of the institutional distribution of power is a greater probability.

The power structures of Negro sub-communities in American cities are in a process of schism and realignment under the impact of desegregation movements and activities. On the practical side, lack of knowledge of the dramatic changes taking place with regard both to the personnel and the tactics of the sub-community leadership on the part of the dominant group power structure invites communication breakdowns which can lead to mutual miscalculations and, ultimately, to civic violence. Within the Negro community, the lack of experience and of a full complement of perspectives to bring to bear on community problems as well as the often wasteful competition among leaders and agencies for power and status (all of which are the heritage of the vicious circle of discrimination and prejudice) further complicate the problem. The challenge this situation presents to social scientists of theoretical as well as of social action persuasion is as pressing as it is obvious.

---

[28] James B. McKee, "Community Power and Strategies in Race Relations: Some Critical Observations," *Social Problems,* VI (Winter, 1958-59), 195-203.

Protest and Negotiation:
A Case Study of Negro
Leadership in Atlanta, Georgia

Jack L. Walker

Since the wave of sit-ins, freedom rides and other demonstrations by Negro college students in 1960 and 1961 there has been considerable speculation, both by journalists and social scientists, that a new, more "militant" type of leadership is emerging among American Negroes. Much attention has been focused on the activities of the students, and on such dramatic "protest leaders" as Martin Luther King, Jr., who, it is asserted, are steadily gaining the allegiance of the Negro masses at the expense of the older, more established community spokesmen.[1]

Reprinted from *Midwest Journal of Political Science*, Vol. VII, no. 2, 1963 by Jack L. Walker by permission of the Wayne State University Press and the author. Copyright 1963 by the Wayne State University Press.
[1]The literature is voluminous, but among the most interesting journalistic efforts are: Hodding Carter, "The Young Negro is a New Negro," *The New York Times Magazine,* May 1, 1960, p. 11; Helen Fuller, "Southern Students Take Over," *The New Republic,* 142: 14-16, May 2, 1960; Louis Lomax, "The Negro Revolt Against the Negro Leaders," *Harper's Magazine,* June, 1960, p. 41; Kenneth Rexroth, "Students Take Over," *The Nation,* 191: 4-9, July 2, 1960; Dan Wakefield, *Revolt in the South* (New York, Grove Press, 1960); Howard Zinn, "Finishing School for Pickets," *The Nation,* 191:71-73, August 6, 1960. Scholarly contributions are not so numerous, but of special interest are: M. Elaine Burgess, *Negro Leadership in a Southern City* (Chapel Hill, University of North Carolina Press, 1962); Tilman Cothran and William Phillips, "Negro Leadership in a Crisis Situation," *Phylon,* Vol. 22 (Summer, 1961), pp. 107-118; Leslie Dunbar, "Reflections on the Latest Reform of the South," *Phylon,* Vol. 22 (Fall, 1961), pp. 249-257; Lewis M. Killian and Charles U. Smith, "Negro Protest Leaders in a Southern Community," *Social Forces* (March, 1960), pp. 253-260.

In this essay certain political attitudes and goals of a group of Negro civic leaders in Atlanta, Georgia, will be described. An inquiry will be made into the motives of the student sit-in demonstrators, and the differences will be explored among Negro leaders of all kinds regarding goals and tactics. Also the socio-economic factors associated with their differing attitudes will be analyzed, and some speculation will be offered, based on the results of this study, about the future development of the leadership of the Negro community in Atlanta.

The description and analysis is based on material gathered during a series of interviews conducted with thirty-six Negro leaders in Atlanta during April and May, 1962.[2] The group selected for interviewing included the Negro leaders who were involved in the controversy over lunch counter segregation which lasted in Atlanta from March, 1960, when the first sit-ins took place, until September, 1961, when the lunch counters, rest rooms and other facilities in the major downtown department and variety stores were opened on a desegregated basis. The list includes all those who either led or helped to organize the sit-in demonstrations, picket lines and economic boycott that took place during the controversy, and all those who figured in attempts, either successful or unsuccessful, to negotiate an agreement to settle the dispute.[3]

The group selected for the study was drawn from almost every segment of Atlanta's Negro middle class, and it includes 10 businessmen, 4 college educators, 4 ministers, 5 lawyers, 4 social workers, 2 physicians, 5 staff members of civil rights groups, 3 student leaders, and 1 housewife. The group does not include, however, any labor leader or government employee, and it does not include a single teacher or administrator in the Atlanta public school system. The first two omissions are understandable since in Atlanta, outside of small segregated locals of the musicians and automobile workers, Negroes do not hold administrative posts in labor unions, and positions above the menial level in either the city, state, or national governments are held by only a tiny handful of Atlanta's Negroes. But the absence of the public school personnel is puzzling. There seems to be some fear among teachers that they might endanger their jobs by becoming involved in controversial public disputes. These apprehensions may or may not be justified. Further investigation suggested, however, that there was nothing about the sit-in controversy in partic-

---

[2]This research was made possible by the support of the Iowa Citizenship Clearing House and the National Center for Education in Politics. Neither of them, of course, is responsible for any errors of fact or interpretation in this study.

[3]The list was compiled from the record of the controversy found in the files of *The Atlanta Constitution, The Atlanta Journal, The Atlanta Daily World,* and *The Atlanta Inquirer.* Each of those identified in the newspaper reports as leaders or important participants was asked to look over the list and add the names of anyone who had led the protest demonstrations, or participated in negotiating sessions of any kind during the controversy. Only two names were added to the list in this way that were not found in the newspaper reports.

ular that discouraged participation by the teachers. This group, which includes
the largest number of college trained professionals in the Negro community,
seems to take little part in political affairs or protest movements of any kind.

This is a study of motives and political tactics; no effort was made to devise
a method of identifying the "real" leaders of the community. The group that
was interviewed does not include, by any means, all those in the Negro community who might have some legitimate claim to influence or leadership in
civic or political affairs. Those who were chosen were the principal actors in
the sit-in controversy, which was the most controversial single incident in the
history of Atlanta's Negro community since World War Two. It is assumed
that by concentrating on this set of dynamic circumstances a significant group
of Negro community leaders has been obtained.

<h2 style="text-align:center">II</h2>

The spontaneous series of protest demonstrations by Negro college students
that swept across the South in 1960 was a most significant manifestation of a
growing impatience among Negroes all over the country with the progress
being made to afford them social, economic, and political equality. Young
Negroes were demonstrating that they were no longer willing to adjust their
aspirations and their behavior to a system in which they were relegated to a
second class status. Very little progress had been made through the regular
channels of democratic decision-making toward removing racial bars to opportunity, even after the 1954 Supreme Court decision in the Brown case.
Negroes were faced with the fact that they were still being denied the right
to vote in some parts of the South, that there was continued, even increased,
resistance from the segregationist whites, and that in the rest of the white
community, all over the country, there seemed to be a general indifference to
their plight. When these circumstances were viewed along with what seemed
to them to be acquiescence to the status quo on the part of the established
Negro leaders, the students became increasingly exasperated and impatient,
and they went into the streets to obtain a hearing for their demands. The
democratic process, the institutions based on discussion, negotiation and compromise, had proved unable to provide them with relief from the deprivations
they suffered.

On February 1, 1960, several Negro students sat down at a lunch counter
in Greensboro, North Carolina, and refused to leave when told that the store
did not serve Negroes. The manager is reported to have said: "They can just
sit there. It's nothing to me." But within a week similar groups were sitting
down in protest all across the South, and on February 17, 1960, the Georgia
legislature responded to the growing movement by passing a special anti-
trespass law.

On the campus of Atlanta University students were planning similar
demonstrations as early as February 4, but they were persuaded by faculty

members and an apprehensive administration to postpone their action until they had drawn up a statement of their grievances. This statement was quickly completed and printed in the form of a full page advertisement in all local newspapers on March 9, 1960, under the title: "An Appeal for Human Rights." The advertisement caused a sensation and it was commented on by politicians and public figures all over the country. This was followed on March 15 by the first widespread sit-in demonstrations in Atlanta in which 77 students were arrested under the new Georgia trespass law.

While their cases were pending in court the students began to work on several other projects. They mounted picket lines against food stores which had large Negro clienteles yet did not hire Negroes above the menial level, they held a series of meetings in Negro churches explaining the student movement and asking for support, they began publishing a weekly news sheet that eventually became a full-fledged weekly newspaper, and on May 17, 1960, they gathered 1400 students together to march on the state capitol in downtown Atlanta to celebrate the Supreme Court's 1954 anti-segregation decision. This march was diverted by Atlanta's Chief of Police to prevent the students from meeting a large, ugly crowd that had gathered at the capitol. When the students left for summer vacation tension was running high in the city.

During the summer the leaders of the student movement remained in Atlanta and continued organizational and propaganda work, and in the autumn, on October 19, 1960, they mounted widespread sit-ins once again, and once again large numbers of the demonstrators were arrested. The students refused to leave the jail on bail, and at this point the Major asked for, and was granted, a 30-day truce period in which he promised to try to reach a settlement of the dispute.

The Mayor was unable even to get all the downtown merchants to meet to discuss the issue, and several other informal efforts to negotiate the dispute also failed. In part this was because of disagreements between the Negro leaders and in part because of the refusal of some white merchants to negotiate at all. The students resumed their sit-ins on November 25, 1960, and also organized a full-scale boycott of the downtown shopping area. A stalemate continued through the months of December and January, during which time most of the lunch counters remained closed and the boycott of the downtown stores remained in effect.

On February 1, 1961, the students, along with many adults, staged a march on the downtown area commemorating the anniversary of the beginning of the sit-in movement. Throughout this three-month period the students, equipped with short-wave radios, had been sitting-in at lunch counters all over the city without incident. Either they had been ignored, or the counters had been closed, but on February 7, 1961, one restaurant manager in a federal office building invoked the trespass law and had the demonstrators arrested, and during the next three days arrests continued daily with the students refusing once again to come out on bail. A protest march and rally was planned to take place in front of the jail on February 19, and there was widespread fear that such a demonstration might result in a riot. At this tense moment the student leaders themselves turned to one of the oldest, most respected Negro leaders who, by utilizing friendships he had with influential white leaders, was able to get negotiations started which eventually led to a settlement of the controversy. The agreement was announced on March 7, 1961, and after a bitter dispute within the Negro community it was accepted. It called for desegregation of the lunch counters after the school desegregation had been completed during the following fall. The counters were actually desegregated on September 27, 1961.

To some degree, the students staged their protest demonstrations because they no longer felt that they were legitimate participants in the democratic process. During the interviews students frequently expressed mistrust and suspicion of all politicians, both white and Negro, and their attitude seemed to be that, for the most part, the legislative bodies at both the state and national levels were simply institutions which had signs over their doors reading "whites only." The sit-in protests opened a new pathway through which these young Negroes could express their demands for equality. That they seized on this method with such enthusiasm and courage in the face of possible violence was a sign of their feeling of impotence within the established political system, and an indication of the depth of their frustrations.

III

One aspect of the student protests that was often commented on in the press was the extent to which the student leaders talked, and frequently acted, as if the adult Negro leaders were as much their enemies as the segregationist whites. This attitude among the students suggests the extent of their impatience with the progress made by the established Negro leaders, but it is also in part an indication of their distaste for the very system in which their leaders are participating. Gunnar Myrdal detected a similar attitude among "common Negroes," many of whom felt that their leaders were, "prepared to barter away their own honor and the interests of the group for a job or a handout." He explained this attitude as a displacement of hatred for the whole segregated society on to those who are participating in it, and seem to be profiting from it in certain ways: "The Negro hates the Negro role in American society, and the Negro leader, who acts out this role in public life, becomes a symbol of what the Negro hates."[4]

---

[4]Gunnar Myrdal, *An American Dilemma* (New York; Harper and Brothers, 1944), p. 744.

In Atlanta the initial sit-in demonstrations took place virtually without the prior knowledge of the adult leaders, and several efforts to begin negotiations failed because of mutual suspicions and recriminations among the Negro leaders. In fact, when the final compromise settlement was announced in Atlanta, the first reaction of large numbers of students and adults was anger and rage expressed in claims that they had been "sold out." There were many baseless accusations that leaders (and at this point the students' leaders were included) had been bribed or had otherwise betrayed them. During the interviews much antipathy toward the adults who engaged in this final settlement of the sit-in controversy was encountered, and students frequently described them as "handkerchief heads," " accommodators," or "Uncle Toms."

In Atlanta, however, the adult Negro leaders do not form a monolithic bloc. Within the community there are divergences of opinion and political styles, and there is much disagreement, sometimes rather bitter in tone, over the proper tactics that should be used in gaining equality. Among the Negro leadership, such terms as "liberals" and "conservatives," "militants" and "accommodators," "young turks" and "old guards" are used to describe the groupings within the Negro civic elite. The Negro leaders display considerable awareness that differences of opinion exist and committees or civic groups within the Negro community tend to be dominated by one or the other grouping. One older, very successful Negro businessman who has been very active in the city's politics describes himself as, "a mature conservative; one of the older heads," while a young physician who has become involved in political and civic work only in the last five years announces that, "I am one of your impatient Negroes."

Although those leaders usually labeled conservative by the community, and frequently by themselves as well, now dominate most of the organizations which deal exclusively with elections and political issues, such as the Atlanta Negro Voters League and the Westside Voters League, several other groups have grown up in recent years which are not under their control, such as the local chapter of the Southern Christian Leadership Council, a group of younger business and professional men called the Atlanta Committee for Cooperative Action, and a student organization called the Committee on an Appeal for Human Rights. Also, in the last two years, the local branch of the NAACP has shifted into relatively more militant hands.

The conservative group is quite aware that its power is being challenged and just as the students and the more militant adults manifest suspicion of the integrity of the conservative leaders, these men frequently question the motives and the honesty of the more militant group. The conservatives generally reject any suggestion that there are ideological differences within the Negro community, but they acknowledged that their authority is being questioned. Those challenging them are described variously as "immature," "unrealistic," "irresponsible," or by one man as: " a bunch of fanatics seeking power for power's sake."

This element of mutual distrust and the widely held impression that there is a contest for power going on showed up quite clearly in the opinions of the Negro leaders interviewed. In answers to the question: "What do you think are the greatest potential dangers to racial progress in the foreseeable future?" only three of the thirty subjects who responded mentioned some development in the white community as a danger. All the rest made reference to some condition in the Negro community. This tendency of Negroes to direct their attention to troubles among themselves rather than to the actions of the segregation forces in assessing the dangers to their continued progress emphasizes the importance of their internal dispute.

The argument seems to revolve around an evaluation of the degree of resistance in the white community to progress toward racial equality, and the stance that ought to be taken by the Negro in fighting this battle. A young physician argued that the drive for the end of racial discrimination was reaching a crucial point:

This thing has begun now and it's like a snowball rolling and picking up speed. This progress will automatically follow *if* we just push hard enough! In the long view, if we just reach out, I think it's impossible to stop. Even the segregation people see this inevitable motion; you can see them beginning to rationalize a lot more than before and to accept defeat much more readily than before.

Seventeen of those responding to the question concerning the dangers they faced held variations on this view. They felt that the greatest danger to racial advancement was the possibility that the Negro community would relax in its drive for equality and be satisfied with only token gains. A lawyer in this group said:

The most important thing by far is stagnation. That is the danger that the Negro will lose his spirit and become satisfied with our present rate of progress; you know, stagnant tokenism.

Ten of the subjects also made reference to a problem within the Negro community, but they identified a different danger. In answer to this question an insurance executive said tersely:

That's simple. The greatest danger is the lack of character in Negro leadership. By that I mean the danger of selfishness and a disregard for the interests of the masses.

Those who shared this opinion were afraid that the wrong kind of leadership would gain control, a leadership not "realistic" enough, and one not dedicated to the interest of the people as they conceive of those interests. A professional social worker, widely known and very influential in politics, identified himself as a "realist above all else. That makes you a conservative in this community." He gave an emphatic answer to this question:

> Without a doubt, the greatest danger is that the wrong people would gain control in the Negro community. We must not have people in control who want power for power's sake, or for personal, commercial or material gain. Now it is no sin to be ambitious and it's very hard to determine just when such conduct becomes improper, but you must not try to get anything for yourself out of political power. I have *never* done that! . . . In fact, I have a very religious commitment that a man will destroy himself if he uses his power selfishly. . . . The only real power is in deeply consecrated people striving to promote the common good. Above all, we must not allow selfish leaders to destroy Negro solidarity in this city. The masses of the people in the Negro community are very poor and uneducated, and they are accustomed to strong, unified leadership.

The respondents who argued that there was a danger from the rise of selfish leaders were apparently expressing a fear of continued and greater Negro militancy and aggressiveness. When they were asked to name a Negro leader who posed such a threat they would usually refer to the most liberal and aggressive leaders in the Negro community. The average age of those who feared that irresponsible leaders might gain control was fifty-four, and they were generally labeled conservative by the community and by themselves. Most of those who expressed a fear that the Negroes in Atlanta might lose their militant spirit were generally thought to be liberal. Their average age was forty-one.

There were some exceptions here; one of those who expressed the most militant attitude and was very active in organizing economic boycotts against firms with discriminatory hiring policies shared the fear of selfish and corrupt leaders, and at the same time one of the best established Negro businessmen in the city, who was generally considered conservative, especially by the students, expressed apprehension that, "we will let up, become complacent with what we've got." Although the lines are blurred in these cases, there is generally found in the responses to this question the outline of conflict; conflict between older men who are established in political and social position and consider themselves mature and realistic, and younger men who call themselves liberals and say that they are impatient for change and tired of compromise and evasion from the whites.

During the interviews no one was asked whether he considered himself to be liberal or conservative, but if in the course of the interview the subject referred to another person or group as conservative, liberal, radical, etc., he was immediately asked to define the term as he was using it. In the course of this line of questioning, he was asked to characterize other community leaders who were to be interviewed and sometimes, though less frequently than was expected, the subject would characterize himself. Of the 36 respondents, seven labeled themselves as liberals and eight labeled themselves as conservatives.

The ages of the self-identified liberals ranged from twenty-one to forty-three and their average age was thirty-one. The self-identified conservatives' average age was fifty-nine; the youngest was fifty and the oldest sixty-five. Although these two groupings are sharply divided by age and although it seems generally true that as age increases militancy decreases among Negro leaders in Atlanta, it should be noted that this is not an invariable rule by any means. This study will show that the differences among those who did not voluntarily identify themselves is not nearly so sharp as among those who did. Also during the interviewing a student leader was encountered who displayed attitudes quite similar to the conservative group, and a minister and college teacher, both in their late fifties, displayed very militant attitudes.

IV

In an effort to establish the nature of the issues over which the Negro leaders are divided, each subject was asked to fill out two cards which were designed to reveal his position on the proper goals of the Negro's political and civic efforts in the city, and the most effective means available to achieve these goals. The cards were used on the assumption, shared by the most thoughtful participants in Atlanta's public life, both white and colored, that the Negro leaders are not in dispute over the goals toward which Negroes should strive, but only over the most effective tactics that should be used to achieve these goals.

The first card[5] with which the respondents were presented contained the following list of preferences:

( ) The chance to purchase homes anywhere in the city without restrictions.

( ) The freedom to use all public parks and to swim in the same places with whites.

---

[5]This first card is a slightly modified version of a card used by Lewis M. Killian and Charles M. Grigg, "Rank Orders of Discrimination of Negroes and Whites in a Southern City," *Social Forces* (March, 1961), pp. 235-239.

( ) The chance at equal job opportunities, pay and promotion based on an individual's work and not on his race.

( ) The freedom to use all hotels and to eat in the same restaurants with whites.

( ) The end of segregation in the public schools.

( ) Equal treatment by the police and the courts.

In reference to this card each subject was asked: "If those changes affecting the way of life of the Negro in this city could come about immediately, which one would you like to see first, next, etc.?" The subject was asked to rank these preferences one through six.

There was reluctance to mark this card on the part of six of the subjects. One of the self-identified liberals objected to the implications that the Negro would agree any longer to obtain his rights piecemeal. Another man, who had been involved in many negotiations in the past, said he had developed the habit of asking for everything all at once, and the others argued that some of the alternatives were of equal importance and thus could not be put in rank order. These respondents were encouraged to mark the card anyway and all except one did so. The subject who refused simply wrote on it: "They are interlaced and interwoven."[6]

The results revealed that there was considerable agreement on the relative desirability of the various preferences presented:[7]

Liberals (N—7)	*Conservatives* (N—8)	*Not Identified* (N—19)	
3	4	3	(Housing)
5	6	5	(Public Parks)
1	1	1	(Job Opportunity)
6	5	6	(Hotels and Restaurants)
2	2	2	(Public Schools)
4	3	4	(Police and Courts)

The most striking thing about the results of this test is the extent to which these groups are in agreement concerning the priority of increased economic

---

[6]None of the respondents said he had no preference or that he did not care about one of the changes, but there were those who said that one of the alternatives was no longer a problem (usually this was equal treatment by the police and the courts) at least within the Atlanta city limits. These subjects were encouraged to assign a number anyway, but two refused. In those cases the number six was arbitrarily assigned to the category the subject had omitted.

[7]To arrive at a group ranking for this test, the responses of each individual to each of the preferences presented on the card were simply added to the responses of all others in this group. A group ranking was assigned to each preference on the basis of this composite score.

opportunity and school desegregation as the two most important goals toward which the Negroes in Atlanta should strive. This result is somewhat in contrast to the findings of James Q. Wilson in Chicago. Wilson found that the protest or militant leaders tended to choose what he calls "status" ends rather than "welfare" ends when faced with a choice. A status end is one which seeks "the integration of the Negro into all phases of the community on the principle of equality — all Negroes will be granted the opportunity to obtain the services, positions, or material benefits of the community on the basis of principles other than race."[8] On the other hand a welfare end is described as "those which look to the tangible improvement of the community or some individuals in it through the provision of better services, living conditions, or positions."[9] The distinction is a subtle one, but Wilson explains it further by saying:

> Welfare and status ends are distinguished by, and defended in terms of, tangible versus intangible benefits, short term versus long-term gains, and specific versus total solutions to the problems of the community. The differences [are] between those who advocate welfare ends, or *things,* and those who urge status ends, or *principles.* . . .[10]

In Atlanta, although the liberals may deal with the problems of the community in moral, absolute terms more frequently than the conservatives, there seems to be a general agreement that welfare type goals are more important than status type goals. Even the liberals agreed that increased employment in city government should be accepted, even if it is placed on a quota basis. Also there was only one respondent who argued that Negroes should refuse to accept increased spending and development of new schools within the Negro community until all the schools were opened on the basis of equality.

There were, however, traces of the preference of status over welfare goals among the liberals. The liberals chose the right to purchase homes anywhere in the city above equal protection by the police which is the third choice of the conservatives. This could be explained by the different historical experience of the two groups. The older men usually talked at length about examples of police brutality and injustice that they had witnessed or experienced in the 1920's or 1930's, and they claim large responsibility for producing the present much more equitable situation through the use of their influence and their management of the political power of the Negro. One of the first breakthroughs they achieved after gaining the right to vote in the

---

[8]James Q. Wilson, *Negro Politics* (Glencoe: the Free Press, 1960), p. 185.
[9]*Ibid.*
[10]*Ibid.,* p. 186.

Democratic primary in 1946 was the obtaining of Negro policemen in the city in 1948. The younger men agree that the police in the city are remarkably fair and efficient, but they seem to take the situation somewhat for granted.

The younger men are more interested in desegregation of housing and, although they felt hopeless about the prospects, some spoke of getting a city ordinance establishing open occupancy. This attitude could be explained in part by a peculiar development in housing in the city, brought about for the most part by the older men. Atlanta is distinguished from most American cities by having extensive Negro suburbs. Large amounts of property on the West side of the town have been taken up by Negroes so that they are not encircled and bound into the central city by white suburban towns, and there are no man-made obstacles to their outward movement in that direction. But the well-kept sub-divisions that have sprung up on the West side since World War Two are a mark of segregation. They are as comfortable as those in the white neighborhoods, but they are part of a ghetto. The older men, in inaugurating the development of the West side gave up efforts to penetrate the dominant white society, but the younger men, although indicating no intention of moving from the West side, were obviously more eager to erase the stigma of the ghetto and the insult of segregated housing.

But the general preference among those respondents for welfare goals was underlined by the fact that the choices involving desegregation of parks, hotels and restaurants were placed at the bottom of the list by all groups. Moreover, none of the respondents took these things very seriously. This was true even of the student leaders whose names appeared as petitioners on a suit against the city calling for park desegregation that was pending in court at the time the interviews took place. The younger men picked the parks above hotels and restaurants, but in discussing the issue they seemed to be as much interested in gaining more parks for Negro neighborhoods as in desegregating all the city's recreational facilities.

When the respondents who marked the cards are arranged according to age the differences just discussed are reduced, and a broad unity of opinion is revealed:

45 years and Under (N—15)	*46 years and Over* (N—18)	
3	3	(Housing)
5	6	(Public Parks)
1	1	(Job Opportunity)
6	5	(Hotels and Restaurants)
2	2	(Public Schools)
4	4	(Police and Courts)

This test indicates that thoughtful local observers are correct when they suggest that there is little dispute among Negroes in Atlanta concerning the goals toward which they should be working. It would seem that among the leaders examined here this is true to a remarkable extent. Although the liberals may find the status differentials between whites and Negroes in Atlanta more galling and frustrating than the older conservatives, all the leaders, both young students and older bankers and business leaders, agree that the economic goals — increased employment opportunity and nondiscriminatory advancement policies — should have the highest priority for action.

V

Once each subject had marked the first card he was presented with a second one on which were listed the following preferences:

(   ) Private negotiations with influential whites.
(   ) Economic Boycotts.
(   ) Efforts to encourage increased voting among Negroes.
(   ) Demonstrations of protest such as sit-ins and marches.
(   ) Civil Rights suits in Courts of Law.

In reference to this card each subject was told: "Listed on that card are various kinds of action that can be used to gain the changes in the Negroes' way of life that were listed on the first card. Which of the methods of bringing about change listed on this card do you think is most effective, next, etc.?" Once again the subject was asked to mark the card one through five.

This test was designed on the assumption that debate among Negro leaders in Atlanta had reached such a stage that those most committed to a political style would mark the card immediately, without extensive consideration. This assumption proved largely correct, again testifying to the emotional intensity of the dispute going on within the Negro community. Those who had voluntarily identified themselves as conservatives or liberals tended to mark this card without hesitation, while those who had been reluctant to mark the first card usually objected even more strenuously to this one.

Eight subjects hesitated or objected to marking this card. One of these was a self-identified liberal who argued that voting should not be included along with the other alternatives because increased voting among Negroes had primarily a long range influence and made very little impact on day to day struggles involving particular issues, especially where private businesses or institutions were involved. The rest argued, in one way or another, that no one tactic was necessarily more effective than any other. The relative effectiveness, they asserted, depended entirely on the particular situation and the issues at stake; therefore, any one of the tactics listed on the card might be the most effective, or the least effective, depending on the circumstances involved. The same gentleman who refused to mark the first card seemed to have this approach to social action, and he refused to mark the second card as well. This time he wrote on it: "All are important and effective."

But the card was marked by most of the subjects without any objections. In fact, several accompanied their marking with such comments as: "This is simple enough," or "Well, I see my first choice right off." The self-identified groups ranked the alternatives in the following way.[11]

Liberals (N—7)	*Conservatives* (N—8)	
5	2	(Negotiation)
1	5	(Boycotts)
2	1	(Voting)
3	4	(Demonstrations)
4	3	(Lawsuits)

The contrasts here are striking and the results of this test offer strong evidence that the dispute between the older, better established group and the younger group is more than simply a struggle for power and prestige. At least among these deeply committed individuals a sharp dispute is in process over the proper tactics that should be used to carry on their fight for equality.

There is not too much disagreement between the two groups over the importance of increasing the number of Negro voters although the more militant group places it second in importance. However, attitudes toward this subject are more divergent than the results of the test reveal. The conservatives usually accompanied their selection of this alternative as their first choice with a lecture on the power of the ballot which was punctuated with stories illustrating how much their situation had changed since the end of the white primary in 1946. One story concerning the mayor's rather contemptuous treatment of their plea for more street lights in the early 1940's which he dismissed with the remark: "Come back to see me when you have 10,000 votes," was frequently repeated.

---

[11]Among those who did not identify themselves as liberal or conservative there was much disagreement on this card. Some individuals in this group placed lawsuits first in effectiveness, and others put voting at the top of their lists. These leaders are not included in this chart because to lump them together in a composite grouping would give a false picture of unanimity among them.

The average rankings of the self-identified liberals and conservatives are close to the actual rankings made by most of the respondents. The range of choices on each alternative was narrow. Negotiations were ranked between 3 and 5 by the liberal respondents and either 1 or 2 by the conservatives. Boycotts were ranked either 1 or 2 by the liberals and either 4 or 5 by the conservatives. Increased voting was ranked either 1 or 2 by the conservatives and between 1 and 5 by the liberals. Demonstrations were ranked from 2 to 4 by the liberals and either 4 or 5 by the conservatives. Lawsuits were ranked from 2 to 5 by the liberals and from 1 to 3 by the conservatives.

The liberal group, however, seemed very reluctant to place voting high on the list although they acknowledged its importance. One of them said:

> Voting is damned important of course . . . but it's over-rated by Negroes, I think. Even with the votes you can't just sit back as some people in this town think. You don't get things without pushing and shoving.

There was a difference of opinion about the efficacy of lawsuits. Both groups thought that lawsuits were important and effective means of gaining civil rights victories, but once again the liberals argue that they are not very useful against privately imposed segregation. One young lawyer, although he was not in the self-identified liberal group, listed lawsuits fourth most effective and stated the objections of the militants quite well by saying:

> The Federal courts seem to be slowly expanding their definition of what constitutes a public activity or function, but they aren't in any hurry to do it. That's a hot one you know — very controversial. Anyway, we are out to get segregation now, not just legal segregation.

The kernel of the dispute between the two groups, however, is their contrasting attitudes toward the possibility of working out compromises with the white community, and in general their attitude toward the present system of settling racial disputes. The conservatives believe strongly in the importance of private negotiations with white leaders, while the liberals place this tactic last on their list. The liberals consider economic boycotts the most effective means of getting their way while the conservatives placed it at the bottom of their list. One member of the conservative group stated flatly: "Man, I just don't like this boycotting — I don't care who's doing it — I just don't think it's right!" The two groups have opposite opinions on the so-called "direct action" techniques. Some of the conservatives seem to reject them almost without qualification, but if such means must be used they prefer protest demonstrations over boycotts. However, the liberals are not even as enthusiastic about protest demonstrations as the results of the test might suggest. They believe that their usefulness in Atlanta is decreasing primarily because the white population is becoming accustomed to seeing Negroes picketing and demonstrating and has begun to ignore them. The leaders of the sit-in demonstrations in Atlanta were quite sensitive to coverage of their activities by the press and they were aware that news of demonstrations was taken off the front page and relegated to the more inconspicuous parts of the newspaper as the controversy dragged on.

When the results of this test from all the respondents are examined the differences between the younger and older leaders is moderated somewhat:

45 and Under (N—15)	*46 and Over* (N—18)	
3	3	(Negotiations)
2	4	(Boycotts)
1	1	(Voting)
5	5	(Demonstrations)
4	2	(Lawsuits)

Differences between the two age groups still exist, but the principal one, the younger groups' preference for economic boycotts over private negotiations with the whites and civil rights suits is less sharply defined than previously. Efforts to increase Negro voting is considered the most effective tactic by both groups, and the older leaders now have a lower rating for private negotiations with the whites and find boycotts more effective than demonstrations, though by a small margin.

VI

Emerging from these interviews is a spectrum of opinion on the effectiveness of various techniques of social action within a significant segment of the leadership of the Atlanta Negro community. There seems to be considerable agreement among these leaders on the goals toward which Atlanta's Negroes ought to strive, but at opposite extremes of the spectrum widely respected leaders exist who disagree very sharply with each other over the tactics to be used in pursuing these goals. These conflicting opinions are a reflection of differences in historical experience between the two groups and also they are a function of their differing positions and occupations within the Negro community.

Of those who identified themselves as conservatives in this study there was one college administrator, one social worker, and six businessmen. These men expressed an aversion for direct action techniques and boycotts and a strong preference for private negotiations with influential whites. They have built up good contacts with the whites over the years, and pride themselves on their ability to speak directly to the top white leaders in the city.

The conservatives feel that their position bars them from taking an active part in protest demonstrations because these public displays of discontent naturally cause bitterness and rancor and tend to destroy the cordial, settled atmosphere which they feel is a necessary pre-condition to effective negotiations. They also have worked hard to build institutions such as the Y.M.C.A., the Urban League and many churches which depend heavily on contributions from influential whites, and during the boycott that accompanied the sit-in affair in Atlanta some of these organizations began to lose white contributors as tension mounted. To some extent the conservatives have each made adjustments to the traditional position of the Negro in Southern society. In varying measures they have given up efforts to penetrate the dominant white society and consequently they have a greater commitment to the institutions of the Negro community.

The businessmen among the conservatives have frequent dealings with influential whites in the city; both the bank and the savings and loan association operated by Negroes in Atlanta have very sizable deposits from white customers. In fact, to a large extent, the power of the conservatives depends on their influence with the white community. They are spokesmen for the Negro community primarily because they have gained white recognition and favor, although their own achievements placed them in a position to be chosen for this role. Because of this process of selection, the liberals regard the conservatives with almost the same hostility they have for the whites, if not more so. They complain that the conservatives' power is based essentially on the Negro's fear of the power of the white man. They think that the established leaders have profited from the injustices of segregation by trading their human dignity for the opportunity to represent the whites within the Negro community.

The younger men are not so directly engaged in activities and institutions that serve the whole community as are the conservatives. Among the group that voluntarily identified themselves as liberals there were two individuals who worked for civil rights or Negro improvement groups, one college teacher, one social worker, one physician, one student leader, and one businessman. These men deal more exclusively with the Negro community than the conservatives, yet at the same time they do not feel as much committed to its maintenance; in fact, they hate all it stands for. Their work brings them into closer contact with the social, economic and political deprivations suffered by the Negro, and they tend to concentrate on these injustices and have fewer reasons to try to protect institutions, both charitable and commercial, that presently exist in the Negro community. They are under less compulsion than the conservatives to act with restraint or to compromise their demands in order to make limited material gains or to promote the fortunes of Negro businessmen. In this sense they stand outside the economic and social life of the established community and they try to keep the dominant leaders, both white and colored, at arm's length, guarding against being too friendly with politicians and certainly never asking them for favors or help of any kind. They try to conduct their affairs strictly on the basis of their moral principles, and for these reasons conservatives frequently regard them as "irresponsible" and find their attitudes toward politics and community leaders "unrealistic" or "hateful." One member of the conservative group, who has a reputation as a good tactician and organizer, acknowledged the importance of the student protests in bringing "more integration in less than two years than we gained in ten," but he argued that "they will never get anything done on their own because they are cut off; they work in a righteous vacuum over there."

The whites also play a large part in selecting the liberal or militant leaders just as they do in choosing the conservative spokesmen. However, it is important to the liberal leaders to become the objects of hostility from the whites, not of their beneficence. At the beginning of the sit-in protests in Atlanta, when student leaders from several organizations on the Atlanta University campus seemed to be competing for control of the new movement, they began vying with each other in making bold, uncompromising public statements, and when they met privately with a leading white merchant they tried to out do each other in challenging him and impressing him with their determination. It is important, to the student leaders in particular, to have the badge of at least one jail sentence for breaking a segregation law, and Martin Luther King, Jr. could have asked for nothing better than to have been bitterly attacked by the Governor of Georgia when he decided in 1960 to move from Montgomery, Alabama, to Atlanta. The liberals thrive on the antagonism of the whites, while the conservatives court their good favor.

The rest of the Negro leaders, those not identified with either the conservatives or liberals, are caught in a maze of conflicting influences stemming from their occupations, their age and historical experiences, their functions within the Negro community and their relations with the whites. These men, spread across the spectrum of opinion between the self-identified liberals and conservatives, display several different combinations of attitudes and action.

Several leaders claimed agreement with the liberals' approach to political tactics yet did not identify themselves as members of the liberal group. During the sit-in controversy these men did not actually involve themselves in the public demonstrations or in advising the student leaders. They marked the attitude cards in a way that suggested their liberal views, but they did not endorse these views with action. Typical of this group was a college teacher in his late fifties who expressed strong approval of the sit-in demonstrations and the boycott. He has been involved in voter registration drives ever since the end of the white primary in 1946 and he is a member of many other community organizations, but he also has close relationships and friendships with many of the leading conservatives. He excused himself for not participating more actively in the sit-in controversy by saying: "They always seemed to schedule meetings when I had obligations at school." Another member of this group is a social worker in his middle forties who has very militant attitudes and is a member of several organizations which are dominated by the liberals, but who works for an agency which depends heavily on financial support from the white community and so he maintains a "realistic" alliance with the conservative leaders and did not participate directly in the protest actions.

On the other side of the spectrum are leaders who hold conservative views but who did not criticize the actions of the demonstrators during the sit-ins or make efforts to bring the protests to an end. A lawyer in his early forties fits into this category. He believed strongly that community disputes should be settled through negotiation and felt that the demonstrators frequently acted unrealistically or recklessly during the sit-in dispute. But he did not have a high regard for the established community leaders, and, since he is a relatively young man who was not born in Atlanta, he does not have a close relationship with the most influential conservatives. He was called on by the students for legal advice at one point during the sit-in controversy, and he gave it, but otherwise he took no part in the dispute.

Standing in the center of the spectrum is a third group of leaders whose attitudes and actions during the sit-in controversy were ambiguous. One such leader is a young, but very successful businessman who has many friends among the liberals, but also has the confidence of several conservatives. He holds high offices in organizations dominated by both sides and a white observer described him as: "the best case of a man over there who has a foot in all camps." This man marked the attitude card concerning tactics three different ways, describing a set of situations that would call for each ranking. Leaders of this sort tended to be least committed to a particular tactical weapon or technique, but not necessarily the less effective in obtaining their goals. When faced with a social or political conflict these men begin thinking of ways to limit the scope of their difficulties and extend the possible alternatives for action. They speak mostly of partial solutions to outstanding disputes and seem to think primarily in terms of the short-run, immediate consequences that might result from their decisions.

This group of leaders in the middle, subject to cross-pressures generated by the ambiguous circumstances in which they find themselves, serve as a balancing force between the more single-minded liberals and conservatives. These men who are not fully committed to either side, through their personal friendships and their memberships in various organizations, tend to moderate the sharp differences of opinion over tactics that exist within the Negro community. Because of their formal and informal efforts, organizational rivalry and bickering is reduced, and the Negro's attack on the institutions of segregation in Atlanta is more unified and effective.

VII

This study of Negro leadership is confined to the description of circumstances existing in Atlanta, Georgia. But unless case studies generate hypotheses which can be examined and tested in other settings they do not make a significant contribution to the study of political behavior. No effort is made in this study to arrive at generalizations concerning the leadership in all Southern Negro communities. In fact, until more progress is made in developing the comparative study of metropolitan political systems all observations concerning the similarities and differences between various communities will necessarily be vague and purely impressionistic. But, even with these reservations, several conclusions are suggested which could be studied fruitfully in other Negro communities:

(1) Liberal and conservative Negro leaders in the South are in essential agreement on the ranking of goals toward which the Negro community should

strive. Although differences of emphasis exist, there seems to be a general concensus that it is more important at this time to improve the welfare of the Negro community and increase the services available to it than to fight to completely eliminate racial discrimination in all phases of the life of the city. Presently welfare goals are more important than status goals.

(2) The disunity presently existing among Negro leaders in Atlanta is not primarily the result of a clash between two generations holding contrasting political attitudes. Although in this study the average age of the self-identified liberals was lower than the average age of the self-identified conservatives, when the data from the attitude cards were tabulated according to age groupings, broad agreement between younger and older leaders was discovered. Age is not the most important factor distinguishing the antagonists among Negro leaders.

(3) Liberal and conservative leaders disagree primarily over the tactics to be employed in achieving their goals. At least when faced with a sharp, emotional community dispute involving the issue of racial discrimination the Negro leaders divide between those who want to use aggressive, "direct action" techniques and those who wish to negotiate "behind the scenes" with influential whites. Caught between these extremes are leaders who act infrequently and reluctantly, or who seem to be called in only to ratify decisions made by others. Some of these men do not take a vigorous and direct role in such controversies because they are not firmly committed to either tactical approach while others find themselves enmeshed in a conflicting web of cross-pressures which restrains them from acting on strongly held opinions.

At the center of the spectrum are leaders who consciously avoid direct identification with any one approach and who endeavor to maintain contact with all parties to the dispute. They measure the circumstances and try to fit their actions to the exigencies of the moment, always trying to maintain their focus on short-run possibilities and solutions.

(4) The isolation of the leadership of the two racial groups, brought on by segregation, is a serious and potentially disruptive weakness in the social structure of a city with a large Negro population. There are no social contacts between white and Negro leaders in Atlanta, and residential segregation places their homes far apart. There are numerous Negro owned businesses, and the institutions within the Negro community are so well developed that it is possible for a Negro to live a distinctly middle class life in Atlanta while having only marginal contacts with the whites. In such a situation, if a crisis arises involving the crucial issue of race, communication between the two racial groups, which is normally rather tenuous and formal, becomes very hard to maintain, and it is even more difficult to establish the conditions in which negotiation of the difficulties that caused the crisis can take place.

During the controversy over the sit-in demonstrations in Atlanta such a breakdown in communications occurred. It was caused in large measure by the inability of the Negroes to agree among themselves, the militant attitude of the student leaders which antagonized many of the whites, and the stubborn refusal of certain white businessmen to discuss the matter at all. It was at this juncture that the student leaders turned to one of the oldest, most respected Negro leaders, who was widely considered to be a conservative although he did not voluntarily identify himself as such when interviewed. He contacted an influential white lawyer with whom he had a cordial relationship, and together these two men were able to initiate negotiations that eventually led to a settlement of the controversy.

(5) Thus when the Negro community becomes involved in a struggle against the institutions of segregation, both the liberal and the conservative leaders can perform useful roles:

(a) The liberal group's function is, literally, to start fights they are unable to finish. They are able to create a crisis, but are frequently unable to resolve it because they have no basis for contact with the dominant white leaders. As James Q. Wilson suggests, one of the inherent difficulties in the use of protest action is: "that the discretion of the protest leader to bargain after he has acquired the resources with which to bargain is severely limited by the means he was forced to employ in order to create those resources."[12] From the beginning of the sit-in dispute in Atlanta the leading merchants refused to negotiate directly with the demonstrators whom they considered to be irresponsible troublemakers.

(b) The conservatively inclined leaders, utilizing their reputations and the connections they have built up with the white community through the years, have the function of resolving the crisis situation created by the protest leaders. In the Atlanta dispute even the antagonism between the two groups was functional because it made the conservatives seem more reliable and responsible in the eyes of the whites, and so they were still able to act as negotiators when both sides were ready to compromise.

(c) Those leaders in the middle, who do not identify completely with either the conservative or the protest leaders, have the function of moderating this conflict over tactics. Some individuals find themselves in this situation because they are subject to cross-pressures which restrain them from becoming attached to either side in the controversy. Others are not committed because they have a flexible attitude toward social action which prompts them to regard all tactical weapons as potentially useful. Regardless of the influences that put them in this position, however, these leaders in the middle provide both formal and informal links between the conservative and protest leaders.

(d) Before the leaders can perform their various functions, of course, the liberal group must create a serious crisis through its actions. Until a

---

[12] James Q. Wilson, "The Strategy of Protest," *Journal of Conflict Resolution* (September, 1961), p. 293.

genuine threat to the public order and reputation of the community exists, the dominant whites are unlikely to be willing to negotiate concessions with the conservative leaders.

VIII

The situation in Atlanta does not seem to have been unique. Something of this same kind of unanticipated cooperation and sharing of functions between liberal and conservative Negro leaders seem to have taken place during the sit-in controversy in Knoxville, Tennessee. Negotiation began initially there without any demonstrations, but broke down after four tedious months of talks. Sit-ins began on June 9, 1960, and a boycott was started five days later on June 14. Merrill Proudfoot describes a meeting of the executive committee of the protest movement which took place on July 2, 1960, after about three weeks of demonstrations. The meeting was attended by the president of Knoxville College, who had not been involved in planning or staging the demonstrations, and he revealed that he had been contacted by an official of the Knoxville Chamber of Commerce who informed him that there was a movement underway to reopen negotiations. Proudfoot rather indignantly comments:

> The circuitous means of communicating with one another has lent a comic-opera aspect to the way this major community problem has been handled. It would seem sensible for one of the merchants to have called Crutcher or James the leaders of the demonstrations and said, "Come on down and let's talk!" Instead the merchants hint to the Chamber of Commerce official that they might be willing; he contacts not Crutcher or James, but Colston — the one person in the Negro community who has the greatest status . . . and he in turn makes the contact within the Negro community.[13]

Also when a negotiating team was created to formulate the final agreement to desegregate, Colston was included once again, but this time he was accompanied by Crutcher. Although the description is not so complete it seems that a similar process operated at Winston-Salem, North Carolina, where the agreement to desegregate the lunch counters was not formulated by the protest leaders. Clarence H. Patrick reports that:

> The demonstrators several times sought unsuccessfully for someone to organize and mediate a meeting between them and the store managers in an attempt to resolve the antisegregation movement on the basis of some mutual agreement. The leaders of the protest never met, as a group, with the managers of the stores where the protests occurred.[14]

[13]Merrill Proudfoot, *Diary of a Sit-in* (Chapel Hill, University of North Carolina Press, 1962), pp. 111-112.
[14]Clarence H. Patrick, *Lunch Counter De-segregation in Winston-Salem, North Carolina* (Pamphlet Distributed by the Southern Regional Council, 1960), p. 7.

The evidence presented here suggests that in some Southern Negro communities a kind of tactical balance presently exists with both conservative and protest leaders playing a part in the fight for equality. However, there is no evidence that the period of change and transition in Negro leadership in Atlanta has ended. In fact, a major unsettling force seems to be developing beneath the level of leadership. Almost all the leaders interviewed, including the conservatives, felt that expectations are rising perceptibly throughout the Negro community as a result of recent successful attacks on the institutions of segregation. The Negro masses, who have traditionally been apathetic toward politics and efforts to fight segregation, seem to be gaining hope that change is possible and are shaking off the mood of cynical resignation that has paralyzed them in the past.

Looking forward, these circumstances suggest a prediction that the drive to break down racial barriers will not stall once a few victories are won, but will continue and intensify in the foreseeable future. The progress toward desegregation which has recently taken place in Atlanta, such as that in the public parks, buses, libraries, and lunch counters, has been in areas which this study has shown are least important to the Negro leaders, while large-scale integration of the public schools, housing segregation and discrimination in employment, which they consider most important, have yet to be approached on a broad scale.

Whatever the prospects for the future, however, the indications are that the issue of racial discrimination will dominate Atlanta's politics for some time to come. In fact, as the younger Negroes begin to look outside the boundaries of the Negro ghetto and yearn for integration into the dominant community, they are not likely to become satisfied until their status or social ranking is arrived at rationally, and until they are judged on the basis of their personal attainments, not merely on the basis of their color. A young lawyer expressed this yearning for community recognition and status when he said: "I want to practice as a lawyer, not as a Negro lawyer." Even more poignantly this mood was expressed by a college teacher who spoke as he gazed out the window of his office at Atlanta University:

You know, I've lived in this town for twenty years now, and I love it here. But the worst thing about it here is the isolation. Why, there are white people who drive by this school every day on their way to work who don't even know what it is. They think it's a hospital or a housing project, and, you know, the very worst thing is they don't take time to find out. They just don't care.

Negro Protest Leaders in a Southern Community*

Lewis M. Killian and Charles U. Smith

One of the significant features of race relations in the past five years has been the emergence of new patterns of Negro leadership in southern communities. Prior to the various court decisions which withdrew legal support from the traditional framework of segregation, Negro leadership gave the appearance of conforming to the pattern of "accommodating" or "compromise" leadership. Analyses of leadership in southern Negro communities, such as the treatment found in Myrdal's *American Dilemma*[1], suggest that the compromise leaders held their positions primarily because they were acceptable to white leaders. They were also accepted by Negroes because accommodation was regarded as the most practical and effective mode of adjustment in the existing power situation.

Reprinted from *Social Forces,* vol. 38, (March 1960), pp. 253-257 with permission of the publisher. Copyright 1962 by the University of North Carolina Press, Chapel Hill, North Carolina.
*The authors are indebted to the Society for the Psychological Study of Social Issues for a Grant-in-Aid which helped make this study possible. This is a revised version of a paper read at the twenty-second annual meeting of the Southern Sociological Society, Gatlinburg, Tennessee, April 17, 1959.
[1]Gunnar Myrdal, *An American Dilemma* (New York: Harper and Bros., 1944) pp. 768-780.

The desegregation decisions of the U. S. Supreme Court, even without extensive implementation, redefined this power situation. In the years following 1954 militant leaders, reflecting the protest motive instead of the theme of patience and accommodation, have moved into the focus of attention of both whites and Negroes. Whereas the accommodating leaders had not been widely known to the white public, largely because they operated in a noncontroversial and often clandestine manner, the new leaders quickly rocketed to fame or notoriety, depending upon the observer's point of view. Martin Luther King, defying the white power structure of his community and being featured on the cover of *Time* magazine, symbolizes this new leadership. Many white leaders have reacted by bewailing the "breakdown of communication" between the races, denouncing the militant Negro leaders as reckless, radical parvenues, and attempting to isolate them by parleys with handpicked, "responsible" leaders. Both practical and theoretical considerations dictate the need for a new appraisal of Negro leadership in the South.

The north Florida community of Tallahassee is one of the southern communities in which a change in the pattern of Negro leadership seemed to accompany a crisis in race relations. The critical situation arose from a challenge to segregation on city buses, culminating in a boycott. Here, too, news media featured daily the names of militant Negroes who previously had been anonymous ciphers in the Negro community as far as most whites were concerned. There were allegations to the effect that "newcomers" had come into the community and stirred up the erstwhile contented population, and that the Negro leadership had "split" with the result that white leaders did not know with whom to deal. Hence this community was well suited for a case study of Negro leadership in crisis.

The situation proved an opportunity to get the answers, for this community, to certain questions. Was the leadership in this Protest Movement actually new to the Negro community, or were the new leaders merely people who had suddenly become known to the white community because of a change of strategy? If they were new to the higher levels of the power structure in the Negro community, had they actually displaced the old group of leaders or was the community split between two competing sets of leaders? A corollary is the question whether these "new leaders" drew their strength from popular support or simply from a tightly organized, activist minority.

Method of Study

The study, executed shortly after the end of the bus boycott, consisted of two related parts. The first was an assessment of the structure of Negro leadership through interviews with a panel of 21 Negroes tentatively designated as "leaders" by social scientists familiar with the community. This list subsequently proved to include what came to be defined as "old" and "new" leaders in almost equal proportions.

A panel of 21 white leaders was also selected. This panel included all of the white leaders who had dealt with the Negro community in connection with the bus protest, in either an official or unofficial capacity. It also included white functionaries who were known to have worked directly with the Negro community in connection with other matters, such as fund drives, civic projects, and community problems, both before and after the boycott. They are the white leaders who most often speak to the Negro community in behalf of the white community. Some of them are high in the power structure. That this group represents fairly the position of the white leadership in Tallahassee is indicated by the absence of opposition to their representations to the Negro community.

The names of the 21 Negroes tentatively listed as "leaders" were placed on a card which was handed to the subject during the interview. Then he was asked a series of questions about Negro leadership *before* and *after* the bus boycott, and told to respond by giving names from the list. The questions which are of interest here were:

1. As best you can recall, which would have identified as "leaders" among Tallahassee Negroes two years ago?
2. At that time, which do you feel were able to influence large numbers of Negroes on important public issues?
3. Which ones were able to express most accurately the feelings of most Negroes in Tallahassee on important public issues?
4. Which ones were able to deal most effectively with white leaders as representatives of the Negro group?
5. Now, at the present time, which do you feel are most able to influence large numbers of Negroes on important public issues?
6. Which are able to express most accurately the feelings of most Negroes, etc.?
7. Which are able to deal most effectively with white leaders, etc.?

Subjects were allowed to give as few or as many responses to each question as they wished, and Negro subjects were encouraged to include their own names if they felt they should.

After the data had been collected, the answers of white and Negro informants were tabulated separately. Each of the 21 potential Negro leaders was given a score and a rank on each question, according to the number of times his name was mentioned in response to the question. Hence each Negro had, for each question, a rank assigned him by the Negro informants and a rank assigned by the white leaders.

The second portion of the study was an attitude survey of a sample of the adult Negro population of Tallahassee. Every fifth address was taken from a list of all the households in blocks occupied only by Negroes. Any adult available at the address was interviewed. A total of 196 usable interviews were obtained. A Likert-type scale of questions concerning attitudes toward segregation in general, the bus boycott, and the leadership of the Bus Protest Movement was used. Key questions for purposes of this study were:

1. The Negro should not boycott to achieve his goals. (Agreement with this statement would represent a repudiation of the militant leaders.)
2. The old, established leaders in Tallahassee were more effective than the ones leading the bus protest.
3. The leadership in the Tallahassee Bus Protest is very good.

Subjects were grouped into three categories on the basis of whether their answers to these three questions reflected approval or disapproval of the leaders who had called for the bus boycott. Those who answered all three of the questions favorably were classified as "Highly favorable," those who answered two favorably were classified as "Favorable," and those who answered only one or none in this manner were placed in the "Unfavorable" category.

Findings

The interviews with the panel of potential Negro leaders revealed that a real change in leadership had indeed taken place between the "Pre-Boycott" and "Post-Boycott" periods. On the basis of high rankings on the answers to the questions "Who were the leaders?" "Who were influential?" and "Who were representative?" two years previously, six individuals were classified as "Pre-Boycott Leaders." Of these six, not one was found in the first five ranked on "influence" and "representativeness" in the Post-Boycott period. None of them were ranked even in the first ten on "influence," although two did remain in the first ten on "representativeness." An indication of how complete the turnover of leadership personnel was is the fact that of the first five ranked as both "influential" and "representative" in the Post-Boycott period, not one was among the first ten named as "leaders" in the Pre-Boycott period.

This change of leadership was also found to involve, as had been postulated, a replacement of Accommodating Leaders by Protest Leaders. Of the six Pre-Boycott leaders, five were ranked by Negroes as being most able to deal effectively with white leaders during this period. Five of the six were also ranked by whites as most able to deal effectively with white leaders. Four, including the three ranked highest by Negroes as "leaders," were ranked in the first five as "emissaries" by both Negroes and whites. This finding bears out the theory that, in the era of accommodation in race relations, leadership in the Negro community was based primarily on acceptability to white leaders and ability to gain concessions from them.

In contrast, none of the five "new leaders" were ranked by either Negroes or whites as among the five Negroes able to deal most effectively with white leaders in the Post-Boycott Period. In fact, none of them ranked in the first ten on acceptability to white leaders as it was perceived by Negroes. Clearly these new leaders were not seen by other prominent Negroes as "Compromise Leaders."

The panel of Negroes interviewed included both the "old leaders" and the "new leaders," plus some individuals who did not receive high rankings for either period. The Negro panel was divided, for purposes of further analysis, into an "old group" of subjects who had ranked in the first ten on the question concerning Pre-Boycott leadership, and a new group. The new group identified as the five most influential leaders in the Post-Boycott period the same five men who had been ranked as "new leaders" by the entire panel. The "old group" ranked four of these five men as the five most influential leaders in this same period, indicating that their perception of the change in leadership was almost the same as that of the "new group." Moreover, none of the "old group," including the "old leaders," gave their own names in response to the question on ability to influence large numbers of Negroes. Although during the course of the boycott some of the old leaders had openly challenged the influence of the new leaders, by the time of this study they seemed to have accepted the fact that they had been displaced. It is accurate, therefore, to say that a change, not a split, in leadership had occurred.

Although no intensive study of the individual characteristics of the old and new leaders was made, certain ones were evident. Even though at the time of the study, the boycott had ended and had obviously failed of its purpose to force desegregation of city buses, all of the New Leaders were strongly identified with it. All were officers of the organization which had led the boycott and all had been arrested and fined for "operating an illegal transportation system" (a car pool). In contrast, not one of the Old Leaders had been active in promoting the boycott, and at least two of them had opposed it as a tactic. Of the six Old Leaders, three were employed in the state-supported school system; none of the five New Leaders were state employees. There were three ministers among the New Leaders, none among the old. Although the Old Leaders had, as a group, indeed lived in the community a longer time than their successors, the shortest time that any of the New Leaders had lived in Tallahassee was three years. One of them had lived there over thirty years. It was only in a limited and relative sense that they could be described as "newcomers."

Since the New Leaders had been identified as synonymous with the leaders of the Bus Boycott, the questions asked in the opinion poll were suited to serve as a measure of their popular support. Were they leaders not only in the eyes of the small panel of prominent Negroes but also in the eyes of the Negro community? The results of the survey indicate that they were. When asked if the leadership in the Bus Protest was very good, 84 percent of the sample agreed that it was. Some inconsistency was found between the answers to this question and the question, "The old established leaders in Tallahassee were more effective than the ones leading the Bus Protest," since only 62 percent of the sample disagreed with this statement. But, to the extent that this sample can be taken as representative, it appears that the New Leaders did have majority support in the Negro community. Subjects were also asked to agree or disagree with the statement, "Should the Negro population of Tallahassee need to develop united action to obtain rights or services not connected with the Bus Protest, the people leading the Protest would probably be selected to lead such action." Again, strong majority support of the New Leaders was indicated, 82 percent of the sample agreeing with this statement.

Using the categories "Highly Favorable," "Favorable," and "Unfavorable," established earlier, an analysis was made of certain differences between Negroes showing greater or lesser support for the boycott and its leaders. The chi-square test of independence was used. Differences significant beyond the .01 level were found in age and education, the more favorably disposed subjects being younger and better educated. Those who were favorably disposed toward the boycott were more likely to own automobiles than those who were not, this difference also being significant beyond the .01 level. This difference may have reflected the fact that the boycott caused less personal inconvenience for car owners than it did for others, or it may have been that car ownership was an indirect measure of socio-economic status. No significant difference in ownership of real property was found between supporters and nonsupporters, however, so the former explanation seems the more likely. This is also suggested by the fact that differences in occupation were not significant at the .05 level.

Summary and Conclusions

In the community studied, the impression that there has been a change in the quality of race relations is borne out. The clearest indication of this change is the replacement of the Old Leaders by New Leaders who clearly reflect the protest motive rather than any spirit of accommodation. These New Leaders have widespread popular support, and the extent of their influence is conceded by the Old Leaders whom they displaced.

Additional findings lent added significance to this shift in Negro leadership. The panel of white leaders were found to perceive Negro leadership in the Post-Boycott period in almost the same way that the Negro leaders did. Of the six men ranked highest by whites as "most influential" in the Post-Boycott period, four were among the Negroes' New Leaders. At the same time, most of these white leaders indicated that they were unwilling to deal with these New Leaders because the militant spokesmen were uncompromising in their opposition to segregation. It is only in this sense that communication has broken down between the races. The New Leaders are unwilling to communicate and negotiate with whites in the circumscribed, accommodating fashion of yesterday. The Old Leaders can no longer claim the support of the Negro population, no matter how acceptable they might be to the whites. As long as this situation prevails, the structure of the situation seems to permit only one kind of communication between the Negro community and the white power structure: formal, peremptory demands, backed by the threat of legal action, political reprisal, or economic boycott. So long as the New Leaders are not accepted as bona fide, albeit antagonistic, emissaries of the Negro community in the same way that the Old Leaders were, this would seem to be the only way in which they can get the attention of the white leaders.

While the present study was principally concerned with a description of the changes in Negro leadership in Tallahassee during the Bus Protest, there is evidence which indicates that the New Leaders and new leadership are permanent in this community. Although they may have been "issue leaders" at first, they have continued to maintain their position of leadership as the sample of the Negro population predicted they would.

In the first place some of the "old" leaders were called upon by the Tallahassee City Commission to get the Negroes to agree to a compromise settlement in the early days of the bus protest. The efforts of the "old" leaders to do this failed completely and ever since they have made no overt efforts to regain the following they had prior to the bus protest. This is apparently due to their belief that neither the Negro population nor the city officials have confidence in them. The Negroes do not trust them because of what they regard as underhanded dealing with the City Commission. The city officials apparently feel that these erstwhile leaders cannot be trusted to gauge Negro sentiment accurately or to deliver results when called upon, because they lack following.

Secondly, the "new" leaders have continued to enjoy reasonable support for their undertakings. Some of them have moved into other areas of leadership, such as the NAACP, the Southern Christian Leadership Conference, and the Florida Council of Human Relations. One of them is president of the Tallahassee Chapter of the NAACP. Another is on the State NAACP Board and on the Board of Directors of the Southern Christian Leadership Conference.

Finally these "new" leaders have sought to keep the Negro community of Tallahassee militant and dynamic by continuing weekly meetings of the ICC, the organization formed to promote the bus protest, conducting institutes on nonviolence, taking preliminary steps toward school integration, working to get more Negroes registered and voting, and making many local and nonlocal public appearances in connection with the uplift of Negroes. Furthermore, the press has done much to contribute to their status as permanent leaders by seeking their opinions and comments on various matters affecting the Negro community in Tallahassee (e.g. the recent rape case).

The writers feel that the "new" leaders are becoming permanent leaders not because of the attractiveness of their personalities or their skill at organizing, but rather because they adhere rigorously to the *form* of militant leadership which is becoming the trend for Negroes throughout the United States. This new leadership is not of the accommodating type. It seeks gains for the Negro community through formal demands and requests, boycotts, lawsuits, and voting. The protest leaders are not concerned with whether or not the whites high in the power structure know, like, or want to deal with them. Until the "old" leaders are willing or able to translate their mode of leadership into a form similar to this, it appears that they will not again rise to prominence as leaders in Tallahassee.

Two Negro Politicians:
An Interpretation

James Q. Wilson

This is an attempt to describe, and in part to account for, the differences between two powerful political leaders, whose constituencies are roughly similar. Although the two congressmen in question are well-known Negroes — Adam Clayton Powell, Jr. of New York and William L. Dawson of Chicago — the analysis of the character of their political life is not meant to explain their idiosyncratic features. It is hoped, rather, that these remarks will illuminate some of the central features of the role of any congressman. By choosing for study two men who, in many ways, are polar opposites but who at the same time share many of the same problems and resources, the contrasts between them can be made more vivid and the argument employed can be sketched in bold strokes.[1]

Reprinted from *Midwest Journal of Political Science,* Vol. IV, No. 1, 1960 by James Q. Wilson by permission of the Wayne State University Press and the author. Copyright 1960 by the Wayne State University Press.
[1]This article is based on interview research conducted in Chicago, New York, and Washington, D. C., on Negro politics. For my larger findings, plus much of the detail which is omitted from this interpretative article, see my book, *Negro Politics* (Glencoe: The Free Press, 1960).

Powell and Dawson are the most famous Negro Democratic congressmen. The former was first elected in 1944, the latter in 1942. Both represent districts that are almost entirely Negro in composition, and which have within them both appalling slums and expensive homes and apartments. Both are relatively senior members of the House of Representatives. Dawson is the chairman of the House Government Operations Committee; Powell is the second-ranking Democrat on the Education and Labor Committee and is a sub-committee chairman on the Interior Committee. Both have received national publicity, Powell more than Dawson, and both are well-known to their colleagues. Both tend to support the Democratic leadership of the House fairly consistently. On "party votes" (i.e., votes which pit a majority of one party against a majority of the other party), neither Dawson nor Powell will as a rule vote against his party in more than two or three per cent of the cases. Neither Dawson nor Powell has an especially good record of voting participation in House roll calls. Although Dawson is better than Powell in most sessions, both are well below the average for the House as a whole. Powell has on occasion been among the very lowest — sometimes *the* lowest — in voting participation, and rarely averages higher than 50 per cent. Dawson has steadily increased his voting participation, rising from 38 per cent in 1947-48 to 83 per cent in 1958.[2]

The similarities between the two men are, however, superficial. The differences are profound. Each has a unique political style which transcends issues, roll calls, or personal fortunes. The one is an orator, the other an organizer; one is flamboyant, the other is conservative; one is militant on the race question, the other is moderate.[3] One seeks publicity and speaks almost always "on the record"; the other shuns publicity and speaks to interviewers only off the record. One is considered by most of his House colleagues to be demagogic and unreliable; the other has the confidence and respect of many influential congressmen. One raises the race issue on every occasion; the other goes out of his way to avoid discussing race or race questions. One is light-skinned, handsome, boyish, gregarious, fun-loving; the other is brown-skinned, aged, reserved, quiet. One spends his free time (of which he has a great deal) in world travel, entertaining, and night life; the other rarely travels, devotes himself completely to politics, and leads a home life

---

[2]See *Congressional Quarterly Almanac,* 1950 through 1958.

[3]On Powell, see Roi Ottley, *New World A'Coming* (Boston: Houghton Mifflin Co., 1943); David Hapgood, *The Purge That Failed: Tammany v. Powell* ("Case Studies in Practical Politics"; New York: Henry Holt & Co., 1959); Will Chasan, "Congressman Powell's Downhill Fight in Harlem," *Reporter,* 20 (July 10, 1958), 24. On Dawson, see John Madigan, "The Durable Mr. Dawson of Cook County, Illinois," *Reporter,* 18 (August 9, 1956), 9; Fletcher Martin and John Madigan, "The Boss of Bronzeville," *Chicago Magazine,* 1 (July, 1955), 22.

carefully screened by privacy and silence. The two most prominent Negro politicians are radically dissimilar, avoid each other's company, speak disparagingly of one another, and elicit the most violent attitudes of love and hate from their many friends and enemies.

An explanation can be offered that will both account for many of these differences and suggest something of interest about the relationship of any political leader to his organization and his constituents. This explanation will endeavor to show that Powell and Dawson are not simply two interesting and perhaps unique men, but that they are also political leaders who have created and who seek to maintain two important kinds of political organizations. The creation and maintenance of these organizations places certain constraints on the actions of the leaders. The leaders' political styles reflect these constraints. It will be necessary, to make this argument plausible, to describe how these organizations were built, the nature of the political systems of which they are part, the maintenance needs these organizations have, and the implications these needs have for the political style of the leader.

We will argue, first, that the most important single factor in creating or modifying the political style of each leader is the character of the organization which supports the leader and the nature of the incentives which he must distribute to sustain it.[4] Each political leader acts so as to maintain the strength of his organization. The strength of the organization is measured in terms of the number and size of the contributions to it, the extent to which a single undisputed leadership can control it, and the extent to which it can attain its collective goal (in this case, the retention of political office). To maintain the flow of contributions (the time, money, and energies of organization workers and the votes of the electorate), incentives must be distributed by the leader. In the case of Powell, these are largely intangible (nonmaterial or "ideal") incentives; in the case of Dawson, these are largely tangible or material.

The second argument will be that the character of the organization which the leader must maintain is largely determined by the nature of the local political system. The aspects of that system most relevant here include the size and composition of the political districts and the relative strength and unity of the city-wide political organization. The maintenance of a Negro political organization is intimately bound up with the maintenance of the political system of the community as a whole.

---

[4] Cf. Chester Barnard, *The Functions of the Executive* (Cambridge: Harvard University Press, 1938). I adopt here the standard methodological dodge of arguing, not that each leader in every case acts so as to sustain his organization, but that he acts *as if* this were his rule. My argument is an assumption, not a law; it is used to order data and give them meaning. The limitations of this assumption will be discussed at a later point. See also Max Weber on "ideal" and "material" benefits in *The Theory of Social and Economic Organization,* trans. A. H. Henderson and Talcott Parsons (Glencoe: The Free Press, 1947), pp. 407-12.

Powell

Adam Clayton Powell, Jr., was not, until the summer of 1959, a member of the regular party organization in New York City. When Powell sought to enter Congress in 1944, Tammany was a weakened machine. Eleven years of rule by LaGuardia, the adoption of a new city charter, and the extension of civil service had left the Tiger in a state of chronic malnutrition. The organization was shot through with factions and internecine warfare, both in Harlem and elsewhere. Rival leaders made competing alliances, broke them, and made new ones. The strength of the Manhattan organization declined, and other forces — such as the Bronx organization of Edward Flynn — rose to power. Few, inside or outside the organization, could depend on machine discipline or machine voting strength. Other bases of political power had to be found by those who sought a permanent and rising career in politics. Powell found his in the pulpit. He built his organization and his political following from outside the city machine. Although he received the endorsement of Tammany when he first ran for Congress in 1944, and subsequently until 1958, he felt he could not rely on either that endorsement or the efforts of the workers in the regular organization. The base of support for Powell was and is the Abyssinian Baptist Church, a church of perhaps 10,000 members that has existed since 1808. It was the church of his father, who retired in 1937. It is independent of any larger organization, and financially self-sustaining. In addition to the church, Powell was co-editor of a Harlem weekly, the *People's Voice*. In the stormy Harlem of the 1930's, Powell was a familiar and dramatic figure in and around the various Negro boycott movements, strikes, and protest demonstrations. He was opposed for the Democratic nomination for Congress in 1944 by the Negro who was then the most important Harlem district leader, but Tammany — either unsure of its ability to elect an alternative candidate, receptive to suggestions from other forces, or desirous of rebuking a rebellious district leader — chose to ignore the leader's protest and endorse Powell.

Powell created a personal organization. In part it was formed because Powell began his career from outside of the established organization, and in part it was necessary because even a position inside the Tammany machine was fraught with dangers and uncertainties. Whether outside or inside the organization, independent political strength was at least an advantage and probably a necessity. A church can be an ideal source of such strength. It directly recruits and organizes the masses, it can be financially independent, it has a variety of channels of communication throughout the community, and it has the luster of an indisputably good institution. In recent elections, Powell has been able to call upon as many as one thousand church workers for his campaigns, mostly volunteers. They are already organized through the elaborate committee structure and social service system of the church, and many of them hear Powell speak every Sunday. The church, in addition, has a paid bureaucracy of workers to provide the necessary staff. The appeals to these supporters are almost entirely intangible. The appeals are even larger than simply the exploitation of established race issues. They are centered around Powell as the personal embodiment, the projective personality, of the Negroes in his congregation. He is the vivid and colorful manifestation of their collective aspirations and expectations.

The use of intangible appeals in political organizations creates a set of constraints upon the user. When appeals are to principle, to lofty moral and racial goals, to the deepest wishes and fears of the listener, they enforce a logic upon the user which is compelling. Three important consequences of this kind of appeal can be mentioned.

First, these appeals tend to be "indivisible"; that is, they cannot easily be reduced to discrete units, given relative priorities, and dealt with apart from other aspects of the leader's career. Rather, they tend to function as a whole, a montage of interrelated ends and means, to which all phases of a leader's life must respond. Powell, for example, does not and probably could not divorce his career in Washington from his career in New York. His role as a congressman is inseparable from his role as a Harlem politician, Negro minister, and colorful personality. Politics for him is not a specific, but a general role, and the appeals upon which it is based are ramified and indivisible. Politics is "functionally diffuse."[5] Powell's position as a congressman is an extension of his position as a Harlem leader. The two offices, in Washington and New York, are systematically related. Both receive a relatively large number of constituents. In Washington, four staff workers are in Powell's office; in New York, three. In Washington, Powell receives as many as five to eight hundred letters a week, perhaps 250 of which state personal problems or requests for information and services. In New York, his congressional office is almost indistinguishable from his church organization, both of which deal with a wide range of the needs and requests of his followers. The church has in its congregation an estimated ten percent of the registered voters in the Sixteenth Congressional District.[6] Powell speaks to some four thousand people every Sunday, and upwards of one thousand persons come to the church or its community house every day of the week. There is little difference between voter and parishioner, between constituency and congregation.

[5]Cf. the treatment by Parsons and Shils of the pattern variables of "specificity" and "diffuseness" as aspects of the role-expectations governing the relevance of social objects. Talcott Parsons and Edward A. Shils, *Toward a General Theory of Action* (Cambridge: Harvard University Press, 1954), pp. 83-84.
[6]Hapgood, *op. cit.,* p. 3.

The generality of Powell's political role is further suggested by the extent to which he intervenes in New York City political affairs in the same manner in which he intervenes in national affairs. Powell frequently makes public charges of race discrimination and injustice in Manhattan and he is not slow to attack the Mayor, the Police Commissioner, Carmine De Sapio, and other officials. Harlem is not simply a constituency which elects Powell to Congress; it is also a source of political issues. Powell's political style in part depends on the existence of an "enemy" — a source of alleged injustice against which Powell can direct his fire. Since his power has not been received from the political organization of the city, the organization is not immune from that fire.

On the other hand, Powell is usually not readily available in his district for receiving constituents. Although he maintains a congressional staff in Harlem which is closely linked with his church staff, he does not personally perform the services usual for a local political leader — hear complaints, requests, and demands from the voters who seek out their politicians directly. These services are provided by lieutenants.

The mingling of political, religious, and civic roles is seen in the organization of his headquarters. The secretary of the church's Board of Trustees acts as financial secretary of Powell's political club (the "Alfred Isaacs Democratic Club"). His congressional administrative assistant, charged with handling local political affairs, has an office adjacent to that of the church's full-time social worker, and the two share the task of dealing with voters-parishioners. The church, a $100,000-a-year enterprise, provided 600 to 1200 political volunteers at various stages of Powell's 1959 campaign for district leader and helped to raise the $30,000 necessary for the 1958 congressional campaign.

Second, intangible appeals tend to be endowed with a sacrosanct quality which renders them difficult to manipulate. This would be true whether the appeal is that of a charismatic leader with the "gift of grace" or of political principles which are invested with a sacred quality. There are undoubtedly elements of both charisma and ideology in Powell's appeal to his followers; how much of each would be difficult to assess. Although there would be important differences in detail, the general effect of either a charismatic or ideological appeal is that the leader becomes ill-suited for a bargaining role. As the manifestation of the private aspirations of individual Negroes, as the assertion of the great public ends of the race, or as the revelation of a prophetic, heroic, or exemplary personality, these appeals are endowed with a sacrosanct quality which makes both the leader and the ends he may represent superior to the leaders and goals of others. To compromise either the position of the leader or the essence of these goals would be to give way to morally inferior persons or demands; in short, it would be to corrupt them. To oppose Powell in an election is to take the side of evil, to be an "Uncle Tom," and to be a "field hand" on the "white man's plantation." Paradoxically, this does not mean that Powell cannot escape his position on issues affecting the race which come before the local or national government. He can, and has, advanced and then dropped causes which involved race ends. Powell has frequently announced a dramatic move in local or national politics, but often little or nothing is in fact done. This was the case with his promised "boycott" of the 1952 presidential election and the independent political organization he promised in 1958. Few followers seem disturbed by this. Powell's own explanation is that such moves, even if only threats, serve to keep Tammany and others "off balance."

It may even be that Powell could reverse himself on some important issue, relying on his personal standing with his followers to justify the move. Charisma would compensate for ideology where the latter had to be sacrificed.[7] Such may have been the case, for example, when he joined with the other three Negro congressmen in voting against a Republican-sponsored civil rights amendment to the 1959 Housing Act on the grounds that it intended to defeat the bill by making it unacceptable to Southerners. Previously, he had sponsored and fought for a civil rights amendment to the federal education bill which, when adopted by the House, was followed by the defeat of the bill as a whole.[8] But considered as a set of appeals, Powell's identification with race issues and aspirations leads to further and further commitments and reduces the opportunity for compromise or the deliberate choice of means. Means, in the words of another student of race and nationalism, always have an "end-component."[9] Means cannot be selected simply on the basis of whether they are efficiently adapted to the attainment of given ends. Means are not valued merely on the basis of utility. Almost all means which might be used toward given ends have a value in and of

---

[7]It will be interesting to discover to what extent Powell's charisma can become "routinized." (Cf., Weber, *op. cit.,* pp. 363 ff.) The accession of Powell to the chairmanship of the House Committee on Education and Labor, predicted for the 87th Congress in 1961, will bring him under a new set of constraints which he may in part accept in hope of enjoying certain of the rewards of chairmanship. At the local level, Powell—by entering Tammany as a district leader—will have a limited amount of patronage and the necessity for creating something more in the way of a specifically political administrative apparatus. These constraints need not be too severe, for Tammany undoubtedly needs Powell more than he needs it. Clearly, Powell is unlikely to trade his non-material appeals for the scanty material ones at the disposal of DeSapio. But marginal adjustments might be expected, all in the direction of routinizing what has been a strictly personal and irregular position.

[8]See *Congressional Record,* 84th Cong., 2d Sess., 1956, CII, Part 9, 11773-883.

[9]See David E. Apter, "Political Modernization in Ghana and Uganda—An Essay in Political Anthropology," 1959 (mimeo).

themselves. Ends react on means, imbue them with value, and render it difficult for a leader to be selective. The means Powell employs are precisely of this character. They involve defying the white man, asserting loudly the rights of Negroes, pressing for liberalizing legislation regardless of the costs to other values held by the society, and keeping the issues alive and hot. Powell's political appeals lend themselves to campaigns based on the Negro ministry. The church is a vital part of Powell's base of support and, even though some ministers individually do not like Powell, most of them can be counted on to campaign in his behalf. It is principally through the mobilized resources of the Harlem ministry that Powell speaks to the people, addressing them from the pulpits of dozens of churches.

Third, Powell indulges his personal wants to an extraordinary extent. Powell stated in 1956 that his income was an estimated $115,000 a year — $40,000 a year earned by him as congressman and minister, and $75,000 earned by his wife (the noted jazz pianist, Hazel Scott).[10] He owns fancy sports cars, several homes, and two boats. Since Powell does not hold his followers and workers by material benefits, they rarely feel cheated by his obvious material success. In part, the lack of resentment is probably due to the feelings of gratification less fortunate Negroes derive from the sight of Powell in expensive restaurants and night clubs. He is doing what many of them understandably would like to do. But in addition, his money and material benefits are not the basis of his political power. Since his organization is not built through the distribution of tangible rewards, Powell can possess an abnormally large share of such rewards without depriving his followers of what they feel ought to be theirs. They support him for other reasons and derive other rewards from his success.[11]

[10]Hapgood, *op. cit.,* p. 3. Powell and his wife are now officially separated, and his worldly possessions may have decreased as a result.

[11]Weber (*op. cit.,* pp. 360-3) comments on various kinds of charismatic leaders who were themselves well rewarded (Germanic kings, Chinese monarchs, etc.) with benefits the followers did not share. The recruiting and paying of workers is part of the process (and problem) of routinization. This may become evident with control, in Powell's case, of a congressional committee and a district organization. Since it would be almost impossible to remove him from the committee chairmanship, and very difficult to attack him as district leader, he may be able to sustain both his personal appeal and his administrative structure. The interesting point thus far is that, contrary to Weber's view, Powell has not had to "deliver" beyond winning successive challenges to his position. (See Weber, *op. cit.,* p. 360: "If he is for long unsuccessful, above all if his leadership fails to benefit his followers, it is likely that his charismatic authority will disappear.") The explanation in Powell's case seems to be that the need for "delivering" in terms of substantive ends and benefits has been in great part obviated by his success in finding and defeating political enemies. This would mean that the existence of an enemy is of crucial significance in permitting intangible, charismatic-ideological politics to function. One "delivers" in a purely formal sense by crushing the opposition.

Dawson

William L. Dawson was at one time an expert and frequent user of many of the same kinds of appeals that now characterize Powell. As an insurgent Republican, seeking to force an entry into the regular organization in Chicago, Dawson was a well-known street-corner speaker with a magnetic personality. He built a personal following outside the machine, in part by holding out to them the hope of eventual material reward, and in part by arousing their interest in the race issues of the day and by appealing to their aspirations. After some success within the Republican Party (he served as an alderman from 1935 to 1939), Dawson joined the Democrats then under the leadership of Edward Kelly and Pat Nash. His entry into the party was the beginning of his first real career as a regular organization man, and it was the beginning of the end of his career as a purveyor of race rhetoric.

Kelly became mayor of Chicago at about the same time that LaGuardia became mayor of New York. The implications of this difference are far-reaching. LaGuardia took over a city administration under heavy attack from the reformers, and proceeded to hasten the rate of reform and further weaken the political machine that he had defeated. Kelly inherited a city administration and a political machine which were intact and in reasonably good health, and he proceeded to strengthen both. At the very time when Tammany was being starved, the Cook County Democracy was being feasted. In New York, the path to political power and success was becoming uncertain and strewn with traps; in Chicago, the same path was more clearly than ever becoming a private road belonging to the Democratic machine. Once inside such an organization, Dawson discovered that rhetorical or other intangible appeals were not only no longer useful, they could be a positive embarrassment. The stock of material incentives which the machine held — patronage and favors — was enormous and growing. Power came to him who could distribute them, and the right to distribute them was reserved to those in good standing with the organization. Remaining in such good standing means, among other things, not dividing or weakening the organization by raising issues which split the machine or which require it to act against its own best interests.

Dawson created an organization in his ward, and extended it to other Negro wards, which attracted and held its workers mostly through the opportunity for jobs. In turn, the organization began the slow and laborious task of altering the voting habits of a Negro population which had been firmly committed to the Republican party. In part the switch of allegiance was accomplished simply by exploiting the national trend among Negroes to the Democratic party, in part it was done by providing services and favors to voters, and in part it was done by bringing them into a complex and thorough set of organizations which clustered about the political machine — women's auxiliaries, youth groups, building and block organizations, and so on. By 1942 the organization was able to send Dawson to Congress by a slim majority (in fact, Dawson was unable to carry his own ward at the time), and then to control an aldermanic election by delivering a winning majority to an organization Democrat who was being challenged by a popular, non-organization Democrat. From that time on, the size of the organization's majorities grew steadily until they reached a stable level of about three-to-one, where they have remained ever since. In the process, Dawson acquired influence over four other Negro ward leaders.

Several consequences flow in part from the character of the organization of which Dawson is a leader and the nature of the rewards which must be distributed to sustain it.

First, tangible rewards tend to be divisible in a sense in which intangible ones are not. The distribution of material rewards can be kept separate from other aspects of the leader's position. His role as a local politician can become a fairly specific one, permitting him to play other roles without creating conflicts. There need be no inevitable connection between local political leadership in Chicago and congressional political activity in Washington, D.C. Few expectations about Dawson's performance and style as a congressman are created among his constituents or his workers. Indeed, Dawson has gone to considerable lengths to divorce his Chicago base of support from his Washington field of action. There is little contact between the Washington and the Chicago office. The staffs are separately recruited and separately organized. The flow of communications between the two centers is relatively small.

The ward headquarters in Chicago performs most of the services to constituents which are necessary; relatively few demands reach Washington. Dawson is to a greater extent than most other congressmen freed from constituency pressures, and he deliberately cultivates this situation. Dawson attends to his constituency assiduously, but in a manner entirely different from Powell. Dawson's Chicago headquarters are located in the very heart of the most depressed Negro area in a modest building. It is drab on the outside and plain on the inside, and deliberately so. It is accessible to the least advantaged constituent and nothing about the office is allowed to make the constituent feel he is out of his element or in unfamiliar surroundings. Dawson, when in Chicago (and he is there frequently), spends almost all his time in his ward office. No appointment is necessary to see him, and the visitor need not state his business to the receptionist. On the bench outside his office on a typical day might be found a police captain, a couple on relief, a young Negro lawyer, an unemployed man, a politician, and a university professor. When Dawson is not in the city, his place is taken by lieutenants who function in the same fashion. His Washington office and its work load are markedly smaller than Powell's, or indeed of other congressmen generally. Where Powell has four staff workers in his Washington office, Dawson has one; where Powell receives five to eight hundred letters a week, Dawson receives one hundred; where Powell replies to 250 "case letters" (requesting information or services) per week, Dawson receives one-third as many. Where Powell mails out large numbers of *Record* reprints and other items, Dawson mails almost none.

Dawson cherishes his reputation as a congressman. He is the chairman of the House Government Operations Committee, one of the three or four largest and most powerful committees in the House. He is highly esteemed by almost all his colleagues, who go out of their way to compliment him and his committee. He enjoys the respect of many southerners as well as large numbers of liberal northern Democrats. He has built his committee since 1949 (when he became its chairman), and his success is measured by the most important yardstick used in government — the size of its budget. In the 81st Congress, it received $300,000; in the 85th, $1,175,000. Its staff is competent and largely free of purely patronage appointments; the proceedings of the committee reflect an attention to business and an aversion to simple publicity that is unusual.

Dawson conceives of his Chicago organization as a base of support which produces, without commitment to issues or similar appeals, automatic majorities for him and his slate. For his role as Chicago ward leader, Dawson has one set of attitudes and action. He is strong, sometimes ruthless; he brooks no rivals; he crushes opposition and the ambitions of men who would challenge him; and he insists on organizational loyalty. In Washington, he plays an entirely different role. There, he is a leader interested in good government and liberal measures. He presides over the committee with authority, but not harshly. He encourages junior colleagues to take on new responsibilities and rise in committee work. He does not feel that he has rivals or opponents, and is friendly with everyone. Although he has considerable power as a congressman, he rarely uses that power for political ends in Chicago. By and large, the political power he has assembled in Washington is used for national goals, and only rarely for Chicago goals. Issues in Chicago affairs have arisen which were in some measure vulnerable to congressional intervention. He did not intervene.

One of the few themes common to both his local and national roles is the avoidance of race as a public issue. As in Chicago, so in Washington, Dawson rarely engages in a *public* discussion of race goals. He has not used his committee staff as a source of "race patronage." Only two of the fifty staff members are Negroes. It is explained that this reflects the shortage of qualified

Negro personnel. The committee has wide jurisdiction, but rarely is its investigative power turned toward explicitly racial issues. Some members of the staff regret this. Many were unhappy about his opposition to the Powell Amendment in 1956. On that occasion he ignored the requests of the NAACP and the numerous representations made to him from people in his district and not only voted but spoke out against the civil rights amendment on the grounds that if it were adopted it would mean southern opposition would be aroused and there would be no federal education bill at all. Dawson, although on friendly terms with two of the three other Negro congressmen, does not confine his association to them. He seems to prefer his wide range of contacts with many congressmen, particularly the House leadership. Although he is not a militant advocate of race ends in Congress, since 1956 he has not voted against such matters on the floor. Dawson, personally, feels that his political power can best be used for the advancement of Negroes in ways other than pressing for legislative correction of racial abuses. He sees himself as promoting Negro interests by intervening on their behalf with the authorities, placing more Negroes in government, and demonstrating the achievements possible for a Negro leader.[12]

The most important single source of controversy about Dawson is whether his political influence and position — which admittedly are rarely used publicly for race ends — are used in a private, unpublicized manner. Dawson and his supporters point to his intervention in many issues involving Negro rights. He has conferred with southern political leaders about Negro registration and segregation in party meetings and functions in the South. He intervened in the Emmet Till lynch case and moved to cut off the hostile, southern-led congressional investigation of school integration in Washington, D. C. All of these facts are difficult to document, given the secrecy which has surrounded them. The truth probably is that Dawson has had more effect than his critics allege and less than his most ardent supporters claim.

The other theme common to both Chicago and Washington is the extent to which Dawson shuns publicity. When Powell grants an interview, it is usually understood to be on the record; when Dawson does, it is almost always specified as off the record. Dawson's aversion to publicity is legendary, and goes far beyond that which is called for simply by prudence. He feels that he has been mistreated by an essentially hostile press, mostly in Chicago, that

---

[12]On this score, Dawson has had a series of conflicts with the executive branch on the distribution of patronage among Negroes. When the Democrats controlled the White House under Truman, Dawson saw himself in competition with the NAACP and similar groups for the right to make decisive endorsements. On occasion he intervened directly with the President on these matters after feeling slighted by presidential assistants who were in charge of patronage. NAACP leaders usually deny that they were attempting to undercut Dawson or that they were involved in patronage matters at all.

even friendly reporters are not allowed to print stories favorable to him, and that publicity invariably ends by embarrassing him or his political allies.

The *second* consequence of Dawson's position in an organization is the high degree of discretion he has on legislative matters, Dawson shuns race issues. His local organization meets weekly to hear Dawson and others speak; rarely is race a theme of their remarks. Dawson's attitude is that race progress must be made from within the party. If the organization can be persuaded to espouse race causes, well and good; if it cannot, then one must accept that fact as the inevitable cost of belonging. Dawson's view of appropriate race ends is largely confined to what has been termed elsewhere "welfare" ends — i.e., ends which are specific, direct, and tangible and which tend to improve the lot of the Negro without necessarily attaining some true measure of integration.[13] Party, not racial unity is stressed.

Dawson has been challenged by individuals and voluntary associations such as the local NAACP for not taking more vigorous *public* stands on race issues such as lynching, the Democratic Party's platform on civil rights, and other matters. Dawson has been criticized in the Negro press. The important fact is that such challenges and criticisms account for little; his electoral strength is barely affected. Dawson, like Powell, is stronger than any single issue which might be used against him. He can survive almost any position he takes on any single issue. But unlike Powell, he need not devote himself to issues and aspirations. His freedom of choice in this matter is much wider. He can be far more deliberate in his choice of ends and means. He can devote himself almost entirely to the pursuit of other, non-racial goals without being penalized. His range of discretion regarding means to any important political ends is broad. This is true in part because he can afford the luxury of little or no publicity, and in part because he need not consider the extent to which the means he uses are endowed with value significance. Means, to Dawson, can be more completely instrumental than to Powell.

Nowhere is the contrast between the Dawson and Powell organizations more striking or important than in the differing roles of the Negro ministry. The ministry is politically significant only in those Negro communities where no independent base of political power exists — i.e., where there is no strong, patronage-oriented machine. Dawson has deliberately worked for twenty years to reduce or eliminate the role of the Negro minister as a political influence in Chicago, and he has in great part succeeded. A fundamental distinction between Negro political systems is whether they must work through existing mass organizations (churches and labor unions) or whether it is possible to

---

[13]See my *Negro Politics,* Chap. VI.

organize the community *directly* for political ends.[14] Dawson, to be sure, has ministerial allies, but he discourages the participation of ministers in politics for the most part. Nor is Powell "dependent" on the ministers. The relationship is symbiotic; each needs the other. The distinction is between one system in which the ends and basis of influence of the politician are relatively *independent* of other ends and bases of influence in the community (as in Chicago) and the alternative system in which political ends and influences are *implicated* in the community (as in New York).

Third, Dawson stands in an entirely different relationship to his followers and workers than does Powell. Because of the character of the incentives used by Dawson to hold their allegiance and maintain discipline, he is subject to a set of constraints from which Powell is largely exempt. The "status gap" between Powell and his supporters is manifestly greater than the disparity between Dawson and his followers. Powell, since he embodies the racial goals and private aspirations of many of his followers, can enrich his own position without weakening his stature — indeed, he may enhance it. Dawson leads a group of men who fundamentally, although not exclusively, are in politics for more tangible rewards. Dawson weakens his position by the extent to which he appears to gain at the expense of his followers. His supporters must be convinced that they can gain in proportion to the gains of Dawson. If Dawson gains disproportionately to his followers, he causes resentment, jealousy, and antagonisms.

This speaks to the question of the nature of Dawson's political skills. In part, of course, they are the skills of any leader of men — the ability to move other men to act in accordance with one's intentions. This requires arranging the situation so that the wants of individuals lead them to act toward the ends of the leader. A typical, but short-sighted, view as to the basis of a machine leader's power is that he "controls patronage." This is an insufficient and in part a misleading explanation. In reality, it says little more than that a man is powerful because he is powerful. The question remains, *why* has *he* been able to grasp and retain control of patronage for the purpose of sustaining his organization? If control of patronage were the only variable, then Negro politics in Chicago might be in a state of constant factional rivalry. The essential element in the use of tangible incentives to sustain political organizations is that the followers must never be allowed to feel that the gains of breaking with the leader outweigh the costs of such a break. The leader ought

---

[14]Cf., Hugh Douglas Price, "The Negro and Florida Politics, 1944-1954," *Journal of Politics*, XVII (May, 1955), 198-220. Price notes the decline in the political importance of Negro ministers and social organizations with the rise in Negro registration and the emergence of specific Negro political roles.

to create a pattern of expectations among his followers which he appears willing to satisfy even at his own expense.

This is made possible when the leader, such as Dawson, derives intangible rewards from a political system that produces tangible rewards for the followers. Dawson's gratifications are not in money and material perquisites, but in prestige, the sense of power, and the fun of the game. He lives austerely, drives second-hand cars, avoids ostentation, spends money freely on others, and generally minimizes the outward or material rewards of his position. He does not appear to be competing with his followers for the scarce material rewards of politics. Perhaps he could afford greater outward display than he does, but it seems clear that the lack of such display enhances his position.[15]

Chicago and New York

These differences between the two organizations can be accounted for largely by the differences in the political systems of which they are parts. In New York, the steady weakening of the Tammany organization which has gone on since 1933 has made it difficult for it to enforce its will on its members and impossible for it to turn back the challenge of a man like Powell. Further, Tammany attempted, during the LaGuardia-Fusion period, to govern Harlem from outside the district, through "absentee" leaders whose influence rested in part on keeping Negro political leadership divided and off balance.[16] Tammany failed — in part through unwillingness and in part through lack of resources — to build a strong, centralized Negro leadership in Harlem. Powell now seeks to fill that void. After his election as a district leader (together with three other leaders allied with him) he sought to create a unified "Leadership Team" for Harlem. In January, 1960, Powell's group received control of the Tammany patronage in Harlem. Although he has now entered the regular organization, Powell's independent base of support and the paucity of the rewards Tammany can offer his followers means that Tam-

---

[15]Cf. Max Weber's description of the creative entrepreneur and his willingness to forgo immediate gain for the sake of investment and ultimate returns which may be only the sense of achievement and power. This can be contrasted to his subordinates or successors who have lost the ethic of work and sense of calling, occupy a bureaucratized position, and derive more material rewards. *The Protestant Ethic and the Spirit of Capitalism*, trans. R. H. Tawney (London: G. Allen and Unwin, 1930). Dawson is not alone in seeking intangible rewards for his political work. Many contemporary leaders such as Richard Daley of Chicago and David Lawrence of Pittsburgh are men for whom politics is not a path to wealth. It would be interesting to analyze past "bosses" to see what rewards attracted the most successful of them, and how the shift in those rewards—in part resulting from closer public scrutiny—from tangible to intangible has altered recruitment patterns and leadership styles. It is likely that even many of the "old line" bosses— like Charles F. Murphy of New York—got less in a material sense out of politics than is commonly believed. Some of the bosses who failed to hold their power were conspicuously men who "took" out of proportion to the gains of their followers.
[16]Cf., *New York Times*, January 10, 1960, p. 1.

many needs Powell more than he needs it. All doubt on this manner was quickly dispelled when Powell made public attacks on New York political leaders for failing to give Negroes more representation in government, for denying Negroes patronage, for persecuting Borough President Hulan Jack (Powell's erstwhile political scapegoat), and for allowing police to drive out Negro numbers racketeers in favor of Italians.

Dawson's organization is a strong portion of a powerful city machine. The possibility of a Powell arising on Chicago's South Side is substantially reduced by this fact. In 1947-1955, an effort was made by a popular minister to become an independent political force in the community. He managed to serve two terms in the City Council as alderman of the Third Ward. But the Dawson organization defeated him in 1955 for several reasons — all of which are indicative of the differences in politics between Chicago and New York. The Dawson organization has available to it perhaps three times the amount of patronage available to comparable districts in Harlem. The independent had to fight, not a group of quarreling factions, but a single, organized opponent who was well-staffed with workers. The independent could gain relatively few civic allies; most were already committed to the strongest force in the community — the Dawson group. Although the independent was a minister, other ministers could not be mobilized as a solid group behind him. Finally, it was necessary in a city where the Democratic primary was invariably dominated by the regular organization for the independent to run as a Republican (where his sympathies happened to lie anyway) and this was a grave weakness in a community overwhelmingly Democratic. (Chicago's aldermanic elections are only nominally nonpartisan.) When the independent attempted to emulate Powell by moving from the city council to Congress, he had again to run as a Republican, and this was fatal.

Thus, the character of the political system into which Powell and Dawson moved in their formative years (the late 1930's and 1940's) was of decisive importance in molding the kind of organization each created. Dawson found a strong, active apparatus in which he had to create a place for himself. Powell encountered a weak, divided organization which it was necessary neither to join nor to defeat.

Some Conclusions

Two important congressmen with roughly comparable constituencies have been compared. Both men, it has been argued, act as if the maintenance of their organizations were their goal. Since the organizations and the incentives necessary to maintain them differ, the political styles of the two men differ.

One organization was created and is sustained by a system of ideal or nonmaterial benefits. This has certain consequences. (1) The benefits are indivisible, and the role of the leader who dispenses them tends to become diffuse and general. All aspects of his career are treated as part of a whole, and all choices relate to a single set of values. (2) The benefits have a sacred component, and thus are difficult to compromise. Means used to attain them share in the moral or sacrosanct quality of the ends themselves; means can only with difficulty be regarded as purely instrumental. (3) The ideal benefits which followers share permit the leader to indulge himself in outward display without alienating them — indeed, he may enhance his position with them. The other organization was created and is sustained by a system of tangible rewards. Among the consequences of this are: (1) The rewards are divisible and may be isolated to the local organization. The role of the leader can be specific and compartmentalized. He may separate his base of support from his national field of action. (2) The absence of race or ideological appeals gives the leader a greater discretion as to the choice of ends to pursue. Means tend to be more thoroughly instrumental. Few of his actions are deliberately imbued with moral significance. (3) The power of the leader in part depends on his ability to satisfy his followers that they gain in proportion to him — that he does not gain at their expense. The "status-gap" between the leader and the led is relatively small.

Further, it has been argued that the character of the two organizations, and hence the nature of their maintenance needs, can be traced to the political systems of which they are parts. One political system (Chicago) has a single leadership which disposes of a large amount of patronage, is unified, and can control its own primaries with ease. The other (New York) has a leadership which constantly must meet challenges, has a short supply of patronage, and cannot invariably control its own primaries. In the latter Powell succeeded; in the former, a Powell-like leader tried and failed.

This mode of analysis has an obvious shortcoming. A political style which may have been, at some early point, functional in terms of the needs of the situation, later tends to become temperamental. Political style tends to become the independent variable, *creating* in part the situation it had formerly served; that is, the image a leader creates of himself inevitably tends to react back on him and modify his behavior apart from what might be considered as the "objective" needs of the situation. Both Dawson and Powell undoubtedly carry many of their attributes to an unusual extreme, and settled habits have now replaced earlier experiments. But we need not linger too long on the problem of untangling the man from the situation, for however subtle a pattern of interaction exists between the two levels, the burden of the analysis remains this: the political style of the two leaders is functional to the organization they must maintain and the position they hold within the larger political system of which they are part.

It is interesting to note the opinion of these men held by prominent Negroes in New York and Chicago. Publicly, both have been criticized and even attacked. The *Chicago Defender* was critical of Dawson in 1956; the New York *Amsterdam News* supported Powell's opponent in 1958. But public criticism is far rarer and much more gentle than the private criticism which can be found directed at both men. The followers are aligned in two intent and mutually exclusive camps. Neither man has anything like universal admiration from the Negro middle class or from Negro intellectuals. Both are criticized by many thoughtful Negroes: Dawson for doing nothing, Powell for being irresponsible. At the same time, both get grudging respect from most Negro civic leaders — Dawson because of his personal position, his stature, and his power; Powell because he is "not afraid of the white man" and because he "stirs things up" and thus makes it easier for civic organizations to gain leverage against influential whites. The important aspect of the private praise and blame heaped on these men is that in the last analysis it is not concerned with ends or accomplishments. Neither leader has "accomplished" much in the way of legislation directed at race goals. Although Powell supporters criticize Dawson for "doing nothing," in fact, of course, Powell has no greater a list of accomplishments. And when pressed, many Negroes will concede this.

This means that most criticism of the two leaders centers on the nature of their political styles. In a situation in which *ends* are largely unattainable (at least by Negro action alone), *means* become all-important. On the basis of the means employed — the political style used — men make judgments as to the worth of the leader and his reputation. Means, in short, tend to become ends in themselves; what is important is not what you do, but how you do it. As pointed out earlier in another content, means acquire an "end-component" either because (a) ends are unattainable or (b) ends are morally endowed.

The relationship of leader to organization in these two cases raises interesting questions concerning the role of congressmen. It has often been assumed that one mark of the statesman is an interest in issues, rather than patronage, as the currency of politics. Schattschneider, for example, censures the "local bosses" because they are irresponsible and because they interfere in national politics to its detriment.[17] The thrust of this paper is that, for a variety of reasons, a "boss" may deliberately separate his local and national roles. Further, he may use his local machine (a) to filter out constituency demands by satisfying them at the local level and (b) to sustain himself in office without extensive or irrevocable commitments on policy matters and

---

[17]E. E. Schattschneider, *Party Government* (New York: Farrar and Rinehart, Inc., 1942), esp. chap. vii. A valuable but neglected challenge to this view is A. L. Lowell, *The Government of England* (3rd ed.; New York: Macmillan Co., 1926), II, 91-5. Lowell presents an analysis of voting in the U. S. Congress among representatives from "machine" constituencies as well as in state legislatures. He concludes that there are few party votes in part because "the machine meddles little with general legislation" (p. 94).

without accepting the support of organized pressure groups. The very position of a person such as Dawson enables him, if he chooses, to disregard both the localistic demands of constituents and the demands of local or national pressure groups. The needs of the constituents can be met largely on an issue-free basis; the demands of the pressure groups can be ignored, as they can do little either to help or harm the leader. In theory, this leaves the congressman free to pursue the public interest, however he chooses to define it. Rather than constraining him and rendering him irresponsible, the existence of the local machine may liberate him and permit him to vote as his conscience dictates. Congressmen without such a powerful and non-ideological base of support may have much less discretion in such matters.[18]

Aside from the theoretical advantages of such a position, there of course remains the empirical question whether a political leader who has risen through the ranks of a local machine would have any elevated view of the public interest. The way of life a machine creates for its members is such that it might render even its best leaders incapable of taking a broad and enlightened view of public affairs even though the organization enforces no constraints that would objectively prevent acting on the basis of such a view. In the psychological dimension of representation, there is a great variation in the roles played. Of all the Democrats in Congress supported by the Cook County organization, some take a narrow and routine view of their functions whereas others (such as Dawson) deliberately endeavor to act on the basis of an enlarged view of the functions of a congressman. No categorical judgments can be made on this point, but the interpretations presented in this study may suggest an approach to the re-examination of the impact of the constituency on the function of representation and a re-evaluation of the role of the local machine in contemporary politics.

---

[18]In fact, both Powell and Dawson can ignore most pressure groups nationally. Neither requires the support of organized labor, and they have frequently made labor lobbyists unhappy by their actions. Powell undoubtedly finds it in his interest to yield to the NAACP on most matters, although he probably could defy it on any single issue. But Powell cannot yield to any temptation to ignore the demands of his constituents for issue agitation on race matters.

Part 3

Enrolling to Vote
in the Sub-Community

On the eve of many elections in America one often hears last minute appeals of the contending candidates to the electorate to "vote as you please, but vote." This appeal to the voters is a reflection of the proposition that high voting participation is a maximization of democratic values. True as this may be, these appeals often come too late because in the American voting system "... two decisions are often required, one to register and another to vote, and the first decision must be made when political issues and activity are at a low point."[1]

---

[1]Seymour Martin Lipset, *Political Man: The Social Bases of Politics,* (Garden City, New York: Doubleday and Company [Anchor Books], 1963), p. 185.

163

The vote is widely considered the Negro's most important weapon in his struggle for full citizenship. This view was the driving force behind the Civil Rights Act of 1957 and 1960 and the Voting Rights Act of 1965. And the numerous Negro registration drives in the South since 1957 testify to the faith of any number of Negro leaders in this assumption. Given these facts it is necessary to examine the extent to which one can expect large Negro registration rolls to become a reality. If Negro registration to vote is as meaningful as the efforts of some would suggest, what stands in the way of greater Negro registration? Do the requirements of the electoral system slow down Negro registration rates? Does the fear of racial reprisal deter Negro enrollment to vote? Does the set of objective personal conditions, both social and economic, under which Negroes have to live affect Negro registration figures?

The first act — the decision to register in America — is made by many people for many different reasons. They have the time; they are aware of the issues; they are familiar with the candidates; or they belong to certain socio-economic groupings and feel they have a stake in society. Some Negroes make the first decision and are prepared to participate in the primary and general elections. Many do not.

This part assesses some of the forces, both internal and external to the Negro sub-community, which make for or militate against Negroes making the first great step in the voting process. Focus is on Negro registration in the South, since it is in this region that race is the crucial factor in the determination of who registers to vote. Many of the factors, of course, which affect Negro registration in the South, especially socio-economic factors, also affect Negro registration in the North.

In the South, as has been stated, race looms large in the determination of who registers to vote. V. O. Key, Jr. in his classic study, *Southern Politics in State and Nation,* found generally that Negro participation in politics was lowest where Negroes were most heavily concentrated in the population. Interestingly enough, however, in the deep South, the presence of the Roman Catholic religion appears to affect Key's general thesis. The first reading presented in this section is a revealing study by Professors John H. Fenton and Kenneth N. Vines reporting the impact of the existence of a high proportion of Catholics in the white population on Negro registration in several Louisiana parishes. Where there was a high proportion of the religious population Catholic, Negroes tended to register to vote in relatively higher proportions than in low Catholic density areas even where there was a heavy concentration of Negroes. The study is significant because, despite the fact that the distribution of the Catholic population in Louisiana and the South is small, any Negro strategy to increase voter registration could assume the acquiescence if not the assistance of Catholic churches and priests in the South where church membership has generally been found to be inversely related to Negro registration. It is a truism of much research that the extent of voter registration corresponds with social status, economic income, and level of education. High social status, high economic income and a high level of education are associated with high voter turnout. Conversely, low social status, low economic income and limited education are associated with low voter turnout. One of the big questions has been: is the correspondence of these variables the same for both whites and Negroes or is race a variable that must be considered? In the second reading Professors Donald R. Matthews and James W. Prothro analyze the significance of socio-economic status for Negro participation. Comparing socio-economic characteristics of whites and Negroes to voter registration, the authors were able to explain much of the variance between white and Negro registration figures, but cited the need for examining political and legal factors in order to refine the explanation of the rate difference. In a follow-up study, the third article reprinted in this section, Professors Matthews and Prothro isolated political and legal factors and found when these factors were included, they could come much closer to predicting Negro voter registration. The political and legal factors — which are barriers to Negro registration — illumine the role of race in southern politics.

Finally, it is important to note that the mere removal of political and legal barriers to Negro participation in the South will not necessarily enhance the Negro's political power. Low social status, relatively small incomes, and a low level of education are the characteristics possessed by the great majority of Negroes in the South and the North. Any student of American politics who attempts to view the vote as a panacea for the Negro in his struggle for equality must keep these facts in mind. Indeed, any present assessment of the Negro's failure to register political gains commensurate with his numbers must be evaluated in light of his overwhelmingly inferior socio-economic position.

Negro Registration
in Louisiana

John H. Fenton and Kenneth N. Vines

The 1944 action of the Supreme Court voiding the white primary ended the last effective legal block to Negro voter registration in the South. After that, resort to legal steps to block Negro registration was either outlawed by the courts or else could only be a delaying device. In the state of Louisiana, however, the decision in *Smith* v. *Allwright* did not result in Negro registration comparable to white registration. In 1956, twelve years later, 30 percent of the potential Negro voting population was registered, compared to 73 percent of the whites. This study is an investigation of some factors in that discrepancy, and in particular, of the differences in registration between Catholic and Protestant areas.

An important characteristic of Negro registration in Louisiana is the extreme range of variation to be found among the several parishes. Table I shows 17 parishes with fewer than 20 percent of the eligible Negroes registered, and 11 parishes with 70 percent or more of the potential Negro vote

Reprinted from the *American Political Science Review*, Vol. LI, (September 1957), pp. 704-713 with permission of the publisher and authors. Copyright 1957 by the American Political Science Association.

registered. Therefore, the statewide "average" percentage of Negro registration[1] has little meaning without more detailed interpretation.

Among the factors responsible for these differences is the religio-cultural variable. Louisiana offers a unique opportunity to study the influence of this variable on the registration aspect of race relations. Catholicism is dominant

TABLE I

LOUISIANA PARISHES BY PERCENTAGE OF NEGROES 21 AND OVER REGISTERED, 1956

Registration Percentage	Number of Parishes
0- 9	7
10- 19	10
20- 29	9
30- 39	6
40- 49	5
50- 59	13
60- 69	3
70- 79	6
80- 89	3
90-100	2

in southern Louisiana and Protestantism in northern Louisiana. The two regions are very nearly separate worlds. Other variables enter, but this one is the focus of this paper.

The material for this study was gathered from Census Reports and from specialized and local sources on the cultural characteristics of Louisiana. Sixteen parishes were visted throughout the state, chosen to represent different degrees of Negro registration, different socio-economic areas, and different religio-cultural areas. Interviews were conducted with state and parish officials and local political leaders, both white and Negro.[2]

---

[1]Current estimates on population figures were obtained as follows: (1) The estimated total population of each parish for 1956 was obtained from *Sales Management Annual Survey of Buying Power,* May 10, 1956. (2) It was assumed that the 1950 ratio of Negroes to the total population in each parish would remain constant. (3) It was assumed that the 1950 ratio of Negroes 21 and over to the total Negro population in each parish would remain constant. (4) Thus by taking percentages of the 1956 total population estimate as derived from the 1950 census, a 1956 estimate was obtained for the potential Negro vote in each parish.

[2]The authors wish to acknowledge the aid of the Southern Regional Council in support of this project. The Louisiana project was part of a Southern-wide survey of Negro registration and voting sponsored by the Council.

I. The Religio-Cultural Variable

Every Louisianian is aware of the religious complications of his state's politics. It has usually been thought, though experience provides exceptions, that only Protestants can be elected to state-wide offices or as congressmen from the north Louisiana districts; and only Catholics can be elected to major offices in south Louisiana. The Catholicism of Louisiana is predominantly French, and it is said that a French name is worth 50,000 votes in south Louisiana in a state-wide election.

Roughly the southern 25 parishes form French Catholic Louisiana while the remaining parishes in the north are predominantly Protestant and Anglo-Saxon. The French parishes remain French-Catholic because of their assimilation of extraneous cultural elements entering the area.

As Table II indicates, Negro registration, in percentages of potential eligibles, is more than twice as great in Louisiana's French-Catholic parishes as in its non-French parishes. In only two of the 25 French-Catholic parishes are less than 20 percent of the eligible Negroes registered, whereas in 13 of the 39 non-French parishes less than 20 percent of the potential Negro vote is registered. In seven of the French-Catholic parishes Negro registration is 70 percent or more, while only four of the non-French-Catholic parishes equal

TABLE II

NEGRO REGISTRATION BY RELIGIO-CULTURAL SECTIONS OF LOUISIANA, 1956

	French-Catholic Parishes[1]	Non-French Parishes[2]
Number of Negroes registered	70,488	90,922
Potential Negro vote	138,000	390,000
Percentage of Negroes registered	51	23
Mean of parishes—percentage of Negroes in total population	32	38
Mean of parishes—percentage of urbanism	30	26
Mean of parishes—percentage of Catholics among all religions[3]	83	12

[1]French parishes: Acadia, Ascension, Assumption, Avoyelles, Calcasieu, Cameron, Evangeline, Iberis, Iberville, Jefferson, Jefferson Davis, Lafayette, LaFourches, Plaquemines, Pointe Coupee, St. Bernard, St. Charles, St. James, St. John the Baptist, St. Landry, St. Martin, St. Mary, Terrebonne, Vermilion, West Baton Rouge. Definition of French parishes taken from T. Lynn Smith and Homer L. Hitt, *The People of Louisiana* (Baton Rouge, 1952), p. 143.
[2]Predominantly Anglo-Saxon Protestant.
[3]From 1926 *Census of Religious Bodies*, the most reliable source available. It is recognized that the figures contain a bias because of the difference between Catholic and Protestant practice in counting children as members of the church. However, the purpose of the figures is to show differences in degree of Catholicism.

or exceed the 70 percent mark. Yet no significant differences exist between the two groups of parishes with respect to Negro-white population balance or to urbanism.

The reasons for the different reaction of French and non-French population groups to Negro registration seem, in large part, to be due to fundamentally different attitudes of each culture toward the Negro. Both Negro and white leaders agree that social attitudes toward the Negro differ in the two cultures.

Some objective evidence of this difference is to be found in these facts: (1) at political meetings in southern Louisiana crowds are often racially mixed, even at indoor meetings, whereas in northern Louisiana such crowds are always segregated; (2) the Citizens' Council organizations have comparatively little support in French-Catholic Louisiana, while in northern Louisiana, as a Madison Council official put it, "Here the Citizens' Councils are the prominent people"; (3) racially hybrid communities occur more frequently in south Louisiana than in north Louisiana.[3]

It should be emphasized that the people of French-Catholic Louisiana are not in favor of integration. Yet they do evidence, people and leaders alike, a permissive attitude toward Negro participation in political affairs that is generally lacking in the northern parishes.[4] These permissive attitudes seem to stem in large part from the social and religious practices of the Catholic Church. The Church looks upon segregation as a sin, and Archbishop Rummel of New Orleans has led the clergy in an all-out doctrinal attack on the practice. Catholic clergy cite the "catholic" character of the Church as the reason for its advanced stand on racial issues and emphasize the fact that the Protestant churches are national in origin and tend to be exclusive in character, whereas the Catholic Church is more universal in both its background and orientation. Many Catholics also point to the effect of the Church on the Negro as a reason for the high percentage of Negro registration in Catholic parishes. According to this argument, the Catholic Negro enjoys religious and ethical training which is identical with that received by the white community, and from a well-educated priest. Therefore, the Catholic Negro's value system more nearly approaches that of the white community than does that of the Protestant Negro, and, accordingly, he is more readily accepted by the greater community.

Since the Catholic Church attempts to build a Catholic culture wherever it exists by providing educational, recreational, and fraternal organizations for

---

[3]See Alvin L. Bertrand, *The Many Louisianas,* Bulletin #46, Louisiana State University, Agricultural Experiment Station, June, 1955, p. 21.

[4]The more "permissive" attitude of the French-Catholic parishes may be demonstrated additionally by comparison of its record on race relations with the northern parishes on such matters as rates of lynching, 1900-1941; and the number of racially integrated state colleges. It was also confirmed in interviews with both Negroes and whites from the two areas.

its members, the influence of the Church as a social institution is great. It appears to be the principal, in many areas the only, unsegregated social institution in Louisiana. In the French parishes where Catholicism has been the major formative factor in the culture for many years, it has been, Catholics say, important in producing the permissive attitudes of the people toward the political and social activities of the Negro.

In north Louisiana, on the other hand, one finds little or no objective evidence that the dominant Protestant religion has aided in the creation of tolerant attitudes toward Negro political activity. Negro leaders in these areas rarely cited white Protestant ministers as friends of the Negro, and seldom referred to a Protestant church as an ameliorative factor in the easing of racial tensions. Although most Protestant national organizations are opposed to racial prejudice and segregation, their position has not effected many changes in the attitudes of local congregations. Protestant churches, in contrast to the authoritative control by the Catholic hierarchy, are dominated by local congregations, and Protestant ministers, though often mindful of national pronouncements on segregation, must remain passive on such matters so as not to offend their flocks.

Although the mean percentage of Negro registration is low in north Louisiana, there are parishes with large Negro registration. As Table III shows, this usually occurs where Negroes are not an important part of the population, that is, where there are few Negroes, little economic tenancy, and no heritage of a plantation society.

When the parishes of northern Louisiana are grouped into areas, this correspondence of a high rate of tenancy and concentration of Negro population to a low Negro registration becomes clearly evident and significant. In the North-Central cut-over pine section where the percentage of Negroes in the

TABLE III

RELATION BETWEEN PERCENTAGE OF TENANCY, PERCENTAGE OF NEGRO POPULATION, AND PERCENTAGE OF NEGROES REGISTERED IN FRENCH AND NON-FRENCH PARISHES OF LOUISIANA, 1956

Percentage of Tenancy	Number of Parishes		Mean Percentage of Negro Population		Mean Percentage of Negroes Registered	
	French	Non-French	French	Non-French	French	Non-French
50 and over	6	11	34	52	65	11
40-49	0	4	—	43	—	23
30-39	7	6	33	39	48	25
20-29	5	6	23	36	67	36
10-19	7	9	34	25	43	53
0- 9	0	3	—	19	—	59

total population (mean of parishes, 24 percent) and prevalence of tenancy (17 percent) is relatively low, there is a great deal of Negro registration (55 percent). In this area, there has been little fear of the Negro as a political force, and the society tends to be pluralistic.[5]

The Mississippi Delta area, in northeast Louisiana, is the section with the highest rate of tenancy (60 percent), the greatest proportion of Negroes (51 percent), and the lowest Negro registration (11 percent) in the state. It remains a plantation society. There are plantation owners in Tensas and Madison parishes who take pride in the resemblance between the plantations of 1856 and 1956, in terms of the physical appearance of the Negro and his cabin, and of the social and economic relationships between Negro and white.

The survival of this kind of society depends upon excluding the Negro from all political and economic power. Outsiders are assured that the Negro happily accepts the existing power structure, and strenuous efforts are made to demonstrate the mutual advantages which accrue from it.

Thus in non-French Louisiana, Negro registration varies with the number of Negroes present and the nature of the economy. In a plantation economy, a tight power structure exists which makes it possible to exclude Negroes from the polls. In addition, the numerical strength of Negroes in such communities arouses real or imagined fears of possible Negro rule if he should obtain the ballot.

As Table III indicates, the economic structure of many of the French-Catholic parishes differs from that of the northern portion of the state. In French-Catholic Louisiana, the Negro is not typically in a tenant-master relationship to the white community. Rather, his position is that of a free wage-earner. The reason is that much of southern Louisiana is engaged in the production of cane sugar, which does not lend itself to the tenant system of farming.

The free wage-earner is more remote from his master than is the tenant farmer, and thus (at least in prosperous times) enjoys greater social and economic freedom. Therefore, the difference in the economies of the two regions undoubtedly exercises an important conditioning effect on Negro registration.

However, even in those French-Catholic parishes where a plantation economy does exist the percent of Negro registration tends to be considerably above that of the northern plantation parishes. In three French-Catholic

---

[5]It should be noted, however, that resistance to Negro registration is stiffening in North-Central Louisiana. Efforts to purge Negroes from the rolls are being vigorously pressed by Citizens Council groups in the section. For a detailed statement of the procedures being used there, see the letter from Assistant Attorney General Olney to Senator Douglas, *Congressional Record,* Vol. 103 (August 1, 1957), pp. 12156-7 (daily ed.); *New York Times,* August 4, 1957, which, however, misplaced the parishes cited as in the southern part of the state.

parishes (St. Landry, Pointe Coupee, and West Baton Rouge), both the percentage of Negro population and the percentage of tenancy is 45 or more. The percentage of Negro registration exceeds 20 in all three parishes and reaches a level of 87 in St. Landry. This highlights the importance of the French-Catholic religio-culture in producing a permissive attitude toward Negro registration.

II. The Effect of Negro-White Population Balance

Perhaps the most widely accepted belief concerning Negro registration in the South is that the amount will vary inversely to the proportion of Negroes in the local population. According to this theory, areas with large Negro populations, (1) were most passionately attached to the cause of the Confederacy, and (2) because of the greater number of Negroes have more reason to fear Negro voting. The theory concludes that the centers of Negro population will be the last to extend the suffrage to the Negro.

Table IV shows that there is certainly no uniform correlation between the proportion of parish population Negro and the proportion of Negroes registered. However, at the extreme ends of the scale, the relationship is significant. The four Louisiana parishes with no Negro registration — Tensas, Madison, West Feliciana, and East Carroll, neighboring parishes in the Mississippi Delta area — are the only parishes with over 60 percent Negro population. In the parishes with less than 29 percent Negro population there is a significant increase in the percentage of Negro registration. However, in ten parishes with a majority of Negro population (50 to 59 percent) the mean percentage of Negroes registered (37 percent) slightly exceeds that for the two intervals with fewer Negroes (40 to 49 percent and 30 to 39 percent).

Table IV also shows that the presence or absence of large numbers of Negroes has a similar effect on Negro registration in French and non-French

TABLE IV

RELATION BETWEEN NEGROES IN TOTAL POPULATION AND NEGRO REGISTRATION IN PARISHES OF LOUISIANA, 1956

Percentage of Negroes in Total Population	Number of Parishes			Mean Percentage of Negroes Registered		
	Total	French	Non-French	Total	French	Non-French
60 and over	4	—	4	0	—	0
50-59	10	4	6	37	44	33
40-49	8	3	5	33	57	19
30-39	19	6	13	32	47	25
20-29	12	6	6	52	51	53
10-19	10	5	5	62	65	59
0- 9	1	1	—	94	94	—

parishes. However, as the table indicates, the range of variation tends to be much narrower in the French than in the non-French parishes. Of course, the degree of economic tenancy is another variable present in this figure, a factor which has already been discussed.

In conclusion, it can be definitely stated that, in Louisiana, the simple fact of the presence of a high proportion of Negroes and a tradition of a planta-tion economy (such as in St. Landry parish) does not necessarily militate against the registration of Negroes in sizeable numbers, especially where a French-Catholic culture predominates.

III. The Effect of Urbanism

Contrary to the widely held belief that Negro registration in the South is concentrated in urban areas, Table V indicates that no clear relationship exists in Louisiana between the degree of urbanism and the extent of Negro regis-tration.

The reason, in all probability, for the stereotype about urbanism and Negro registration is that those few Negroes who were registered to vote prior to 1944 resided in the large urban centers. In addition, the first increases in Negro registration after 1944 largely occurred in urban areas. The urban areas of the state contain the largest concentration of professional and business Negroes, equipped to provide leadership toward registration; and the cities provide, one might imagine, an environment of political competition better suited to encourage Negro political participation.

As Table V indicates, however, Negro registration in Louisiana is, if any-thing, lower in the large urban centers than in the more rural portions of the state. The table also shows that an identical though more pronounced pattern

TABLE V

RELATION BETWEEN URBANISM AND WHITE AND NEGRO REG-ISTRATION, FOR STATE AND BY RELIGIO-CULTURAL SECTIONS, LOUISIANA, 1956

Percentage of Urbanism	Number of Parishes			Mean Percentage Registered of Potential Vote					
				Negro			White		
	Total	Fr.	Non-Fr.	Total	Fr.	Non-Fr.	Total	Fr.	Non-Fr.
70 and over	5	2	3	29	43	20	64	70	60
50-69	4	3	1	45	48	35	75	78	69
40-49	8	2	6	27	67	13	78	79	77
30-39	10	3	7	46	54	42	84	84	84
20-29	14	8	6	49	61	33	90	91	88
10-19	6	3	3	28	43	13	88	89	87
0- 9	17	4	13	43	53	40	92	93	90

obtains for white registration too. Taking the religio-cultural areas of the state separately, the same relationship between urbanism and registration exists in both regions as in the state as a whole, but with both Negro and white registration in the French parishes tending to be either equal to or higher than registration in the non-French parishes.

Negro registration tends to be lower in the urban than the rural areas for a variety of reasons. Many an urban Negro is rootless, and tends to feel little identification with his community or his fellow Negroes; his leadership often works at cross purposes, and is particular rather than general. In addition, local interest in registration and voting tends to be more intense in Louisiana's rural areas, where the election of a sheriff is an important event, than in the urban areas. All of these factors tend, also, to operate on the level of white registration.

Even though the urban centers do not provide favorable environments for securing a high proportion of Negro registration, the "pilot" role of activities in urban centers toward launching Negro registration is important. In all parishes studied the registration of Negroes was initiated by business and professional Negroes residing in the major urban center of the parish. In the event resistance to Negro registration made it necessary to resort to legal and political action, the city provided the resources and locus for suits against the registrar, for requests to the F.B.I. to investigate reluctant registrars, and for bargains which might be negotiated with courthouse politicians.

IV. The Political Factor

The first concern of every politician is to be elected and reelected to office. Therefore, the existence in any community of a reservoir of untapped voters tends to act as a magnet on politicians in search of votes. The Negro vote in Louisiana, however, was not exploitable until the Supreme Court declared the white primary laws unconstitutional. After 1944, Louisiana politicians could legally pursue the Negro vote.

In all the Louisiana parishes except those with the very largest cities, political power and interest center in the courthouse of the parish seat. The dominant figure in the courthouse is the sheriff, whose election occasions the most interest and largest voter turnout in the parish. Where Negro registration has occurred in large numbers, the sheriff has almost invariably been friendly to the idea.

The process by which this political variable helps bring Negroes to the polls works generally as follows: community attitudes must, first of all, be permissive with respect to Negro registration. If the white community is strongly and unalterably opposed to Negro voting, the sheriff or other politician will rarely venture to seek the Negro vote. Instead, as in the Mississippi parishes with no registration, the sheriff will help keep the Negroes away from the polls. This is true because the politician fears the reaction of his townspeople to Negro registration and because he, too, generally shares the dominant attitude.

Secondly, the sheriff, by the very nature of his office, is subject to manifold temptations relating to law enforcement, particularly, in Louisiana, to the classic "payoff" to permit gambling. When a sheriff permits gambling, he is charged with corruption of his office by the good government, middle-class voters of his community. In this event the sheriff is compelled to turn to lower socio-economic groups or to marginal groups in the community for support.

After Negro leaders have initiated the movement for registration and thus demonstrated their group's potential voter strength, the sheriff or other official can then use to his own profit the power of his office to prevent interference with registration, or else later encourage registration drives and voter turnout campaigns. In many parishes the Negro vote has become a "balance of power" factor.

Finally, the reward of the Negro for his vote is respect from the politicians and attendance at Negro political meetings, cessation of police brutality, and promises made and often kept regarding such matters as street improvements and better school facilities. It is ironical that this advance may thus result from an alliance of shady white and underdog Negro elements against the more "respectable" white segment of the community.

The political factor is also important as an inhibiting influence. For example, in the two French parishes (Terrebonne and Plaquemines) with a rate of Negro registration below 20 percent, the local sheriff has been instrumental in keeping the Negroes from the polls. In these cases, the sheriff is unalterably opposed to Negro voting, primarily out of fear that it will cost him the election, and, consequently, he uses the power of his office to prevent registration. In all probability, a different sheriff could permit Negro registration without suffering a serious reaction from the white community.

V. Conclusions

This paper is concerned with the problem of differences in the political behavior of the South toward the Negro. These differences have been studied, here, through an analysis of Negro registration for voting in Louisiana. Negro registration is basically related to Southern politics not only because it is the fundamental step for the Negro toward the power of the ballot box but also because it appears to be vitally related to the willingness or unwillingness of specific societies to allow the Negro an equal place in the community. The evidence indicates that Southern attitudes and practices toward the Negro are in large part a function of the culture in which the relationships occur.[6] Our inquiry here is whether religio-cultural variables in the South, long celebrated as the "Bible-belt" of the nation, are related to Negro-white political relationships insofar as these can be defined by practices and attitudes toward Negro registration.

The findings of this study emphasize the importance of religio-cultural factors in defining white attitudes and practices toward Negro registration. In the southern French-Catholic parishes, the percentage of Negroes registered is more than twice as great as in the northern Anglo-Saxon Protestant parishes. Socio-economic factors, urbanism, and Negro-white population balance, account for some of the difference. Yet where non-religious cultural factors are held constant, as in cotton plantation areas with large Negro populations, the religio-cultural variable emerges as a clearly influential factor in Negro registration.

First-hand observations in the parishes of Louisiana support the statistical evidence that Negro registration is related to the type of religio-cultural area involved. Permissive attitudes toward Negro registration in French-Catholic parishes seem expressive of the basic value that the Negro is spiritually equal in a Catholic society. Such a view of man's relation to man, a scheme of elementary justice implicit in a Catholic society, some Catholics maintain, is sustained by traditional Catholic theology and actively promoted by the Church in Louisiana. There is little evidence in the Protestant parishes of cultural values assigning the Negro a spiritually equal place in the community or of activity by the church itself toward these values.

Dr. Frank Tannenbaum has written a brilliant exposition of the comparative treatment of the Negro in North and South America, maintaining that differences are in large part a function of the respective Protestant and Catholic cultures.[7] Curiously, the religio-cultural analysis has been largely neglected in race-relations analysis of the United States, even though the role of the Protestant ethic, for instance in economic behavior and intellectual development, has been well stated.

It is not the intention of the authors to urge religious determinism in this paper but to maintain that, on the evidence, the politics of Negro registration in Louisiana can be understood only by consideration of religio-cultural variables with other relevant factors. In consequence we suggest that religio-cultural analysis may be useful in understanding the whole of Southern politics. Excepting Maryland, possibly, the type of analysis employed here

---

[6]See, for example, V. O. Key, Jr., *Southern Politics* (New York, 1949); and Hugh Douglas Price, *Negro and Southern Politics, A Chapter of Florida History* (New York, 1957).

[7]*Slave and Citizen: The Negro in the Americas* (New York, 1947).

would not be possible in other Southern states due to the lack of distinctive religio-cultural areas. Some attention could be given, however, to the general problem of the Protestant ethic in the South and its involvement with political behavior.

Social and Economic Factors and Negro Voter Registration in the South*

Donald R. Matthews and James W. Prothro

The vote is widely considered the southern Negro's most important weapon in his struggle for full citizenship and social and economic equality. It is argued that "political rights pave the way to all others."[1] Once Negroes in the South vote in substantial numbers, white politicians will prove responsive to the desires of the Negro community. Also, federal action on voting will

Reprinted from the *American Political Science Review,* Vol. LVII, (March 1963), pp. 24-44 with permission of the publisher and authors. Copyright 1963 by the American Political Science Association.

*This study has been supported by a grant from the Rockefeller Foundation to the Institute for Research in Social Science of the University of North Carolina. The first named author holds a Senior Award for Research on Governmental Affairs from the Social Science Research Council. We wish to express our gratitude to these organizations for providing the resources needed to engage in this analysis. Professors V. O. Key, Jr., Warren E. Miller, and Allan P. Sindler have commented generously upon an earlier version of this paper. Professor Daniel O. Price afforded us the benefit of his counsel on statistical problems throughout the preparation of the article. While we have learned much from these colleagues, neither they nor the organizations named above should be held responsible for the contents of this article.

[1]*New York Times,* January 7, 1962. See also H. L. Moon, *Balance of Power: the Negro Vote* (Garden City, N. Y., Doubleday, 1949), p. 7 and *passim.*

be met with less resistance from the white South — and southerners in Congress — than action involving schools, jobs, or housing.

Such, at least, seems to have been the reasoning behind the Civil Rights Acts of 1957 and 1960, both of which deal primarily with the right to vote.[2] Attorney General Robert F. Kennedy and his predecessor, Herbert Brownell, are both reported to believe that the vote provides the southern Negro with his most effective means of advancing toward equality, and recent actions of the Justice Department seem to reflect this view.[3] Many Negro leaders share this belief in the overriding importance of the vote. Hundreds of Negro registration drives have been held in southern cities and counties since 1957.[4] Martin Luther King, usually considered an advocate of nonviolent direct action, recently remarked that the most significant step Negroes can take is in the "direction of the voting booths."[5] The National Association for the Advancement of Colored People, historically identified with courtroom attacks on segregation, is now enthusiastically committed to a "battle of the ballots."[6] In March, 1962, the Southern Regional Council announced receipt of foundation grants of $325,000 to initiate a major program to increase Negro voter registration in the South.[7] The Congress of Racial Equality, the NAACP, the National Urban League, the Southern Christian Leadership Conference, and the Student Nonviolent Coordinating Committee are among the organizations now participating in the actual registration drives.

While the great importance of the vote to Negroes in the South can hardly be denied, some careful observers are skeptical about the extent to which registration drives can add to the number of Negroes who are already registered. Southern Negroes overwhelmingly possess low social status, relatively small incomes, and limited education received in inferior schools. These attributes are associated with low voter turnout among all populations.[8] The low voting rates of Negroes in the South are, to perhaps a large extent, a result of these factors more than a consequence of *direct political* discrimination by the white community. Moreover, the low status, income, and education

---

[2]71 Stat. 635; 74 Stat. 86. *Cf.* U.S. Commission on Civil Rights, *1959 Report* (Washington, 1959); *1961 Report,* Vol. I, "Voting" (Washington, 1961).

[3]*New York Times,* January 7, 1962; Louis E. Lomax, "The Kennedys Move in on Dixie," *Harpers Magazine,* May 1962, pp. 27-33.

[4]*Wall Street Journal,* November 6, 1961; *New York Times,* July 10, 1961.

[5]Baltimore *Afro-American,* October 7, 1961; *New York Times,* August 17, 1961.

[6]The 1962 Atlanta, Georgia, national convention of the NAACP had the "Battle of the Ballots" as its theme. Raleigh (N.C.) *News and Observer,* June 24, 1962.

[7]*New York Times,* March 29, 1962. Louis E. Lomax, *op. cit.*

[8]For useful summaries of the literature see Robert E. Lane, *Political Life* (Glencoe, Ill.: The Free Press, 1959), ch. 16; and Seymour M. Lipset *et al.,* "The Psychology of Voting," in G. Lindzey, (ed.), *Handbook of Social Psychology* (Cambridge, Mass.: Addison-Wesley Publishing Company, 1954), Vol. II, pp. 1126-1134.

of southern whites foster racial prejudice.[9] Thus poverty and ignorance may have a double-barrelled effect on Negro political participation by decreasing the Negroes' desire and ability to participate effectively while increasing white resistance to their doing so. Negro voting in the South is not, according to this line of argument, easily increased by political or legal means. A large, active, and effective Negro electorate in the South may have to await substantial social and economic change.

Despite the current interest in the political participation of southern Negroes, the literature of political science tells us little about the factors which facilitate or impede it. A theoretical concern as old as political science — the relative importance of socio-economic and political factors in determining political behavior — is raised when one addresses this problem. Can registration drives, legal pressures on the region's voter registrars, abolition of poll taxes, revision of literacy tests, and similar legal and political reforms have a significant impact on Negro registration in the former confederate states? Or do these efforts deal merely with "super-structure," while the social and economic realities of the region will continue for generations to frustrate achievement of Negro parity at the ballot box? Social scientists owe such a heavy, if largely unacknowledged, debt to Karl Marx that most would probably assume the second alternative to be more valid. But the tradition of James Madison, recognizing the importance of social and economic factors but also emphasizing the significance of "auxiliary" governmental arrangements, offers theoretical support for the former possibility.

A single article cannot hope to answer such a broad question, but we can attack part of it. In this article we offer a detailed analysis of the relationships between variations in rates of Negro voter registration in southern counties and the social and economic characteristics of those counties. While we shall not be directly concerned with political variables, the analysis has an obvious relevance for their importance. The more successful the explanation of the problem with socio-economic variables, the less imperative the demand to examine political and legal factors. Alternatively, if we can account for only a small part of the variance with socio-economic factors, the stronger the case

---

[9]Herbert H. Hyman and Paul B. Sheatsley, "Attitudes Toward Desegregation," *Scientific American,* Vol. 195 (1956), pp. 35-39; B. Bettelheim and M. Janowitz, *The Dynamics of Prejudice* (New York, 1950); Melvin M. Tumin, *Desegregation: Resistance and Readiness* (Princeton University Press, 1958), p. 195 and *passim.* James W. Vander Zanden, "Voting on Segregationist Referenda," *Public Opinion Quarterly,* Vol. 25 (1961), pp. 92-105, finds the evidence in support of the relationship in voting on segregationist referenda in the South "inconsistent and even contradictory . . . this study seems to suggest that the socio-economic factor may not play as simple or as critical a role as some of us doing research in this field have been prone to assign it" (p. 105).

for abandoning socio-economic determinism and adding political and legal variables to the analysis.[10]

I. The Data and the Approach

While the literature offers no comprehensive effort to account for variations in Negro voter registration in the South, previous studies of southern politics suggest a number of specific influences. Drawing upon this literature, we collected data on 20 social and economic characteristics of southern counties (counting Virginia's independent cities as counties). Some of these items, such as per cent of population Negro or per cent of population urban, could be taken directly from the U.S. Census. Others, such as per cent of nonwhite labor force in white-collar occupations or white and nonwhite median income, were derived from census figures but required calculations of varying degrees of complexity for each county. Still other items, such as per cent of population belonging to a church or the number of Negro colleges in each county, came from noncensus sources.[11] Since our focus is on Negro registration, 108 counties with populations containing less than one per cent Negroes were excluded from the analysis. All other counties for which 1958 registration data were available by race were included.[12] This selection procedure gave us a total of 997 counties for the analysis of Negro registration and 822 for the consideration of white registration.[13]

While this represents the most massive collection of data ever brought to bear upon the problem of political participation by southern Negroes, it is subject to several limitations.

To begin with, the measure of the dependent variable is two steps removed from a direct measure of the voting turnout of individuals. Registration

---

[10]In addition to the problem of the relative importance of political variables, we are postponing consideration of still another possibility — that variations in state systems (social, economic, and political) account for a significant proportion of the variation in Negro registration among southern counties.

[11]A complete list of sources used to obtain county frequencies for the independent variables used in this analysis would be too lengthy to reproduce here. A mimeographed list will be supplied by the authors upon request. We are indebted to the following research assistants for their help in collecting these data: Lawton Bennett, Lewis Bowman, Barbara Bright, Jack Fleer, Donald Freeman, Douglas Gatlin, and Richard Sutton. All told, the collection and coding of these data took one man-year of work.

[12]Voter registration rates, by race, are presented in U.S. Commission on Civil Rights, *1959 Report* and *1961 Report*, Vol. I, "Voting." The 1958 registration data, contained in the *1959 Report,* are more complete and were used for all states except Tennessee. The 1960 figures, printed in the *1961 Report,* are the only ones available for Tennessee.

[13]There are 1136 counties in the 11 southern states, 1028 of which have populations containing at least 1 per cent Negroes.

rather than voting figures had to be employed because they are available by race whereas the number of Negroes actually voting is not known. This tends to exaggerate the size of the active Negro electorate since, for a number of reasons, some registered Negroes seldom if ever exercise their franchise. Moreover, voting lists in rural areas are often out of date, containing the names of many bonafide residents of New York, Detroit, and Los Angeles, to say nothing of local graveyards. In some states, the payment of a poll tax is the nearest equivalent of voter registration and numerous exemptions from the tax make lists of poll tax payers not strictly comparable to the enfranchised population. Finally, statewide statistics on voter registration (or poll tax payment) by race are collected only in Arkansas, Florida, Georgia, Louisiana, South Carolina, and Virginia. In the remaining states, the number of registered Negro voters must be obtained from estimates made by county registrars, newsmen, politicians, and the like. Nonetheless, when analyzed with caution, the sometimes crude data on Negro voter registration can throw considerable light on Negro voting in the South.

The measure of the dependent variable is further removed from the actual behavior of individuals in that it consists of the percentage of all voting age Negroes who are registered to vote in each southern county. This employment of *areal* rather than *individual* analysis narrows the question we can examine. Rather than an unqualified examination of the relationship of social and economic characteristics to Negro registration, the effort must be understood to focus on the relationship of social and economic characteristics of given areas (counties) to variations in Negro registration among those areas. Accordingly, the data furnish no evidence of the sort afforded by opinion surveys directly linking political behavior to individual attributes. But they do permit conclusions linking varying registration rates to county attributes. Compensation for the loss of the former type of evidence is found in the acquisition of the latter type, which cannot be secured from surveys because they are conducted in a small number of counties. Our approach maximizes what we can say about counties, then, at the same time that it minimizes what we can say about individuals.

Another limitation stems from the fact that our measures capture an essentially static picture of both the characteristics of southern counties and of the relationship of their characteristics to variations in Negro registration. If data were available on Negro registration at the county level, for earlier points in time, the analysis could be geared principally to rates of change. Only since the creation of the Civil Rights Commission, however, have adequate county registration data become available. We are necessarily limited, therefore, to an analysis based on *areal* rather than *temporal* variation.

A final limitation lies in the statistical approach employed here, which is that of correlation and regression analysis.[14] The coefficient of correlation (r) is a measure of the association between different variables when each variable is expressed as a series of measures of a quantitative characteristic. The value of the measure varies from 0 (no association between independent and dependent variables) to 1.0 (one variable perfectly predicts the other). A positive correlation indicates that as one variable increases the other also increases; a negative correlation indicates an inverse relationship — as one variable increases, the other decreases. We shall first consider simple correlations, describing the association between per cent of Negroes registered and each of the social and economic characteristics of southern counties. In order to make a better estimate of the independence of these relationships, we shall also present partial correlations, which measure the remaining association between two variables when the contribution of a third variable has been taken into account. Finally, we shall employ multiple correlation (R) in order to determine the strength of association between all our independent variables and Negro registration.

While these measures are efficient devices for determining the strength and direction of association between the variables with which we are concerned, a caveat is in order. Correlations do not reflect the *absolute level* of the variables. Thus, a given amount and regularity of change in Negro registration will produce the same correlation whether the actual level of Negro registration is high or low. Only for the more important variables will we look beneath the correlations to examine the level of Negro registration.

In the analysis which follows, we shall first consider the development of Negro registration and compare the distribution of white and Negro registration rates. Then we shall examine the correlations between a battery of social and economic variables and Negro voter registration in order to determine the extent to which the former are predictive of the latter for the South as a whole. The same social and economic factors will be correlated with the registration rate of whites to ascertain the extent to which the factors are related to voter registration in general, rather than to Negro registration alone. Finally, the multiple correlation between all the social and economic variables and Negro voter registration will be presented, and conclusions and implications will be drawn from the analysis.

II. Negro Voter Registration: An Overview

Immediately after *Smith* v. *Allwright* declared the white primary unconstitutional in 1944, the number and proportion of Negro adults registered

---

[14]For a good discussion of correlation analysis see M. J. Hagood and D. O. Price, *Statistics for Sociologists* (New York, 1952), chs. 23 and 25.

to vote in the southern states increased with startling speed (Table I). Before this historic decision, about 250,000 Negroes (5 per cent of the adult nonwhite population) were thought to be registered voters. Three years after the white primary case, both the number and proportion of Negro registered voters had doubled. By 1952, about 20 per cent of the Negro adults were registered to vote. Since then, however, the rate of increase has been less impressive. In 1956, the authoritative Southern Regional Council estimated that about 25 per cent of the Negro adults were registered. Four years, two Civil Rights Acts, and innumerable local registration drives later, the proportion of Negro adults who were registered had risen to only 28 per cent. Of course, the fact that Negroes held their own during this period is a significant accomplishment when one considers such factors as heavy outmigration, increased racial tensions stemming from the school desegregation crisis, the

TABLE I

ESTIMATED NUMBER AND PER CENT OF VOTING AGE NEGROES
REGISTERED TO VOTE IN 11 SOUTHERN STATES, 1940-60

Year	Estimated Number of Negro Registered Voters	% of Voting Age Negroes Registered as Voters
1940	250,000	5%
1947	595,000	12
1952	1,008,614	20
1956	1,238,038	25
1958	1,266,488	25
1960	1,414,052	28

Sources: Derived from U. S. Census data on nonwhite population and Negro registration estimates in G. Myrdal, An American Dilemma (New York, 1944), p. 488; M. Price, The Negro Voter in the South (Atlanta, Georgia: Southern Regional Council, 1957), p. 5; Southern Regional Council, "The Negro Voter in the South—1958," Special Report (mimeo.), p. 3; U. S. Commission on Civil Rights, 1959 Report and 1961 Report, Vol. I, "Voting."

adoption of new voter restrictions in some states, and the stricter application of old requirements in other areas.

Figure 1 shows the 1958 distribution of southern counties according to level of voter registration for Negroes and whites. The point most dramatically demonstrated by the figure is that Negro registration is still much lower than white registration. In 38 per cent of the counties, less than 20 per cent of the adult Negroes are registered, whereas less than 1 per cent of the counties have so few whites registered. Indeed, the most common (modal) situation for Negroes is a registration below 10 per cent of the potential; the most common situation for whites is a registration in excess of 90 per cent. Nevertheless, the range of Negro registration in the South is sizeable; in a significant minority of cases, the level of Negro registration compares favorably with that of white southerners.

III. Social and Economic Correlates of Negro Registration

What accounts for the wide variation in Negro voter registration rates? The simple correlations between the per cent of the voting age Negroes registered to vote and 20 social and economic characteristics of southern counties are presented in the first column of Table II.[15]

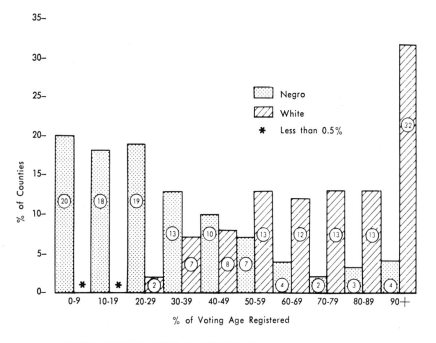

FIGURE 1. WHITE AND NEGRO REGISTRATION RATES IN SOUTHERN COUNTIES.

Negro Concentration

In most political settings, the concentration of an ethnic or occupational group in a geographical area provides reinforcement of common values suffi-

---

[15]All computations were made on the University of North Carolina's UNIVAC 1105 high-speed digital computer. The inaccuracy of some of the registration figures tends to reduce the magnitude of all correlations obtained by this analysis. The assumption of linearity underlying the computation of *r* also reduces the size of the correlations where the relationship between dependent and independent variables is, in fact, a curvilinear one. It is therefore safe to assume that the *r's* reported in this article err in the conservative direction.

cient to produce more active political participation. But southern Negroes are in a peculiarly subordinate position. And the larger the proportion of Negroes in an area, the more intense the vague fears of Negro domination that seem to beset southern whites. Thus in virtually every study of southern politics, the proportion of Negroes in the population has emerged as a primary explanatory variable.[16]

It is not surprising, therefore, that the per cent of Negroes in the county population in 1950 is more strongly associated with the county's rate of Negro registration than any other social and economic attribute on which we have data. The negative value of the simple correlation (−.46) verifies the expectation that smaller proportions of Negroes register in those counties where a large percentage of the population is Negro. This does not mean, however, that the decline in Negro registration associated with increasing Negro concentration occurs at a constant rate. If the relationship between these two variables is examined over the entire range of southern counties, we see that increases in the proportion Negro from 1 per cent to about 30 per cent are not accompanied by general and substantial declines in Negro registration rates (Figure 2). As the proportion Negro increases beyond 30 per cent, however, Negro registration rates begin to decline very sharply until they approach zero at about 60 per cent Negro and above. There would seem to be a critical point, at about 30 per cent Negro, where white hostility to Negro political participation becomes severe.

One reason Negro concentration is such a powerful explanatory factor in analyzing southern politics may be that it is related to so many other social and economic characteristics of the region's counties. The simple correlation between per cent Negro in 1950 and per cent of farms operated by tenants is +.49; the correlation with nonwhite median income is −.40; with nonwhite school years completed, −.47; with per cent of the labor force in agriculture, +.30; with per cent of the total population belonging to a church, +.38. Such characteristics as these are in turn related to variation in rates of Negro voter registration. It is possible that these related factors rather than Negro concentration, viewed largely as an index of white attitudes,

[16]V. O. Key, Jr., *Southern Politics* (New York, 1949) gives little attention to Negro voting since it was of little importance at the time he wrote (see, however, p. 518). His stress upon the overriding importance of Negro concentration for all aspects of southern politics makes his study highly relevant, nonetheless. Other works specifically on Negro voting which stress the importance of Negro concentration include: James F. Barnes, *Negro Voting in Mississippi,* M.A. thesis, University of Mississippi, 1955; Margaret Price, *The Negro and the Ballot in the South* (Atlanta, Georgia: Southern Regional Council, 1959); H. D. Price, *The Negro and Southern Politics: A Chapter of Florida History* (New York: New York University Press, 1957); Donald Strong, "The Future of the Negro Voter in the South," *Journal of Negro Education,* Vol. 26 (Summer, 1957), pp. 400-407; United States Commission on Civil Rights, *1961 Report,* Vol. I, "Voting."

TABLE II

CORRELATIONS BETWEEN COUNTY SOCIAL AND ECONOMIC
CHARACTERISTICS AND PER CENT OF VOTING AGE NEGROES
REGISTERED TO VOTE, BY COUNTY, IN 11 SOUTHERN STATES

County Characteristics	Simple Correlations (r)	Partial Correlations, Controlling for Per Cent Negro, 1950
Per cent of nonwhite labor force in white-collar occupations	+ .23	+ .15
Nonwhite median school years completed	+ .22	+ .01
Nonwhite median income	+ .19	+ .02
Per cent of total church membership Roman Catholic	+ .15	+ .10
Per cent increase in population, 1940–50	+ .08	.00
Per cent of labor force in manufacturing	+ .08	+ .09
White median income	+ .08	— .03
Per cent of population urban	+ .07	— .02
Percentage point difference in per cent population Negro, 1900–50	+ .04	— .02
Per cent of total church membership Jewish	+ .004	+ .01
Difference in white-nonwhite median school years completed	— .02	— .02
Difference in white-nonwhite median income	— .02	— .05
Number of Negro colleges in county	— .05	+ .01
Per cent of total church membership Baptist	— .10	— .07
Per cent of population belonging to a church	— .17	+ .01
Per cent of labor force in agriculture	— .20	— .07
White median school years completed	— .26	— .15
Per cent of farms operated by tenants	— .32	— .13
Per cent of population Negro in 1900	— .41	— .01
Per cent of population Negro in 1950	— .46	—

Note: No tests of significance are reported in this paper since the correlations are based upon a complete enumeration rather than a sample.

account for the —.46 correlation between per cent Negro and per cent registered to vote.

The partial correlations between Negro registration and Negro concentration, controlling separately for the contribution of all other county characteristics, reveals that this is not the case: Negro registration in southern counties goes down as the proportion of Negroes goes up regardless of the other characteristics of the counties. Only one county characteristic is so closely related to both Negro registration in 1958 and Negro concentration in 1950 that the strength of their association drops when its contribution is taken into account — and this characteristic is an earlier measurement of the same independent variable. Controlling for per cent of Negroes in the population in 1900 reduces the correlation between 1950 Negro concentration and regis-

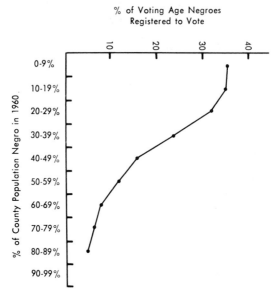

FIGURE 2. MEDIAN % OF VOTING AGE NEGROES REGISTERED TO VOTE BY % OF COUNTY POPULATION NEGRO IN 1950: 11 SOUTHERN STATES.

tration to —.21. Even with this control, the independent tendency of Negro registration to decrease in counties currently containing more Negroes is not eliminated, though it is reduced substantially.

Let us be clear on what a partial correlation does. It is designed to give us, as indicated above, the strength of association between two variables that remains after the contribution of a relevant third variable is taken into account. But when the third variable is introduced into the equation, so are all of the additional hidden variables that are associated with it. The magnitude of the partial correlation will accordingly be reduced not only by any contribution of the third variable to the association between the two original variables, but also by any contribution of factors that are associated with the third variable. This means that, when we attempt to examine the contribution of a third variable by computing partial correlations, we can be certain about its contribution only when the results are negative. That is, if the partial correlation is not much smaller than the simple correlation, we can be sure that the third variable is not responsible for the magnitude of the simple correlation. When the partial correlation is substantially smaller, however, we cannot conclude that the third variable *alone* is responsible for the magnitude of the simple correlation. It happens in the present instance that almost all of the county characteristics are similarly associated with Negro concentration in both 1900 and 1950. As a result, virtually all of the factors that contribute slightly to the correlation of Negro registration with 1950 Negro concentration are added to the contribution that 1900 Negro concentration makes to the correlation. The result is that Negro concentration in 1900 *and the hidden factors related to it* account for about half of the magnitude of the association between 1950 Negro concentration and Negro registration.

Before we conclude that Negro concentration at the turn of the century is as important as mid-century Negro concentration for current variations in Negro registration, we need to consider both the nature of the two measures and the detailed relationships of the variables. The two measures are of the same county characteristic, differing only in the point in time from which they were taken. And the characteristic they reflect cannot reasonably be thought to act directly on Negro registration. Today's lower rates of Negro registration in counties where Negroes constitute a larger portion of the population certainly do not stem from any tendency of Negroes to crowd one another out of registration queues! Even more evident is the fact that the percentage of Negroes in a county's population over half a century ago cannot have a direct effect on current rates of Negro registration. Both measures appear to be indexes of county characteristics (most importantly, white practices and attitudes on racial questions) that are of direct consequence for Negro registration.

The 1900 measure was included in the analysis on the assumption that practices and attitudes produced by heavy Negro population may persist long after the Negroes have died or left for more attractive environs. Earlier research has suggested that Negro concentration around the turn of the century — when southern political practice was crystallizing in its strongly anti-Negro pattern — may be as important as current Negro concentration for rates of Negro political participation.[17] Since the proportions of Negroes in different southern counties have not decreased at uniform rates (and have even increased in some counties), the measures at the two points in time afford an opportunity to test this hypothesis. And it seems to be supported by the fact that Negro concentration in 1900 is almost as highly (and negatively) correlated with Negro registration ($-.41$) as is Negro concentration a half century later. This large simple correlation, added to the decrease in the correlation between 1950 Negro concentration and registration when 1900 Negro concentration is controlled, is impressive evidence of the stability of southern racial practices. The virtual absence of correlation ($+.04$) between Negro registration and the percentage point difference in the proportion of population Negro between 1900 and 1950 seems to point to the same conclusion.[18]

---

[17]On this point see H. D. Price, *op. cit.*, p. 41ff.
[18]See H. D. Price, *op. cit.*

It would be a mistake, however, to conclude either that 1900 Negro concentration is as important as 1950 Negro concentration for Negro registration, or that decreases in Negro concentration are not associated with increasing Negro voter registration. When we reverse the partialling process, and control for Negro concentration in 1950, the correlation between current Negro registration and 1900 Negro concentration disappears (it becomes —.01). The 1900 simple correlation accordingly seems to come from stable racial practices that in turn reflect a large measure of stability in Negro concentration and related county characteristics. The 1900 Negro concentration in itself has no autonomous relationship to present rates of Negro registration.

Moreover, decreases in Negro concentration are not as inconsequential as they would appear from the small simple correlation obtained from percentage point decreases. The lack of correlation seems to be an artifact of our crude measure. The largest percentage *point* decreases in Negro population have occurred in counties with very high Negro proportions in 1900, and most of these counties still have heavy concentrations of Negro population. When one looks at the relationship between registration and decreases in Negro concentration, holding constant the proportion of the population Negro in 1900, several heretofore hidden relationships emerge (Figure 3). (1) In counties with heavy (over 70 per cent) Negro concentrations in 1900,

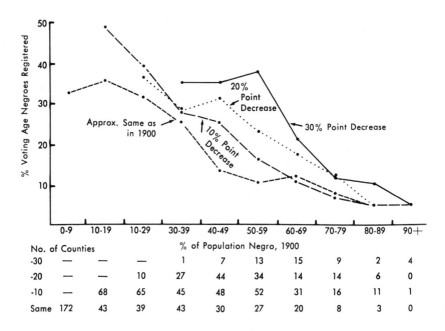

FIGURE 3. MEDIAN % OF VOTING AGE NEGROES REGISTERED TO VOTE, BY COUNTY NEGRO CONCENTRATION IN 1900 AND % POINT CHANGE SINCE 1900.

decreases in the proportion Negro seem to make little difference — their Negro concentration was still relatively high in 1950 and the proportion of Negroes registered is negligible. (2) In counties with relatively few (less than 30 per cent) Negroes in 1900, rates of Negro registration tend to be high whether a decline in the proportion Negro was experienced or not. A decline in Negro concentration in these counties, however, is associated with a somewhat higher rate of Negro registration than in those counties where the division of the two races remained approximately the same between 1900 and 1950. (3) In counties with moderate (30 to 70 per cent) Negro concentrations in 1900, a decline in Negro concentration is clearly related to higher Negro voter registration. Moreover, the larger the decrease in the Negro population percentage, the higher the registration. The average county in this moderate group with a 30 percentage point decrease in Negro proportions has a voter registration rate double or triple that of the average county which did not experience significant change in the numerical balance between colored and white inhabitants.

The proportion of the county population which is Negro is the single most important social and economic factor for explaining its rate of Negro voter registration. The —.46 correlation accounts for about 20 per cent (r^2) of the variation in Negro registration rates, an unusually high explanatory power for any variable in the complex world of political and social relationships. But it leaves room for considerable fluctuation in registration rates unrelated to the per cent of Negroes in the population. The "unexplained" fluctuation may be the result of random and idiosyncratic factors, of political variables[19] which have been excluded from this analysis, or the result of the operation of other social and economic factors. In the remainder of this paper we shall examine this last possibility.

Negro Attributes

The higher the educational level, occupation, or income of a person, the more likely he is to participate actively in politics: these are among the more strongly supported generalizations in contemporary research on political par-

---

[19]In view of the relatively high associations between Negro concentration and a wide variety of political phenomena (including Negro registration rates), it might be argued that Negro concentration is, in fact, a "political" rather than a "demographic" variable. But Negro concentration is as strongly associated with many social and economic characteristics of southern counties as it is with their political peculiarities. And while the correlations of Negro concentration with political characteristics are relatively large, they fall far short of a 1.0 correlation. As we shall demonstrate in a subsequent article, a number of political variables have an association with Negro registration that is independent of Negro concentration. Under these circumstances, to call Negro concentration a "political" variable would be distinctly misleading.

ticipation.[20] Moreover, these three factors are probably a pretty good index of the size of the county's Negro middle class. It is widely believed by students of Negro politics that the low rate of voter registration by southern Negroes is partly the result of a lack of leadership.[21] Only when there is a pool of educated and skillful leaders whose means of livelihood is not controlled by whites can sufficient leadership and political organization develop to ensure a relatively high rate of Negro registration in the South.

Our data support both lines of argument. The three largest positive correlations with Negro voter registration are per cent of the nonwhite labor force in white-collar occupations ($+.23$), the median number of school years completed by nonwhites ($+.22$), and the median income of nonwhites ($+.19$). These are simple correlations, however, and fairly small ones at that. It is quite possible that they are largely, if not entirely, the result of some third factor associated both with Negro registration rates and with Negro education, occupation, and income. The large negative correlation of Negro concentration with Negro registration suggests that the percentage of the population Negro in 1950 is the most likely prospect as a key third variable. This expectation is heightened by the fact that it is also substantially correlated with Negro school years completed ($-.47$), income ($-.40$), and white-collar workers ($-.23$). When controls are introduced for per cent of Negroes in the population (see the second column of Table II), the positive association of Negro registration with both income and education is reduced almost to the vanishing point. Thus Negro income and education levels are intervening variables, which help to explain why more Negroes are registered in counties with fewer Negroes in their population. But in themselves, they have no independent association with Negro registration; in the few counties with large Negro concentrations but high Negro income and education, no more Negroes are registered than in similar counties with lower Negro income and education.

The explanatory power of our occupational measure — the per cent of the nonwhite labor force in white-collar occupations — is also reduced when per cent of Negroes is taken into account, but to a much lesser degree. It becomes $+.15$. While this is a small partial correlation, it is one of the higher partials

---

[20]See Lane, *op. cit.;* Lipset *et al., op. cit.;* Angus Campbell, Philip E. Converse, Warren E. Miller, and Donald E. Stokes, *The American Voter* (New York, 1960), ch. 13; V. O. Key, Jr., *Public Opinion and American Democracy* (New York, 1961), ch. 6. For a study of these variables and political participation among southern Negroes, see Bradbury Seasholes, "Negro Political Participation in Two North Carolina Cities," Ph.D. dissertation, University of North Carolina, 1962.

[21]For an extreme statement of this position, see E. Franklin Frazier, *Black Bourgeoisie: The Rise of a New Middle Class in the United States* (Glencoe, Ill.: The Free Press, 1957). Less exaggerated statements to the same effect may be found in the literature cited in *n.* 16, above.

obtained in this study while controlling for the important factor of Negro concentration. The proportion of the employed Negroes in white-collar jobs does, therefore, have a small but discernible independent association with Negro voter registration.

Moreover, small increases in the proportion of Negro white-collar workers are associated with large increases in Negro voter registration (Figure 4), and these higher rates cannot be simply attributed to the registration of the white-collar workers themselves. A very small increase in the size of the Negro middle class seems to result in a substantial increase in the pool of qualified potential leaders. Middle class Negroes are far more likely to register, and they in turn appear to stimulate working class Negroes to follow their example. The average southern county with 1 per cent of its nonwhite labor force in white-collar jobs has only 4 per cent of its voting age Negroes registered to vote; at 5 per cent white-collar, 15 per cent of the Negroes are registered, and so on, each percentage point increase in white-collar occupation being associated with a 3 to 4 percentage point increase in voter registration. This trend continues until 12 per cent of the nonwhites are in white-collar jobs and 42 per cent of the potential Negro electorate is registered. After this point, additional increases in the proportion of Negroes in white-collar jobs are no longer associated with increases in voter registration; indeed, voter registration actually declines as per cent white-collar increases. Perhaps when the Negro middle class becomes fairly large, it tends to become more isolated from other Negroes, more preoccupied with the middle class round of life, less identified with the black masses.[22] A sharpening of class cleavages within the Negro community may lead to some loss of political effectiveness. Even so, this decline in effectiveness is not enough to wipe out the added increment from jobs to registered votes; it merely declines from 3 or 4 votes for every white-collar job to about 2.

Despite the independent association of Negro white-collar employment with voter registration, the correlations between Negro registration and Negro education, income, and occupation are far smaller than many of the correlations between Negro registration and the characteristics of the white-dominated community. The level of Negro voter registration in southern counties is far less a matter of the attributes of the Negro population than of the characteristics of the white population and of the total community. The rest of our correlations, therefore, are with community and white characteristics rather than with Negro attributes.

---

[22]This is the basic argument of Frazier, *op. cit.* A more mundane explanation would be called for if counties from particular states were clustered at particular points on the curve in Figure 4, but examination of the same relationships for each state reveals no such state-by-state clustering.

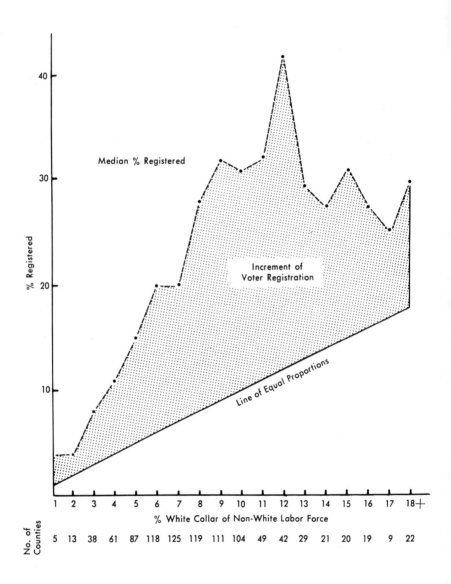

FIGURE 4. MEDIAN % OF VOTING AGE NEGROES REGISTERED TO VOTE, BY % OF NONWHITE LABOR
FORCE IN WHITE-COLLAR OCCUPATIONS.

The Agrarian Economy

It is widely believed that the South's relatively poor agricultural economy contributes to the low levels of Negro political participation in the region.[23] People living in poverty are unlikely candidates for active citizenship anywhere. The Negroes' economic dependence upon local whites in the rural South serves as a potent inhibition to those few who are not otherwise discouraged from voting. Rural whites are both more hostile to Negro voting and in a better position to do something about it than their urban kin. Our correlations tend to support this line of reasoning. Two measures included in the analysis reflect the degree to which a county has an agrarian economy — the per cent of labor force in agricultural employment and the per cent of farms operated by tenants.[24] The negative relationship of both these attributes to Negro voter registration (—.20 and —.32, respectively) indicates that Negro registration is lower in the old-style agrarian counties. But the region's Negro population is still primarily rural: the simple correlation between per cent in agriculture and per cent Negro is +.30; between farm tenancy and Negro concentration, +.49. Are these two characteristics of the counties still associated with low Negro voter registration when Negro concentration is controlled? The partial correlation between farm tenancy and Negro registration is —.13 when Negro concentration is controlled; between per cent in agriculture and registration it is reduced even further to —.07. There is, therefore, some tendency for Negro voter registration to decline as agricultural employment and farm tenancy increase which holds true even when differences in Negro concentration from one county to the next are taken into account. Nonetheless, it is a far less important factor than Negro concentration and is no more important than the size of the Negro middle class as a factor explaining Negro participation and non-participation.

Urbanization and Industrialization

If the South's agrarian economy tends to discourage Negro registration and voting, then industrialization and urbanization should facilitate them. The urban-industrial life is more rational, impersonal, and less tradition-bound; both Negroes and whites enjoy more wealth and education; the Negroes benefit from a concentration of potential leaders and politically relevant organizations in the cities. The urban ghetto may provide social reinforcement to individual motivations for political action. Many other equally plausible

---

[23]See especially, U.S. Commission on Civil Rights, *1961 Report,* Vol. I, "Voting," pp. 143–199.
[24]This and other measures of county-wide characteristics might better be considered separately for Negroes and whites, but they are not separately reported in the census.

reasons might be suggested why urbanization and industrialization should foster Negro registration.[25] Our southwide correlations, however, cast serious doubt upon the entire line of reasoning.

The simple correlations between the per cent of the county population living in urban areas and Negro registration is a mere $+.07$; between per cent of the labor force in manufacturing and Negro registration the correlation is $+.08$. When partial correlations are figured, controlling for Negro concentration, the association between urbanization and Negro registration completely disappears, a fact which suggests that the initial $+.07$ simple correlation may be largely the result of the low proportion of the urban population which is Negro and associated factors. The partial correlation between per cent in manufacturing and Negro registration goes up slightly to $+.09$ when controls for Negro concentration are added. Partial correlations figured after controlling for many other social and economic variables do not significantly increase either correlation.

What accounts for these surprising findings? One possible explanation is the imperfections of the statistical measures we have employed. The 1950 census definition of "urban," for example, includes all places of 2,500 plus the densely settled fringe around cities of 50,000 or more. Many "urban" places in the South are therefore exceedingly small. From the potential Negro voter's point of view, it may make little difference whether he lives in a town of 5,000 or in the open country, but one place is classified as "urban" and the other as "rural." Moreover, a county with a relatively small population concentrated in two or three small towns may possess a higher "urban" percentage than a very large county with a medium-sized city in it. A more meaningful classification of counties along an urban-rural dimension might possibly lead to different results.

It seems plausible to assume, however, that if urbanization does facilitate Negro voter registration, the effect should be particularly clear in the region's largest urban complexes. If the Negro registration rates of the 70 counties contained in the South's Standard Metropolitan Areas[26] are compared with

---

[25]On Negro voting in urban settings see Charles D. Farris, "Effects of Negro Voting Upon the Politics of a Southern City: An Intensive Study, 1946–48," Ph.D. dissertation, University of Chicago, 1953; George A. Hillery, "The Presence of Community Among Urban Negroes: A Case Study of a Selected Area in New Orleans," M.A. thesis, Louisiana State University, 1951; Leonard Reissman *et al.,* "The New Orleans Voter: A Handbook of Political Description," *Tulane Studies in Political Science,* Vol. II (1955), pp. 1–88; Cleo Roberts, "Some Correlates of Registration and Voting Among Negroes in the 1953 Municipal Election of Atlanta," M.A. thesis, Atlanta University, 1954; Harry J. Walker, "Changes in Race Accommodation in a Southern Community," Ph.D. dissertation, University of Chicago, 1945.

[26]The Bureau of the Census defines Standard Metropolitan Areas as a county or group of contiguous counties which contains at least one city of 50,000 inhabitants or more. The contiguous counties must be socially and economically integrated with the central city to be included in the SMA.

TABLE III

MEDIAN PER CENT OF VOTING AGE NEGROES REGISTERED TO
VOTE IN COUNTIES WITHIN STANDARD METROPOLITAN AREAS
AND ALL OTHER COUNTIES, BY LEVEL OF NEGRO
CONCENTRATION

% Negro in pop. 1950	Counties in SMAs of over 200,000 pop.	Counties in SMAs of less than 200,000 pop.	Counties not in SMAs
%	%	%	%
0–9	25.0(6)	28.8(11)	37.8(236)
10–19	45.0(11)	30.0(12)	35.7(133)
20–29	30.0(6)	35.0(6)	32.2(153)
30–39	24.0(6)	23.8(7)	23.8(142)
40–49	—	15.0(5)	15.9(110)
50–59	—	—	12.0(78)
60–69	—	—	8.1(50)
70–79	—	—	5.8(22)
80–89	—	—	5.0(4)
Total Counties	(29)	(41)	(928)

registration rates for non-metropolitan counties (Figure 5), we note that the "metropolitan" counties are far more likely to have from 20 to 40 per cent of their voting age Negroes registered than the other counties. Moreover, there is a tendency for counties in larger metropolitan areas to have slightly higher registration rates than counties in less populous SMAs. However, the metropolitan counties have smaller concentrations of Negroes than the rural and small town counties. Do these relationships hold true when comparisons are made between metropolitan and non-metropolitan counties with approximately the same proportion of Negroes within their boundaries? Table III indicates that the answer is no: there is no meaningful difference in the rate of Negro registration between metropolitan and non-metropolitan counties when Negro concentration is controlled. Thus, neither "urbanism" nor "metropolitanism," as crudely defined by the census categories, appears to be independently related to high Negro voter registration.

The very low correlation between per cent of the labor force in manufacturing employment and Negro voter registration appears to be the result of other considerations. The word "manufacturing" conjures up images of the "New South" — with belching smokestacks, booming cities, and bulging payrolls. For the South as a whole, this is a quite misleading picture. While manufacturing in 1950 was associated with somewhat higher income for both Negroes

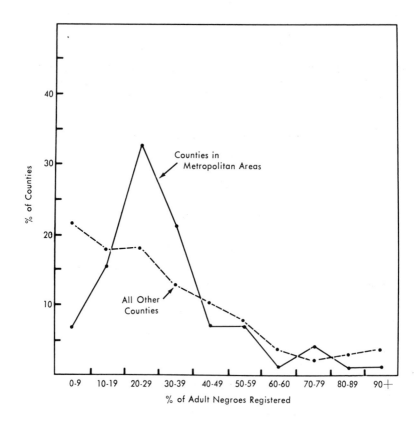

FIGURE 5. MEDIAN % OF VOTING AGE NEGROES REGISTERED TO VOTE IN METROPOLITAN AND OTHER AREAS.

and whites (the correlation between per cent in manufacturing and median income was $+.19$ for both races), it was not primarily an urban phenomenon (the correlation between per cent in manufacturing and per cent urban was $+.08$), nor was it associated with rapid population growth (the correlation with population increase between 1940 and 1950 is $+.05$). Manufacturing was negatively correlated with school years completed by both whites and Negroes ($-.14$ and $-.05$, respectively). This kind of low-wage manufacturing centered in relatively stable, small towns is not very strongly associated with growing Negro voter registration. It is possible that the recent industrialization of the region — electronics as opposed to home production of chenille bedspreads, for example — may be quite differently related to Negro participation. So few counties have this new type of industry that they tend to be hidden by the bedspreads in a county-by-county correlation.

While our analysis should not be taken as the last word on the subject, it does strongly suggest that urbanization and industrialization are vastly over-rated as facilitators of Negro voter registration. Urbanization and industrialization may provide necessary conditions for high levels of Negro political participation but, by themselves, they are not sufficient to insure them.

White Educational Levels

If, as we have argued, Negro registration rates in the South respond far more to the characteristics of the white community than to the attributes of the Negroes themselves, then it seems reasonable to expect Negro voter registration to be positively correlated with white educational levels. Numerous studies have shown that racial prejudice and discrimination tend to be related to low levels of formal education.[27] Where the whites are relatively well educated, there should be less resistance to Negro political participation and, therefore, more Negro voter registration.

Just the opposite is the case for the South as a whole. The correlation between median school years completed by whites and Negro voter registration is —.26, one of the largest negative correlations obtained in this study. When the education of whites in a county increases, Negro voter registration in the county tends to decrease.

How can we account for this unexpected finding? In view of the surprising nature of the relationship, the first expectation would be that it is merely a reflection of some third variable which happens to be related both to Negro registration and to white education. If so, it should disappear when other factors are held constant. But the correlation holds up surprisingly well when other variables are controlled: only one of the other social and economic characteristics of southern counties reduces the correlation at all. The third variable is, once again, Negro concentration in the population. With Negro concentration in 1950 controlled, the partial correlation between white educational level and Negro registration is —.15; controlling for Negro concentration in 1900 produces a partial correlation of —.16. While these are substantial reductions, the partial correlations are among the largest obtained after controlling for the extraordinarily important factor of Negro concentration. The strong correlation (+.30) between Negro concentration and median school years completed by whites is almost as unexpected as the correlation between Negro registration and white education. The whites in the black belt counties tend to be better educated — at least quantitatively — than other white southerners. And, regardless of the percentage of Negroes in the popu-

---

[27]See the literature cited in *n.* 9, above.

lation, fewer Negroes are registered in counties where whites have more education.

A second explanation for the negative relationship between white education and Negro registration might be that their relationship is curvilinear: at the lower educational levels, increases in white median school years might be associated with declining rates of Negro registration but, at higher educational levels, the relationship might be reversed. If this were the case, then the overall negative relationship would be a result of the generally low educational levels of the South, concealing the fact that the few counties with high white educational levels had the highest rates of Negro registration. Figure 6 suggests only a moderate tendency in this direction. As the number of school years completed by whites goes up through the primary and secondary grades, the proportion of voting age Negroes registered declines.[28] In the very few counties in which the average white adult has completed high school or received some higher education, the trend reverses and Negro registration

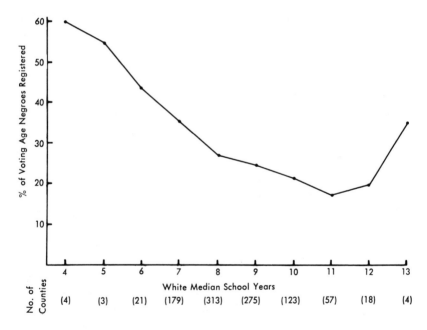

FIGURE 6. MEDIAN % OF VOTING AGE NEGROES REGISTERED TO VOTE, BY MEDIAN SCHOOL YEARS COMPLETED BY WHITES IN COUNTY.

[28]Eleven of the 28 counties in which the average white adult has completed less than seven years of schooling are French-Catholic parishes in Louisiana. Even if those parishes are eliminated, the trend shown in Figure 6 remains the same. The partial correlation between white school years and Negro registration, controlling for per cent Roman Catholic, is — .25.

rates begin to increase. But the reversal is not sharp enough for the counties with the highest white education to reach as great a Negro registration as the counties with the lowest white education. Southern counties with extremely high white educational levels have only about average rates of Negro registration. The impressive fact revealed by Figure 6 is the near uniformity with which an increase in white school years is associated with a decrease in Negro registration.

Being unable to "explain away" our finding entirely, either by examining the correlation for hidden third variables or by examining the regularity of the association, we must conclude that white education in southern counties is independently and negatively associated with Negro registration. Short of the highest levels, the more educated the whites the more actively and effectively they seem to enforce the traditional mores of the region against Negro participation in elections. The usual effect of an increase in average schooling for whites in the South as a whole appears to be to give the white people more of the skills that are needed to express effectively their anti-Negro sentiment. For example, the correlation between median school years completed by whites and the presence or absence of a White Citizens Council or similar organization is +.32. It seems to take considerably more formal education than the average southern white receives to *alter* his attitude toward the Negro's place in southern politics.

White Religious Affiliation

A variety of studies suggest that religion plays some role — either as independent or intervening variable — in the racial politics of the South. Church-goers have been found to be less tolerant than non-attenders,[29] and the South is a church-going region. Studies of Louisiana politics have found substantial political differences between the Catholic and Protestant sections of the state.[30] It seemed worthwhile, therefore, to examine the correlation between white religious affiliation and Negro registration rates for the South as a whole.

We find that Negro registration rates are depressed as church membership among whites[31] increases (—.17), despite the fact that white membership

---

[29]Samuel A. Stouffer, *Communism, Conformity, and Civil Liberties* (New York, Doubleday, 1955).

[30]Allan P. Sindler, *Huey Long's Louisiana* (Baltimore: The Johns Hopkins Press, 1956); V. O. Key, Jr., *op. cit.*, ch. 8; John H. Fenton and Kenneth N. Vines, "Negro Registration in Louisiana," this REVIEW, Vol. 51 (1957), pp. 704–13.

[31]The most recent attempt to compile county-by-county figures on church membership is reported in a census by the National Council of Churches of Christ, *Churches and Church Membership in the U.S.*, Series C, 1956. Negro churches are not included in this census, and the figures reported for many white churches appear to be incomplete.

in different churches has different functions — Baptist membership is negatively related to Negro registration (—.10) while Catholic membership is positively related (+.15). On a southwide basis, the percentage of Jews in the county's total church membership is not significantly associated with Negro registration.

Granted that Catholicism is positively related to Negro registration, we can partial out the influence of Catholicism in order to determine the correlation between non-Catholic white church membership and Negro registration. This partial correlation is, as expected, slightly greater (—.23) than the simple correlation. But the negative correlation between white church membership and Negro registration disappears when Negro concentration is held constant. (The partial correlation is +.01.) Greater church membership among whites accordingly appears to be a reflection of other county attributes rather than an independent factor in relation to Negro registration. When we examine the correlations between church membership and all of our other measures of county attributes, we find very low correlations with all other variables except Negro concentration (+.38) and Catholicism (+.31). Apparently, then, white church membership *per se* is unimportant for Negro registration. White people in the kinds of counties with more Negroes and in predominantly Catholic counties are more often members of churches. In the former kinds of counties, fewer Negroes will vote regardless of non-Catholic church membership. Most non-Catholic churches presumably take on the racial attitudes of their localities; or, if they do not, they have little effect on those attitudes in so far as the attitudes are reflected in rates of Negro registration.

Per cent of Roman Catholics in the white church population appears to be by far the most important of our religious attributes of southern counties. And the relationship between Catholicism and Negro voter registration does not disappear when Negro concentration is controlled. (The partial correlation is +.10.) The presence of Roman Catholics, then, does seem to facilitate Negro voter registration on a southwide basis. Roman Catholic churches and priests presumably react less directly to other county attributes than most Protestant churches and their ministers; in any case, Catholicism is independently and positively related to Negro voter registration.

However, the concentration of Catholic population in Louisiana and the small number Catholics in most other parts of the South dictate caution in accepting this explanation. For one thing, the distribution of Catholic percentages deviates so far from the assumption of normal distribution underlying correlation analysis that our southwide correlations may have been curiously and unpredictably affected. In the second place, the atypical political patterns of Louisiana — rather than Catholicism *per se* — may account for a large part of the correlation obtained. Only state-by-state analysis of the correlations can indicate if Catholicism is a genuinely independent and significant factor facilitating Negro registration throughout the entire South.

IV. Negro Versus White Registration Rates

We have assumed that our analysis is of *Negro* voter registration rather than of voter registration *in general*. But this assumption might be incorrect: while Negroes register to vote in the South at a much lower rate than whites (Figure 1, p.185), the registration rates of the two races could be highly correlated with one another, both responding to the same social and economic characteristics of southern counties. The data permit two tests of this possibility: (1) an examination of the relationship between Negro and white registration; (2) a comparison of the relationships between county attributes and white registration with the relationships found between the same attributes and Negro registration.

The Relationship Between Negro and White Registration

To a limited extent, Negro registration does increase as white registration increases; their simple correlation is +.24. Figure 7 presents the relationship

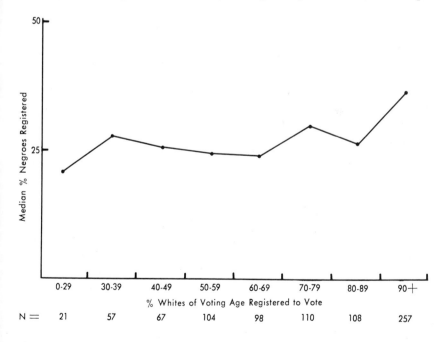

FIGURE 7. MEDIAN % OF VOTING AGE NEGROES REGISTERED TO VOTE, BY % OF WHITES REGISTERED IN SAME COUNTY.

of Negro to white registration for every level of white registration. The detailed relationships depicted by the graph reveal that the lowest and the highest levels of white registration contribute most of the small correlation between the registration rates of the two races; if both of the extreme points were eliminated, the curve would be virtually horizontal, indicating that Negro registration had no relationship at all to white registration. Only when white registration is extremely high or extremely low, then, is it associated with the rate of Negro registration. For the broad middle range of counties with from 30 to 89 per cent of the whites registered — a group which contains over 70 per cent of all southern counties — Negro registration appears to be independent of white registration.

TABLE IV

CORRELATIONS BETWEEN COUNTY SOCIAL AND ECONOMIC CHARACTERISTICS AND PER CENT OF VOTING AGE WHITES REGISTERED TO VOTE, BY COUNTY, IN 11 SOUTHERN STATES

County Characteristics	Simple Correlations (r)	Partial Correlations, Controlling for:	
		% Negro, 1950	% Urban, 1950
Per cent of nonwhite labor force in white-collar occupations	— .26	— .24	— .15
Nonwhite median school years completed	— .34	— .34	— .28
Nonwhite median income	— .19	— .17	— .08
Per cent of total church membership Roman Catholic	— .09	— .08	— .03
Per cent increase in population, 1940–50	— .06	— .04	+ .08
Per cent of labor force in manufacturing	+ .05	+ .05	+ .07
White median income	— .19	— .19	— .05
Per cent of population urban	— .25	— .24	
Percentage point difference in per cent population Negro, 1900–50	+ .10	+ .11	+ .05
Per cent of total church membership Jewish	— .03	— .03	+ .04
Difference in white-nonwhite median school years completed	+ .11	+ .07	+ .14
Difference in white-nonwhite median income	— .12	— .13	— .03
Number of Negro colleges in county	— .10	— .11	— .04
Per cent of total church membership Baptist	+ .20	+ .19	+ .15
Per cent of population belonging to a church	+ .06	+ .02	+ .07
Per cent of labor force in agriculture	+ .21	+ .19	+ .06
White median school years completed	— .08	— .11	+ .03
Per cent of farms operated by tenants	+ .09	+ .05	+ .05
Per cent of population Negro, 1900	+ .03	— .12	+ .02
Per cent of population Negro, 1950	+ .10		+ .06

Note: County characteristics are listed above in the same order as in Table II in order to facilitate comparison of Negro and white correlations.

The Relationships Between Socio-Economic Factors and Negro and White Registration

Table IV presents the correlations between the per cent of eligible whites registered to vote and the same 20 social and economic factors utilized in our effort to explain Negro registration. While these factors were chosen for their presumed relevance for Negro registration, the magnitude of the simple correlations in the first column of the table suggests that they are as strongly related to white as to Negro registration. When these simple correlations for whites are compared with those for Negroes in Table II, however, we see that the direction of the correlation is reversed for 15 of the 20 social and economic factors. Not one of the 20 variables is substantially and consistently related to both Negro and white rates of voter registration.

The reversal of relationships is so regular that social and economic attributes might appear to have opposite meanings for Negro and white registration.[32] Closer inspection reveals, however, that the relationships are disparate rather than opposite.

The crucial variable for Negro registration is Negro concentration in the population, which not only furnishes the strongest simple correlation but is also the variable that most consistently accounts for other apparent "influences" on Negro registration. Indeed, Negro concentration has generally been cited as the critical factor in all dimensions of southern political behavior. Hence, one immediately suspects that all of the variables which facilitate white registration must be positively correlated with concentration of Negro population, which would thereby stand as the dominant third factor for both Negro and white registration. While this familiar interpretation would conveniently account for the striking discrepancy between correlates of white and Negro registration, it is not supported by our findings. On the contrary, *Negro concentration has a negligible relationship to white voter registration.* Moreover, the small simple correlation of Negro concentration and white registration (+.10) drops to the vanishing point (+.06) when urbanism is controlled.

No single variable is as important for white registration as Negro concentration is for Negro registration, but urbanism emerges as particularly significant. Per cent of population urban — which proved inconsequential in the analysis of Negro registration — furnishes one of the strongest negative correlations with white voter registration, a correlation that is not affected when Negro concentration is controlled. And the same relationship is found if, instead of per cent of population urban, we use Standard Metropolitan Areas

---

[32]A simple Kendall tau rank order correlation of the two distributions of correlations in Tables II and IV is — .54.

as our index of urban-rural difference; white registration is consistently higher in rural than in urban counties. Other county characteristics associated with urbanization — such as high income and education levels for whites and Negroes — are similarly related to low white registration. Perhaps the rural white resident finds politics more meaningful in a one-party region, where personality plays such an important role in elections.[33] In any event, urban-rural differences are a key factor in variations in white voter registration.

Similar variations are found in the relationships of white and Negro registration rates to the other social and economic characteristics of southern counties. Average white education, for example, manifested a strong negative association with Negro registration — an association that held up under various controls so well that it led to novel conclusions. White education is also negatively related to white registration, but the correlation is extremely small and it is reversed when per cent of population urban is controlled.

Without an extended consideration of white registration, then, we can conclude that our analysis does apply to Negro voter registration in particular rather than to voter registration in general. The social and economic characteristics of southern counties have widely different meanings for Negro and white registration.

V. Conclusions

The proportion of voting age Negroes registered to vote in the former confederate states has increased more than 500 per cent since *Smith* v. *Allwright* was decided in 1944. Today, 28 per cent of the voting age Negroes are registered voters, a rate which is about half that of white adults in the South. In this article we have examined the statistical associations between selected social and economic characteristics of southern counties and Negro registration in an effort to ascertain the extent to which variations in Negro registration can be explained by the social and economic realities of the region.

The personal attributes of Negroes — their occupations, income, and education as reflected in county figures — were found to have relatively little to do with Negro registration rates. The size of the Negro middle class does appear to have an independent and positive correlation with Negro registration, but this correlation is small compared to those between Negro registration and the characteristics of the whites and of the total community.

The largest single correlation (−.46) was between the per cent of the population Negro in 1950 and Negro registration. Differences in the proportion of the population Negro up to about 30 per cent are not associated

---

[33]Urban counties in the South undoubtedly purge their registration lists with greater regularity than the more rural ones. How much effect this may have on these correlations cannot be ascertained.

with drastic reductions in the per cent of Negroes registered, but increasing Negro concentration above this figure seems to lead to very rapid decreases. Negro concentration in the past seems almost as important as Negro concentration today until one discovers that the close association of past with present Negro concentration accounts for the finding. Indeed, declines in Negro proportions in counties with populations from 30 to 70 per cent Negro in 1900 are associated with substantial registration increases over similar counties which have not experienced such change.

The presence of an agricultural economy and farm tenancy were found to have a small, independent, and depressing effect on Negro registration rates. Neither urbanization nor industrialization, on the other hand, seems to be associated with Negro registration increases when other factors are controlled.

White educational levels were of about equal importance to the size of the Negro middle class and the existence of an agrarian economy. The more highly educated the whites in a county, the lower the rate of Negro registration — until the average white adult was a high school graduate or possessed some higher education. In these few counties, the rate of Negro registration was moderate. Up to the highest levels, increases in white educational levels apparently lead to more effective enforcement of the region's traditional mores against Negro participation in elections.

Another factor of about equal importance to all the others save Negro concentration is Roman Catholicism. The larger the proportion of Roman Catholics in a county, the higher the rate of Negro registration regardless of what other factors are controlled.

When the same social and economic characteristics of southern counties are analyzed for their relationships to white voter registration, a radically different pattern is discovered. The direction of the relationship is reversed for most of the attributes with the shift from Negro to white registration, but more than a simple reversal is involved. The magnitudes of the correlations with white registration (disregarding direction of correlation) are quite different, and a different variable emerges as the most consistent independent correlate. Whereas Negro registration tends to increase in the counties — rural or urban — that have smaller portions of Negroes in their populations, white registration tends to increase in the more rural counties — regardless of the portions of Negroes in their populations. We can accordingly have some confidence that we are dealing with an autonomous set of relationships in our analysis of Negro registration in the South.

In all of the preceding analysis, we have examined the association between selected social and economic factors and Negro registration one at a time. While controls for the impact of one social and economic factor on another have been introduced, we have not yet attempted to estimate the extent of the association between all the social and economic factors taken together and

Negro registration. In order to do this, we have computed the multiple correlation coefficient between all 20 social and economic factors (plus the size of the Standard Metropolitan Area, if any, within which the county is contained — a qualitative variable for which simple correlations could not be obtained) and Negro voter registration. The correlation between all of the social and economic variables and county registration rates of Negroes is .53, which explains about 28 per cent (R^2) of the variation in Negro registration.

A multiple correlation of this magnitude demonstrates the great importance of social and economic characteristics for Negro registration.[34] To explain over one-fourth of the variance in Negro registration — or any other significant political phenomenon — is no mean achievement in the current state of political science. But almost three-fourths of the variance remains to be accounted for. This leaves room for significant variation independent of social and economic forces that have been considered here. If political variables were added to the analysis, could still more of the variance in Negro registration be explained? If political variables do emerge as having an autonomous set of relationships to Negro registration, what is the comparative importance of political and demographic variables? Finally, if variations in state systems (social, economic, and political) were taken into account, could still more explanatory power be gained? A social and economic analysis has taken us a long way in our effort to understand Negro registration rates, but we still have a lot further to go. The massive bulk and complexity of our data require that an analysis of political and legal factors, of the relative importance of demographic versus political variables, and of variations in state systems be reported separately. Our expectation is that, by an analysis of these additional factors, we can reduce the range of unexplained variation still further.

The application of our findings to the contemporary policy problem of how best to increase Negro voting in the South must be approached with the utmost caution. Our analysis deals with registration, not voting, and these are not identical forms of political participation. Our data deal with the characteristics of counties, not individuals, and the leap from the areal to the individual level is hazardous. Third, the analysis has been of variations in rates of registration and not of factors which determine its absolute level. To find that an independent variable accounts for some of the variation in the dependent variable gives us no direct information on the size of the dependent variable. Fourth, correlations are not "causes" but merely associa-

---

[34] Indeed, it was on the basis of a roughly equal multiple correlation, based on survey data rather than aggregate county data, that an early voting behavior study concluded that "social characteristics determine political preference." Paul F. Lazarsfeld, Bernard Berelson, and Hazel Gaudet, *The People's Choice* (New York: Columbia University Press, 1948), p. 27. This work reports a multiple correlation between voting preference and social factors of "approximately .5" (p. 25).

tions; attributing causal relationships to variables which are correlated with one another is to engage in the drawing of inferences, which sometimes are spectacularly wrong. Finally, the bulk of our analysis has been restricted to one point in time so that it does not directly produce predictions in which time is a key factor.

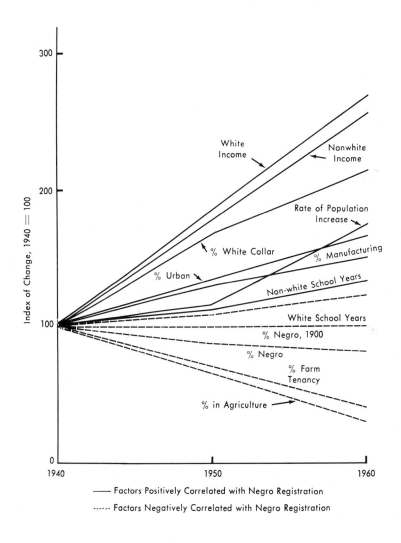

FIGURE 8. RATES OF SOCIAL AND ECONOMIC CHANGE IN THE SOUTH 1940-1960.

If these caveats are not forgotten but merely set aside, our correlations suggest that reformers should not expect miracles[35] in their efforts, through political and legal means, to increase the size and effectiveness of the Negro vote in the South. The Negro registration rate is low, in rather large part, because of the social and economic characteristics of southerners — both Negro and white. These facts are not easily and quickly changed by law or political action. One cannot help but be impressed by the massive indications of stability in the situation — the extremely high negative correlation between per cent Negro in 1900 and Negro registration in 1958, the apparent failure of urbanization and industrialization to provide sufficiently favorable conditions for Negro political participation, the negative correlation between white educational levels and Negro registration, and so on.

At the same time, Negro registration has increased rapidly since 1944 and the social and economic factors we have considered account for only about 28 per cent of its 1958 variation. Changes in the southern society and economy strongly argue that Negro registration will continue to increase. In Figure 8, the trend since 1940 is presented for the variables we found to be most strongly related to Negro voter registration.[36] *Every one of the variables positively associated with Negro registration is on the increase —* some have doubled in 20 years and all but one have increased by at least 50 per cent. Only one of the factors associated with low Negro registration — white school years completed — is also increasing, and there is reason to believe that a good many southern counties will soon reach the stage where this factor may tend to facilitate rather than hinder Negro political participation.[37] All the other factors negatively correlated with Negro registration (except, of course, per cent Negro in 1900) are declining rapidly.

The South's social and economic structure may be the reformer's major barrier — but it may also be a long-run cause for hope.

---

[35]For example, Martin Luther King's statement in a speech to the 1962 NAACP annual convention about southern Negroes being "able to elect at least five Negroes to Congress in the next few years" seems to underestimate wildly the social and economic barriers to Negro political participation. *New York Times,* July 6, 1962. See also the sanguine expectations of Lomax, *op. cit.*

[36]No trend data were available on religious affiliation. Median income figures, by race, were not available for 1940. In Figure 8, it is assumed that median income for both races increased at the same rate between 1940 and 1950 as between 1950 and 1960.

[37]If white school years completed continues to increase at the 1950-60 rate, the average southern white will have completed 11.4 years of schooling by 1970 and many southern counties will have average white school years completed of 12 years or more. Assuming that the relationship presented in Figure 6 continues to hold true, the effect of white education on Negro registration may gradually reverse.

Political Factors and Negro Voter Registration in the South*

Donald R. Matthews and James W. Prothro

A recent Herblock cartoon in the *Washington Post* depicts three bare-footed backwoodsmen. The oldest and most tattered of them (labeled "poll tax") lies wounded, his head propped against a boulder, his rifle abandoned near his side. As the other rifle-bearing rustics — identified as "literacy tests" and "scare tactics" — bend sorrowfully over him the older man says, "I think them Feds got me, boys, but I know you'll carry on." Perhaps it is premature to anticipate the ratification of the anti-poll tax amendment proposed by the 87th Congress as the newest addition to the federal constitution. No doubt the cartoonist is correct, however, in picturing both "literacy tests" and "scare tactics" as less vulnerable to federal government attack. These presumed barriers to equal participation by Negroes in the politics of the South may "carry on" for some time to come.

Reprinted from the *American Political Science Review*, vol. LVII, (June 1963), pp. 355-367 with permission of the publisher and authors. Copyright 1963 by the American Political Science Association.
*Grants from the Rockefeller Foundation [to UNC's Institute for Research in Social Science], and a Senior Award for Research on Governmental Affairs from the Social Science Research Council made this research possible and are gratefully acknowledged. A portion of this paper was presented at the Duke University Conference on "The Impact of Political and Legal Changes in the Postwar South," Durham, N. C., July 12-14, 1962.

Yet at present political scientists are not able to say how much difference these and other political and legal arrangements and practices make in the rate of Negro voting in the states of the former Confederacy. About 28 per cent of the voting age Negroes in the South were registered to vote in 1958, as compared to about 60 per cent of the voting age whites.[1] It would be a gross error to attribute this substantial disparity to legal and political discrimination alone, though unquestionably official discrimination is a factor. For southern Negroes overwhelmingly possess the historical heritage of low social status, relatively small incomes, and limited educations received in inferior schools. These attributes are associated with low voter turnout among *all* populations, regardless of skin color or region. Moreover, the low status, income and education of many southern whites foster racial prejudice. Thus poverty and ignorance may have a double-barrelled effect on Negro political participation by decreasing the Negroes' motivation and ability to participate while increasing white resistance to their doing so. The low voting rates of Negroes in the South may result to a large extent from these factors, as well as from direct political or legal discrimination by the white community. So far, the methods of political science have not been successfully applied to the problem of sorting out these various factors and ascertaining their relative importance.

In an earlier paper,[2] we analyzed the relationships between a wide gamut of social and economic factors and the rates of Negro voter registration in the South. Twenty-one census-type demographic characteristics of southern counties were correlated with the per cent of the counties' voting age Negro populations registered to vote. A multiple-correlation coefficient of 53 was obtained, which means that these 21 variables statistically "explain" about 28 per cent (R^2) of the variation in Negro registration rates. While the magnitude of this correlation indicates that social and economic conditions have a powerful influence, it still leaves much room for significant variation independent of these forces. In this paper we shall attempt to isolate and measure the impact of political and legal factors on Negro voter registration in the 11 states of the Confederacy.

I. The Data and the Approach

We start with an analysis of a large number of characteristics of southern counties (counting Virginia's independent cities as counties) obtained or

---

[1]U.S. Commission on Civil Rights, *Report* (Washington, G.P.O., 1959), pp. 40-41.
[2]"Social and Economic Factors and Negro Voter Registration in the South," this REVIEW, Vol. 57 (1963), pp. 24-44.

derived from the U. S. Census and other standard sources.[3] Since our focus is on Negro registration, 139 counties were excluded because their populations contained less than 1 per cent Negroes, or because their registration data were not available from the U. S. Commission on Civil Rights. The 997 other southern counties are included in the analysis.[4]

These data suffer from a number of limitations. While our interest is in Negro *voting*, we have had to employ *registration* figures since they are available by race as well as county, as voting totals are not. Registration figures vary in accuracy from one state to the next and in some cases are little more than informed estimates. Our unit of analysis is the county, not individuals, and it is often hazardous to transfer conclusions drawn from one level of analysis to the other. Finally, our data are for one point in time. We are therefore limited to the analysis of variations in the rate of Negro registration of southern counties in 1958.[5]

Our basic approach is that of multiple regression and residual analysis.[6] In computing the multiple correlation coefficient between the 21 demographic characteristics and Negro registration rates previously reported, we obtained an equation — called a multiple regression equation — which represents the typical relationship between these 21 variables and Negro registration rates for the South as a whole. By entering the values of these 21 social and economic attributes for each county into this equation, a "predicted" rate of Negro registration is obtained for every southern county. This is the proportion of voting age Negroes who would be registered if the relationships in that county between socio-economic structure and Negro registration corresponded exactly to those for the South as a whole. Some counties have just the level of Negro registration they "ought" to have on that basis, while others have registration rates above or below the predicted level. By examining the pattern of these deviations — called "residuals" in statistical par-

---

[3]A complete list of sources used to obtain county frequencies for the independent variables used in this analysis is too lengthy to reproduce here. A mimeographed list will be supplied by the authors upon request. We are indebted to the following research assistants for their help in collecting these data: Lawton Bennett, Lewis Bowman, Barbara Bright, Jack Fleer, Donald Freeman, Douglas Gatlin, and Richard Sutton. All told, the collection and coding of these data took one man-year of work.

[4]The 1958 registration data contained in the 1959 *Report* of the Commission on Civil Rights are more complete than the 1960 registration data contained in the Commission's 1961 *Report* (Washington, 1961), Vol. I, "Voting," and were used in all states except Tennessee, for which 1958 data were not available. There are 1136 counties in the 11 southern states (counting Virginia's independent cities as "counties"), of which 1028 had populations containing at least 1 per cent Negroes in 1950. Negro registration figures are not available for 31 of these.

[5]For a more extended discussion see Matthews and Prothro, *op. cit.*

[6]Computations were made on the University of North Carolina's UNIVAC 1105 high-speed digital computer.

lance — we are able to control the effects of socio-economic structure on Negro registration, and thereby to ascertain whether political and legal factors have any independent association with Negro registration; and if so, how much. A residual of 0.0 indicates that the rate of Negro voter registration is exactly what the county's social and economic attributes would lead one to expect; the positive or negative value of other residuals indicates whether the county's actual Negro registration is above or below the level expected from its socio-economic characteristics. The larger the residual, the more likely it is that other factors are needed to explain the county's Negro registration rate.

II. State Variations in Negro Voter Registration Rates

Perhaps the most important political and legal fact about the South is its division into eleven states. The rates of voter registration by adult Negroes vary widely among these states.

In Table I the former Confederate states are ranked according to the average per cent of the voting age Negro population registered to vote in their counties. In Mississippi, the average county has only about 3 per cent of its potential Negro electorate registered to vote. The average county in South Carolina has about 12 per cent. In Tennessee, on the other hand, the typical county has 72 per cent of the voting age Negroes registered, a figure which is no doubt inflated by the state's casual approach to the niceties of electoral administration.

TABLE I

MEAN PERCENTAGE OF VOTING AGE NEGROES REGISTERED TO VOTE, BY COUNTY, IN SOUTHERN STATES, COMPARED TO MEAN PERCENTAGE PREDICTED BY 21 DEMOGRAPHIC VARIABLES (1958)

State	Actual Mean Per Cent	Predicted Mean Per Cent	Residual	Actual Mean as Percentage of Predicted Mean
Mississippi	3.4	17.7	— 14.3	19.2
South Carolina	12.5	19.4	— 6.9	64.4
Alabama	20.5	26.8	— 6.3	76.5
Virginia	24.1	34.3	— 10.2	70.3
Arkansas	27.6	32.3	— 4.7	85.4
Georgia	30.4	24.9	+ 5.5	122.1
Louisiana	31.2	31.2	0.0	100.0
North Carolina	36.0	32.8	+ 3.2	109.7
Texas	36.8	36.7	+ 0.1	100.3
Florida	39.1	32.6	+ 6.5	119.9
Tennessee	72.3	39.7	+ 32.6	182.1

What accounts for these wide variations among the states? We have already shown that a part of the explanation lies in the differences in the social and economic structure of the states. Mississippi and South Carolina, for example, have a larger proportion of Negroes in their populations than the other southern states, and this has a major depressing effect on Negro registration.[7] But our ability to predict, by means of a multiple regression equation, what the rate of registration ought to be on the basis of social and economic characteristics indicates that this is only a partial explanation, not the full story.

The second column of Table I presents the predicted Negro registration percentage for the average county within each of the southern states. Mississippi not only has the lowest and Tennessee the highest actual rates of Negro registration but they also "ought" to have the lowest and highest rates on the basis of their social and economic attributes. If this were a sufficient explanation, however, the predicted and the actual rates of registration should be the same. This is very nearly the case in two states — Louisiana and Texas — but all the others have either more or less Negroes registered than the expected rate. In Mississippi, for example, about 18 per cent of the voting age Negroes ought to be registered if Mississippi counties responded to socio-economic factors as other southern counties do; but instead, only about 3 per cent are actually registered. The Negro registration rate is about 7 percentage points below the expected in South Carolina, 6 points below in Alabama, 10 points below in Virginia, and 5 points below in Arkansas. On the other hand, Tennessee (+32.6 residual), Florida (+6.5), Georgia (+5.5), and North Carolina (+3.2) have more Negroes registered to vote than expected.

These state contrasts persist, accordingly, even after we minimize the possibility of finding differences by controlling for 21 social and economic factors. Raw differences in registration rates show a wild variation — the range of difference reaching 69 percentage points between Tennessee and Mississippi (Column 1). But much of this difference clearly stems from the fact that Mississippi has so many more Negroes and is both more rural and less industrialized. When such factors are controlled the difference of 69 points between the two states is reduced to 47 (Column 3). Or, if we take less extreme cases and compare South Carolina with Florida, the raw difference of 27 points is reduced to a residual difference of 13. By the same token, residual analysis may reveal a small raw difference to be more meaningful than it appears. Georgia counties, for example, have an average Negro registration rate 3 percentage points higher than Arkansas counties. But, allowing for the social and economic attributes of these counties, one would

[7]See Matthews and Prothro, *op. cit.*

expect the Arkansas average to be higher than Georgia's; hence, the raw difference of 3 points becomes a residual difference of 10 points.

The contrasts revealed by residual analysis demonstrate that the state political systems must be an independent influence on Negro voter registration. To say that these contrasts result from different state political systems is not to say very much. What aspects of state politics account for these differences? We turn now to this problem.

III. Legal Requirements for Voting

Around the turn of the century, southern Bourbons led a movement to restrict the suffrage in response to the twin threats of the Negro and of populism. In the process they developed a "variety of ingenious contrivances to inconvenience the would-be voter."[8] Some of these contrivances survive to this day, despite the intervening rise and fall of the white primary, changing political attitudes and conditions, and the efforts of the U. S. Supreme Court. Just how effectively these electoral obstacles — today primarily the poll tax and literacy tests — serve to disenfranchise potential Negro voters is not known. In northern discussions of southern politics, these devices are often cast in "the role of chief villain."[9] Detailed analyses by Key and Ogden suggest that their impact on the turnout of *white* voters is fairly modest. "The chances are," Key writes, "that if other things remain equal (and they rarely do), elimination of the poll tax alone would increase voting in most southern states by no more than 5 to 10 per cent of the potential number of white voters."[10] Our multiple regression analysis enables us to make a similar estimate for potential Negro voters.

Five southern states — Alabama, Arkansas, Mississippi, Texas, and Virginia — still levy poll taxes. They vary in amount from Mississippi's $2.00 to Arkansas's $1.00 and must be paid one to nine months before election day. The tax is cumulative in Mississippi, Alabama, and Virginia; new voters are required to pay the tax for the preceding two or three years before they are enrolled. Most states exempt members of the armed forces, and some also exempt veterans, the elderly, the blind, the deaf or dumb, the maimed, Indians, and other miscellaneous categories of citizens.

All the southern states save Arkansas, Florida, Tennessee, and Texas require potential voters to pass literacy tests. A recitation of the language of these requirements is scarcely necessary: "Whether a person can register

---

[8]V. O. Key, Jr., *Southern Politics in State and Nation* (New York, 1949), p. 531.
[9]*Ibid.*, p. 579.
[10]*Ibid.*, p. 617. See also F. D. Ogden, *The Poll Tax in the South* (University, Ala., University of Alabama Press, 1958), ch. 5.

to vote depends on what the man down at the courthouse says, and he usually has the final say. It is how the tests are administered that matters."[11] In one North Carolina county, for example, the registrant is regarded as literate even if he requires help in reading the following words: solemnly, affirm, support, Constitution, inconsistent, therewith, resident, township, precinct, ward, general, election, and registered. In a Mississippi county, on the other hand, the registrar of voters frankly told the authors that the literacy test was administered so that no Negro could pass.

To what extent are differences in formal voting requirements — despite variations in their administration — related to differences in registration rates, after controlling for social and economic structure? The answer is given in Table II.

TABLE II

**STATE VOTER REQUIREMENTS AND NEGRO VOTER REGISTRA-
TION RESIDUALS, BY COUNTY, 1958**

Voter Requirements	Mean Residual of Counties
Poll Tax and Literacy Test	
Mississippi	— 14.3
Virginia	— 10.2
Alabama	— 6.3
All counties in group	— 10.5
Poll Tax Only	
Arkansas	— 4.7
Texas	+ 0.1
All counties in group	— 1.0
Literacy Test Only	
South Carolina	— 6.9
Louisiana	0.0
North Carolina	+ 3.2
Georgia	+ 5.5
All counties in group	+ 2.3
Neither Literacy Test Nor Poll Tax	
Florida	+ 6.5
Tennessee	+ 32.6
All counties in group	+ 18.1

County registration rates within the three states with both the poll tax and the literacy test are, on the average, 10.5 percentage points below the predicted value. Counties in the two states with neither a poll tax nor a literacy test have registration rates 18.1 percentage points higher than expected. The pattern is not perfect. South Carolina, with only a literacy

---

[11]Key, *op. cit.*, p. 460.

test, has a lower residual than Alabama, with both a fairly substantial poll tax and a literacy test. Texas has a small plus residual (+0.1) while Arkansas has a sizeable negative one (—4.7); both are poll tax states without a literacy requirement. Nonetheless, the tendency for the states with stringent formal voter requirements to have lower registration rates than those with more liberal requirements is impressive, even after controlling for 21 social and economic factors. If we were able to take account of the way these formal requirements are variously administered by different local officials within each state, the relationship in Table II would undoubtedly be even closer.

A survey of county registration officials made by the North Carolina Advisory Committee to the U. S. Commission on Civil Rights suggests the extremely wide variety of ways in which the same legal requirements are actually administered.[12] Some county registrars reported administering tests which involved the taking of oral dictation, extensive reading aloud, quizzing applicants on the meaning of words and phrases, and the like, while others settled for an ability to fill out an application form properly and to sign one's name. Several county registration officials reported that they did not enforce the constitutionally required literacy test at all. The following counties — all in the northeastern black-belt area of the state — reported literacy tests which appeared to be unusually difficult or arbitrary:

County	County Residual	Residual Adjusted for State Mean
Bertie	— 1.0	— 4.2
Camden	— 9.1	— 13.3
Currituck	— 15.1	— 18.3
Franklin	+ 3.2	0.0
Gates	— 22.1	— 25.3
Greene	— 6.1	— 9.3
Halifax	— 2.8	— 6.0
Northampton	+ 0.7	— 2.5
Warren	+ 1.8	— 1.4
Mean	— 5.6	— 8.9

Their Negro registration rate is, on the average, more than 5 percentage points below the expected and almost 9 percentage points below that expected for North Carolina counties with their social and economic characteristics.

---

[12]The returns of an Advisory Committee questionnaire mailed to county registrars are reported, in part, in "Voting and Voter Requirements in North Carolina" (mimeographed), June 4, 1961.

The North Carolina counties which do not administer literacy tests are all in the mountainous west. They and their residuals are:

County	County Residual	Residual Adjusted for State Mean
Catawba	+ 23.5	+ 20.3
Wilkes	+ 32.6	+ 29.4
Yancey	+ 12.9	+ 9.7
Mean	+ 23.0	+ 19.8

On the average, these counties have 23 percentage points more Negroes registered than predicted, and almost 20 percentage points more than the state average.

Crude as these data are, they still suggest that formal voter requirements and their administration have a far larger impact on Negro voter registration than they do on white registration. Even so, other political factors are obviously at work. The structure of party and factional competition and the presence or absence of race organizations and of racial violence are less formal political variables that have been cited as offering possible explanations for Negro participation in particular localities. The remainder of this article is devoted to an examination of the importance of these variables for south-wide variations in rates of Negro voter registration.

IV. The Structure of Competition: Party Systems

The South differs from the rest of the United States in so many ways that it is tempting to assume that all forms of distinctiveness are functionally linked. Thus southerners register and vote in smaller proportions than other Americans, and the South is the country's largest one-party region. Hence, the one-party politics of the South must decrease voter participation. Much can be said for this interpretation. When the results of general elections are foreordained in favor of Democracy — and despite important changes in recent years this is the most common situation for most offices in the South — general election campaigns are tepid affairs, party organizations make little if any effort to increase registration or to get out the vote, and the act of voting in general elections becomes little more than a ritual.

Furthermore, though the Democratic primaries may be hotly and regularly contested, this form of electoral competition seems less effective in stimulating political interest and activity than partisan competition. Contrary to a popular assumption, the turnout for primary elections in the South, where the primary may be the real election, is no greater than in the parts of the country where the real election comes later.[13] A sizeable group of candidates running without party labels is harder to choose between, and the likely pay-off from the election of one candidate rather than another is difficult to determine. Without the mental shorthand of party identification to structure the situation, the voter is presented with more vexing cognitive problems to solve than in a partisan contest. It is more difficult to ascertain where one's self-interest lies and the effort or "costs" of voting are correspondingly increased. While Democratic factions seek to improvise get-out-the-vote organizations in behalf of their candidates, these are transient affairs, relatively impotent even when compared to the eroded efficacy of local party organizations outside of the South. All these characteristics of one-partyism have their greatest impact on poorly educated, "have-not" groups in the southern electorate, of which the Negro is conspicuously one.

The difficulty with this explanation, as applied to voter registration or general election turnout, is the dearth of supporting data. While we do have evidence to support the argument that primaries stimulate less voter interest than more structured general elections, Robert Lane argues that it is nothing more than a "common-sense view of the causes of high or low participation" to say that "a close election, where the issue was in doubt, would bring more people to the polls than one in which the result was determined from the beginning."[14] As for the non-southern parts of the United States, Lane reports that, "When we eliminate regional factors by dropping the South (as a region with a special sub-culture) and examine counties instead of states, the relationship between turnout and closeness of vote disappears. . . ."[15]

From this point of view, registration and voting are seen as satisfying needs of the citizen unrelated to the closeness of election contests, so that only a small correlation can be expected between one-partyism and political participation. Which line of interpretation holds up when variations within the "special sub-culture" of southern counties are examined?

Figure 1 appears to support the earlier line of reasoning: Negro voter registration increases in southern counties as party competition increases. It seems safe to assume that the counties in which Eisenhower polled less than 40 per cent of the vote for President in 1956 are Democratic in presidential as well as other electoral contests. Relatively few Negroes tend

[13]Key, *op. cit.,* ch. 23.
[14]Robert E. Lane, *Political Life* (Glencoe, Ill., 1958), p. 308.
[15]*Ibid.,* Lane's conclusion is based primarily upon an analysis by Warren E. Miller, "One-Party Politics and the Voter," this REVIEW, Vol. 50 (1956), pp. 707-725. Additional support may be found in James A. Robinson and William H. Standing, "Some Correlates of Voter Participation: The Case of Indiana," *Journal of Politics,* Vol. 22 (1960), pp. 96-111.

to be registered in these counties, compared to the more competitive counties (defined as those with 40-59 per cent for Eisenhower). But the rates of Negro registration seem as high in heavily Republican counties (60 per cent and over for Eisenhower) as in the competitive counties. The difficulty with these findings, as with those cited by Lane, is that we do not know whether these differences are the result of competitive elections or of the tendency for presidential Republicanism to be strongest in areas where the social and economic inhibitions against Negro voting are most attenuated.

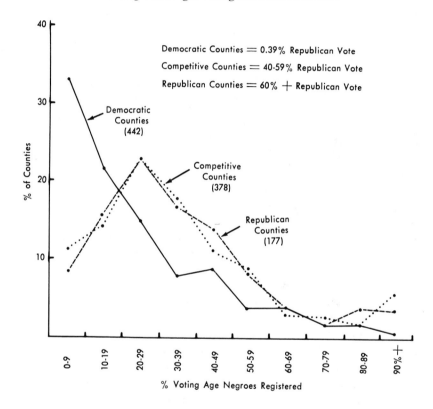

FIGURE 1. PARTY COMPETITION IN PRESIDENTIAL ELECTION OF 1956 AND NEGRO VOTER REGISTRATION RATES, BY COUNTY.

Table III, which shows the mean residuals for Democratic, competitive, and Republican counties, demonstrates that most of the tendency for Negro registration to increase with levels of competition in presidential voting is the result of social and economic factors. Republican counties have slightly fewer Negroes registered than would be expected on the basis of their social and economic characteristics, and Democratic counties likewise. The com-

TABLE III

PARTY SYSTEMS AND NEGRO VOTER REGISTRATION RESIDUALS, BY COUNTY, 1958

	Mean Residual	Number of Counties
Democratic counties	— 0.9	442
Competitive counties	+ 1.3	378
Republican counties	— 0.9	177

Note: Democratic counties defined as those in which Republican presidential vote in 1956 was from 0-39% of total vote; in competitive counties the Republicans polled 40-59%; in Republican counties, 60% and over.

petitive counties, on the other hand, have 1 percentage point more Negroes registered than their social structure suggests. The existence or absence of partisan competition is associated with variations in Negro registration rates, then, but once we go beyond that simple co-variation we discover that the variations of both are largely accounted for by the social and economic characteristics of southern counties.

V. The Structure of Competition: Factional Systems

The vast bulk of all political competition in the South takes place within the Democratic party. We have already seen that this form of politics seems, in general, to have a small inhibiting effect upon Negro registration rates. But the structure of Democratic factionalism varies a good deal from one southern state to the next and this may affect the meaning of voting to southern Negroes.

Repeatedly confronted with a choice between an incumbent like Senator Eastland and a challenger attempting to outdo the senior Senator from Mississippi at his own game, thousands of potential Negro voters may never have any incentive to attempt to register. Given a choice between Frank Porter Graham and Willis Smith, they might be expected to turn out in droves — as they did. The southern Negro vote is "issue-oriented," and race is the important issue. In some southern states, all the candidates for public office are unsatisfactory from the Negro's point of view; in other states, it is usually possible for the Negro to distinguish one or more candidates as favorably disposed to Negro interests — despite the candidate's best efforts to avoid being labeled by whites as the "Negro candidate" — and these candidates have some chance of winning. Before 1958, this normally seems to have been the case in Tennessee, North Carolina, Louisiana, Florida and Texas but rarely so elsewhere.

Southern state political systems vary in other ways which may affect the nature of the choice confronting potential or actual Negro voters. In some states, two fairly clear-cut factions battle it out on rather even terms and these factions tend to persist from one election year to the next. In others, Democratic factionalism is more fluid and unstructured, the number of serious candidates tends to be larger, and there is little relationship between one electoral contest and the next. The extent to which the Democratic party divides into two party-like factions, or tends instead toward splintered factionalism, is suggested by the following figures on the percentage of the total vote polled jointly by the two highest candidates for governor, in the initial Democratic primaries (excluding run-offs) held in each election year between 1948 and 1960:[16]

	Median Per Cent
Virginia	100.0
Tennessee	95.8
Georgia	94.7
South Carolina	89.8
Arkansas	81.5
North Carolina	77.9
Texas	69.3
Florida	60.5
Louisiana	58.6
Alabama	58.1
Mississippi	44.4

In Virginia, Tennessee and Georgia, electoral battles appear to be dominated by one or two major factions which manage to attract virtually all the vote. In Mississippi, Alabama, Louisiana (of the post-Long era), Florida and Texas, state politics follows the "every man for himself" style of fluid multifactionalism. The other states fall into an intermediate group, closer to bifactional than multifactional politics.

The relative strength as well as the number of factions is important. A better way to assess the competitiveness of Democratic factionalism is to

---

[16]Primary election returns were compiled from Richard M. Scammon (ed.), *Southern Primaries '58* (Washington, Governmental Affairs Institute, 1959); from various issues of the *Congressional Quarterly Almanac,* and *Congressional Quarterly Weekly Report;* legislative manuals and Reports of Secretaries of State; and the *New York Times.* Contests involving incumbents in Arkansas and Texas — the only southern states in which governors may succeed themselves — and uncontested races were omitted in computing medians.

look at the median per cent of the total vote polled by the leading candidate for governor in the first Democratic primary during the same span of years considered above. The percentages are:

	Median Per Cent
Virginia	65.8
South Carolina	61.3
Tennessee	55.6
Georgia	49.3
Arkansas	47.7
North Carolina	46.7
Texas	39.9
Florida	34.7
Alabama	34.1
Louisiana	33.1
Mississippi	28.1

Factional struggles were unusually uneven in Virginia and South Carolina. During the fifties, these were not so much bifactional states as states in which one faction dominated without serious challenge.

From a logical point of view, the citizen should have less reason to vote where one dominant faction runs the show; there is no realistic choice to be made. It is a good deal easier for a voter of limited political interest and skill to determine where his self-interest lies in a bifactional state than in one characterized by fluid multifactionalism. Candidates can be identified as belonging to the Long faction, or Talmadge faction, or Kerr Scott faction, and these labels have at least some policy meaning.

We expect, therefore, that both the number and strength of Democratic factions and the extent to which candidates are identified with different racial views should be associated with different rates of voter registration among Negroes. When the 11 southern states are classified according to these criteria, and the mean county residuals of each type of state are examined, we see that this is indeed the case (Table IV). Two states, Virginia and South Carolina, have been dominated by one faction since 1948 and neither offers candidates favorable to Negroes. The mean county residual for the two states is −9.3. Alabama and Mississippi have multifactional systems combined with white racial consensus: their mean county residual is −10.7. Arkansas and Georgia have had bifactional Democratic politics but it has been difficult for Negroes to ascertain significant differences on racial policy between them: their mean county residual is +2.7. Louisiana, Florida, and Texas have had multifactional politics in recent years, but they have offered candidates with discernible differences from the Negro point of view. Taken together, they have a residual of +1.4. Finally, North Carolina and Tennessee have had both bifactional politics and perceptible differences on racial matters between the factions. The mean county residual for these two states is $+13.7$.

Thus the structure of competition does seem to make a difference, and these differences are in the expected direction. The presence of observable differences in the racial views of candidates is associated with about 10

TABLE IV

THE STRUCTURE OF FACTIONAL COMPETITION IN SOUTHERN STATES, 1948-60, AND NEGRO VOTER REGISTRATION RESIDUALS*

Type of Factionalism	Generally No Major Candidate Favorable to Negroes		Generally 1 or More Major Candidates Favorable to Negroes		All Counties in Group
One Dominant Faction	Virginia	$-$ 10.2			$-$ 9.3
	South Carolina	$-$ 6.9			
	All Counties in Group	$-$ 9.3			
Two Competitive Factions	Arkansas	$-$ 4.7	Tennessee	$+$ 32.4	$+$ 7.3
	Georgia	$+$ 5.5	North Carolina	$+$ 3.2	
	All Counties in Group	$+$ 2.7	All Counties in Group	$+$ 13.7	
Multifactionalism	Alabama	$-$ 6.3	Louisiana	0.0	$-$ 2.4
	Mississippi	$-$ 14.3	Florida	$+$ 6.5	
	All Counties in Group	$-$ 10.7	Texas	$+$ 0.1	
			All Counties in Group	$+$ 1.4	
All Counties in Group		$-$ 4.9		$+$ 5.3	

*The numbers in the table are the mean residuals of counties in states or groups of states.

TABLE V

MEAN NEGRO VOTER REGISTRATION RESIDUALS BY EXTENT OF RACE ORGANIZATION IN SOUTHERN COUNTIES, 1958

Extent of Negro Organization in County	White Race Organization in County	No White Race Organization in County	All Counties
Local organization and NAACP chapter	$+$ 11.4 (14)	$+$ 1.0 (10)	$+$ 7.0 (24)
NAACP chapter only	$+$ 0.8 (74)	$-$ 0.3 (214)	$-$ 0.01 (288)
No Negro organization, no data	$-$ 10.5 (125)	$+$ 0.4 (551)	$-$ 1.6 (676)
All counties	$-$ 5.5 (221)	$+$ 0.3 (776)	

Note: Too few counties have local organizations but no NAACP chapters to permit computation of means. They have been included, however, in the means for "all counties." The number of counties upon which means are based are in parentheses.

percentage points more Negroes registered to vote than in states where such distinctions cannot be drawn. The surplus of Negro voter registration in bifactional states is even larger, especially when compared to states generally dominated by a single faction. Thus the structure of Democratic factionalism appears to have a major impact on Negro registration rates.[17]

VI. Race Organization

If neither party nor factional organizations are particularly effective in structuring electoral choice or stimulating electoral activity in the South, other kinds of organizations may seek to fill this void.

The South has seen a plethora of new racial organizations created since *Smith* v. *Allwright* and *Brown* v. *Board of Education.* Scores of Negro voters' leagues, civic leagues, community betterment organizations, ministerial alliances, etc., have been organized in local communities. The Southern Christian Leadership Conference, Student Non-Violent Coordinating Committee, and Congress of Racial Equality have entered the lists along with the National Association for the Advancement of Colored People and the Urban League as instruments of Negro protest. Local chapters have been established in the South by some of these national organizations. Among the white majority, the White Citizens Councils, sometimes by different names in different areas but all dedicated to the defense of white supremacy, have sprung up and have largely supplanted the Ku Klux Klan. Most of these racial organizations are involved in electoral politics, either quite directly and explicitly or, at a minimum, as a provider of cues in the confusing atmosphere of southern factional politics. It seems reasonable to expect these groups to have some impact on rates of Negro voter registration.

We have made strenuous efforts to ascertain — through correspondence and a systematic search of newspaper files[18] — the location of all Negro and white race organizations and their local chapters. Our list is no doubt incomplete, but we are reasonably confident that the counties we think have such organizations do have them — at least on paper.

---

[17]The above is not intended to imply a single direction of causality: a meaningful choice may lead more Negroes to register, the registration of more Negroes may lead candidates to take positions more favorable to Negroes, or both. So far as bifactional as opposed to unifactional or multifactional politics is concerned, however, one can conceive of the pattern of factionalism as the independent variable associated with Negro registration but one can hardly imagine the registration rates of Negroes as the independent variable. [18]The *New York Times* was consulted from January, 1945, to February, 1961, and the Southern Educational Reporting Service's "Facts on Film," Rolls 1-40, first supplement Rolls 1-3, second supplement Rolls 1-11, were examined in a search of news about these organizations. Letters of inquiry were addressed to known national and statewide organizations seeking the location of their local chapters. Persons known to be knowledgeable about the racial politics of specific states and localities also were contacted.

Table V shows the relationships between the extent of race organization in the counties and their Negro registration residuals. Looking first at the marginal distributions at the far right and bottom of the table, we can readily see that extensive Negro organization is associated with a substantial (7 percentage points) surplus of Negro registered voters over the registration rate predicted by social and economic structure alone. Counties with white race organizations have about 5.5 percentage points fewer Negroes registered than predicted. Both types of race organizations thus seem to be related to Negro registration rates to a fairly sizeable extent.

The partial distributions in the center of the table are even more interesting. A local Negro organization, rather than an NAACP chapter, seems to have the greater impact on Negro registration. Most of these local organizations are explicitly political in orientation whereas NAACP chapters are often little more than fund-raising agencies. Forty-three per cent of the counties with such local organizations have had at least one Negro public official, either elective or appointed, in recent years; whereas only 13 per cent of the counties with only NAACP chapters have had one or more Negro public officials. Only 0.3 per cent of the counties with no known Negro organizations have had a Negro appointed or elected to public office.

Negro registration is not seriously inhibited by the existence of white race organizations, except in the areas where there are no Negro organizations at all; then the dampening effect is substantial, more than 10 percentage points. In areas where both Negroes and whites are organized, the Negro registration rate is actually higher than in counties where only the Negroes are organized along racial lines. Under these circumstances, the organization of a white counter-organization may actually have a boomerang effect, by drawing the Negroes closer together in their own organizations than they might otherwise have been. Local Negro political organizations seem to thrive on competition; white organizations upon its absence. Both, however, help account for a fair share of the variation in Negro voter registration rates in the contemporary South, even after controlling for social and economic factors.

VII. Racial Violence and Intimidation

The South has had a violent history. Before the Civil War, much of the region was thinly-settled frontier in which vigilantism and a "hell-of-a-fella' " tradition flourished.[19] The region's "peculiar institution" — slavery — was, by definition, based upon force. A bloody civil war, fought largely on southern soil, and an anarchistic Reconstruction served to reinforce this

---

[19] W. J. Cash, *The Mind of the South* (New York, Vintage [reprint], 1960), p. 52.

tradition of violence. The subsequent re-establishment of white supremacy and the disfranchisement of the Negro were achieved primarily by force, threats, and intimidation. Constitutional and legal devices — such as the grandfather clause, poll tax, white primary, and legally enforced racial separation in other realms of life — followed the *de facto* realization of racial segregation and served to reinforce, maintain, and legitimize the arrangement. Most of these constitutional and legal defenses have now crumbled, a few of them voluntarily abandoned by the white South, more of them as a result of Supreme Court decisions. But even in the absence of these "legal" and "constitutional" barriers, many southern Negroes are reluctant to exercise their newly re-established franchise and to participate fully in the political life of the region. Some of these nonvoting Negroes are undoubtedly and understandably afraid of possible violence or economic reprisal from a hostile white community.

Negroes living in areas characterized by unusual racial violence could be expected to be particularly reluctant to attempt to register and vote. Unfortunately, reliable and complete data on the incidence of racial violence in southern counties are hard to come by. Most compilations of such incidents are based upon newspaper accounts, probably adequate for the larger cities but spotty in their coverage of racial violence in rural areas. They are confined to overt acts and rarely deal with threats or the subtler forms of intimidation. Two such compilations will be used in this analysis, the Tuskegee Institute's records of lynchings in the South between 1900 and 1931 and the Southern Regional Council's listing of acts of violence occurring between 1955 and 1960 in the wake of *Brown v. Board of Education.*[20]

Racial violence in the South during these two periods was rather different. Lynching was most common ". . . in the newer and more sparsely settled portions of the South, where cultural and economic institutions [were] least stable and officers of the law [were] farthest apart, poorest paid, and most dependent upon local sentiment."[21] Victims were almost invariably Negro and the cause of the mob action was an alleged crime by an individual Negro against a white person. In 1930, for example, the alleged reasons for that year's 21 lynchings were: murder (5), rape (8), robbery or theft

---

[20]The Tuskegee data are reported, by county, in Charles S. Johnson (ed.), *Statistical Atlas of Southern Counties* (Chapel Hill, University of North Carolina Press, 1941). The reports on racial violence, 1955-59, may be found in *Intimidation, Reprisal, and Violence in the South's Racial Crisis,* published jointly by American Friends Service Committee, Southeastern Office, High Point, N. C.; National Council of Churches of Christ, Department of Racial and Cultural Relations, New York; Southern Regional Council, Atlanta, Georgia, 1960.

[21]A. F. Raper, *The Tragedy of Lynching* (Chapel Hill, University of North Carolina Press, 1933), p. 1.

(3), attempted rape (2) and bombing a house (1). No crime at all was alleged in the case of two lynchings.[22]

The new style racial violence since the *Brown* decision tends rather to occur in urban areas (Figure 2). Most recent violence has been triggered by collective efforts by Negroes to take advantage of their newly found legal rights. The targets of white violence and destruction are frequently institutions — churches, schools, temples — and include presumed white sympathizers toward the Negro cause. (Of the 29 persons reported shot and wounded in racial incidents between 1955 and 1960, 11 were white. All six fatalities, however, were Negro.[23]) Counties with high rates of lynching

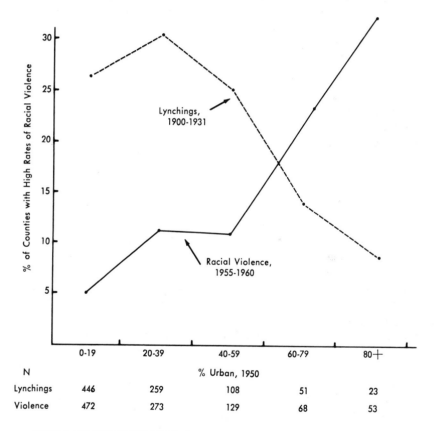

FIGURE 2. PER CENT OF COUNTIES WITH HIGH RACIAL VIOLENCE, BY PER CENT URBAN, 1950

---

[22]*Ibid.*, p. 4.
[23]*Intimidation, Reprisal, and Violence*, p. 15.

in the early decades of this century have *not* been the areas with the most spectacular incidents of racial violence in recent years. Most of the new-style racial violence has occurred in areas with peaceful race relations in the past, at least insofar as lynchings are concerned (Table VI).

Table VII presents the mean percentage of the voting age Negro population registered to vote in southern counties, according to their rate of lynchings from 1900 to 1931 and to the amount of racial violence reported to have occurred in them from 1955 to 1960.

TABLE VI

RELATIONSHIP BETWEEN LYNCHING RATE, 1900-31, AND ACTS OF RACIAL VIOLENCE, 1955-60, FOR SOUTHERN COUNTIES

Lynchings Per 100,000 Total Population, 1900-31	Acts of Racial Violence, 1955-60				Number of Counties
	None	1 or 2	3+	Total	
	%	%	%	%	
0–9	88	9	3	100	656
10–19	90	10	0	100	144
20–29	98	2	0	100	39
30–39	95	5	0	100	19
40 +	100	0	0	100	30

The very few counties with both a history of lynching *and* recent racial violence have low rates of Negro registration, about 7 per cent. The next lowest group of southern counties are those with generally peaceful race relations, and the highest rates of Negro registration are found in counties with either heavy lynching in the past or present day racial incidents, but not both. This same rank order of counties is maintained when we control for 21 socio-economic variables by examining Negro voter registration residuals (Table VIII). The counties with both high lynching and high contemporary racial violence scores have about 11 percentage points fewer Negroes registered to vote than we would expect on the basis of their social and economic characteristics. Those with either some contemporary racial violence or a history of lynching have about 2 or 3 percentage points more registered Negroes than anticipated, while the counties with little or no violence have about the expected rate.

Apparently, to speculate a bit, race violence nowadays must be extremely massive indeed in order to have a depressing effect on Negro voter registration. Save in the most violent one or two per cent of southern counties, racial violence seems to be more an indication of white weakness than of strength. Far lower rates of Negro registration are found in counties with little if any racial violence. Here Negro subordination may be so total that

TABLE VII

MEAN PER CENT OF VOTING AGE NEGROES REGISTERED TO VOTE IN SOUTHERN COUNTIES, BY AMOUNT OF RACIAL VIOLENCE

Lynching Rate, 1900-31	Amount of Racial Violence, 1955-60					
	None		Some		Total	
Low	14.8%	(576)	29.3%	(80)	16.1%	(656)
High	26.6%	(216)	6.9%	(16)	25.3%	(232)
Total	18.1%	(792)	25.6%	(96)		

Notes: A "low" lynching rate is less than 10 lynchings per 100,000 population in 1930. The numbers in parentheses are the total number of counties upon which the percentages have been based.

TABLE VIII

MEAN NEGRO VOTER REGISTRATION RESIDUALS OF SOUTHERN COUNTIES, BY AMOUNT OF RACIAL VIOLENCE

Lynching Rate, 1900-31	Amount of Racial Violence, 1955-60					
	None		Some		Total	
Low	− 0.2	(575)	+ 2.0	(80)	+ 0.1	(655)
High	+ 3.2	(216)	− 11.3	(16)	+ 2.2	(232)
Total	+ 0.7	(791)	− 0.1	(96)		

Notes: A "low" lynching rate is less than 10 lynchings per 100,000 population in 1930. The numbers in parentheses are the total number of counties upon which the percentages have been based. No residual figure was obtained for one county for which the percentage of voting age Negroes registered to vote was not known. Hence this table is based on one less case than Table VII.

violence is not required to keep the Negro "in his place" and outside of the polling booths. Racial violence, standing alone, is overestimated as an inhibition to Negro political participation. Save in a tiny fraction of southern counties, its effects, if any, seem to be to contribute to Negro militancy, solidarity, and political activity — to say nothing of Justice Department investigations.

Summary and Conclusions

In this paper we have attempted to determine the relationships between political and legal factors and variations in the rate of Negro voter registration in the southern states. In order to control the substantial effects of social and economic factors on Negro registration, we employed a multiple-regression equation containing the typical relationships between 21 social and economic variables and Negro registration rates in the counties of the region. From this equation, we predicted what the Negro registration rate in each county ought to be on the basis of its social and economic structure alone. Variations of the actual rate above and below this predicted figure — residuals expressed in percentage points — were viewed as largely the result of political and legal variations from county to county within the South.[24]

The most important political and legal fact about the South is its division into 11 states. The counties of some states have far higher average rates of Negro voter registration than they ought to have on the basis of their social and economic characteristics, while others are far below the predicted levels. The range in the residuals between the highest (Tennessee) and lowest (Mississippi) states amounts almost to 50 percentage points. No other political factor examined is nearly so important. On the other hand, the meaning of these figures is not particularly clear until we probe salient features of the formal and informal political systems of the states.

Three such factors were found to have a moderate relationship with Negro voter registration rates. These were formal voter requirements (the range of residuals was 28.6 percentage points), state factional systems (24.4 percentage point range), and the amount and kind of racial organizations in the counties (21.9 percentage point range).

Two other political factors — the extent of partisan competition and of racial violence in southern counties — had very small relationships with Negro voter registration rates.

The analysis up to this point thus provides some ranking in relative importance of the various political and legal factors we have been able to consider. But it does not tell us the relative importance of these political and legal factors, taken together, in comparison with the social and economic factors considered in our earlier article.

From that study we reported, as noted, that the multiple correlation between all 21 social and economic variables and Negro registration was .53, which means that they explain about 28 per cent (R^2) of the variation in Negro registration. If we add 10 political variables[25] to the equation and calculate the multiple correlation between all 31 variables — socio-economic

---

[24]These variations are, of course, also the result of chance factors and of the fact that the 21 social and economic variables do not reflect all of the complex social and economic realities of the world. Moreover, the 21 measures we did employ were not themselves perfect measures of the variables they represented.

[25]These 10 political variables are (1) states; (2) per cent of presidential vote States' Rights, 1948; per cent of presidential vote Republican (3) in 1928, (4) in 1948 and (5) in 1956; (6) per cent of vote Republican in race for statewide office in year of highest Republican vote, 1950-59; (7) presence or absence of Negro race organization in county; (8) presence or absence of white race organization in county; (9) presence or absence of desegregated school in county; and (10) number of incidents of racial violence in county.

plus political — we obtain a multiple correlation of .70, which explains about 50 per cent of the southwide variation in Negro registration figures. The addition of the political variables almost doubles the explanatory power of the analysis. Insofar as statistical analysis will answer such a broad and complex question, it would appear that political variables are nearly as important as socio-economic factors in explaining Negro registration in the South.

Part 4

Negro Politics in the South

V. O. Key, Jr. has written, "In its grand outlines the politics of the South revolves around the position of the Negro."[1] This has meant in practice a politics of race. At the base of Southern white politics, the greatest single goal and effort has been to keep the races separate. Accordingly, the majority effort has been made to proscribe the political arena to Negro citizens. Given this kind of framework, the question which may be rightfully asked is: what can we say about Negro political response — the politics of the Negro in the South — to this challenge?

Negro political activity in the South has grown rapidly since the Supreme Court decision in 1944 holding the white primary invalid.[2] This activity

[1]*Southern Politics in State and Nation,* (New York: Vintage Books, 1949), p. 5.
[2]*Smith v. Allwright,* 321 U.S. 649 (1944).

235

and its growth has been irregular over the South. In 1947, estimates of Negroes registered to vote ranged from a low of one per cent in Mississippi to a high of twenty-five per cent in Tennessee. Five years later, in these same states estimates ranged from four per cent to twenty-seven per cent respectively. By 1960 these same states had registrations ranging from six per cent to forty-eight per cent. With the emergence of Goldwaterism in American politics in 1964, Negro registration rates were 6.7 per cent in Mississippi and 69.4 per cent in Tennessee.

This section is an effort to answer some of the "whys" in uneven Negro political activity and to place in perspective the initiatives and responses of the Negro in the South to a political system which has had as its highest value his exclusion.

Professor Everett Carll Ladd, Jr., in a chapter from his book, *Negro Political Leadership in the South,* describes the overall place of Negroes in the Southern political process. One of the recurring themes in Negro political behavior, namely, Negro powerlessness before World War II and Negro migration out of the South and the acquisition of power since that migration, is succinctly stated here. This selection is followed by Professor Hugh Price's "The Negro and Florida Politics, 1944-1954" which carefully discusses the differential impact of urban and rural living on Negro participation.

The extent of political participation by Negroes in the South is often influenced by economic, political, and cultural arrangements of the community as well as by the extent of its urbanness or ruralness. Birmingham, Alabama, for example, is a very urban community; yet Negroes experience a great deal of hostility when they attempt to participate in the political process. In short, commonplace sociological understandings about urban community behavior do not always hold, especially in the South, where Negroes are involved. In the third selection reprinted in this section, Professors Clubok, De Grove, and Farris show how a complex of factors coincide either to vitiate or complement sociological truisms. The development of different economic, political, and social patterns determine the development of various majority-minority relations in the community which in turn influence Negro registration, voter turnout, and the gains derived from political participation.

It has long been accepted that participation in groups and group life has a decided impact on political behavior.[3] In the fourth selection, Professors McConaughy and Gauntlett describe the impact of organization membership on Negro political participation in one southern state.

---

[3]See, for example, Robert E. Lane, *Political Life: Why People Get Involved in Politics,* (New York: The Free Press of Glencoe), chap. 14; James C. Davies, *Human Nature in Politics,* (New York: John Wiley and Sons, 1963), chapters 5 and 6; Nelson W. Polsby, Robert A. Dentler, and Paul A. Smith, *Politics and Social Life: An Introduction to Political Behavior,* (Boston: Houghton-Mifflin Company, 1963), chapter 3.

Negro Politics in the South: An Overview

Everett Carll Ladd, Jr.

In the South the Negro's person and property are practically subject to the whim of any white person who wishes to take advantage of him or to punish him for any real or fancied wrongdoing or 'insult.' A white man can steal from or maltreat a Negro in almost any way without fear of reprisal, because the Negro cannot claim the protection of the police or courts, and personal vengeance on the part of the offended Negro usually results in organized retaliation in the form of bodily injury (including lynching), home burning or banishment. . . . Physical violence and threats against personal security do not, of course, occur to every Negro every day. . . . But violence may occur at any time, and it is the fear of it as much as violence itself which creates the injustice and the insecurity.

Gunnar Myrdal, *An American Dilemma*[1]

The one word which better than any other describes the position of Negro Americans in the South from the 1890's until the outbreak of World War II

Reprinted from Everett Carll Ladd, Jr., *Negro Political Leadership in the South*, pp. 17-47. Copyright 1966, Cornell University. Used by permission of Cornell University Press.
[1]New York, 1944, p. 530.

is *powerless*. In 1900 the nearly eight million Negroes in the states of the old Confederacy had no voice in the important social, economic, and political decisions which affected them and the life and future of their region. And the South which Negro G.I.'s left in 1942 was not very different. The symptoms of this powerlessness were everywhere. Negroes were totally excluded from positions of decision making in all institutions which served the entire, as opposed to solely the Negro, population. All public facilities in the region, including city parks and playgrounds, theaters, hotels, and restaurants were rigidly segregated — as was, of course, the entire school system. The disenfranchisement of Negroes was virtually complete and was accomplished through such practices and vehicles as the white primary, the poll tax, a biased application of voting requirements, and a variety of pressures directed at discouraging Negroes from even attempting to participate in electoral politics.[2] When the United States entered World War II, only 5 per cent of her Negro citizens in the South were registered. In only a few localities — principally in cities of Tennessee, North Carolina, and Virginia — was voting by significant numbers of Negroes accepted. And even in these cities, local Negro organizations often played ball with the dominant white political organization as a price for the privilege of voting.[3] Or — as in Nashville, Charlotte, and Raleigh — the Negro vote lacked solidarity (primarily because no candidate would make any significant appeals or promises to it), and splintered much as the white electorate.[4]

The worst expression of this powerlessness, however, was the vulnerability of Negroes to assaults on their personal safety and well-being. The introductory quotation from Myrdal's *Dilemma* in no way exaggerates this vulnerability. Because in large parts of the region the Negro could not expect white law enforcement officials to protect him and because courts of law were in fact (as far as he was concerned) instruments for maintaining white

---

[2]Since most of the South in this period was solidly Democratic, with the only genuine contests for public office occurring in the nominating primaries of that party, the exclusion of Negroes from membership in the Democratic party was a very convenient means of excluding them from politics. After two decades of litigation, the Supreme Court condemned finally the white primary in the landmark *Smith v. Allwright* decision. 321 U.S. 649 (1944). The Court ruled that the conduct of a primary election under no circumstances can be considered purely private activity. Because of the central position of primaries in the electoral process, state delegation to a party of the power to determine qualifications for primaries is the delegation of a state function, thus making the party's action state action. And the Fifteenth Amendment, of course, forbids the states to deny any citizen the right to vote "on account of race, color, or previous condition of servitude."

[3]The late E. H. Crump, the political boss who ruled Memphis for more than a quarter of a century until his death in 1954, used the Negro vote to keep his candidates in office. V. O. Key notes that local outposts of the Byrd organization in certain Virginia cities used the Negro vote in a similar manner (*Southern Politics in State and Nation* [New York, 1950], p. 649).

[4]*Ibid.*, p. 649.

supremacy, he frequently had to endure whatever harassments and brutalities which whites chose to mete out. At least 3,275 Negroes were lynched in the American South between 1882 and 1936.⁵ We have no way of determining how many Negroes met other forms of violent death at the hands of whites in this period. And as Myrdal pointed out, although violence, intimidations, and frauds occurred only sporadically, the fears created were ever-present. The old biracial system stood as full testimony to the powerlessness of southern Negroes. Encompassing all the elements cited above, and more, this was a pervasive pattern of discrimination, rooted in law and custom, and enforced by legal and extralegal violence. It assigned one position in society to whites, and another — distinctly subordinate and inferior — to Negroes. This biracial system is now disintegrating. Discrimination remains, but not the system which until two decades ago stood securely as part of the "southern way of life."

To understand what has happened, we must look to several central precipitating factors: changes in the definition(s) held by white Americans of the proper or legitimate pattern of race relations; changes in the expectations of Negro Americans and in certain basic demographic facts of southern Negro life; and, resulting from these, changes in the power position of southern Negroes.

Historically many white Americans have objected to the flagrant injustices within the old biracial system — lynchings, the appalling inferiority of Negro schools, economic exploitation. But until the last two decades the legitimacy of the system itself was not seriously challenged by any powerful segment of white America. The challenge has developed within the last twenty years, and it has two main bases: (1) that the biracial system is without intellectual or moral justification (the ideological basis), and (2) that however right or wrong it may be it is not expedient (the political basis). These obviously overlap and interact, but we will not attempt to untangle the "chicken or the egg" causality question.

Four factors seem to be particularly important in explaining the erosion of the ideological defense of segregation. White (and Negro) Americans were long treated to a view of Africa as one massive steaming jungle where naked black savages were regularly made fools of by one naked white man called Tarzan. This "Tarzan image" of the black man was widely disseminated, and it reinforced the biracial system. It strengthened the view of the Negro as little more than a beast, distinctly inferior to white *Bwanas*. And it made the forced move of Negroes from their homeland to the United States appear a distinctly liberating experience. But in the postwar period we have witnessed the emergence of independent black African nations. Whatever one thinks

⁵E. Franklin Frazier, *The Negro in the United States* (New York, 1957), p. 160.

of Tshombe and Kenyatta, they obviously are quite above the savages Tarzan regularly outwitted and overpowered. They are *men*.

The falsity of the charge that Negroes are biologically inferior is now clearer than ever before. The Negro middle class is much larger. The accomplishments of Negro Americans are much more impressive and better publicized. Social prestige is affected by the roles which individuals play, and white America slowly is becoming accustomed to the performance of Negroes in roles far above those which have been theirs historically.

In addition, within the United States, the cumulative effect of social science research has been felt. As late as the 1920's, the biracial system was not seriously challenged by legitimate scholarship. The weight of the scholarship of the last three decades, however, has precluded any intellectually respectable defense of the system. Prejudices remain strong, of course, but they are now *known* as prejudices rather than as *facts*. Moreover, even among the less well educated there is recognition that the "environment" may have a good bit to do with the way people are. The popular statement of Social Darwinism — that the good guys will win, that the virtuous will be rewarded, that the industrious and talented will be served; and concomitantly, that those who are not getting along well are receiving their just deserts — clearly has been weakened, though certainly not replaced, by the social science based concept of social guilt or responsibility.

Finally — and this is a product of the first three factors — there is the factor of numbers. Two decades ago proponents of the old biracial system could be confident of the rightness of their stand. Who was questioning it? Today, they find themselves attacked on all sides — from other countries, by northern whites, by Negroes North and South, and even by a small but growing number of southern whites. The southern white majority is acutely sensitive to this, and we should not be deceived by all the brave talk that the rest of the world can be damned. We have only to note how hungrily the white South devoured Carleton Putnam's very meager offering, *Race and Reason: A Yankee View,* to see how starved for outside approbation it is. Beliefs are strongest when they are uncontradicted. The belief in Negro inferiority is being contradicted with constantly increasing power. For all these reasons, the white South is much less certain of the legitimacy of its cause than it was twenty years ago.

The old biracial system is also under attack for political reasons. Some Americans seem more sensitive to the charge that the system is "helping the Communists" than to the criticism of segregation as ethically wrong and intellectually unjustifiable. Our position as a world leader together with the challenge of Communism has made segregation a distinct embarrassment. But purely internal considerations are of much greater importance. The mass migration of Negroes to the urban North in the last five decades has helped persuade increasing numbers of northern politicians to be more solicitous of Negro interests.[6] More than 3.5 million Negroes were registered to vote outside the South in the 1964 presidential election, and these voters were strategically concentrated in the major cities of the large industrial states:

California	550,000	Pennsylvania	412,000
Ohio	298,300	New Jersey	80,000
Illinois	540,000	Michigan	353,520[7]
New York	580,000		

In 1960, the 6.2 million Negroes living in these states constituted 8.1 per cent of the total population of these states. Negroes make up at least 10 per cent of the population in fifty-seven congressional districts outside the South. The migration has, in brief, added enormously to the strategic distribution of the Negro population in the country, and must be considered in any explanation of the factors committing the federal government to a policy of eradicating certain forms of discriminatory treatment in the South.

And there have been important changes within the South. The establishment of branch plants of northern corporations and a consequent influx of Yankees, industrialization and urbanization of the region, and, again in a circular fashion, the increasing economic and political power of southern Negroes have brought the Negro a motley collection of allies.[8] Businessmen not infrequently have used their influence to bring about a limited accession to Negro demands, probably in no small part because continued resistance would mean racial tension — bad for business. Atlanta's experience remains the best illustration of this. Negro voting on a fairly large scale in some parts of the South has made it good politics for white politicians to avoid an anti-Negro position even if it is still bad politics to be identified as pro-Negro.

---

[6]The scope and timing of the Negro migration is indicated by the percentage of the total Negro population of the United States living in the eleven states of the old Confederacy in selected years:

1830	92.8	1930	78.7
1870	90.6	1960	52.3
1920	85.2	1964 (est.)	49.0

[7]These are estimates furnished by the NAACP in a report issued on October 9, 1964, and again — in somewhat revised form — on October 31, 1964.

[8]Northerners moving South with branch plants rarely crusade against "the southern way of life." Many, perhaps most, sympathize with the white southerners, but they are not wedded to the traditions, values, and style of the old biracial system. Confronted with the choice of obeying a court order or closing the schools, transplanted northerners generally favor the former. In this way they have become allies of sorts of southern Negroes. Some, of course, bring genuinely liberal attitudes.

The action of the United States Supreme Court represents a unique blend of the ideological and the political aspects of the challenge within white America to the legitimacy of the biracial system. The frontal assault by the Court in the last two decades on that system reflects the growing conviction that segregation is wrong. It is also true that the Court, a political institution, has responded to a new alignment of political power.

The Supreme Court has also contributed to the rise in Negro expectations. By placing the structure of American law against the institutions of white supremacy, the Court has encouraged large numbers of southern Negroes to expect that the American democracy can give them much more than they have been getting.

It seems safe to say that Negro Americans never regarded the old biracial system as right or natural. But it seems equally clear that until two decades ago few saw any possibility that things could be much different in the short run. Their expectations precluded any assault on the system. Negroes wore the mask of passivity to survive through a period in which no significant segment of white America gave aid and comfort to any attack on white supremacy. There has been, then, a revolution in expectations. In discussing the relationship of economic development to democracy, S. M. Lipset makes the point that "stable poverty" does not produce pressures for change. On the contrary, "individuals whose experience limits their significant communications and interactions to others on the same level as themselves will . . . be more conservative than people who may be better off but who have been exposed to the possibilities of securing a better way of life. The dynamic in the situation would seem to be *exposure to a better way of life.*"[9] And Marx, with characteristic insight, observed:

> A house may be large or small; as long as the surrounding houses are equally small it satisfies all social demands for a dwelling. But let a palace arise beside the little house, and it shrinks from a little house to a hut.[10]

Negro Americans have been exposed to the palace which is full acceptance in the American democracy. The central element in their exposure to a better way of life is not, of course, simply seeing it. The peasant in 1700 could *see* the palaces of the nobles. What he could not see was the possibility of the life therein *ever being his.* The "new Negro" expects to get some of the

[9]S. M. Lipset, *Political Man* (Garden City, N.Y., 1960), p. 63. The italics are mine.
[10]Karl Marx, "Wage-Labor and Capital," in Marx and Engels, *Selected Works* (Moscow, 1958), I, 93.

things which his father believed beyond reach.[11] All of the changes which have led a segment of white America to question and in some cases to actively oppose the old biracial system have increased Negro expectations that the system can and will be altered in their interest. The change in white attitudes has resulted in a weaker application of the sanctions — formal and informal, legal and extralegal — which sustained the system.

Accompanying these developments, and essential as a basis for the revolution, are certain long-term changes of a demographic nature. The level of those skills necessary for significant and continuous political participation has risen steadily in the southern Negro population. Specifically, southern Negroes have become better educated. The pool of leadership talent is bigger. Also, their economic position has been strengthened. Particularly important here is the creation of a Negro middle class economically independent of whites — dentists, optometrists, lawyers, and so on, in addition to ministers. The urbanization of the Negro population *within the South* has played a part. Certainly the revolution could never have occurred in the kind of scattered, rural population that southern Negroes formed in 1910.

Together, these factors — the ideological and political challenges within white America, the marked increase in Negro expectations, and the demographic changes — have served to extend and expand Negro political power. It should be clear, of course, that Negro political power itself has contributed to the establishment of the conditions which have furthered it: changes in each area set the stage for further changes in the others — a snowball effect. One does not need to spend many days in a southern city in which Negroes make up 25 per cent of the electorate — that is, of those registered and voting — to see that the behavior and to a lesser but still significant degree the attitudes of whites become more permissive when Negroes actually possess

---

[11]See, for example, William Brink and Louis Harris, *The Negro Revolution in America* (New York, 1964), p. 238. They wanted to know whether Negroes expected to find their situation better, worse, or about the same five years from now.

	Total rank and file %	Leaders %
Pay		
Better off	67	81
Worse off	2	7
About the same	14	11
Not sure	17	1
Housing accommodations		
Better off	62	52
Worse off	2	4
About the same	24	44
Not sure	12	—

significant sanctions. (The result may be exactly the opposite when there is merely an unrealized potential for significant political power — as in Mississippi.) "Ideology," Mr. Dooley might have said, "follows th' iliction returns." This aside, the revolution in American race relations must finally be understood as a revolution in political power.

Evidence of a strengthened political position is everywhere. In September 1964 the Reverend K. L. Buford and Dr. Stanley Hugh Smith won positions on the Tuskegee, Alabama, city council, and in doing so became the first Negroes elected to public office over white opponents in Alabama in almost a century. Three out of every ten registered voters in Winston-Salem are Negroes; and in three successive elections between 1957 and 1961, the victorious mayoralty candidate received a distinct minority of the white vote. Negroes throughout the South, pushed on by their fears of Goldwater, recorded electoral advances in the 1964 elections. November 1964 saw election results in the South that were — from a civil rights standpoint — mixed, because a white backlash produced in some sections an unusually large and anti-Negro white vote. Turnout in the five states of the deep South increased from 2.5 million in 1960 to 3.5 million in 1964, and analysis makes it clear that Goldwater-supporting whites accounted for much of this increase. Still, it is also clear that Negroes themselves registered impressive gains in electoral participation. Between 1952 and 1962, Negro registration increased by only about 400,000, from a little more than 1,000,000 to 1,414,000. By the Fall of 1964, however, 2,250,000 Negroes were registered in the eleven states of the old Confederacy. And the largest part of this increase was recorded in the eight months preceding the November 1964 election. The rapidity of the expansion is indicated by the data in Table 1.

It is clear that if all votes cast by Negroes were simply subtracted, Johnson would have lost Florida, Virginia, Tennessee, and Arkansas. And the result in North Carolina would have been very close. In Florida, for example, the Democratic nominee won by only 37,800 votes, while an estimated 211,000 Negro voters gave him between 97 and 99 per cent of their votes. (It should be recognized, however, that if the race issue had been kept out of the campaign, Johnson probably would have won all eleven southern states by landslide majorities. The race issue was the one factor producing mass defections from the first southerner to occupy the White House in almost a century.)

The higher turnout of registered Negro voters was perhaps the most impressive single aspect of the generally heightened Negro political participation in 1964. Estimates of the number of Negroes voting November 3, 1964, necessarily are not precise, and state-by-state estimates vary greatly — more one suspects than actual performance — from a high of 86 per cent in Texas to a low (excluding Alabama and Mississippi) of 61 per cent in North Carolina. We do have *precise* data, however, for certain cities. In Winston-

TABLE 1

EXPANSION AND DISTRIBUTION OF NEGRO REGISTRATION IN ELEVEN SOUTHERN STATES*

State	Negroes of voting age	Negro† registration Feb. 1964	% of voting-age Negroes† registered Feb. 1964	Negro† registration Nov. 1964	% of voting-age Negroes† registered Nov. 1964
Texas	649,512	300,000	46.1	375,000	57.7
Tenn.	313,873	202,974	64.6	220,000	70.0
Florida	470,261	213,128	45.5	299,964	63.8
N.C.	550,929	233,773	42.3	276,000	50.1
Virginia	436,720	108,312	24.8	200,000	45.7
Arkansas	192,626	80,000	41.5	90,000	46.7
S.C.	371,104	111,628	30.0	181,050	48.7
Georgia	612,910	221,919	36.2	285,000	46.4
La.	514,589	162,084	31.4	184,000	35.7
Alabama	481,320	90,000	18.6	111,000	23.0
Miss.	422,256	28,000	6.6	28,000	6.6
Totals	5,016,100	1,751,813	34.9%	2,250,014	44.9

*Data on the voting-age population in each state are from the *U.S. Census of Population, 1960.* The Southern Regional Council furnished the estimate of the number of Negroes registered as of February 1964. The estimates for November 1964 were released by the National Association for the Advancement of Colored People. The Southern Regional Council estimated that 2,164,200 Negroes were registered for the November elections in the South, 86,000 less than the NAACP estimate of 2,250,014 cited here. Precise figures, of course, are not available, but these estimates are broadly reliable.
†The figures given for Texas are for "nonwhites" rather than for Negroes.

Salem, for example, over 80 per cent of the registered Negroes went to the polls and cast valid ballots for President, a turnout far in excess of the highest ever before achieved. At least 70 per cent of the 2.25 million Negro voters in the South cast valid ballots in the 1964 Presidential election.

Negro candidates have continued to have relatively little success winning elections. Only three were elected to southern state legislatures in 1964, two in Georgia (one the incumbent Leroy Johnson) and one in Tennessee (the first to serve in that state's legislature since Reconstruction). In Forsyth County, where Winston-Salem is located, a Negro candidate for the state legislature, the Reverend William Crawford, was defeated by a Republican opponent although his two white Democratic colleagues won by substantial margins. Crawford's defeat is important because it illustrates the very great obstacles still confronting Negro candidates seeking city- or county-wide (to say nothing of state-wide) office in the South — Negro candidates, that is, who must win the votes of substantial numbers of whites. Although the elections of 1962, 1963, and 1964 saw for the first time a sizable scattering

of Negro candidates for city councils, county school boards, and state legislatures, few won who had to depend on white support. With few exceptions,
Negro officeholders in the South represent the relatively few electoral districts
which are overwhelmingly Negro.

The election of Negroes to public office in the old Confederacy is important and notable because for a full six decades from the 1890's to the 1950's
almost *no* Negroes were elected. But the drama of the "first Negro elected"
is deceiving. Certainly the most important results of the heightened participation in electoral politics lie elsewhere — in helping to defeat white candidates clearly anti-Negro, in making it good politics for white officials to meet
at least some of the political demands of the Negro citizenry, and, more
broadly, in changing the climate of race relations. A group with the kind of
sanction which large-scale voting provides generally will not be exploited to
the same degree as one essentially powerless. Voting has meant that some
streets in Negro neighborhoods have been paved, some Negro policemen
have been appointed, schools in Negro areas have received more funds, recreational facilities in the ghetto have been improved, and the city fathers
have shown somewhat more respect. There have been few miracles, but substantial gains have and will continue to be recorded. As the Southern Regional
Council put it in a recent report:

> Effective Negro registration and participation in elections is the best
> assurance that race will be eliminated as a politically profitable issue
> . . . and that all the southern states will be freed from the demagogic
> appeals to racism.[12]

Gains in Negro registration and voting have occurred unevenly. The concerted efforts of civil rights workers in the Mississippi "Freedom Summer"
project of 1964 added few Negro voters to the rolls in that state. But this
failure must be put in perspective. Wiley Branton, director of the Voter Education Project of the Southern Regional Council, reported that voter registration efforts for the twenty-one months up to December 31, 1963, succeeded
in expanding the Negro electorate in Mississippi by only 3,228. Twenty-eight
thousand Negroes were registered in Mississippi for the 1964 elections, only
a few thousand more than were on the books in 1960. Mississippi, in short,
has successfully resisted all attempts to build a substantial Negro electorate
out of the state's 422,000 voting-age Negroes — who make up 36 per cent
of the total number meeting the age requirement for voting.

Registration efforts have been far more successful in urban areas than in
the rural South, both in terms of the numbers registered and the uses to
which the registered electorate is put. The Director of the Voter Education

---

[12]Report released November 15, 1964: "What Happened in the South?"

Project estimated that 90 per cent of the 265,000 Negroes who registered between April 1962 and December 1963 were urban dwellers.[13] Sixty thousand Negroes are on the rolls in Memphis, Tennessee, and are an important force in the city's politics. But efforts to register Negroes in the nearby rural Tennessee counties of Fayette and Haywood have met determined resistance.[14] While it should be noted that these Western Tennessee counties border on Mississippi and have Negro majorities (Fayette is 68 per cent Negro, Haywood 61 per cent) and hence that white resistance is particularly strong, Negroes throughout the rural South are far more vulnerable to economic sanctions and to threats to life and liberty. Rural Negro populations are more widely dispersed and hence harder to organize. They are poorer. And, in general, they have been drained of their most talented and best educated members, and hence do not have human resources comparable to those of urban populations. Once registered, Negroes in rural areas have a much more difficult task making their votes count.

We can profitably examine the basic demographic facts of life of Fayette County Negroes, because they unfortunately are essentially similar to those of rural Negro populations throughout the South.[15] The median age of Fayette's Negro males in 1960 was 16.3 years, against 27.4 for white males in the county, 28.0 for all Tennessee residents, and 33.1 for New York residents. This indicates, of course, the extent to which Negroes are fleeing the rural Tennessee county. In 1959, when the median family income for the United States as a whole was $5,660, for Tennessee $3,949, and for Memphis Negroes $2,666, the median family income of Fayette Negroes was $854. More than two-thirds (72.7 per cent) of all Negro-occupied housing units in the county were described by the 1960 *Census of Housing* as either *deteriorating* or *dilapidated*. Only 10.4 per cent of the units had all plumbing facilities. Fayette Negroes are particularly disadvantaged in their educational background. The chasm between Charlotte, North Carolina, Negroes, 9.1 per cent of whom in 1960 had some college education and half of whom had at least an eighth-grade education — close to the average for the urban South — and Fayette Negroes, only 2.3 per cent of whom ever attended anything called a college and half of whom had a fifth-grade education or less (and that in one-room Negro schools) is wide indeed. And these figures become even

---

[13]*New York Times,* Feb. 17, 1964.
[14]In May 1959 only 58 Negroes were registered in Fayette County. Shortly thereafter, however, 1,500 Negroes were registered as a result of a local drive and the intervention under the 1957 civil rights act by the Justice Department. Whites then retaliated. Many Negroes lost their jobs. A list of those who had registered was circulated, and those on the list found their credit cut off, loans called. The "offending" Negroes found themselves unable to buy even the necessities of life. These retaliatory actions were ended only when the Justice Department intervened vigorously. The situation was the same in Haywood County.
[15]The source for the data which follows is the *U.S. Census of Population, 1960.*

more striking when one remembers that urban-South Negroes themselves are seriously disadvantaged. Add to these grinding deprivations the wide dispersal of Fayette Negroes throughout the county, the relative lack of transportation, the absence of the anonymity which the ghetto provides, and the greater strength of virulently anti-Negro attitudes in the county's homogeneous white population, and one has gone far toward explaining the fact that despite concerted efforts to register Negroes between 1959 and 1964, only 2,000 — fewer than 30 per cent of those of voting age — were on the rolls for the 1964 county election. After five years of continuous work in a county in which nearly 70 per cent of the population is Negro, the candidates for county office supported by the Negro citizenry were defeated in August 1964 by 2-1 margins. Such are the political problems of Negroes in much of the rural South.

The cities, and particularly those of the rim-South, are a different political world. Attaching Negro support to a candidate in Winston-Salem or Jacksonville is not automatically a "kiss of death." The "Negroes' candidate" will lose white support as a result of his association with Negro interests, but he will gain votes as well. Whether he will be damaged or helped depends on other aspects of his base of support, his personal attractiveness, and the specific time and setting for his candidacy. But certainly being anti-Negro is not a magical formula with which a candidate can automatically gain victory.

Negro voting in the South frequently has been bloc voting, with landslide proportions going to the favored candidate. We should not be surprised, given the overriding importance of race advancement, that when one candidate can be readily identified as more responsive to the interests of Negroes, large numbers of Negro voters will support him. The Negro voter cannot afford the luxury of being cross-pressured. There is no *series* of issues and orientations to make conflicting demands on his loyalties. What will the candidate do for the race? All else can and must be subordinated to this. Still, the cohesion frequently attained is impressive, and particularly so because of the fairly low level of political awareness of many Negro voters. Richard Bolling, the liberal Missouri Congressman, was opposed in his district's 1964 Democratic primary by a coalition of several Kansas City Democratic party factions. Bolling's district is 17.4 per cent Negro. A number of influential Negro ward and precinct leaders in Kansas City were allied with the anti-Bolling factions. They believed — as have Congressman William Dawson and members of his Negro Democratic organization in Chicago — that they had a stake in the success of the party "machine."[16] But although Negro voters followed these ward leaders in local races, they voted overwhelmingly for Bolling. The

---

[16]This development — Negro politicians who are at times willing to subordinate immediate race interests to strengthen their positions in the party organization — is an important one. Thus far it is confined largely to northern and border-state cities, although it can now be found in embryonic form in certain southern cities.

heavily Negro 14th ward was carried by Mr. Bolling, 2,924 votes to 426. In short, Negro voters would not follow their politicians in rejecting a Congressman whose record as a supporter of civil rights and social welfare legislation was so strong.[17] The opposition of Negro ward and precinct leaders did not significantly reduce Bolling's strength in Negro areas, to say nothing of defeating him.

When Negro leaders are united behind a man with a good civil rights record, the cohesion of the Negro electorate approaches unanimity. Dan Moore and Richardson Preyer faced each other in the second, or runoff, Democratic primary in North Carolina in June 1964. Preyer's civil rights position from the viewpoint of Negro voters was good, that of Moore very bad. Preyer carried the Negro precincts of Winston-Salem by such margins as 778 to 1, 1,883 to 2 and 1,581 to 13.[18]

This cohesion of the Negro electorate, however, is a source of weakness as well as of strength. Politicians are able to exploit fears of Negro "bloc voting," and candidates can suffer badly in white hands when they are clearly the recipients of the "bloc" support. Richardson Preyer, although backed by Governor Terry Sanford and a fairly efficient organization, was overwhelmingly defeated by Dan Moore in the 1964 North Carolina runoff primary. I. Beverly Lake, an extreme segregationist, had been eliminated in the first primary. Preyer lost in the second because he was identified as the Negro-supported "racial liberal," while Moore wore the mantle (in the eyes of North Carolina whites) of the moderate. Negro voters, an embattled minority, necessarily and properly demonstrate cohesion. Yet the cohesion which makes them a balance of power in some races produces greater white cohesion against their favored candidates in others.

The Negro vote in the South now is largely a Democratic vote. At precisely the time Negroes are being driven from positions which they traditionally have held in southern state Republican parties they are entering in large numbers the organizational hierarchy of the Democratic party, from which historically they have been excluded throughout much of the South. Many "new" Republicans in the South, Goldwater Republicans, want a white man's party. They are not violently anti-Negro on the model of "Pitchfork Ben" Tillman or Theodore Bilbo. But they see a bright future for the Republican party in offering an alternative to Democrats unhappy about the direction of their party in recent years — particularly the direction in civil rights.[19] There are many exceptions to this. Some southern Republicans diligently court Negro support. But looking to the South as a whole, Negroes have been pushed still further into the Democratic camp by the rise of the "new" Republicans.

[17] *New York Times,* August 6, 1964.
[18] *Winston-Salem Journal,* June 28, 1964.
[19] A number of Republican leaders in North and South Carolina were interviewed in late 1962 and in 1963.

The Negro electorate in the South is not irrevocably Democratic, however; but rather potentially is highly fluid. It can be captured by any candidate who is demonstrably "better" on civil rights issues than is his opponent. Indeed, the Negro vote appears to be potentially less stable than that of virtually any other demographic group. White voters, of course, will leave their party for another if they become convinced that their interests are not finding expression. Senator Barry Goldwater, as the Republican nominee in 1964, carried 87 per cent of the vote in Mississippi — so strong was the white reaction in that state to the civil rights movement and the identification of the national Democratic party with the movement. But the "embattled" psychology of Mississippi whites is exceptional. Given the strength and persistence of party identification, it takes a crisis of major proportions to push many voters from their party home; and such crises for white voters in affluent America are few.[20] But the Negro vote exists in a state of perpetual crisis. Race advancement necessarily dominates Negro electoral participation as no issue dominates the participation of white voters. No other group ever has had to look to government for so much assistance affecting such vital interests as Negro Americans must at present.

Some observers have equated Negro loyalty to the Democratic party with that shown by "newer" ethnic groups such as Polish Americans. In fact, with the exception of a few large northern cities like Chicago, where Negro voters are thoroughly enmeshed in a Democratic electoral machine and where ghetto politics resembles that of other ethnic minorities at a similar point in their trek along what Samuel Lubell has called the "tenement trail," Negro voters are much less firmly attached to the Democratic coalition. Louis Gerson chronicled the continued efforts of Republicans in the first decade after World War II to find issues — for example, the 1952 platform promise to "repudiate all commitments contained in secret understandings such as those of Yalta which aid Communist enslavements" — that could win over Americans of east European ancestry.[21] He concluded that these efforts were largely unsuccessful. The most significant ethnic defections of the last two decades appear to be products of slow demographic changes — such as the movement to the suburbs and middle-class respectability — rather than of success in manipulating an issue. The Negro American differs from other hyphenates, then, in

---

[20]Bone and Ranney concluded that "party identification is one of the most stable of all forces in American politics. The evidence of history is that large masses of voters switch their basic loyalties only in times of great crisis" (*Politics and Voters* [New York, 1963], p. 10). Campbell *et. al.* found that 85 per cent of the "Strong Democrats" stayed with Stevenson in 1956, as did 63 per cent of the "Weak Democrats" (*The American Voter* [New York, 1960], p. 160).

[21]Louis Gerson, *The Hyphenate in Recent American Politics and Diplomacy* (Lawrence, Kans., 1964), pp. 178-220.

that he is continually involved with an issue strong enough to produce defections.

The fluidity inherent in a vote so completely dominated by a single issue of transcendent importance to the group occasionally produces very dramatic shifts in voting. Lyndon Johnson carried Negro precincts in Pine Bluff, Arkansas, with 97.8 per cent of the total vote. But Orval Faubus, the Democratic gubernatorial candidate, received only 11.5 per cent of the vote in these precincts even though he and his supporters had made some effort in this campaign to secure Negro support. Faubus' anti-Negro image had been too firmly established, while the record of his opponent (Winthrop Rockefeller) in support of Negro aspirations was generally good. In 1956 Dwight Eisenhower carried Forsyth county, North Carolina, with 64 per cent of the two-party vote. Eight years later Senator Goldwater lost the county by a narrow margin, gaining 49 per cent of the vote. The Democratic share of the county vote was 15 per cent higher in 1964 than in 1956 — 51 per cent as opposed to 36 per cent. Voting by whites was remarkably stable over the 1956, 1960, and 1964 elections, fluctuating from 34 per cent Democratic in 1956 and 1960 to approximately 40 per cent Democratic in 1964. But though Eisenhower received 47 per cent of the Negro vote in the county in 1956, Goldwater's share of this vote in 1964 was about 1 per cent.[22]

The Negro vote in recent elections has been faithfully Democratic, and certainly a large majority of Negro Americans vote for Democratic candidates when they are unable to see a decisive difference on racial questions. "Other things being equal," most Negro voters support Democrats. But Republicans who wish to tap the Negro vote, and who find it politically feasible to make a clear appeal for Negro electoral support, can get it. We should expect the southern Negro electorate to remain overwhelmingly Democratic in its voting habits, because many "new" Republicans in the South have little interest in making their party a home for the Negro. Many are committed to building a party which appeals to white disenchantment with the Negro revolution. But with a vote so responsive to even subtle differences in approach to racial questions — a vote so inherently fluid — we can expect occasional sharp fluctuations in the shares of the vote won by Republican and Democratic candidates.

The Negro electorate in the South has doubled in size, then, in the last decade. More than 40 per cent of the five million voting-age Negroes in Dixie were registered to vote in the Novemeber 1964 elections. The Negro

---

[22]The Republican share of the two-party vote for President was much lower in 1964 than in 1956 in many parts of the country, of course; but as great as was the defection of white voters — Goldwater received only 44 per cent as many votes in New England as Eisenhower did in 1956 — the *rate* of defection by whites did not approach that by Negroes.

electorate has become large enough and active enough to make itself felt in state politics — except in Alabama and Mississippi. It has become a significant electoral force in most of the urban South, if in only a few of the rural areas and small towns of the region. Expansion of this electorate will continue, although certainly at a slower rate in much of the rim-South as the core of nonregistrants is reduced to those severely disadvantaged in socio-economic terms, and hence those who, quite apart from race, tend to be the least active and conscious politically.

The Negro's access to the ballot box is still very recent, and we can expect higher levels of participation as legal barriers fall and extralegal harassment and intimidation diminish: more Negroes seeking public office; more gaining appointment to governmental boards and commissions such as school boards; and more attaining lower- and middle-level positions in city, county, and state Democratic (and in certain areas Republican) party organizations. There will be more Negro voting organizations producing larger electorates, bargaining more effectively with white candidates.

Developments in electoral politics give ample basis for both optimism and pessimism. Certainly, the level of Negro participation has increased greatly in the last decade and particularly in the last three years, and important benefits have been realized. Two decades ago Negroes were a cipher in virtually all of the South; today they are a force to be considered. Nothing should obscure the revolutionary nature of this development. But at the same time, emphasis on what has been accomplished should not obscure the fact that the political position of Negroes in the South remains very weak, and that substantial obstacles confront any attempt to strengthen it. The rapid migration of Negroes from the South continues. Only 20 per cent of the voting-age population in the eleven states of the old Confederacy is Negro, and this figure will decline further before it stabilizes. There is little prospect that Negro voters will be able to enter into an effective and continuing coalition comparable to the one which, for example, Polish Americans entered into in the urban North three decades ago. It will remain bad politics for white politicians to become associated too closely with the political interests of Negro Americans.

The expansion of Negro electoral power, so dramatic in the last decade, has meant or will soon mean for much of the South an impressive change in the style of politics. The militantly segregationist politician is becoming a figure of the past. The Negro vote is entering an evolving balance as two-party politics becomes a reality in state and local, as well as presidential, elections. But the white South is waking from its long political stupor, and large numbers of white voters will continue to oppose candidates identified with the Negro's cause, and particularly Negro candidates. Relatively few positions can be won by the Negro vote alone, and the vigorous participation by Negroes will continue to produce reactions — the backlash — in favor of racially conservative candidates. Parts of the South already have left, and many more soon will leave, an era characterized by the powerlessness of Negroes. The Negro no longer is a cipher in southern politics — no longer merely a "threat" to be evoked or a thing to be exploited. But achievement of a position as an equal participant in the American democracy belongs to another era still far distant.

The increased political power of Negroes in the South manifests itself in areas other than electoral politics. Race-advancement organizations, now infinitely better organized than two decades ago, have more members and possess a variety of techniques ranging from economic boycotts to direct action demonstrations with which to compel recognition of their interests. NAACP membership in the states of the old Confederacy has increased by 1800 per cent in the last twenty-five years. CORE chapters now are active throughout the South. The Southern Christian Leadership Conference has affiliates in many regional cities, such as the Danville (Virginia) Progressive Christian Association. Peak community organizations have been established in every southern state, and range from the very effective — such as Durham's Committee on Negro Affairs (CONA) — to the relatively weak and struggling — such as the Edenton (North Carolina) Movement or the Alabama Civic Affairs Association. The significance of the 1964 Freedom Summer in Mississippi is that the project was *possible at all.* The development observed in electoral politics has its parallel in all levels of political participation.

We have tried here to suggest something of what this revolution has meant for Negroes who must live their lives in Dixie. Comparison of the position of Negroes in Winston-Salem — a rim-South city in which Negroes are perhaps as strong politically as anywhere in the region — with that of their counterparts in Greenville — where Negroes remain far weaker politically — will provide us with a much more detailed picture of this development.

This expansion of Negro political power necessarily comes to a focus at the level of leadership, and the changes in southern Negro leadership are profound. We now hear much of a greater militancy of Negro leaders — a response viewed with both alarm and surprise by segregationists and with a curiosity tinged with concern by many other whites. But the cause of this new militancy should be obvious. Negroes now expect much more than they did two decades ago and their leaders have the power to do things which at that time would have been either impossible or highly dangerous. When we speak of a greater militancy of Negro leadership in the South we are in fact saying that within the last two decades the basis for leadership protest "outside the *status quo*" has been established. Charles Johnson was correct when he wrote in 1944 that southern Negro leadership, insofar as it protested against discrimination in work opportunities, schools, libraries, and other public facilities, did so within the "separate but equal" framework.[23] The change in the structure of race relations now permits the dominant thrust of southern Negro leadership to be against that principle and all its implications.

Negro leadership in the South from the end of Reconstruction to World War II was extremely weak. What influence Negro leaders had in this period was indirect, channeled through a white intermediary. They could not directly influence race relations. Since the Negro was not viewed as an immediate threat, Negro leaders at times enjoyed small successes with divided whites. Lewis describes the activity of Negro leaders in a small South Carolina town in the late 1940's in the appointment of a principal for a Negro school. A white school official favored one candidate, the Negroes backed another. Several Negroes spoke to influential whites in behalf of their candidate and the school official yielded. The attitude of some whites was indicated by the remarks of one: "I guess your preachers are satisfied now with the appointment."[24] But the important point is that in day-to-day activity Negro leaders in the South twenty years ago had *no other means* of attaining their objectives.

This was the period of the "Uncle Tom," the "handkerchief head," the "white man's nigger." Whites wanted passive Negroes who would be faithful servants and efficient workers. They rewarded "good" Negroes who said the right things and who showed proper respect for the system of race relations. The rewards, as in the case described by Lewis, took the form of consulting with these "good" Negroes, listening to their appeals for help, and then channeling certain tangible benefits through to the Negro community.

In this way Negro leaders were "made." Negro communities accepted these white-designated leaders because they had no choice. They needed people who could talk to influential whites and secure from them certain goods and services, and who could obtain small favors and personal protection in a white-dominated society. Negroes also accepted this white-selected political leadership because, under the old biracial system, the white community had the preponderance of status-conferral power. The Negro with access to whites gained in status in his own community (and this, in turn, furthered his position with whites). Myrdal observed that

> the Negro hates the Negro role in American society, and the Negro leader who acts out this role in public life becomes the symbol of what the Negro hates.[25]

Frazier, Myrdal, and others describe the hostility between the brown upper-strata Negroes who furnished the preponderance of accommodating leader-

---

[23]Charles Johnson, *Patterns of Negro Segregation* (New York, 1943), p. 251.
[24]Hylan Lewis, *Blackways of Kent* (Chapel Hill, 1955), p. 171.
[25]*Op. cit.*, p. 574.

ship, and the black masses. Still, southern Negroes in this period were without political power. Recognition of this lack of power, together with the low level in skills necessary for political participation and low expectations about the possibility of change, produced inactivity and passivity, and a general acceptance of the "white man's nigger."

To summarize, and this is a generalization so broad that it necessarily admits exceptions, Negro political leadership in the South in the last decades of the nineteenth century and the first four decades of the present century was not Negro-selected leadership. The ability of these leaders to effect the patterning of political behavior within their communities did not rest upon their control of institutional structures which in a major way affect social, political, and economic life; nor did it rest upon a charismatic relationship with the Negro masses or upon the adoption of positions on race-related issues that articulated the deep sense of frustration and hostility which southern Negroes felt. Crucial for the maintenance of a position of leadership was a favorable relationship with influential whites. The majority of southern Negroes, caught up in the biracial system, without effective political power, and without expectations that the system could be altered significantly in the near future, necessarily accepted those leaders able to gain the most within the system. This is *out-group based* leadership. The term does not imply that a group of influential whites would sit around a table in City X and decide who would be Negro leaders. Such a model would be ridiculously simplistic. There were only a limited number of Negroes with sufficient interest, time, skills, industry, and community respect to be leaders. But given the overwhelming preponderance of political, social, and economic power of the white majority, it is hardly surprising that the decision of influential whites as to which of the "eligible" Negroes were to be leaders was accepted by the Negroes themselves. The out-group determination thus was binding on the in-group. Whites had patronage (social, economic, and political) to bestow. White support of thoroughly disreputable and incompetent Negroes would not have given such people authority in their community. But this was not an issue. Whites wanted to reward "solid" Negroes of the Booker Washington model.

The rise over the last two decades in Negro skills and expectations, and above all in political power, has made possible a Negro leadership in the South whose effectiveness rests not on white support or tolerance, but on support within the Negro community. The significance of this shift from white-based to Negro-based leadership can hardly be overemphasized here. Southern Negroes no longer are political blanks. Their newly achieved ability to apply significant — though far from sufficient — sanctions has enabled them to sustain leadership responsive to their interests. This new leadership is issue-oriented, and the one issue that matters is race advance-

ments. Its authority is dependent upon subcommunity approval of its promotion of race advancement.

This shift in the basis of authority of Negro leaders to something closer
to the model of sustained popular selection and away from out-group
selection has had important ramifications. Negroes who by their very prox-
imity to whites had influence in the past frequently have lost it. Hylan
Lewis in his South Carolina study observed that under the old system
Negroes with intimate access to influential whites — certain cooks, for
example — were looked upon as important people in the subcommunity.
He quoted a Negro as saying: "You can get along all right just so you
don't cross one of these white folks' cooks."[26] All this has changed.

More importantly, under out-group selection Negro leadership was splintered and fragmented. What reason was there for organization or unity?
The maintenance of a leadership position demanded access to influential
whites. Negroes who had achieved this had every reason to seek to exploit
it and to handle matters individually and informally. The charge was
often made by Negroes that they suffered from not "sticking together."
But "sticking together" makes sense only when the group has sufficient
political power to sustain leadership of its own choosing. With the transition to in-group selected leadership, an extremely self-conscious attempt
has been made to bring disparate elements together for the great struggle.
A new Negro leadership drawing its authority from the support of the
Negro masses has seen the necessity of attempting to weld together the
entire community. There are few medium- or small-sized cities in the South
in which an attempt has not been made in the last decade to create effective
community-wide race-advancement organizations. Many of these attempts
have failed, but the effort goes on.

That the objectives of Negroes and the means which they use have
changed greatly can scarcely — in view of the developments sketched above
— be considered surprising. The new goals-means orientation is simply
testimony to the dramatic alteration of the position of southern Negro
leaders. Twenty years ago the NAACP had a monopoly of Negro "radicalism" — radicalism meaning little more than keeping the flag of protest
flying in the South while the slow assault on discriminations went on in
the courts. Today, the Association is under attack for its "moderate and
legalistic" approach to race relations.[27]

Today, Negro leadership in the South is emphasizing goals on which,
historically, southern whites have been most sensitive. Myrdal observed in
An American Dilemma that certain types of discrimination were "more

[26]*Op. cit.,* p. 168.
[27]See, for example, Louis E. Lomax, *The Negro Revolt* (New York, 1962).

important" to southern whites, and that the importance corresponded to the relationship to the "anti-amalgamation doctrine." Ranking just below opposition to sexual intercourse between Negro males and white females was opposition to "dancing, bathing, eating, drinking together; and social intercourse generally. . . . Thereafter follows the segregations and discriminations in the use of public facilities such as schools, churches and means of conveyance." After these came discrimination in voting, in courts of law, and by police and other public officials, and discrimination in securing land, jobs, and public relief.[28] The thrust of the activity of the major protest organizations is now aimed at goals which stand near the top of this "rank order of discriminations."

And the means so frequently used to promote these goals — direct action demonstrations, from sit-ins to picketing to freedom rides — are considered particularly objectionable by many whites, North and South. The physical confrontation, the physical defiance, the possibility of violence, the very invitation to mass involvement, have introduced into southern race relations a distinctly new element. Before that chilly December 5, 1955, when Mrs. Rosa Parks refused to give up her seat in the front of a bus to a white man and in so doing precipitated the Montgomery Movement, Negro leaders in the South had been limited in their promotion of race goals to one or more of three other means: (1) requests presented by individuals to whites considered not hostile, (2) requests presented by Negro organizations such as voting leagues with the implicit threat of "withholding" such support as the vote, and (3) the lawsuit. Direct action has been a major addition to the arsenal of race leaders, and together with the expansion of the franchise has provided them with the significant sanctions which they lacked previously. Although some proponents of the 1964 Civil Rights Act emphasized the need for such legislation to "get the civil rights struggle off the streets and into the courts," there is no indication that direct action will cease to be a major weapon, although the objectives for which it is used have changed and will continue to change.

The more specific developments in race leadership are set in this profound change — revolution — in the structure of race relations in the American South. The old biracial system — based on and perpetuating the political powerlessness of southern Negroes — has been shattered. Negro leaders throughout Dixie are operating in the new and still evolving setting which this revolution has produced.

---

[28]Myrdal, *op. cit.*, pp. 60-61.

The Negro and
Florida Politics, 1944-1954

Hugh Douglas Price

In the excitement over the Supreme Court's recent decision against segregation in the public schools another important landmark in the history of the South has been overlooked: 1954 also marked the tenth anniversary of the historic *Smith* v. *Allwright*[1] decision which spelled the beginning of the end for the "white primary." With the current discussion of widespread changes or of violent reaction due to the school decision it is doubly interesting to trace the result of federal court intervention to secure Negro rights

---

Reprinted from *Journal of Politics*, Vol. 17, (May, 1955), pp. 198-220 with permission of the publisher. Copyright 1955 by the Southern Political Science Association.
[1]321 U.S. 649 (1944). The possibility of large-scale evasion was largely precluded by *Rice* v. *Elmore*, 165 F 2d 387 (1947), certiorari denied. The various schemes for disfranchisement are described in V. O. Key, Jr., *Southern Politics in State and Nation* (New York: Alfred A. Knopf, 1949), chapters 25-31. In the 1953 case involving the "Democratic Jaybird Club" in Texas, *Terry* v. *Adams,* 345 U.S. 461 (1953), the Supreme Court held that the Fifteenth Amendment applies even to a pre-primary election if it is the controlling step in the election process.

in the political sphere.[2] This study seeks to show what effect the 1944 court decision has had in one southern state, the rôle which the Negroes of that state have assumed as voters, and the consequences of these changes on the use of the Negro as a political issue.

The choice of Florida as a laboratory for the study of Negro voting is not accidental. Although a comprehensive survey of the whole South would obviously be desirable, Florida is the only state in the South which publishes registration figures broken down by race for each party.[3] Without the basic information as to how many Negroes register, where they register, and how the precincts composed largely of Negroes actually vote, only fragmentary and impressionistic accounts are possible. Moreover, on the basis of the best available estimates of Negro registration in the South, a higher percentage of Negroes register and vote in Florida than in any other Southern state.[4]

The outstanding fact indicated by the tremendous growth of Negro registration since 1944 is that "a revolution which will rank second only to Reconstruction in the emancipation of the Southern Negro"[5] has occurred. By 1954 a total of 128,329 Negroes were registered in Florida. These Negroes, representing 64 of the state's 67 counties, accounted for over ten per cent of the state's total registration.[6] By contrast, in 1944 no Negroes were registered in 36 Florida counties and the remainder had a total of

---

[2]Although the public school and primary voting situations are not completely parallel, there has been the same loose talk of "blood in the streets" in connection with both. Thus, in regard to Negro voting, one South Carolina legislator was quoted in *The Southern Frontier,* VI, No. 11 (November, 1945) as saying that "we'll fight him at the precinct meeting, we'll fight him at the county convention, we'll fight him at the enrollment books, and, by God, we'll fight him at the polls if I have to bite the dust as did my ancestors." In 1952, however, the Southern Regional Council estimated that there were 115,000 Negroes registered in South Carolina, and some observers credited Stevenson's narrow margin in the state to the Negro vote.
[3]Louisiana publishes state and parish registration totals by race, but does not break the party registration down by race. For Virginia some information can be drawn from local poll tax records, and in all southern states rough estimates can be made on the basis of total registration in precincts predominantly inhabited by Negroes.
[4]Official registration figures of May, 1952, indicated that 33 per cent of Florida's adult Negroes, as reported in the 1950 census, were registered. The Southern Regional Council's estimates of Negro registration for November, 1952, work out to the following percentages of adult Negroes: Florida, 34.1; Texas, 30.0; South Carolina, 29.5; Arkansas, 28.0; Tennessee, 26.7; Georgia, 25.6; Louisiana, 20.8; North Carolina, 18.2; Virginia, 16.6; Alabama, 9.6; and Mississippi, 4.0. Except for the low percentages of Alabama and Mississippi this rank order shows little connection with increasing percentage of Negro population in the individual states.
[5]William G. Carleton, "The Fate of Our Fourth Party," *The Yale Review,* XXXVIII, No. 3 (March, 1949), 451.
[6]The three counties with no Negro registrants — Lafayette, Liberty, and Union — are sparsely populated rural counties with less than one half of one per cent of the state's adult Negro population.

about twenty thousand, all registered as Republicans and hence ineligible to participate in the decisive Democratic primaries.[7] Table 1 indicates the tremendous growth of Negro registration, and the rapid shift of party affiliation.

TABLE 1

NEGRO REGISTRATION AND PARTY AFFILIATION IN FLORIDA: 1944-1954 (AS OF MAY IN EACH YEAR)

Date	Number of Negro Democrats	Number of Negro Republicans	Total Negro Registration
1944	0[a]	20,000[a]	20,000[a]
1946	32,280	15,877	48,157
1948	53,368	8,647	62,015
1950	106,420	9,725	116,145
1952	112,868	8,045	120,913
1954	119,975	8,354	128,329

[a]In 1944 Negroes were ineligible for registration as Democrats by stipulation of the State Democratic Executive Committee. Since the 1944 registration figures were not published separately by race, the Republican figure is an estimate arrived at on the basis of the earliest 1945 segregated returns and by tracing the drop in total Republican registration from 1944 to 1946.

The figures in Table 1[8] are significant in several ways: the rapidity until 1950 of the rise in Negro registration, the decisive Negro "crossing of the Jordan" from Republican to Democratic affiliation, and the marked slow-down in the rate of increase of Negro registration since 1950. The slow-down since 1950 can be accounted for on several grounds. In the early years the most aggressive Negroes were those in counties where there was least white opposition registered; since 1950 the registration drive has had to work with the less aggressive and more apolitical Negroes, and it has had to seek gains in those areas of most intense white opposition. Also, after 1950 a more conservative trend in public affairs set in, both locally with

[7]In 1944 Negroes made up about one half of the Republican registration in the state, and much more in some counties. Thus the 1944 total Republican registration in Duval County (Jacksonville) was 6,089, but the 1946 figures — broken down by race — indicated only 654 white Republicans. In Jackson County the corresponding figures were 600 in 1944 and 12 in 1946. As might be expected, Negro leaders had played an important role in the state Republican Party's leadership with Negroes from Jacksonville and Miami serving as delegates and alternates to Republican national conventions. Prior to 1944 the actual Negro voters had been of importance only in municipal politics in a few cities, such as Gainesville and Daytona Beach.
[8]Unless otherwise noted all statewide and county registration and election returns for Florida are based on the *Biennial Report of the Secretary of State* for the appropriate year. Precinct data was personally obtained by the author from supervisors of registration in numerous counties.

the defeat of Senator Pepper and nationally, so that fewer issues of real concern to the Negro have been raised. Finally, the white organization for Stevenson went to pieces in Florida in the 1952 presidential campaign, and in 1954 none of the gubernatorial candidates made any major drive to register additional Negro voters.

The biggest increase in Negro registration in any of the two-year periods came in 1948-1950. Much of this increase can be attributed to the concerted drive for Negro votes made on behalf of Senator Pepper, but Negro interest in local elections and in the 1948 Presidential election are also of importance. The latter factor is emphasized by the fact that a breakdown by race of the registrants for the November, 1948, election showed a total of 85,180 Negroes, thus accounting for 23,165 of the 54,130 increase over the May, 1948, to May, 1950, period. That the bulk of the currently eligible Negroes likely to register have by now enrolled is apparent from the small changes reported in most counties for the most recent two-year period, 1952-1954: most counties showed only tiny increases in Negro registration, and there was even a decline in 19 counties. Nevertheless, total Negro registration for the state continues to mount, slowly but surely. This should continue for a number of years since the present state-wide average of adult Negroes registered, 35.0 in May, 1954, is still only about one half the average of registration for adult whites.

In general, the commonly accepted idea that Negroes participate in politics most heavily in the urban areas is correct; however, the sharp increase in total Negro registration is by no means entirely caused by large-scale registration in the cities. As Table 2, which classifies the number of counties

TABLE 2

PERCENTAGE OF ELIGIBLE NEGROES REGISTERED IN FLORIDA, BY COUNTY: 1946-54

Per cent of Adult Negroes Registered	Number of Counties in Each Class, as of May of Each Year				
	1946	1948[a]	1950	1952	1954
None	4	4	5	4	3
0.1-9.9	30	15	10	8	5
10.0-19.9	20	16	10	5	8
20.0-29.9	9	11	16	14	14
30.0-39.9	2	6	9	11	11
40.0-49.9	1	5	8	12	11
50.0-59.9	1	7	6	5	8
60.0 and over	0	1	3	8	7

[a]Two counties unreported by race in 1948. All 67 reported in each of the other years indicated.

in each range of Negro registration by years, shows, there has been general state-wide acceptance of Negro registration.[9] In fact, the highest percentages of registration are in relatively small counties where a single particularly able Negro leader[10] can encourage registration in a way that cannot be done in a large city where there are thousands of Negroes. The largest concentration of Negro voters in the state, however, is in Duval County (Jacksonville) where 25,774 were reported registered in 1954. Dade County (Miami) had 20,179 Negro registrants; Escambia (Pensacola) reported 6,545; and Volusia (Daytona Beach), 4,537. In each case this represents between forty and fifty per cent of the county's 1950 adult Negro population; however, this relatively high level of registration is not found in all major Florida cities.[11] In 1954 Hillsborough County (Tampa) reported only 4,003 Negro registrants, or 16.0 per cent of its adult Negroes; Pinellas (St. Petersburg) reported 3,408, or 28.1 per cent; Palm Beach (West Palm Beach) reported only 5,198, or 23.4 per cent; and Orange (Orlando) reported only 2,687, or 18.8 per cent.[12] Since two-thirds of the adult Negroes in the state live in the twelve most populous counties, the low levels of registration in some of the cities are quantitatively more important in state-wide elections than is the lack of significant numbers of Negro registrants in some of the rural counties with the highest proportion of Negroes in their total population.

Another commonly accepted idea, that Negroes are least active where the proportion of Negro to white population is highest, and the whites

---

[9]Detailed comparison of the percentage of adult Negroes registered as compared with whites is impossible for many of the smaller counties, where laxity of the supervisors of registration has resulted in rolls with more registrants than there were adults reported in the 1950 census. In 1952, for example, there were 28 Florida counties reporting more white registrants than there were white adults in 1950. This distortion, which results from failure to purge the rolls, pads white Democratic totals, but probably has relatively little effect on the Republican and Negro figures since they represent mostly recent additions to the rolls. A check of total votes cast in the counties concerned gave no indication of "graveyard voting" — the turn-out was about what would be expected on the basis of the census figures.

[10]Thus Brevard County, home of the late Harry T. Moore — the leading NAACP worker in the state after the war — had over fifty per cent of its total adult Negro population registered by 1950. The importance of such personal and organizational factors lessens the possibility of finding clear-cut social or economic correlates to Negro political participation.

[11]Of the 14 counties in Florida with cities of 25,000 or greater population in 1950 there are 8 above the state average in percentage of Negroes registered (as of 1954) and 6 below. The considerable differences are quite clearly *not* due to differences in percentage of Negro population: of the 7 such counties with a higher percentage of Negroes than the state as a whole 5 have a higher proportion of Negroes registered than does the state as a whole; for the 7 such counties with a lower percentage of Negroes than the state 4 have a lower percentage of Negroes registered than does the state as a whole.

[12]In most of these cities the Negro middle class is smaller and local white politicians have made less effort to win Negro votes than in the previously mentioned cities.

consequently most resistant, is not entirely borne out by the facts in Florida. Table 3 indicates the percentage of eligible Negroes registered in 1952 in the seven Florida counties with over forty per cent Negro population, and in the six counties with less than ten per cent Negro population. Two of the "black belt" counties had levels of Negro registration above that of the state average, and two of the counties with a small percentage of Negro population reported a total Negro registration of ten in one case and none in the other. Thus the extent of Negro participation is not a mechanical reflex of the proportion of Negroes to whites in a county. Sometimes it is a matter of Negro leadership, of white candidates seeking Negro support, or both. The extent of Negro registration in a given area appears to depend upon a cultural complex of mores, folkways, habits, prejudices, and beliefs.

For the South as a whole the correlation between "black-belt" counties and low Negro registration is probably quite high, but the deviations — where counties have recently become concentrations of Negro population, as

TABLE 3

PERCENTAGE OF NEGRO ADULTS REGISTERED AND PERCENTAGE OF NEGRO POPULATION IN FLORIDA COUNTIES OVER FORTY PER CENT NEGRO AND IN COUNTIES UNDER TEN PER CENT NEGRO

County	Per Cent of Negroes in County Population as of 1950	Per Cent of Adult Negroes Registered as of 1952
Florida Counties over Forty Per Cent Negro		
Flagler	45.6	0.2
Gadsden	56.1	0.1
Glades	40.8	44.9[a]
Hamilton	42.2	8.6
Jefferson	62.5	3.8
Madison	45.6	0.0
Seminole	44.4	47.2[a]
Florida Counties under Ten Per Cent Negro		
Gilchrist	9.9	0.1[b]
Hardee	7.4	69.3
Holmes	4.4	47.8
Lafayette	9.4	0.0[b]
Okaloosa	8.0	26.0
Santa Rosa	8.5	55.6
State Average	21.8	33.0

[a]These two deviations from the expected "black belt" pattern are both located outside the Suwannee-Apalachicola River "Old South" region.
[b]These two deviations from the expected pattern in counties with small Negro populations are both located within the Suwannee-Apalachicola River region.

in parts of South Florida, or where much of the Negro population has drifted away — show that the correlation need not mean causation.[13] The percentage of Negroes in the Florida population, by counties, is shown in Figure A. Comparison of this map with Figure B, which indicates the percentage of adult Negroes registered, by county, illustrates the difference in behavior in counties with approximately equal percentages of Negro population. Particularly striking is the location of the four counties whose 1952 percentages deviate from the pattern of Table 3. The two counties with high levels of Negro registration despite the presence of over forty per cent Negroes are both located outside the old antebellum planter area, which roughly included the 18 counties bordering or between the Suwannee and Apalachicola Rivers. And the two counties of low Negro concentration but almost no Negro registrants are both located within the Suwannee-Apalachicola "Old South" region. Thus the resistance to Negro voting is explicable not as an automatic result of the percentage of current Negro population, but as a manifestation of a whole culture and way of life which, a century ago, rested upon large numbers of Negro laborers.

   Three of the four counties which had no Negro registrants from 1944 through 1952[14] are located within the Suwannee-Apalachicola region, and 15 of the 18 counties in the area have a smaller proportion of registered Negroes in 1954 than does the state as a whole. These counties have in common a high proportion of rural population, low income level, static or declining total population, a virtual absence of registered Republicans, and

---

[13]Such areas are particularly evident in Florida, and the inverse correlation between percentage Negro population and percentage of adult Negroes registered is consequently rather low: — .35 on the basis of the most recent registration and census figures. Of the 42 counties with a higher percentage of Negroes than the state as a whole 22 have a higher percentage of Negroes registered than the state as a whole and 20 are below the state average. Of the 25 counties with a smaller share of Negro population than the state average 13 are above the state average for percentage of adult Negroes registered and the remaining 12 are below. The importance of cultural-historical factors is shown by a comparison between the nonurban Suwannee-Apalachicola counties (excluding only Leon County, which has a city of over 25,000) and the remaining counties with no city of over 25,000. About two-thirds of the counties in each category are above the state average in percentage Negro population, but the nonurban Suwannee-Apalachicola counties divided 14 below and 3 (plus urbanized Leon) above the state average for percentage of Negroes registered; the other nonurban counties divided 12 below and 24 above the state average for Negro registration. Thus in the "Old South" area there are approximately five counties *below* the state average in percentage of Negroes registered for every one above the average. In the remaining nonurban counties the ratio is two counties *above* the average for every one below.

[14]Liberty, Lafayette, and Madison are the three counties within the area; Union county is an isolated cultural holdover of the "Old South" way of life still remaining in the north-central part of the state, most of which has been transformed by migration and urbanization. Within the Suwannee-Apalachicola region proper only Leon County, site of the state capitol at Tallahassee, has been greatly changed by recent trends.

intense devotion to "white supremacy."[15] Where migration of the rural Negro population to the North or to Southern cities has left a lower percentage of Negro population, in such counties the intense opposition to Negro "pretensions" has continued; but in the new centers of Negro population outside this area there has been relatively little opposition to Negro voting. The remarkable thing, however, about the political revolution taking place in the South since 1944 is not the white resistance to Negro voting in a few areas, but the widespread acceptance of Negro voting by southern whites. Although many regard it as a "necessary evil," they see it as an inevitable fact and accept it.[16]

The registration of large numbers of Negro Democrats has raised delicate problems for both the white candidates and for Negro leaders. Although the Negroes are in the Democratic Party of the South, they are not of it; to date they have been successfully "Jim-Crowed" within the party. In Florida this has helped to preclude any mass exodus of white voters from the Democratic Party. Despite the fact that Eisenhower carried the state in 1952, the Republican Party in 1954 still could claim only somewhat less than ten per cent of the registered voters in the state. What increases there have been in Republican registration can be accounted for by the gradual drift of economic conservatives to the Republican Party and by the continuing northern migration into the state. In the rural "white supremacy" counties, where resentment over Negro political activity is strongest, the increase in Republican registration has been least.[17] Moreover, the fact that most local

---

[15]This is the area where the Ku Klux Klan may also be a factor in preventing Negro registration. When Bill Hendrix resigned as Grand Dragon of the Florida Klan and ran for governor in the 1952 Democratic primary, this was the region giving him the most support. Hendrix, who polled only 1.52 per cent of the state-wide vote, received 18.00 per cent in Wakulla County, 15.03 in Liberty, 10.80 in Jefferson, 9.26 in Madison, 7.61 in Suwannee, 6.40 in Lafayette, 6.16 in Franklin, 4.10 in Gadsden, and 3.65 in Taylor. All nine of these counties are in the area bordering or between the Suwannee and Apalachicola Rivers, and Liberty, Lafayette, and Madison were three of the four counties with no Negro registrants from 1944 through 1952. Before the 1954 primaries, 586 Negroes went *en masse* to the Madison County courthouse and were registered (558 as Democrats and 28 as Republicans). All previous attempts to register by individual Negroes had been successfully "discouraged" by Klan parades, threats of intimidation, or persuasion. It is not strange that Negroes are somewhat slow to press their rights in an area where one out of every ten whites will throw away his vote on behalf of a Klan candidate.

[16]Here again the Dixiecrat movement, which can be regarded as the counterrevolution to check not only Negro civil rights but the social and economic implications of Negro voting, failed. The reasons behind the Dixiecrat failure are analyzed by Emile B. Ader, in "Why the Dixiecrats Failed," THE JOURNAL OF POLITICS, 15, No. 3 (August, 1953), 356-69.

[17]Leon was the only county of the 18 in the Suwannee-Apalachicola region where the 1952 Republican registration accounted for over one per cent of the county total. Only three counties in the whole West Florida "panhandle" had over one per cent Republican registration, and none of these reached the five per cent level.

FIGURE A. PERCENTAGE OF NEGRO POPULATION IN FLORIDA BY COUNTIES, 1950

and state contests are still settled in the Democratic primaries operates powerfully to prevent voters from joining the Republican Party.

Negroes are generally excluded from participation in the organization
of the Democratic Party. A few Negroes have been elected to the Democratic county committees in Florida, but predominantly Negro precincts usually
elect whites to the Democratic county committee or go unrepresented. The
shift of Negro voters from the Republican to the Democratic ranks has been
so complete that the old Negro Republican leaders can no longer exercise
a real voice in the state Republican organization, and yet the state Democratic organization is controlled by those who oppose extension of Negro
influence or the mixing of the races in any sort of relation. And to date
Negro voters themselves have shown an almost total indifference to party

FIGURE B. PERCENTAGE OF ADULT NEGROES REGISTERED IN FLORIDA, BY COUNTIES, IN 1954

primary elections for county, state, and national committee members and — what is more significant — to elections for delegates to the national convention.[18]

Segregated rallies have become a common practice. Frequently the county Democratic committee will schedule Negro rallies for the Negro neighborhood. All the Democratic candidates are invited to appear, and most usually do so. Negroes regard the segregated rallies as a definite gain even in areas where they freely attend mixed rallies. Facing an all-Negro audience the candidates have to speak on some matters of genuine concern to Negroes.

---

[18]Despite the tremendous Negro support for Kefauver in the 1952 Presidential preference primary, only a fraction of those Negroes voting in the second primary (when the actual delegates were elected) indicated choices for the Democratic convention delegates.

Also, present political mores allow the candidates to take stands at such rallies on many local issues of concern to the Negro, although to give a proportionate amount of time to such questions at a general rally would alienate many white voters. Under such circumstances the candidates are tempted to make, and often do make, promises they would not make before a mixed audience.

In addition, Florida Negroes have developed a large number of local voters' organizations and political leagues to work within the Democratic Party and to designate the candidates deserving of Negro support in the Democratic primaries. With the rise of these political organizations the Negro ministers, church organizations, fraternal orders, and community morticians have declined in political influence, especially in the cities. The new leaders are more ideological, less in the "accommodating" tradition, and more conscious of the critical attention with which many Southern whites view Negro voting. Besides endorsing a slate and holding rallies, the local political leagues distribute literature, facilitate Negro registration, personally solicit the voters, and get out the Negro vote on election day. On paper the Florida Progressive Voters' League, organized by NAACP leaders in 1944, speaks for all the state's Negro voters, but actually its influence is largely limited to a few counties where the state officers are also the local Negro leaders. The really effective Negro organizations are local, and in the larger cities — Jacksonville, Miami, and Tampa, for instance — there are several competing Negro political leagues.

Since the essential function of the Negro political league is to endorse a slate of candidates, the key position in the organization is that of chairman of the endorsing committee. This group meets with the various candidates, studies their past records, asks their position on pending issues, and sometimes even submits a written list of questions on specific issues. The subject of money may or may not become important. Some groups are so sensitive on this point that they refuse any contribution from candidates even for expenses; others frankly operate on a fee basis with endorsements going to the candidates they believe best, provided that these pay the minimum assessments.[19] A few groups apparently have endorsements "for sale" to the highest bidder, but such organizations quickly lose their position in the Negro community and are seldom able to swing many Negro voters. The

---

[19]The money collected from candidates is not so much an additional source of income for Negro political leaders as it is a means of meeting the inevitable operating overhead of an effective organization. The more effective groups have purchased voting machine mockups, maintain card files listing the Negro voters in each district, print their own literature, and hire additional workers for election eve and election day. All this costs money. As a matter of fact, a candidate regarded as particularly desirable but with limited funds may receive a "free ride" endorsement.

recommendations of the endorsing committee are generally accepted by the league. The final slate is usually kept secret as long as possible up to the last minute before the election since Negro endorsements have repeatedly been reprinted in various forms by the unendorsed candidates for use in gaining white support by picturing the endorsed candidates as "nigger-lovers." The most effective method seems to be that of personally delivering endorsement cards with the names and voting machine lever numbers of the endorsed candidates to Negro homes the night before the election — the more powerful leagues have regularly organized groups of ward, precincts, and block workers for this purpose.[20]

The importance of the Negro political leagues can be seen in the voting patterns of Florida Negroes. Although the percentage of registered Negroes who actually vote is generally from ten to twenty per cent below that of the white registrants, the leagues play an important part in getting out the vote. For another thing, the league endorsements are an additional factor contributing to the much-discussed "block voting" in which eighty-five, ninety, or even ninety-five per cent of the Negro vote goes to one candidate. Finally, Negroes display a much greater inclination to "single shot" or "double shot" the key contests and to fail to indicate a choice in the others than do white voters. And where they do vote in only one or two races, they tend to vote for the candidates heading the locally endorsed slate and not necessarily for the candidates appearing first on the ballot.[21]

Negro participation has been highest and "block voting" most marked in opposition to avowed "white supremacy" candidates, in support of municipal and county officials such as mayor, sheriff, or school superintendent who are regarded as favorable in their treatment of Negroes, and in national races where integrated liberalism or Negro rights were an issue. In such races Negro political league endorsements have occasionally been made for the "wrong" candidate — in such cases the Negro voters have overwhelmingly repudiated the league endorsements and have voted in terms of their

---

[20]An alternate method frequently used in smaller communities is for the Negro voters' league to hold a rally the night before the election. At the rally only the endorsed candidates are invited. Obviously this is a much less democratic method than having a segregated party rally at which all candidates appear.

[21]In the April, 1951, Jacksonville municipal election, for example, the precinct organization of the largest Negro precinct in the city (with over 2,000 Negro voters) endorsed candidates in each of the five races for the city council. The candidate in the contest appearing first on the ballot was also first on the endorsed list, and 1,913 votes were cast in the race. The second highest number of votes, 1,398, was cast in the race which was fourth on the ballot but second on the league endorsement cards. The race which was second on the ballot but third on the endorsement cards involved only 1,222 votes. Here again, however, the correlation need not indicate causation. It is usually a case of the Negro leaders anticipating the reactions of the Negro voters, and not of the voters blindly following the league endorsements.

own self-interest. In more routine elections the league endorsements generally prove decisive, although the multiplicity of competing groups in the larger cities has sometimes resulted in differing slates and a factionalized Negro vote. That Negroes vote as much as twenty to one against "white supremacy" candidates is hardly surprising. What is often overlooked in discussions of "block voting" is that the die-hard opponents of Negro rights in the "Old South" rural counties often vote *for* "white supremacy" candidates by even heavier margins than the Negroes turn in for their opponents. Table 4, for example, shows the percentage of votes cast in Jacksonville Negro precincts for Senator Kefauver and three local candidates strongly supported by Negroes in the 1952 first primary. None of the four carried the county, but their majorities in the Negro precincts are impressive. But, while Kefauver was winning 80-85 per cent of the Negro vote in the Presidential preference primary, his opponent, Senator Russell, won 93.2 per cent of the Madison County vote and outran Kefauver by better than three to one in 17 of the 18 counties of the Suwannee-Apalachicola area! Incidentally, the candidate receiving the lowest Negro support of the four listed in Table 4 (Mr. Taylor) was a Negro.[22]

TABLE 4

DEGREE OF NEGRO SUPPORT FOR SELECTED CANDIDATES IN DUVAL COUNTY (JACKSONVILLE) FIRST DEMOCRATIC PRIMARY, MAY 6, 1952

Precinct Number	Percentage of Negroes in Precinct Democratic Registration	Percentage of Precinct Vote Cast for Each Candidate[a]			
		Kefauver for President	Sweat for Sheriff	Boyd for School Superintendent	Taylor for Justice of Peace, in District 2
2-G	95.6	82.3	78.4	83.9	79.6
2-H	98.2	84.9	79.3	87.2	——[b]
3-A	99.9	86.5	79.4	87.4	75.4
3-B	99.8	88.2	89.4	88.3	83.2
3-F	99.2	87.0	80.4	86.2	79.6
5-A	99.9	81.0	77.9	87.5	76.7
5-C	99.9	85.4	77.8	84.2	70.1
5-D	98.9	79.9	80.8	82.1	78.1
5-F	99.7	81.4	81.8	85.9	——[b]

[a]All four candidates listed failed to win a majority in the first primary in the county as a whole.
[b]Taylor's district did not include these two precincts.

[22]He was defeated in the first primary. The candidates for sheriff and school superintendent listed in Table 4 had both built up favorable reputations with Jacksonville Negroes and, in the second primary, each received over ninety per cent of the vote in each of the precincts listed. Mr. Sweat, the candidate for renomination as sheriff, won his run-off, but Mr. Boyd was defeated in the school superintendent's race despite his heavy Negro support.

Analysis of the returns from the state's predominantly Negro precincts indicates that Truman in 1948, Pepper in the Senatorial race of 1950, and Stevenson in 1952 each received Negro support of ninety per cent or more. Due to the confused pattern of residential segregation very few counties have precincts composed solely of Negro voters;[23] however, there were four such precincts in Palm Beach County. Although Smathers carried the county by almost two to one, the four Negro precincts turned in from 90.4 to 95.7 per cent of their votes for Pepper. The percentage of registrants voting for the county as a whole was 70.1, but for the four Negro precincts it ranged from 33.4 to 64.8. By 1952 most of the urban counties had a number of precincts composed almost wholly of Negroes. Table 5 shows the mean percentage of Negro registrants in the predominantly Negro precincts of six Florida counties in 1952. Comparison of the percentage vote for Stevenson in those precincts and in the counties as a whole shows that, although Eisenhower was the choice of a majority of the white voters in each of the counties except Escambia, the Negroes voted overwhelmingly for Stevenson.

TABLE 5

COMPARISON OF SUPPORT FOR STEVENSON AND PERCENTAGE OF REGISTRANTS VOTING IN NOVEMBER, 1952, IN SIX FLORIDA COUNTIES AT LARGE AND IN THE PREDOMINANTLY NEGRO PRECINCTS IN THOSE COUNTIES

County (and City)	Electoral Constituency	Per Cent Negro Registrants[a]	Per Cent for Stevenson	Per Cent of Registrants Voting
Dade	4 precincts	79.6	71.6	46.0
(Miami)	county-at-large	6.4	43.2	74.7
Duval	9 precincts	99.1	89.5	72.1
(Jacksonville)	county-at-large	19.7	51.8	81.1
Escambia	6 precincts	68.1	78.5	71.6
(Pensacola)	county-at-large	13.0	62.7	69.1
Orange	2 precincts	57.3	63.3	68.6
(Orlando)	county-at-large	5.8	28.9	81.8
Pinellas	2 precincts	75.0	68.2	70.5
(St. Petersburg)	county-at-large	4.8	28.6	79.6
Volusia	5 precincts	71.8	72.0	55.8
(Daytona Beach)	county-at-large	15.0	37.5	79.9

[a]Mean percentage of Negro precincts; per cent of total for the county-at-large.

[23]During 1946 and 1947 some counties experimented with the use of separate voting machines for whites and for Negroes. Although the practice had been upheld by the state attorney-general, it was quickly abandoned because of the needless delay in having whites wait while the Negro machines were empty and vice versa. For elections where the practice did prevail, exact information on the Negro turn-out and vote could be obtained by checking the vote for the machines used by the Negroes. Since abandonment of the attempt to use segregated voting machines, the only way to check on Negro voting is by studying the returns for those precincts where Negroes make up most of the registration.

Considering that most of the predominantly Negro precincts still contained some white voters, the differences between white and Negro performance were even greater than the figures of Table 5 indicate. Also noticeable is the markedly lower per cent of registrants voting in the predominantly Negro precincts in each county except Escambia. Again the actual difference in participation rate between white and Negro registrants is greater than the figures indicate, not only because of the effect of the whites in the predominantly Negro precincts but because the county-at-large figure is influenced by the performance of the Negro precincts within the county.[24]

Negro voters as a whole have been least interested in the gubernatorial and other state races. For one thing there have been no strongly anti-Negro candidates for governor nor any candidates raising issues of vital concern to the Negro. Other factors which have tended to a lower level of Negro interest in state politics than in national and local races include: the blandness of one-party politics, the meaningless factionalism, the failure to raise basic issues, the weakness of the Florida governor as popular and legislative leader, and the seeming lack of relevance of most state issues to the concrete problems of the Negro. Thus in 1948 there were fewer votes cast in the predominantly Negro precincts in the hotly contested Governor's race than in the largely unorganized Presidential election; the reverse was true in most white precincts. In the absence of basic issues the Negro voter tends to be influenced in state elections by local white voting trends and by the endorsements made by the local Negro leagues.

In several southern states Negro candidates for public office have been elected in recent years, but this has not yet happened in Florida. Negroes have qualified as candidates in the Democratic primaries, carried on active campaigns, and even succeeded in getting into the second primary run-off, but none has yet been elected, at least not since around the turn of the century. This is caused in part by the fact that most local officials — even city councilmen — are now elected at large rather than from districts and

---

[24]The lower rate of voter turn-out among Negro registrants is also apparent in the estimates of Negro voting in the 1954 primaries which have been compiled by the Attorney-General of Florida (see appendix to Florida's *amicus curiae* brief filed pursuant to discussion of implementation of the May 17, 1954, segregation decision). For whatever they may be worth (and such estimates of aggregates must be treated with caution) estimates of the number of Negroes voting in the first primary were received from supervisors of registration in 59 of the 67 counties. These 59 counties reported 98,833 Negro registrants, but estimated that only 44,531 Negroes (45.1 per cent of those registered) voted in the first primary. Remarkably, the brief suggests, page 179, that either the estimates are "poor guesses," or that "any Negro who dares register is determined to exercise his right to vote." This evaluation is made since — according to the brief — "the percentage of registered Negroes who vote is much higher than one would estimate on the basis of the socio-economic levels which correlate with voting interest." This is the exact opposite of what the estimates — and other data — clearly indicate.

wards. Also, the Negro candidates who have run in Florida have not been the outstanding leaders of the Negro communities. Several have been "promoters" or newspapermen apparently interested in the publicity, and a few have had suspicious encouragement from the extreme left. Several of these factors combined to prevent the election of a Negro city councilman in Jacksonville in 1947, when councilmen were still elected from districts.[25]

The political weaknesses of the Negro in the South are remarkably similar to those of organized labor, another relatively new major factor in American politics, on the national scene. By substituting "Negro" for the word "labor" one can paraphrase most of the outstanding weaknesses of organized labor, as they have been summarized by Samuel Lubell,[26] and apply them to the southern Negro. (1) An overly militant campaign to register Negro voters or to gain Negro support provokes so much fear and opposition that it produces an anti-Negro reaction. (2) The Negro and the Democratic Party are still uneasy allies; in fact, in many Florida counties the formal Democratic Party organization and the local Negro voters are political opponents. (3) Negro leaders have been unable to deliver the Negro vote as a block except in the direction it was already inclined to go.

The Southern Negro is also under some handicaps which do not plague labor. There is the continued general prejudice against Negro voting, and the tremendously important and generally underestimated factor of the existence of the one-party system. Although Florida has the makings of both a liberal and a conservative group within the Democratic Party,[27] the issues are rarely raised or are so blurred and blended with personalities and factionalism that the power of a cohesive minority group such as the Negro is minimized.[28] Finally, the context of primary contests is wholly different from that of general elections: there can be no appeal to party loyalty and consequently no effective restraint on demagogic use of the race issue.

---

[25]The candidate was a thirty-five dollar a week mortar mixer, who was taken to the city office to qualify by a white merchant seaman alleged to have been the executive-secretary of the Florida Community Party. Most of the qualifying fee was said to have been paid by the left-wing National Negro Congress. The long-standing Negro community leaders, most of middle class background, did not appreciate the intrusion. In the run-off between the Negro and a white candidate the Negro leaders "went fishing" and only about thirteen per cent of the Negro registrants, who outnumbered whites in the district, voted. The Negro was defeated, and the next session of the legislature amended the Jacksonville city charter to make councilmen elected at large. A sequel to the incident, which is instructive of the sort of horse-trading common in politics, was the construction of a municipal swimming pool for Negroes in the district where the leaders had failed to rally behind the self-appointed Negro candidate.
[26]*The Future of American Politics* (New York: Harper and Brothers, 1951), p. 190.
[27]See Herbert J. Doherty, Jr., "Liberal and Conservative Voting Patterns in Florida," *The Journal of Politics*, 14, No. 3 (August, 1952), 403-17.
[28]Talk of "balance of power" politics is obviously inappropriate when, as in most primary races, there are no fixed centers of power to be balanced.

The various factors inhibiting the political influence of the Negro in the South make it imperative to consider not only the behavior of the Negro as a voter, but the rôle of the Negro as a political issue. Can the strength which a candidate gains from Negro voters be offset or turned into a net loss by reducing his support among race-conscious whites? Florida experience over the past ten years indicates that such can but need not necessarily be the result in a Democratic primary contest, but that it will generally not be the case in a general election. The most striking illustration of the differing importance of the racial issue in a primary as compared to a general election is provided by the Kefauver and Stevenson votes in May and November of 1952. In the Presidential preference primary, where Kefauver was saddled with the stigma of FEPC and deprived of the protecting mantle of traditional party loyalty, he lost every one of the 25 counties bordering or west of the Suwannee River. In the general election just six months later Stevenson, also under fire because of FEPC, won every single one of these same 25 counties, and by almost as heavy margins as had Russell.[29]

The impact which the development of a two-party system, where the real decisions are made in general elections, would have on the rôle of the Negro voter can hardly be overestimated. Within a statewide Democratic primary, when the Negro question is raised, the Negro precincts vote ten to one for the liberal candidate (Pepper in 1950; Kefauver in 1952), but many of the "Old South" counties are alienated or closely divided. However, in a national election between the Democratic and Republican parties, the predominantly Negro precincts will go ten to one for a Truman or a Stevenson; and the "Old South" rural counties, true to their Democratic Party tradition and favoring high federal crop supports, will at the same election likewise pile up heavy majorities for the Democratic Presidential nominee, at least under broad conditions similar to those existing in 1952. Thus in a primary contest *within* the party the Negro urban precincts and the "white supremacy" rural counties are apt to be enemies; but in a general election contest *between* the two parties the Negro precincts and the "Old South" counties tend to be allies, each piling up large majorities for the

---

[29]Prejudice designed to work against a Democratic *candidate* may actually result in an increased vote for the Democratic *party* in a general election. Thus in 1928 Al Smith, an economic liberal, should have had appeal to the entire West Florida "panhandle," but he lost six of the seven counties in the extreme western half. He might well have done as poorly, because of the religious issue, in the eastern half but for the long-standing identification of "white supremacy" with the Democratic Party. As it happened, however, Smith carried 17 of the 18 counties in the Suwannee-Apalachicola region, but only 9 in the rest of the state. Truman in 1948 and Stevenson in 1952 also carried every county in the Suwannee-Apalachicola region. The outcome in a Democratic primary, as evidenced by the 1952 Kefauver-Russell contest, is apt to be the reverse with the liberal candidate losing this area.

Democratic Party.[30] So long as the Negro voters and the poor whites of the rural counties tend to neutralize each other in the primaries, the way is made clear for victory for the candidates supported by the conservative counties and more prosperous urban classes. Since the chief beneficiaries of the present one-party system are the economic conservatives who would have to pull out of the Democratic Party to establish a two-party system — there being no place for the liberals to go — it is doubtful that anything short of a liberal victory, both in the state and nation, will greatly hasten the rise of a two-party system in the state.

The classic example, to date, of the genuine appeal for Negro support and widespread use of the Negro as an issue in Florida was the Pepper-Smathers campaign of 1950. Samuel Lubell has written that "the defeats of both Pepper and Graham [in North Carolina] can be credited largely to heavy Negro voting, which spurred an even heavier anti-Negro outpouring."[31] While this seems to have been the case with Senator Graham, it is not the sole or even the main explanation for the defeat of Pepper. Unlike Graham — who had polled within one per cent of a clear majority in the first primary, before the race issue became dominant — Pepper was defeated in the first primary by 67,561 votes out of approximately seven hundred thousand. Pepper's greatest loss of strength, in comparison to his successful 1944 campaign, was not in the racially sensitive Suwannee-Apalachicola region, but in the towns and small cities of central Florida and the East Coast.[32] As another writer has pointed out, the Smathers pattern of victory over Pepper "is much the same as the Hoover-Dewey-McCarty [1948] pattern, only more extensive."[33] This pattern, which the Eisenhower victory also followed, is primarily one of economic conservatism, not — as in the 1952 Russell pattern — one of "white supremacy."

The combined effect of heavy Negro Democratic registration and of the potentially explosive race issue has been to cause a certain ambivalence on the part of the candidates. The Negro vote is too large for conservative candidates to risk indulging in undiluted Negro-baiting, but neither do liberal candidates dare expose a too pro-Negro program or make too open a bid

---

[30]Thus Samuel Lubbell's suggestion, *op. cit.,* p. 122, that "in state politics in the South the Negro's interests parallel more closely those of the urban Republicans in their struggle against the anti-Negro rural areas" has proved partially correct in Florida. It applies to Democratic primary contests when Negro rights become the dominant factor; it does not apply to general elections or to primary contests where the basic division is economic rather than racial.

[31]Lubell, *op. cit.,* p. 120.

[32]Of the 18 counties in the Suwannee-Apalachicola region Pepper and Smathers each carried nine, with Pepper losing four of the eleven he had carried in 1944, but winning two which he had lost in 1944. Pepper carried 13 of the 21 counties west of the Suwannee River; he won in only 7 of of the remaining 46 in the state.

[33]Doherty, *op. cit.,* p. 414.

for Negro support. Even in the Pepper-Smathers campaign both candidates faced both ways: Pepper denounced compulsory FEPC, and Smathers emphasized that his own record was not that of a Negro-baiter. In the gubernatorial campaign of 1952, Dan McCarty, in the absence of any overt raising of the Negro question and with the aid of most of the urban Negro political leagues, was able to pile up heavy majorities in most Negro precincts and also carried 15 of the 18 counties in the "Old South" region. The special gubernatorial primary of 1954, occasioned by the death of Governor McCarty in office, posed a dilemma to Negro voters. Acting Governor Charley Johns had been one of the five state senators supporting a private "white primary" bill in 1947,[34] but was regarded as pro-labor and promised more generous old-age pensions. Johns' opponent in the run-off, LeRoy Collins, who ultimately won the nomination, was a middle-of-the-road candidate who made few popular promises, but Collins had fought in the state senate against the "white primary" and in support of a bill to unmask the Klan. Under this cross pressure the Negro vote split, with an unusually large number of Negroes staying away from the polls.

The long-run effects of the one-party system on Negro voting and on the Negro as an issue can be traced through a number of stages. By its tendency toward meaningless factionalism it makes effective Negro "balance of power" politics most difficult. By its transfer of most real political contests from the general election to the party primary it removes the restraining factor of party loyalty and makes Negro-baiting much more tempting. By increasing the likelihood of use of the Negro as an issue it makes it much more difficult for a candidate to make a public appeal to the Negro as a voter; the difficulty of appealing to the Negro as a voter frequently makes it necessary that appeals for Negro support be made privately to Negro leaders. This, in turn, opens the possibility of "deals" and actual buying of support rather than giving more incentive to the Negro voters to make a rational choice on issues.

Despite all the handicaps, the lack of experience, white opposition, the one-party system, and a shortage of middle-class leaders, Negroes in Florida have won impressive gains from their re-entry into politics. At the local level the Negro community in many places is getting better police protection,[35]

---

[34]Although the bill was sponsored by a senator from Jacksonville, each of the other four voting or paired in favor of the measure had one of the four counties with no Negro registrants in his district. Of the eleven counties which the five senators collectively represented, eight are in the Suwanee-Apalachicola River region. The sponsor of the measure, incidentally, was defeated in the 1948 Democratic primary.

[35]Much of the Negro dissatisfaction on this score has been due to the extreme laxity of Southern white police, juries, and judges in regard to Negroes accused of committing crimes against other Negroes. "Rough stuff" and unnecessary severity in dealing with Negro suspects has also caused dissatisfaction. See Gunnar Myrdal, *An American Dilemma* (New York: Harper and Brothers, 1944), chapters 25-26. The rapid rise in the number of Negro policemen in Florida cities, from 5 in 1940 to 30 in 1946 to 96 in 1952, has done much to alleviate both these situations.

and Negroes accused of offenses against white people seem to be receiving more just treatment. Street lights, sidewalks, and paved streets are more common in communities where Negroes vote in substantial numbers. Such things as Negro civic centers, bandshells, playgrounds, libraries, hospital annexes, and even swimming pools are found in increasing numbers of Florida cities. To date these developments have been within the context of "separate but equal" facilities. Thus special "reserve days" for Negro use of municipal golf courses and auditoriums have also been within this pattern. The importance of federal aid in providing low-rent housing projects for Negroes, and the impetus of federal court decisions in the education field in providing more Negro schools and better pay for Negro teachers cannot be overlooked. All these developments are farthest advanced in those communities where Negroes register and vote in large numbers.

At the state level the Florida legislature has steadily refused to enact measures designed to circumvent the *Smith* v. *Allwright* decision. In 1953 a proposal to cut off all state funds for public schools in the event of a Supreme Court decision abolishing segregation in the Florida public schools was dropped. An expensive state detention home for Negro girls, the Forrest Hills Correctional Institute, has recently been opened. Also, for the first time in history, the Florida Farm Colony for the feeble-minded recently opened several wards for Negroes.

The possible influence of the Southern Negro on national politics is hard to gauge, particularly because of the conservative trend in the past several years. But the overwhelming vote in the Negro precincts for Truman in 1948, for Kefauver in the preferential primary of 1952, and for Stevenson in the Presidential election of 1952 shows that Southern Negroes think politically along the same lines as do Negroes in Detroit, Chicago, Pittsburgh, and New York. Of all the Florida groups responsible for Truman's victory in the state in 1948 and for Stevenson's large vote in 1952, the Negroes were the most solid in their support.

A review of the rôle which Negroes have played in Florida politics during the past ten years indicates that they, like Americans everywhere, are interested in tangible benefits for themselves, a high standard of living, and a greater share of the good things which American society has to offer. Very few Florida Negroes have shown any interest at all in a separate political party, extreme left-wing movements, or selling their votes. To date they have relied largely on Negro middle-class leadership and have participated in local, state, and national politics with traditional American aims and values in mind and within the framework of traditional American party and political institutions. The real revolution in the South during the past decade has been not the quadrennial histrionics of the Dixiecrats, but the successful entry into politics of that long-excluded American — the southern Negro. The increasing participation of Negro voters in the South, already estimated to be over a million strong,[36] should be watched for its effects both upon political behavior within the one-party system and for its rôle in producing conditions which will hasten the development of a two-party system.

---

[36]As of the end of 1952 the Southern Regional Council estimated total Negro registration for the eleven ex-Confederate states to be 1,040,000. *Pittsburgh Courier*, February 21, 1953.

The Manipulated Negro Vote: Some Pre-Conditions and Consequences*

*Alfred B. Clubok, John M. De Grove
and Charles D. Farris*

The subject of this paper is one aspect of our recently completed field research on political leadership in the "face-to-face" community. We selected six small Florida towns for interviewing, ranging in population from approximately 4,000 to 15,000. Two towns were selected in each of three major geographical areas of the State: the old South agricultural and pine tree area of northern Florida; the citrus, cattle, vegetable area of the central portion of the peninsula; and the light industry, tourism, retirement area of southern coastal Florida. The towns in the northern tier of counties are still little different from their counterparts in neighboring Southern states. On the other hand, the dynamic economic and population growth in peninsular Florida afforded an excellent opportunity for assessing political leadership and Negro political participation in a wide variety of economic, political, and cultural settings.

Reprinted from *Journal of Politics,* Vol. 26, (February, 1964), pp. 112-129 with permission of the publisher. Copyright 1964 by the Southern Political Science Association.
*We gratefully acknowledge a grant from the Rockefeller Foundation which made this research possible. Of course, we accept full responsibility for all interpretations.

A research team of two professors spent approximately six weeks in each town, and from 40 to 60 individuals, both white and Negro, were interviewed.[1] Interviewing began with present public office holders and was then expanded to include other white political influentials as they were identified. The purpose of these interviews was to develop a picture of the political structure of the white community from the end of World War II to the time of interviewing. The interview guide was also designed to obtain white conceptions of the political structure of the Negro community and to uncover the relationship between these two structures. During the white interviews a partial list of Negro leaders was developed which was later expanded during the Negro interviews. The Negro interview guide was designed to obtain information concerning the leadership structure of the Negro community, factionalism within this community, and the relationship of the Negro community to the white political structure over a 15-year time period.

The findings reported in this paper are consistent, we think, with the Matthews-Prothro findings on Negro political participation in the South.[2] Using multiple correlation and regression analysis these two authors found that 21 selected socio-economic variables "stastistically 'explain' about 28 per cent (R^2) of the variation in Negro registration rates."[3] Adding to the 21 variables ten explicitly "political variables," the research team found that they could explain, in a stastistical sense, about 50 per cent of the Southwide variance in Negro voting registration. In the social sciences a statistical explanation of approximately 50 per cent of the variance of a dependent variable is by no means a negligible accomplishment.

On the basis of our recent field research, we suggest that an examination of the political relationship of the white and Negro communities at the local level might have high explanatory value, vis-à-vis Negro registration and turnout, in the more rural towns and counties of the South and, therefore, might significantly reduce the unexplained variance of the Matthews and Prothro analysis. Data of this type are, of course, time consuming to gather since the conceptual framework underlying the analysis requires a field investigation, not only of the structure of the Negro political community, but of the white as well.

We conceive of five possible relationships between the two political communities — the Non-Voting town; the Low Voting, Unorganized town; the

---

[1]Interview schedules were open-ended, and their construction represented a blending of the "attribution" and "issue" techniques.
[2]Donald R. Matthews and James W. Prothro, "Political Factors and Negro Voter Registration in the South," *American Political Science Review,* Vol. LVII (1963), pp. 355-367.
[3]Matthews and Prothro, *op. cit.,* p. 355.

Manipulative town; the Independent Bargaining town; and the Office Holding town.[4]

Negroes do not register and vote in the Non-Voting town, normally because of active hostility on the part of the white political structure. However, we can conceive of a possible variant of this type where active hostility has disappeared but, out of fear, indifference, or inertia, Negroes do not register.

In the Low Voting, Unorganized town, either because of a policy of the white political structure which permits only a few selected and presumably "safe" Negroes to vote or because of fear and/or indifference, only a relatively small number of Negroes register and vote. No attempt is made either by the whites or Negroes to organize politically a significant proportion of the Negro community.

Towns in which the Negro community has been politically organized and controlled to a large degree by white political leadership we conceive of as Manipulative towns. In the Manipulative town the electoral activists — those responsible for turning out the Negro vote — are primarily the agents of members of the white political structure, and the preponderance of voting Negroes are responsive to the activists as agents of the whites.

We distinguish the Independent Bargaining town from the Manipulative town. In the Independent Bargaining town electoral activists in the Negro community tend to be independent of the white political structure and bargain with white politicians for gains, either for the Negro activists or for the Negro Community as a whole. The Negro voter tends to respond either to the activist as an individual or to the activist as a representative of the Negro community interests.

Our final category, the Office Holding town, is similar to the Independent Bargaining town in all respects except that Negro gains through independent organization and bargaining have resulted in Negroes' appointment or election to public offices.

We conceive of a town undergoing a transformation when the pattern of structural relationships change. For instance, in Prospect Bluff, a white political clique which had organized and manipulated a sizeable number of Negro votes ceased to function in the town. The Negro community remained unorganized for several years, after which Negro leadership, rather than white, emerged to reorganize the Negro political community. In this case,

[4]Three major concepts were used in constructing this typology: (1) voting or non-voting as a characteristic of the Negro community, (2) the degree of political organization of the Negro community, and (3) the bargaining or manipulative nature of the relationship between the two communities.

then, we would speak of transformations from "Manipulation" to "Low Voting, Unorganized" to "Independent Bargaining."
The following tables summarize the characteristics of the six towns.[5]

TOBACCO HILL

LOCATION — North Florida (Roth County)

Population		Percentage Non-White	
1940	6337	1940	32
1950	8072	1950	34
1960	9966	1960	32

Economic Base............Service, trade, and county seat
Style of White Politics

1945-47	no data
1947-51	competition
1952-56	monopoly
1956 to date	competition

Negro Community:
Structural relations with white community
Percentage white 20 years + registered (1959)   85
Percentage Negro 20 years + registered (1959)   54
Negro percentage total registered vote (1959)   22

1945-47... Non-Voting
1947 to date .. Manipulative

PROSPECT BLUFF

LOCATION — North Florida (Hawkins County)

Population		Percentage Non-White	
1940	7641	1940	49
1950	9677	1950	45
1960	11529	1960	43

Economic Base............Manufacturing, service, trade, county seat
Style of White Politics

1945-57	monopoly
1957 to date	competition

---

[5] In the following tables under the category of "Style of White Politics" we note two types of politics. "Monopoly, according to our definition, prevails when one leadership clique regularly wins all, or practically all council seats regardless of the changing identity of candidates backed by the clique and when there is no continuing opposition from a rival leadership clique that regularly sponsors candidates or coopts successful candidates. A monopoly style of politics, indeed, can prevail under the following conditions: no opposition; 'personal' opposition by candidates not affiliated with a clique; or formation of a temporary opposition group constituted for a particular election and either dissolved upon its defeat or disintegrated by cooptation of its successful candidates into the ruling leadership clique. . . . Competition, as a style of politics, exists when at least two leadership cliques compete on a continuing basis for elective office. We do not require an alteration in the political control of the community. One clique could consistently win control of the city council but, as long as the opposition clique exists and challenges in elections, we use the term 'competition' to describe the communities' style of politics." See Gladys M. Kammerer, Charles D. Farris, John M. De Grove, and Alfred B. Clubok, The Urban Political Community (Boston, 1963), p. 6.

Negro Community:
Structural relations with white community

pre-1945 ... Manipulative
1945-48 .. Low Voting, Unorganized
1948 to date .... Independent
Bargaining, low level
importance

Percentage white 21 years + registered (1960)   65
Percentage Negro 21 years + registered (1960)   21
Negro percentage: total registered vote (1960)   18

ANGUSVILLE

LOCATION — Central Peninsula (Call County)

Population

		Percentage Non-White	
1940	3726	1940	23
1950	4801	1950	24
1960	7346	1960	19

Economic Base .... Service, trade, retirement, county seat

Style of White politics

1945-48 .... monopoly
1948-54 .... competition
1955-60 .... monopoly
1961 to date .. competition

Negro Community:
Structural relations with white community

1945-mid 1950s .. Low Voting, Unorganized
mid 1950s to date....Manip-
ulative, low level of
importance and
organization

Percentage white 20 years + registered (1962)   65
Percentage Negro 20 years + registered (1962)   33
Negro percentage: total registered vote (1962)   9

HAMLIN

LOCATION — Central Peninsula (Ward County)

Population

		Percentage Non-White	
1940	3062	1940	35
1950	4307	1950	34
1960	5260	1960	29

Economic Base..........Citrus, manufacturing, service, trade, county seat

Style of White Politics

1945-55 ....monopoly
1956 to date.... competition

Negro Community:
Structural relations with white community

1945-46....Low Voting,
Unorganized
1946 to dale....Manipulative

Percentage white 20 years + registered (1959)   51
Percentage Negro 20 years + registered (1959)   20
Negro percentage: total registered vote (1959)   14

LISA CITY

LOCATION — South Florida (Reid County)

Population

1940	2482
1950	4566
1960	13046

Percentage Non-White

1940	24
1950	23
1960	43

Economic Base............Suburb (heavy Negro); Retirement (heavy trailer court)

Style of White Politics

1947-49	competition
1949-59	monopoly
1959 to date	competition

Negro Community:
Structural relations with white community

1945-48	Non-Voting
1948-61	Independent Bargaining
1961 to date	Office Holding

Percentage white 21 years + registered (1961)	79
Percentage Negro 21 years + registered (1961)	60
Percentage Negro: total registered vote (1961)	28

BOUGAINVILLE

LOCATION — South Florida (Reid County)

Population

1940	4238
1950	6813
1960	12731

Percentage Non-White

1940	44
1950	45
1960	44

Economic Base........... Retirement, winter tourism

Style of White Politics

1945-53	competition
1954-55	monopoly
1956 to date	competition

Negro Community:
Structural relations with white community

1945-50	Manipulative
1950 to date	Independent Bargaining

Percentage white 21 years + registered (1962)	57
Percentage Negro 21 years + registered (1962)	22
Negro Percentage: total registered vote (1962)	22

Because of obvious space limitations we will treat only the Manipulative town in this paper and, in particular, the relationship of law enforcement agencies to the Negro vote in the Manipulative town.

II

In five of the six towns in which we interviewed, Negro registration and voting was or had been encouraged, facilitated, and, to varying degrees, organized by members of the white political structure. In four of these five

Manipulative towns the agencies of the law played key roles in the relation-ship between the white and the Negro political structure. White encourage-ment of Negro voting in these towns did not stem from abstract concepts of civil liberties, nor from fears of racial disturbances. Direct contact with the United States Civil Rights Commission or concern over its activities was entirely lacking in these towns. The attitude of the white political structure in Tobacco Hill towards the activities of the Civil Rights Commission was summarized when a county judge stated: "Hell, the Federals are interested only when you try to keep the colored from voting, and we're voting them to the hilt." Our data suggests that the white politicians' encouragement of Negro registration was based either on actual or anticipated competition for public office. Organization and manipulation of a Negro vote was conceived of as a means of either obtaining or retaining control of public policy-making positions.

That the agencies of the law should be interested in election returns and, therefore, actively engaged in obtaining a "proper" outcome by securing votes should surprise very few. However, law enforcement as a political tool is often far removed from the life experience of a member of the American middle class — whether the individual is an insurance salesman or a political scientist. If we were to judge the state of knowledge within the discipline by the textbooks, then we would have to conclude that political considerations are at most aberrations in the law enforcement process. We must admit that few law enforcement officers were as openly political as a Tobacco Hill judge when he stated: "In my type of operation [he is describing the office of county judge] you have to politic every day. Favors get votes, and you have to do favors." Even so, we find the judge's position far closer to "reality" than the textbooks are.

We define law enforcement agencies broadly by including not only the police and sheriff's departments but also the courts and lawyers of the town. The political role of sheriffs, judges, or lawyers needs little further comment at this point. Lawyers traditionally have been part of the American political scene. Sheriffs and local judges run for office and, periodically at least, they must appeal to the voter. The law enforcers' membership in political parties, factions, cliques, or crowds and the attendant protection of various interests — whether they be low taxes, the office itself, or the rackets — are part of the informational backlog of any student of politics. The political ties and activities of a police chief are often hidden behind the appointive rather than the elective nature of the office; yet, in our experience, chiefs are usually members of political cliques either because the chief is indebted to the clique for his appointment and support or because the clique is beholden to the chief for favors and votes.

III

Varied techniques are used to turn out the Negro vote in the Manipulated town. In Hamlin the city judge and sheriff, along with the police chief who is recognized as a subordinate of the sheriff, handle the actual organization of the Negro vote. Before an election barbecues are held for the Negro voters on the ranch of the city judge. Negroes are driven to the ranch in trucks, and barbecue, fish, liquor, and beer are apparently in plentiful supply at this type of election meeting. On the day of the election the organization swings into high gear. A hired crew of Negro "street walkers" canvasses in the Negro community as agents for the whites.[6] The street walkers are provided with a list of registered Negro voters, and it is their job to produce the voters at the polls. The street walker is usually provided with money, some of which may be passed on to voters, but it was our impression that the money was used to defray the cost of mobilizing the vote and, of course, for the street walker's own commission.

The middle class Negro in Hamlin deplores the barbecue-liquor-street-walker complex but often finds himself in the same voting camp as the manipulated Negro. At the suggestion of the white manipulative leadership, middle class Negroes formed a Negro Civic Association and, by means of registration campaigns, increased the proportion of registered middle class and lower class Negroes. The Association does not ordinarily hold meetings with candidates prior to an election, since the contact of the middle class Negro with the white politician is still at the level of individual personal contact. Some members of the Civic Association expressed the feeling that they had been "used" by the whites simply to increase the size of the manipulated vote and yet, although they expressed bitterness, they have so far remained loyal to the manipulative camp.

In Tobacco Hill similar techniques are used. Barbecues and fish fries are held before elections. Taxis are hired to take Negroes to the polls, and city owned cars have been used on occasion for the same purpose. The police and the sheriff's deputies openly campaign. Many of the credit groceries in the Negro section of the town are tied to the manipulative camp in the town, and these are used to remind the Negro patrons of their civic duty to vote and, most important, for whom to vote. An election meeting is normally held in one of Tobacco Hill's Negro churches prior to the local election. Candidates are invited to speak before the group and usually do so. A substantial sum of money is normally spent during a Tobacco Hill election. Apparently, some of the money makes its way to the voter — there appears to be a semi-

---

[6]These people are not female prostitutes. We were surprised to find this term used in several towns.

professional group of vote-sellers in the town, both Negro and white — but most of what is spent is used to defray the cost of mobilizing the vote.

In Angusville where the Negro vote is relatively small and where the organization of the Negro vote has been far less thorough than in either Hamlin or Tobacco Hill, white leadership has, nevertheless, given some thought to the mechanics of manipulation. The primary white political contact with the Negro community is made through a law firm. A lawyer in this firm divides the Negroes into four groups. The first are the more successful old line Negro families of the community. Although they are small in number and formally unorganized, they do have recognized leadership. The leadership of this segment of the community is approached and, according to the lawyer: "You ask them to go your way and more than likely they will." The second group is the Negro "working class." The approach to this segment of the Negro community is made through those in the Negro community who have partaken of the services of the law firm and also through the activities of the third group, that is, those who are involved in bolita, moonshine, and other rackets.[7] This lawyer believes, and we think correctly, that the people involved in the rackets are probably the best organized segment of the Negro community in Angusville. The fourth group contacted are the so-called transients — those who work as hands in the pulpwood industry or as citrus and vegetable pickers. Negroes in this category are difficult to organize because of the transient nature of their work, but a few votes can be obtained by contacting their employers and/or foremen. Little money is spent, as far as we can tell, in organizing the vote. Although taxis are hired on election day to take Negro voters to the polls and some private white cars are used, the machinery to turn out the Negro vote is not elaborate. Even though some effort is made to turn out the Negro vote, it is not considered to be a crucial factor in Angusville elections.

IV

Although the actual techniques of organization and manipulation of the Negro vote by law enforcement agencies were varied, law enforcement in the Manipulative town shared certain characteristics which we conceive of as *preconditions for manipulation.* Their existence promotes an atmosphere which makes the Negro susceptible to manipulation and control. In no case did we find that violence or hostility was characteristic of law enforcement in the Manipulative town. Rather, it was the absence of such stereotyped white behavior which we believe provided a favorable climate for manipulation by law enforcement agencies. In Tobacco Hill and Hamlin, the two towns where manipulation of the Negro vote was most evident, the agents

---

[7]Bolita is a Spanish word used widely in Florida to indicate the numbers racket.

of the law had the reputation among the Negroes of being "good men," of treating the "colored man just as they would treat a white man." Negro prisoners were not mistreated nor were they intimidated. The fair and decent treatment accorded Negroes by these manipulative law enforcement agencies was in direct contrast with the behavior of previous regimes. In both towns the memory of brutality by previous police chiefs and sheriffs was still strong among our Negro respondents. A middle class Negro respondent in Tobacco Hill described the change in law enforcement when he stated that "there are many things that happen in town between the colored and white that 20 years ago would have seen Negroes being run out of town, but this doesn't happen any more." The sheriff stopped his deputies from "beating up" Negroes when he took office in 1945, just as the mayor stopped police brutality when he took office in 1947.

The memory of a shift in the treatment of the Negro was accomplished in these two towns by what we would label a "dramatic event." Following an incident in the mid-1940's in Tobacco Hill when Mayor Nobb, with the police standing by, horsewhipped a group of Negroes including several women, he was defeated for re-election by Sam Turner, who immediately replaced the chief of police and instituted a continuing period of fair and decent treatment of Negroes by the police of the town.

Similarly, a "dramatic event" occurred in the late 1940's in Hamlin when the "High Sheriff" very firmly intervened in a rape case by refusing to allow a Negro to be "framed" for the offense of a white man. These dramatic events, combined with relatively decent treatment of Negro prisoners, have left lasting impressions on the Negroes in these towns. While we are not suggesting that fair and decent treatment of Negroes by itself provides a law enforcement agency with significant manipulative leverage, we do suggest that it is an important, and probably necessary, pre-condition for manipulation.

The favorable response of the Negro to fair law enforcement does not appear to be limited to those Negroes who have had direct experience with officers of the law nor to those whose behavior might lead to such an encounter. The middle class Negro in the Manipulative town, whose chances of a hostile encounter with the law are probably no greater than his counterpart in the white community, also appears to be favorably impressed and responsive to fair and decent law enforcement. It is our impression that middle class Negroes tend to view fair law enforcement from an abstract racial standpoint. We think, then, that the middle class Negroes' racial commitment leads them to converge with the poorer, less educated Negro in supporting the manipulative white politicians.

Just as decent treatment of prisoners makes an impression on Negroes, a friendly attitude on the part of law enforcement officers when dealing with Negroes in a nonofficial capacity appears to have a significant impact upon a number of Negroes. For instance, middle class Negro respondents in Hamlin appeared to be impressed by the friendly behavior of the "High Sheriff" who would lean out of his car window, wave and call to them by name as he drove by, or stop and talk to them for an hour on a street corner. The friendliness of the sheriff had been affirmed on several occasions when he voiced his support for Negro requests to use city recreational facilities. The Negro middle class in Hamlin, as far as we can ascertain, supports the sheriff in his own campaigns and, at a minimum, listens sympathetically when he approaches them as individuals on behalf of other candidates.

Negroes in Tobacco Hill also were responsive to friendly behavior. Not only did Mayor Turner keep the police under control, he was considered to be the Negroes' friend — they could bring their problems to him and be treated "almost as equals." Mayor Turner had solid Negro support, not only for himself, but for other candidates as well.

The support given a sheriff or mayor by middle class Negroes appears incongruous during a period of militant Negro action on a nationwide scale. Yet we would speculate that there are many small towns in the South where Negroes are still convinced that this really is a "white man's world." In this particular type of environment, friendly behavior can easily elicit political support.

Aside from fair and friendly treatment, law enforcement agencies can provide another "service" for at least part of the Negro community which we conceive of as a pre-condition for manipulation. Following Dollard, we label this particular service "impulse freedom."[8] The freedoms to which we refer are in the realm of sexual behavior, public drunkenness, gambling, and aggressive behavior *within* the Negro community. Of course, freedom in the expression of impulse is judged by an idealized white middle class norm.

Impulse freedom is difficult to discuss in 1964 without offending the sensibilities of the national Negro movement — which tends to reflect, in large measure, middle class values and aspirations — or without providing ammunition for the Southern segregationist. However, for whatever historical or sociological reasons, the normative system, as well as the external behavior, of the lower class Negro diverges sharply from the idealized code of the white middle class.

The enforcement of white middle class values is, to a degree, placed in the hands of the law enforcement agencies of the town, but the agencies have, within limits, a "choice" as to how rigorously the law shall be enforced. This particular choice can be expressed, from the Negro standpoint, by the distinction between a "hard police chief" and a "good man" as police chief. The "hard police chief," from the Negroes' point of view, "goes out of his way"

---

[8]John Dollard, *Caste and Class in a Southern Town* (Garden City, 1949), pp. 390-433.

to discover infringements of the law and, once infringements are discovered, they are not overlooked. The hard law enforcement agency patrols the Negro community "laying for drunks." However, the "hard chief" should be distinguished from the "brutal chief." The "hard chief" is fair to the Negro once he is apprehended and, accordingly, not brutal, but he is considered "hard" because he interferes with the Negroes' freedom. In a town which has a "good man" as the police chief or sheriff, the Negroes are left alone. Law enforcement is lax — gambling, moonshine, other rackets, and aggression *within* the Negro community are tolerated. The police do not "pick on" the Negro.

The acceptance of the rackets as part of the way of life of a town is well illustrated by a story, probably apocryphal, but revealing, about the bolita racket. According to an interviewee, for a number of years in Tobacco Hill a major bolita operation was housed in Joe's Bar. On Friday afternoon when a large number of phone calls were made to the Bar to learn the winning number, the line to the Bar was often busy. Prior to the installation of a dial telephone system, the operator would inform the caller that the line was busy and then continue by saying "but the number for today is xxx."

In a town which tolerates a high degree of impulse freedom the courts, as well as the police, can be involved. Negroes before the courts, given this particular environment, might tend to receive shorter sentences than a white in similar circumstances. Lax law enforcement tends to be rationalized by the phrase "after all it's only a nigger." We by no means intend to imply that the set of attitudes which calls forth this particular rationalization is confined to manipulative law enforcement agencies. We found this attitude evident among many of our white interviewees. However, we are implying that the level of law enforcement, vis-à-vis the Negro community, is, at times, the product of a calculated choice based on strategic consideration of the Negro vote. An interesting example of this type of calculation can be found in Tobacco Hill. When Sam Turner, after having served 14 years as Mayor of Tobacco Hill, was defeated by Lewis Alger in the 1961 mayoralty election, Alger inherited a community in which, for a number of years, the rackets and police corruption were prevalent and, we might add, readily discussed by many of our interviewees.

The Negro vote in Tobacco Hill is sizeable. In 1959 is comprised 22 per cent of the registered voters in the town, and in the mayoralty election that year 21 per cent of the voters were Negroes. When Turner became mayor in 1947, Tobacco Hill was a Non-Voting town although the sheriff elected in 1944 had already begun to organize the registered Negroes for county elections. However, it was the Turner administration which openly encouraged and organized Negro registration and voting in the town. The advent of the Turner administration brought an end to police brutality in Tobacco

Hill and, from the lower class Negroes' point of view, to police interference in the life of the Negro community. Asked why Negroes voted for Turner, a Negro answered "we're just satisfied. . . . Nobody bothers us and we just ain't going to have a change, 'cause we don't know what it might be like."

When Turner was defeated in 1961 the new mayor was faced with a strategic problem; to curtail the impulse freedom of the Negro would mean the probable alienation of a large number of Negroes whose friendship and votes he might need at the next election. After interviews with the new mayor and his political allies and enemies, we are convinced that he made a calculated decision to minimally increase the level of law enforcement — just enough to impress his white middle class supporters but not enough to alienate the Negro vote.

A decision of this sort, of course, must take into account the political strength and attitude of the Negro middle class in the town. In both Tobacco Hill and Hamlin we found members of the Negro middle class who were quite concerned about the low level of law enforcement in the Negro community. Moreover, their concern was not simply at the abstract level of Negro middle class morality; they were concerned about the physical safety of their families and themselves within the Negro community. A Negro middle class respondent in Tobacco Hill stated that it was dangerous to complain of the activities of ones' neighbors to the police because, although the police might talk to the individual, they would also tell him who had registered the complaint and, accordingly, reprisals might occur. While we have some evidence which indicates that middle class Negroes are concerned about the low level of law enforcement within the Negro community, we also have evidence indicating that many middle class Negroes whom we interviewed tend to interpret strict law enforcement as discriminatory from a racial standpoint. The middle class Negro, then, may be caught in the conflict of two value systems. His middle class morality and desires for personal safety clash with his racial ideology.

Segments of the Negro middle class are often tied to law enforcement agencies by their particular economic interest. In the small town, independent Negro businesses, if they exist, often are limited to taxi service, funeral homes (which often include ambulance service), and the ownership of bars and "juke joints."[9] Each of these businesses is, to a varying degree, vulnerable to decisions made by the law enforcement agencies of the town. The bar and juke joint operators are, perhaps, most vulnerable since strict law enforcement in the immediate vicinity of their establishment would substantially reduce

---

[9] A "juke joint" is an establishment which sells beer and/or whiskey, legally or illegally, and often has a coin-operated record player (juke box) on the premises used for dancing or listening. In our towns, juke joints were segregated, some for whites and others for Negroes.

trade. Taxi operators are, of course, susceptible to strict enforcement of traffic regulations and to licensing procedures. Undertaking and ambulance services are less vulnerable to the activities of law enforcement agencies than the other businesses listed. However, the sheriff and the police do control a lucrative trade in ambulance service for accident victims, and the proprietors of such a service, as was the case in Tobacco Hill, can be tied economically to these law agencies. Astute and manipulative white politicians under these circumstances are likely to ignore the problems of middle class Negroes. They are economically vulnerable, their value orientations toward whites are not completely consistent, and they are not numerous.

A Negro minister in Tobacco Hill who was bitter and disturbed by what he called the "immorality and disorganization" of the Negro community estimated the "immoral vote" — that is the vote directly controllable by the police and other agents of the white political structure by means of whiskey, fish fries, money and other techniques — at about 75 per cent of the voting Negroes. The county attorney, a member of the court house clique of Roth County, and, in our view, an astute professional politician, also estimated the "riff raff" Negro vote — the directly controllable Negro vote — at 75 per cent of the voting Negroes. There was agreement among most of our interviewees in Tobacco Hill that the directly manipulated Negro vote ran somewhere in the range of 75 per cent. In Hamlin there was less agreement over actual percentages. Estimates of the "immoral" vote ran from 90 per cent down to 60 per cent. Whatever the actual distribution of these two populations is, the strategy of the law enforcement agencies appears to be to ignore the potential problems of middle class Negroes while still remaining on friendly terms with them.

While we have mentioned the rackets previously, we will deal with them briefly here. Some testimony concerning bolita, moonshine, and prostitution was forthcoming in every town in which we interviewed. However, in only three of the six towns do we have enough data to warrant our judgment that the agencies of the law were directly connected to the rackets, either through payoff or by ownership. All three of these towns were or had been Manipulative towns. In Bougainville the police chief protected the bolita operation and controlled Negro voting in large measure until the early 1950's when Negro veterans re-organized the Civic League and began to bargain with members of the white political structure. The chief later made several attempts to elect "bolita men" to the board of the Civic League but failed. In Tobacco Hill the law enforcement agencies protected the bolita operation, while in Hamlin the data point to ownership of the rackets by the law enforcement officers. We tend to think that the significance of the rackets lies not so much in the actual number of votes which, for instance, a bolita peddler or moonshine distributor can influence as an individual, but rather in the complex we labeled impulse freedom — that is, the voter is responsive to the lawman because the latter facilitates activity desired by segments of the Negro community, and, in order that the rackets may flourish, law enforcement agencies are willing to permit a wide range of impulse freedom.

To the unsophisticated, lower class Negro in the small town the law is complicated and, usually, something to be feared. When he is in trouble he often needs someone to explain, defend, and, hopefully extricate him from his difficulties. Help from a sophisticated member of the Negro middle class, preferably a Negro lawyer, would be desirable. However, such help is, in our experience, often unobtainable. The Negro community in most of the towns in which we interviewed is too small and probably too poor to support a Negro attorney so that the Negro in need of legal aid is forced to turn to a white lawyer. Moreover, we speculate, based on interview materials, that many Negroes, whether with reason or not, believe that a Negro attorney would be in a disadvantageous position compared to his white counterpart in local courts.

In Angusville where the Negro community is politically disorganized as compared to other Manipulative towns, the attempt to organize and direct the Negro vote by the whites originated in the family law office of a member of the political clique which had controlled that town's elected offices for a number of years. The firm handles most of the legal problems of the Negroes in the town. The senior partner is the trial lawyer of the firm and his performance in court is geared to a Florida cracker audience and jury. Amidst shouting, whispering, crying, and statements of "after all the defendant is only a nigger," the Clarence Darrow of Angusville is able to retrieve a number of Negroes from the clutches of the law.[10]

The law firm has gained in a number of ways from its endeavors for the Negro. First, it has acquired the property of some Negroes in lieu of payment of legal fees. Second, since many of its Negro clients cannot pay the fees for services rendered, the firm has "allowed" them to work off their indebtedness on the family farm. Third, the most important from our standpoint, the lawyers of the firm are looked upon by many Negroes as friends and possible saviors. Therefore, when the time of a local election approaches a series of letters and personal contacts flow from the law office to the Negro community suggesting who the firm feels is best qualified to hold public office and, apparently, many are responsive. A white lawyer, then, willing to handle Negro cases, and with the added attraction of a reputation as a winner in court, can have manipulative value at the time of an election.

[10]The statement "after all the defendant is only a nigger" implies that if the damaged party were white, "what would you expect from a Negro"; or if the damaged party were another Negro, "what difference does it make."

V

On the basis of our case studies of various towns in their Manipulative phase, it seems clear to us that manipulation of the Negro vote by white politicians as a structural feature of a town's politics helps to account for part of the unexplained variance in the Matthews and Prothro study. Given usual abstract conceptions of civil rights, it is ironical that in our case study towns Negro registration and voting were usually initiated by the white political structure.

What has the Negro in Manipulative towns, such as Tobacco Hill or Hamlin, gained after more than 10 years of voting? Police harassment and brutality have disappeared. The Negro community in these towns is, in a relative sense, "let alone." From the standpoint of integration there were no gains. When freedom riders passed through Tobacco Hill the signs in the bus station were removed and the riders were served, but once the freedom riders were satisfied and continued their journey, signs were replaced. No Tobacco Hill or Hamlin Negro has enjoyed integrated service. The schools, restaurants, motels, and public recreational facilities all remain segregated in both towns. From the standpoint of municipal services Negroes received occasional promises but little fulfillment. In Tobacco Hill a few blocks of streets were paved in the Negro section. In Hamlin Negroes have not been able to obtain paving on the streets leading to the Negro schools. From an economic standpoint, also, gains have been minimal. In Tobacco Hill the Turner administration hired some Negroes for unskilled city work, and two Negro policemen were put on the force. In Hamlin economic gains have been even fewer than in Tobacco Hill.

Why have the Negro communities gained so little? We would suggest that the weakness of the Negro middle class in these towns prevents effective Negro leadership from emerging which might have organized the Negro community to bargain with the white political structure. In Hamlin and Tobacco Hill the Negro middle class is small and, to a degree, economically dependent upon the whites. The largest numerical segment of the Negro middle class — the school teachers — provide little or no leadership. Although the teachers are theoretically protected by a state merit system, they are still vulnerable to action by local white leadership. Furthermore, political leadership implies skills in bargaining and coalition-making which are *learned.* There are few ways that the Negro can obtain the requisite training in a small town. What political training the local Negro obtains usually has been given by whites, but this is training only in taking orders and, perhaps in a limited fashion, in individual bargaining. Negroes who acquire skills in the outside world and, therefore, would be potential leaders of the Negro community seldom return to towns like Tobacco Hill or Hamlin because of the limited number of job opportunities.

For the Negro community to successfully bargain its votes for gains, a coalition is probably necessary between the educated Negro middle class and the uneducated, but numerically larger, lower class. But as we have indicated previously, the values, life patterns, and goals of the two strata diverge. To bring them together, then, is not a simple task. The gains from Negro voting in the Manipulative town might be small from the viewpoint of the white liberal or race-conscious middle class Negro, but the uneducated, unsophisticated Negro in the Manipulative towns tends to view his gains from a different frame of reference. The voting situation in the Manipulative town, from a racial standpoint, contains a number of ambiguous elements which, we believe, makes the transformation from a Manipulative to an Independent Bargaining situation difficult. Obviously, we are not arguing that a transformation from Manipulation to Independent Bargaining is impossible, for we do have evidence of such a transformation in some of the towns we studied.[11] However, we do believe that the difficulty of effecting such a transformation helps to explain the success of the street demonstration technique as a device for bringing the two sections of the Negro community together as an effective Independent Bargaining unit. To build a voting coalition requires skill, time, and patience. Demonstrations are immediate, dramatic, and, from a racial standpoint, unambiguous. Moreover, demonstration or the threat of demonstration occurs in a situation which, unlike voting, is not structured by the white political community and, therefore, is not easily controlled or manipulated by the whites.

---

[11]In a forthcoming book, we will examine not only the politics of the Manipulative town, but also the other elements of the typology which we developed at the beginning of our paper — the Non-Voting town; the Low Voting, Unorganized town; the Independent Bargaining town; and the Office Holding town.

The Influence of the S Factor
upon the Voting Behavior of
South Carolina Urban Negroes

John B. McConaughy and John H. Gauntlett

Aristotle stated that man is a political animal. The authors decided to investigate by means of the survey method the S or social factor among a sample of 530 urban Negroes of voting age in South Carolina during the summer of 1958. The S factor was defined as the type or amount of activity in which an individual engaged with respect to organizations. This factor can be measured qualitatively by the type of organization, or quantitatively by the number of organizations to which the individual belongs. It was decided to compare the influences of the type of organization with the influence of the number of organizations in order to determine whether the social factor was more important qualitatively or quantitatively in influencing vote participation, party orientation, and party loyalty among South Carolina urban Negroes.

The respondents were asked to list the names of the organizations to which they belonged. They were also asked questions concerning their voting participation, the candidates for whom they voted, and their attitudes concerning certain political questions. The respondents were assured of their anonymity

Reprinted from *Western Political Quarterly,* Vol. XVI, (December, 1963), pp. 973-984, by permission of the University of Utah, copyright owners.

in order to obtain frank and truthful answers to the questions asked. Negro interviewers were used in order to establish better rapport with the respondents. Five cities in South Carolina were selected for the study. One ward in each, containing the greatest percentage of Negroes, was selected for the interviews.

Each ward was divided into five sections of approximately equal Negro population and a separate interviewer was assigned to each section. The interviewers were instructed to take every "Nth" house depending upon the number of houses in his section. They were told to select only one person from each house for interviewing and to return another time if no one was home. The interviewers were college students or teachers with a good educational background. The five cities included two from the Piedmont or northern section, one from the center, and two from the Low Country or southern part of the state. Table I gives the characteristics of the total sample.

In order to make the qualitative study, Negro organizations were grouped into four classifications: political, social, religious, and business-professional. Church membership was discarded since practically all of them stated that they belonged to some church, but sub-organizations within a church were counted. Political organizations were defined as any organization which attempts to influence either elections or the political attitudes of persons. Social organizations were those which had as their principal object the fostering of friendly feelings among their members. Religious organizations were those within the church or outside the church whose principal purpose was to

TABLE I

CHARACTERISTICS OF SAMPLE BY WARDS

Cities	Number	Mean Age in Years	Mean Education in Years	Mean Annual Income
Spartanburg	93	43.90	9.15	$2,082
Greenville	101	43.80	10.33	$3,192
Columbia	140	42.16	12.31	$3,180
Darlington	98	36.00	9.92	$2,662
Charleston	98	39.00	10.19	$2,872
Total or Mean	530	42.41	10.44	$2,861

Cities	Sex Per Cent Male	Per Cent Protestant (Church Members)	Median Residence Years	Per Cent Registered
Spartanburg	50.53	92.5	Over 20	58.06
Greenville	38.60	90.2	Over 20	77.22
Columbia	54.26	93.0	Over 20	79.97
Darlington	57.40	99.0	Over 20	81.63
Charleston	52.04	83.7	Over 20	75.48
Total or Mean	50.75	91.7	Over 20	75.09

foster religious activity. Business organizations and professional associations were those which had a business or professional purpose or objective. These were grouped together because their members showed similar voting behavior. Table II gives the distribution of Negroes in these different organizations. It will be seen that about half of those answering belonged to no organization. The social and religious groups had about a third each of those Negroes belonging to organizations and the remaining third was distributed among political and business-professional groups. The Negroes were grouped in the type of organization which they listed first. This was done in order to avoid duplication where a person belonged to more than one organization and because it was thought that the respondent would mention first the organization which he considered most important. Table III gives the quantitative distribution of organizational membership.

It should be noted that if we start with the number that belonged to three organizations and continue to those who belong to no organizations, we obtain something close to a geometric ratio: if we multiply by two, we obtain the next frequency. A perfect geometric ratio would be 32, 64, 128, 256. Whether this is a general principle or true only in our sample would be an interesting investigation for other political or social researchers. In the quantitative classification, Negroes were placed in the category of the number of organizations they belonged to regardless of whether it was political, social, religious or business-professional. The attempt here was to determine the quantitative effect regardless of the type of organization.

Table IV gives the percentage vote participation by Negroes according to type of organization to which they belonged but disregards the number of

TABLE II

QUALITATIVE PARTICIPATION IN ORGANIZATIONS

	Total Sample		Those Answering		No Organization
Number	530		449		223

	Political	Social	Religious	Business	Total Organization
Number	32	88	80	26	226
Per Cent Membership	14	39	35	12	100

TABLE III

QUANTITATIVE PARTICIPATION IN ORGANIZATIONS

	Total Sample	Those Answering	Membership	One	Two	Three
Number	530	449	226	130	64	32
Percentage			100	58	28	14

organizations of which they were members. Six elections were studied: three presidential elections, 1948, 1952, and 1956; and three gubernatorial, 1954, the first Democratic primary of 1958, and the second Democratic primary of 1958 which was the gubernatorial run-off election. In most Southern states, including South Carolina, if no candidate receives a majority of the popular vote for governor in the first Democratic primary, all but the two highest candidates are eliminated and the run-off election decides who shall be the Democratic nominee. This system of two primaries if no candidate receives a majority in the first is considered necessary because the general election is unimportant since the Democratic nominee always wins. It would seem from the recent presidential election that the general election has become important so far as presidential elections are concerned in the formerly one-party states. This presidential Republicanism has not as yet, however, been transferred to gubernatorial elections.

It can be seen that there is a certain consistency in three of the four groups of organizations. Of all the groups, the Negroes who belong to political organizations participated most in five out of six elections. Those who belong to social organizations were the second most active group in four out of six elections. The religious group was the least active of the four groups in five out of six elections. The business-professional group, however, is quite inconsistent. It was first once, second twice, third twice, and fourth once. The percentages of difference between the groups which participate the most and the group which participates the least is from a low of 21 per cent in the first gubernatorial primary of 1958 to a high of nearly 33 per cent in the 1956

TABLE IV

VOTING PARTICIPATION ACCORDING TO THE QUALITATIVE S FACTOR
(rank order and percentage voting)

| | PRESIDENTIAL ELECTIONS | | | | | | GUBERNATORIAL ELECTIONS | | | | | |
| | 1948 | | 1952 | | 1956 | | 1954 | | 1958 (1) | | 1958 (2) | |
Group	Rank	Per Cent	Rank	Per Cent	Rank	Per Cent	Rank	Per Cent	Rank	Per Cent	Rank	Per Cent
Political	1	73.06	3	69.99	1	93.54	1	81.25	1	90.31	1	100.00
Social	2	69.49	2	79.25	3	83.75	3	66.26	2	80.93	2	91.42
Business-Professional	3	54.16	1	83.33	2	87.50	2	70.83	3	79.16	4	70.83
Religious	4	42.64	4	59.99	4	60.80	4	55.55	4	69.20	3	86.27
Percentage Difference		30.42		23.34		32.74		25.70		21.11		29.17
P		.02		.05		.01		.20		.10		N.S.*

*N.S. means not suitable for chi square because of a zero in one cell.

presidential election. If we use the chi square method with the raw numbers to determine the probability of the distribution happening by chance in each election, we find that P is significant at the 1 per cent level in only one of the five elections in which the chi square method was used. There is very little likelihood that such consistency of the rank order for three of the four groups in six elections could happen by chance; and it indicates so far as these groups are concerned that the type of organization is an important influence in voting participation. In the business-professional group, the voting participation order is so erratic that in the opinion of the authors, its distribution might be due to chance or the erratic political behavior of the group. The P's are more significant in the presidential than in the gubernatorial elections. This greater significance in the former would indicate that the type of organization to which the Negroes belong has more influence on their voting participation in a presidential election than in a gubernatorial election.

In Table V, the influence of the quantitative S factor is examined. The South Carolina urban Negroes are grouped according to the number of organizations to which they belong regardless of the type.

If we examine the rank order of voting participation according to Table V, we find a remarkable consistency. Those Negroes who belong to no organization vote the least of all groups in all six elections. Those who belong to one organization participate next to last in voting. Those who belong to two organizations have the second highest percentage in voting activity in four elections and have the highest activity in two elections. Those who belong to three or more organizations have the highest voting activity in four of the six elections and are second in two elections. In one of these, the 1948 presidential election, the percentage difference between the most active and second

TABLE V

VOTING PARTICIPATION ACCORDING TO THE QUANTITATIVE
S FACTOR
(rank order and percentage voting)

	PRESIDENTIAL ELECTIONS						GUBERNATORIAL ELECTIONS					
	1948		1952		1956		1954		1958 (1)		1958 (2)	
Number of Groups	Order	Per Cent	Order	Per Cent	Order	Per Cent	Order	Per Cent	Order	Per Cent	Order	Per Cent
None	4	37.36	4	48.52	4	53.73	4	39.80	4	57.63	4	53.36
One	3	51.30	3	63.63	3	69.74	3	57.85	3	69.60	3	60.00
Two	1	70.68	1	85.71	2	85.00	2	71.66	2	82.25	2	73.43
Three	2	70.00	2	74.19	1	93.75	1	84.37	1	96.87	1	84.37
Percentage Difference between 0 and 3												
organizations	32.64		25.67		40.02		44.57		39.24		31.01	
P	.001		.001		.001		.001		.001		.001	

most active groups in voting is less than one per cent. The percentage differences between the most active and least active groups is consistently higher for each election than it was for the qualitative groups shown in Table IV. The probability is for each of six elections significant at the .001 level. Since the quantitative social factor shows greater consistency in rank order, a higher percentage of difference between the lowest and highest groups and a much more significant probability for all six elections, we must come to the conclusion that so far as South Carolina urban Negroes are concerned, the number of organizations to which they belong is a much more important factor in their voting participation than the type of organization to which they belong. All organizations to which they belong are political in the sense that they increase voting participation. The authors believe that this is due to greater social interaction which is more important than the type of social interaction. The stimuli received from more interactions is more effective in stimulating voting than a single interaction even though it be with a political organization.

The qualitative and quantitative S factors were then examined for their influence upon party allegiance. The respondents were asked to indicate whether they considered themselves Republicans, Democrats, or Independents. Table VI gives the qualitative S factor.

It can be seen that the social group which has the highest percentage of Republicans is the political group. This may well be due to the fact that there is a strong Republican organization working with Negroes in South Carolina. The religious group has the lowest percentage of Republican votes. This is probably caused by the greater conservativeness of the religious groups. Although one might think that the Republican party is more conservative than the Democratic party, yet in a state such as South Carolina which has only recently become a two-party state in presidential elections, the conservative and traditional approach to party politics would be Democratic. The

TABLE VI

THE QUALITATIVE S FACTOR AND PARTY ALLEGIANCE
(rank order and percentages)

Group	REPUBLICAN Order	REPUBLICAN Per Cent	DEMOCRAT Order	DEMOCRAT Per Cent	INDEPENDENT Order	INDEPENDENT Per Cent
Political (32)	1	37	3	47	3	16
Social (88)	3	20	1	68	4	12
Religious (80)	4	17.5	2	64.9	2	17.5
Business-Professional (24)	2	21	4	46	1	33
Percentage Difference between highest and lowest		19.5		22		21
Sum of percentage differences = 62	P = .13					

social group has the highest percentage of Democratic members, although it is closely followed by the religious group. Less than a majority of both the political group and the business-professional group consider themselves Democratic. Both the religious and the social groups would seem to be more traditional-minded than the political and business-professional groups.

Table VII compares the influence of the quantitative S factor upon party allegiance. It can be seen from the table that a definite pattern appears.

As the number of organizations to which the Negro respondents belong increases, the percentage belonging to the Democratic party decreases. This, then, is an inverse relationship. There is a direct relationship between the organizational membership and the percentage considering themselves Independents: that is, as membership in organizations increases the percentage of Independents increases. The Republican percentages show a direct relation also with the number of organizations to which the respondents belong. In the latter case, however, those who belong to three or more organizations tend to vote more Independent than Republican. Organization membership leads to diversity of ideas. In the market place are many ideas. The old traditional conservative ideas are challenged by new ideas which are competing for legitimacy. The voter when challenged by these new ideas must make a choice and often this choice is a new idea which has been presented to him by his increased social interaction. Those who have been faced with the bleak discomfort of a common uniformity whether it be from authoritarianism or democracy may draw some warm comfort from these results.

Although the P is significant only at the .13 level which would indicate that the number of organizations has little influence on party allegiance, yet the chi-square method does not take into account the consistent pattern that develops according to the number of organizations to which the respondents belong. If this were to be taken into consideration, the influence would seem

TABLE VII

THE QUANTITATIVE S FACTOR AND PARTY ALLEGIANCE
(rank order and percentages)

Organization Membership	REPUBLICAN		DEMOCRAT		INDEPENDENT	
	Order	Per Cent	Order	Per Cent	Order	Per Cent
No Organization (140)	4	16.42	1	75.00	4	8.57
One Organization (99)	3	20.20	2	66.66	3	13.13
Two Organizations (60)	1	25.00	3	56.66	2	18.33
Three Organizations (30)	2	23.33	4	50.00	1	26.67
Percentage Differences between 0 and 3 organizations		6.91		25.00		18.10
Sum of percentage differences = 50	P = .13					

to be an important one. The differences in percentages between the party allegiance is sufficient to determine an election even in the case of the Republican percentage which is the lowest, amounting only to about 7 per cent. In the case of the Democratic percentage, the difference between party allegiance is 25 per cent. In comparing the importance of the qualitative and the quantitative S factors, it would seem from the percentage differences and the P's that they are of about equal influence in determining party allegiance.

Although party allegiance is extremely important in determining voting behavior, it is clear, especially after the 1960 presidential election in South Carolina, that the mere statement that one is a Democrat does not mean that he is going to vote Democratic in a presidential election. We have in both Southern and Northern states people who consider themselves Democrats but switch votes and vote for Republican presidential candidates at times. This phenomenon occurred also in the recent presidential election in California where, in spite of a surplus Democratic registration, the Republican candidate carried the state. The Negro respondents were asked whether they had ever voted for a candidate of a party different from the one to which they belonged. Table VIII gives the results of the qualitative S factor in regard to party switching.

If we compare Table VIII with Table VI, we can see that although only 33 per cent of the business-professsional group declared that they were Independents, yet 53 per cent of this group stated that they had switched party candidates. Another 20 per cent therefore switched who considered themselves to be either Democrats or Republicans. This latter group is the most nonconformist and independent of the four groups studied. The business-professional group is followed closely by the members of the political group in percentage switching. The groups which switch parties the least are the religious and social groups. As pointed out above, these are the ones which have the highest percentages of Democratic members. The two groups which

TABLE VIII

THE QUALITATIVE SOCIAL FACTOR AND PARTY SWITCHING
(rank order and percentages)

Group	SWITCHED		NO SWITCH	
	Order	Per Cent	Order	Per Cent
Political (32)	2	50	3	50
Social (88)	3	37	2	63
Religious (80)	4	25	1	75
Bus.-Prof. (24)	1	53	4	47
Percentage Difference between highest and lowest		28		28
P = .10				

switched the most have the highest percentage of Republican members. Therefore, we can assume that there tends to be an inverse ratio between the
percentage of groups which are Democratic and vote-switching. The higher
the percentage of the group which is Democratic, the less vote-switching
occurs. Group solidarity is an adverse factor in vote-switching. An individual
tends to vote with the majority of the group of which he is a member. If a
large majority of the group is Democratic, the social pressures of the group
encourage conformity and most of the vote is Democratic. If, however, the
majority of the group is either Republican or Independent and only a minority
is Democratic, a switch of votes to the Republican party or Independent electors would be encouraged. The social pressures of the organization indeed
encourage such diversity. This vote-switching among South Carolina urban
Negroes must take place only in presidential elections since the Republicans
had never, until 1961, put up any slate of state officers. There had been no
Republican state officers or members of the South Carolina legislature since
1900, until the election of a Republican representative from Richland County
to the state legislature in a 1961 special election.

It will be noted that again a pattern develops. As the number of organizations to which the Negroes belong increases, the party switching increases.
In the case of those who belong to three or more organizations, half of them
report that they have switched their votes in presidential elections. The uniformity of the pattern is remarkable and indicates that the quantitative S
factor is very important in determining vote-switching (see Table IX). The
P which is significant at the .001 level also indicates the great influence of
this factor. Because of the high significance of the P and the progressive pattern of party switching, it would seem that the quantitative S factor is much
more important than the qualitative S factor in determining party switching.

TABLE IX

THE QUANTITATIVE S FACTOR AND PARTY SWITCHING
(rank order and percentages)

Organization Membership	SWITCHED		NO SWITCH	
	Order	Per Cent	Order	Per Cent
No Organization (140)	4	17.80	1	82.20
One Organization (99)	3	30.43	2	69.56
Two Organizations (60)	2	39.58	3	60.41
Three Organizations (30)	1	50.00	4	50.00
Percentage Difference between highest and lowest		32.2		32.2
P = .001				

It might be thought that the relationship between the quantitative social factor and voting participation, party allegiance and party switching is an artifact. The argument would be that there is a high correlation between income and the number of organizations to which the voter belongs and that therefore, one might be measuring income rather than the influence of the quantitative social factor upon voting behavior. If the income factor is held constant, it can be seen, however, that the quantitative social factor is an independent factor in voting behavior.

In order to study the relationship between the income factor and the quantitative social factor, the voters were divided into three classes according to family income: (1) Low Income: 0–$1,999; (2) Middle Income: $2,000–$3,999; and (3) High Income: $4,000 and over. The distribution of organization membership and voting behavior was then studied in each income class. Table X shows the organization membership and voting participation in each of the three income classes.

It can be seen from Table X that organization membership does increase as income rises. If we look at the percentage distribution of organization membership by income groups, we can see that the percentage who belong to no organizations decreases from 70 per cent in the Low Income group to 38 per cent in the High Income group. Likewise, the number who belong to three or more organizations increases from 3 per cent in the Low Income group to 18 per cent in the High Income group. In spite of this relationship, however, it would seem clear that the quantitative social factor is an independent factor in voting participation in the six elections. For instance, in the Low Income group in the first gubernatorial primary of 1958, only 30 per cent of those who belonged to no organization voted while 100 per cent of those who belonged to three or more organizations voted. In the same election, 69 per cent of those in the Middle Income group who belonged to no organization voted, but 100 per cent of those who belonged to three or more organizations voted. In the High Income group in the same election, 79 per cent of those who belonged to no organization voted while 94 per cent of those who belonged to three or more organizations voted. The quantitative S factor would seem to have the greatest influence in the Low Income group and the least influence in the High Income group. Those who belong to three or more organizations show the greatest deviation from the general pattern in the High Income group.

Table XI shows the influence of the income factor and the quantitative S factor upon party allegiance.

If we consider the income factor alone, it would seem that as income increases there is a slightly higher Democratic percentage. In the Low Income group only 69 per cent of those who belong to no organization consider themselves Democratic, while 74 per cent of the Middle Income and 73 per cent of the High Income group consider themselves Democratic. It is believed that the Low Income group is less Democratic than the Middle or High Income group because the Low Income group is a protest group. It therefore follows that in a state which is one-party Democratic in state elections, those who are opposed to the *status quo* would tend to vote Republican in a presi-

TABLE X

VOTING PARTICIPATION AND ORGANIZATION MEMBERSHIP WITH INCOME CONSTANT

	LOW INCOME 0–$1,999				
Organization Membership	0	1	2	3	Total
Number	109	33	10	4	156
Percentage					
Distribution of Vote	70	21	6	3	100
1948 Presidential	19	36	40	100	
1952 Presidential	29	45	70	100	
1956 Presidential	33	42	70	100	
1954 Gubernatorial	23	33	40	100	
1958 1st Gubernatorial	30	36	90	100	
1958 2nd Gubernatorial	27	30	70	100	

	MIDDLE INCOME $2,000–$3,999				
Organization Membership	0	1	2	3	Total
Number	113	50	31	12	206
Percentage					
Distribution of Vote	55	24	15	6	100
1948 Presidential	40	50	74	67	
1952 Presidential	53	68	90	83	
1956 Presidential	57	84	90	83	
1954 Gubernatorial	41	66	71	50	
1958 1st Gubernatorial	69	82	81	100	
1958 2nd Gubernatorial	63	82	74	100	

	HIGH INCOME $4,000 AND OVER				
Organization Membership	0	1	2	3	Total
Number	34	29	11	16	90
Percentage					
Distribution of Vote	38	32	12	18	100
1948 Presidential	56	72	82	56	
1952 Presidential	71	86	100	69	
1956 Presidential	76	97	91	100	
1954 Gubernatorial	71	76	75	88	
1958 1st Gubernatorial	79	90	91	94	
1958 2nd Gubernatorial	59	79	91	81	

dential election. Although the income factor would tend to produce a greater Democratic percentage in the Middle and High Income group, the S factor acts in opposition to this trend and indeed overcomes it. In the Middle Income group 74 per cent of those who belong to no organization consider themselves Democratic while only 50 per cent of those who belong to three or more organizations consider themselves Democratic. In the High Income group, while 73 per cent of those who belong to no organizations consider themselves Democratic, only 40 per cent of those who belong to three or more organizations consider themselves Democratic. In the Low Income group, there is a difference of 19 per cent in the Democratic percentage between those who belong to no organization and those who belong to three or more organizations. In the Middle Income group there is a difference of 24 per cent and in the High Income group a difference of 33 per cent.

TABLE XI
PARTY ALLEGIANCE AND ORGANIZATION MEMBERSHIP WITH INCOME CONSTANT

	LOW INCOME 0–$1,999				
Organization Membership	0	1	2	3	Total
Number	55	21	8	2	86
Percentage					
Republican	20	29	63	0	
Democratic	69	67	29	50	
Independent	11	4	8	50	
Total	100	100	100	100	

	MIDDLE INCOME $2,000–$3,999				
Organization Membership	0	1	2	3	Total
Number	76	47	29	12	164
Percentage					
Republican	17	15	21	25	
Democratic	74	74	62	50	
Independent	9	11	17	25	
Total	100	100	100	100	

	HIGH INCOME $4,000 AND OVER				
Organization Membership	0	1	2	3	Total
Number	30	26	11	15	82
Percentage					
Republican	17	38	18	27	
Democratic	73	50	55	40	
Independent	10	12	27	33	
Total	100	100	100	100	

The highest influence of the S factor would seem to be in the High Income group in regard to party allegiance. These differences caused by the quantitative S factor are much greater than those caused by the income factor since the greatest difference in those who belong to no organizations in the Democratic percentage is only 5 per cent.

According to Table XII, the income factor seems to have little influence upon party switching.

The greatest difference in party switching of those belonging to no organization is only 2 per cent on the three income levels. The percentage differences between those who belong to no organization and those who belong to three or more organizations in respect to party switching are: Low Income, 35 per cent; Middle Income, 50 per cent; and High Income, 15 per cent. This would seem to indicate that the greatest influence of the quantitative S factor in party switching is in the Middle Income group.

TABLE XII

PARTY SWITCHING AND ORGANIZATION MEMBERSHIP WITH INCOME CONSTANT

	LOW INCOME 0–$1,999				
Organization Membership	0	1	2	3	Total
Number	62	20	5	2	89
Percentage					
Switching Parties	15	25	60	50	
Not Switching	85	75	40	50	
Total	100	100	100	100	

	MIDDLE INCOME $2,000–$3,999				
Organization Membership	0	1	2	3	Total
Number	82	40	25	9	156
Percentage					
Switching Parties	17	33	32	67	
Not Switching	83	67	68	33	
Total	100	100	100	100	

	HIGH INCOME $4,000 AND OVER				
Organization Membership	0	1	2	3	Total
Number	25	21	9	3	58
Percentage					
Switching Parties	16	33	56	31	
Not Switching	84	67	44	69	
Total	100	100	100	100	

In summary, it would appear that the income factor is important in determining voting participation of South Carolina urban Negroes but of minor importance in determining party allegiance and party switching. The quantitative S factor is an independent factor in determining voting participation and a much more important factor than the income factor in determining party allegiance and party switching among South Carolina urban Negroes.

In respect to voting participation, party allegiance, and party switching, both the qualitative and quantitative social factors seem to have an important influence among South Carolina urban Negroes. The quantitative S factor seems to be much more important in determining voting participation and party switching in presidential elections. The qualitative and quantitative social factors seem to be about equally influential in determining party allegiance. Further research needs to be done among Northern Negroes and white voters in order to determine if the same results would be obtained from diverse groups. The authors believe that this is the first time that qualitative and quantitative factors have been compared and their importance evaluated among Negro voters. They believe that this is also the first time that the influence of the social factor upon party allegiance and party voting has been studied.

Part 5

*Negro Politics in the North**

The political position of the Negro sub-community in the North differs considerably from that of the Negro sub-community in the South. There are no legal barriers to Negro involvement in Northern politics, and the great cities of the North in which Negroes live dominate their respective states.

This part is an effort to place in perspective the nature of Negro politics in the North and some of the consequences of such politics for the Negro and the political system.

*North for our purposes is meant to include western as well as northern urban centers in which the legal and population relations of Negroes to the larger community are decidedly similar.

Negro Politics in the North

Professor James Q. Wilson in a chapter from his book, *Negro Politics: The Search for Leadership,* describes Negro political behavior in northern and western urban communities and the nature of Negro political organizations which influence that behavior.

As has been stated in earlier readings, Negro migration into the North has been taking place at a rapid pace. Today almost fifty per cent or half of America's Negroes live in the North. The Negro population in a number of northern and western states now exceeds the Negro populations of any number of southern states. There are more Negroes in the state of New York than in Louisiana, more in Illinois than in Mississippi, more in California than in Florida. The five states of the deep South — Alabama, Georgia, Louisiana, Mississippi, and South Carolina — together have only one-sixth of the nation's Negro population whereas Illinois, Pennsylvania, and New York together have a slightly larger fraction. Most of the increase in Negro population in the North occurred in the central cities of the twelve largest metropolitan areas — New York, Chicago, Los Angeles, Philadelphia, Detroit, Baltimore, Cleveland, Washington, St. Louis, San Francisco, Boston, and Pittsburgh.[1]

The Negro's concentration in the urban centers of the North and West at once increases his political effectiveness and shapes his political attitudes. This is so especially in Presidential contests, because Presidential candidates stand for office before a national constituency which is likely to be closely divided. A Presidential candidate can win without the electoral votes of the South, but he cannot be successful without a substantial portion of the heavily populated states of the northeast, midwest, and far west which carry large electoral votes.[2] Those states contain the great urban centers of the nation in which the citizen's survival needs are likely to be seen in terms larger than those of racial separation. In a voting system that delivers the vote of a state to the presidential candidate with a mere plurality or at best a simple majority, Negro voters in the central cities of such states often hold the political balance of power. In the second article reprinted in this part, Professor Oscar Glantz empirically documents just how strategic the Negro vote is in the North.

Race, we have said, is no barrier to who registers and votes in the North. However, race as a factor in northern Negro politics cannot be discounted.

---

[1]See *Congressional Quarterly,* August 21, 1964, (Washington, D. C.: Congressional Quarterly Inc., 1964), p. 1839.
[2]See, for example, the cogent arguments of Lewis A. Froman, Jr., *People and Politics: An Analysis of the American Political System* (Englewood Cliffs, New Jersey: Prentice Hall, Inc., 1962), pp. 87-88; and Nelson W. Polsby and Aaron B. Wildavsky, *Presidential Elections: Strategies of American Electoral Politics* (New York: Charles Scribner's Sons, 1964) pp. 28-29.

Northern Negroes as well as southern Negroes are American citizens first and are influenced by the same forces and considerations which affect the outlook and attitudes of other Americans, but they often are bound to act together politically because they have a common goal if not common problems. Where there has been sharpened conflict over the Negro's status in American society, Negroes have tended to band together to support the party or politicians which least oppose their equality in the political system. Thus in the 1956 campaign when civil rights was a major issue and the Democrats failed to adopt a strong civil rights plank,[3] there was considerable Negro defection from the voting ranks of the Democratic party. Henry Moon in the third article of this part analyzes the Negro vote in the presidential election of 1956 and finds that there is considerable flexibility in the Negro vote, and that the assumption may be false that Negroes are permanently wed to the Democratic party.

It has been argued that the attachment of the Negro in the North to the Democratic party is less flexible than Moon's study shows, because that attachment is the product of a compound of economic as well as racial attitudes.[4] Thus, it is assumed, Negro support of the Democratic party would not be altered considerably even where the party fails to take as strong a stand on civil rights as most Negroes would desire. A good case is made for this argument by Professor William McKenna in the fourth article reprinted in this part. McKenna's study of the Negro vote in Philadelphia elections shows that Negro exodus from the Democratic party from time to time has been only slight and ephemeral even where civil rights questions have been at issue.

---

[3] See *Revolution in Civil Rights* (Washington, D. C.: Congressional Quarterly Service, 1965), p. 26.

[4] See, for example, Elmer W. Henderson, "Political Changes Among Negroes in Chicago During the Depression," *Social Forces,* XIX, (May 1941), pp. 538-546.

Negro Politics in the North

James Q. Wilson

Chicago, Detroit, Los Angeles, and New York are important centers of Negro population. Although the proportion of Negroes living in these cities is not as high as elsewhere, in total numbers they are among the very largest.[1]

Reprinted with permission of The Free Press and the author from *Negro Politics* by James Q. Wilson. Copyright 1960 by The Free Press, a Corporation.

[1] The Negro population of these four cities, during the period 1955-1957 for which the last estimates are available, is approximately as follows:

City	Negro Population	Per Cent of City Total	Per Cent Increase, 1950-56
Chicago	631,750	18.0	22.1
Detroit	400,000	22.0	24.1
Los Angeles	254,595	11.3	32.8
New York	948,196	12.2	21.2

Sources: Chicago — Otis Dudley Duncan and Beverly Duncan, *The Negro Population of Chicago* (Chicago: University of Chicago Press, 1957), p. 29. The estimate is for 1955. *Detroit* — average of estimates supplied by the Human Relations Commission and Professor Albert Mayer of Wayne State University. *Los Angeles* — the figures are from the 1956 Special Census of Los Angeles. *New York* — the figures are from the 1956 Special Census of New York City (all five boroughs). The data, in each case, are for the *city* (not the Standard Metropolitan Area) and for *Negroes* (not non-whites). Other sources of estimates are Morton Grodzins, "Metropolitan Segregation," *Scientific American,* October, 1957, pp. 33-41, and R. Norgren et al, *Employing Negroes in American Industry* (New York: Industrial Relations Counsellors, Inc., 1959), p. 161.

Political activity in these Negro communities is generally high. Three of the four cities have sent a Negro to the United States House of Representatives.[2] In two of the cities, the Negro political leader is a nationally known figure — William L. Dawson in Chicago and Adam Clayton Powell, Jr., in New York. In each city except Los Angeles at least one Negro sits on the City Council, and in Chicago there are six. Each city sends at least one, and usually more, Negroes to the state legislature. Negro judges sit on the bench in each of the four cities. In every case except Los Angeles, the Negro voters comprise one of the largest single ethnic groups in the central city electorate and a group that is rapidly growing both in absolute size and as a proportion of the total population. This growth, accompanied by the retreat of whites from the periphery of Negro areas, means, among other things, that the size of Negro political representation at all levels of government will continue to grow. In just the four cities under consideration, there are at least six Congressional districts in which substantial numbers of Negroes already live and which are generally expected to elect Negro politicians in the near future.

The growing number of Negroes in northern cities suggests the increased possibility that Negro political power will become a decisive factor in the quest for race goals. Political leadership, based on this large electorate, might presumably be a potent force for change. This chapter will discuss the general features of Negro political leadership in several large northern cities. We shall suggest that Negro political influence has not grown in proportion to the numbers of Negro voters, that the emerging Negro political leadership has thus far (in most cases) not been an effective agent for social change, and that the reasons for this are to be found in the nature of political organization itself. The limitations on political influence are a product, first, of the political system of the particular city, and second, of the constraints imposed by the requirements for maintaining a political organization.

The Structure of Negro Politics

The most important single conclusion that emerges from a survey of Negro politics in large northern cities is that, in all cases, the structure and style of Negro politics reflect the politics of the city as a whole. Politics for the Negro, as for other ethnic groups before him, can be viewed as a set of "learned responses" which he acquires from the distinctive political system of the city in which he lives.

---

[2]William L. Dawson of Chicago, first elected in 1942; Charles Diggs, Jr., of Detroit, first elected in 1954; and Adam Clayton Powell, Jr., of New York, first elected in 1944. Before Dawson, there were two Negro Congressmen from Chicago: Oscar de Priest (1928-34), and Arthur W. Mitchell (1934-42).

Negro politics cannot be understood apart from the city in which it is found. This suggests, happily, that by examining Negro politics on a comparative basis we are at the same time examining American city politics. It also implies that research on this topic must be much broader than the subject itself indicates. The student must cast a wide net; inquiry must begin with the city as a whole in order to understand fully the actions and problems of Negro politicians in that city. This point, obvious by itself, takes on added significance when one considers the nature of the organization and the means by which it induces workers and voters to contribute to it, the pattern of Negro registration and voting, and the relative strength and unity (or weakness and disunity) of the organization.

The Negro political organization is created and shaped by the political organization of the city. The existence of a Negro machine, as in Chicago, is dependent upon the existence of a white machine. Machine politics requires a centralization of leadership, a sizeable stock of tangible incentives with which to reward contributors, a large group of people in the city who would be attracted by the kinds of rewards a political machine can distribute, and (usually) a ward or district system of selecting party leaders, aldermen, and candidates for public office. The prior existence of a machine, operating under such conditions, means that the entry of Negroes into politics will take place under the forms and rules already established. Where various factors have weakened the city organization and produced a situation of factional rivalry and imperfect solidarity, the Negro political organization will be similarly gripped by internecine warfare and competing leaders. This is the case in Manhattan, where the city organization is weak — i.e., it cannot enforce its rules on its members or maintain an undisputed single leadership. There, the elements of machine politics have been decaying rapidly, and the results are evident in white and Negro areas. In Los Angeles and Detroit, where almost none of the elements of machine control exists, the politics of the city as a whole is characterized by *ad hoc* groupings which come into being in election years to elect good-government, economy-minded leaders whose appeal must be largely based on personality, issues, and newspaper influence. Negroes, where they can enter this kind of political system at all, are forced to do so on its own terms and with the limited resources at hand. No Negro "boss" can spring up where there is not already a white boss. When a strong civil service system, a mobile and prosperous electorate, and a long tradition of "public relations politics" exist as in Los Angeles, Negroes must play the game by the same rules and under the same conditions. In doing so, of course, they are placed at a profound disadvantage.

The most important modification of the statement that Negro politics in northern cities is a reflection of the politics of the cities as a whole is the general time lag in the entry of Negroes into positions of political influence.

Contributing to this lag is the operation of those same factors which have delayed the entry of other, earlier ethnic groups. Big city politics often takes the form of a succession of new arrivals each trying to scale the same ladder of political achievement by pressing those above them for "recognition." Resistance to Negroes is not, in part, different from the general resistance put up by (for example) the Irish political leadership of the big city to the demands for political recognition expressed by Poles, Italians, or Germans. Little is given without a struggle, even when the maintenance needs of the political organizations as a whole would seem to require it. The personal interests of those who hold the higher positions inevitably tend to override the organizational interests of the machine which provides them with those positions. In the case of the Negro, however, this resistance is intensified by the frequent operation of personal prejudice and hostility. Negro entry into politics thus far has been less than proportional to their numbers, as expressed in the size of their contribution to the Democratic vote in city elections. Often, as in Chicago's 24th Ward, Los Angeles' 55th and 63rd Assembly Districts, and parts of New York's 13th Assembly District, Negroes can be the largest group in the political unit long before they manage to take control of the leadership of that unit.[3] This is true, again, because Negro voters — unless they are made the objects of really intense, well-led organizational campaigns — will not vote along strictly racial lines in a Negro-white contest, especially when it occurs at the bottom of the ticket in the seemingly unimportant race for ward committeeman or district leader.

In addition to political resistance stiffened by personal hostility and prejudice, another factor works to delay Negro entry into political organizations. Negroes — whose income and educational levels are almost always among the lowest in the city and whose rural background deprives them of sophistication in the ways of the city — are often hard to organize for political ends. Many of them doubt that politics offers any real opportunities. The difficulty in building a Negro organization *from outside the machine* which will then make a bid for recognition and power has been discovered many times in all four cities. This obstacle makes all the more remarkable the achievement of William Dawson of Chicago in rising to power in the 1930's from a powerless base. The aid of Mayor Edward Kelly, valuable as it may have been, was no guarantee of success — if only because of the large number of Negro rivals to Dawson whose factional fights could easily have paralyzed all attempts at coherent organization. In non-machine or weak-machine cities, the active intervention of another strong force which has a vested interest in mobilizing Negroes seems to be necessary to bring them into important poli-

---

[3]For example, in St. Louis in 1959, six wards returned Negro aldermen but only two of these had Negro ward leaders (wards 18 and 19).

tical roles. In Detroit, this has been the function of the CIO. In Los Angeles, where no machine and no intervening organization exists, Negro political organization becomes an immensely difficult task.

The time lag characterizing Negro entry into northern politics has not been uniform in all cities. Negroes held important political offices in Chicago long before they did in New York, and Negroes emerged in New York before they were active in Los Angeles or Detroit. To account for these differences, three factors, in addition to the political organization of the city, appear to be important: (a) the rate of in-migration, (b) the density of the Negro area, and (c) the size of the basic political unit.

In Chicago, Negro entry occurred as early as 1915 when a Negro was elected to the City Council, and later (in 1920) another became a ward committeeman (the real center of political power in the Chicago wards). The powerful city machine was at that time firmly in the hands of the Republicans, and thus the Negro political leaders were at first Republicans. Their entry was partly a reflection of the need of the city organization to insure its strength in the Negro wards by co-opting Negro leaders, and it was partly a product of a bitter struggle by Negroes to gain "recognition" in politics against the opposition of established non-Negro leaders. The machine system in the Negro wards solidified as early as 1920, and by 1928 Negroes were able to elect a member of their own race to Congress.

The relatively early date by which Negroes were able to gain elective office in Chicago, as compared to other northern cities, can be explained by the fact that (a) the concentration of Negroes in one or a few all-Negro areas was, from the first, higher in Chicago and (b) the Chicago political system was based on a large number of relatively small wards usually drawn to conform to the racial, nationality, or religious character of the neighborhood. This demographic concentration in small political units facilitated the entry of Negroes into politics in Chicago, while relatively less concentrated Negro population centers in cities with large districts (or, in some cases, no districts at all) meant that Negro entry was greatly delayed. This was the case in New York, and to an even greater extent in Detroit and Los Angeles.

New York, with even more Negroes than Chicago, and with a political system somewhat comparable, did not have a Negro district leader in Tammany Hall until 1935, and it did not have a second until 1941. In part, this reflected the relatively larger size of New York districts as compared to Chicago wards. This size facilitated a process of gerrymandering that worked to exclude Negroes from important posts. Furthermore, New York districts have been, and still are, divided into halves or even thirds for leadership purposes in order to find compromises between the competing claims of various ethnic groups residing in the district. Thus, a district containing significant numbers of Negroes, Italians, and Jews would be split into three parts, and each part given to a Negro, an Italian, and a Jewish leader. In turn, the single vote which that district had in Tammany Hall would be split into three one-third votes. This often worked to weaken the influence of Negroes even after they had captured a leadership. For this and other reasons which will be taken up later, Negro influence in Tammany was less and increased more slowly than Negro influence in the Cook County Central Committee in Chicago. The first Negro Congressman from New York was not chosen until 1944, after redistricting had created a new Congressional District with a Negro majority. Other things being equal, Negro political strength in city organizations tends to be directly proportional to the size and density of the Negro population, and inversely proportional to the size of the basic political unit.

In Los Angeles, where the growth of the Negro population has been more recent (largely since World War II, rather than World War I as in the case of Chicago and New York), Negro entry into politics has really not occurred at all. The only Negro holding elective office is one member of the State Assembly. No Negroes are on the City Council, and no Negroes are in its Congressional delegation. Los Angeles politics are largely nonpartisan. There are no wards, and no ward leaders. City Councilmen are elected from large heterogeneous districts which must, by law, be reapportioned every four years. Considerable pains have been taken to insure that such redistricting will operate to exclude Negroes from the Council. Civil service is strong in Los Angeles, and there are few material incentives with which to construct a political organization. There is no city-wide organization with a need to attract all segments of the population to support a complete slate of candidates, and hence no group which would have a vested interest in constructing a "balanced ticket" and distributing "recognition" to ethnic, religious, and other easily identifiable groups. Politics is largely the province of white, middle-class, Anglo-Saxon Protestants. Although the sole Negro elective official is formally a Democrat, he has supported Republican Mayor Norris Poulson in both the 1953 and 1957 elections, despite Poulson's stand against public housing. Neither race nor party are clear determinants of political positions in Los Angeles.

One additional factor should be mentioned. The density of Negroes in Los Angeles has been markedly lower than in either Chicago or New York. Los Angeles, for example, has a comparative absence of apartments and tenements in the central city and instead an immense number of small, single-family homes and duplexes. It has, as a result, a Negro population which is spread over a much greater territory than in Chicago. This relative dispersion has many consequences, but one which is important at this juncture is the greater ease with which district lines can be drawn to exclude Negroes. A widely spread (but generally contiguous) Negro area can more easily be broken up in such a way that Negroes are in a minority in each district. This would be less feasible in a small but densely-populated area.

Detroit is, in many ways, comparable to Los Angeles. City politics is nonpartisan, and genuinely so. Members of the Common Council are elected at-large from the city as a whole. Each voter has nine votes which he may give to as many as nine different candidates, but no more than one vote per candidate. In the primary, eighteen men are selected from a wide-open field frequently of more than one hundred aspirants. The eighteen compete in a run-off election from which nine emerge. There are no ward leaders, and civil service has put an end to almost all patronage at the city and county level. In such a situation it is not surprising that it was not until 1957 that a Negro was first elected to the Common Council.

The Detroit situation differs from that in Los Angeles because of the existence of a large and powerful labor movement in the former city which has tried to operate as a political organization, endorsing slates of candidates and attempting to organize workers in most of the election precincts. Although this organization, in co-operation with other liberal groups and with the regular Democratic party, has been strikingly successful in electing a Governor and two Senators, as well as a host of other state-wide offices (where the elections are openly *partisan*), it has had much less success in the city itself. It was never able to defeat four-time Mayor Albert E. Cobo, a conservative, nor could it dominate the Common Council.[4]

The CIO United Auto Workers, which was first confronted with Negro laborers in Detroit when they were used as strikebreakers in the 1930's,[5] has since succeeded in incorporating them into the union movement with considerable success. Unlike many craft-oriented unions, the UAW has not segregated the Negroes into separate, all-Negro locals. Rather, Negroes are to be found in all the locals in sizeable numbers. Perhaps one-fourth to one-third of the membership of the average local in Detroit is now Negro.[6] In political action, the CIO has concentrated heavily on Negro areas — often with remarkable effect. For example, Negroes are becoming very numerous in the First and Fifteenth Congressional Districts which now return

---

[4]Negro voters were strongly opposed to Mayor Cobo and always voted heavily for his opponent. Many Negro leaders, and some liberal whites, believe that part of Cobo's appeal, especially to middleclass whites who felt threatened by Negro residential expansion, was what they considered to be Cobo's anti-Negro policies in public housing, real estate, and other areas.

[5]See Walter F. White, *A Man Called White* (New York: Viking Press, 1948), pp. 212-19.

[6]In 1952, Negroes were 19 percent of a random sample of Detroit UAW members. Cf. Arthur Kornhauser, *et al., When Labor Votes* (New York: University Books, 1956), p. 24. At the time, there were about 290,000 UAW members in Detroit or about 30 per cent of both the labor force and the eligible voters (p. 22).

two white Democratic Congressmen, Thaddeus M. Machrowicz and John D. Dingell. Negro Democrats challenged each incumbent in the 1958 primary, but the white leaders — with CIO endorsement — were able to defeat their Negro opponents by substantial margins. Most Negroes voted the CIO ticket rather than on the basis of race.

Negroes and whites share high offices in the AFL-CIO Wayne County Council (a Pole and a Negro are the two vice-presidents) and Negroes hold office in UAW locals. This has had political advantages and disadvantages for the Negroes. The CIO appeal to Negroes has been reflected in the strong CIO backing which Negro goals usually receive in public affairs. At the state level, a strong FEPC (Fair Employment Practices Commission) statute was passed and implemented. This has been attractive to Negroes while alienating relatively few white workers. The CIO, particularly the UAW, has been a strong supporter of the Detroit NAACP, although the Negro leadership of the NAACP prefers to maintain an image of independence as much as possible. In Chicago, by way of contrast, the labor movement has not been dominated by any single union giant. Individual unions have tended to exclude Negroes altogether (as in certain building trades and railroad unions), relegate them to all-Negro locals (as in many AFL craft unions), or permit Negroes to take over a union almost entirely (as with several packinghouse workers' locals). The politics of Chicago labor are infinitely complex, but the end result is that there is usually no strong union force placed behind various race causes.

There has been a price for the strong Detroit alliance between labor and Negroes. The closer to home a race issue is, the less vigorous the union can afford to be on its behalf. Championing legislation which, if passed, would have few immediate effects on the white workers living in Detroit may be one thing. Championing a law which would, for example, end discriminatory practices in the private housing market is quite another thing. Other groups in the CIO (or who follow CIO leadership politically) must be considered. One of these is the Poles; another is the southern whites. In this very tense area, having an ally as powerful as the Detroit CIO is not enough for the Negro. Lily-white neighborhood "improvement associations," created to keep Negroes out of certain residential areas, often share members with a CIO union.[7]

The other cost has arisen out of the fact of integration in labor. Some Negroes, including some leaders, would prefer to have certain things — such as offices in a union local — given to them as a matter of race recognition rather than as a result of competition on relatively equal terms with white groups for a common set of offices. Negroes cannot control any single

---

[7]Polish and German UAW members expressed more hostility towards Negroes in a sample survey than did native Americans. Cf. *ibid*, p. 180.

local, and although they are present in very large numbers in the union as a whole, many have felt frustrated by what they consider to be a shortage of official positions. If the Negroes were grouped into a few Negro locals, there would at least be some Negro union presidents; as it is, often the Negroes must be content with, for example, the position of recording secretary in each of several locals.

Some Detroit Negro leaders speak of the mixed feelings they have toward their labor ally. On the one hand, a single industrial structure, organized by a single powerful union, has aided the NAACP in reaching Negroes and recruiting them as members. It has provided a source of stability which has given to the local NAACP leadership an unusual freedom from bitter internal struggles. But at the same time, as one Negro leader said, the union "has dulled the effectiveness of Negro leadership to some extent":

> Twenty-five years ago when the UAW was a baby we had strong Negro leadership here. It's still remembered. People still talk about the three or four Negro ministers who were so influential at that time in leading the Negro community. . . . I believe it was true. The UAW has reduced the size of this Negro leadership and reduced its importance by providing a more significant, more influential, more comprehensive liberal leadership in the community. It may be a good thing. But it has happened.

On the whole, however, integration into a large and powerful union undoubtedly has worked to the net advantage of most Negroes. The level of conflict between hostile ethnic groups — for example, between Negroes and Poles — might be very much higher if each group controlled its own set of locals and was isolated from the other group. Under the present system, competition for recognition and position between the two groups in the union must proceed within a common organization, much as such competition occurs within a city-wide political machine. Neither side can afford to press too hard for fear of alienating other supporters or even the leadership; neither side can afford to jeopardize the chances for success of the organization as a whole in either union bargaining or political campaigns. The CIO in Detroit acts, in part, as a political machine with two important differences: it has relatively few tangible rewards with which to attract workers and supporters,[8] and it is out of power in the city. Being out of power, and forced to rely on inducements other than material, it has become skilled in raising and agitating various issues which appeal to many of its constituent

---

[8]The CIO partially reimburses some union political workers for time lost on the job. Further, some members combine political work with the position of shop steward, and thus in a sense have a "job" with political overtones. But by and large, precinct politics is a volunteer operation.

elements. This, of course, does not deny the evident sincerity of the union leaders who espouse these causes.

An interesting variation of the impact of the system of at-large elections on Negro political fortunes is found in Cincinnati. From 1925 until 1957, councilmen were elected at-large under proportional representation. PR modified the effect of the at-large system to the extent that one or two Negroes were usually elected to the city council by receiving as little as 10 per cent of the total vote. After PR was abolished in 1957 and a system of at-large elections for nine councilmen was instituted, the leading Negro politician was defeated. An important factor in the campaign against PR was the presumed threat posed by the possibility of Negro political power in the city. Theodore M. Berry, the Negro councilman who had been elected Vice-Mayor in 1955 after running second in a field of twenty-one candidates, was the target of much of this attack. In urging Negroes to vote to retain PR, Berry made explicit reference to the Detroit situation as a warning of what would happen to Negro political representation should PR be rejected.[9] The at-large, nonpartisan election system has similarly helped to exclude Negroes from the Boston Common Council. Negroes held office in Boston for over a century beginning in 1776, but by 1910 they had all been displaced. In the 19th century, Negroes were often elected from predominantly white districts by Yankees who, like the Negroes, were Republicans. After the turn of the century, with the entry of new immigrant groups into political life, particularly as members of the Democratic party, this benevolence ceased. Districts were redrawn to split the Negro vote. In 1949, the district system was abolished altogether, and the nine Council members were elected at large. A Negro running for the Council in 1958 finished fifteenth out of eighteen candidates, although he ran first in the most important Negro ward.[10]

The structure of political competition in these northern areas has implications for the responsiveness of white politicians to Negro goals as well as for the organization of Negro politics itself. The relative success in enacting laws embodying Negro race ends in Michigan and New York, for example, has been due to a large number of factors, including the presence of powerful allies for Negro causes. One factor upon which some speculation seems worthwhile at this point concerns the distribution of Negroes in electoral districts. Although no conclusive evidence can be offered, it is interesting to conjecture about the differences in white politicians' attitudes toward race ends which may be related to a large-district political system (such as New York) as compared to a small-district system (such as Chicago).

---

[9]For a complete account of the impact of the Cincinnati electoral system on Negro politics, see Ralph A. Straetz, *PR Politics in Cincinnati* (New York: New York University Press, 1958), esp. chap. viii.
[10]I am indebted to the researches of Ralph Ottwell, former Nieman Fellow at Harvard, for most of my facts on Boston.

Manhattan, which was over 21 per cent Negro in 1957, has elected a Negro as borough president. Negro voters in just the four "recognized" Negro districts produced from one third to one half of the majorities won by the top of the Democratic ticket between 1954 and 1958.[11] As the strength of Tammany declines, the pressure mounts on city officials, such as the mayor, to move more and more in the direction of meeting the demands of organized minority groups. Mayor Wagner, for example, was a steady supporter of the proposed "open occupancy" ordinance barring discrimination in private housing even though the *Negro* politicians (with one exception) were silent or unenthusiastic. Here we see the Negro bene-fiting from what may have been the by-product of political and civic action engaged in by entirely different actors and in part for different purposes. White political leaders, it might be hypothesized, meet demands for race ends in such a situation only in part to attract the Negro vote. Their goal is also to attract and hold liberal *white* voters (for example, Jews) who judge a politician in part on the basis of his contribution to the goals of integration and social justice.[12] The Negro may be the unintended bene-ficiary of such a process. But whatever the audience to which the politician appeals, there is little doubt that in New York — in contrast to Chicago — an appeal must be made. Politics in the former city are more nearly two-party (opponents of the Democratic organization can and do win), and hence greater efforts must be expended to be certain of victory.

Furthermore, New York political units (the districts from which council-men and borough presidents are elected) are relatively large. Sizable num-bers of Negroes live in many of these districts and boroughs.[13] Many white

---

[11]The four districts are the 11th, 12th, 13th, and 14th Assembly Districts in Harlem. The difference between the Democratic and Republican totals in the four districts is divided by the difference between the Democratic and Republican vote for Manhattan as a whole. The results are: 1954 — 32.46 per cent; 1956 — 55.57 per cent; 1958 — 49.05 per cent.

[12]On Jewish tendencies to vote split tickets, see Lawrence H. Fuchs, *The Political Behavior of American Jews* (Glencoe, Ill.: The Free Press, 1956), pp. 131-49.

[13]The six Manhattan Council districts had, in 1957, an average population of slightly less than 300,000. By comparison, the average size of a Chicago ward (in 1950) was about 72,000 persons. At least four of the six Manhattan Councilmen have sizable Negro areas in their districts, and Negroes are to be found in scattered locations in the other two. There are, in addition, important Negro population centers in the Bronx (134,767), Brooklyn (307,796), Queens (116,193), and Staten Island (8,372). The distribution of Negroes in the various New York City boroughs is of great importance. The Board of Estimate on which the Borough Presidents sit has substantially greater power than the City Council. It is composed of the Mayor, the Comptroller, the Council President (all elected city-wide) with four votes each and the Borough Presidents from Manhattan, Brooklyn, Queens, the Bronx, and Richmond (with two votes each). Thus, with twelve votes among them, the city-wide officials can dominate the Board and the important deci-sions it makes, although the necessary unity can be difficult to achieve. The lack of such unity and its consequences are described in Wallace S. Sayre and Herbert Kaufman, *Governing New York City* (New York: Russell Sage Foundation, 1960), chaps. xvii and xviii.

politicians must anticipate the reaction of Negroes to city issues affecting the race. What may be more important, *opponents* of race goals find it harder to gain the support of their political representatives against such measures when the districts these leaders represent are so large and diversified. The larger political unit is a factor which works to deter or delay Negro entry into politics, but it may also be a factor which makes it harder for anti-Negro forces to block race legislation which has strong civic backing. Smaller units in Chicago, on the other hand, facilitate Negro entry into politics but also make it easier for anti-Negro elements in local neighborhoods to mobilize support from their politicians to oppose race measures.

The Style of Negro Politics

The style of Negro politics in northern cities can be viewed as a function of the felt needs of the organization (its goals and the incentives it must have in order to generate action to attain these goals) and of the character of the constituency to which the electoral appeal must be made.[14] The Negro political organization, like all organizations, has maintenance needs which both arise from within and are imposed from without. One index of the differential effect of internal and external needs on a Negro political organization is the extent to which it finds it in its own interest to use racial appeals in its activities — i.e., appeals to Negroes to realize race ends and elect "race men."

Organizational Needs

The first set of factors involves the needs and position of the organization itself. Negro political action is modified by the answers Negro leaders give to these questions: How can I attract workers to my organization? How can I attract voters to my campaign? Usually, the answer to both these questions is the same for the Negro leader as for his white colleague, but there are interesting variations. Racism, or, more broadly, ideology in Negro politics is often a product of a position outside the established organization, a position of weakness within the established organization, or an absence of material incentives with which to attract and reward Negro supporters. Political conservatism and an avoidance of race issues, on the other hand, often reflects the fact that the Negroes are part of a strong and cohesive political organization.

Some of these differences can be suggested by a comparison of the organizational bases of Negro politics in Chicago and Manhattan. In Chicago, Negro Democrats are part of a powerful political machine; in Manhattan,

---

[14] Cf. Chester Barnard, *The Functions of the Executive* (Cambridge: Harvard University Press, 1938), and his notions of "effectiveness" and "efficiency," esp. chap. iii.

they work within a weak machine. The position of Dawson as leader of at least five of the six Negro wards in Chicago and the seven Negro Democrats in the Illinois state legislature is thus far unchallenged. In Manhattan, not only the position of any given Negro leader, but of many white leaders as well, is often precarious and fraught with uncertainty and weakness. The Chicago organization benefits from a reservoir of funds and patronage that, although reduced from the early 1940's, has not been seriously weakened as yet. The Manhattan organization — or coalition of factions which attempts to operate as an organization — has had many of its sources of strength seriously curtailed. These differences, and the consequences for Negro political style, can be seen in a brief historical comparison.

In Manhattan, Negroes began to enter the Tammany Democratic organization at the district level at a time when the city organization was already under heavy attack. Fiorello LaGuardia had already led a successful Fusion movement which placed him in the City Hall, and he was going out of his way to create difficulties for the Sachems of Tammany.[15] The great, restless ferment of the Depression years which expressed itself in Harlem, in Chicago's Bronzeville, and in other Negro communities in various protest and separatist movements left a permanent mark on New York. Tammany for years has had to deal with a series of insurgents and dissidents. This history of insurgency had an effect in New York unlike that in Chicago. In the latter city, the Negroes had already forced an entry *before* the Depression began; many of them were committed to the political status quo before a crisis could develop. The regular Cook County Democratic organization was able to sweep the Republicans out of office and install a strong Democratic mayor — Edward Kelly — who promptly cast about for a means to cement his alliance with the strongest Negro leaders. Dawson, until then a maverick Republican, switched parties and became, through his skill and Kelly's support, the new Democratic leader in the Negro wards. These years of dramatic change left, in Chicago, a newly strengthened Democratic organization in power — a power it has never surrendered. In New York, essentially the same upheavals placed a reform mayor in office whose appeal was personal and direct. Negroes broke into Tammany just as the posts for which they were fighting were rapidly decreasing in value. The 1930's in New York stimulated a pattern of contention and insurgency within the regular organization from which it has never fully recovered, and one that has caught up Negroes and whites alike.

No strong, single Negro leadership ever developed in Harlem. Negroes were used, one against the other, by forces in the steady struggle for place

---

[15]La Guardia was elected Mayor in 1933. His election, and the revelations of the Seabury investigation, led to the adoption of a new city charter in 1937 which centralized power in the hands of the Mayor and the Board of Estimate.

and power; and, in turn, the Negroes made separate and competing alliances to further their own interests. The arrival on the scene of Adam Clayton Powell, Jr., was certainly not the cause of the political debility of Tammany in Harlem, but it was symptomatic of the malaise and in time served to deepen it. When the 22nd Congressional District was, in 1944, created in order to be handed over to a Negro, the principal Negro Democratic district leader in the area was unable to choose the nominee, and in fact was overruled in favor of Powell by Tammany. The weakness of the organization in Harlem continued. In 1958-59, Powell and his followers were able to beat regular organization candidates in the Democratic Congressional primary and in three district leader contests.

Dawson, before being co-opted into the Democratic Party, was an outspoken and vigorous champion of racial causes. Once inside an organization that was strong and which manifestly held the key to the future, race matters were subdued. He was able to provide a plausible, and in many ways correct, rationale to account for the change: The future of the Negro was bound up with political advancement and power. This could best be obtained by working within the Democratic Party and accepting, as a cost, what one could not immediately change. In contrast to this, Herbert Bruce, the first Democratic Negro leader in Harlem, fought the established white leader on the grounds that most of the political jobs were going to whites who no longer lived in the district. Few were left for the Negroes who remained. On entering, however, he discovered a machine which was weak and divided, and it was necessary to fight a steady stream of challengers from within and without. To Bruce, and others like him, race appeals never really became outmoded because the struggle for position never really ended.

In Los Angeles, the forms and nature of city politics are reflected in the politics of the Negro area. The single Negro elected official has a base of support that is personal and of long duration. The attempt by liberal Democrats to revitalize the party in the city and the state through the Democratic Club movement has elicited comparable attempts in the Negro areas. But here the obstacles have been far greater. Negroes have proved to be much more difficult to organize with the intangible incentives and middle-class appeals characteristic of the Club movement. In the 63rd Assembly District, for example, which is about 50 per cent Negro, there are ten Democratic Clubs. Until recently, nine of these were white and only one Negro. The Club movement is not active in the single assembly district (the 62nd) which elects a Negro State Assemblyman. To stimulate political organization among Negroes in the apolitical atmosphere of Los Angeles, a group of Negroes called the Democratic Minority Conference has had to rely more heavily on strictly racial appeals and the demand for race ends such as Negro representation in government. A leader of the Conference explained that it must use a "frankly racial appeal" because Negroes distrust the Democratic Party and feel that the white-led Democratic Clubs can give them little more than the regular organization. The Conference, although allied with the Club movement, has discouraged Caucasians from membership in it. Led by Negroes, it has endeavored to attract Mexicans and Japanese as well.

The Nature of the Constituency

The perceived character of the constituency to which an electoral appeal must be made can condition several aspects of the campaign. Some cities have an electorate thoroughly conditioned and deeply committed to the goal of nonpartisanship. In Los Angeles, this has been carried to the point where until recently the political parties as formal organizations have been almost non-existent. In Detroit, where at least one strong party operates, it is still essential to appeal to the voters in a manner that does not seem to do violence to the ideal of nonpartisanship.

Further, the nature of the constituency conditions the extent to which issues are believed to be relevant. In Chicago, issues in city elections are conspicuous by their rarity. In New York, they are somewhat more common. In Detroit and Los Angeles, candidates often must go to considerable lengths to *generate* issues in order to attract interest to their campaigns for public office. Little else can be offered the voter to induce him to participate in the election than an appeal to his civic or personal interests.

Finally, the nature of the constituency modifies the quality of the candidates offered. Where the organizational strength is weak or declining, it is thought to be more important to offer candidates who are thoroughly presentable and of considerable civic luster — i.e., "blue ribbon" candidates. For example, when Negroes entered Detroit politics, they found none of the common kinds of patronage available to sustain their position. Conditions seemed to be ripe for a political campaign based on the demand for race issues. But city councilmen and county judges are elected at large. Only a small portion of the whole constituency is Negro. The selection of the Negroes to run, and the decision as to the style in which their campaign would be waged, had to take this into account. The support of labor unions and of the daily press seemed to be essential. The result was the election of a handful of very able, eminently presentable men of moderate views and unimpeachable character to sit, as Negroes, on the Council and the bench.[16]

In Los Angeles, the strongest effort made by Negroes to place a man on the City Council required the mobilization of a broad cross-section of the

---

[16]Negro judges in Detroit were first *appointed,* to fill vacancies, by party leaders. High-calibre men were deliberately selected in each case. They then stood for election as incumbents.

Negro community to provide the necessary support in terms of time, effort, and money. Negro Democratic clubs which demanded more Negroes in public office were mobilized. But in appealing to the electorate of the district as a whole, which has a very large number of whites, a sober, "good government" platform was devised stressing taxes and city services. Two separate and different sets of inducements had to be employed: one to attract Negro support for the campaign, and one to attract white votes for the candidate.

Having said this, it is important to consider precisely how important to Negro leaders such racial appeals may be. Assuming the existence of conditions which lead the politicians to adopt their use, it is by no means certain that they will always have the intended effect. It has been shown in many studies in a variety of cities that the "Negro vote" is not *simply* a racial vote. Negroes do not vote for other Negroes merely because of race. The divisions of the Negro community along lines of party, class, and status are much too profound and pervasive to allow for the operation of any such uncomplicated response as a "race vote." Morsell has shown, in his study of Negro politics in New York, that the Negro tends to register and to turn out to vote in about the same proportions as whites, and that general party alignments are often more important than are specific racial considerations.[17] The problem of information is undoubtedly crucial in accounting for much of the absence of a "race vote." Many Negroes cannot identify Negro candidates in an election.

The Efficacy of Organization

These considerations raise squarely the question of the efficacy of political organization among Negroes in northern cities. For instance, what difference does the existence of a strong organization make in the political behavior of Chicago Negroes? What are the consequences of the absence of such organization or the presence of a weak and attenuated organization in other cities? No conclusive answers to these questions can be given, but some suggestions can be made. We shall compare the four cities in several areas of political behavior to see what important discrepancies, if any, exist, and then we shall attempt to relate these discrepancies to the nature of the political organization in the city.

---

[17] John Morsell, "The Political Behavior of Negroes in New York City" (PhD dissertation, Columbia University, 1950). See also Harold Gosnell, *Negro Politicians* (Chicago: University of Chicago Press, 1935); St. Clair Drake and Horace R. Cayton, *Black Metropolis* (New York: Harper & Bros., 1945); and Henry L. Moon, *Balance of Power: The Negro Vote* (Garden City, N. Y.; Doubleday & Co., 1948). On Negroes in New York, see Oscar Handlin, *The Newcomers* (Cambridge: Harvard University Press, 1959).

A complete treatment of this subject would require a precinct-by-precinct survey of the relative effectiveness of machine and non-machine politics. Failing that, only a general pattern can be adduced from the over-all data we have. The existence of a strong political machine among Negroes in a northern city has little detectable effect on the size of the vote delivered to Negro candidates, the percentage of the total vote polled by the winning candidate, or the number of straight-ticket votes. Strong organization has greater effect on the ability of the leadership to control the primary vote and to produce a sizable vote for ballot propositions. Finally, the strength of the organization seems unrelated to, and in some cases hinders, the ability of Negroes to secure important appointive offices in the state and local governments.

The size and percentage of the vote won by leading Negro candidates in four cities is shown in Table 1. Few important differences are apparent. No significant advantage seems to accrue to Dawson for having a strong organization as compared to Hawkins, who has a relatively weak one. If anything, these data suggest that Powell has been able to do slightly better than Dawson in most cases, and that Hawkins has often done much better. All Negro political leaders, by the fact of being Democrats and incumbents, have had little trouble in turning back Republican challengers.

Similarly, there is little evident difference in the ability of the various Negro leaders to deliver a straight party vote in their districts. If the elections are partisan, there will be a relatively small "spread" between the vote received

TABLE 1

AGGREGATE VOTE OF LEADING NEGRO POLITICIANS IN FOUR
CITIES AND PERCENTAGE OF TOTAL VOTE CAST

Politician	1958	1956	1954	1952	1950
Dawson	60,778	66,704	71,472	96,354	69,660
(Chicago)	(72.21%)	(64.41%)	(75.56%)	(73.45%)	(62.64%)
Diggs	57,354	87,383	64,716	*	*
(Detroit)	(73.01%)	(69.76%)	(66.14%)		
Hawkins†	19,085	19,367	16,518	20,914	14,260
(Los Angeles)	(84.75%)	(100%)	(70.78%)	(79.07%)	(82.05%)
Powell‡	56,383	59,339	43,545	72,562	35,233
(New York)	(90.81%)	(69.72%)	(77.55%)	(69.84%)	(69.84%)

*Diggs first elected to Congress in 1954.

†Hawkins' vote is for the primary in all cases. Under California law, he has been able to cross-file and has invariably won the nomination of both parties. In 1956, he was unopposed in the primary. Cross-filing was abolished in 1959.

‡In 1958 Powell won both the Democratic and Republican nominations. He was opposed in the general election only by the Liberal candidate, Earl Brown. In 1944 Powell won the nomination of all three parties and was unopposed in the general election. Since 1944, Powell has never received Liberal Party endorsements.

by the top of the ticket (the most popular candidate on the slate) and the bottom of the ticket. The Negro candidate will do neither better nor worse except in unusual cases. The vote will be racially stable; it will not discriminate between Negro and white candidates, nor between whites favorable to Negroes and whites hostile to Negroes. In Table 2 is shown this "spread" in three Negro areas: Chicago's second ward, Detroit's first ward, and New York's eleventh assembly district. The Table suggests that there are few important differences between cities except that Powell has recently (in 1956 and 1958) done better than the rest of his party. Negro voters in all three cities tend to be straight-ticket voters. To a slight extent, the Dawson organization can produce more straight-ticket votes than the Detroit organization. No data for Los Angeles can be presented owing to the absence of voting returns tabulated by Assembly Districts for any office other than that of Assemblyman.

One special case should be noted. The extent of straight-ticket voting varies, not with the strength of the political organization, but with the presence or absence of partisan elections. A straight-ticket vote can be found in roughly the same proportion in all four cities where the elections are partisan. Where they are nonpartisan, significant discrepancies exist between the votes of different individuals with the same endorsements (by labor unions, newspapers, citizens' committees, etc.). These discrepancies occur most frequently along ethnic and national lines. It can be assumed that one

TABLE 2

VOTE FOR NEGRO LEADER AND FOR BOTTOM OF DEMOCRATIC TICKET AS A PERCENTAGE OF TOP OF TICKET VOTE

	Chicago Ward 2	Detroit Ward 1	New York* 11th Assembly Dist.
1958			
Percentage for Negro Leader	99.12	96.21	126.49
Percentage for Bottom of Ticket	97.83	92.69	97.06
1956			
Percentage for Negro Leader	97.06	93.99	103.76
Percentage for Bottom of Ticket	95.32	90.28	93.42
1954			
Percentage for Negro Leader	97.83	91.43	88.27
Percentage for Bottom of Ticket	96.57	91.34	86.89

*The Powell vote is shown as a percentage of the vote of the leading Democratic candidate. Since the leading Democratic candidate in New York has had in these elections the nomination of the Liberal Party as well, his total vote would be higher than that used here. If one included the Liberal Party vote, Powell's percentage of the top of the ticket would be lower in all cases: 1958, 116.98 per cent; 1956, 91.87 per cent; 1954, 81.56 per cent.

goal of a political organization (either a machine or an endorsing committee) is to produce a winning vote for an entire slate of candidates, resisting the practice known as "ticket-cutting." Ideally, a Negro should do about as well in a Polish area as a Pole, and vice versa. If he does not — if the Polish voters "cut" the Negro candidate on the slate in favor of the Polish candidate — then the organization can be considered less effective than desired. This situation can be illustrated with data drawn from contests in ethnically-heterogeneous, multi-member districts or in at-large contests with large slates of candidates. Chicago and Detroit can usefully be compared in this regard. The conclusion seems to be that there is relatively little ticket-cutting in Chicago (where all elections are in fact partisan) and relatively little in those Detroit elections which are partisan. In nonpartisan Detroit elections, ticket-cutting is widespread.

In Chicago, ten members of the Board of County Commissioners are elected at large, and one Negro has been on the regular Democratic ticket since 1938. Judges of the Municipal and Superior courts are likewise elected at large, and Negro candidates have usually been entered in recent years. In Detroit, members of the Common Council and judges of the Circuit Court are elected at large and Negroes have participated in these nonpartisan races.

Even a cursory inspection of the election returns clearly indicate that ticket-cutting in Chicago's wards is minimal in races for County Commissioner and Superior or Circuit Court Judge, while in Detroit, a very high level of voter discrimination is evident in Common Council and Circuit Court contests. A Negro running for County Commissioner in Chicago, one of ten Democrats on the party slate, will receive 94 per cent of the votes of the leading Democratic candidate (a popular Irishman) in the city as a whole. In Negro wards, he will do slightly better than the Irishman (perhaps 1 or 2 per cent at the most) while in wards where anti-Negro sentiment is notoriously strong he will be somewhat weaker than the Irishman (2 to 15 per cent). A Negro running for Circuit Court Judge in Chicago has shown even less susceptibility to ticket-cutting. In the city as a whole, his vote has been less than 0.5 per cent under the top of the ticket vote, and in anti-Negro wards his vote never sags by so much as 5 per cent. It is important to note that this pattern holds true even in those wards where the machine has historically been weak. In the fifth ward (which is the site of the University of Chicago) and the fiftieth ward (a generally well-to-do north shore residential area), there is hardly any more voter discrimination than in the "river wards" where the machine is powerful. Although neither ward consistently votes Democratic — in fact, the fiftieth is usually Republican — those Democratic votes that are cast tend to be straight-ticket votes.

In Detroit, the situation is completely reversed. Although the Wayne County totals show the Negro Circuit Court candidate lagging less than 9 per cent behind the top of the ticket (an Irishman), in individual wards and cities the variation is extreme. In the Negro wards, the Negro will receive a vote almost four times as large as that given to the top of the ticket, and he will do even better against a liberal Jewish candidate who is well-known for his activities on behalf of Negro causes. In the Polish city of Hamtramck, on the other hand, the Negro received only about one-fourth of the vote received by the Polish candidate.

In contests for the Detroit Common Council, a Negro was elected for the first time in 1957. He ran eighth in a race for nine seats. In the city as a whole, the Negro received about 56 per cent of the total vote cast, while the most popular candidate (a woman) received almost 90 per cent. The disparity in the over-all totals is far surpassed by the variation in the ward returns. In the Negro wards, the Negro did three or four times as well as in the city as a whole, and twice as well at the top of the ticket. In the white middle-class wards, on the other hand, the Negro received only one-fourth the votes of the top of the ticket. In the Negro wards, the cutting against white candidates was widespread. One man, widely believed to be anti-Negro, was of course heavily cut, receiving only one-fourth the vote he received on the average in the wards. But also cut was a liberal, UAW-sponsored candidate who had worked on behalf of many Negro causes.

Where Negroes have run in *partisan* elections (as candidates for Congressman, State Representative, State Senator, and member of the Board of Governors of Wayne University), they have done about as well as their white colleagues. The results approximate those obtained by Negroes in Chicago, and differences in organizational strength have relatively little impact. Where Negroes have run in nonpartisan contests in Detroit, ticket-cutting is pronounced. The value of partisanship, then, lies not simply in the strength of the machine but more in the traditional party allegiances of the voter, in the greater ease of straight-ticket voting, and by the presence of well-known state and national figures at the top of the ticket.

This situation raises two questions. The first is whether part of the machine's role in facilitating Negro entry into politics may be due to nothing more than the ability of the organization to bestow on the Negro candidate the official party label. That label alone may be enough to enable the Negro to take advantage of the straight-ticket voting which characterizes most Negro areas regardless of differences in machine strength. The additional services it provides may amount, in the last analysis, to little more than relieving the candidate of the financial and organizational burden of getting the sure vote to the polls. The second question involves the political position of white liberal allies of the Negro. In partisan elections, Negroes do not discriminate against candidates on the party ticket who are personally hostile to Negro interests. In nonpartisan elections, on the other hand, Negroes frequently "cut" white candidates who are widely known as liberal supporters of Negro causes. In the former case, partisan elections work against the Negro's punishing his enemies, while nonpartisan elections reduce the likelihood of the Negro's rewarding his friends. White liberal candidates who had suffered from this situation in Detroit's nonpartisan elections have privately expressed disappointment after the race. "Why stick your neck out for them on race issues if you only get it cut off in the election?"

The electoral advantage of strong machine organization is more evident in primary contests and, to a lesser extent, in the voting for ballot propositions. Here, the evidence is very skimpy, for Powell and Dawson rarely meet serious challengers in their primaries. What limited data there are, however, indicate that the Dawson organization is better able to turn out a large vote in primary contests than the Powell organization. In 1958, Dawson was unchallenged in the Democratic primary. Little interest was shown in the campaign, either in the city as a whole or in his district. His organization, nonetheless, produced a vote of 31,706 for him with no real effort. The same year, Powell faced a vigorous and strongly-backed primary opponent in his New York district. Earl Brown, a well-known Negro leader and one of the two Negroes on the New York City Council, was given Tammany support in the primary in an effort to "dump" Powell. The campaign was intense and dramatic, it received wide local and national publicity, and a maximum effort was made to turn out an overwhelming vote for Powell. Yet in a district similar in size to Dawson's, Powell received only 14,935 votes — less than half Dawson's total — while his opponent received 4,959. The total vote cast was less than three-fourths of the vote Dawson alone received in Chicago. In Detroit the situation parallels that in New York except that Diggs is more regularly challenged in the primary. In 1958 he defeated one opponent by receiving 82.3 per cent of 23,933 votes; and in 1954 (the first year he ran) he defeated three opponents by receiving 61.4 per cent of 33,530 votes.

The absence of real primary contests is probably as good an indication as any of the power — both actual and imputed — of the machine. Such contests are rare for any office held by a Negro member of the Dawson organization in Chicago. If there is an opponent at all, he is usually a weak one who entered simply to gain publicity for himself or his business. Serious contenders are either persuaded to drop out, sometimes with compensation in the form of money or an offer of another political job, or they are defeated by large majorities. In New York, on the other hand, scarcely a year passes without a real challenge being offered to a district leader or state assemblyman in the primaries. Rival Democratic clubs spring up in Harlem with remarkable frequency and important posts change hands regularly. Here again, machine strength or weakness in primaries in Negro areas is a reflection of such strength or weakness in city-wide primaries. In 1955, Democratic party leader Richard J. Daley challenged incumbent Martin Kennelly for the mayoral nomination in Chicago. The four Negro wards then led by Dawson voted for Daley by over 86 per cent, contributing more than 40 per cent of Daley's city-wide majority. Machine strength in the Negro areas is thus not only an historical product of machine strength in the city, but also one of its most important contemporary supports.

Machine strength may also be a determining feature of the Negro vote for referendum measures. Once more, the evidence is very fragmentary. But Chicago and New York can be compared by the degree to which a sizeable vote from Negroes can be produced on behalf of ballot propositions which would be of benefit to Negroes and which have Democratic Party endorsement. Here the differences, for the few comparable cases at hand, are striking. In Chicago's second ward, in the period 1953 through 1958, a bond proposal to provide additional street lighting received 49.8 per cent of the top of the ticket vote; a proposal to increase County Hospital facilities received 63.8 per cent; and a proposal to pay benefits to Korean War Veterans received 51.3 per cent. During the same period in New York's eleventh assembly district, a proposal to increase the state subsidy to public housing received only 13.8 per cent of the top of the ticket vote, and a proposal to finance additional public housing through a bond issue received only 9.8 per cent. Many qualifications must be made to this picture, not the least of which is that party machines rarely press vigorously for a large vote on the propositions because of the greater importance of concentrating on key elective offices. Nevertheless, the differences between Chicago and New York are so great as to suggest that the Chicago city organization can rely to a much greater extent on a positive Negro attitude toward propositions than can the New York machine.

Presumably one of the important goals of a political organization is to place its members in public office. The appointive offices captured by Negroes in northern cities vary greatly in number. In Los Angeles and Detroit there are probably the fewest, and this would seem to argue for the desirability of organized political strength. But when New York and Chicago are compared, it is quickly seen that machine strength is, if anything, in inverse correlation to the number of Negroes in important posts. Chicago, having about 750,000 to 850,000 Negroes, has only three Negro judges, one Traffic Court Referee, and one assistant to the Probate Court Judge.[18] New York, having about one million Negroes, has seventeen Negro judges: two Supreme Court Justices, one General Sessions Judge, four city Magistrates, three Domestic Relations Court Judges, six Municipal Court Judges, and one City Court Judge. In addition, in New York City (unlike Chicago), many Negroes hold administrative positions at the cabinet and sub-cabinet level. Several factors might account for this discrepancy. One would undoubtedly be the more liberal ethos of New York and the lessened resistance to the entry of Negroes into many areas of public life. Another factor is related to the uncertainty of white political leaders as to the presumed "Negro vote," and the need they feel to develop greater appeals to it in a situation of declining organizational strength. Negro political organization does not necessarily contribute to the placement of Negroes in important public offices; it may actually work against it. The Mayor of New York may believe, for example, that the civic leaders actually speak "for" the Negro community with greater authority and political power than do the politicians, and it thus becomes necessary to gratify them by co-opting some into the administration and by paying heed to the recommendations of others.

The importance of political organization among northern Negroes is, thus, a complex question. The machine seems to make little difference in the size of the Democratic vote or in the number of straight-ticket votes (in partisan elections). It may, in some cases hamper the entry of Negroes into prestigious appointive positions. At the same time, it provides for stronger control of party primaries and perhaps a higher turnout on referen-

---

[18]The Chicago *Daily Defender,* August 18, 1959, carried an editorial on this subject, written on behalf of Chicago Negro lawyers who were anxious to gain greater representation on the bench. The editorial, in a manner characteristic of much Negro thought on the subject of the political goals of the race, spoke of the need for "recognition" of the race in proportion to its numbers. It provided a table with the Chicago population of several major ethnic and nationality groups together with the number of judges drawn from each group. To this I have added another column, showing judges per 100,000 population:

Group	Population	Judges	Judges per 100,000 population
Irish	400,000	33	8.25
Jews	285,000	20	7.02
Poles	500,000	10	2.00
Italians	175,000	6	3.43
Negroes	900,000	3	0.33

The editorial was based on a report of the all-Negro Cook County Bar Association, prepared by its Committee on Public Affairs (June 29, 1959). The report also listed 38 Negro lawyers who held administrative posts in city, state, and federal agencies in Illinois, including about 16 Democrats and 19 Republicans. (The population figures here should not be considered accurate.)

dum measures. The deeper significance of organization is probably not evident from election analyses, however. The real impact of strong party organization is in the set of constraints it places on the leaders and members. An organization such as a political machine develops maintenance requirements, and these predispose it to treat issues, candidates, platforms, and election appeals in a manner distinct from that which might be employed by organizations of a different character. The primary importance of the machine lies in the way of life it creates for its members. The fundamental differences between machine and non-machine or weak-machine Negro areas consists not so much in the final election results, but in what must be done to produce those results, what obligations members acquire for having benefited by them, and what rewards exist for those who have contributed to their attainment. The machine conditions political life by the characteristic manner in which it recruits, elects, maintains, and disciplines the politicians.

The Negro Voter in
Northern Industrial Cities

Oscar Glantz

The political role of Negro citizens in northern industrial cities has been described and discussed in numerous reports and commentaries on Negro political behavior, particularly in reference to presidential and gubernatorial elections.[1] In presidential elections, for example, the best available data

Reprinted from *Western Political Quarterly,* Vol. XIII, (December 1960), pp. 999-1010, by permission of the University of Utah, copyright owners.

[1]See, for example, Ernest M. Collins, "Cincinnati Negroes and Presidential Politics," *Journal of Negro History,* XLI (1956), 131-37; Oscar Glantz, "Recent Negro Ballots in Philadelphia," *Journal of Negro Education,* XXVIII (1959), 430-38; Harold F. Gosnell, "The Negro Voter in Northern Cities," *National Municipal Review,* XXX (1941), 264-67 and 278; Edward H. Litchfield, "A Case Study of Negro Political Behavior in Detroit," *Public Opinion Quarterly,* V (1941), 267-74; Robert E. Martin, "The Relative Political Status of the Negro in the United States, *Journal of Negro Education,* XXII (1953), 363-79; J. Erroll Miller, "The Negro in Present Day Politics," *Journal of Negro History,* XXXIII (1948), 303-43; and Henry Lee Moon, "The Negro Voter in the Presidential Election of 1956," *Journal of Negro Education,* XXVI (1957), 219-30. For representative articles in the popular literature, see Robert Bendiner, "The Negro Vote and the Democrats," *Reporter,* May 31, 1956, pp. 8-12; R. H. Brisbane, "The Negro's Growing Political Power," *Nation,* September 27, 1952, pp. 248-49; Carl Rowan, "Who Gets the Negro Vote?" *Look,* November 13, 1956, pp. 37-39; and Walter White, "Win Our Vote or Lose," *Look,* October 7, 1952, pp. 18-19 and 21-22.

indicate that Negro voters have been supporting the Democratic party since
1936, by contrast to a history of strong allegiance to the Republican party
in the seventeen elections from Reconstruction through 1932.[2] Moreover,
it is evident that the northward migration of southern Negroes, plus the
accelerated migration to California,[3] has served to enlarge the numerical
force of the Negro body politic. In the single decade from 1940 to 1950, for
example, Negro migrants accounted for more than 50 per cent of the
increase in potential Negro voters in various northern cities (Table I). In
several outstanding cases, Negro migrants accounted for no less than 80
per cent of the increment.[4]

As a consequence of such increments, Negro voters in northern and
western industrial cities have achieved a balance-of-power position in local,
state and national elections.[5] On the national level, this position was notably
effective in contributing to Mr. Truman's dramatic victory in the presidential
election of 1948. When one recalls that his victory would not have been
possible without the electoral votes of California, Illinois, and Ohio, and
that he managed to carry those states by narrow margins of 17,000, 33,000,
and 7,000 votes respectively, it is readily apparent that the overwhelming
pro-Truman preference of Negro voters was indispensable in placing the
three states in the Democratic column.[6] One political commentator has
suggested that "less than a fifteen per cent switch in the Negro vote would

---

[2]In 1932, Mr. Roosevelt received only 23 per cent of the Negro vote in Chicago and 29
per cent in Cincinnati. Gosnell, *op. cit.,* and Collins, *op. cit.*
[3]For a discussion on the Negro voter in California and other western states, see Loren
Miller, "The Negro Voter in the Far West," *Journal of Negro Education,* XXVI (1957),
262-72.
[4]A rough indication of demographic developments during the decade from 1950 to 1960
can be obtained from John M. Maclachan, "Recent Population Trends in the Southeast,"
Social Forces, XXXV (1956), 147-54. He has calculated the possible net loss of migrants
from the southeastern region (eleven states) and has concluded that "the projected loss
of 2,950,000 would be comprised of about 980,000 white and 1,970,000 nonwhite net
migrants" (p. 150). For critical comments on Maclachan's data, see Homer L. Hitt,
"Migration Between the South and Other Regions." *Social Forces,* XXXVI (1957), 9-16.
[5]The leading treatise on this subject can be found in Henry Lee Moon, *Balance of Power:
The Negro Vote* (Garden City: Doubleday, 1949). For several early comments on the
relationship between Negro migration and political power, see Emmett J. Scott, *Negro
Migration During the War* (New York: Oxford University Press, 1920), especially the
optimistic editorial from the *Philadelphia Christian Recorder* (February 1, 1917) which
is reproduced on pp. 164-65.
[6]"The records show," according to R. H. Brisbane, "(1) that of the 100,000 Negroes who
went to the polls in California, 70,000 voted for Truman . . . (2) that of the 119,000
votes cast in three Negro wards in Chicago, 85,000 went to Truman . . . [and] (3) that
in Ohio 130,000 of 200,000 Negroes voted for Truman." *Op. cit.,* p. 249. Indeed, data
in the current study suggest that Mr. Truman received a percentage of Negro ballots in
Ohio which exceeds the percentage suggested by Brisbane.

TABLE I

CONTRIBUTION OF NET NEGRO MIGRATION, 1940-1950, TO THE INCREASE IN POTENTIAL NEGRO VOTERS, 1940-1950

			Net Migrants, 21+, 1940-1950	
	Number of potential voters, 1950*	Increase in potential voters, 1940-1950	Number†	As percentage of increase in potential voters, 1940-1950
Chicago	331,825	140,107	110,500	78.9
Cincinnati	52,491	15,235	13,100	86.3
Cleveland	97,757	41,811	24,500	58.7
Detroit	202,101	102,231	89,700	87.8
Kansas City	39,722	9,062	4,200	46.9
New York City	511,538	194,183	160,700	82.8
Pittsburgh	53,508	12,842	9,200	71.9
St. Louis	101,911	26,761	10,900	40.9

*With the exception of New York City, the number of Negroes in the non-citizen category is a fraction of one per cent. In New York, it is approximately two or three per cent. No adjustment was made for this factor.

†To estimate the net intercensal migration of Negroes in the eight cities, the writer utilized statewide data available in Everett S. Lee, *et al., Population Redistribution and Economic Growth* (Philadelphia: The American Philosophical Society, 1957), Vol. I, Table 1.14, pp. 87-90. For the task at hand, the "census survival!" estimate for a given state (e.g., Illinois: 215,300) was divided proportionally according to the percentage of Negroes in the state who were resident in the city under review (e.g., Chicago: 215,300 × 76.2 = 164,058). The number allocated to the given city was then multiplied by an age standard for that city (percentage of Negroes in the 21+ age-group in 1950) in order to estimate the number of potential voters gained through net migration (e.g., Chicago: 164,058 × 67.4 = 110,575). Some refinement in this procedure was possible, of course, but the purpose of the current study did not warrant it.

have delivered all three of those states to Dewey, enough to have slipped him into the White House and made Korea a 'Republican war.' "[7]

This is not to say that the Negro vote is sufficient in itself to assure political success to this or that candidate in any given election. For example, various cursory estimates of the Negro vote in 1952 and 1956 indicate that northern Negroes continued to return varying majorities to the Democratic party, thereby playing a negative role in the two elections. In the event of a close election, however, it is evident that a large turnout of Negro voters and a substantial proportion of ballots for one of the candidates can lead to the margin of victory in at least nine important states.[8] It must be said, of course,

---

[7]Bendiner, *op. cit.,* p. 8. To show that the Truman-Dewey contest was extremely close, it should also be noted that Dewey carried New York State, Michigan, and Indiana by 60,000, 35,000, and 13,000 votes respectively.

[8]The nine states and their current electoral votes are as follows: California, 32; Illinois, 27; Indiana, 13; Michigan, 20; Missouri, 13; New Jersey, 16; New York, 45; Ohio, 25; and Pennsylvania, 32.

that such margins are meaningful only when one compares the Negro vote with the white vote taken collectively. Obviously, certain subgroups within the white group (e.g., organized labor) are capable of contributing heavily to one particular candidate or the other, but when the white group is treated as a single group, these subgroup contributions may be counterbalancing, an effect which creates a close election.

Yet it should be noted that a close election is not an *automatic* condition whereby Negro voters gain the balance of power.

In addition to a close election, this would require the overwhelming majority of all potential Negro voters to be registered, highly organized and flexible. This is a large order, requiring most sharply drawn issues. Cohesiveness of the Negro vote increases greatly where his rights and aspirations are at issue. However, even though there is an unusually high feeling of group identity among Negroes, there are strong class differentiations and complete political solidarity is quite unlikely where both parties make any real effort to secure their support.[9]

Purpose of the Current Study

In view of the possibility of an exceedingly close presidential election in 1960, and in view of the increasingly important role of Negro voters in such elections, it was the purpose of the current study to gain a precise measure of developments in Negro political participation and preference in eight industrial cities, namely the ones which are listed in Table I.[10] Stated as questions which can be answered on the level of empirical observation: (1) to what extent, if any, has the Negro body politic altered its pattern of political participation in the last three presidential elections, and (2) to what extent, if any, has the Negro body politic altered its pattern of political preference in the last three presidential elections?[11]

The data on political participation will refer to the percentage of registrants who exercised their political franchise by voting for a presidential candidate. The data on political preference will refer to the percentage of voters who voted for the candidate of the Democratic party. To sharpen the focus of the report, the participation and preference data for Negroes will

---

[9]Martin, *op. cit.*, p. 378.

[10]The study was supported, in part, by a grant from the All-University Research Fund, Michigan State University.

[11]Evidence on the second question is also available in Moon's study of "The Negro Voter in the Presidential Election of 1956," *op. cit.*, Tables I, II, and III. Moon presents estimates which compare the vote in 1952 to the vote in 1956 in 39 northern and 23 southern cities. Many of his figures for northern cities are related to ecological areas which are relatively heterogeneous in population composition, thereby providing us with estimates which are too imprecise for the historical record. From the vantage point of the current study, Moon's data tend to underestimate the amount of pro-Democratic preference on the part of northern Negroes.

be compared to similar data for the total population of each city. Unfortunately, it was impossible to distinguish between the total population and the white population within it. Thus, in examining the comparative data in Tables IV and V, one should recall that the differences would always be larger if Negro and white behavior had been compared directly.[12] Nonetheless, by placing the trends of Negro participation and preference within the context of general trends, it will be possible to draw additional inferences from the data.

Procedures

The measurement of Negro political behavior was accomplished by utilizing official data for rigorously selected sample areas in each city. On the basis of a severe "90 plus" criterion, these areas were located according to the following procedures:

1. (a) For Chicago, Cleveland, Detroit, Kansas City, Pittsburgh, and St. Louis, the writer selected all census tracts in which the Negro population exceeded 90 per cent of the total population in 1950. This approach yielded a total of 134 tracts for the six cities, ranging from 4 tracts in Kansas City to 77 in Chicago.[13]

1. (b) In the case of New York City, the selection was limited to Manhattan (New York County) so as to reduce the burden of collecting the necessary political data. Moreover, the selection was limited to all census tracts in which the Negro population exceeded 90 per cent of the total population in 1940 as well as in 1950. Nonetheless, there were 14 tracts which met the double "90 plus" criterion, with approximately 157,000 Negroes in 1950.

1. (c) In Cincinnati, the sample was limited to the 16th Ward, where the Negro proportion of the total population was 92.1 per cent in 1940 and 94.5 per cent in 1950.[14]

---

[12]See Glantz, *op. cit.,* for an example of a direct comparison between Negro and white political behavior in Philadelphia. Needless to say, direct comparisons add a certain amount of depth to the analysis.

[13]In five of these cities, the selection included one or two tracts in which the Negro population was somewhat less than 90 per cent of the total population in 1950. In order to enlarge the samples in Kansas City and Pittsburgh, one tract in each city which fell below the "90 plus" criterion (85.5% in Kansas City and 84.3% in Pittsburgh) was added to the tracts which met the "90 plus" criterion. Two tracts were added in Chicago (89.8% and 87.3%), in Cleveland (89.9% and 89.2%), and in St. Louis (88.1% and 86.9%) in order to establish contiguous areas and thereby to facilitate the collection of political data.

[14]In selecting the sample for Cincinnati, the writer followed the procedure marked out by Collins, *op. cit.*

2. (a) For the seven cities other than Cincinnati, the census tracts were plotted on maps containing political subdivisions. All precincts which fell within the census tracts *at the time of each election* were taken as the basic political units for the study. Inasmuch as precinct boundaries are changed from time to time, it should be noted that the number of precincts in each sample area varied from one election to the next.

2. (b) The same procedure was not necessary for Cincinnati, where the sample area and the basic political unit were coterminous.

One last note concerns the procedure which was employed to collect the necessary political data. They were assembled from official records in the offices of registration and election commissioners in each city.[15]

Adequacy and Representatives of the Sample Areas

In Table II, it can be observed that the number of Negroes in each sample area accounted for an adequate proportion of the total Negro population. The lowest figures are for New York City (21.1 per cent) and Cincinnati (23.7 per cent). The remaining percentages vary from 31.3 in Pittsburgh to 67.7 in Chicago.

TABLE II

POPULATION COMPOSITION OF SAMPLE AREAS, 1950*

| | Sample Area | | | Negroes in S.A. as percentage of Negroes in city |
	Total	Negro	Per cent Negro	
Chicago	339,854	333,488	98.1	67.7
Cincinnati†	19,625	18,547	94.5	23.7
Cleveland	76,355	73,135	95.8	49.5
Detroit	110,267	106,013	96.1	35.3
Kansas City	21,259	20,028	94.2	36.0
New York City	159,311	157,828	99.1	21.1
Pittsburgh	27,866	25,841	92.7	31.3
St. Louis	85,693	80,202	93.6	52.2

*Source: U.S. Bureau of the Census, *Seventeenth Census of the United States,* 1950, Volume III, Census Tract Statistics, Table 1, P-D Bulletins 10, 12, 17, 27, 37, 43 and 47; selected tracts.
†Collins, *op. cit.,* Table 2, p. 133.

[15]The writer gratefully acknowledges his indebtedness to numerous persons in the various registration and election offices. Without their co-operation, it would have been impossible to assemble the data.

To test the representativeness of each sample area, the non-white labor force, by sex, in the non-white population of each sample area was compared to the non-white labor force, by sex, in the city-wide non-white population. It was impossible to make a comparison of this sort for the Cincinnati sample, but in the other seven cities the sample areas appear to be representative (Table III). In 10 of the 14 available comparisons, it can be seen that the difference is one per cent or less. The other four comparisons point to differences of −2.2 per cent for males in the Cleveland sample, −3.2 per cent for males and −4.0 per cent for females in the Detroit sample, and +4.7 per cent for females in the New York sample. The minus signs indicate underrepresentation of male workers in the Cleveland sample and both male and female workers in the Detroit sample, while the plus sign indicates overrepresentation of female workers in the New York sample. To the extent that workers and non-workers differ in political behavior, the accuracy of the political data for Cleveland, Detroit, and New York may be slightly impaired.

Political Participation in 1948, 1952, and 1956

Although presidential elections fail to involve large percentages of the adult population in any region of the United States,[16] they tend to attract relatively large percentages of the registered population, particularly in urban places. The latter point is evident from the data in the three columns on the left-hand side of Table IV, where the reader may note that the turnout of all registrants was typically in the range from 75 to 85 per cent in 1948 and from 80 to 90 per cent in 1952 and 1956. Thus, an individual's intention to vote in a presidential election is initially a function of his earlier motivation to get on or remain on the registration roster. In the registration-to-participation nexus, however, it is obvious that the first event is a necessary legal antecedent to the second event, so that the question of final motivation for the turnout of registrants still goes unanswered in the current study. Fortunately, several interview-studies have provided reasonable answers to the latter question by utilizing the panel technique, i.e., by conducting pre- and post-election interviews. One writer, for example, has reported recently that "the greater the feeling of involvement in the

---

[16]In 1948, for example, the participation rates for the adult population (presidential ballots) were as follows: 60.2 per cent in the northeastern states, 61.3 per cent in the north-central states, 56.9 per cent in the western states and 30.0 per cent in the southern states. U.S. Bureau of the Census, *Current Population Reports*, Series P-25, Population Estimates, No. 63, August 31, 1952, Table 2. The reader may compare these percentages with the ones in Table IV (current paper) on the turnout of the registered population in the cities under review.

election campaign, the more likely the voter will fulfill a positive intention to vote."[17]

TABLE III

REPRESENTATIVENESS OF SAMPLE AREAS*
NON-WHITE PERSONS IN THE LABOR FORCE, 14 YEARS OLD AND OVER, AS PERCENTAGE OF ALL NON-WHITE PERSONS 14 YEARS OLD AND OVER

	Males		Females	
	City	Sample Area	City	Sample Area
Chicago	79.1	78.7	40.6	39.9
Cincinnati†	—	—	—	—
Cleveland	80.2	78.0	37.0	36.6
Detroit	81.9	78.7	29.4	25.4
Kansas City	76.2	75.4	42.7	42.8
New York City	76.6	77.0	47.6	52.3
Pittsburgh	75.4	74.4	28.7	28.5
St. Louis	72.5	73.2	37.7	37.7

*Source: U.S. Bureau of the Census, *Seventeenth Census of the United States*, 1950, Volume II, Characteristics of the Population, Chapter C, Parts 13, 22, 25, 32, 35 and 38 (city-wide data) and Volume III, Census Tract Statistics, Table 4, P-D Bulletins 10, 12, 17, 27, 37, 43 and 47 (S.A. data, selected tracts).
†Sample area is 16th Ward. Labor force data unavailable.

TABLE IV

PERCENTAGE OF REGISTRANTS WHO VOTED FOR A PRESIDENTIAL CANDIDATE

	Of All Registrants*			Of Negro Registrants†		
	1948	1952	1956	1948	1952	1956
Chicago	84.6	84.8	83.3	72.8	71.5	72.5
Cincinnati	77.9	82.9	83.6	61.4	66.4	63.1
Cleveland	70.9	83.2	85.0	66.0	71.0	77.5
Detroit	76.7	82.3	81.7	68.7	73.4	78.2
Kansas City	87.2	93.5	87.4	81.7	83.5	78.2
New York City‡	—	—	—	—	—	—
Pittsburgh	78.7	85.7	83.3	71.3	80.4	73.7
St. Louis	84.4	89.8	83.8	73.7	80.9	78.3

*City-wide data.
†Based on data for sample areas.
‡Registration data unavailable for New York City.

[17]William A. Glaser, "Intention and Voting Turnout," *American Political Science Review*, LII (1958), 1032. The relation between involvement and turnout is further elaborated by Glaser in his analysis of the sociological and psychological conditions under which differential involvement leads to differential turnout (pp. 1033-40).

It would be injudicious to assume that a given turnout rate is likewise a measure of group-wide psychological involvement in a given election campaign, inasmuch as numerous uninvolved persons manage nonetheless to vote on election day.[18] However, to the extent that *differential turnout* is a reflection of *differential involvement,* comparative turnout rates can be taken as rough measures of group-wide *differences* in psychological involvement. Indeed, differential turnout can be attributed to differences in various psychological factors which are related presumably to political participation, e.g., the "interest complex"[19] and the "sense of political efficacy"[20] and that old-fashioned tag known as "political apathy."[21] In these terms, differential turnout rates for two cities, e.g., 84.6 per cent for all registrants in Chicago (1948) and 77.9 per cent for all registrants in Cincinnati (1948), or differential turnout rates for two population groups, e.g., 84.6 per cent for all registrants in Chicago (1948) and 72.8 per cent for Negro registrants in Chicago (1948), or differential turnout rates for a single population group in two elections, e.g., 72.8 per cent for Negro registrants in Chicago (1948) and 71.5 per cent for Negro registrants in Chicago (1952), can be taken as indications of a higher feeling of involvement, higher interest, a higher sense of political efficacy, less political apathy, and so on. In the current study, the writer will exercise the option of favoring the concept of political efficacy.

Along this line, a consistently lower group-wide sense of political efficacy on the part of Negro registrants, by contrast with the registered population in general, can be inferred from the comparative data in Table IV. Although the level of Negro participation varied from city to city and from one election to the next, it never matched the level of total participation in any of the city-by-city comparisons in any of the three presidential elections under review. On a more generalized basis, it can be noted that the turnout of Negro registrants was typically in the range from 65 to 75 per cent in

---

[18]*Ibid.,* Table IV, p. 1037. It should be added that some persons who are highly involved in the election campaign nonetheless fail to vote on election day.

[19]See Paul F. Lazarsfeld, *et al, The People's Choice* (New York: Duell, Sloan and Pearce, 1944), pp. 40-45. For example, "as the level of interest decreases . . . the lower the index of participation and activity in the campaign."

[20]See Angus Campbell, *et al, The Voter Decides* (Evanston: Row, Peterson, 1954), pp. 187-94. For example, "the higher one's sense of political efficacy, the higher the level of his participation in the 1952 election." Parenthetically, it can be noted that Campbell and associates, in examining the relationship between demographic components and political efficacy, reached the conclusion that "Negroes feel more politically impotent than the rest of the population."

[21]See Morris Rosenberg, "Some Determinants of Political Apathy," *Public Opinion Quarterly,* XVIII (1954), 349-66. For example, "the individual may be a member of a group in which political apathy is a positive group norm — a group which would discourage political action."

1948 and from 70 to 80 per cent in 1952 and 1956. When one recalls that the turnout of all registrants was typically in the range from 75 to 85 per cent in 1948 and from 80 to 90 per cent in 1952 and 1956, a continuous discrepancy of approximately ten percentage points is evident. Thus, by failing to match the turnout of the total population, Negro registrants fail to enhance their position as a balance of power.

In connection with the 1952 election, however, it is appropriate to emphasize the upward trend in the level of Negro participation at the ballot box. With the exception of the turnout in Chicago (where there was a small decrease of 1.3 percentage points), the activity of Negro registrants increased by approximately two points in Kansas City (where the rate was relatively high in 1948), five points in three additional cities (Cincinnati, Cleveland, and Detroit), seven points in St. Louis and nine points in Pittsburgh. The upturn continued into the 1956 election in Cleveland and Detroit,[22] but it was not sustained in the other cities. Nonetheless, there is some suggestion in the data for 1952 that Negro registrants are approaching a new level of political consciousness, and in these terms, a new sense of political efficacy. Under certain circumstances, of course, there is always the possibility that a significant portion of the Negro body politic may decide to boycott both parties in a given presidential election, but it is much more plausible to suggest that the concomitants of urbanization, such as educational and re-educational opportunities, intensified communications, machine politics and convenient polling places, will tend eventually to maximize political participation on the part of the Negro people. This is not to say that the aforementioned discrepancy between the total body politic and the Negro body politic will be narrowed in the immediate future. As it happens, there were parallel increments in political activity on the part of the total registered population in each of the cities which have been examined here.

Political Preference in 1948, 1952 and 1956

It is not uncommon, particularly in the popular literature, for publicists and political analysts to describe the Negro vote in terms which imply racial solidarity, e.g., "en masse voting" and "en bloc voting." In such terms, various writers have claimed that "Negroes must be appealed to en masse,"[23] that "Negroes, on the sole issue of civil rights, voted almost

---

[22]To give the reader some idea of differential estimates, it is interesting to note that Henry Lee Moon, in his study of the 1956 election, *op. cit.*, points to a *decrease* of 6.4 percentage points in Cleveland (p. 228), whereas the current study points to an *increase* of 6.5 percentage points. Additional disparities are evident when Moon's data are compared with the current data for Chicago (−12.0 vs. +1.0) and Pittsburgh (−15.4 vs. −6.7).

[23]Brisbane, *op. cit.*, p. 249.

en masse [in 1948],"[24] and that "Negroes have in fact tended to vote en bloc, as a few simple statistics will testify."[25] It is not the purpose here to question these claims, but it should be said that there are some logical objections concerning the applicability and utility of this notion of bloc voting as a means of characterizing the Negro vote or the vote of any other single group. For example, in a specific reference to the Negro vote, one commentator posed the issue as follows: "In what degree . . . [is it] a function not of racial-bloc voting but of socio-economic status?"[26] Moreover, in a generalized reference to the voting behavior of any group, a leading pollster suggested recently that "there is no such thing as bloc voting," a term which is "too often used to describe what is just a tendency on the part of a particular group to vote more unilaterally than does the general public."[27]

With these objections in mind, the analysis of Negro voting behavior in the current study will be phrased in terms of voting strength rather than racial solidarity. From the balance-of-power standpoint, such strength can be measured in terms of two calculations, the first of which is based on four factors which determine the size of a given candidate's margin of victory among Negro voters. These factors are (1) the number of potential Negro voters in a given city or state; (2) the level of registration; (3) the level of participation at the polls; and (4) the level of support for the candidate in question. The second calculation is simply the size of the candidate's margin of victory among all voters. If the first figure is larger than the second, it can be said that the Negro body politic had sufficient strength to play a decisive role in the election.

To use the Negro vote in Chicago as an example (1948), the first calculation can be obtained on the assumption that the number of potential Negro voters was approximately 303,000 in 1948 (note in Table I that the number was 331,000 in 1950, with an average increase of 14,000 each year from 1940 to 1950), that the level of registration was approximately 70 per cent,[28]

---

[24]White, *op. cit.,* p. 17.

[25]Bendiner, *op. cit.,* p. 17.

[26]Comment by Professor David B. Carpenter in his discussion of my paper at the 1958 Meeting of the Population Association of America. See Oscar Glantz, "Political Implications of Negro Migration: Summary and Discussion," *Population Index,* XXIV (1958), 222.

[27]Comment by Elmo Roper at the 1957 Meeting of the American Association for Public Opinion Research. See Richard S. Halpern's report in "Interpretations of the 1956 Election," *Public Opinion Quarterly,* XXI (1957), 448.

[28]With a few exceptions, registration offices in northern industrial cities do not compile registration data on the basis of race. One of these exceptions is the office in Philadelphia, where the record indicates that 69.8 per cent of the potential Negro voters (all Negroes 21 years old and over) were registered for the gubernatorial election in 1950. A reliable estimate indicates that 70.3 per cent were registered for the presidential election in 1948.

that the level of participation at the polls was 73 per cent (see Table IV), and that the level of support for Mr. Truman was 70 per cent (see Table V). Thus, the number of registrants was 303,000 × .70 = 212,000; the number of voters was 212,000 × .73 = 154,833 (say 154,000); the number of votes for Truman was 154,000 × .70 = 107,800 (say 107,000); the number of votes for Dewey was 154,000 − 107,000 = 47,000; and the margin of victory for Truman was 107,000 − 47,000 = 60,000. In the entire state of Illinois, Mr. Truman's margin among all voters was 33,000, indicating clearly that the Negro vote in Chicago (to say nothing of the Negro vote in other districts of Illinois) was responsible for the statewide victory, at least when the white vote is viewed collectively. An additional example of decisive voting strength in 1948 is provided by the data for two cities in Ohio, a state where Mr. Truman's margin among all voters was only 7,000. Among Negro voters, however, his margin was approximately 10,000 in Cincinnati and 18,000 in Cleveland, more than enough in either city to change the statewide decision in an election which was otherwise closely contested.

This is not to say that Mr. Truman received his strongest support from Negro voters in Chicago (70 per cent), Cincinnati (75 per cent) and Cleveland (71 per cent), but rather to indicate that these levels were crucial in the sense that they served to tip the balance in favor of a given candidate. As the reader may observe in Table V, the level of pro-Truman support among Negro voters in the other cities under review was roughly as high in St. Louis (68 per cent) and New York (72 per cent) and higher in Kansas City (77 per cent), Pittsburgh (77 per cent) and Detroit (84 per cent). Insofar as political cohesiveness influences the general drift of social and economic decisions in various branches of government, each of these levels was significant. However, they were not crucial from the balance-of-power standpoint.[29]

On the assumption that the 1960 presidential election will be closely contested, thereby providing the Negro body politic with another opportunity to exercise the balance of power in a number of states, it is the further task of this paper to examine the extent to which Negro voters have altered their pattern of political preference since 1948. Specifically, to what extent did Negro voters endorse Mr. Stevenson's candidacy in 1952? To what extent was this endorsement withdrawn in 1956? And of greatest importance, to what extent and in which direction did the pattern in 1956 differ from the pattern in 1948?

---

[29]In view of Mr. Truman's margin of 262,000 among all voters in his home state of Missouri, the Negro vote in Kansas City and St. Louis was not crucial in the sense that it was not decisive. In 1952, however, the Negro vote was responsible for Mr. Stevenson's slim margin of 30,000.

From the data in Table V, it can be seen that the peak of Negro allegiance to the Democratic party was reached in 1952, which is to say that Mr. Stevenson polled a larger percentage of Negro ballots in 1952 than Mr. Truman had polled in 1948, and probably a larger percentage than Mr. Roosevelt had polled in any of the previous four elections. The level of support for Mr. Stevenson was 75 per cent in Chicago, from 78 to 83 per cent in six additional cities, and one-tenth of one percentage-point short of 90 per cent in Detroit. In a year which marked the end of the New and Fair Deals for thousands of white voters, this pro-Democratic increment on the part of the Negro body politic can be taken as an outstanding example of political fidelity. As a consequence, the pro-Democratic gap between the Negro vote and the general vote ranged from 17 percentage points in St. Louis to 38 in Cincinnati.

However, when Mr. Stevenson altered his political posture in 1956, he lost some of the ardent support which had developed among Negro voters in his first campaign. Although there was less alienation than one might have expected in three of the cities (a decrease of approximately five percentage points in Detroit, Pittsburgh, and St. Louis), the downturn was significant in a majority of cases.[30] There was a loss of 9 points in Cincinnati,

TABLE V

PERCENTAGE OF VOTERS WHO VOTED FOR THE PRESIDENTIAL
CANDIDATE OF THE DEMOCRATIC PARTY

	Of All Voters*			Of Negro Voters†		
	1948	1952	1956	1948	1952	1956
Chicago	58.2	54.2	48.6	70.4	74.7	62.6
Cincinnati	48.3	43.4	37.5	75.0	81.2	72.2
Cleveland	64.5	59.9	54.6	71.3	78.8	62.7
Detroit	59.3	60.2	61.7	83.9	89.9	84.4
Kansas City	61.1	51.6	53.1	77.3	81.8	70.0
New York City‡	51.5	58.4	55.7	71.8	83.2	68.9
Pittsburgh	59.6	55.7	52.2	77.6	82.0	76.9
St. Louis	64.2	62.1	61.1	68.4	79.6	74.8

*City-wide data.
†Based on data for sample areas.
‡Limited to Manhattan (New York County). Data include Liberal vote, Democratic candidate.

[30]It can be noted that Negro voters in the South, by contrast with their compatriots in the North, defected from the Democratic party to a much greater extent. In Henry Lee Moon's article on "The Negro Voter in the Presidential Election of 1956," *op. cit.,* Table III, p. 224, estimates for 23 southern cities suggest that Mr. Eisenhower received a majority of Negro ballots in 13 of them. In some of these places, the Democratic loss was greater than 50 percentage points.

12 points in Chicago and Kansas City, 14 points in New York, and 16 points in Cleveland. Moreover, when the data for 1956 are compared with the data for 1948, it can be seen in Table V that Negro voters in six of the eight cities gave Mr. Stevenson less support in 1956 than they had given Mr. Truman in 1948. The largest downturns are evident in the comparative data for Chicago (-7.8) Cleveland (-8.6) and Kansas City, (-7.3), while downturns of less significance are recorded for Cincinnati (-2.8) New York (-2.9) and Pittsburgh (-0.7).

From the balance-of-power standpoint, these developments suggest that the Democratic candidate in 1960 will have only a slim chance of gaining the electoral votes of Illinois and Ohio if the current level of Negro support in Chicago, Cleveland, and Cincinnati remains unaltered or continues downward, assuming of course that the next election will be as closely contested as was the one in 1948. With the exception of Michigan, where the current level of Democratic preference on the part of Negro voters in Detroit is extremely high, a similar conclusion can be reached for Missouri (given contradictory trends in St. Louis and Kansas City) and possibly New York and Pennsylvania. It should be noted, however, that this conclusion presupposes a relatively static situation from 1948 to 1960. In the event that the Negro body politic in these places has been augmented considerably by continuing in-migration, and in the event that this body politic manages to raise its level of participation at the polls, the current pro-Democratic level, even if it continues downward to a small extent, may be sufficient nonetheless to tip the balance in favor of the Democratic candidate. By way of illustration, if it is necessary to obtain 70 per cent of the ballots of 150,000 Negro voters in order to overcome a lead of 59,000 votes among all other voters, the same lead of 59,000 can be overcome by 60 per cent of 300,000 Negro ballots.

In summary, the leading observations and inferences from the current study are as follows: (1) There was a consistently lower group-wide sense of political efficacy on the part of Negro registrants, by contrast with the registered population in general. Although the level of Negro participation at the polls varied from city to city and from one election to the next, it never matched the level of total participation in any of the city-by-city comparisons in any of the three presidential elections under review. (2) At the same time, the participation data for 1952 indicate that there was an increase in Negro activity at the polls in seven of the eight cities examined here. These increments suggest that Negro registrants are approaching a new level of political consciousness, and in these terms, a new sense of political efficacy. (3) From the balance-of-power standpoint, Negro voters in Illinois (represented here by Chicago) and Ohio (Cleveland and Cincinnati) played a decisive role in tipping the balance in favor of Mr. Truman in 1948.

(4) The peak of Negro allegiance to the Democratic party in each of the eight cities was reached in 1952, when Mr. Stevenson polled a larger percentage of Negro ballots than Mr. Truman had polled in 1948. In a year which marked the end of the New and Fair Deals for thousands of white voters, such allegiance on the part of the Negro body politic serves as an outstanding example of political fidelity, comparable perhaps to the high level of Negro allegiance to Mr. Hoover in 1932. (5) When Mr. Stevenson posed as a moderate in 1956, he lost varying amounts of support among Negro voters in each of the eight cities. These losses were within a range from five percentage points in three of the cities to 16 points in Cleveland. (6) Moreover, Negro voters in six of the eight cities gave Mr. Stevenson less support in 1956 than they had given Mr. Truman in 1948. The largest downturns occurred in Chicago, Cleveland, and Kansas City. (7) From the balance-of-power standpoint, these downturns suggest that the Democratic candidate in 1960 will have only a slim chance of gaining the electoral votes of Illinois, Ohio and Missouri (and possibly New York and Pennsylvania) if the current level of Democratic preference remains unaltered or continues downward, assuming of course that the next election is closely contested. (8) However, to the extent that the Negro body politic has been augmented to any substantial degree by continuing northward migration, and to the extent that Negro registrants participate in greater force in the next election, the current level of Democratic preference, even if it turns downward slightly, may be sufficient to change the verdict of a closely contested election. In any event, neither party can afford to ignore the numerical weight of the Negro vote. In the next campaign, the Democratic candidate will have the responsibility of reversing the changing image of the Democratic party,[31] while the Republican candidate will have the responsibility of enlarging the social and economic appeal of the Republican party.

[31]For example, Mr. Roy Wilkins, executive secretary of the NAACP, told a Chicago audience in 1956 that "we Negroes have got to consider whether we want to swap the known devil for the suspected witch." Reported by Rowan, *op. cit.,* p. 39.

The Negro Vote in the
Presidential Election of 1956

Henry Lee Moon

Long before the ballots were counted on the night of November 6, 1956, it was apparent that Negro voters, who for 20 years had been strongly attached to the Democratic party, were no longer satisfied with what they were getting, or believed that they could hope to get, out of the political coalition which Franklin D. Roosevelt had fashioned from dissimilar and, sometimes, hostile elements of the electorate.

The New and Fair Deals to which Negro voters had given ardent support had passed into history. President Roosevelt, the leader of the New Deal, was dead. Harry S. Truman, his successor, was retired. Adlai Stevenson, the Democratic party standard bearer, who inherited the political goodwill of his predecessors in 1952 was handicapped by his futile pursuit of an illusory party unity which alienated not only many Negro voters but also Southern whites.

By Election Day, 1956, there was ample evidence of a sizeable break-away of Negro voters from the Democratic party. Partisan as well as non-political spokesmen for the race had warned that resurgence of racial bigotry in the

Reprinted from *Journal of Negro Education,* Vol. **XXVI**, (Summer 1957), pp. 219-230 by permission of the publisher.

South endangered the old alliance. Polls had indicated that the Democrats could not count on the overwhelming majorities from Negro districts which had been returned consistently during the past 20 years. The Republicans, sensing the disillusionment of Negro voters, made cautious overtures inviting them to return to the party of their fathers which they had abandoned, almost *en masse,* in the mid-Thirties.

There remained only the counting of the ballots to determine the extent of the defection and the post-election analyses to assay the causes and interpret the significance of the switch.

A Gallup poll reported on January 16, 1957, that "of all the major groups of the nation's population, the one that shifted most to the Eisenhower-Nixon ticket last November was the Negro voter." According to this poll, the vote for the Republican candidates in the nation's Negro districts was up 18 percentage points from that of 1952 when only a fifth of the Negro voters cast their ballots for General Eisenhower. Samuel Lubell, the political analyst, placed the Eisenhower gain at 11 percentage points in his series of Sidney Hillman lectures at Howard University in February, 1957.

A survey by the National Association for the Advancement of Colored People of the election returns from predominantly Negro areas of 63 cities in all' sections of the country and of varying sizes indicates a gain of 19.9 percentage points for the Republican presidential candidate. Negro voters in 23 Southern cities increased their vote for the President by 36.8 percentage points. In the 40 non-Southern cities, the NAACP survey shows, the Eisenhower vote was up 9.9 percentage points.

Of the 63 cities, the Republican candidate in 1952 carried the Negro precincts only in Leavenworth, Kans., and Zanesville, Ohio. Four years later, the majority of Negro voters in 12 Southern and 10 Northern cities cast their ballots for the Eisenhower-Nixon Republican team. In 1952, the Democratic candidate made a complete sweep of the Negro districts in 47 cities from which the NAACP obtained election returns. His percentage of the total vote cast in these precincts ranged from 55 in Rochester, N.Y., to 99 in Darlington, S.C., in one ward of which he received 509 votes out of a total of 514.

While the swing to the Republican standard bearer in 1956 was widespread, it was not universal. There are four Northern cities covered by the 1956 survey in which the Eisenhower ticket sustained losses up to five percentage points among Negro voters. In ten other non-Southern cities his gain in percentage points was five or less. The President received 1,437 fewer votes in three Negro wards of Detroit than in 1952. His percentage points were down five. He also lost ground in Wilmington, Del.; Saginaw, Mich.; and Albany, N.Y. He gained five or less percentage points in Kansas City, Mo.; Leavenworth, Kans.; Milwaukee; Minneapolis; Paterson, N.J.;

Portland, Ore.; Freeport, Ill.; Toledo; St. Louis; Trenton, N.J.; and Phila-delphia. In no Southern city covered by the survey was the President's gain less than five percentage points.

The 15 cities, all Northern, in which Negro voters deviated five per-centage points or less from their 1952 support of the Republican candi-dates are indicated in Table I. Although sustaining losses, the Democratic presidential candidate carried the majority of Negro voters in most Northern cities. However, in nine of the cities from which the NAACP received reports, Negro districts which gave substantial majorities to Stevenson in 1952 returned majorities for the President in the 1956 election. The Eisen-hower majorities in these cities ranged from 50.6 in Columbus, Ohio, to 61.1 in Montclair, N.J. Negro districts in Baltimore; New Haven; Middle-town, Ohio; and Atlantic City, Montclair, East Orange and Union Township in New Jersey also switched to President Eisenhower in his second election.

Elsewhere in the North and West, the Democratic candidates won, but by reduced majorities. Even in cities whose Negro voters remained in the Democratic fold, the count revealed increases in the Eisenhower vote up to 21 percentage points. Table II indicates 24 non-Southern cities in which there was a shift to the Republican candidates amounting to more than five per-centage points.

It was in the Southern states that the Republicans made their most notable gains among Negro voters. In many precincts throughout the region, the vote was reversed from that of 1952. In 1952 the Stevenson-Sparkman ticket received as high as 75 to 90 per cent of the vote in these precincts. In 1956, the Eisenhower-Nixon ticket swept many of these districts with impressive majorities. A Charleston, S.C., precinct which returned only 38 votes for the Republicans in 1952 gave the ticket 618 votes in 1956. Two wards in Darlington, S.C., which returned 722 votes for Stevenson in 1952 to six for Eisenhower, in 1956 gave the President 497 votes to 193 for the Democratic candidate. In 1952 the solidly Negro Scarboro 4th District in Oak Ridge, Tenn., cast only 19 votes for the President as compared with 319 for Gov. Stevenson. In 1956, President Eisenhower carried the district, 128 to 87. Thirty-eight precincts in Memphis which returned 68 per cent of their votes for the Democratic candidate in 1952 gave 54 per cent of their votes to the President in the second election.

In 1952 the Illinois governor carried the Atlanta Negro precincts better than 2 to 1. Four years later he received less than 15 per cent of the vote in these precincts. The Democratic candidate did even better in Norfolk, receiving 87 per cent of the vote in the earlier election. In 1956 his vote in the same precincts was only 20 per cent of the total. The story was similar in Richmond — Stevenson's 1952 and 1956 percentages standing at 78 and 27, respectively. A Birmingham precinct which had overwhelmingly sup-

TABLE I

VOTE IN NEGRO AREAS DEVIATING 5 OR LESS PERCENTAGE POINTS, 1952 TO 1956
(Northern Cities)

CITY	1952		1956		% Eisenhower		Eisenhower
	Eisenhower (R)	Stevenson (D)	Eisenhower	Stevenson	1952	1956	% gain
Albany, N. Y., Wards 6, 8	869	3,201	725	2,853	21.3	20.2	—0.1
Detroit, Mich., Wards 3, 5, 7	4,467	26,862	3,030	29,787	14.2	9.2	—5.0
Freeport, Ill., Precincts 14, 15; Lancaster 2	629	853	592	733	42.4	44.7	2.3
Kansas City, Mo., Wards 2, 4, 14	7,344	21,535	6,849	16,132	25.4	29.8	4.4
Leavenworth, Kans., 13 Precincts	5,384	3,802	5,316	3,373	58.6	61.1	2.5
Milwaukee, Wards 6, 8	5,517	11,298	5,160	9,770	32.8	34.5	1.7
Minneapolis	2,990	5,725	2,315	3,587	34.2	39.2	5.0
Paterson, N. J., 9 Precincts of Ward 4	2,881	4,553	1,582	2,473	38.7	39	0.3
Philadelphia, 14 Wards	54,028	142,210	48,114	121,070	27.5	28.4	0.9
Portland, Oregon	2,176	3,812	1,789	3,050	36.3	37	0.7
Saginaw, Mich.	464	2,054	561	2,905	18.5	16.2	—2.3
St. Louis, Wards 4, 5, 6, 18, 19, 20, 26	19,799	62,378	18,947	50,827	24.1	27.1	3.0
Toledo, Ohio, Wards 6, 7, 8, 9	6,658	13,599	5,874	11,208	32.8	34.3	1.5
Wilmington, Del., Wards 1, 2, 4, 6, 8	4,443	4,838	3,399	4,327	47.8	43.9	3.9
Trenton, N. J., 13 Election Districts	2,370	3,974	1,944	3,121	37.2	38.3	1.1

TABLE II

VOTE IN NEGRO AREAS WITH SUBSTANTIAL INCREASE IN EISENHOWER VOTE, 1952 TO 1956

(Northern Cities)

CITY	1952		1956		% Eisenhower		Eisenhower % gain
	Eisenhower (R)	Stevenson (D)	Eisenhower	Stevenson	1952	1956	
Atlantic City, N. J., 27 precincts	2,647	5,420	3,599	2,872	32.8	55.6	22.8
Baltimore	30,776	61,253	28,548	23,580	33.1	54.7	21.6
Boston, Ward 9	3,058	7,827	3,811	3,970	28.1	48.9	20.8
Chicago, Wards 2, 3, 4, 6, 20	48,441	116,849	54,224	91,197	29.5	37.2	7.7
Cleveland, Wards 11, 12, 16, 17, 18, 24, 25	23,732	51,187	33,670	36,423	31.6	48	16.4
Columbus, Ohio, Wards 6, 7, 8, 13	8,142	15,691	11,767	11,467	34.2	50.6	16.4
Denver, Precincts 1801, 1802	898	3,797	1,408	3,442	19.1	29	9.9
Gary, Ind., 39 Precincts	5,413	15,360	8,386	11,977	26.0	41.1	15.1
Grand Rapids, Mich., Ward III—Precincts 5, 7, 9, 10, 11, 14, 23, 25, Ward II—Precinct 12	1,411	3,504	1,524	2,900	28.7	34.4	5.7
East Orange, N. J., Ward 4, Districts 2, 3, 12	923	1,188	1,181	838	43.7	58.4	14.7
Johnstown, Pa., Ward 4, Ward 12, Precincts 1, 2	293	807	452	551	26.6	45	18.4
Joliet, Ill., Precincts 37, 38, 45, 46	825	1,779	1,027	1,229	31.3	45.5	14.2
Los Angeles, 27 Sample Precincts	1,364	5,138	2,040	3,827	20.9	34.7	13.8
Middletown, Ohio, Precincts 1A, 26, 2D, 27, 2I, 4D, 46	715	1,761	895	842	29.6	51.5	21.9
Montclair, N. J., Ward 4	1,418	2,465	2,148	1,362	36.5	61.1	24.6
Passaic, N. J., Ward 1 — Districts 2, 3, Ward 2—Districts 4, 5, 6, Ward 4—Districts 1, 2, 3	1,563	2,743	1,957	2,142	36	47.7	11.7
New Haven, Conn., Ward 19	719	1,709	1,002	883	29.6	53.1	23.5
New York City, Brooklyn 6 AD, EDS 1-8; 12-25; 27-31	5,326	16,833	7,803	11,986	24	39.4	15.4
Manhattan, ADS 11, 12, 13, 14	29,435	110,458	44,450	88,182	21	33.5	12.5
Pittsburgh, Pa., Wards 3, 5	4,627	17,319	5,105	13,559	20.9	27.3	6.4
Union Township, N. J., EDS 6, 7, 8	843	1,100	1,160	772	43.4	60	16.6
Youngstown, Ohio, 62 Precincts	3,488	14,387	5,393	10,850	19.5	33.2	13.7
Zanesville, Ohio, Precincts 1E, 2E, 36, 44C, 4E, 5D, 5K, 5N	1,410	1,128	1,605	663	55.5	70.7	15.2
Camden, N. J., 12 Election Districts	1,401	4,547	1,960	3,401	23.8	36.5	12.7

ported the Democratic candidate in 1952 gave the President 898 votes to 480 for Stevenson in 1956.

Of 23 Southern cities in the NAACP survey, President Eisenhower carried the Negro districts in 13 in the 1956 election. In none of these 23 cities did the majority of the Negroes vote for him in 1952. Even in the cities which he failed to carry, the President registered gains ranging from 11.2 percentage points in Knoxville, Tenn., to 43.8 in Winston-Salem, N. C. In six of these latter cities he received at least 45 per cent of the vote in the Negro areas. The vote as cast in Negro areas in 23 Southern cities in 1952 and in 1956 is tabulated in Table III.

The election returns validated the predictions of a switch in the voting pattern of Negro citizens. In a measure the 1952-56 elections repeated the experience of 1932-36. In the earlier period, Negro voters followed the national trend four years later. Although President Herbert Hoover was not popular with Negroes who were among the first to feel the full impact of the depression, the majority of these voters cast their ballots for the Republican candidate more out of tradition and habit than out of any confidence in Hoover. It was not until 1936 that the swing to the Democrats got under way. Of 15 predominantly Negro wards in nine cities studied by Myrdal, President Roosevelt carried four in 1932, nine in 1936 and 14 in 1940.[1] Thereafter, the proportion of Negro citizens casting their ballots for Democratic candidates rose steadily. This trend continued unabated in 1952 at a time when the nation gave overwhelming endorsement to the Republican candidates. In 1956, Negroes, although still giving the major share of their votes to the Democrats, began to catch up with the national trend as they had done 20 years previously.

Any study of the political behavior of the Negro voter must begin with the recognition that he is an American citizen first and is basically influenced by the same kind of political considerations which motivate other American voters. But because of disabilities peculiar to the Negro as a racial group there are additional factors which condition his voting habits. Other groups, of course, are also influenced by considerations affecting their special interests. Certainly this is true of Southern white voters. Also of farmers, industrialists and trade unionists. It is no accident that Jewish voters, by and large, supported Roosevelt who, even before World War II, was known to oppose Hitler. These voters also backed Stevenson because, among other reasons, they believed that his position on Israel was more in accord with their own than that of President Eisenhower.

When Charles E. Wilson declared: "What's good for General Motors is good for the country," he aroused widespread indignation. Yet he was

---

[1]Gunnar Myrdal, *An American Dilemma.* (New York: Harper & Bros., 1944), p. 496.

TABLE III

VOTE IN NEGRO AREAS, PRESIDENTIAL ELECTIONS, 1952 AND 1956
(Southern Cities)

CITY	1952 Eisenhower (R)	1952 Stevenson (D)	1956 Eisenhower	1956 Stevenson	% Eisenhower 1952	% Eisenhower 1956	Eisenhower % gain
Atlanta, 11 Precincts	2,134	4,764	9,565	1,640	30.9	85.3	54.4
Charleston, S. C. Ward 9 (43 votes for Independents, 1956)	284	439	354	234	39.2	56.1	16.9
Charlotte, N. C., 7 Precincts	1,368	6,975	2,105	3,361	16.3	38.5	22.2
Chattanooga, Tenn., 4 Wards plus 3 Precincts	769	2,969	1,889	1,943	20.5	49.3	28.8
Columbia, S. C.—Ward 9 (56 for Independents in 1956)	109	1,250	504	551	8	45.4	37.4
Darlington, S. C., Wards 4, 5	6	722	497	193	.08	72.02	71.94
Durham, N. C., Pearson Precinct	106	1,168	655	407	8.3	61.6	53.3
New in 1956—Whitted, Burton, Horners			1,649	1,466		52.9	
Greensboro, N. C., Precincts 5, 9	475	3,037	1,437	895	13.5	61.6	48.1
Houston, Texas, 7 Wards	2,665	22,589	8,278	15,481	10.5	34.8	24.3
Jacksonville, Fla., 20 Precincts	2,983	15,964	6,781	9,783	15.7	40.9	25.2
Knoxville, Tenn., 8 Precincts	1,254	2,955	1,610	2,322	29.7	40.9	11.2
Mobile, Ala., Ward 7	129	902	1,129	1,273	12.5	47	34.5
Memphis, Tenn., 50 Precincts	12,173	26,020			34.4	54	19.6
Nashville, Tenn., Ward 5, Precincts 1, 2, 3	564	1,878	1,576	982	23	61.6	38.6
New Orleans, La., 21 Precincts, 1952; 32 Precincts, 1956	2,575	10,148	9,204	7,476	20.2	55.1	34.9
Norfolk, Va., 6 Precincts	240	1,451	1,726	439	14.2	79.7	65.5
Oak Ridge, Tenn. Scarboro, 4th District	19	319	128	87	5.6	59.5	53.9
Pine Bluff Ark., Ward 4	389	1,366	862	923	22.2	48.2	26.0
Raleigh, N. C., 3 Precincts	310	2,177	1,136	648	12.4	63.1	50.7
Richmond, Va.—Precincts 1, 4, 5, 18, 19, 46, 55, 63, 64, 65	1,172	4,165	3,495	1,301	21.9	73	51.1
Tampa, Fla.—Precincts 11, 13	299	970	791	1,013	23.5	43.8	20.3
Tuskegee, Ala.—4 Boxes	237	558	649	235	29.8	73.4	43.6
Winston-Salem, N. C.—3 Precincts	184	5,370	1,808	2,028	3.3	47.1	43.8

merely, if rashly, asserting aloud what every group believes of its own special interest. Trade union leaders certainly think that what's good for the labor movement is good for the country. The oil men of Texas and the farmers of Iowa are convinced that what's good for them benefits the country. So, also, do Negro voters. Each believes that a government that gives due consideration to his special interest is good government for the whole American people.

Negro voters in 1956, like other citizens, were concerned about peace and prosperity, taxes and the atom bomb. School desegregation and other civil rights issues were also vital issues with them as they were with white Southerners. All of these concerns found some measure of expression at the polls on November 6. Ironically, the civil rights issue was a factor which, in many localities in the South, united opposing groups behind the same candidate.

What happened between 1952 and 1956 to sharpen the civil rights issue? To what extent did this issue motivate the Negro break-away from the Democrats? Would there have been a decline in the Negro vote for the Democrats if this issue had remained the same as it had been in 1952? These questions are vital to any consideration of the factors involved in the sizeable switch of Negro voters away from the Democratic party in 1956.

The United States Supreme Court ruling of May 17, 1954, banning racial segregation in public education had a profound impact upon the thinking of Negroes throughout the country and upon Southern whites. The decision clearly indicated that the nation's No. 1 domestic problem is that of human rights. It spurred the demands of Negroes for an early end to the inequity of segregation. It placed the white South on the defensive, galvanized extremist elements into hardcore resistance to the Court's order, silenced and inactivated the so-called moderates. It placed a new responsibility upon the federal government to implement constitutional guaranties of equal rights.

The May 17th decision was followed by Supreme Court rulings which held that segregation in public recreation and in local transportation is also unconstitutional. There was, in addition, an Interstate Commerce Commission order banning segregation in interstate travel. Southern resistance to these rulings precipitated a crisis which continues. It brought to the surface the ancient sectional split within the Democratic party. Roosevelt had succeeded in creating and maintaining a successful political coalition composed of hostile elements. Stevenson's efforts to maintain party unity cost him votes both among Northern liberals and Negroes and among Southern whites. The result was disaster.

Civil rights was most certainly an important consideration in the minds of Negro voters. It is noteworthy that in the South where this issue was sharp and inescapable, their switch was most pronounced. Southern Negroes in 1952 had voted more strongly for Gov. Stevenson than had their kinsmen in the North. Four years later they led the flight from the Democratic camp. There were exceptions, as Houston, Texas, Chattanooga, Tenn., and other cities whose Negro districts again went Democratic, though by reduced majorities as in the North.

Responses to the NAACP survey indicate that the upsurge of the Republican vote among Negroes stemmed more from the failings of the Democrats than from the performance of the Republicans. It was neither the candidate nor the party which lured large numbers of Negro voters back to the political house of their fathers after 20 years. President Eisenhower's popularity and the Republican record were cited only occasionally in the NAACP reports. Rather it was the hostile antics of the Dixiecrats that drove them away, the NAACP correspondents reported.

In the South, certainly, and to a lesser extent elsewhere, the credit for the Negro switch to the Republicans may rightly be claimed by Senators James O. Eastland of Mississippi and Herman Talmadge of Georgia, Congressman James C. Davis of Georgia, the signers of the Southern Manifesto, Gov. Luther Hodges of North Carolina, the instigators of anti-NAACP legislation in Southern states, the White Citizens Councils, the Ku Klux Klan, and the mobs which drove Autherine Lucy from the campus of the University of Alabama and threatened the lives of colored school children in Clinton, Tenn., and Clay and Sturgis, Kentucky. The slogan: "A vote for the Democrats is a vote for Eastland" proved effective.

It was in protest against these outrages that Negro voters reacted. There were, of course, other factors. Among these were the relatively high employment level, the stepped-up Republican campaign within Negro areas, and the increasing economic stratification within the Negro community with the development of a more stable and substantial middle class with Republican leanings. Undoubtedly, many of these would have voted for President Eisenhower even had there been no civil rights issue.

Significantly, the closer the Negro lived to the resurgent terror, the sharper was his defection from the dominant party in his area. However, it was not distance from the violence alone which held the majority of Negro voters in the North within the Democratic camp. Unlike the South, many Northern Negroes have a vested interest in the local Democratic machine, sharing in the patronage, actively participating in the local and state party organizations, cooperating in the selection of local and state candidates, and receiving other benefits. Such participation is rare in the South. Equally rare in the region are candidates and officeholders with liberal racial views.

The success of the Democratic party in the Negro districts of Detroit was due in large measure to the popularity of Governor G. Mennen Williams who was a candidate for reelection. There was also the powerful influence of the United Automobile Workers with its large Negro membership. The union leadership strongly endorsed the Democratic candidates. Similarly the candidacies of such liberal Democrats as Thomas C. Hennings of Missouri and Joseph S. Clark of Pennsylvania enabled the party to hold the Negro vote in St. Louis and Kansas City, Philadelphia and Pittsburgh. Nowhere in the South was there any such Democratic candidate for Congress or governor.

The potential Negro vote, on the basis of the 1950 census, exceeded 9,200,000, of which 5,700,000 were in the South. The estimates of the number of Negroes registered to vote in 1956 vary from 4,300,000 to 6,000,000. Obviously there can be no really accurate figure for only a few states maintain registration records by race, among these Florida and Louisiana. The only other means of checking on the number of Negroes is through knowledge of the precincts in which these voters reside. Even such knowledge would give only an approximation as many voting districts, in the North as well as in the South, include both Negro and white voters.

Data compiled by the NAACP indicate a registration of 1,300,000 Negroes in the Southern states. In the North where there are no obstacles to Negro voting an estimated 3,000,000 Negroes were registered to vote. Of the total of 61,700,000 ballots cast in the 1956 election, it is unlikely that Negro voters accounted for as many as 4,000,000. The significance of the Negro vote derives not so much from its size as from its strategic distribution. This vote was certainly a vital factor in the election of President Truman ، in 1948. Negro districts in Ohio, Illinois and California provided majorities for the Democratic candidate in excess of the slim majorities by which he carried these pivotal states. In 1952, the strong support given to Gov. Stevenson by Negro voters in the South contributed to his success in five of the nine states he carried — Arkansas, Kentucky, Louisiana, South Carolina and West Virginia.

A 1956 *Congressional Quarterly* study indicated that potentially Negro voters exercised a balance of power in 61 congressional districts in 21 Northern and Western states.[2] These are districts in which the potential Negro vote exceeded or approximated the margin by which the winning candidate was elected to Congress in 1954. Thirty-two of these districts were then represented in Congress by Democrats and 29 by Republicans.

Nationally there was a slight increase in the total vote cast in 1956 over the 1952 total. However, there was a sharp decline in balloting in many Negro districts throughout the country, but particularly in Northern industrial centers from which, in previous years, the Democrats had received huge majorities. This, despite an increased Negro population in most of these

---

[2]*Congressional Quarterly:* Fact Sheet on Negro Voting, April 30, 1956.

cities. In Philadelphia, 27,000 fewer votes were cast than in 1952 for a loss of 14.7 per cent. Voting in the Negro wards of Kansas City, Mo., was off a fifth for a decline of 5,900 in the number of ballots cast. The percentage loss was even higher in Boston where the vote was down 28.5. The Negro vote declined 19 per cent in Atlantic City; 15.6 in Toledo; 15.4 in Pittsburgh; 12 in Chicago; 9.3 in Brooklyn; 9.1 in Youngstown, Ohio; 6.4 in Cleveland; and 5.9 in Harlem.

The Negro wards of Detroit, which Stevenson carried by a bigger majority than in 1952, were an exception. There was a slight increase in the total number of votes cast in those districts. There were increases also in such Southern cities as Atlanta, Norfolk, Charlotte, Chattanooga and Tampa.

Many factors may have contributed to the decline in the Negro vote in these selected areas. Population shifts may well have placed more Negroes in predominantly white precincts. Newcomers replacing them may have not been registered to vote. These and other considerations may be taken into account. Nevertheless, the poor turnout in many of these districts seems to have stemmed from a sort of indifference to the outcome of the election. In short, it may be interpreted as a stay-at-home strike against the Democrats who suffered most by this inaction.

Unlike the white Southerners who bolted the head of the Democratic ticket to vote for President Eisenhower, Negro voters of the region also voted heavily for congressional and state Republican candidates wherever the opportunity was afforded. Atlanta Negroes who cast 85.3 per cent of their votes for President Eisenhower in 1956 did even better by the Republican congressional candidate from that district. They gave him 86.2 per cent of their vote. The Democratic incumbent, James C. Davis, was particularly obnoxious to Negro voters because of his role in the congressional attempt to discredit school desegregation in the District of Columbia.

The experience was similar in North Carolina and Virginia. Republican candidates for governor and Congress ran ahead of President Eisenhower in the predominantly Negro wards of Charlotte, N. C. The Republican gubernatorial candidate also carried the Negro precincts in Durham. In Norfolk, The Virginian Pilot reports, the only precincts carried by the Republican congressional candidate were those "shown by registration records as Negro voting centers." The Memphis Commercial Appeal reported on November 7 that "local Republicans ran strongest in Negro communities like Orange Mound, where in the second precinct of the 29th Ward every Democrat on the ballot was second best." In Kentucky and Maryland Negro voters gave strong support to Republican senatorial candidates.

The unanticipated support given to Republican candidates by Southern Negroes imparted new significance to speculation about the possibility of reviving the two-party system in the South. C. A. Scott, publisher of the

South's only Negro daily, the Atlanta *Daily World,* cited a "desire to contribute to the development of a two-party system in this area," as one of the
reasons why Atlanta Negroes voted down the line for the Republican candidates for President and Congress. In North Carolina, C. A. McKnight, editor
of the Charlotte *Observer,* expressed the opinion that "if the GOP can hold
its Southern Negro voters, and collect more, the development of a two-party
system in the South will be speeded up substantially."

Republicanism among Southern whites is growing as industrialism spreads
through the region. There is an increasing number of white Southerners who
are politically homeless because of the one-party system. A strong Republican
party in their area is the answer to their need. The Negro switch provides
a base upon which to build such a party. There is, however, no future in
the South for a Republican party which conforms to present racial attitudes.
Nor is there any future for an all-Negro Republican party in the South.
The party may remain conservative in the field of economics but, in order
to grow, it must be liberal in the area of human rights. The problem the
party faces is whether it can hold its Negro supporters and attract a sufficient
number of white voters to assure permanent local and state organizations.
Thomas L. Stokes, the Washington correspondent, foresees the possibility of
"a combination of Negroes and white conservatives who are numerous in
the South and now seem willing to vote their Republican convictions."

The 1956 election also thrust into the forefront the most serious problem
confronting the Democratic party. It is the issue of liberalism. By now it
must be clear that the party can succeed nationally in normal times only as
a liberal party. And it cannot be a liberal party as long as it attempts to
embrace with equal fervor Senator Eastland and Senator Herbert Lehman;
Representative Davis of Georgia and Representative James Roosevelt of
California; Governor Hodges of North Carolina and Governor Williams of
Michigan. It cannot continue to claim the support of liberals and race-baiters
alike. The time has come for the party to make a choice. It must decide
whether to seek to be a national party based upon liberal principles or to
sink to the level of a provincial political clique dedicated to the perpetuation
of the myth of white supremacy.

Significantly, the election demonstrated anew that decisions in national
elections do not depend upon the vote of the Solid South. If Stevenson had
carried all of the Southern states, as he had hoped, he still would have lost
the election. Only once in this century has the Solid South been essential
to the election of the successful presidential candidate. That was in 1916
when Woodrow Wilson would have been denied a second term had he
failed to carry the South.

This suggests a reappraisal by the Democrats of the role of the South in
presidential elections. How far should the party accede to the demands of

its most backward elements? How much discipline can it exercise over the Eastlands and Talmadges? Shall it, in the name of party unity, jeopardize its appeal to Negro and other liberal voters in order to appease a faction which cannot deliver the necessary votes on election day?

The Negro Vote in
Philadelphia Elections

William J. McKenna

Bloc voting[1] has been evident in the pattern of Philadelphia politics for many years. The strength of the Democratic party in Philadelphia has been concentrated in the Italian, Polish, Jewish, and Negro blocs in most of the elections since the election of President Franklin D. Roosevelt in 1932.[2] Religion,[3] economics, and political philosophy[4] have been important factors in the bloc voting pattern of Philadelphia.

The foundation of the strength of the Democratic party in Philadelphia, however, is in the voting behavior of the seventeen so-called Negro wards.

Reprinted from *Pennsylvania History,* Vol. XXXII, (October 1965), pp. 406-415 by permission of the publisher and author. Copyright 1965 by The Pennsylvania Historical Association.
[1]In 1960 there were approximately 300,000 Jews and 530,000 Negroes in Philadelphia. There were also 700,000 Catholics out of a total population of 2,002,512.
[2]The heavily Jewish wards (49th and 50th) have voted Democratic in all Presidential elections since 1936. They have also voted Democratic in almost all elections since the victory of Joseph S. Clark in the controller election of 1949. This has also been true of the Italian and Polish wards.
[3]In 1928 the nomination of Alfred E. Smith as the Democratic candidate for President resulted in a total Democratic vote in Philadelphia of 276,000. In 1932 the total Democratic vote in Philadelphia decreased to 260,000. In 1960 Senator Kennedy received approximately 75% of the vote of the Catholic Italian wards.
[4]The Jewish wards vote consistently for liberal Democratic candidates even though economically these wards are upper middle class.

This paper will examine this pattern and discuss the factors that have influenced the pattern.

The Negro Population of Philadelphia

Since 1940 the Negro population of Philadelphia has increased by 303,620 — from 250,880 in 1940 to an estimated 554,400 in 1963.[5] The Negro population of Philadelphia is largely concentrated in the areas immediately east and west of the Schuylkill River. This area is one of overcrowded housing, inadequate schools, and industrial plants. It contains many of the families who are on relief and other assistance programs. The rate of unemployment in this area is more than double that of the rest of the city. Public housing has been built in the area but this has not greatly lessened the concentration of Negro population in the region.[6]

The Political Pattern of Philadelphia

Prior to the election of President Franklin D. Roosevelt in 1932, Philadelphia was definitely a one-party Republican city. As late as 1931 the Democratic candidate for mayor received a total vote of only 30,821 compared to a Republican total of 367,344 — a Republican landslide majority of 336,523 or 90.1% of the total vote.[7] In 1932, however, the Republican candidate for President carried the city by only 70,766 votes. The subsequent elections witnessed a further weakening of the strength of the Republican party in Philadelphia for all city, state, and national offices. In Philadelphia the Republican party barely won the elections for United States Senator in 1934 and 1938, and has lost all such elections since 1940 with the exception of the national Republican swing of 1946.[8] Since 1950

---

[5]This 554,400 estimate is that of the Philadelphia Chamber of Commerce (see the 1964 Edition of *Greater Philadelphia Facts,* Chamber of Commerce of Greater Philadelphia, December, 1963, p. 48). The 1950 Negro population of Philadelphia was 376,041. If the growth of the Negro population of Philadelphia continues, it may reach 40% of the city population by 1980. It is now 27.2%.

[6]The areas surrounding the University of Pennsylvania and Temple University are areas of heavy Negro population concentration. The redevelopment of these areas is gradually encroaching upon the heavily populated Negro residential areas. These areas have been described as "slum areas" because of the large number of residential dwellings containing from four to six separate apartments.

[7]In the mayoralty election of 1927 the total Democratic vote was approximately 10,000 and the Republican vote 296,551.

[8]The Republicans won the United States Senate race in 1934 by only 3,012 votes and the 1938 election by 17,167 votes. The 1946 election for United States Senator went Republican by 108,853 votes. All such elections since 1946 have been won by the Democratic party by heavy margins.

the Republican party has lost every election for Governor by substantial margins. Again, since 1932 the Republican party has suffered defeat in all Presidential elections. The climax in the Republican decline in Philadelphia occurred in the Presidential election of 1960, when that party was defeated by 331,544 votes. A similar pattern of Republican decline is evident in all local elections in Philadelphia since 1932. Although the Republican party won the mayoralty elections in 1935-1947, the majorities were far from impressive,[9] when compared with the pre-1935 majorities.[10] Since 1951 the Democrats have won every mayoralty election.[11]

The principal architects of the rise of the Democratic party in Phildelphia were two unusual men: Joseph S. Clark and Richardson Dilworth. In 1947 these two former Republicans spearheaded the reform movement in Philadelphia. Dilworth ran for mayor in 1947 but was defeated by a Republican ward leader, Bernard Samuel, by 91,622 votes. In 1949 Clark was elected city controller by a Democratic majority of 112,000 votes.[12] The history of the Democratic party since 1947 has largely been the history of these two men. They were reformers. They were both graduates of "Ivy League" colleges (Harvard and Yale), and each was wealthy in his own right. Both men were committed to the elimination of political corruption and political bossism which had characterized Republican politics in Philadelphia for many years. In 1951 Clark was elected mayor by 125,000 votes. Since that date the Democratic party has dominated practically all elections in Philadelphia.[13]

The Negro Vote in Philadelphia

For the purpose of this study the term "Negro Ward" is applied to those wards which in 1960 had a total Negro population of 50% or more. There are sixteen of these wards. The 38th Ward has also been included in this study because in 1960 it had a Negro population of 24,505 (33.3%), and it is contiguous with the other heavily populated Negro wards.

These seventeen wards in 1960 had a total Negro population of 414,864, or 78.4% of the 529,239 Negro population of Philadelphia. Sixteen of

---

[9]The mayoralty Republican majorities were: 1935, 45,478; 1939, 30,006; 1943, 63,465; and 1947, 91,622.

[10]In 1927 the Republican majority was 285,903 (96.4%) and in 1931 the majority was 336,523 (90.1%).

[11]Joseph S. Clark won in 1951 by nearly 125,000, and Richardson Dilworth by 132,000 in 1955. He was reelected in 1959 by 208,000 votes. In 1963, James H. J. Tate was elected mayor by a 68,268-vote majority.

[12]In the same year Dilworth was elected city treasurer. He also ran for Governor in 1950 and, although he carried Philadelphia by 77,000 votes, he was defeated in the state.

[13]In 1953 the Republicans won the city controller election by the narrow margin of 15,579 votes in a very light election of 565,799 total votes.

these wards had a 1960 Negro population varying from approximately 50.0% to 95.8% (see Table I).

TABLE I

NEGRO POPULATION: 17 SO-CALLED NEGRO WARDS, CITY OF PHILADELPHIA, 1950 AND 1960.

Ward	Negro Population			
	1950		1960	
	Total	Percent	Total	Percent
4	4,294	42.7	4,055	58.2
13	7,859	59.3	5,070	70.2
14	9,604	67.8	8,560	82.7
20	25,559	58.3	24,110	74.4
24	36,741	58.0	45,666	80.8
28	20,040	39.6	46,230	91.3
29	12,594	41.2	23,095	81.3
30	23,789	87.4	21,587	91.4
32	44,872	73.7	52,191	95.8
36	22,623	43.0	23,542	52.0
37	4,372	20.2	11,284	60.2
38	6,132	8.7	24,505	33.3
44	23,398	56.3	28,598	78.0
46[1]	2,297	2.6	40,171	50.0
47	27,690	76.5	28,173	90.2
52	20,059	35.4	27,975	53.6
17 Wards[1]	291,923	77.6	414,864	78.4
City	376,041		529,239	

[1]In 1961 the 46th ward was divided into the new 46th and 60th wards.
SOURCE: *Greater Philadelphia Facts*, Chamber of Commerce of Greater Philadelphia, 1962 Edition, p. 46. Percentages calculated.

Even before the Democratic party succeeded in winning municipal elections in Philadelphia, these seventeen Negro wards had provided a significant basis of support for the Democratic party. For example, in the Presidential elections of 1940-1948, these wards had provided a Democratic majority that was 44.3%, 52.6%, and 457.5% of the total city-wide Democratic majority.[14] A similar trend prevailed in the elections for the United States Senator and Governor in 1950.[15]

Since 1952 the seventeen Negro wards in Philadelphia have consistently given a still heavier percentage of their votes to the Democratic party. The

[14]The unusual percentage for 1948 reflects the 30,806 Democratic majority given by these seventeen Negro wards to President Truman in the face of a city-wide majority for Truman of 6,737.
[15]See Table IV.

percentages for each of the seventeen Negro wards for the three Presidential elections since 1952, the three Gubernatorial elections since 1954, and the three mayoralty elections since 1955 are shown in Table II.

There is a very high Democratic registration among the Negro population of Philadelphia. It has increased from 170,491 in 1950 to 231,308 in 1962.[16] As is to be expected, there is a large concentration of the Democratic Negro registration in the seventeen Negro wards of the city. The Democratic registration in these seventeen Negro wards has increased from 132,848 in 1950 to 179,013 in 1962, but the percentage of registration has remained constant (see Table III).

TABLE II

DEMOCRATIC PARTY, PERCENTAGE OF TOTAL VOTE, 17 SO-CALLED NEGRO WARDS OF PHILADELPHIA. SELECTED ELECTIONS, 1952-1963. DEMOCRATIC VOTE, PERCENTAGE OF TOTAL VOTE.

Wards	President			Governor			Mayor		
	1952	1956	1960	1954	1958	1962	1955	1959	1963
4	59.4	61.7	72.8	51.4	56.0	57.1	57.0	57.9	76.8
13	44.8	74.5	81.1	46.0	74.1	78.0	57.4	76.0	81.3
14	60.7	71.2	80.3	54.8	73.6	76.1	62.8	77.4	78.5
20	67.8	73.7	83.3	59.2	76.2	77.9	61.6	77.5	79.6
24	71.2	71.1	79.9	63.2	75.8	73.4	73.8	79.2	76.0
28	73.6	73.8	83.6	68.4	78.0	69.4	70.2	79.4	80.3
29	68.3	68.3	79.6	67.3	73.4	74.2	69.2	77.4	77.1
30	74.3	69.0	79.7	65.9	71.5	70.8	70.6	72.9	76.9
32	81.3	78.7	83.1	75.8	79.1	72.9	76.7	78.2	79.7
36	76.8	71.3	83.2	75.4	78.2	74.2	74.4	78.8	74.1
37	58.7	61.2	73.5	58.8	71.1	71.5	63.1	76.4	76.4
38	59.3	57.4	71.8	60.7	63.1	57.0	60.5	66.9	57.8
44	74.8	68.7	80.0	67.6	74.2	70.3	71.4	75.8	78.0
46	55.7	58.7	70.7	59.1	65.8	62.9	61.0	72.1	71.0
47	76.7	74.0	84.0	68.8	76.5	76.6	72.4	78.6	81.6
52	72.1	72.2	76.5	70.1	75.1	70.8	72.9	77.2	72.6
60	—	—	—	—	—	67.8	—	—	73.7
All 17 Wards	68.3	68.0	78.0	65.2	72.6	69.4	67.9	75.2	73.8
City-Wide	58.5	57.6	68.1	57.7	61.7	56.7	59.3	65.6	54.6

SOURCE: Richard M. Scammon, *America Votes,* Volumes I-IV (Governmental Affairs Institute, New York: Macmillan Company, 1956; Governmental Affairs Institute, Pittsburgh: University of Pittsburgh, 1958-1962). Percentages for mayoralty elections taken from data in City of Philadelphia election returns, *Annual Report of the Registration Commission for the City of Philadelphia,* 1956-1962. Percentages for 1963 calculated from unofficial sources.

---

[16]In the 1963 mayoralty election the total Negro registration in the city was estimated at 233,000.

As the Democratic margin of victory decreases in city-wide elections, the Democratic majority of the seventeen Negro wards becomes a more significant factor in the Democratic victory. This is evident in the figures presented in Table IV. Thus, in the close election for city controller in 1961, the 61,033 Democratic majority of the seventeen Negro wards accounted for 107.9% of the total Democratic city-wide majority. In the Gubernatorial election of 1962, a Democratic majority in the Negro wards was 68.7% of the city-wide Democratic majority. And in the mayoralty election of 1963 the 85,214 majority of the Negro wards was 123% of the total city-wide Democratic majority of 69,310.[17]

Factors Affecting the Negro Vote in Philadelphia

Many complicated factors influence the voting pattern of any bloc of voters. In Philadelphia there are several factors which seem to have influenced the Negro to vote and to remain Democratic. Among these factors are the following:

(1) The identification of the Democratic party with the Roosevelt policies and philosophy. With the advent of the "New Deal" the Democratic party initiated many programs which have directly benefited the Negro. Social and economic legislation of the 1933-1940 period has laid the basis of much

TABLE III

NEGRO DEMOCRATIC REGISTRATION IN PHILADELPHIA, CITY-WIDE AND THE 17 SO-CALLED NEGRO WARDS. SELECTED YEARS, 1950-1962.

Year	City-wide	17 Negro Wards	Percentage
1950	170,941	132,848	77.7
1952	178,365	138,196	77.4
1954	173,281	134,200	77.4
1956	195,469	152,278	77.9
1958	210,517	164,618	77.7
1960	219,232	170,569	77.7
1962	231,308	179,013	77.8

SOURCE: *Annual Report of the Registration Commission for the City of Philadelphia,* 1950-1962.

[17] James H. J. Tate, acting mayor of Philadelphia, was the Democratic candidate. He had become acting mayor as a result of the resignation of Mayor Richardson Dilworth, who resigned to run for Governor. The Philadelphia City Charter of 1951 provides that any elected official of the city government must resign from his office in the event he files for another elective office. Tate, as the president of the City Council, became acting mayor in February 1963.

assistance to the Negro, because it was the group which was the most depressed. Although all administrations since Roosevelt have followed to some extent the social welfare policies of President Roosevelt, the Negro in Philadelphia seems to associate these policies with Roosevelt.[18]

TABLE IV

DEMOCRATIC MAJORITIES IN PHILADELPHIA, CITY-WIDE AND 17 SO-CALLED NEGRO WARDS. SELECTED ELECTIONS, 1940-1963.

Office	Democratic Majority		Democratic Majority of 17 Negro Wards as Percent of City-wide Majority
	City-Wide	17 Negro Wards	
President			
1940	177,409	78,656	44.3
1944	149,987	78,983	52.6
1948	6,737	30,826	457.5
1952	160,867	101,694	63.2
1956	123,875	86,366	69.7
1960	331,544	130,233	39.2
U. S. Senator			
1950	63,995	35,018	54.7
1956	170,164	94,033	55.2
1958	133,413	80,809	60.5
1962	180,379	87,071	48.2
Governor			
1950	77,078	42,197	54.7
1954	118,273	63,471	53.6
1958	177,998	87,399	49.1
1962	106,738	73,316	68.7
Mayor			
1951	124,680	43,518	34.3
1955	132,706	68,866	51.9
1959	208,406	85,174	40.9
1963	69,310	85,214	123.0
City Controller			
1949	111,404	33,169	29.8
1957	77,523	50,544	65.2
1961	56,581	61,033	107.9

SOURCE: Compiled from data in *Annual Report of the Registration Commission* for the City of Philadelphia, 1954-1962; also *Pennsylvania Manual,* various years.

---

[18]Late in the mayoralty campaign of 1963 the Democratic leadership in Philadelphia had James Roosevelt make a campaign appearance in the Negro areas. This was in recognition of the lasting influence of President Roosevelt among the Negroes.

(2) Economic factors. The solidity of the Negro vote behind the Democratic party in Philadelphia is largely based upon economic factors. These include jobs, housing, and educational opportunities. The Negro in Philadelphia has in recent years been confronted with an unemployment rate of 10-20%. This is, of course, partly related to the lack of skilled occupations among the Negro group. But it is also affected by the slow rate of hiring of Negro workers by employers and the discrimination against qualified Negroes by certain unions.[19]

The Negro leadership of Philadelphia in the past two years has pursued a determined policy of lessening housing discrimination in Philadelphia. These leaders have felt that the local Democratic leadership has been more sympathetic to this goal than the Republicans.[20]

In order to increase the educational opportunities of the Negro population of Philadelphia there has been a concerted drive to transfer Negro pupils to predominantly white schools. This drive has taken the form of transferring Negro pupils to white schools by school buses. The policy has been opposed by the Republican leaders in Philadelphia as the wrong approach to the improvement of educational opportunities for the Negro.[21] At present there seems to be little likelihood that the Negro voter in Philadelphia will end his allegiance to the Democratic party until the Negro feels that the Republican party will offer at least an equal opportunity for the Negro to improve his economic status.

(3) Government jobs. The Democratic administration in Philadelphia has been especially active since 1951 in providing jobs for Negroes in the city government. No published figures are available, but it has been estimated that Negroes hold from 8,000 to 10,000 jobs in the Philadelphia city government.[22] In addition, the Democratic Governors of Pennsylvania from 1954 to 1962 have appointed Negroes to positions in the various state government agencies. Since 1960 a similar policy has been pursued by the Kennedy and Johnson administrations in Washington. The net effect of these policies has been to retain the loyalty of the Negro leaders and their following in Philadelphia.

---

[19]Under the leadership of 400 Negro ministers in Philadelphia there has been a successful drive to place Negroes in jobs in many Philadelphia industries. This result has been attained by a policy of general boycott and picketing of firms which allegedly practiced job discrimination. Cecil B. Moore, the leader of the Philadelphia Chapter of the NAACP, has also aggressively pursued a policy of ending job discrimination.

[20]This drive for integrated housing has met with some opposition in the so-called "white wards," and they have tended to vote Republican in recent elections.

[21]James T. McDermott, the Republican candidate for mayor in 1963, publicly opposed the policy of "busing" Negro pupils to white schools. He believed it was a sounder policy to improve the Negro schools and their facilities.

[22]An attempt was made by certain Negro leaders to secure an actual census of Negro jobholders in the city government, but such a census was refused on the ground that color is not included in job applications.

(4) Public Housing. The Negro housing situation in Philadelphia is one of the blights of the city. Since improved public housing has been initiated under national Democratic administrations, there is a belief among Philadelphia Negroes that the Democratic party is more committed to a policy of improved public housing than is the Republican party. The advances in public housing under the Eisenhower administration did not materially change this attitude among Negroes in Philadelphia.

(5) Civil Rights. Rightly or wrongly, the Negroes in Philadelphia seem to feel that the Democratic party is the best hope for the improvement of civil rights. In recent years this issue has become a very emotional one in Philadelphia. The Negro leaders of Philadelphia are determined to secure full civil rights in housing, in schools, and in jobs. Until the Republican party in Philadelphia is able to convince the Negro voter on the issue of civil rights, there is little chance that the Republican party can make any headway among the Negro voters.

(6) "Writing off the Negro Vote." There was a definite feeling among the Negro leadership in the mayoralty campaign of 1963 that the Republican party had "written off the Negro vote."[23] This belief, whether it had a logical basis or not, tended to strengthen the Negro support behind the Democrats. The Republican candidate for mayor in 1963, James T. McDermott, vigorously denied the allegation that the Republican party had "written off the Negro vote."[24] He asserted that the issues in the campaign were political bossism and political corruption, and that local economic conditions were dominant in the campaign.

The Future

The issues of political bossism, political corruption, or inept municipal leadership have not been effective in winning the Negro voter to the Republican side in Philadelphia. Nor are they likely to do so in the immediate future unless these issues become far more explosive. The Negro in Philadelphia has a much greater identity with the national Democratic party and its leaders than it does with the local Democratic leaders. The Negro wards will, in my opinion, continue to stick with the Democratic party in Philadelphia until there is a material improvement in the economic position of the Negro; until the Negro feels that equal job opportunities are his;

[23]This was one of the reasons given by Cecil B. Moore of the Philadelphia NAACP for his support of the Democratic candidate for mayor in 1963.
[24]It is of interest that a Republican candidate for the state General Assembly from an almost 100% "white ward" in a conversation with me stated that: "When a voter asked him how he should vote, he replied, 'Vote white.' "

until housing is improved substantially; until educational opportunities and facilities are equal; in other words, until the Negro is convinced that he is guaranteed all his rights by both parties, not by word alone but by performance. Emotions may govern his political behavior, but he is convinced that the Democratic party offers him the realization of his hopes. This, in essence, is the challenge that confronts the Republican party in Philadelphia.

Part 6

Governmental Outputs
to the Sub-Community

In both the North and the South the growing political power of Negroes is having an impact on the governmental decisions made for the society. The inputs (demands) of the Negro into the political system during the past decade and a half have been many: legal activity in the courts, moral appeals in the streets, sit-ins at the lunch counters, boycotts of the schools, lobbying in the legislatures, and marches on the U.S. capitol. The question which may be asked is: Has the political system responded meaningfully to the demands made on it? A review of some of the outputs (policies) made by the political system reveals that to a large extent it has. The school desegregation decision of 1954 reversing the separate-but-equal policy established in 1896, the Civil Rights Act of 1957 which further secured and protected the right to vote, the Civil Rights Act of 1960 which provided for direct court protection of voting rights on request of the Attorney General, the sweeping provisions of the Civil Rights Act of 1964 and the Voting Rights Act of 1965, and, more recently, at the state level, the California Supreme Court decision striking down as violative of the United States Constitution, a California constitutional amendment which would prohibit the state of California from denying to any person the right to decline to sell or rent his property to whomsoever he chooses, are manifestations of the governmental response. To be sure, the policies of the political system in the field of civil rights have been the product of a compound of the values of the political system and the values of a great many white people, North and South, as well as Negro political activity. But the Negro's own participation has been crucial because as Dr. Martin Luther King succinctly puts it, " . . . it is a historical fact that privileged groups seldom give up their privileges voluntarily."[1]

The selections reprinted in this section are illustrative of the responses of the governmental system to the demands made by, at least, one part of the system. The Civil Rights Act which President Johnson signed into law July 2, 1964, was the subject of some of the most effective lobbying in modern legislative history. The overwhelming 290 to 130 and 76 to 18 margins by which the House and Senate respectively approved the bill testified to the superior resources and talent the civil rights forces were able to muster.[2] The first selection, "The Civil Rights Act of 1964" is, perhaps, the most crucial piece of action taken by the government recently in the direction of changing the status of Negroes favorably in American society. It opened the doors to social areas hitherto closed to Negroes in both Northern and Southern life. Most of the rights which the average white American takes for granted have been extended to and guaranteed to the Negro.

The 1964 Civil Rights Act was intended to take the civil rights struggle out of the streets and into the courts. In many respects—except notably voting—the law was successful. In several states Negroes were still denied the vote chiefly through literacy tests administered by local officials. The campaign for voting rights returned to the streets. After a series of events in Selma, Alabama in the winter of 1964 in which state and local officials interfered with Negro demonstrations protesting discriminatory practices, the government in Washington became gravely concerned. On March 17, 1965, President Johnson submitted a bill to Congress designed to strike down

[1]"Letter From Birmingham Jail" *Christian Century,* Vol. LXXX, Nr. 24, (June 12, 1963), p. 768.
[2]For a list of the organizations and forces which backed the bill see Congressional Quarterly Service. *CQ Guide to Current American Government,* Spring 1965. (Washington, D.C.: Congressional Quarterly Service, 1965) pp. 27-29.

voting restrictions against Negroes in federal, state, and local elections. The second selection, "The Voting Rights Act of 1965," is a powerful piece of value allocation by the Congress because it at once provides the means for overriding virtually all legal barriers to Negro political participation and sets the stage for further changes in the political system.

In 1959 the California legislature passed the Unruh Civil Rights Act which prohibited discrimination by business establishments of every kind on grounds of race, color, religion, ancestry, or national origin. The Act was interpreted by the California Supreme Court[3] to include real estate brokers as well as businesses which sold or leased residential housing. During the same session the California legislature passed the Hawkins Act prohibiting racial discrimination in publicly supported housing. In 1963 the California legislature passed the Rumford Fair Housing Act barring racial discrimination by an owner in the sale or rental of any private dwelling of more than four units or by an owner-occupier of a single-family, publicly assisted dwelling. The State Fair Employment Practices Commission was empowered to prevent violations.

In reaction to the passage of the Rumford Act an initiative measure— Proposition 14—was placed on the ballot in the general election of 1964. Proposition 14 was designed to amend the California Constitution to give property owners absolute discretion over the choice of persons to whom they would sell, lease, or rent. The Proposition was approved by an overwhelming majority of the California electorate and became article I section 26 of the California Constitution.

In May 1963, prior to the passage of Proposition 14, Mr. and Mrs. Lincoln W. Mulkey, both Negroes, tried without success to rent an apartment in Santa Clara from the owner, Neil Reitman. They were refused. The Mulkeys brought suit under the fair housing laws asking that Reitman be restrained from refusing to rent. The trial court ruled in favor of Reitman on the grounds that sections 51 and 52 of the Civil Code had been rendered null and void by the passage of Proposition 14. The Mulkeys appealed. The final selection, *Mulkey* v. *Reitman,* the California Supreme Court decision overturning a California constitutional amendment which would have allowed discrimination in the sale or rental of privately owned housing is unique because it places a state supreme court at the cutting edge of progress on a crucial question in American politics—the question of open occupancy. The state court decision is all the more important because it may mark the beginning of a new consensus by state high courts, relieving some of the burdens of litigation and legislation, so far, placed on the federal courts and Congress.

---

[3]See *Lee* v. *O'Hara,* 20 Cal. Rptr 617; 370 P. 2d 321.

Civil Rights Act of 1964

Congress and the President

AN ACT

To enforce the constitutional right to vote, to confer jurisdiction upon the district courts of the United States to provide injunctive relief against discrimination in public accommodations, to authorize the Attorney General to institute suits to protect the constitutional rights in public facilities and public education, to extend the Commission on Civil Rights, to prevent discrimination in federally assisted programs, to establish a Commission on Equal Employment Opportunity, and for other purposes.

(Key Sections)

TITLE I — VOTING RIGHTS

Section 101.

. . . .

(a) (2) No person acting under color of law shall —

(A) in determining whether any individual is qualified under State law or laws to vote in any Federal election, apply any standard, practice, or pro-

Public Law 88-352; 78 Stat. 241.

cedure different from the standards, practices, or procedures applied under such law or laws to other individuals within the same county, parish, or similar political subdivision who have been found by State officials to be qualified to vote;

(B) deny the right of any individual to vote in any Federal election because of an error or omission on any record or paper relating to any application, registration, or other act requisite to voting, if such error or omission is not material in determining whether such individual is qualified under State law to vote in such election; or

(C) employ any literacy test as a qualification for voting in any Federal election unless (i) such test is administered to each individual and is conducted wholly in writing, and (ii) a certified copy of the test and of the answers given by the individual is furnished to him within twenty-five days of the submission of his request made within the period of time during which records and papers are required to be retained and preserved. . . .
. . . .

TITLE II — INJUNCTIVE RELIEF AGAINST DISCRIMINATION IN PLACES OF PUBLIC ACCOMMODATION

Section 201.

(a) All persons shall be entitled to the full and equal enjoyment of the goods, services, facilities, privileges, advantages, and accommodations of any place of public accommodation, as defined in this section, without discrimination or segregation on the ground of race, color, religion, or national origin.

(b) Each of the following establishments which serves the public is a place of public accommodation within the meaning of this title if its operations affect commerce, or if discrimination or segregation by it is supported by State action:

(1) any inn, hotel, motel, or other establishment which provides lodging to transient guests, other than an establishment located within a building which contained not more than five rooms for rent or hire and which is actually occupied by the proprietor of such establishment as his residence;

(2) any restaurant, cafeteria, lunchroom, lunch counter, soda fountain, or other facility principally engaged in selling food for consumption on the premises, including, but not limited to, any such facility located on the premises of any retail establishment; or any gasoline station;

(3) any motion picture house, theater, concert hall, sports arena, stadium or other place of exhibition or entertainment; and

(4) any establishment (A) (i) which is physically located within the premise of any establishment otherwise covered by this subsection, or (ii) within the premises of which is physically located any such covered establishment, and (B) which holds itself out as serving patrons of such covered establishment.

(c) The operations of an establishment affect commerce within the meaning of this title if (1) it is one of the establishments described in paragraph (1) of subsection (b); (2) in the case of an establishment described in paragraph (2) of subsection (b), it serves or offers to serve interstate travelers or a substantial portion of the food which it serves, or gasoline or other products which it sells, has moved in commerce; (3) in the case of an establishment described in paragraph (3) of subsection (b), it customarily presents films, performances, athletic teams, exhibitions, or other sources of entertainment which move in commerce; and (4) in the case of an establishment described in paragraph (4) of subsection (b), it is physically located within the premises of, or there is physically located within its premises, an establishment the operations of which affect commerce within the meaning of this subsection. For purposes of this section, "commerce" means travel, trade, traffic, commerce, transportation, or communication among the several States, or between the District of Columbia and any State, or between any foreign country or any territory or possession and any State or the District of Columbia, or between points in the same State but through any other State or the District of Columbia or a foreign country.

(d) Discrimination or segregation by an establishment is supported by State action within the meaning of this title if such discrimination or segregation (1) is carried on under color of any law, statute, ordinance, or regulation; or (2) is carried on under color of any custom or usage required or enforced by officials of the State or political subdivision thereof; or (3) is required by action of the State or political subdivision thereof.

(e) The provisions of this title shall not apply to a private club or other establishment not in fact open to the public, except to the extent that the facilities of such establishment are made available to the customers or patrons of an establishment within the scope of subsection (b).

Section 202.

All persons shall be entitled to be free, at any establishment or place, from discrimination or segregation of any kind on the ground of race, color, religion, or national origin, if such discrimination or segregation is or purports to be required by any law, statute, ordinance, regulation, rule, or order of a State or any agency or political subdivision thereof.

Section 203.

No person shall (a) withhold, deny, or attempt to withhold or deny, or deprive or attempt to deprive, any person of any right or privilege secured by section 201 or 202, or (b) intimidate, threaten, or coerce, or attempt to intimidate, threaten, or coerce any person with the purpose of interfering with any right or privilege secured by section 201 or 202, or (c) punish or attempt to punish any person for exercising or attempting to exercise any right or privilege secured by section 201 or 202.

Section 204.

(a) Whenever any person has engaged or there are reasonable grounds to believe that any person is about to engage in any act or practice prohibited by section 203, a civil action for preventive relief, including an application for a permanent or temporary injunction, restraining order, or other order, may be instituted by the person aggrieved and, upon timely application, the court may, in its discretion, permit the Attorney General to intervene in such civil action if he certifies that the case is of general public importance. Upon application by the complainant and in such circumstances as the court may deem just, the court may appoint an attorney for such complainant and may authorize the commencement of the civil action without the payment of fees, costs, or security.

. . . .

(c) In the case of an alleged act or practice prohibited by this title which occurs in a State, or political subdivision of a State, which has a State or local law prohibiting such act or practice and establishing or authorizing a State or local authority to grant or seek relief from such practice or to institute criminal proceedings with respect thereto upon receiving notice thereof, no civil action may be brought under subsection (a) before the expiration of thirty days after written notice of such alleged act or practice has been given to the appropriate State or local authority by registered mail or in person, provided that the court may stay proceedings in such civil actions pending the termination of State or local enforcement proceedings.

(d) In the case of an alleged act or practice prohibited by this title which occurs in a State, or political subdivision of a State, which has no State or local law prohibiting such act or practice, a civil action may be brought under subsection (a): Provided, That the court may refer the matter to the Community Relations Service established by title X of this Act for as long as the court believes there is a reasonable possibility of obtaining voluntary compliance, but for not more than sixty days: Provided further, That upon expiration of such sixty-day period, the court may extend such period for an additional period, not to exceed a cumulative total of one hundred and twenty days, if it believes there then exists a reasonable possibility of securing voluntary compliance.

Section 205.

The Service is authorized to make a full investigation of any complaint referred to it by the court under section 204 (d) and may hold such hearings with respect thereto as may be necessary. The Service shall conduct any hearings with respect to any such complaint in executive session, and shall not release any testimony given therein except by agreement of all parties involved in the complaint with the permission of the court, and the Service shall endeavor to bring about a voluntary settlement between the parties.

Section 206.

(a) Whenever the Attorney General has reasonable cause to believe that any person or group of persons is engaged in a pattern or practice of resistance to the full enjoyment of any of the rights secured by this title, and that the pattern or practice is of such a nature and is intended to deny the full exercise of the rights herein described, the Attorney General may bring a civil action in the appropriate district court of the United States by filing with it a complaint (1) signed by him (or in his absence the Acting Attorney General), (2) setting forth facts pertaining to such pattern or practice, and (3) requesting such preventive relief, including an application for a permanent or temporary injunction, restraining order or other order against the person or persons responsible for such pattern or practice, as he deems necessary to insure the full enjoyment of the rights herein described.

(b) In any such proceeding the Attorney General may file with the clerk of such court a request that a court of three judges be convened to hear and determine the case. Such request by the Attorney General shall be accompanied by a certificate that, in his opinion, the case is of general public importance . . . and it shall be the duty of the judges so designated to assign the case for hearing at the earliest practicable date, to participate in the hearing and determination thereof, and to cause the case to be in every way expedited. An appeal from the final judgment of such court will lie to the Supreme Court.

. . . .

Section 207.

(a) The district courts of the United States shall have jurisdiction of proceedings instituted pursuant to this title and shall exercise the same without regard to whether the aggrieved party shall have exhausted any administrative or other remedies that may be provided by law.

(b) The remedies provided in this title shall be the exclusive means of enforcing the rights based on this title, but nothing in this title shall preclude any individual or any State or local agency from asserting any right based on any other Federal or State law not inconsistent with this title, including any statute or ordinance requiring nondiscrimination in public establishments or accommodations, or from pursuing any remedy, civil or criminal, which may be available for the vindication or enforcement of such right.

TITLE III — DESEGREGATION OF PUBLIC FACILITIES
Section 301.

(a) Whenever the Attorney General receives a complaint in writing signed by an individual to the effect that he is being deprived of or threatened with the loss of his right to the equal protection of the laws, on account of his race, color, religion, or national origin, by being denied equal utilization of any public facility which is owned, operated, or managed by or on behalf of any State or subdivision thereof, other than a public school or public college as defined in section 401 of title IV hereof, and the Attorney General believes the complaint is meritorious and certifies that the signer or signers of such complaint are unable, in his judgment, to initiate and maintain appropriate legal proceedings for relief and that the institution of an action will materially further the orderly progress of desegregation in public facilities, the Attorney General is authorized to institute for or in the name of the United States a civil action in any appropriate district court of the United States against such parties and for such relief as may be appropriate, and such court shall have and shall exercise jurisdiction of proceedings instituted pursuant to this section. The Attorney General may implead as defendants such additional parties as are or become necessary to the grant of effective relief hereunder.

(b) The Attorney General may deem a person or persons unable to initiate and maintain appropriate legal proceedings within the meaning of subsection (a) of this section when such person or persons are unable, either directly or through other interested persons or organizations, to bear the expense of the litigation or to obtain effective legal representation; or whenever he is satisfied that the institution of such litigation would jeopardize the personal safety, employment, or economic standing of such person or persons, their families, or their property.

. . . .

TITLE IV — DESEGREGATION OF PUBLIC EDUCATION
Section 407.

(a) Whenever the Attorney General receives a complaint in writing —
(1) signed by a parent or group of parents to the effect that his or their minor children, as members of a class of persons similarly situated, are being deprived by a school board of the equal protection of the laws, or
(2) signed by an individual, or his parent, to the effect that he has been denied admission to or not permitted to continue in attendance at a public college by reason of race, color, religion, or national origin, and the Attorney General believes the complaint is meritorious and certifies that the signer or signers of such complaint are unable, in his judgment to initiate and maintain appropriate legal proceedings for relief and that the institution of an action will materially further the orderly achievement of desegregation in public education, the Attorney General is authorized, after giving notice of such complaint to the appropriate school board or college authority and after certifying that he is satisfied that such board or authority has had a reasonable time to adjust the conditions alleged in such complaint, to institute for or in the name of the United States a civil action in any appropriate district court of the United States against such parties and for such relief as may be appropriate, and such court shall have and shall exercise jurisdiction of proceedings instituted pursuant to this section provided that nothing herein shall empower any official or court of the United States to issue any order seeking to achieve a racial balance in any school by requiring the transportation of pupils or students from one school to another or one school district to another in order to achieve such racial balance, or otherwise enlarge the existing power of the court to insure compliance with constitutional standards. The Attorney General may implead as defendants such additional parties as are or become necessary to the grant of effective relief hereunder.

. . . .

TITLE V — COMMISSION ON CIVIL RIGHTS

Section 104.

(a) The Commission shall —
(1) investigate allegations in writing under oath or affirmation that certain citizens of the United States are being deprived of their right to vote and have that vote counted by reason of their color, race, religion, or national origin; which writing, under oath or affirmation, shall set forth the facts upon which such belief or beliefs are based;

(2) study and collect information concerning legal developments constituting a denial of equal protection of the laws under the Constitution because of race, color, religion or national origin or in the administration of justice;

(3) appraise the laws and policies of the Federal Government with respect to denials of equal protection of the laws under the Constitution because of race, color, religion or national origin or in the administration of justice;

(4) serve as a national clearing house for information in respect to denials of equal protection of the laws because of race, color, religion or national origin, including but not limited to the fields of voting, education, housing, employment, the use of public facilities, and transportation, or in the administration of justice;

(5) investigate allegations, made in writing and under oath or affirmation, that citizens of the United States are unlawfully being accorded or denied the right to vote, or to have their votes properly counted, in any election of presidential electors, Members of the United States Senate, or of the House of Representatives, as a result of any patterns or practice of fraud or discrimination in the conduct of such election; and (a) Nothing in this or any other Act shall be construed as authorizing the Commission, its Advisory Committees, or any person under its supervision or control to inquire into or investigate any membership practices or internal operations of any fraternal organization, any college or university fraternity or sorority, any private club or any religious organization.

(b) The Commission shall submit interim reports to the President and to the Congress at such times as the Commission, the Congress or the President shall deem desirable, and shall submit to the President and to the Congress a final report of its activities, findings, and recommendations not later than January 31, 1968.

Section 506.

(f) The Commission, or on the authorization of the Commission any subcommittee of two or more members, at least one of whom shall be of each major political party, may, for the purpose of carrying out the provisions of this Act, hold such hearings and act at such times and places as the Commission or such authorized subcommittee may deem advisable. Subpenas for the attendance and testimony of witnesses or the production of written or other matter may be issued in accordance with the rules of the Commission as contained in section 102 (j) and (k) of this Act, over the signature of the Chairman of the Commission or of such subcommittee, and may be served by any person designated by such Chairman. The holding of hearings by the Commission or the appointment of a subcommittee to hold hearings pursuant to this subparagraph, must be approved by a majority of the Commission, or by a majority of the members present at a meeting at which at least a quorum of four members is present.

(g) In case of contumacy or refusal to obey a subpena, any district court of the United States or the United States court of any territory or possession, or the District Court of the United States for the District of Columbia, within the jurisdiction of which the inquiry is carried on or within the jurisdiction of which said person guilty of contumacy or refusal to obey is found or resides or is domiciled or transacts business, or has appointed an agent for receipt of service of process, upon application by the Attorney General of the United States shall have jurisdiction to issue to such person an order requiring such person to appear before the Commission or a subcommittee thereof, there to produce pertinent, relevant and non-privileged evidence if so ordered, or there to give testimony touching the matter under investigation; and any failure to obey such order of the court may be punished by said court as a contempt thereof.

TITLE VI — NONDISCRIMINATION IN FEDERALLY ASSISTED PROGRAMS

Section 601.

No person in the United States shall, on the ground of race, color, or national origin, be excluded from participation in, be denied the benefits of, or be subjected to discrimination under any program or activity receiving Federal financial assistance.

Section 602.

Each Federal department and agency which is empowered to extend Federal financial assistance to any program or activity, by way of grant, loan, or contract other than a contract or insurance or guaranty, is authorized and directed to effectuate the provisions of section 601 with respect to such program or activity by issuing rules, regulations, or orders of general applicability which shall be consistent with achievement of the objectives or the statute authorizing the financial assistance in connection with which the action is taken. No such rule, regulation, or order shall become effective unless and until approved by the President. Compliance with any requirement adopted pursuant to this section may be effected (1) by the termination of or refusal to grant or to continue assistance under such program or activity to any recipient as to whom there has been an express finding on the record, after opportunity for hearing, of a failure to comply with such requirement, but such termination or refusal shall be limited to the particular political entity, or part thereof, or other recipient as to whom such a finding has been made and, shall be limited in its effect to the particular program, or part thereof, in which such non-compliance has been so found, or (2) by any other means authorized by law: Provided, however, That no such action shall be taken until the department or agency concerned has advised the appropriate person or persons of the failure to comply with the requirement and has determined that compliance cannot be secured by voluntary means. . . .

Section 604.

Nothing contained in this title shall be construed to authorize action under this title by any department or agency with respect to any employment practice of any employer, employment agency, or labor organization except where a primary objective of the Federal financial assistance is to provide employment.

TITLE VII — EQUAL EMPLOYMENT OPPORTUNITY

Section 701.

For the purpose of this title
. . . .

(b) The term "employer" means a person engaged in an industry affecting commerce who has twenty-five or more employees for each working day in each of twenty or more calendar weeks in the current or preceding calendar year, and any agent of such a person, but such term does not include (1) the United States, a corporation wholly owned by the Government of the United States, an Indian tribe, or a State or political subdivision thereof, (2) a bona fide private membership club (other than a labor organization) which is exempt from taxation under section 501 (c) of the Internal Revenue Code of 1954: Provided, That during the first year after the effective date prescribed in subsection (a) of section 716, persons having fewer than one hundred employees (and their agents) shall not be considered employers, and during the second year after such date, persons having fewer than seventy-five employees (and their agents) shall not be considered employers, and during the third year after such date, persons having fewer than fifty employees (and their agents) shall not be considered employers. Provided further, That it shall be the policy of the United States to insure equal employment opportunities for Federal employees without discrimination because of race, color, religion, sex or national origin and the President shall utilize his existing authority to effectuate this policy.

. . . .

(d) The term "labor organization" means a labor organization engaged in an industry affecting commerce, and any agent of such an organization, and includes any organization of any kind, any agency, or employee representation committee, group, association, or plan so engaged in which employees participate and which exists for the purpose, in whole or in part, of dealing with employers concerning grievances, labor disputes, wages, rates of pay, hours, or other terms or conditions of employment, and any conference, general committee, joint or system board, or joint council so engaged which is subordinate to a national or international labor organization.

(e) A labor organization shall be deemed to be engaged in an industry affecting commerce if (1) it maintains or operates a hiring hall or hiring office which procures employees for an employer or procures for employees opportunities to work for an employer, or (2) the number of its members (or, where it is a labor organization composed of other labor organizations or their representatives, if the aggregate number of the members of such other labor organization) is (A) one hundred or more during the first year after the effective date prescribed in subsection (a) of section 716, (B) seventy-five or more during the second year after such date or fifty or more during the third year, or (C) twenty-five or more thereafter, ...

. . . .

Section 703.

(a) It shall be an unlawful employment practice for an employer —

(1) to fail or refuse to hire or to discharge any individual, or otherwise to discriminate against any individual with respect to his compensation, terms, conditions, or privileges or employment, because of such individual's race, color, religion, sex, or national origin; or

(2) to limit, segregate, or classify his employees in any way which would deprive or tend to deprive any individual of employment opportunities or otherwise adversely affect his status as an employee, because of such individual's race, color, religion, sex, or national origin.

(b) It shall be an unlawful employment practice for an employment agency to fail or refuse to refer for employment, or otherwise to discriminate against, any individual because of his race, color, religion, sex, or national origin, or to classify or refer for employment any individual on the basis of his race, color, religion, sex, or national origin.

(c) It shall be an unlawful employment practice for a labor organization—

(1) to exclude or to expel from its membership, or otherwise to

discriminate against, any individual because of his race, color, religion, sex, or national origin;

(2) to limit, segregate, or classify its membership, or to classify or fail or refuse to refer for employment any individual, in any way which would deprive or tend to deprive any individual of employment opportunities, or would limit such employment opportunities or otherwise adversely affect his status as an employee or as an applicant for employment, because of such individual's race, color, religion, sex, or national origin; or

(3) to cause or attempt to cause an employer to discriminate against an individual in violation of this section.

(d) It shall be an unlawful employment practice for any employer, labor organization, or joint labor-management committee controlling apprenticeship or other training or retraining, including on-the-job training programs to discriminate against any individual because of his race, color, religion, sex, or national origin in admission to, or employment in, any program established to provide apprenticeship or other training.

(e) Notwithstanding any other provision of this title, (1) it shall not be an unlawful employment practice for an employer to hire and employ employees, for an employment agency to classify, or refer for employment any individual, for labor organizations to classify its membership or to classify or refer for employment any individual, or for an employer, labor organization, or joint labor-management committee controlling apprenticeship or other training or retraining programs to admit or employ any individual in any such program, on the basis of his religion, sex, or national origin in those certain instances where religion, sex, or national origin is a bona fide occupational qualification reasonably necessary to the normal operation of that particular business or enterprise, and (2) it shall not be an unlawful employment practice for a school, college, university, or other educational institution or institutions of learning to hire and employ employees of a particular religion if such school, college, university, or other educational institution or institutions of learning is, in whole or in substantial part, owned, supported, controlled, or managed by a particular religion or by a particular religious corporation, association, or society, or if the curriculum of such school, college, university, or other educational institution or institutions of learning is directed toward the propagation of a particular religion.

. . . .

(j) Nothing contained in this title shall be interpreted to require any employer, employment agency, labor organization, or joint labor-management committee subject to this title to grant preferential treatment to any individual or to any group because of the race, color, religion, sex, or national origin of such individual or group on account of an imbalance which may exist with respect to the total number of percentage of persons of any race, color, religion, sex, or national origin employed by any employer, referred or classified for employment by any employment agency or labor organization, admitted to membership or classified by any labor organization or admitted to, or employed in, any apprenticeship or other training program, in comparison with the total number or percentage of persons of such race, color, religion, sex, or national origin in any community, State, section, or other area, or in the available work force in any community, State, section, or other area.

Section 704.

. . . .

(b) It shall be an unlawful employment practice for an employer, labor organization, or employment agency to print or publish or cause to be printed or published any notice or advertisement relating to employment by such an employer or membership in or any classification or referral for employment by such a labor organization, or relating to any classification or referral for employment by such an employment agency, indicating any preference, limitation, specification, or discrimination, based on race, color, religion, sex, or national origin, except that such a notice or advertisement may indicate a preference, limitation, specification, or discrimination based on religion, sex, or national origin when religion, sex, or national origin is a bona fide occupational qualification for employment.

Section 705.

(a) There is hereby created a Commission to be known as the Equal Employment Opportunity Commission, which shall be composed of five members, not more than three of whom shall be members of the same political party, who shall be appointed by the President by and with the advice and consent of the Senate. One of the original members shall be appointed for a term of one year, one for a term of two years, one for a term of three years, one for a term of four years, and one for a term of five years, beginning from the date of enactment of this title, but their successors shall be appointed for terms of five years each, except that any individual chosen to fill a vacancy shall be appointed only for the unexpired term of the member whom he shall succeed. The President shall designate one member to serve as Chairman of the Commission, and one member to serve as Vice Chairman. . . . .

. . . .

(d) The Commission shall at the close of each fiscal year report to the Congress and to the President concerning the action it has taken; the

names, salaries, and duties of all individuals in its employ and the moneys
it has disbursed; and shall make such further reports on the cause of and
means of eliminating discrimination and such recommendations for further
legislation as may appear desirable.

. . . .

(g) The commission shall have power—

(1) to cooperate with and, with their consent, utilize regional, State,
local, and other agencies, both public and private, and individuals;

. . . .

(4) upon the request of (i) any employer, whose employees or some
of them, or (ii) any labor organization, whose members or some of them,
refuse or threaten to refuse to cooperate in effectuating the provisions of
this title, to assist in such effectuation by conciliation or such other remedial
action as is provided by this title;

(5) to make such technical studies as are appropriate to effectuate the
purposes and policies of this title and to make the results of such studies
available to the public;

(6) to refer matters to the Attorney General with recommendations
for intervention in a civil action brought by an aggrieved party under
section 706, or for the institution of a civil action by the Attorney General
under section 707, and to advise, consult, and assist the Attorney General
on such matters.

(h) Attorneys appointed under this section may, at the direction of the
Commission, appear for and represent the Commission in any case in court.

. . . .

Section 706.

(a) Whenever it is charged in writing under oath by a person claiming to
be aggrieved, or a written charge has been filed by a member of the Commission where he has reasonable cause to believe a violation of this title
has occurred (and such charge sets forth the facts upon which it is based)
that an employer, employment agency, or labor organization has engaged
in an unlawful employment practice, the Commission shall furnish such
employer, employment agency, or labor organization (hereinafter referred
to as the "respondent") with a copy of such charge and shall make an
investigation of such charge, provided that such charge shall not be made
public by the Commission. If the Commission shall determine, after such
investigation, that there is reasonable cause to believe that the charge is
true, the Commission shall endeavor to eliminate any such alleged unlawful
employment practice by informal methods of conference, conciliation, and
persuasion. Nothing said or done during and as a part of such endeavors

may be made public by the Commission without the written consent of the
parties, or used as evidence in a subsequent proceeding. . . . .

. . . .

(c) In the case of any charge filed by a member of the Commission
alleging an unlawful employment practice occurring in a State or political
subdivision of a State, which has a State or local law prohibiting the practice
alleged and establishing or authorizing a State or local authority to grant
or seek relief from such practice or to institute criminal proceedings with
respect thereto upon receiving notice thereof, the Commission shall, before
taking any action with respect to such charge, notify the appropriate State
or local officials and, upon request, afford them a reasonable time, but not
less than sixty days (provided that such sixty-day period shall be extended
to one hundred and twenty days during the first year after the effective
day of such State or local law), unless a shorter period is requested, to act
under such State or local law to remedy the practice alleged.

. . . .

(e) If within thirty days after a charge is filed with the Commission
or within thirty days after the expiration of any period of reference under
subsection (c) (except that in either case such period may be extended to
not more than sixty days upon a determination by the Commission that
further efforts to secure voluntary compliance are warranted), the Commission has been unable to obtain voluntary compliance with this title,
the Commission shall so notify the person aggrieved and a civil action may,
within thirty days thereafter, be brought against the respondent named in
the charge (1) by the person claiming to be aggrieved, or (2) if such charge
was filed by a member of the Commission, by any person whom the charge
alleges was aggrieved by the alleged unlawful employment practice. Upon
application by the complainant and in such circumstances as the court may
deem just, the court may appoint an attorney for such complainant and may
authorize the commencement of the action without the payment of fees, costs,
or security. Upon timely application, the court may, in its discretion, permit
the Attorney General to intervene in such civil action if he certifies that
the case is of general public importance. Upon request, the court may, in its
discretion, stay further proceedings for not more than sixty days pending
the termination of State or local proceedings described in subsection (b)
or the efforts of the Commission to obtain voluntary compliance.

(f) Each United States district court and each United States court of
a place subject to the jurisdiction of the United States shall have jurisdiction
of actions brought under this title. . . . .

(g) If the court finds that the respondent has intentionally engaged in
or is intentionally engaging in an unlawful employment practice charged
in the complaint, the court may enjoin the respondent from engaging in

such unlawful employment practice, and order such affirmative action as may be appropriate, which may include reinstatement or hiring of employees, with or without back pay (payable by the employer, employment agency, or labor organization, as the case may be, responsible for the unlawful employment practice). Interim earnings or amounts earnable with reasonable diligence by the person or persons discriminated against shall operate to reduce the back pay otherwise allowable. No order of the court shall require the admission or reinstatement of an individual as a member of a union or the hiring, reinstatement, or promotion of an individual as an employee, or the payment to him of any back pay, if such individual was refused admission, suspended, or expelled or was refused employment or advancement or was suspended or discharged for any reason other than discrimination on account of race, color, religion, sex, or national origin or in violation of section 704 (a).

. . . .

(i) In any case in which an employer, employment agency, or labor organization fails to comply with an order of a court issued in a civil action brought under subsection (e), the Commission may commence proceedings to compel compliance with such order.

. . . .

Section 707.

(a) Whenever the Attorney General has reasonable cause to believe that any person or group of persons is engaged in a pattern or practice of resistance to the full enjoyment of any of the rights secured by this title, and that the pattern or practice is of such a nature and is intended to deny the full exercise of the rights herein described, the Attorney General may bring a civil action in the appropriate district court of the United States by filing with it a complaint . . . requesting such relief, including an application for a permanent or temporary injunction, restraining order or other order against the person or persons responsible for such pattern or practice, as he deems necessary to insure the full enjoyment of the rights herein described.

(b) The district courts of the United States shall have and shall exercise jurisdiction of proceedings instituted pursuant to this section, and in any such proceeding the Attorney General may file with the clerk of such court a request that a court of three judges be convened to hear and determine the case. . . . it shall be the duty of the judges so designated to assign the case for hearing at the earliest practicable date, to participate in the hearing and determination thereof, and to cause the case to be in every way expedited. An appeal from the final judgment of such court will lie to the Supreme Court. . . . .

Section 709.

(a) In connection with any investigation of a charge filed under section 706, the Commission or its designated representative shall at all reasonable times have access to, for the purposes of examination, and the right to copy any evidence of any person being investigated or proceeded against that relates to unlawful employment practices covered by this title and is relevant to the charge under investigation.
. . . .

(c) Except as provided in subsection (d), every employer, employment agency, and labor organization subject to this title shall (1) make and keep such records relevant to the determinations of whether unlawful employment practices have been or are being committed, (2) preserve such records for such periods, and (3) make such reports therefrom, as the Commission shall prescribe by regulation or order, after public hearing, as reasonable, necessary, or appropriate for the enforcement of this title or the regulations or orders thereunder. The Commission shall, by regulation, require each employer, labor organization, and joint labor-management committee subject to this title which controls an apprenticeship or other training program to maintain such records as are reasonably necessary to carry out the purpose of this title, including, but not limited to, a list of applicants who wish to participate in such program, including the chronological order in which such applications were received, and shall furnish to the Commission, upon request, a detailed description of the manner in which persons are selected to participate in the apprenticeship or other training program. . . . .

(d) The provisions of subsection (c) shall not apply to any employer, employment agency, labor organization, or joint labor-management committee with respect to matters occurring in any State or political subdivision thereof which has a fair employment practice law during any period in which such employer, employment agency, labor organization, or joint labor-management committee is subject to such law, except that the Commission may require such notations on records which such employer, employment agency, labor organization, or joint labor-management committee keeps or is required to keep as are necessary because of differences in coverage or methods of enforcement between the State or local law and the provisions of this title. . . . .

(e) It shall be unlawful for any officer or employee of the Commission to make public in any manner whatever any information obtained by the Commission pursuant to its authority under this section prior to the institution of any proceeding under this title involving such information. . . . .

Section 710.

(a) For the purposes of any investigation of a charge filed under the authority contained in section 706, the Commission shall have authority to examine witnesses under oath and to require the production of documentary evidence relevant or material to the charge under investigation.
. . . .

Section 711.

(a) Every employer, employment agency, and labor organization, as the case may be, shall post and keep posted in conspicuous places upon its premises where notices to employees, applicants for employment, and members are customarily posted a notice to be prepared or approved by the Commission setting forth excerpts from or, summaries of, the pertinent provisions of this title and information pertinent to the filing of a complaint.
. . . .

TITLE X — ESTABLISHMENT OF COMMUNITY RELATIONS SERVICE

Section 1001.

(a) There is hereby established in and as a part of the Department of Commerce a Community Relations Service (hereinafter referred to as the "Service") which shall be headed by a Director who shall be appointed by the President with the advice and consent of the Senate for a term of four years. . . . .
. . . .

Section 1002.

It shall be the function of the Service to provide assistance to communities and persons therein in resolving disputes, disagreements, or difficulties relating to discriminatory practices based on race, color, or national origin which impair the rights of persons in such communities under the Constitution or laws of the United States or which affect or may affect interstate commerce. The Service may offer its services in cases of such disputes, disagreements, or difficulties whenever, in its judgment, peaceful relations among the citizens of the community involved are threatened thereby, and it may offer its services either upon its own motion or upon the request of an appropriate State or local official or other interested person.

Section 1003.

. . . .

(b) The activities of all officers and employees of the Service in providing conciliation assistance shall be conducted in confidence and without publicity, and the Service shall hold confidential any information acquired in the regular performance of its duties upon the understanding that it would be so held. . . . .

TITLE XI — MISCELLANEOUS

Section 1101.

In any proceeding for criminal contempt arising under title II, III, IV, V, VI, or VII of this Act, the accused, upon demand therefor, shall be entitled to a trial by jury, which shall conform as near as may be to the practice in criminal cases. Upon conviction, the accused shall not be fined more than $1,000 or imprisoned for more than six months.

This section shall not apply to contempts committed in the presence of the court, or so near thereto as to obstruct the administration of justice, nor to the misbehavior, misconduct, or disobedience of any officer of the court in respect to writs, orders, or process of the court. No person shall be convicted of criminal contempt hereunder unless the act or omission constituting such contempt shall have been intentional, as required in other cases of criminal contempt.

Nor shall anything herein be construed to deprive courts of their power, by civil contempt proceedings, without a jury, to secure compliance with or to prevent obstruction of, as distinguished from punishment for violations of, any lawful writ, process, order, rule, decree, or command of the court in accordance with the prevailing usage of law and equity, including the power of detention.

Voting Rights Act of 1965

Congress and the President

AN ACT

To enforce the fifteenth amendment to the Constitution of the United States and for other purposes.

(Key Sections)

Section 2.

No voting qualifications or prerequisite to voting, or standard, practice, or procedure shall be imposed or applied by any State or political subdivision to deny or abridge the right of any citizen of the United States to vote on account of race or color.

Section 3.

(a) Whenever the Attorney General institutes a proceeding under any statute to enforce the guarantees of the fifteenth amendment in any State

Public Law 89-110; 79 Stat. 437.

or political subdivision the court shall authorize the appointment of Federal examiners by the United States Civil Service Commission in accordance with section 6 to serve for such period of time and for such political subdivisions as the court shall determine is appropriate to enforce the guarantees of the fifteenth amendment (1) as part of any interlocutory order if the court determines that the appointment of such examiners is necessary to enforce such guarantees or (2) as part of any final judgment if the court finds that violations of the fifteenth amendment justifying equitable relief have occurred in such State or subdivision: Provided, That the court need not authorize the appointment of examiners if any incidents of denial or abridgement of the right to vote on account of race or color (1) have been few in number and have been promptly and effectively corrected by State or local action, (2) the continuing effect of such incidents has been eliminated, and (3) there is no reasonable probability of their recurrence in the future.

(b) If in a proceeding instituted by the Attorney General under any statute to enforce the guarantees of the fifteenth amendment in any State or political subdivision the court finds that a test or device has been used for the purpose or with the effect of denying or abridging the right of any citizen of the United States to vote on account of race or color, it shall suspend the use of tests and devices in such State or political subdivisions as the court shall determine is appropriate and for such period as it deems necessary.

(c) If in any proceeding instituted by the Attorney General under any statute to enforce the guarantees of the fifteenth amendment in any State or political subdivision the court finds that violations of the fifteenth amendment justifying equitable relief have occurred within the territory of such State or political subdivision, the court, in addition to such relief as it may grant, shall retain jurisdiction for such period as it may deem appropriate and during such period no voting qualification or prerequisite to voting, or standard, practice, or procedure with respect to voting different from that in force or effect at the time the proceeding was commenced shall be enforced unless and until the court finds that such qualification, prerequisite, standard, practice, or procedure does not have the purpose and will not have the effect of denying or abridging the right to vote on account of race or color: Provided, That such qualification, prerequisite, standard, practice, or procedure may be enforced if the qualification, prerequisite, standard, practice, or procedure has been submitted by the chief legal officer or other appropriate official of such State or subdivision to the Attorney General and the Attorney General has not interposed an objection within sixty days after such submission, except that neither the court's finding nor the Attorney General's failure to object shall bar a subsequent action to enjoin enforcement of such qualification, prerequisite, standard, practice, or procedure.

Section 4.

(a) To assure that the right of citizens of the United States to vote is not denied or abridged on account of race or color, no citizen shall be denied the right to vote in any Federal, State, or local election because of his failure to comply with any test or device in any State with respect to which the determinations have been made under subsection (b) or in any political subdivision with respect to which such determinations have been made as a separate unit, unless the United States District Court for the District of Columbia in an action for a declaratory judgment brought by such state or subdivision against the United States has determined that no such test or device has been used during the five years preceding the filing of the action for the purpose or with the effect of denying or abridging the right to vote on account of race or color: Provided, That no such declaratory judgment shall issue with respect to any plaintiff for a period of five years after the entry of a final judgment of any court of the United States, other than the denial of a declaratory judgment under this section, whether entered prior to or after the enactment of this Act, determining that denials or abridgments of the right to vote on account of race or color through the use of such tests or devices have occurred anywhere in the territory of such plaintiff.

An action pursuant to this subsection shall be heard and determined by a court of three judges in accordance with the provisions of section 2284 of title 28 of the United States Code and any appeal shall lie to the Supreme Court. The court shall retain jurisdiction of any action pursuant to this subsection for five years after judgment and shall reopen the action upon the motion of the Attorney General alleging that a test or device has been used for the purpose or with the effect of denying or abridging the right to vote on account of race or color.

If the Attorney General determines that he has no reason to believe that any test or device has been used during the five years preceding the filing of the action for the purpose or with the effect of denying or abridging the right to vote on account of race or color, he shall consent to the entry of such judgment.

(b) The provisions of subsection (a) shall apply in any State or in any political subdivision of a state which (1) the Attorney General determines maintained on November 1, 1964, any test or device, and with respect to which (2) the Director of the Census determines that less than 50 per centum of the persons of voting age residing therein were registered on

November 1, 1964, or that less than 50 per centum of such persons voted in the presidential election of November 1964. . . . .

(c) The phrase "test or device" shall mean any requirement that a person as a prerequisite for voting or registration for voting (1) demonstrate the ability to read, write, understand, or interpret any matter, (2) demonstrate any educational achievement or his knowledge of any particular subject, (3) possess good moral character, or (4) prove his qualifications by the voucher of registered voters or members of any other class.

(d) For the purposes of this section no State or political subdivision shall be determined to have engaged in the use of tests or devices for the purpose or with the effect of denying or abridging the right to vote on account of race or color if (1) incidents of such use have been few in number and have been promptly and effectively corrected by State or local action, (2) the continuing effect of such incidents has been eliminated, and (3) there is no reasonable probability of their recurrence in the future.

(e) (1) Congress hereby declares that to secure the rights under the fourteenth amendment of persons educated in American-flag schools in which the predominant classroom language was other than English, it is necessary to prohibit the States from conditioning the right to vote of such persons on ability to read, write, understand, or interpret any matter in the English language.

(2) No person who demonstrates that he has successfully completed the sixth primary grade in a public school in, or a private school accredited by, any State or territory, the District of Columbia, or the Commonwealth of Puerto Rico in which the predominant classroom language was other than English, shall be denied the right to vote in any Federal, State, or local election because of his inability to read, write, understand, or interpret any matter in the English language, except that in States in which State law provides that a different level of education is presumptive of literacy, he shall demonstrate that he has successfully completed an equivalent level of education in a public school in, or a private school accredited by, any State or territory, the District of Columbia, or Commonwealth of Puerto Rico in which the predominant classroom language was other than English.

Section 5.

Whenever a State or political subdivision with respect to which the prohibitions set forth in section 4 (a) are in effect shall enact or seek to administer any voting qualification or prerequisite to voting, or standard, practice, or procedure with respect to voting different from that in force or effect on November 1, 1964, such State or subdivision may institute an action in the United States District Court for the District of Columbia for a declaratory judgment that such qualification, prerequisite, standard, practice, or procedure does not have the purpose and will not have the effect of denying or abridging the right to vote on account of race or color, and unless and until the court enters such judgment no person shall be denied the right to vote for failure to comply with such qualification, prerequisite, standard, practice, or procedure: Provided, That such qualification, prerequisite, standard, practice, or procedure may be enforced without such proceeding if the qualification, prerequisite, standard, practice, or procedure has been submitted by the chief legal officer or other appropriate official of such State or subdivision to the Attorney General and the Attorney General has not interposed an objection within sixty days after such submission, except that neither the Attorney General's failure to object nor a declaratory judgment entered under this section shall bar a subsequent action to enjoin enforcement of such qualification, prerequisite, standard, practice, or procedure. Any action under this section shall be heard and determined by a court of three judges in accordance with the provisions of section 2284 of title 28 of the United States Code and any appeal shall lie to the Supreme Court.

Section 6.

Whenever (a) a court has authorized the appointment of examiners pursuant to the provisions of section 3 (a), or (b) unless a declaratory judgment has been rendered under section 4 (a), the Attorney General certifies with respect to any political subdivision named in, or included within the scope of, determinations made under section 4 (b) that (1) he has received complaints in writing from twenty or more residents of such political subdivision alleging that they have been denied the right to vote under color of law on account of race or color, and that he believes such complaints to be meritorious, or (2) that in his judgment (considering, among other factors, whether the ratio of nonwhite persons to white persons registered to vote within such subdivision appears to him to be reasonably attributable to violations of the fifteenth amendment or whether substantial evidence exists that bona fide efforts are being made within such subdivision to comply with the fifteenth amendment), the appointment of examiners is otherwise necessary to enforce the guarantees of the fifteenth amendment, the Civil Service Commission shall appoint as many examiners for such subdivision as it may deem appropriate to prepare and maintain lists of persons eligible to vote in Federal, State, and local elections. . . . Examiners and hearing officers shall have the power to administer oaths.

Section 7.

(a) The examiners for each political subdivision shall, at such places as the Civil Service Commission shall by regulation designate, examine applicants concerning their qualifications for voting. An application to an examiner shall be in such form as the Commission may require and shall contain allegations that the applicant is not otherwise registered to vote.

(b) Any person whom the examiner finds, in accordance with instructions received under section 9 (b), to have the qualifications prescribed by State law not inconsistent with the Constitution and laws of the United States shall promptly be placed on a list of eligible voters. A challenge to such listing may be made in accordance with section 9 (a) and shall not be the basis for a prosecution under section 12 of this Act. The examiner shall certify and transmit such list, and any supplements as appropriate, at least once a month, to the offices of the appropriate election officials, with copies to the Attorney General and the attorney general of the State, and any such lists and supplements thereto transmitted during the month shall be available for public inspection on the last business day of the month and in any event not later than the forty-fifth day prior to any election. The appropriate State or local election shall place such names on the official voting list. Any person whose name appears on the examiner's list shall be entitled and allowed to vote in the election district of his residence unless and until the appropriate election officials shall have been notified that such person has been removed from such list in accordance with subsection (d): Provided, That no person shall be entitled to vote in any election by virtue of this Act unless his name shall have been certified and transmitted on such a list to the offices of the appropriate election officials at least forty-five days prior to such election.

(c) The examiner shall issue to each person whose name appears on such a list a certificate evidencing his eligibility to vote.

(d) A person whose name appears on such a list shall be removed therefrom by an examiner if (1) such person has been successfully challenged in accordance with the procedure prescribed in section 9, or (2) he has been determined by an examiner to have lost his eligibility to vote under State law not inconsistent with the Constitution and the laws of the United States.

Section 8.

Whenever an examiner is serving under this Act in any political subdivision, the Civil Service Commission may assign, at the request of the Attorney General, one or more persons, who may be officers of the United States, (1) to enter and attend at any place for holding an election in such subdivision for the purpose of observing whether persons who are entitled to vote are being permitted to vote, and (2) to enter and attend at any place for tabulating the votes cast at any election held in such subdivision for the purpose of observing whether votes cast by persons entitled to vote are being properly tabulated. Such persons so assigned shall report to an examiner appointed for such political subdivision, to the Attorney General, and if the appointment of examiners has been authorized pursuant to section 3 (a), to the court.

Section 9.

(a) Any challenge to a listing on an eligibility list prepared by an examiner shall be heard and determined by a hearing officer appointed by and responsible to the Civil Service Commission and under such rules as the Commission shall by regulation prescribe. Such challenge shall be entertained only if filed at such office within the State as the Civil Service Commission shall by regulation designate, and within ten days after the listing of the challenged person is made available for public inspection, and if supported by (1) the affidavits of at least two persons having personal knowledge of the facts constituting grounds for the challenge, and (2) a certification that a copy of the challenge and affidavits have been served by mail or in person upon the person challenged at his place of residence set out in the application. Such challenge shall be determined within fifteen days after it has been filed. A petition for review of the decision of the hearing officer may be filed in the United States court of appeals for the circuit in which the person challenged resides within fifteen days after service of such decision by mail on the person petitioning for review but no decision of a hearing officer shall be reversed unless clearly erroneous. Any person listed shall be entitled and allowed to vote pending final determination by the hearing officer and by the court.

(b) The times, places, procedures, and form of application and listing pursuant to this Act and removals from the eligibility lists shall be prescribed by regulations promulgated by the Civil Service Commission and the Commission shall, after consultation with the Attorney General, instruct examiners concerning applicable State law not inconsistent with the Constitution and laws of the United States with respect to (1) the qualifications required for listing, and (2) loss of eligibility to vote.

(c) Upon the request of the applicant or the challenger or on its own motion the Civil Service Commission shall have the power to require by subpena the attendance and testimony of witnesses and the production of documentary evidence relating to any matter pending before it under the authority of this section. . . . .

Section 10.

(a) The Congress finds that the requirement of the payment of a poll tax as a precondition to voting (i) precludes persons of limited means from voting or imposes unreasonable financial hardship upon such persons as a precondition to their exercise of the franchise, (ii) does not bear a reasonable relationship to any legitimate State interest in the conduct of elections, and (iii) in some areas has the purpose or effect of denying persons the right to vote because of race or color. Upon the basis of these findings, Congress declares that the Constitutional right of citizens to vote is denied or abridged in some areas by the requirement of the payment of a poll tax as a precondition to voting.

(b) In the exercise of the powers of Congress under section 5 of the fourteenth amendment and section 2 of the fifteenth amendment, the Attorney General is authorized and directed to institute forthwith in the name of the United States such actions, including actions against States or political subdivisions, for declaratory judgment or injunctive relief against the enforcement of any requirement of the payment of a poll tax as a precondition to voting, or substitute therefor enacted after November 1, 1964, as will be necessary to implement the declaration of subsection (a) and the purposes of this section.

(c) The district courts of the United States shall have jurisdiction of such actions which shall be heard and determined by a court of three judges in accordance with the provisions of section 2284 of title 28 of the United States Code and any appeal shall lie to the Supreme Court. It shall be the duty of the judges designated to hear the case to assign the case for hearing at the earliest practicable date, to participate in the hearing and determination thereof, and to cause the case to be in every way expedited.

Section 11.

(a) No person acting under color of law shall fail or refuse to permit any person to vote who is entitled to vote under any provision of this Act or is otherwise qualified to vote, or willfully fail or refuse to tabulate, count, and report such person's vote.

(b) No person, whether acting under color of law or otherwise, shall intimidate, threaten, or coerce, or attempt to intimidate, threaten, or coerce any person for voting or attempting to vote, or intimidate, threaten, or coerce, or attempt to intimidate, threaten, or coerce any person for urging or aiding any person to vote or attempt to vote, or intimidate, threaten, or coerce any person for exercising any powers or duties under section 3 (a), 6, 8, 9, 10, or 12 (a).

Section 12.

(a) Whoever shall deprive or attempt to deprive any person of any right secured by section 2, 3, 4, 5, 7, or 10 or shall violate section 11 (a) or (b) shall be fined not more than $5,000, or imprisoned not more than five years, or both.

(b) Whoever, within a year following an election in a political subdivision in which an examiner has been appointed (1) destroys, defaces, mutilates, or otherwise alters the marking of a paper ballot which has been cast in such election, or (2) alters any official record of voting in such election tabulated from a voting machine or otherwise, shall be fined not more than $5,000, or imprisoned not more than five years, or both.
. . . .

(d) Whenever any person has engaged or there are reasonable grounds to believe that any person is about to engage in any act or practice prohibited by section 2, 3, 4, 5, 7, 10, 11, or subsection (b) of this section, the Attorney General may institute for the United States, or in the name of the United States, an action for preventive relief, including an application for a temporary or permanent injunction, restraining order, or other order, and including an order directed to the State and State or local election officials to require them (1) to permit persons listed under this Act to vote and (2) to count such votes.

(e) Whenever in any political subdivision in which there are examiners appointed pursuant to this Act any persons allege to such an examiner within forty-eight hours after the closing of the polls that notwithstanding (1) their listing under this Act or registration by an appropriate election official and (2) their eligibility to vote, they have not been permitted to vote in such election, the examiner shall forthwith notify the Attorney General if such allegations in his opinion appear to be well founded. Upon receipt of such notification, the Attorney General may forthwith file with the district court an application for an order providing for the marking, casting, and counting of the ballots of such persons and requiring the inclusion of their votes in the total vote before the results of such election shall be deemed final and any force or effect given thereto. The district court shall hear and determine such matters immediately after the filing of such application. The remedy provided in this subsection shall not preclude any remedy available under State or Federal law.

(f) The district courts of the United States shall have jurisdiction of proceedings instituted pursuant to this section and shall exercise the same without regard to whether a person asserting rights under the provisions of this Act shall have exhausted any administrative or other remedies that may be provided by law.

Section 13.

Listing procedures shall be terminated in any political subdivision of any State (a) with respect to examiners appointed pursuant to clause (b) of section 6 whenever the Attorney General notifies the Civil Service Commission, or whenever the District Court for the District of Columbia determines in an action for declaratory judgment brought by any political subdivision with respect to which the Director of the Census has determined that more than 50 per centum of the nonwhite persons of voting age residing therein are registered to vote, (1) that all persons listed by an examiner for such subdivision have been placed on the appropriate voting registration roll, and (2) that there is no longer reasonable cause to believe that persons will be deprived of or denied the right to vote on account of race or color in such subdivision, and (b), with respect to examiners appointed pursuant to section 3 (a), upon order of the authorizing court. A political subdivision may petition the Attorney General to request the Director of the Census to take such survey or census as may be appropriate for the making of the determination provided for in this section. The District Court for the District of Columbia shall have jurisdiction to require such survey or census to be made by the Director of the Census and it shall require him to do so if it deems the Attorney General's refusal to request such survey or census to be arbitrary or unreasonable.

Mulkey v. Reitman

The California Supreme Court

Lincoln W. Mulkey *et al.*, Plaintiffs and Appellants

v

Neil Reitman *et al.*, Defendants and Respondents
Supreme Court of California, In Bank, May 10, 1966.,
As Modified on Denial of Rehearing, June 8, 1966.

(Major Sections)

Plaintiffs appeal from a summary judgment entered upon the granting of a motion therefor in an action for relief under sections 51 and 52 of the Civil Code.[1]

Published as 413 P. 2d 825; 50 Cal. Rptr. 881.
[1]Civil Code, section 51, provides as follows:
"All persons within the jurisdiction of this state are free and equal, and no matter what their race, color, religion, ancestry, or national origin are entitled to the full and equal accommodations, advantages, facilities, privileges, or services in all business establishments of every kind whatsoever."
Civil Code, section 52, provides as follows:
"Whoever denies, or aids, or who incites such denial, or whoever makes any discrimination, distinction or restriction on account of color, race, religion, ancestry, or national origin, contrary to the provisions of section 51 of this code, is liable for each and every such offense for the actual damages, and two hundred fifty dollars ($250) in addition thereto, suffered by any person denied the rights provided in section 51 of this code."

Plaintiffs complaint sets forth that they are husband and wife, citizens of the United States and residents of the County of Orange; that they are Negroes; that defendants are the owners and managers of a certain apartment building in Orange County; that in May 1963 at least one apartment therein was unoccupied and was being offered by defendants for rent to the general public; that plaintiffs offered to rent any one of available apartments and were willing and able to do so; that defendants refused to rent any of the available apartments to plaintiffs solely on the ground that plaintiffs were Negroes; that because of such refusal plaintiffs were unable to rent a suitable place to live; that they suffered humiliation and disappointment and endured mental pain and suffering; that defendants will continue to refuse to rent to plaintiffs and other members of their race solely on the ground of such race unless restrained by order of the court; that plaintiffs have no adequate remedy at law because the discrimination practiced by defendants is also practiced by other real estate brokers, and home and apartment landlords and owners in Orange County.

The motion for judgment was made and granted solely on the ground, as stated by the trial court, "that the passage of Proposition 14 has rendered Civil Code sections 51 and 52 upon which this action is based null and void." The reference is to the initiative measure which appeared as Proposition 14 upon the statewide ballot in the general election of 1964. Following its approval by the voters it was incorporated into the California Constitution as article I, section 26.

Plaintiffs unsuccessfully opposed the motion on the ground that article I, section 26, is void for constitutional reasons under both the state and federal constitutions. This contention presents the sole question on appeal.

Proposition 14, as now incorporated into the California Constitution, provides in full as follows:

"Neither the State nor any subdivision or agency thereof shall deny, limit or abridge, directly or indirectly, the right of any person, who is willing or desires to sell, lease or rent any part or all of his real property, to decline to sell, lease or rent such property to such person or persons as he, in his absolute discretion, chooses.

" 'Person' includes individuals, partnerships, corporations and other legal entities and their agents or representatives but does not include the State or any subdivision thereof with respect to the sale, lease or rental of property owned by it.

" 'Real property' consists of any interest in real property of any kind or quality, present or future, irrespective of how obtained or financed, which is used, designed, constructed, zoned or otherwise devoted to or limited for residential purposes whether as a single family dwelling or as a dwelling for two or more persons or families living together or independently of each other.

"This Article shall not apply to the obtaining of property by eminent domain pursuant to Articles I, sections 14 and 14½ of this Constitution, nor to the renting or providing of any accommodations for lodging purpose by a hotel, motel or other similar public place engaged in furnishing lodging to transient guests.

"If any part or provision of this Article, or the application thereof to any person or circumstance, is held invalid, the remainder of the Article, including the application of such part or provision to other persons or circumstances, shall not be affected thereby and shall continue in force and effect. To this end the provisions of this Article are severable." (Cal. Const., art. I, section 26.)

A state enactment cannot be construed for purposes of constitutional analysis without concern for its immediate objective. . . . . To determine the validity of the enactment in this respect it must be viewed in light of its historical context and the conditions existing prior to its enactment. . . . .

In 1959, the State Legislature took the first major steps toward eliminating racial discrimination in housing. The Unruh Civil Rights Act. (Civ. Code, sections 51-52) prohibited discrimination on grounds of "race, color, religion, ancestry, or national origin" by "business establishments of every kind." On its face, this measure encompassed the activities of real estate brokers and all businesses selling or leasing residential housing. . . . .

At the same session the Legislature passed the Hawkins Act (formerly Health and Saf. Code, sections 35700-35741) that prohibited racial discrimination in publicly assisted housing accommodations. In 1961 the Legislature broadened its attempt to discourage segregated housing by enacting proscriptions against discriminatory restrictive covenants affecting real property interests (Civ. Code, section 53) and racially restricted conditions in deeds of real property. (Civ. Code, section 782.)

Finally in 1963 the State Legislature superceded the Hawkins Act by passing the Rumford Fair Housing Act. (Health and Saf. Code, sections 35700-35744.) The Rumford Act provided that "The practice of discrimination because of race, color, religion, national origin, or ancestry is declared to be against public policy" and prohibited such discrimination in the sale or rental of any private dwelling containing more than four units. The State Fair Employment Practice Commission was empowered to prevent violations.

Proposition 14 was enacted against the foregoing historical background with the clear intent to overturn state laws that bore on the right of private sellers and lessors to discriminate, and to forestall future state action that might circumscribe this right. In short, Proposition 14 generally nullifies both the Rumford and Unruh Acts as they apply to the housing market.

Prior to its enactment the unconstitutionality of Proposition 14 was urged to this court in *Lewis* v. *Jordan,* Sac. 7549 (June 3, 1964). In rejecting the petition for mandamus to keep that proposition off the ballot we stated in our minute order "that it would be more appropriate to pass on those questions after the election . . . than to interfere with the power of the people to propose laws and amendments to the Constitution and to adopt or reject the same at the polls . . . ." But we further noted in the order that "there are grave questions whether the proposed amendment to the California Constitution is valid under the Fourteenth Amendment to the United States Constitution . . . ." We are now confronted with those questions.
. . . .

It is now beyond dispute that " . . . among the civil rights intended to be protected from discriminatory state action by the Fourteenth Amendment are the rights to acquire, enjoy, own and dispose of property. Equality in the enjoyment of property rights was regarded by the framers of that Amendment as an essential pre-condition to the realization of other basic civil rights and liberties which the Amendment was intended to guarantee." (*Shelley* v. *Kraemer,* 334 U.S. 1, 10; see also *Buchanan* v. *Warley* (1917) 245 U.S. 60, 62; *Brown* v. *Board of Education* (1954) 347 U.S. 483; *Barrows* v. *Jackson* (1953) 346 U.S. 249; *Jackson* v. *Pasadena City School Dist.* (1963) supra, 59 Cal. 2d 876; *Sei Fujii* v. *State of California* (1952) 38 Cal. 2d 718.)

The question of the fact of discrimination, by whatever hand, should give us little pause. The very nature of the instant action and the specific contentions urged by the defendants must be deemed to constitute concessions on their part that article I, section 26, provides for nothing more than a purported constitutional right to *privately* discriminate on grounds which admittedly would be unavailable under the Fourteenth Amendment *should state action* be involved. Thus, as a complete and only answer to plaintiffs' allegations which irrefutably establish a discriminatory act, defendants urge that section 26 accords them the right as private citizens to so discriminate. The only real question thus remaining is whether the discrimination results solely from the claimed private action or instead results at least in part from state action which is sufficiently involved to bring the matter within the proscription of the Fourteenth Amendment. For reasons stated below we have concluded that state action is sufficiently involved to fall within the reach of the Constitutional prohibition.
. . . .

However subtle may be the state conduct which is deemed "significant," it must nevertheless constitute action rather than inaction. The equal protection clause and, in fact, the whole of the Fourteenth Amendment, is prohibitory in nature and we are not prepared to hold, as has been urged, that it has been or should be construed to impose upon the state an obligation to take positive action in an area where it is not otherwise committed to act. . . . .

To conclude that there is state action in the instant circumstances we are not limited to action by one who, cloaked with the authority of the state, acts as its designated representative. In the broad sense, state action has been consistently found where the state, in any meaningful way, has lent its processes to the achievement of discrimination even though that goal was not within the state's purpose. . . . .

Shelley, and the cases which follow it, stand for the proposition that when one who seeks to discriminate solicits and obtains the aid of the court in the accomplishment of that discrimination, significant state action, within the proscription of the equal protection clause, is involved. The instant case may be distinguished from the *Shelley* and the *Abstract* cases only in that those who would discriminate here are *not seeking* the aid of the court to that end. Instead they are in court only because they have been summoned there by those against whom they seek to discriminate. The court is not asked to enforce a covenant nor to eject a tenant, but only to render judgment denying the relief sought in accordance with the law of the state. Thus, it is contended by defendants that the isolated act of rendering such a judgment does not significantly involve the state in the prior act of discrimination.

It must be recognized that the application of *Shelley* is not limited to state involvement only through court proceedings. In the broader sense the prohibition extends to any racially discriminatory act accomplished through the significant aid of any state agency, even where the actor is a private citizen motivated by purely personal interests. (See *Burton* v. *Wilmington Pkg. Auth.,* supra, 365 U.S. 715, 722.) Thus, in *Marsh* v. *State of Alabama,* 326 U.S. 501, an entire town was owned by a purely private company, the agents of which caused the arrest for trespass of persons engaged in exercising their constitutional freedom of speech. Although no government officials or agents were involved, the Supreme Court found sufficient state action to invoke the Fourteenth Amendment. This was based on the view that the company managers were performing a governmental function of managing and controlling a town wherein persons resided who were entitled to Fourteenth Amendment protections: " . . . In our view the circumstances that the property rights to the premises where the deprivation of liberty, here involved, took place, where held by others than the public, is not sufficient to justify the State's permitting a corporation to govern a community of citizens so as to restrict their fundamental liberties . . . ." (*Marsh* v. *State of Alabama, supra,* at p.509.) There, as contended by defendants in the instant case, the state did not participate except to condone private action.

Even more applicable in the instant circumstances are the so-called "white primary cases." (*Smith* v. *Allwright,* 321 U.S. 649; *Terry* v. *Adams,* 345 U.S. 461; *Nixon* v. *Condon,* 286 U.S. 73; *Baskin* v. *Brown,* 174 F. 2d 391; *Rice* v. *Elmore,* 165 F. 2d 387.) In those cases private action infringing the right to vote was held to be the equivalent of state action where accomplished with the culpable permission of the state. In *Nixon* v. *Condon, supra,* 286 U.S. 73, for instance, a state statute which forbade voting by Negroes in primaries was declared to be unconstitutional. It was thereupon repealed and a substitute measure enacted which was wholly permissive, that is, political parties were allowed to prescribe the qualifications for membership and voting rights in the party's primaries. A local political party thereafter barred Negroes from voting in its primaries and it was held that the permissive private action was chargeable as action. (See also *Baskin* v. *Brown, supra,* 174 F. 2d 391, 394.)

A similar abdication of a traditional governmental function for the obvious purpose of condoning its performance under color of private action has recently been struck down by the Supreme Court in *Evans* v. *Newton, supra,* 382 U.S. 296. There, a park for the enjoyment of white persons was owned, managed and maintained by the City of Macon, Georgia, as trustee under the 1911 will of Senator August Bacon. When a question was raised whether the city could continue to maintain the segregated park consistent with the Equal Protection Clause, it purported to transfer the park to private trustees with the intent that it would continue to be maintained for the enjoyment of white persons only. The foregoing conduct on the part of the municipality was held to be proscribed by the Fourteenth Amendment.

It is contended by defendants, however, that the foregoing cases, in the main, involved some recognized governmental function which, although undertaken by private persons, nevertheless was required to be performed in the same non-discriminatory manner as would be required in the case of performance by the state. Such contention fails to recognize the basic issue involved. Those cases are concerned not so much with the *nature* of the function involved as they are with *who* is responsible for conduct in performance of that function. If the function is traditionally governmental in nature unquestionably the state is responsible. But this cannot be the only instance wherein the state assumes responsibility — it is also responsible when, as we have stated, it becomes significantly involved in *any* discriminatory conduct. (See *Burton* v. *Wilmington Pkg. Auth.,* supra, 365 U.S. 715, 722.)

Going to the question of what constitutes significant involvement, it is established that even where the state can be charged with only encouraging discriminatory conduct, the color of state action nevertheless attaches. Justice Black, in writing for the majority on *Robinson* v. *State of Florida,* 378 U.S. 153, 156, and for the dissenters in *Bell* v. *State of Maryland,* 378 U.S. 226, 334, asserted that private racial discrimination violated the Fourteenth Amendment once the state in any way discourages integration or instigates or encourages segregation. In *Barrows* v. *Jackson,* supra, 346 U.S. 249, in holding that a racially restrictive convenant could not constitutionally support a suit for damages, the court explained at page 254: "The result of that sanction by the State would be to encourage the use of restrictive convenants. To that extent, the State would act to put its sanction behind the convenants. If the State may thus punish respondent for her failure to carry out her covenant, she is coerced to continue to use her property in a discriminatory manner, which in essence is the purpose of the covenant. Thus it becomes not respondent's voluntary choice but the State's choice that she observe her convenant or suffer damages."

Proscribed governmental encouragement of private discrimination has not been confined to the courts. *Anderson* v. *Martin,* 375 U.S. 399, involved racial labelling of candidates on ballots. Although the state practice did not *require* discrimination on the part of individual voters, it was struck down because it *encouraged* and assisted in discrimination. (See also *Baldwin* v. *Morgan,* 287 F. 2d 750.) Similarly, as early as 1914, in *McCabe* v. *Atchison, T and S. F. Ry.,* 235 U.S. 151, it was stated at page 162 that the denial of equal railroad facilities to Negroes by a private railroad was unconstitutional state action on the ground that the right to discriminate was authorized by a local statute and that should the carrier perpetuate such discrimination, it would be acting under "the authority of a state law.' The court reasoned that the state *authorization* to discriminate was no less state action than state *imposed* discrimination. (See also *Boman* v. *Birmingham Transit Company,* 280 F. 2d 531.)

The Supreme Court has recently spoken out against state action which only authorizes "private" discrimination. In *Burton* v. *Wilmington Pkg. Auth.,* supra, 365 U.S. 715, the court had before it the question of whether the State of Delaware discriminated against a Negro who was excluded from a privately operated restaurant leased from a public agency of that state. The court stated at page 725, that the state "not only made itself a party to the refusal of service, but has elected to place its power, property and prestige behind the admitted discrimination. The State has so far insinuated itself into a position of interdependence ... that it must be recognized as a joint participant in the challenged activity...." In a concurring opinion Justice Stewart, concluding that the state enactment involved, as construed by the state court, *authorized discrimination,* stated at page 727: "I think, therefore, that the appeal was properly taken and that the statute, as authoritatively construed by the Supreme Court of Delaware, is constitutionally invalid." Even the dissenting justices agreed that if the state court had construed the state enactment as authorizing racial discrimination, there was a denial by the state of equal protection of the laws, Justice Frankfurter stating at page 727: "For a State to place its authority behind discriminatory treatment based solely on color is indubitably a denial by a State of the equal protection of the laws in violation of the Fourteenth Amendment."

In a case involving a fact situation similar to *Burton,* and clearly pertinent to our present inquiry, a Tennessee statute renounced the state's common law cause of action for exclusion from hotels and other public places and declared that operators of such establishments were free to exclude persons for any reason whatever. In the particular circumstances of that case the statute was deemed to bear on the issues "only insofar as" it "expressed an affirmative state policy fostering segregation." The court stated that: "our decisions have foreclosed any possible contention that such a statute . . . may stand consistently with the Fourteenth Amendment." (*Turner* v. *City of Memphis* (1962) 369 U.S. 350, 353.)

The instant case presents an undeniably analogous situation wherein the state, recognizing that it could not perform a direct act of discrimination, nevertheless has taken affirmative action of a legislative nature designed to make possible private discriminatory practices which previously were legally restricted. We cannot realistically conclude that, because the final act of discrimination is undertaken by a private party motivated only by personal economic or social considerations, we must close our eyes and ears to the events which purport to make the final act legally possible. Here the state has affirmatively acted to change its existing laws from a situation wherein the discrimination practiced was legally restricted to one wherein it is encouraged, within the meaning of the cited decisions. Certainly the act of which complaint is made is as much, if not more, the legislative action which authorized private discrimination as it is the final, private act of discrimination itself. Where the state can be said to act, as it does of course, through the laws approved by legislators elected by the popular vote, it must also be held to act through a law adopted directly by the popular vote. When the electorate assumes to exercise the law-making function, then the electorate is as much a state agency as any of its elected officials. It is thus apparent that while state action may take many forms, the test is not the novelty of the form but rather the ultimate result which is achieved through the aid of state processes. And if discrimination is thus accomplished, the nature of proscribed state action must not be limited by the ingenuity of those who would seek to conceal it by subtleties and claims of neutrality.

Contrary to defendant's claims, the state's abstinence from making the decision to discriminate in a particular instance does not confer upon it the status of neutrality in these circumstances. Justice Byron R. White's view of the facts in *Evans* v. *Newton,* supra, 382 U.S. 296, poses an almost identical issue to that here presented. In his view the majority in *Evans* was not justified on the record in concluding that the City of Mason was continuing to operate and maintain the park there involved after transfer to private trustees, and he grounded his conclusion of proscribed state action on 1905 legislation which did not compel but would nevertheless make it possible for the maintenance of segregated private parks for either white or colored persons. His reasoning and resolution of the issue are stated at page 306 in the following language: "As this legislation does not compel a trust to condition his grant upon use only by a racially designated class, the State cannot be said to have directly coerced private discrimination. Nevertheless, if the validity of that racial condition in Senator Bacon's trust would have been in doubt but for the 1905 statute and if the statute removed such doubt only for racial restrictions, leaving the validity of nonracial restrictions still in question, the absence of coercive language in the legislation would not prevent application of the Fourteenth Amendment. For such a statute would depart from a policy of strict neutrality in matters of private discrimination by enlisting the State's assistance only in aid of racial discrimination and would so involve the State in the private choice as to convert the infected private discrimination into state action subject to the Fourteenth Amendment."

From the foregoing it is apparent that the state is at least a partner in the instant act of discrimination and that its conduct is not beyond the reach of the Fourteenth Amendment.

The question remains whether section 26 in whole or in part must be struck down. . . . .

It is immediately apparent from the operative portion of the instant constitutional amendment that it is mechanically impossible to differentiate between those portions or applications of the amendment which would preserve the right to discriminate on the basis of race, color or creed, as distinguished from a proper basis for discrimination. The purported preservation of the right to discriminate on whatever basis is fully integrated and under the rule of *Blaney,* not severable. Moreover, while we can conceive of no other purpose for an application of section 26 aside from authorizing the perpetration of a purported private discrimination where such authorization or right to discriminate does not otherwise exist, any such other purpose clearly "entails the danger of an uncertain or vague future application of the [enactment]" and would thus require that it be struck down. (*Franklin Life Ins. Co.* v. *State Board of Equalization* (1965) 63 A. C. 221, 227.)

For the foregoing reasons the severability clause is ineffective in the instant case, and the whole of the constitutional amendment must be struck down.

Article I, section 26, of the California Constitution thus denied to plaintiffs and all those similarly situated the equal protection of the laws as guaranteed by the Fourteenth Amendment to the federal Constitution, and is void in its general application.

The judgment is reversed. Peek, J.

Traynor, C. J., and Peters, J., Tobriner, J., and Burke, J., concur.

White, J., and McComb, J., dissent.

. . . .

Part 7

The Future of Negro Politics

If there is one large fact which emerges out of these readings, it is the dual understanding that Negroes in America have made great strides in the political system while at the same time not making as great an impact as some of the sound and fury on the present scene would suggest. The Negro in America remains *en masse* at the bottom of the socio-economic totem pole. This fact perhaps circumscribes Negro political behavior far more than any legal facts. Accordingly, a Negro political strategy which would change radically the Negro's position in American society is a long way off.

In addition, "Because of the structure of American politics . . . Negro politics will accomplish only limited objectives."[1] Among other things, the existence of several political cultures in the American political system precludes government from behaving with a single response to Negro needs and demands.[2] Thus, if, in the future, the Negro's new found political rights are not to be construed as a panacea and his frustrations are not to grow, the meaning of these new political rights must be made clear. In the first article reprinted in this section Professor Sindler places the Negro's new political power in balanced perspective in both North and South.

For the present the impact of Negro politics in America is obviously likely to be more visible in the South than elsewhere. The result of greater Negro participation in the South is likely to have at least two consequences: a growth of two-party politics and a change in the political behavior of Democrats who desire to remain Democrats. The former is treated in the second selection by Professor Gerald Pomper, "Future Southern Congressional Politics"; the latter in the final selection, "A Moderate's Victory in A Southern Congressional District," by Professors Jennings and Ziegler.

Beyond the conclusions arising from the selections reprinted in this book it appears defensible to add that for the foreseeable future, Negro politics will continue to be a relatively more distinctive minority group politics: more visible and more volatile throughout the country than the politics of other minorities. This is likely because the Negro's low socioeconomic position and his strategic geographic location uniquely give him the power to create political chaos even where he does not possess the power to persuade. The extent to which Negro politics will retain a special political identity will depend upon the speed with which greater numbers of Negroes begin to play a larger role in the American political system and share more equitably in the American dream. This need not await an increase in Negro political power; the process can be speeded up by a greater acceptance, on the part of those with the most political power in the country, of a fairer concept of justice which assumes the subordination of the discomforts of practicing equality in everyday life to the larger principle of equality which has been broadly accepted.

---

[1] James Q. Wilson, "The Negro in Politics" *Daedalus,* Vol. 24, Nr. 4 (Fall, 1965), p. 970.

[2] For, perhaps, the best and most recent discussion of the impact of various political cultures in America on governmental action, see Daniel J. Elazar, *American Federalism: A View From the States.* (New York: Thomas Y. Crowell Company, 1966), especially chapters 4 and 5.

Protest Against the
Political Status of the Negro

Allan P. Sindler

ABSTRACT: The complexity of the many interrelated problems making up
what is popularly termed "the Negro problem" creates difficulties both for
adequate analysis and social action. The usual solution is to segmentize
the problems, in the manner done by this symposium, which runs the risk
of partial analysis and implicit single-cause explanations and remedies.
Negro political rights is a prime example of this risk because of the widespread agreement on the criticality of voting rights to Negro achievement
of equal status. The argument on voting rights has "psychological" and
"practical" dimensions. On the former, it is here agreed that Negro possession of political rights is a necessary precondition of his full acceptance
as an equal citizen. On the latter, the attempt is made to demonstrate that,
for a wide variety of reasons, Negro political influence will be neither as
extensive nor as facilitative of the solution of other Negro problems as
the proponents of Negro voting rights assume. Adoption of a more modest
view of the capabilities of Negro political power should be helpful to the

Reprinted from *The Annals of the American Academy of Political and Social Science,*
Vol. 357 (January 1965), pp. 48-54, with permission of the publisher and author.
Copyright 1965 by the American Academy of Political and Social Science.

planning of Negro strategy and should minimize the risk of civil disorder attendant upon a growing Negro disillusionment with alleged inadequacies of working through the political process.

Now that we Americans finally have acknowledged the rightness and necessity of furthering Negro advance, we find ourselves almost overwhelmed by the magnitude and depth of the problems produced by our past gross repression of our Negro citizens. As governmental officers at all levels can testify, in our time the determination of virtually every important domestic public policy has become intimately involved with some aspect of Negro deprivation. There is no single "Negro problem," but instead an almost inexhaustible number of separate yet related problems, the cumulative impact of which is numbing no less to the social science analyst than to the social activist and public official. Hence it is natural that participants in and commentators on the struggle for Negro equality choose, rather than to permit the complexity of the problems to overwhelm them into inaction or into advocacy of impractiable "total" solutions, to concentrate on one or another facet of it. Yet, however necessary it is to segmentize the Negro problem into components congenial to the requirements of objective analysis and of social action, there should be no blinking the fact that for this simplification of reality we pay a price.

Advocacy of Single Causes

To cite but one example, the intense specialization within the social science disciplines promotes a multiplicity of compartmentalized appraisals of the Negro plight. The standing temptation to the academic analyst is to overemphasize the one component integral to his disciplinary commitment or approach — be it, for example, law, economics, or ideology — as *the* key to *the* problem. The decorous nod to other aspects of the problem does not stop this approach from all too often skirting the thin edge of advancing a unicausal explanation and of pushing for a panacea. Since any such unidimensional analysis must be wide of the mark, the contribution of such an approach to the development of an effective strategy of Negro protest is gravely limited.

In light of these observations, it comes as no surprise to note the existence of competing unicausal claims and groups in the contemporary movement for Negro equality. Some see housing as the critical factor; others point to education or to religion and the "hearts of men," and still others opt for employment as the nub of the matter. Some plump for litigation and legislation as the means, while others urge demonstrations, boycotts, and other forms of direct action. Some advocate that the Negro "go it alone" without reference to the views of white allies; others counsel an alliance with white liberals, with union labor, or with other minority ethnic groups.

Given this disputatious context, it is perhaps remarkable to be able to come up with one aspect which has received virtually universal endorsement as a critical handicap, the full and rapid remedying of which merits the highest of priorities. That aspect is political rights, the subject of this paper. Our comments on the limits and risks of a compartmentalized assessment of the Negro problem suggest, notwithstanding the broad consensus in support of the centrality of political rights to the struggle for Negro equality, that we critically review the proposition rather than automatically confirm it. What follows attempts essentially to suggest that the panacealike consequences often assumed to flow from achieving this goal are, in fact, unrealistic expectations.

Psychological Dimensions

It is no accident that voting rights were the focus of the Civil Rights Acts of 1957 and 1960 and of the proposed civil rights legislation of the Kennedy Administration prior to the Birmingham disorders in the Spring of 1963. This stress reflected in part the high place accorded political rights in the effort to strengthen the Negro's capacity to help himself, a "practical" perspective about which much more will be said shortly. This stress also reflected the high place accorded political rights in the democratic ethos of the nation, providing what may be termed a "psychological" dimension to voting guarantees.

This psychological dimension operated in several complementary and reinforcing ways. By the mid-1900's, the right to vote was fully accepted as an unchallengeable part of widely held democratic values. Hence, on the one hand, the Negro could not begin to aspire to equal status until and unless his political rights were on the same footing as those of white men. The psychological symbolism of the possession of the right to vote, in other words, became so critical to the Negro search for a self-respecting personal and social identity that the Negro cause had to assign to the securing of political rights the very highest and most urgent priority. And, on the other hand, those who for whatever reasons were committed to the enactment of federal protective legislation for the Negro found that they could marshal the broadest public and legislative support, and arouse the least conflict with other values and interests, by concentrating on the issue of voting. Negro and white concerns thus neatly meshed in the promotion of Negro political rights.

The attempt, in the summer of 1964, by white and Negro volunteers to register Negroes in Mississippi and that of the biracial Freedom Party to challenge the regular Mississippi delegation at the Democratic national convention should be understood in large part in terms of the psychological meaning of both voting rights and of Mississippi to the Negro protest movement. That state has richly earned its symbolic position as the last-ditch bastion of white supremacy, and Negroes quite properly regard its intransigence as a standing mockery of their recent gains in law and practice. The Negro compulsion to "crack Mississippi" is thus easily understandable, and given that compulsion, its tactical implementation by a focus on voting rights — involving the expectation of federal intervention and protection and of arousing an affirmative national public opinion — made good sense. Although the tangible gains of the project in terms of Negro voter registration were meager, the effort succeeded in communicating to the nation the plight of the Negro in Mississippi and the necessity for federal enforcement and other action to make effective in that state the rights recently won by American Negroes.[1] Taking the not-so-long view, the willful resistance of areas like Mississippi at best can delay, but not defeat, Negro advance when backed by national law, the commitment of the national government, and the courageous persistence of the Negro protest movement. The direction of public policy on the matter of basic political rights for the Negro is clear and irreversible.

The Leverage of the Vote

The "practical" as distinguished from the "psychological" argument for the overriding importance of political rights to the Southern Negro is what most concerns this paper. The belief that an enlarged Negro franchise more or less automatically paves the way to Negro achievement of numerous other important rights and equal opportunities is shared by an impressive grouping, including the Attorney General and virtually all segments of the Negro protest movement. There can be no doubt, of course, that an enfranchised Negro population has greater self-protection and influence than an unenfranchised one, but the proponents of the thesis of the centrality of Negro voting rights mean much more by their argument than that. In most cases, the proponents assume that since skin color is irrelevant to the purely quantitative democratic formula of "one man, one vote," Negro possession of

---

[1] The pervasive harassment of these volunteers and the murder of three of them should lie heavily on the consciences of white Mississippians. At the same time, the sponsors of this project — the Council of Federated Organizations, an umbrella organization made up, with reference to this project, mostly of SNCC and CORE with, one suspects, less than enthusiastic backing from the NAACP and SCLC — might well be asked a few hard questions. The morality of the project would depend greatly on the extent to which the young student volunteers clearly understood and accepted the risks they would run in coming as outsiders, without protection, to Mississippi communities in which all influential local forces would be hostile to their presence and activities.

the power of the ballot in the South will invariably lead to the same degree of group acceptance and group benefits as that earlier enjoyed by other minority voting blocs in the nation. It is this set of expectations which warrants closer examination, to the end that a more realistic appraisal of the probable limits of the efficacy of Negro political power may be had.

As of 1960, only 28 per cent of Negro adults were registered voters in the eleven-state South — the former Confederacy — as compared with 60 per cent of white adults. No small part of the explanation relates to varied patterns of white intimidation and circumvention or violation of law, particularly in rural counties with high proportions of Negro population. But, even wrongly assuming that the repressive effects of all such white hostility could be countered by litigation and law enforcement, the gap between racial proportions of registered voters would still remain sizeable. The hard general fact is, as has been verified by numerous analyses of voting behavior, that low registration and turnout rates are associated with low socio-economic status — and the great majority of Negroes belong to that class status. This should not be taken to imply that current efforts to enforce the law on behalf of Negro voting rights or to conduct Negro registration drives should be abandoned — quite the contrary, since both the psychological and the practical aspects of the voting-rights factor compel persistent attention to increasing the number of Southern Negro registrants. This is to say, however, that the effective guarantee of Negro political rights will not result in Negro registration rates comparable to those of whites, and for reasons not remediable by law or federal enforcement.[2]

Handicaps to Negro Politics

Just as the size of the Southern Negro vote will be less than hoped for, so, too, will the restrictions on the application of Negro political power on behalf of racial advance be greater than supposed. Since space limits prohibit a detailed elaboration of this position, the burden of the argument should be stated clearly at the outset. It cannot be disputed that one of the important conditions sensitizing the nation and the parties to the justice of the Negro cause is the political presence of Negroes — who migrated from the South — in the cities of industrialized non-South states. The utility of Negro political influence to the Negro pursuit of equality could be illustrated by countless

[2]Space limits preclude any discussion of the major factors associated with variations in Negro registration rates in the South. For a recent and thorough investigation of that subject, see Donald R. Matthews and James W. Prothro, "Negro Voter Registration in the South," in Allan P. Sindler (ed.), *Change in the Contemporary South* (Durham, N. C.: Duke University Press, 1963), pp. 119-149. Data on Negro registration and on the denial of voting rights to the Negro may be found in the 1959 *Report* and the 1961 voting study of the U.S. Commission on Civil Rights.

other examples at all governmental levels. But there is no need to do so since the point is here cheerfully granted and the focus of the argument lies elsewhere. That argument is simply that the customary expectations on the probable consequences of Negro balloting overlook or underestimate the force of a number of important conditioning factors which are likely to confine Negro political influence. Some — not all — of these factors are briefly discussed in what follows.

In playing the game of pressure group and party politics, Negro leaders often allude to the existence of a cohesive Negro vote which is capable of shifting flexibly from party to party depending upon the civil rights record of each. While the bloc character of the Negro vote is a generally accurate description, the implication of flexibility is not. Since 1936, as Samuel Lubell, among others, has pointed out, the Negro vote in national politics — and in most states and localities as well — has been closely aligned to the Democratic party, for reasons at least as heavily economic as racial.[3] Studies of voting behavior have demonstrated the durability of party attachment of most Americans, further reinforced in the Negro case by their common lower-class standing, so that notwithstanding the greater utility of a shifting bloc vote it is not likely to come about in the near future.[4]

The wedding of Negroes to the Democrats has paid off for the Negro more with reference to the Presidency than to the Congress — where Democratic majorities place Southerners in control of many committees — but its chief drawback lies in the possibility that the party may come to discount Negro demands on the expectation that the Negro vote has nowhere else to turn. That possibility would be heightened if some of the other elements of the Democratic coalition exhibited restiveness over the rate of Negro advance. Contemporary discussion of the white "backlash" in response to the Civil Rights Act of 1964 and to militant direct action tactics of some Negro protesters provides ample testimony to the existence of such white restiveness on a national scale.

Resistance by Whites

Mention of the backlash serves to remind that the response of politicians to Negro demands will not be one of automatic accommodation because of the size and cohesion of the Negro vote. The reaction of whites to Negro

---

[3]Samuel Lubell, "The Negro and the Democratic Coalition," *Commentary,* Vol. 38 (August 1964), pp. 19-27.
[4]The importance of an individual's party identification to his voting behavior has been most fully explored by the Survey Research Center of the University of Michigan. See, for example, Angus Campbell *et al., The American Voter* (New York: John Wiley & Sons, 1960).

political pressures will sharply delimit the range of concessions to Negroes politicians can afford, for whites constitute the majority of voters, not to mention the white near-monopoly of other attributes of political power. And while the mood of the nation defies uniform characterization, it may safely be said that nowhere near a white majority would be in support of the content and timetable of Negro progress as put forth by the more militant Negro spokesmen.

The impact of resistant or adverse white reaction, while by no means restricted to the South, is most dramatically illustrated within that region. In many jurisdictions, including those in which the right of the Negro to vote has long been unquestioned and an important Negro bloc vote exists, Negro political leaders continue to operate covertly in deference to the attitudes of the white community. Negro "demands" tend to be framed in moderate terms, and to be pressed through secret rather than public understandings. The beneficiary of the Negro vote always runs the risk of his opposition making a major issue of that support and, as part of the same pattern, Negro leaders often find themselves forced to support the least racist of the available candidates, with no chance of putting into office an affirmative and influential advocate of the Negro position.

It is no slight to the significance of the benefits Southern Negroes have wrung from this sort of covert politics to emphasize that Negro gains are seldom commensurate with Negro impact on election outcomes. The root reason is that the political process still operates mostly within, and does not transcend, the racial mores. While rising Negro political power in a hypothetical Southern community can perhaps be expected to reduce, let us say, police brutality toward Negroes, it cannot soon be expected to bring about the enactment of an "open housing" ordinance. In sum, the ability and willingness of whites to use the political process to resist and confine Negro political influence will make of the latter something less than *the* critical lever for racial advance it is assumed to be.

Northern Politics

In the markedly less covert Negro politics of the North, the belatedness of the political coming-of-age of the Negro — relative, for instance, to that of minority ethnic groups — handicaps the achievement of Negro goals. For one thing, the Negro now stands virtually alone, not merely lacking an alliance with a variety of minority groups sharing a common purpose — in the manner of the 1930's — but in many instances opposed by them because of the latter's fears that their rising but still insecure middle-class position is threatened by Negro aspirations. For much the same reasons, the necessary Negro stress on welfare-state measures will find fewer receptive ears in our

time than it would have several decades ago. Again, the style of Negro
politics, which is that of the older ethnic politics of "recognition" and
material benefits, is increasingly out of touch with middle-class values and
with the ideological stance of political liberals with whom the Negro
normally would seek alliance.[5] Moreover, as the Chicago experience testifies,
the loyalty of Negroes to big-city Democratic machines may come to serve
party and organizational and leadership needs more than mass racial needs.
It might be mentioned in passing that Negro leadership ranks are today
no better developed for purposes of politics than for other pursuits. As a
final example, in a listing which could be multiplied greatly, consider the
fact that the growing concentration of Negroes within city boundaries, in
conjunction with that of whites in the suburbs, tends to make the metropolitan
and the Negro problem virtually one and the same. The possibility that
such a merged identification will decrease rather than heighten popular
and governmental willingness to tackle metropolitan problems — even allowing for Negro and big-city gains through reapportionment based on the
population factor — is at least as plausible as the reverse.

It may be suggested, in short, that there is a rough political analogy to
the serious economic problem of attempting to find employment for large
numbers of untrained Negroes in an economy increasingly unable to provide
the requisite number of such unskilled jobs. Negroes may find that in
politics also their adherence to the older ways places them at a competitive
disadvantage relative to other, and not necessarily friendly, groups.

Conclusions

No part of this paper quarrels with the proposition that securing the
voting rights of Negroes merits the high priority assigned to it by both
the federal government and the Negro protest movement. Political rights are
critical in the psychological sense that Negroes cannot pretend to equal
citizenship in the absence of those rights. Political rights are highly significant
in the practical sense as well, since they arm the Negro with a legitimate
group weapon for both self-protection and the exercise of influence over
others and over public policy.

This paper has been concerned with what seems to the writer to be the
overly optimistic assumptions held by those who advocate the centrality of
Negro voting rights to the larger struggle for Negro equality. Many important Negro problems are not amenable to political solutions at all, and of

---

[5]These points are among the central theses advanced in James Q. Wilson, *Negro Politics:
The Search for Leadership* (Glencoe, Ill.: Free Press, 1960), and in Edward C. Banfield
and James Q. Wilson, *City Politics* (Cambridge, Mass.: Harvard University Press, 1963).

those that are the political process will operate in a manner more complex, for reasons here discussed, than merely reflecting the one new dimension of an enlarged Negro vote.

It is of some importance to achieve a balanced view of the capabilities of Negro political influence. Otherwise, there is the danger on the one hand that other essential Negro strategies may be overlooked and, on the other, that Negro disillusionment with working through the political process may become pervasive. The first pitfall would jeopardize the quest for Negro equality while the second would jeopardize the maintenance of civil order. Neither danger should be permitted to become an actuality because of well-intentioned but unrealistic conceptions of the gains realizable through the Negro vote.

Future Southern
Congressional Politics

Gerald Pomper

I.

Southern alienation from the national Democratic party has been evident since the 1928 Presidential election.[1] The 1960 contest showed increased disaffection: the Republican party won thirty-three electoral votes in Virginia, Tennessee and Florida, while fourteen electors from Alabama and Mississippi used their legal discretion to cast ballots for Senator Harry F. Byrd. In the other states of the former Confederacy, the Democratic margin was comfortable only in Georgia.

At the present time, however, Republican strength is largely confined to the Presidential level. Even after the great effort made in the 1962 elections,

Reprinted from *Southwestern Social Science Quarterly*. Vol. 44 (June 1963), pp. 14-24, with permission of the publisher and author. Copyright 1963 by the Southwestern Social Science Association.
[1]See V. O. Key, Jr., "Hoovercrats and Dixiecrats," in *Southern Politics* (New York: Alfred A. Knopf, Inc., 1949), pp. 317-344, and Allan P. Sindler, "The Unsolid South: A Challenge to the Democratic National Party," in Alan F. Westin, ed. *The Uses of Power: 7 Cases in American Politics* (New York: Harcourt, Brace and World, 1962), p. 239.

the GOP holds only one Senate and eleven House seats in the eleven Southern states. While flirting with "free elector" plans and Presidential Republicanism, Southern leaders have not attempted to destroy one-party control in other elections.

Through the one-party system, a variety of interests have been served. Office-holders generally have been grateful for the absence of competition. Conservative economic groups have been able to dissipate the energies that might become organized through a competitive political system. "A loose factional system lacks the power to carry out sustained programs of action, which almost always are thought by the better element to be contrary to its immediate interests."² Segregationists have been able to prevent, at least until now, the full participation of the Negro in the political battle and the egalitarian demands that would follow. Even some Republican leaders have been wary of two-party politics, fearing a loss of the scraps of patronage and prestige which they have long monopolized.³

The long-term trend is certainly toward a two-party South. As elaborated by Alexander Heard, competition is being stirred by major changes in the Southern economy and society. They include the immigration of Northerners and the emigration of Negroes, the abolition of racial restrictions on voting, industrialization and urbanization. They are leading to "a clearer identification of economic interest with political action."⁴ As economic and social issues claim priority over racial questions, the Republican appeal will grow.

The specific timing of party competition depends on the perceptions of dominant Southern groups. They will become Republican when forced or persuaded to see this as in their interests. That time may now be near. The pressures against the one-party system can be seen in the case of Congressional elections, which probably are the most crucial for the national political system.

II.

The Southern one-party system is now sustained chiefly by the advantages accruing to the region in Congress. The rules of seniority give "the occupants of safe Southern seats an outpost on the Potomac for sniping and breaking

---

²Key, p. 308. See Duane Lockard, *New England State Politics* (Princeton: Princeton University Press, 1958), chap. 12, for a discussion of the effect of party competition on social policy.
³See William Buchanan, "Cracks in Southern Solidarity," *Antioch Review*, 15 (September, 1956), pp. 351-364, and V. O. Key, Jr., "The Erosion of Sectionalism," *Virginia Quarterly Review*, 31 (Spring, 1955), especially pp. 170-174.
⁴Alexander Heard, *A Two-Party South?* (Chapel Hill: University of North Carolina Press, 1952), pp. 144-156. See also Harry Ashmore, *An Epitaph to Dixie* (New York: W. W. Norton & Company, Inc., 1957).

up incipient attacks."[5] Aside from relatively infrequent primary challenges,[6] these Senators and Congressmen are virtually guaranteed tenure at the Capitol. From their positions of power, they can benefit their particular constituencies,[7] while also defending the region against attacks on segregation.

The usefulness of Congressional seniority depends on the absence of a Republican threat to Democratic office-holders. There is considerable evidence that Southern Congressmen will not long enjoy this political immunity. In the last three Presidential elections, there has been a tendency for the number of districts uncontested by the Republicans to decrease and for the Republican Congressional vote to increase. This is shown in Table 1, in which the five rim states are listed separately.[8] By contrast, the party vote in these elections generally decreased in the previous thirty years.[9]

TABLE 1

SOUTHERN REPUBLICAN CONGRESSIONAL VOTE

	Number of Districts*					
	Rim South			All South		
Republican Vote	1952	1956	1960	1952	1956	1960
0% [Uncontested]	36	27	30	72	61	62
Below 20%	3	5	5	9	9	13
20%–32.2%	7	7	8	8	10	13
33.3%–49.9%	9	15	11	11	19	11
50% and over	6	7	7	6	7	7

*In 1952 and 1956, the 8th and 22nd districts of Texas were combined. For purposes of comparison, they are considered as separate districts in all computations.

It is evident that the increase in Republican strength was considerable from 1952 to 1956 and that a slight decline followed in 1960. The latter is to be expected, given the general Democratic upswing. However, it is apparent that there is a significant Republican residue from the elections and events of 1952 to 1960, and that the previous declining trend has been reversed. As was to be expected, Republican strength is concentrated in the rim South.

---

[5]Buchanan, pp. 351-352.

[6]It is estimated that nearly half of Southern Congressmen face neither primary nor general election contests. See Julius Turner, "Primary Elections as the Alternative to Party Competition in 'Safe' Districts," *Journal of Politics,* 15 (May, 1953), p. 201.

[7]It is not coincidental that the major share of the space agency's expenditures will be made in Southern states. See *The National Observer,* February 4, 1962.

[8]The data for all tables is from U.S. Bureau of the Census, *Congressional District Data Book (Districts of the 87th Congress)* (Washington: Government Printing Office, 1961), Tables I, III. The "rim South" includes Florida, North Carolina, Tennessee, Texas and Virginia. Contrary to tradition, I have included Arkansas in the Deep South, on the basis of resistance to school integration, along with Alabama, Georgia, Louisiana, Mississippi and South Carolina.

[9]Heard, chap. 4, especially pp. 70-73.

Another tabulation indicates more thorough Republican growth. If attachment to the GOP is reaching below the Presidential level, there should be increasing correspondence between the votes for President and the votes for Congressmen. A truly converted Southerner will vote for the entire ticket, not just for its leader. As shown by Table 2, the trend in fact is toward a closer relationship, and it is particularly marked in the five rim states.

There appears to be some definite long-term growth in the Republicans' strength below the Presidential level. This would be even clearer except for the large number of uncontested Congressional districts. Obviously, the

TABLE 2

REPUBLICAN CONGRESSIONAL AND PRESIDENTIAL VOTE

	Rim South			All South		
	1952	1956	1960	1952	1956	1960
(A) Congressional Vote (1,000s)	790	1458	1601	909	1672	1769
(B) Presidential Vote (1,000s)	2987	3148	3533	4090	4213	4724
Correlation of (A) and (B)	.26	.46	.45	.22	.40	.37

GOP Congressional vote cannot increase, either in absolute numbers or in relation to the Presidential vote, unless there are Republicans actually running for the House of Representatives. In many states, the progress of the party has been slowed by the inability or reluctance of the local parties consistently to present Congressional candidates.[10] Where such men are offered, however, there is an undoubted and uniform tendency for the Congressional vote to increase in total numbers and to approach the Presidential vote. This is shown by Table 3.[11]

In every temporal comparison, the later Republican Congressional vote more closely approximates the Presidential vote. The rise in Republican strength in the South is not merely the growth of "Presidential Republicanism." It is being accompanied, indeed led, by the development of firm party strength. Thus, in districts contested in all elections, the Congressional GOP vote increased 20% from 1952 to 1956 and another fifth from 1956 to 1960. In the same period, the Presidential vote rose by only 12% and 15%.

Table 3 also indicates the payoff for persistence. The deepening of Repub-

---

[10]Local "deals" are one reason. In Tennessee, "trading across party lines has been notorious . . . The state's political sophisticates take it for granted that agreement exists between Democratic and Republican leaders to minimize political strife — to create, in effect, two one-party systems." See Heard, p. 108.

[11]To avoid distorted percentages resulting from very small numbers, a contested district is here considered one in which the Republicans get at least 10% of the Congressional vote. However, the Mississippi third district is counted as contested in 1960, although the Republican vote was below this figure. This is because the district did meet the criterion in 1952, and a valid comparison requires its inclusion.

TABLE 3

SOUTHERN REPUBLICAN VOTE IN CONTESTED DISTRICTS

Districts Contested:	Correlation of Republican Congressional and Presidential Vote		
	1952 (N=28)	1956 (N=42)	1960 (N=41)
In Given Years	.67 (28)	.69 (42)	.74 (41)
In All Three Elections	.73 (15)	.79 (15)	.83 (15)
In 1956 and 1960	....	.72 (28)	.78 (28)
In 1952 and 1960	.70 (22)	....	.80 (22)
In 1952 and 1956	.69 (20)	.76 (20)	....
Only in 1956 and 1960	....	.63 (13)	.69 (13)
Only in 1952 and 1960	.58 (7)	....	.66 (7)
Only in 1952 and 1956	.50 (5)	.65 (5)	....

lican loyalties occurs after a number of elections in which party candidates for Congress have been available. If nominees are continuously advanced, the local organization gradually gains practice, knowledge, and funds. At the same time, the voters become accustomed to the existence of a Republican ticket, rather than a Republican Presidential candidate alone. Analysis of districts contested in 1960, as in Table 4, shows the results. The closest ticket correlation exists in those districts in which competition has been most frequent and most persistent. Lack of these qualities results in a loss of Republican votes.

TABLE 4

REPUBLICAN VOTE IN CONTESTED DISTRICTS, 1960

Type of Districts	Correlation of Congressional and Presidential Vote, 1960
Newly Contested in 1960 (N=6)	.45
Only Contested in 1952 and 1960 (7)	.66
Only Contested in 1956 and 1960 (13)	.69
Contested in Three Elections (15)	.83
All Contested in 1960 (41)	.74

Of course, the increase in Republican votes is not due to changes in voter habits alone. Congressional candidates are generally being named only in those districts in which the party believes it has some fundamental strength. The point is still valid, however, that there are such areas and that the GOP has a substantial and increasing number of followers in those districts.

This recent strength appears to be substantially based. Transient causes, such as Eisenhower's personal popularity in 1952 and 1956, and anti-Catholic feeling in 1960, have had some effect, to be sure. However, these factors cannot explain the steady and significant increase in the GOP Congressional vote. Neither do temporary rebellions by frustrated segregationists account for the changes in voting patterns.

The new and permanent strength of the Republicans is in the rim South and in urban areas, in which a GOP vote is based on economic rather than racial issues. Included in the districts showing strong support for the party are Arlington and Richmond in Virginia, Houston and Dallas in Texas, Tampa and Cape Canaveral in Florida. In 1960, of thirty-one districts showing a high correlation between the Republican Presidential and Congressional vote, sixteen were wholly or partially composed of major cities.[12]

Republican progress in Southern Congressional contests is slow but apparently secure. Increasingly, Southern Democratic Congressmen will be forced to make a choice. If they wish to remain Democrats in office, they will find themselves in need of support from the national party and its Presidential ticket. They will no longer be able to be completely independent, secure against any electoral threat. The result of these needs is likely to be increased cooperation and policy agreement with the national leaders. If they refuse cooperation they must face a rising Republican challenge without significant support from the national party.

At the same time, there is less reason for the national Democratic party to accept Southern defiance and defection. It can now actually bargain with the Southern Congressmen. He is no longer politically invulnerable. Failing in party loyalty, he may find himself facing, unaided, a formidable Republican opposition and, possibly, bearing the additional burden of attacks by loyal Democrats in his own constituency.[13] The choice increasingly will be between Democratic loyalty, with a degree of acceptance of party policy and candidates, or outright and consistent support of the Republican party.

The national Republican party too is likely to demand a clear choice of loyalty. In the past, the GOP could present no real threat to Southern legislators. Making a virtue of necessity, the party accepted the nominal Democratic allegiance of the South and hoped for no more than a Dixiecrat revolt in support of the Republican Presidential candidate and for policy agreements in Congress. Now the Republicans can and must attempt to win Congressional seats in the South in their own name.

In order to win control of Congress, the party has no alternative but to

---

[12]Analyzing the 1952 election, Donald S. Strong concluded that urban, and particularly higher-income, endorsement of the GOP was "the most consistent and persuasive finding." He predicted correctly that segregationist support of the Republicans would decline, but that the vote of higher-income urban dwellers would become more definitely Republican. See "The Presidential Election in the South, 1952," *Journal of Politics,* 17 (August, 1955), pp. 343-389.

[13]In Texas, loyal Democrats in 1961 were reported to support Republican John Tower for the Senate rather than a conservative and anti-Kennedy Democrat, William Blakely, who was subsequently defeated. See *Wall Street Journal,* May 25, 1961.

honestly contest Southern elections. In recent years, Democrats have invaded many traditionally Republican areas, from Maine to Hawaii. Outside of the South, the two-party vote has been closely divided, yet the GOP has won control of Congress only once since 1946, and then only by the narrowest margin and with the aid of a Presidential landslide. For its own self-interest, the Republican party will be putting increased pressure on the Southerners, either by inviting them to change parties openly or by challenging them at the polls.

In state politics, it has been noted that even small opposition parties promote "a degree of cohesion and responsibility that is almost completely lacking in the dominant parties of the one-party systems, and thus clarify the choice that the voter must make."[14] The Republican party is clearly growing in the South. As it becomes organized more extensively, the outcome is likely to be increased Democratic party unity and, consequently, more persistent and meaningful two-party competition in the region.

III.

The choice between support of the Democratic or Republican party must be made by individual Congressmen, present and future. Each will consider a number of factors, including the electoral division of his district, party traditions, and the public policies of the national groups. Some will be most interested in the preservation of segregation. Insofar as this is their objective, it will not be served by continued membership in the Democratic party.

This is not just because of the commitment of the "presidential wing" of the party to civil rights. Southerners in Congress have often shown ability to block the programs of a Democratic President. Rather, the cause of future segregationist alienation is to be found in Congress itself, particularly in the increasing numbers and influence of Negro legislators.

Among Democrats in Congress, there are really two large groups from one-party areas: legislators from the South and legislators from the core areas of the large non-Southern cities. Although, unlike most Southerners, big-city Democrats usually face Republican opposition, they are easily elected and re-elected. Like their fellow partisans from the South, they are able to accumulate seniority and status.[15]

Democratic dominance of big-city elections is significant for the South because this party control is becoming, or can become, Negro control. In recent years the metropolitan centers have come to include a large and

---

[14]Austin Ranney and Willmore Kendall, *Democracy and the American Party System* (New York: Harcourt, Brace and Company, 1956), p. 197.
[15]Turner, *loc. cit.,* indicates that primary challenges in "safe" districts in the Northeast occur in only 29.7% of elections, compared to 57.5% in the South.

increasing percentage of Negroes, who now comprise a fifth of the population of the twenty-five largest cities,[16] and often a majority of the population in at least one Congressional district.

The city cores have long been Democratic. They are now becoming Negro as well, while remaining Democratic. Table 5 below indicates two things.

TABLE 5

DEMOCRATIC VOTE IN NON-SOUTHERN DISTRICTS, BY NEGRO
POPULATION*

Negro Percentage of Population	Number of Districts	Democratic Vote (%)		
		1952	1956	1960
20%–25.0%	5	53	53	63
25.1%–29.9%	5	57	57	66
30.0%–39.9%	6	64	65	70
40.0%–49.9%	5	70	73	77
50% and over	5	65	65	74

*Not included in this table are three California districts in the 30% range and one with 23% Negro population. All of these districts were technically non-contested in 1952 because of the cross-filing primary system. Comparisons with the 1956 and 1960 elections are therefore impossible.

The areas with large Negro concentrations are increasingly Democratic, on the average giving some two-thirds of their vote to the party. Secondly, the Democratic percentage generally increases as the Negro proportion in the areas increases.[17]

It is likely that the Congressmen elected from these areas will be both Negro and Democratic. All but one of the five districts now containing an absolute majority of nonwhites do, in fact, have Negro Congressmen. A fifth Negro was elected in 1962 from a new Los Angeles district. Legislators elected from these districts will probably be relatively safe from primary challenges, since the most efficient urban machines now in existence are those in the Negro wards.[18]

The influence of Negro voting in big-city districts is already apparent. Of only four Negroes in the 87th Congress, two were committee chairmen — William Dawson of Government Operations and Adam Powell of Education and Labor. In the not-distant future, more Negroes will be Congress-

[16]*The New York Times,* April 15, 1962.
[17]These two trends are related. The districts are classified here by the percentage of Negro population in the 1960 census. It is likely that the proportion of nonwhites increased in each of these areas during the three Presidential elections involved. As this change in population occurred, the areas became more firmly Democratic.
[18]See James Q. Wilson, *Negro Politics* (Glencoe, Illinois: The Free Press, 1960), particularly chaps. 2, 3, and David Hapgood, *The Purge That Failed: Tammany v. Powell* (New Brunswick: Eagleton Institute, 1959).

men and some will survive long enough to become chairmen. In 1960, Negroes constituted a majority of the population in two districts in Chicago and one each in Detroit, New York and Philadelphia. They represented over 40% of the population in five additional districts in Baltimore, Detroit, New York and Cleveland. It would not be too difficult for Negroes to win and retain these ten seats.[19] Proper placement on committees, combined with continued local victories and Democratic Congressional majorities would result in substantial influence. For the longer future, there are an additional nine districts with 30 percent or more Negro population, and eleven with 20 to 30 percent Negro population. Given nonwhite population growth, and the natural political strength of a unified minority, these districts too might have Negro legislators within a foreseeable time.

As the Negro population in the core cities increases, the result will be that more Negroes will be elected to Congress and will serve for longer periods. They will rise, through the seniority system, to positions of influence and to committee chairmanships when the Democrats are in control of Congress. The institution of seniority, long noted for its conservative and prosegregationist effects, may well come to serve opposite objectives. Democratic majorities in Congress now result in increased influence for those opposed to integration and civil-rights legislation. By helping to elect Democrats in the North, Negroes are in the anomalous position of advancing Howard Smith to chairman of the House Rules Committee.

Ironically, the opposite may soon be true. Southern Democratic votes will help to elevate Negroes to positions of power. Indeed, the situation has already occurred. Despite Southern unhappiness, the inexorable workings of seniority have enabled Congressman Powell to investigate and attack segregation in education, employment and labor unions. When this occurs, the value of the one-party system to Southerners, or at least to segregationist Southerners, has become questionable, if not totally illusory. In addition to civil-rights action, liberal legislation in general is likely to be advanced by Negro Congressmen. Elected by low-income and disadvantaged voters, they will usually endorse programs of governmental welfare and economic regulation.

It should be noted that the Senate represents a different situation. Negroes are not likely soon to be elected, and continuously re-elected, to the upper chamber and obviously cannot gain seniority there. This can provide only limited comfort to the South. The Republican threat is probably greater in the Senate, because it is simpler to challenge 22 seats there than 106 in the House. Moreover, since Negroes cannot yet rise from the House to the

---

[19] A Negro candidate for Congress from Cleveland was defeated in 1962, in part because of the Republican sweep in that state. It is likely that a Negro will soon represent the district, however.

Senate, their seniority in the lower chamber will accumulate more rapidly. In any case, the close battles between liberals and conservatives today occur in the House. Thus, increased Negro strength there is most significant. In the past, conservative Democratic Southerners enjoyed the best of two possible worlds. In a Democratic Congress, they held influential positions which could be used to block or delay measures they considered obnoxious, such as civil-rights legislation. In a Republican Congress, they lost their positions, but could usually remain assured that no legislation repugnant to them would be passed.

In the future, Southerners may find both their positions and their policies endangered in a Democratic Congress. Continued support of the party would subject Southerners to increased competition by the Republicans at home, and to increased pressure to support the legislative program of the national Democratic party. Continued allegiance would also require them to support Northern Negroes for seniority posts.

Because it would overcome some of these disadvantages, membership in the Republican party will be more attractive to Southerners than in the past. By joining the GOP, the Southern representative would be able to ride the rising political tide. Insofar as he favors more conservative domestic policies, he would find substantial support among Republicans.[20] While he would not be assured of any privileged consideration on seniority, he would not be required to vote for Negroes as committee chairmen, since none are likely to be elected continuously as Republicans.

It is not likely that all Southern Democrats will become Republicans. Many are too committed, by tradition, belief, and political necessity, to change their party label. Others will find the defense of segregation too unimportant to justify a metamorphosis, or will regard the Republican party as inadequate to its defense. Some will remain Democrats while relying on remaining devices, such as the Senate filibuster, to defend their interests. In the long run, the South will lose some of its power in Congress and in the nation.

In any case, Southerners cannot expect to defend segregation permanently. Neither of the national parties is likely to adopt a segregationist position as the price of Southern adherence in Congress. Instead, the choice of party must be made on other grounds. Many Southern representatives will be attracted to the GOP by its relative conservatism and by its increasing political strength in the region. Others will be urged on this course by the rising Negro strength in the Democratic party and in Congress.

The full realization of these trends will probably require the removal of

---

[20]See Austin Ranney, "Republicans and Democrats: Principles and Perversities," in Alfred Junz, ed., *Present Trends in American National Government* (New York: Frederick A. Praeger, 1961), p. 52.

the integration issue from national politics. Now that a Democratic, as well as Republican, Administration has used military force to support school desegregation, the way may be open for the full development of two-party politics in the South. This trend in turn may lay the basis for a party system with limited but distinct differences between the parties and for increased central authority within the parties. Contrary to some views, these effects do not require "changes in current institutions and procedures which would deprive nominal Southern Democrats of those advantages that make them loathe to shed their Democratic label."[21] These shifts will come about through the continuation of political trends now evident and likely to continue for a considerable period. One hundred years after the Civil War, the outlook is for a truly national political system.

---

[21]Sindler, p. 280.

A Moderate's Victory in a
Southern Congressional District*

M. Kent Jennings and L. Harmon Zeigler

Social, economic, and political changes continue to gain tempo in the
South. Urbanization, increasing Negro political participation, growing Republicanism, and legislative redistricting are hallmarks of the changes. One
possible consequence will be the emergence of political officeholders —
especially at the congressional level — more in step with thier Northern
counterparts. This article presents an electoral analysis of the efforts of one
"new style" Southern Democratic congressional aspirant.

Basically, the strategy of insurgent Southern Democrats is to offer attractive, moderate opponents in the Democratic primaries who would make a
clear distinction between themselves and the conservative incumbents or new
office seekers. They would identify themselves more with the national Democratic Party and its aims. The strategy would be particularly effective, they
argue, if there is strong Republican opposition in the offing, because the
lack of contrast between the conservative Democrat and the Republican

Reprinted from *Public Opinion Quarterly,* Vol. XXVIII, (Winter 1954) pp. 595-603
with permission of the publisher. Copyright 1964 by Princeton University Press.
*The research reported in this paper was supported by a grant to Professor Zeigler from
the Emory University Graduate Research Committee.

candidate could be pointed out. With Negro voting on the rise, they also stress that moderate Democrats will be needed to keep these votes from going Republican.

The 1962 congressional election in the Fifth District of Georgia offered a chance to study the consequences of this kind of thinking. This oversized district consisted of highly urbanized Fulton County (primarily Atlanta) with a population of 536,000, suburban DeKalb County with 257,000, and tiny rural Rockdale County with slightly under 11,000. Prior to the judicial invalidation of Georgia's county unit system in 1962, a combination of DeKalb's six unit votes and diminutive Rockdale's two votes could, and on some occasions did, outweigh Fulton County's six votes — even though the latter carried with them a greater popular vote. With the abolition of the county unit system, the electoral position of Atlanta and Fulton County was tremendously improved, while the pivotal role of sparsely populated Rockdale was eliminated. Candidates would now essentially be running in only two counties.[1]

These two counties, however, differ significantly in socio-economic characteristics, as shown by these 1960 census figures:

	Fulton	DeKalb
Median education (years)	10.6	12.2
Median family income	$5,207	$6,873
Per cent working outside county of residence	6.4	62.7
Per cent Negro (nonwhite)	34.8	8.7

Politically, one of the big differences between the counties is the high electoral participation of Negroes in Fulton County. They are registered in rather high proportion (around 40 per cent), and reliable estimates indicate that they match or exceed whites in turning out at the polls.

We are making no case that the Atlanta area and the Fifth District are typical of even very many urbanized districts in the South, to say nothing of other kinds of districts. Yet, given the socio-economic and political forces at work, it is likely that several more districts (and other political units as well) will follow in this direction. Therefore, it is useful to consider the Georgia Fifth as a possible prototype of what may lie ahead in the areas where these forces are in motion.

The congressional election of 1962 found a young Atlanta lawyer, Charles Weltner, opposing incumbent James C. Davis in the initial Democratic

---

[1]Rockdale is omitted from further discussion not only because it is so small but because census tract data are lacking and the whole county comprises but one voting precinct. Since 1962, districts have been reapportioned.

primary. The two differed sharply in their platforms. Davis, an eight-term veteran from DeKalb County, based his appeal (as in the past) on segregation, economy in government, and states' rights. Weltner, while no flaming liberal, assumed a "moderate" stance on civil rights for Negroes. In general, he was more in harmony than Davis with the dominant views of the national Democratic Party and had been an active campaigner for John F. Kennedy in the 1960 presidential contest. In fact, it is widely believed that the Democratic National Committee and the AFL-CIO's COPE provided aid to Weltner in his primary struggles with the conservative Davis. Although Weltner slightly outdrew Davis in the first primary (47 versus 46 per cent), two minor candidates polled enough votes to force a run-off primary. Weltner won this contest with 55 per cent of the 135,000 votes cast, running up enough of a majority in Fulton County to offset his losses in DeKalb. Under the unit system Davis would have won. It is difficult to tell what happened to the small minor candidate votes of the first primary, but it appears that Weltner received the majority of them.

In the general election Weltner faced James O'Callaghan, choice of the Republican nominating convention. The Republicans had made a fairly strong showing in 1956, but their strength had faded since that time. In 1962, however, a vigorous local Republican organization was using the congressional election to establish a permanent beachhead in the district. O'Callaghan's platform was similar to that used earlier by the conservative Davis — minus the segregation issue — but his major call was for the establishment of a two-party system. In the general election Weltner defeated O'Callaghan with 55 per cent of 108,000 votes registered.

Thus the moderate, more nationally oriented Democrat prevailed, a seeming confirmation of the moderate strategy for displacing arch-conservatives. But what were the electoral components of this victory? How did they vary from the primary to the general election? And what do the results suggest for other congressional districts in the urban South? To answer these questions we ascertained the voting patterns in the run-off primary[2] and general elections according to selected socio-economic and political variables. In this report we deal only with former.[3]

As part of the analysis, the following information was compiled for all precincts in Fulton and DeKalb Counties: per cent Negro, median education, median family income, and ratio of managers to managers and laborers com-

[2]The run-off primary was used for analysis because the distribution of the vote in the run-off closely resembled that of the first primary, and the run-off was a direct clash between Davis and Weltner.
[3]A discussion of the political variables and campaign strategies will be found in M. Kent Jennings and L. Harmon Zeigler, eds., *Essays in the Electoral Process,* Englewood Cliffs, N. J., Prentice-Hall, forthcoming.

bined. The simple and partial correlations of these variables with the vote for Weltner in the primary and general elections were then calculated for each county.[4] It should be noted that voters do not register by party in Georgia. Hence, the "Democratic" primary is an open one. There is little doubt that Republican identifiers as well as only nominal Democrats vote along with Democratic Party regulars in these primaries.

As Table 1 shows, there are substantial differences in the correlations on the basis of election and of county. Considering briefly the simple correlations first, it is apparent that Weltner's primary vote in Fulton County was negatively related to education, income, and proportion of managers, while just the opposite was the case in more affluent and heavily white DeKalb County. In the general election, however, with the introduction of party labels, the signs of r assume the same negative direction in both counties, although the magnitudes are considerably greater in Fulton than in DeKalb. Significantly,

TABLE 1

SIMPLE AND PARTIAL CORRELATIONS BETWEEN VOTE FOR
WELTNER AND SOCIO-ECONOMIC FEATURES OF PRECINCTS
IN FULTON AND DEKALB COUNTIES

	Primary		General	
	Simple	Partial*	Simple	Partial*
Fulton County:†				
Per cent Negro	.88	.81	.56	.27
Median education	—.34	.27	—.73	—.39
Median income	—.37	—.13	—.69	—.26
Ratio managers to laborers	—.63	.17	—.65	.23
DeKalb County:‡				
Per cent Negro	.42	.08	.28	.05
Median education	.70	.54	—.37	—.28
Median income	.48	.42	—.39	—.33
Ratio managers to laborers	.60	—.23	—.33	.18

*Partials are of the third order and involve the variables listed in the table.
†Sixty-six precincts.
‡Forty-nine precincts.

---

[4]Since the demographic data are reported by census tract rather than precinct, it was necessary to estimate the degree of overlap and weight each variable accordingly. Several outlying precincts in Fulton County were combined to form larger units more comparable in size to most other precincts. The total number of precincts used in the analyses is 66 from Fulton County and 49 from DeKalb. In Fulton, 53 precincts (80 per cent) in the primary and 49 (73 per cent) in the general election, with individual voting totals between 500 and 2,500, supplied roughly 80 per cent of the total vote in each election. For DeKalb, 40 precincts (82 per cent) in the primary and 39 (80 per cent) in the general election, with individual voting totals between 500 and 1,600, cast approximately 95 per cent of the total ballots in each contest.

of the four socio-economic indicators only per cent Negro shows a positive relationship with Weltner's vote for each election in both counties, and the correlation is much higher in Fulton than in DeKalb.

But let us turn to the partial correlations, where the individual importance of the variables can be assessed. By all odds the single most impressive partial in the primary is the .81 figure for per cent Negro in Fulton County, where the bulk of the Fifth District's Negroes reside and vote. This variable alone accounts for about two-thirds of the variance of the Weltner vote with three other measures of socio-economic status controlled. Evidently, Weltner's moderate stand on civil rights struck a much more responsive chord as the proportion Negro increased. DeKalb County, with less than 10 per cent Negro population, shows a very poor partial correlation between this factor and the Weltner vote. But education and income show rather strong correlations with the vote in DeKalb, especially in contrast to the Fulton pattern. By inference, it seems that the Negro component in Fulton mitigates the association of income and education with the vote.

It is important to observe what happens to the high partials when we move to the general election. With the intrusion of a Republican candidate and an interparty fight, the partial correlation for per cent Negro drops appreciably in Fulton County, although it is still definitely on the positive side. In both counties education and income now show moderate *negative* correlations, with the manager-laborer ratio having a very modest positive valence. The pattern of support now resembles what we might expect to find in some non-Southern constituencies. We shall return to a consideration of these interelection changes shortly.

Taken together, these four socio-economic indicators go a surprisingly long way toward explaining the moderate Democrat's victory. The coefficients of multiple correlation (R) between these factors and per cent Weltner vote are as follows: Fulton — primary, .93, general, .78; DeKalb — primary, .76, general, .49. The R for the Fulton primary is extremely high, explaining as it does 86 per cent of the variance in the Weltner support. Notice that R is much higher in Fulton than in DeKalb and in the primary election than in the general.[5] One of the prime reasons for the contrast between counties in the primary is the differential Negro composition. R is almost the same (about .75) in each county until per cent Negro is added to

---

[5]Both the partial and multiple correlations suggest a caveat to the general contention that socio-economic indicators are better predictors of general than of primary elections (see, for example, Peter H. Rossi and Phillips Cutright, "The Impact of Party Organization in an Industrial Setting," in Morris Janowitz, ed., *Community Political Systems,* New York, Free Press of Glencoe, 1961, pp. 97-98). The apparent explanation for the pattern described in the Georgia Fifth is that the electorates in the primary and general contests in all probability overlapped considerably. This would not be the case in the more customary two-party electoral situation.

the equation. While the effect of adding the race variable in Fulton County is to increase R considerably, it has virtually no effect in DeKalb. The drop-off in the multiple correlations in the general election may be attributed primarily to the influence of partisan considerations.

Apparently, then, Weltner's winning electoral combination underwent substantial transformation from primary to general election. In addition to the evidence already presented, this can be shown by examining the rank order correlations (Kendall's tau) derived from arranging precincts in the order of their support for Weltner in two pairs of elections, as shown below:

	Fulton	DeKalb
First primary and run-off	.73	.81
Run-off and general	.19	—.11

While the rank order of support remained rather stable moving from the first primary to the run-off, it dropped precipitously in both counties from the run-off to the general. Shifts in support may have originated, of course, both from changed votes of the same voters and from changes in the population of voters.

The drastic shuffling in rank order adds further confirmation to the thought that the introduction of partisanship contributed to a recombination of electoral support for the moderate Democrat between the run-off primary and the election. Further explication of this shift may be gained from a closer look at types of precincts. In terms of who received the majority of the precinct's vote, here is the interelection pattern:

Majority Received by	Number of Precincts
Conservative Democrat in primary and moderate Democrat in general	49*
Moderate Democrat in both primary and general	37*
Conservative Democrat in primary and Republican in general	13
Moderate Democrat in primary and Republican in general	16

*Includes one precinct giving Weltner exactly one-half the vote in the general.

We can gain an idea of what kinds of precincts shifted and in what direction by grouping the precincts according to socio-economic status (SES), with a control for race in Fulton County. Dividing all the precincts into three roughly equal categories of low, medium, and high SES levels reveals two opposing trends in the white precincts of both counties (Table 2). Going from the run-off to the general election, Weltner made a large net increase in the low SES precincts and a moderate one in those of the middle range. (Significantly, this pattern also prevailed in tiny Rockdale County, with its rural, white, and low- to middle-class population.) Both types, on the average, returned solid majorities for him in the general election. Notice, however, that he actually suffered a net loss among the high-status precincts and received, on the average, less than half the vote. But the most startling contrasts in Table 2 are those between the low-status Negro precincts of Fulton County and comparable white precincts in both counties. The Negro

TABLE 2

RELATIONSHIP BETWEEN PRECINCT SES LEVEL AND MEAN PERCENTAGE WELTNER VOTE IN RUN-OFF PRIMARY AND GENERAL ELECTION IN FULTON AND DEKALB COUNTIES

| SES Level* | No. of Precincts | Weltner Percentage | | |
		Run-off Primary	General Election	Net Difference
Low:				
Fulton:				
White	(16)	46.2	64.7	+18.5
Negro†	(16)	89.2	70.3	—18.9
DeKalb	(9)	35.9	57.1	+21.2
Medium:				
Fulton	(19)	49.0	60.9	+11.9
DeKalb	(15)	40.3	56.1	+15.8
High:				
Fulton	(15)	52.5	43.9	—8.6
DeKalb	(25)	51.8	47.8	—4.0

*The SES index was constructed by averaging the percentages of persons over twenty-five years of age with less than nine grades of education, families whose incomes were $5,000 or less, and males over fourteen years of age employed in non-white collar jobs and then subtracting the average percentage from 100.

†Negro precincts were defined as those with over 50 per cent Negro population. Out of 16 "Negro" precincts, 7 had a Negro percentage from 90 to 100 per cent, 4 from 80 to 89 per cent, 3 from 70 to 79 per cent, and only 2 from 50 to 69 per cent.

precincts have an average drop of close to 20 percentage points, versus an increment of about the same order for the white precincts, so that the over-all disparity is about 40 percentage points. Significantly, the attrition of Weltner's vote in the Negro precincts follows the pattern of the high-status white precincts. Nevertheless, the Negro precincts still return the highest average support for Weltner of all groupings shown in Table 2.

Combining the correlational and index analyses leads to several important conclusions (or, to be more cautious, inferences):

1. The support of predominantly Negro electorates was crucial in Weltner's victory. Even though Negro support dropped off in the general election, it nevertheless supplied the moderate Democrat with a key base of support.

Given the present socio-economic conditions and political attitudes of Southern Negroes,[6] it is likely that they will support moderate Democrats, if offered the chance, in other districts also.[7]

2. Lower-class whites supported the more conservative Democrat when given the choice. Perhaps of greater significance, their partisan loyalties permitted them to "transfer" their allegiance to a more moderate Democrat, despite seeming ideological differences in the civil rights area, rather than vote for a Republican. This transfer gave Weltner another key segment of support in the general election. Evidently, if the moderate Democrat can survive the intraparty fight, he may rely on this pool of "traditional" Democrats in much the same way that Democratic candidates in other regions may.

3. Higher-status white electorates appeared to give the moderate Democrat more support in the Democratic clash than did the lower-status electorates. However, this support was not manifested in the general election. Indeed, the support the Republican O'Callaghan received among precincts of this type was impressive. It lends credence to the notion that the nascent Republicanism of the urban South can be tapped in the same social strata as in other regions for more than just presidential elections.

4. The association of socio-economic factors with voting cannot be denied. This was particularly apparent in the Democratic primary. That the association was considerably weaker (though still of sizable proportions) in the interparty election attests to the impact of partisanship factors on the relationship between socio-economic status and voting behavior.

5. To the extent that the Georgia Fifth is not atypical of a changing South, the strategy of the moderate, more nationally oriented Southern Democrats appears to be shrewd but not without hazards. Surviving the intraparty scrap will be particularly difficult. Furthermore, the delicate job of recombining the components of support from a primary to a general election will be no mean accomplishment. The challenge from the right, in the form of conservative Democrats in primaries and Republicans in general elections, is likely to be formidable and in some cases victorious.[8]

---

[6]See Donald R. Matthews and James W. Prothro, "Southern Images of Political Parties: A Comparison of White and Negro Attitudes," *Journal of Politics,* Vol. 26, February 1964, pp. 82-111.

[7]Some confirmation for this may be found in the 1962 contest in Tennessee's Fifth District (Nashville), where Negroes appeared to support moderate Richard Fulton over conservative Carlton Loser. By the same token, when Negroes had little to choose between a conservative Democrat and a conservative Republican in the Virginia Third (Richmond), they backed the Republican as a protest against the conservative Byrd machine. It should also be noted, though, that Republicans apparently did very well among Negro voters in the Tennessee Third (Chattanooga), where moderate Democrat Wilkes T. Thrasher was defeated by William E. Brock III.

[8]In addition to the Georgia Fifth and the Tennessee Fifth, the strategy seems to have paid off in the Florida Third and Tenth Districts in 1962. It failed in such areas as the Texas Seventh and Twenty-second, however.

Index

Abu-Laban, Baha, 72, 88, 101, 106, 107n, 109n.
Abyssinian Baptist Church: as base of support for Adam Powell, 147.
Ader, Emile B., 265n.
Alabama: and Negro electorate, 251-252; and 1960 electoral vote, 430; and party factionalism, 223-225; and poll taxes, 216.
Alabama Civic Affairs Association, 253.
Almond, Gabriel, 38n.
Amendments to United States Constitution:
Thirteenth, 2.
Fourteenth, 2, 19-20, 412-414, 416-417.
Fifteenth, 2, 14-15, 20, 23-24, 26, 399.
Nineteenth, 20.
American Council on Race Relations, 7.
American Dilemma, An, 7n, 136, 237-238, 256.
American Men of Science, 74-76.
Anderson v. *Martin,* 415.
"Anti-Amalgamation doctrine," 257.
Anti-Catholic feeling in 1960 election, 434.
Anti-NAACP legislation in southern states, 361.
Anti-Semitism, 9.
Apathy: and absence of Negro leadership, 68-69.
Apter, David, 150n.
Arkansas: and poll taxes, 216; and voter registration by race, 182.
Arnold, Thurman W., 7n.
Ashmore, Harry, 431n.
Atlanta (Ga.): and large Negro vote, 241; Negro leadership in 113-135.
Atlanta Committee for Cooperative Action, 118.
Atlanta University: civil rights organizations on campus, 130.

Backlash: and impact of on Johnson election in South, 244; and range of concessions to Negroes, 426; and

vigorous participation by Negroes in South, 253.
Bacon, August, 414.
Baldwin v. *Morgan,* 415.
Ball, Harry V., 104n.
Banfield, Edward C., 55, 69n, 428n.
Baptists: proportion Negro, 81.
Barber, Bernard, 88.
Barnard, Chester, 146n, 325n.
Barnes, James F., 186n.
Barrows v. *Jackson,* 412, 415.
Barth, Ernest A. T., 72, 88, 101, 102, 106, 107n, 109n.
Bartlett, Irving H., 102n.
Baskin v. *Brown,* 414.
Baumgardt, David, 11.
Bell v. *State of Maryland,* 415.
Bell, Wendell, 72n.
Bentham, Jeremy, 11, 12.
Berelson, Bernard, 208n.
Berry, Theodore M., 323.
Bertrand, Alvin L., 169n.
Bettelheim, B., 180n.
Bilbo, Theodore, 240.
Biracial system, 239-240, 242-243, 254-255, 257.
Birmingham (Ala.): and hostility toward Negroes, 236; and riots of 1964, 52.
Birthplaces: of Negro leaders, 85.
Black, Hugo, 25, 415.
"Black Cabinet," 30.
Bloc voting, 249, 269-270, 425-427.
Blumberg, Leonard U., 92n.
Bolling, Richard, 248-249.
Boman v. *Birmingham Transit Company,* 415.
Boston Common Council: and exclusion of Negroes through at-large elections, 323.
Boston (Mass.): and Negro officeholding, 323.
Boswell Amendment, 32.
Boycott, 51, 127, 130, 377.
Branton, Wiley, 246.
Breedlove v. *Suttles,* 20.

449

70
71
72
74
75
76
77
79
81
83
85
88